C000143161

1 MONTH OF
FREE
READING

at

www.ForgottenBooks.com

By purchasing this book you are
eligible for one month membership to
ForgottenBooks.com, giving you
unlimited access to our entire
collection of over 1,000,000 titles via
our web site and mobile apps.

To claim your free month visit:

www.forgottenbooks.com/free97875

* Offer is valid for 45 days from date of purchase. Terms and conditions apply.

ISBN 978-0-483-46254-0
PIBN 10097875

This book is a reproduction of an important historical work. Forgotten Books uses
state-of-the-art technology to digitally reconstruct the work, preserving the original format
whilst repairing imperfections present in the aged copy. In rare cases, an imperfection in
the original, such as a blemish or missing page, may be replicated in our edition. We do,
however, repair the vast majority of imperfections successfully; any imperfections that
remain are intentionally left to preserve the state of such historical works.

Forgotten Books is a registered trademark of FB &c Ltd.
Copyright © 2018 FB &c Ltd.
FB &c Ltd, Dalton House, 60 Windsor Avenue, London, SW19 2RR.
Company number 08720141. Registered in England and Wales.

For support please visit www.forgottenbooks.com

THE
ELEMENTARY SCHOOL TEACHER

Journal

VOLUME VII

SEPTEMBER, 1906—JUNE, 1907

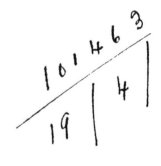

CHICAGO
The University of Chicago Press
1907

Published
September, October, November, December, 1906
January, February, March, April, May, June, 1907

Composed and Printed By
The University of Chicago Press
Chicago, Illinois, U. S. A.

INDEX TO VOLUME VII

INDEX TO ARTICLES

INDEX TO AUTHORS

INDEX TO BOOK REVIEWS

VOLUME VII   NUMBER I

THE ELEMENTARY SCHOOL TEACHER

SEPTEMBER, 1906

A SERIES OF PRIMARY READING-LESSONS. I

JENNIE HALL
Francis W. Parker School

Weaving, as an industry for primary children, has widely proven itself of value, and interesting work in textiles is being done in many schools.   The time has come, moreover, when teachers demand of manual work, not only that it shall keep the children busy, but that it shall pay for this expenditure of time and energy in physical development, intellectual training, and moral habits.   We insist that our industry shall be educational, not manufactural.   We recognize, too, that a mind under the stimulus of a new and interesting manual activity is eager and plastic toward associated intellectual influences.   Therefore we try to link this little school activity with the great world-industries.   We try to show our child-weaver his place in a long, world-wide, and time-diversified procession of textile workers. We try to translate his loom, his weaving, into terms of history, art, and poetry.   In these efforts we bring materials into the schoolroom—an Indian blanket, an oriental rug, a Cashmere shawl, spinning-wheels, spindles, pictures.   We make excursions to textile museums and factories.   We tell stories of shepherds— Abraham, David, Endymion, James Hogg.   We study conditions of shepherd life.   We read poems of shepherds and weavers.   We make reading-lessons to convey information and story.   The children express their newly gained knowledge and emotions by writing, painting, modeling, and acting.

The following reading-lessons were made and printed at the

Francis W. Parker School for the use of the second grade in connection with weaving. The methods of using them have been various, since the children differ widely in their reading ability. Sometimes the story has been read aloud by one child. Frequently the class has read silently, using the information acquired in writing, drawing, modeling, and discussion. Sometimes the story has been simplified and written upon the board. Often one group has prepared a lesson and has read it orally to the other children. At times various children have read aloud different parts of a lesson, and thus together have made the whole story. The pupil's interest in the reading is a strong plea for correlated reading-matter, and their widening images and interests in connection with their handwork make a plea for developing the intellectual matter associated with a manual activity.

The collection is far from complete. Descriptions of other skilful weavers are needed—Swedish, Japanese, East Indian. There should be more poems—upon spinning and weaving. Cotton- and linen-working are untouched. Nothing has been done with embroidery and lace-making. But the writer hopes that the present material may be of use to the readers of the *Elementary School Teacher*, and that many people will help to complete the collection.

SECOND-GRADE READING LESSONS
A SHEPHERD'S LIFE

It must be pleasant to be a shepherd in Greece.
Early in the morning it is cool.
The sky is golden around the sun.
The mountains are rosy.
The sheep move slowly over the hill.
Their bells tinkle sweetly.
The shepherd lies on a rock.
He plays his pipe.
The sound floats far away.
His dog lies beside him.
But at noon it is very hot.
The shepherd drives his sheep slowly to a well.
He draws water, and the sheep drink.

Then he drives them to a shelter.
It is a little flat roof of brush.
It stands on short poles.
It makes a little shade.
Here the sheep lie close together and sleep.
There is another smaller roof for the shepherd.
Here he and his dog lie down and sleep.
After a few hours it grows cool.
The shepherd and the sheep wake.
The sheep go out again to eat.
The shepherd follows slowly.

(Used by the teacher; parts of poems committed by the children)

THE SHEPHERD

How sweet is the shepherd's sweet lot;
    From the morn to the evening he strays;
He shall follow his sheep all the day,
    And his tongue shall be filled with praise.

For he hears the lamb's innocent call,
    And he hears the ewe's tender reply;
He is watchful while they are in peace,
    For they know when their shepherd is nigh.
                              —WILLIAM BLAKE.

THE PASSIONATE SHEPHERD TO HIS LOVE

Come live with me and be my love.
    And we will all the pleasures prove
That hills and valleys, dale and field,
    And all the craggy mountains yield.

There will we sit upon the rocks
    And see the shepherds feed their flocks,
By shallow rivers, to whose falls
    Melodious birds sing madrigals.

There will I make thee beds of roses
    And a thousand fragrant posies,

A cap of flowers, and a kirtle
  Embroider'd all with leaves of myrtle.

A gown made of the finest wool,
  Which from our pretty lambs we pull,
Fair linèd slippers for the cold,
  With buckles of the purest gold.

A belt of straw and ivy buds
  With coral clasps and amber studs:
And if these pleasures may thee move,
  Come live with me and be my love.

Thy silver dishes for thy meat
  As precious as the gods do eat
Shall on an ivory table be
  Prepared each day for thee and me.

The shepherd swains shall dance and sing
For thy delight each May morning:
If these delights thy mind may move,
Then live with me and be my love.
                                —C. MARLOWE.

A SHEPHERD'S VILLAGE

It is lonely work being a shepherd.
The sheep wander on day after day.
Sometimes they go miles from home.
The shepherd does not see his people for weeks.
He is far up in bare hills.
But there are other shepherds in those hills.
They all grow lonely.
Sometimes they hear one another's pipes far away.
"There are other shepherds," they say to themselves.
They drive their sheep in the direction of the music.
When they meet they are very glad.
"Let us camp together," they say.
So they build sheds for themselves and their sheep.

They make them of brush or of rushes.

The sheep-shed is a big ring with a roof around the edge.

The men's sheds are like beehives.

Inside is a shelf for the men to lie on.

On the ground in the middle burns a little fire.

Here the shepherds all live for weeks.

When the grass is gone they move on to a new camp.

A LOST SHEEP

A shepherd stood on the mountain-side.

He was counting his sheep.

One was gone.

Across the valley was another mountain-side.

Here was another shepherd with his sheep.

The first shepherd called across to him.

He had to call very loudly and slowly, because it was far away.

He said: "I have lost a sheep. Is he with you?"

"I will see," called the other shepherd.

He counted his sheep.

There was one too many.

Now, all sheep look very much alike.

How could he tell which one was not his?

The sheep all had their heads down eating.

The shepherd gave his call.

All his sheep knew that call.

They raised their heads.

But one sheep kept on eating.

The shepherd shouted: "Yes, I have one strange sheep."

Then the other shepherd gave his call.

It floated softly across the valley.

The strange sheep heard it and lifted its head.

"He is yours," called the man who was watching.

Then the other shepherd left his dog to guard his herd.

He came across the valley, and got his lost sheep.

> Would that my father had taught me
> The craft of a keeper of sheep;
> For so, in the shade of an elm tree,

Or under a rock on the steep,
Piping on reeds I had sat
And had lulled my sorrow to sleep!

—Moschus.

GOATS

Goats are very useful to men.
People drink their milk.
They make cheese from the milk.
They eat the meat of goats.
They make pails and bottles from the skin.
They make cloth from the hair.
They can make pretty cloth without any dye.
That is because goat hair is of so many colors.
Some goats are black.
Some are white.
Some are dark brown.
Some are light brown.
Some are blue-gray.
A herd of goats on a mountain-side is very pretty.
The rocks are big and rough and gray.
Little green plants grow in the cracks.
The goats, brown and black and white and gray, jump from
rock to rock and eat these plants.
The shepherd with his crook sits on a rock.
He has a bright handkerchief on his head.
These goats do not belong to him.
Down the mountain is a little village.
The goats belong to the people of this village.
Early in the morning the shepherd walks through the village.
The goats are waiting for him at their own doors.
He whistles, and the goats walk on ahead of him.
In the evening he drives them home.
When a goat comes to her own door she turns in.
Sometimes she has to go upstairs to be milked.
Up she goes without any fuss.

GIOTTO

There was a shepherd boy called Giotto.

He lived in Italy long ago.

His father had a little stone house on a hillside.

It was a little village of stone houses.

Below it were green fields beside a river.

Above it was the rocky hill.

The father worked in the fields by the river.

The boy Giotto tended the sheep on the hill.

There he lay, while the sheep ate.

He looked at the clouds in the blue sky.

He saw the little houses and the green fields.

He watched the sun set behind the hills.

He looked at his sheep with their heads down, eating.

He had nothing to do, so he took a little stone and scratched on a big smooth rock.

Sometimes he made only crooked marks.

Sometimes he made pictures of his sheep.

He made them lying down.

He made them running.

He made them eating.

One day a stranger came up the hill on a horse.

He saw the boy lying down scratching with his stone.

He rode near and stopped.

He looked at the pictures on the rock.

He watched the boy at work.

At last he said: "These are good sheep, my boy.

"I make pictures myself, I am an artist.

"I have a work shop down in the city.

"Come down and work with me.

"I will teach you to use brush and paints.

"I will show you how to make pictures of Christ and of angels."

Giotto leaped up with joy.

Of course he wanted to go.

He and the stranger went to his father.

They talked for a long time.

At last the father said "Yes."

Then Giotto tied some clothes into a bundle.

He kissed his father and mother and started for the city.

There he worked for years.

He learned how to paint.

He made very beautiful pictures of Christ and of Mary and of angels.

But he could do other things also.

He could carve marble.

He could make buildings.

He built a beautiful tower for bells.

He made it of marble—green, white, pink.

Into it he put little pictures carved in marble.

One of them is a picture of a man plowing.

Another is a picture of a man sitting in his tent-door.

In front of him are his sheep.

His dog is watching them.

I think that when Giotto made those pictures he was thinking of his old home, his sheep, his father's fields.

MY MOTHER'S STORY OF SHEEP-SHEARING

When I was a little girl, I used to like sheep-shearing time.

It was in spring.

The days were warm.

The sheep did not need their thick winter wool.

It began to come out.

When I played in the woods, I often found locks of it on the bushes.

"We must not lose any more wool," my father said when he saw it.

"We must do our shearing."

The men put on their high rubber boots and went down to the creek.

We children ran along to watch.

We liked the fun.

The brook ran through the woods pasture.

The sheep were running among the trees.

There was a little pen near the brook.

The men drove the sheep into this pen and shut them in.

One man waded out into the brook.

"All ready," he said.

Then another man opened the gate of the pen.

He drove one sheep out and into the water.

The man in the brook caught it.

He held it between his knees in the water.

He washed the wool and squeezed it in his hands.

He pulled out burrs and straws and sticks from the wool.

The sheep in the water was very still.

When the man thought the sheep was clean, he let it go.

Off it ran, baaing into the woods.

The man in the pen sent out another sheep into the water.

Soon the sheep were all washed and were running about in the woods.

We children liked that time best.

What a noise!

What a running-about!

Mothers had lost their lambs, and lambs had lost their mothers.

They ran about the woods bleating to call each other.

When they met they were very happy.

The mothers rubbed the little ones with their noses.

The lambs danced around their mothers.

It was a very pretty sight.

We children laughed with joy.

After some days, the sheep's wool was dry.

The boys swept the barn floor clean.

They drove all the sheep into the front barn-yard.

It was clean there.

Father took down the sheep-shears from the shed and went to the barn.

"Come on,' he called when he was ready.

The boys drove a sheep into the barn.

Father caught it and put it between his knees.

Sometimes the sheep tried to get away.

Then father tied its legs together.

Then it had to lie quiet on the floor.
"Clip, clip," went the shears.
The thick wool began to roll off.
It was matted together.
So it came off in one piece.
It looked like a whole skin, as it lay on the floor.
When it was all cut off, one of the boys took it.
He tied it into a roll.
Father untied the sheep's legs.
It ran out into the other barn-yard, baaing for its friends.
The boys drove another one in.
Off came his wool.
The sheared sheep looked very funny.
Their legs were like little sticks.
Their pink skin showed through their short hair.
My father looked at the pile of wool in the barn.
"Well," he said, "that will make us all the clothes we need.
"I think we shall have some to sell."

THE SHEEP

"Lazy sheep, pray tell me why
In the grassy fields you lie,
Eating grass and daisies white
From the morning till the night?
Everything can something do,
But what kind of use are you?"

"Nay, my little master, nay,
Do not serve me so, I pray;
Don't you see the wool that grows
On my back to make your clothes?
Cold, ah! very cold, you'd get,
If I did not give you it.

"Sure it seems a pleasant thing
To nip the daisies in the spring,
But many chilly nights I pass
On the cold and dewey grass,

Or pick a scanty dinner where
All the common's brown and bare.

"Then the farmer comes at last,
When the merry spring is past,
And cuts my wooly coat away
To warm you in the winter's day;
Little master, this is why
In the grassy fields I lie."

—ANN TAYLOR.

UP! UP! YE DAMES AND LASSES GAY!

Up! Up! ye dames and lasses gay!
To the meadows trip away.
'Tis you must tend the flocks this morn,
And scare the small birds from the corn,
Not a soul at home may stay;
    For the shepherds must go
    With lance and bow
To hunt the wolf in the woods today.

Leave the hearth and leave the house
To the cricket and the mouse:
Find grannam out a sunny seat,
With babe and lambkin at her feet,
Not a soul at home may stay:
    For the shepherds must go
    With lance and bow
To hunt the wolf in the woods today.

—S. T. COLERIDGE.

SHEPHERD PICTURES

Shepherds on the hillside, playing pipes,
Calling to each other through your pipes,
Looking at your sheep and at the rocks,
Looking at the hills and at the trees,
Looking at the valleys down below,
   And making up tunes on your pipes.

Looking at the craggy mountain-side
And looking at the stars at night,
Looking at the deep blue sky,
And looking at the moon among the clouds—
 How sweet is the life of the shepherd!
     —Second Grade, 1904.

KINDERGARTEN AND PRIMARY GAMES

ANNE ELIZABETH ALLEN
University Elementary School

Until the effort is made one can never know the difficulty of the task of trying to write out children's games. The baldness and bareness of mere words, minus the music, the charming. unconscious action of the children, and the thousand subtilties that add to the rounding-out of a game, tempt one, even after putting his hand to the plow, to turn back. Besides, one never plays a game exactly the same the second time. Different children, different days, different conditions in many ways, combine to make changes to "fit." Hence only an artist could put before a reader an adequate description of many of the games that grow directly out of the work in hand.

The introduction of a new game is an art, a fine art built upon long experience. To make it go, it must take hold of the children's interest in a practical way. The leader must know where to turn for help among the children who have strength in taking the initiative and whose interest will at once become active. Again, the leader must be able at a moment's notice to change her plan or modify it according to the suggestions of the children.

By dramatizing the industrial life around us we are soon able to select the dramatic incidents in a story, and "act them out"—mostly in pantomime, to be sure, but in a way most satisfactory and pleasing to the children.

From time to time I hope to make the attempt to put before the readers of this magazine some of the plays and games as we have played them in our kindergarten, asking always leniency for the manner and style of the bare outlines I am forced to give.

GAME I

CLOUDS AND RAIN

Time: A cloudy, rainy day.

Music: "Plump Little Baby Clouds," from *Primary and Kindergarten*

Songs, Part II, by Eleanor Smith; "Pit-a-Pat," from *Songs of the Child World*, Part I, by Jessie Gaynor.

Watch the clouds to see if the wind is blowing them. Choose one child to show how fast or how slowly the clouds are moving. Ask if they are making any noise as they move, and insist upon very quiet movement. Suggest that the eyes be covered with the arms, so that everything will seem dark as the clouds make it seem. Choose one child at a time, giving all who ask a chance to show, and then "magically" change them all into "plump little baby clouds, dimpled and soft," and play and sing softly as they creep softly around the room. Try this a number of times, until the children get into the spirit of it. Next play "Pit-a-pat," and let them lower their arms and run in time to the music, pattering their feet to represent the pattering of the rain. Play slowly and softly, then more rapidly, and still more rapidly and louder, asking that they follow the lead of the piano. Suddenly the music will stop, indicating that the shower is over, beginning again and stopping at intervals. (An excellent opportunity is thus afforded for alert attention and instantaneous obedience.) If there is a thunderstorm, the arms may be thrown away from the eyes and back again to indicate lightning, and the feet make a noise to represent thunder.

Over and over again this may be played with the deepest interest on the part of the children—just so long as the teacher is herself interested and will insist upon absolute obedience to the piano's dictates.

GAME II

GAME OF THE FIRE FAIRIES

Dramatizing a story: Tell the story of "Ted and the Fire Fairies," *Course of Study*, January, 1901.

Ask the children to watch a fire burn, noticing how it dances and plays around a piece of paper that it devours. Call the flames "the fire-fairies," and ask who could show with his arms the way they dance. Gradually the children will develop a movement with their arms, darting them up and down slowly and rapidly, as the music will suggest. (The "Fire Music" from *Siegfried* is the best, but any staccato music may be used by adapting the tempo to the darting movement of the flames. Beginning with a slight movement of the arms upward, with the hand held straight, and increasing in rapidity, the children may rise gradually to their feet, and with arms still darting upward may very realistically represent the "fire-fairies," as they softly dance up and down on their toes. As the "fuel" gives out, the children may gradually sink to the floor, and finally drop entirely down, pushing out a tiny flame occasionally, as one sees in a dying fire. Several children may group themselves on the floor to represent a heap of coals. One child may clap his hands to represent the striking of a match, and a fire will thus be started. Another child may play that he is a log of wood, and be started in the same way. The fairy-ring may also be started as told of in the story.

A fireplace may be made of several chairs, and someone may play grandmother sitting near the fireplace knitting. (A child in the fireplace represents the fire.) Ted comes in at the door shivering as he plays that he takes off his wraps and lies down in front of the fire to get warm. He asks his grandmother what becomes of the flames as they go up the chimney, and she replies that she thinks they go back to the palace of the fire-king. Ted goes off to sleep, the fairy jumps out of the fire, takes him by the hand, and leads him through the land of the fire-fairies, showing him the fairy-ring, red-hot stove, log of wood, etc. He then takes him to the palace of the fire-king; and the play thus progresses as the story winds along, until Ted is brought back by the fairy and is wakened by the dinner bell and his grandmother's voice.

Naturally this subject must be handled most carefully. The story and play emphasize constantly that little children must let fire alone. Ted was sent for because he played with the fire. It may be made a very helpful or a most harmful thing, and is given to show that a doubtful subject may be handled in such a way as to benefit rather than harm little children. Most children are brought in contact with fire every day, and learning how to let it alone seems to me to be a very important lesson.

THE MACDONALD CONSOLIDATED SCHOOL, AT GUELPH, ONTARIO

J. W. HOTSON, M.A.
Principal

There is nothing, it seems to me, that is of more vital importance in molding the destiny of a nation than its method of education in its rural districts. This is markedly true in the case of Ontario, where the majority of the population depends directly upon the soil for their livelihood. If education means anything, it should mean a preparation for real life; it should prepare men and women better to live, better to live among the surroundings in which they find themselves, better to battle with the problems of life that meet them on every side, so that they may become more and more part of their environment, and thus become contented and useful citizens. In order to be contented with their lot, humble though that lot may be, they must be interested in it. As a rule, a person is most interested in the things that he knows the most about. It is one of the chief aims of the Macdonald Consolidated School at Guelph—and it should be of all rural schools—to engender such an interest and love for country life that the boys and girls will not be lured away by the attractions of the city.

I have great faith in the rural school, in its power to mold and build up a national character; but new educational methods must be used in order to secure the best results. In order to compete with our rivals in the world's markets, in order to equalize the advantages of country and city life, in order to make our country life attractive enough to keep our bright boys and girls on the farm, and thus maintain an intelligent, prosperous, progressive, and contented rural people, we must give immediate and effective attention to the needs of the rural school. A consolidated school makes it possible so to modify the curriculum that the development of the child is the ultimate aim, and not the cramming of the mind with mere facts.

In the Consolidated School at Guelph an attempt is being made "to adapt education to need." All the children who attend this school are country children; none from the city are accepted. The teachers are reminded, first, that they are dealing solely with rural children; second, that the majority of these children are going to spend their lives on the farm. Keeping these two facts in mind, an effort is made to adapt the teaching and what is taught to the special needs of the rural people.

The improvement of rural education is attempted along a line of what is taught. Besides the regular subjects, that are usually taught in the rural school, there are taught manual training, domestic science including sewing, nature-study, and school garden work. That phase of nature-study is emphasized that tends toward agriculture.

In Canada the greatest industry is essentially agriculture. Nearly 70 per cent. of its population live in rural districts and are dependent directly upon the farm for a livelihood, and their children are being educated in the rural school. There are about 10 per cent. of the population who are educated for the so-called "higher professions." Of these the greatest number come from the farm. When we reflect for a moment on the amount of money that is expended in the preparation of this 10 per cent. for their life-work, we cannot help but feel disappointed, not that so much money is spent in their education, but that so little is expended in the preparation of the 70 per cent. who live in rural districts, to carry on scientifically and well the greatest of all industries—the cultivation of the soil.

In Ontario, as in many states of the Union, the educational system does not tend to produce the best results in the lives of the boys and girls of the country. The whole system tends to lead toward professional life rather than toward the farm. City things are being taught rather than country things. The farm and the farm home have been neglected; the greatest industry, farming, and the noblest institution, the farm home, have been discredited; and consequently the rural districts are being drained of their best young men and women. The present system of education does not prepare the rural children sufficiently for the life they are to live.

It is a mistaken idea that some people have that anyone can be a successful farmer. To be a successful farmer—that is, to make a profession of it—requires as much systematic training and careful experience as any other profession. The cause of so many failures in farm life is largely due to lack of early training along a line that would prepare them for this kind of work. Who is responsible for this lack of early training? If the rural people are to be so strong a factor in molding the character and destiny of the nation, does it not behoove every truly loyal citizen, whether he lives in a palatial dwelling or in the humblest cot in the land, to guard well the education of the rising generation?

Many of our rural people live in very humble circumstances. In many cases it is impossible for them ever to get away from these conditions. Why not lead them into a more sympathetic relation to their daily life by getting them interested in the numberless things around them in nature, and thus tend to make them more contented and better citizens?

It is one of the objects of the Macdonald Consolidated Rural School to teach the common things with which the child comes in contact every day, and in this way to lead him into a more sympathetic relation to his environment.

The Macdonald Consolidated School at Guelph is an experiment for the purpose of trying to improve rural education. It was established in the autumn of 1904, and is financed by Sir William Macdonald, of Montreal.

As Sir William's time is largely taken up with his business, the preliminary arrangements and inauguration of the enterprise were intrusted to Professor J. W. Robertson, LL.D., C.M.G., president of the Macdonald College of Agriculture at Ste. Anne de Bellevue, near Montreal. This school is situated on the grounds of the Ontario Agricultural College, Guelph, Ont., and is capable of holding 300 pupils. It is well furnished and equipped. To this school are brought all the children of school age in five surrounding school sections. These are brought in every morning, and taken out in the evening, in eight large, comfortable, covered vans. After the preliminary arrangements were made, the management of the school was vested in a local board, which consists of the three trustees from each of the sections being consolidated.

The rate of taxation is the same as it was before the inauguration of the scheme. All the additional expense is met by the Macdonald fund. This agreement lasts for three years, or until sufficient time has elapsed to give it a fair trial. At the end of that time the building and equipment will be handed over to the local board, and they may either continue the work or go back to the old district schools as they see fit. But it is firmly believed that the advantages of consolidation will be so great that they will not wish to return to the old system.

To show how the general public looks upon the work being done, another school section applied to be allowed to join the Consolidated School, and was admitted last August.

One of the great aims of this school is to interest the children, not only in country life, but in agricultural problems. The school garden has been found to be a potent factor in accomplishing this end. Every child in the school has a little plot of ground for himself, which is his very own. Here he is given instruction as to planting and caring for vegetables and flowers. The produce is his, and is either sold or taken home. Each class has a plot in which they work together. There are also some illustration plots in which the whole school works. These are for the purpose of experimenting with good and poor seeds, spraying, fertilizers, rotation of crops, etc.

Our point of view cannot be expressed better than in the words of Professor Bailey, of Cornell.

In the rural districts the school must become a social and intellectual center. It must stand in close relationship with the life and activities of its community. It must not be an institution apart, exotic to the everyday lives; it must teach the common things, and put the pupil into sympathetic touch with his own environment.

WOMAN'S PART IN PUBLIC-SCHOOL EDUCATION

MRS. A. E. HYRE
Member of School Board, Cleveland, O.

The thought of the day seems to be that a child shall be educated in a way that will enable him to live a worthy life; that less stress shall be placed upon the development of his intellectual powers, and more upon his qualities of character; that the school life shall be a continuation and enlargement upon the true home life, and not a training separate and apart.

In the light of these views, the question of "Woman's Part in Public-School Education" is of more than ordinary interest and deserves the thoughtful consideration of every one who is interested in school affairs. The work that woman has done, and the success that has obtained along humane, philanthropic, and educational lines, in the past twenty-five years, indicate that she has a sympathy and patience with children, and an understanding of them, that fit her to take an important part in public-school education.

I believe that woman has a part in public education because she possesses certain natural qualities peculiar to her sex, that are essential elements in the rounded up education of a boy or girl.

I shall not take your time to discuss the political or legal right of woman to a part in public education, but desire simply to call your attention to the moral duty and inherent right of woman to live out her own individuality and up to the best talent within her. Because of this, woman finds her work where children's interests are.

It is not a trade or a business that woman has learned. It is the intuitive insight into child-life and child-nature that God Almighty has given her. Woman knows a hundred ways to reach a child. It may be through his pride, his reason, his intellect or his affection, or by means of her individual tact; but whatever method is used, there are always back of it the patience and interest of woman in youth. And so, wherever children are concerned,' wherever their safeguards or development are involved, the woman view-point should have expression. It is not only in a general and abstract way that woman should enter into the public education of our youth, but in a material and practical way.

Woman has a part in public education as a student, as a teacher, as a patron, and as a member of boards of education. Woman's love and understanding of children are a natural instinct that exists in the most primitive and ignorant woman; but if we would have the larger benefits of that knowledge in our citizenship, we must educate the possessor to use it in an intelligent manner. The evolution of woman has been and is wonderful. Every year large numbers who are to be the mothers of the coming generation are filling our educational institutions. Half of our public-school population are girls, while women constitute nearly 30 per cent. of all college students.

Occasionally someone will denounce the higher education of women. Recently a woman physician said that the mental development of woman is destroying her ability to carry out her proper functions. In answer to this, let me quote Dr. J. M. Taylor, dean of Vassar College, who has made careful study of this subject:

The bearing of the higher education of women on the health of women and their attitude toward the home is of perennial interest. It has been abundantly shown, over and over again, by the most careful investigation, that the health of college women improves during the four years' college course. While that is not true in all cases, it is certainly not true in the cases of all men. Only three of 153 graduates of 1903 of Vassar did not improve in general health after entering college. The first ten years' history of Vassar shows that half the total number of graduates married, and that the proportion of children to each was from three to four. There is nothing in the college training of American women to contribute to abnormal results. A healthy mind, a natural body, and absolutely healthy and natural sentiments toward life are the general product. No work in America promises more for its future than the thorough education of its girls.

But woman's part in public-school education has its greatest manifestation, at the present time, in the large number of women teachers in the public-schools. In 1880 the percentage of women teachers was 57. In 1903 it had increased to 74, and we naturally ask why this has come about. I venture one suggestion. At one time in the history of teachers the only equipment necessary was a certificate. If an applicant before a board of examiners maintained an average of 70 per cent., he was a teacher, and nothing could prevent him, if he could delude some weak board of education into giving him a school. The time is not so far distant when physical strength was of greater value to the schoolmaster than intellectual power. It was necessary for him to control and break the spirit of the biggest boy in his room, or else he had not been a success. Experience has taught us that this influence did not stimulate the pupil's respect for law and order, but destroyed it. But there came a change in the sentiment of the public; they began to wonder if there was not some other way to reach children. Here and there a slight little woman would succeed in a school where a strong man had been employed and failed. By moral suasion, by studying the boy, by giving her woman-nature full sway, she would capture the boy's heart, perhaps touch his pride, secure his co-operation, stimulate his gallantry—in a word, win him. Educators and the thinking public at last realized that woman's way was the best way of reaching children.

At this period moral suasion supplanted the birch whip. The sentiment of the public became so strong against physical punishment that laws prohibiting it were placed upon the statute-books of a number of states. The teacher, in preparing for his calling today, does not have to measure his professional value by his ability to administer corporal punishment. The teacher of the present, who makes a success of his work, loves it. He studies and trusts his pupils, and by that very faith wins their love and confidence. He has an understanding of and sympathy with child-life, and he has tact to manage it.

The teacher must also have the ability to discriminate. The doctor, as he goes about his practice, cannot send out a general prescription to apply to all cases; he must have the skill to discriminate. The commercial man who is a successful one must study his men; he must approach them in as many different ways as there are minds; he cannot commit a speech and repeat it to every business man he may approach; he must have the acuteness to discriminate. The nurse who goes into a sickroom fully determined to put into effect the theories she has learned, without considering whether the case is one of typhoid fever or a critical operation, will soon find out that she has mistaken her calling. She, too, must have the quality of discrimination. The teacher is no exception to the general rule. He must surpass the others in tact; he must have the ability to find out each child's individual make-up and temperament; he must discover the avenue through which he may influence him; he must reach down and interest the child-mind; he can lift it up to his own mentality only as he leads it on, year after year. This requires a comprehension of childhood; and woman's nature fits her peculiarly to enter into a sympathetic relationship with children and to teach them properly.

But the business man complains of lack of confidence and individuality in our city-taught boys. Educators themselves are somewhat disturbed over the apparent shortcomings. Some of them give as a reason that there are too many women teachers in the city schools, and that boys, as they enter the adolescent age, need, in greater degree, masculine influences. I believe this is true; but that does not prove anything, because the average boy at that age is in high-school work and comes under the direct influence of both men and women. In substantiation of this it is a fact, interesting to note, that out of a canvass of the 60 grammar buildings in Cleveland, the average age of the graduating classes of 1905, or 3,222 grammar pupils, was found to be 14.08 years. There was only one building where the average age of the class was 15 years. In 23 buildings the average age was 13+, and in the other 36 buildings the class age average was 14+.

It is in the cities that there is complaint of a lack of individuality among pupils, but I believe this is not because there are so many women teachers, but on account of the close organization and the lack of freedom for each teacher to work out his own problems. Technical training is the foundation of a teacher's work, but it depends upon his individual interpretation and application of that training whether or not he shall succeed. I believe that it is the teacher, irrespective of sex, who goes on, year after year, surrounded by limitations and restrictions, that makes him little more than a machine to grind out so much work per day, that fails to create individuality in pupils or instil into boys any vigorous manhood.

It is, however, not only as a student and teacher that woman has a part in public education, but as a patron also. We cannot get far in advance of the people in any movement; and so, if we would secure the best equipment for our public schools, and the greatest benefits for the youth who attend them, we must keep the patrons alive to their needs.

It is the duty and mission of the school to develop a child, but the greatest work lies in bringing him into harmony with the community interests in which he lives; and I believe this can best be done by correlating the work of the home and the school. No teacher can do this, however, unless she has the cordial interest and support of the parent. It is to be regretted that so few fathers have an opportunity to familiarize themselves with the daily working conditions of the schoolroom. The average father is absent from home during the hours that the school is in session; he is usually so engrossed in the efforts of securing ways and means that the work of straightening out the "tangles" falls to the mother. This fact brings her into close touch with the teacher and the schools, and makes the mother a factor as a patron.

Realizing the benefits to their children, to be derived from this contact of mother and teacher, "mothers' clubs" exist in almost every school district in many cities. These clubs study and discuss many questions pertaining to children, and co-operate with and support the teachers in carrying out their plans for better and broader results.

In our own city of Cleveland the women are thoroughly alive to the interests of the schools. Besides mothers' clubs, there are other organizations of women that contribute to their welfare. The Needle-Work Guild, through information obtained from the principals of some of the poor districts, each fall furnishes a change of underwear, stockings, and other necessaries, to needy children, so that they may come to school in a presentable and cleanly manner. The Denison Patrons' League is an organization composed of the patrons of the school. Its officers are the leading citizens of the community. The league furnishes four free entertainments or lectures each year in the auditorium of the school building to the parents of the district, at which are discussed the relationship of the home and the school. The Free Day Nursery and Kindergarten Association support four summer vacation schools, and by their interest and effort stimulate the carrying out and enlargement of the work. The Daughters of the American Revolution appropriated a sum of money the past winter and gave, in conjunction with the school authorities, a series of patriotic lectures in the school auditoriums, where the population was largely foreign. The title of the lecture was "The Story of America." It was given in simple English, and was supplemented with stereopticon slides and patriotic music. This work was a grand success from every standpoint. These are only a part of the numerous efforts of Cleveland women in the interest of good schools. Other cities are working along similar lines, and it will only be a matter of time when the work of woman as a patron will be considered an essential part of every successful school.

But it is equally important that woman should have representation in the administrative department of our public schools as in the educational. Far be it from me to say that all women are fitted for school-board members, or that women should be upon every board for the sake of having a woman. But I do believe that the right woman should be upon every board, whether in a large or small system, because broader results will be obtained by adding the woman viewpoint of school administration; because the right woman, when it comes to children, is unselfish and has no interests which supersede those of the child; because the interest of the teacher and patron can always have expression with a woman representative upon the administrative board.

Two of the distinctive features that mark the services of women upon school boards are their close attention to detail and their willingness to hear the patron's side of the question. The public schools are the closest to the people of all public institutions, and through the members of its school board only can the people have representation. I therefore consider this public service and close attention to detail splendid qualifications for any member of a school board, and especial qualifications for women. The public has poor service from a member of a public board who, willing to sacrifice himself for the dear public before election, after election places himself upon a pedestal and draws the ."awful circle" about himself so that no one can approach him. Women members are interested in the questions of hygiene and sanitation, and especially in those questions of education which carry with them moral influences which go to make better boys and girls. The married women serving on school boards, as far as I have been able to learn are women who have had years of contact with children. The one experience that makes a mother valuable is that she has gone through that period of rearing her children, studying their natures, sympathizing with their weaknesses, and realizing their worth.   By this time what she knows about children is not "theory," but experience; and if she is an educated, broad-minded woman, she can do much good in addition to being a fond mother and grandmother.   The unmarried women who have been upon school boards are those who have dealt with children in a large way, and on account of that experience are quite as valuable.

In order that I might not discuss this part of my subject from a theoretical standpoint, I have written to prominent citizens in several cities where women are serving upon boards of education, and asked for opinions in reference to the value of their services.   The answers received show that these women are not only acceptable members of their respective boards, but that they are rendering special, and almost invaluable, service to the schools because they are women.   I give a few extracts.

In speaking of the woman who is a member of the board of education, the commissioner of schools at Rochester, N. Y., says:

She has made a constant contribution of suggestions and intelligent discussion equal to that of any other member; she has done more visiting than all the other members together.   She has interested herself in the music, decoration, and sanitation of the schools, and has brought to these subjects an experience, good taste and special knowledge which are quite exceptional.   She has been greatly interested in all that concerns the teacher, and by her remarkable gift as a public speaker she has been a force in the discussion of school questions at meetings of parents—a work of education of public sentiment which has made the progress of our schools possible through steadfast popular support.   I doubt if her knowledge in the matter of selecting supplementary reading for children is surpassed by that of any other woman in the country.

Another writes as follows:

Of the two women members at Warren, Ohio, one has been for a number of years at the head of the building committee, with excellent results, and the other has been chairman of the teachers' and textbook committee.   The first work they did was to renovate the schoolrooms.   At the end of the first year that these women were on the board the city board of health, in making its report to the state, spoke of the splendid sanitary condition of the schoolhouses, and gave the women of the board the credit.

The member at Grand Rapids, Mich., is serving her tenth year upon the board.   In these years she agitated for manual training until it was established in the grammar grades.   She has been chairman of summer-school work, and it is considered a success from

every standpoint. She was a teacher, is the mother of children now
in school, and is thoroughly in sympathy with the work of keeping
the patron interested in the school. She is independent in her thought
and action, and I should say, from the splendid commendation of her
I have received, that the public of Grand Rapids feel that she is one
of the most valuable members of the board.

Toledo, Ohio, boasts for the first time of a woman upon its board,
and the following are extracts concerning her work:

> She has brought about a better feeling between teacher and parent by giving
> one afternoon a week to hear the patron's side of the question. She is more
> earnest and conscientious than most of the members of the board, inasmuch as
> she has "no ax to grind." She is conscientious and independent in her action,
> as has been demonstrated in several instances, but always yields gracefully when
> defeated. She is doing fine work, and has the admiration of the board and com-
> munity for her splendid poise and tact.

Cleveland has had a woman on the school board for ten years.
The first one found the board renting rooms over saloons to relieve
the overcrowded condition of the public schools. She protested; they
insisted. She threatened to call to her aid the public press, and never
since then has such a thing been proposed. These women advocated
and advanced the department of kindergarten, manual training, and
domestic science, and were the ardent supporters of the present day
deaf school. They also did much toward abolishing the use of basement rooms.

The member who served upon the board from 1901 to 1904 was a
splendid business woman, having large business interests of her own.
These women, who were upon the Cleveland board from 1894 to 1904,
were women of education and had had an experience with children,
either as mothers or as teachers. They were conscientious and
enthusiastic, and always for whatever seemed to be for the best interests of the children. So efficiently have these women served the
public that I believe it to be the fixed policy of the people of my own
city to keep at least one woman on the board of education.

This question of woman's part in public education is no longer
unsettled. It has been demonstrated in many cities that she has a
part in the administrative department as well as in the educational.
It is only a matter of time when every community will realize its

importance, and when every superintendent will urge that he be given this aid. When this time comes, *one woman—the right woman*—will be a member of every board of education, whether in a large or small city.

In a little drawer in my desk is a daguerreotype picture of a woman. It is an old picture, taken perhaps in the forties. The shawl that covers the shoulders of the subject is an old-style Paisley, and the bonnet would be an heirloom today. The hair, jet-black, is parted in the middle, and is carefully smoothed upon the forehead. It is a plain face, but to me beautiful—beautiful to me because it is the face of my mother. As I sit and look at that picture, it recalls to me the influence that has come down the years and molded my life. But the devotion, the patience, the sacrifice, that shine forth from the face of that daguerreotype picture are as old as woman herself. It is this spirit of love and unselfishness that is needed everywhere today. It should permeate our commercial and business life, and should enter into the public education of every child, to the end that he may become a better citizen and a more lovable neighbor.

When this moral element shall become a permanent influence in our public schools, health will supersede discipline; the heart will lead the will; knowledge for knowledge' sake will give place to knowledge of life and its human relations; and industrial and political strife will be gradually eliminated by the brotherhood of man. For, after all, what is the purpose of education? Is this life a wager to see how much information can be accumulated and stored in the human brain; or, rather, is it a grand privilege to study and understand our relations to God, to nature, and to our fellow-man? To set a lower or a narrower standard for the public schools of our country is to deprive our youth of the best elements of good citizenship, and to lessen their opportunities for a higher life.

STANDARDS IN EDUCATION

A. H. CHAMBERLAIN
Throop Polytechnic Institute, Pasadena, Cal.

More than a century past, our fathers, single minded to the best interests of education, essayed to enunciate what to us still seems to be a fundamental principle, that "religion, morality, and knowledge being necessary to good government and the happiness of mankind, schools and the means of education shall forever be encouraged." At all times and in all places education of one sort or another has been held to be a necessity, looking toward the best and fullest development of the individuals in a tribe, community, or nation. The question has never been: "Shall we educate?" The query, rather, has been put: "What shall we study, and how?"

But a hundred years in the study of educational thought and achievement is but as yesterday. In early Egypt, in Arabia, in Babylon, the dwellers in Assyria, and Phoenicia, the Persian and the Roman, the Greek and the Hindu, the Jew and the Japanese; each country and each people has endeavored in its own way, to work out its individual problems, and consciously or unconsciously to follow Paul's admonition: "Prove all things; hold fast that which is good."

Education has long been defined, but as we today glance back over the centuries we find it difficult to true the definition of any particular people to the practices of their educational doctrine; much less are we able to square the practice of yesterday with the theory of tomorrow. And whatever may be said of the needs and necessities of those who have so worthily preceded us, or of the broad strides education has taken, there can be no doubt that today, as never before, we are looking for the prophet to lead us, and more than ever before do we realize that the mighty dynamic changes in our industrial and social atmosphere demand a deeper and more significant interpretation be placed upon our

definition of education, and that the practices thereof be laid in
accordance with such interpretation.

Here and there the worth of a system is exemplified in the
life and achievement of a great soul.   More than four centuries
before Christ and upon the plains a short call from Rome, a product of the education of the day left his plow in the furrow and
with the sword of the soldier and the robe of the dictator, between sunset and sunset, saved the Roman army from defeat.
Then leaving power and glory and the acclaim of the multitude,
Cincinnatus returned to the occupation of his fathers.   Lincoln
at Gettysburg, Washington at Valley Forge, where—

> Dumb for himself, unless it was to God,
> But for his barefoot soldiers eloquent,

Mary A. Livermore and Julia Ward Howe, Florence Nightin-
gale in the Crimea, and Horace Mann in Massachusetts; as
teachers of men the work of these and countless others is clearly
traced upon the pages of history and reflected in the lives of our
fellows.

Often enough do we listen to the words of the philosopher on
the meaning of the school, to the ideal utterances of the theorist,
to the academic statements of the narrow-minded and conservative, and often enough do we condemn the results achieved in the
past as spiritless and formal.   What call, however, have we to
criticise the work of an Aristotle, or a Herbart, a Luther or an
Erasmus?   For has it not been written as much for the educa-
tionalist as for the money changers, "who shall ascend into the
hill of the Lord?"   And the answer: Not the rich, necessarily,
or the powerful or the gifted, but "he that hath clean hands and a
pure heart."

How difficult then to analyze the word or, work of another.
For Plato education must make only for spiritual growth, and
with him spiritual development had nothing in common with the
material world.   To think of the present was not to be tolerated,
for he tells us in the Republic that, "practical arts are degrading."
Hence all training must be of that ideal character that shall consider only a future state.   The philosophy of Plato here seems to
be narrowing in that too little is made of our everyday existence.

But as Putnam points out, it was after all Plato whose writings seem to have forecast the modern kindergarten and the doctrine of "learning to do by doing."

Aristotle, on the other hand, seems to be the warm humanist who plans to meet the requirements of everyday life, and who insists that perfect citizenship is the goal toward which education should tend. We gather from Aristotle's *Politics* that if a man prove virtuous in character, no further concern need be felt for his future. Nevertheless the practical, so-called, does not cover the whole of the Aristotelian philosophy. Note what he says: "To be always in quest of what is useful is not becoming to high-minded men and freemen." And in a study of other great minds, Socrates and Seneca, Agricola and Sturm, Ascham, Rabelais, Bacon, Comenius, Francke, Rousseau, Froebel, Speucer and Locke, all have agreed, and disagreed, and as yet no one has entirely erected the superstructure of the education needed today.

It is held by some that education is the reconstruction of experience. They say that neither preparation for life, nor information is the goal, and believe with Aristotle that to work toward an ultimate moral character simply is to stop short of the desired end. It is always necessary, I believe, in such undertaking as the one in which we are now engaged, to pause and to follow the lead of Daniel Webster by returning to the original point of departure, that we may be sure of having an established premise.

The question then is: For what does the school stand? What is education? Education, say some, is training for life, to which answer is made that it is more than a training for life; it is life itself. To meet such a requirement education should bring into action all the abilities of the pupil, or, as O'Shea puts it, the ideal attributes that exist *in potentia* in the human spirit, it should develop in him all essential qualities and virtues; it is to make him master of himself mentally, physically, and morally; it is to help him appreciate and value only the good and discard the relatively bad; it is to prepare him for more complete living; is, in short, the means by which he shall be enabled to take his place in the great world of life and action as a unit in a complete social order. And if it be true, as has been affirmed, that "to teach men how they may grow independently and for themselves is perhaps the greatest service that one man can do for another," then education should look toward teaching men how to best perform this service.

It seems to be plain that any education worthy the name, considers the present as well as the future of the individual, or, to put it in another way, considers the present, and hence the future, of the individual. Characters must be formed, not alone that ultimate good may be accomplished, but that the standards of society may be raised here and now. This brings us at once to the dual nature of our problem—the individual upon the one hand and society upon the other—and hence, the psychological and sociological elements are both to be considered. The relation of the individual to society gives us the sociological view, while the psychological aspects are determined by the relation of the individual to himself.

Society is made up of a group of individuals. The individual lives in society, is a part of society, is responsible to society, and helps to determine and mold the tone or character of the social atmosphere. Society, however, sets the standards, and the individual must conform, in great measure, to these standards as set. On the other hand, while being responsible, and owing duties, to society, the individual must demand something of himself as well. But while these two sets of duties, of individual to society and of individual to self, are distinct and may be segregated, the one from the other, there is no sharp line of demarcation between the two. That is, the one cannot be considered practically without the other, for what is best for the individual is best for society, and conversely what is for the best interests of society, will prove of greatest value to the individual.

Professor MacVannel points out that just as the individual is a unity whose life is in the process of making, of organization, so is he also a unity in, or an intrinsic part of, the larger unity of society which is in the process of organization as well. If society is to perpetuate and strengthen itself, and if the individual is to exist and prosper, the latter must, many times, merge his desires in the will of society, and to a greater or less degree forsake personal or selfish ends for the common well-being.

In the material world this dualism of psychological and sociological elements is noted. Society demands an article, brick it may be, or a dynamo, or a bucket. Society needs the article and thereby sets the standards. The *what* is the social phase of our problem. How to produce the article, to carry it over in the various processes of manufacture from the raw material to the completed state, to transport from place to place, the cheapest and most effective methods of advertising—these have to do with the psychological phase.

That the raw materials of the average present-day curriculum are not designed to touch deeply the sociological element in experience can readily be shown. The evolutionary process, the unfoldment of the child's powers, presupposes a widening of the child's experience—a growth from within, through the presentation of certain study materials. But the boy or girl, the product of the school, has little opportunity to react upon society. Or perhaps one might better say, the individual has not gained that which will enable him to react with profit upon society. Knowledge is *not* power, unless knowledge can be transformed into terms of power-reducing energy. The mere knowing a thing is not always significant in itself. The thing known must have some relation to the conditions, the needs, the desires, the life, of the society of which the individual is only one of the component parts. The facts of knowledge must be capable of application looking toward the satisfying of needs and the raising of standards, and the training of the individual must be such as to make possible the interpretation of such application.

But the question is here raised: How does it happen that the raw materials of which we have been speaking, the school studies, have not been such as to meet the sociological and psychological demands? Have the schoolmen of the past been blind to the interests of society? Has too little thought been used in considering the best development of the individual? Have we not held the lesson of mutual helpfulness to be a necessity? Are we prompted by unworthy ideals or basing our work upon principles that are of our own making?

According as we hold one or another view of the underlying principles of education and of the real province of the school do we translate the school studies into terms of value, and attribute to them relative worths. To some the school stands for culture, and the curriculum should be so ordered as to promote this culture side of the child's life. Some think rather in terms of discipline, and insist that school studies should make for this end. Others again would place information as the chief element to be considered. Shall the value of school studies, however, be found to exist within the studies themselves, or be determined by the nature of such studies? If society sets the standard, how can there be several possible values? With several standards set up, there is, as Dr. Dewey says, "no conception of any single unifying principle . . . the extent and way in which a study brings the pupil to consciousness of his social environment, and confers upon him the ability to interpret his own powers from the standpoint of their possibilities in social use, is the ultimate and unified standard."

It is, of course, unsafe to say that mathematics and the languages make for discipline chiefly, that the study of English brings culture, that history lends itself to the informational side of development. The fact is that, under the best conditions, mathematics is cultural and informational as well as disciplinary in value; the English group of studies may be made to cover as wide a field as mathematics and Latin, while history may bring as complete a development as any school subject. To say that one study makes for culture and another for discipline simply means that the standard for culture or for discipline comes from the individual, not from society. Culture, in the terms of our discussion, means possibilities for development, open-mindedness, honesty, the sense of service awakened, not merely varnish and veneer. Information implies knowledge to be sure, but knowledge that not only can be used, but that is carried over and made a part of the lives of others to the end that all are advantaged thereby. Discipline suggests, not only the analytic mind and the trained muscle, but the sympathetic soul and teachable spirit as well.

Method, too, is a determining element in the value of studies, for the compositive worth of any given subject-matter to the individual or to society is determined, in no small degree, by the manner of presentation. While it is true that subject-matter and method are not distinct, but exist as the two sides of experience, the psychological and the social, it remains to be said, however, that, for the practical purposes of the teacher and the school, it is eminently necessary that they be clearly distinguished, the one from the other. It has long been insisted by some, and assumed by others, that in a course of training, for example, the method was of chief concern; that if the teacher in embryo could secure a knowledge of method, and understanding of how to do the given thing, that a knowledge of subject-matter itself, of the definite facts connected with the particular line of work, could be somehow grasped at a later time. The fallacy of this view is apparent to all who consent for a moment seriously to consider the issues involved. How utterly inconsistent to endeavor to formulate a method, or to act intelligently under one, until a knowledge is had of that upon which method is based. Many of our normal schools have this lesson yet to learn and educational schools the country over, both elementary and secondary in character, would do well to select the subject-matter of the curriculum with more care than has been manifest in the past. Indeed, the necessity for a knowledge of subject-matter before training or method work is attempted is one of the strongest possible arguments in favor of normal and professional schools admitting as students only those who have had a thorough, previous academic training.

Once subject-matter has been selected in any school, the work should be made more intensive than we now find it—more intensive from the standpoint of thought-values, and also from the side of execution.

All this does not in any manner whatsoever contradict what has been said previously regarding thought and expression being paramount. It simply means that a knowledge at first hand of

things that have a valid place in society, not only for the future
but in the present, is to be the first essential. It means, as Doctor Dewey tells us, that "The present has its claims. It is in
education, if anywhere, that the claims of the present should be
controlling;" and this in accord with the words of President Butler: "Education is the adjustment of the individual to the spiritual possessions of the race." It means what Browning means
when he says:

> Let things be—not seem,
> I counsel rather, do and nowise dream!
> Earth's young significance is all to learn;
> The dead Greek lore lies buried in the Urn,
> Where he who seeks fire finds ashes.

And self-control, leadership, responsibility. It is the duty of
the school to undertake the task of inculcating in its pupils these
elements so essential to success? Must the time be placed and
the thought of education be centered upon these factors, when
it might be troubling itself with the real facts of knowledge?
The question is put only to have one answer returned. What
of the city where the members of the police number as great as
the teachers engaged in the schools, of the houses of correction,
of the institutions of reform, the prisons, the courts of justice,
and to a lesser extent the hospitals, asylums, and homes for the
unfortunate and distressed? Lack of self-control, inability properly to interpret the demands of society or to perform the duties,
having learned them, unstableness in character, to the end that
the right is lost sight of and the stronger powers of leadership
in others prevail. Could the school teach effectively the lesson
of self-control, she need have little fear of results when the product of her system is thrown among the currents of the world.
And here the tact and ability of the teacher shows itself. It
is the teacher who, at his best, stands between the child and the
various experiences which await him. The teacher, from his
larger store of knowledge, directs the child toward, and introduces him to, these forms of experience which are especially
adapted to bring out and develop the element of control, pointing the way that the pupil may, in the *shortest possible time* and

with the *least expenditure of misdirected energy,* adjust himself to his environment.

Rigid traditionalism, extreme rulings, and deeply-furrowed acceptances of the past do not lend themselves to initiative, to open-mindedness, to leadership, to self-control. What would have been the achievements of a Michael Angelo or a Raphael, a Wagner or a Beethoven, a Goethe or an Emerson, a Franklin or a Newton, a Gladstone or a Garrison, had these minds not felt free to reach forth in any direction, free to accept all the inspiration that came to them from the past, free to ignore all the narrowing influences so apparent in the life and work of most of us, free to express themselves naturally and clearly and without restraint?

Alfred Russell Wallace, in his lectures and essays on *Natural Theology and Ethics,* gives us as clear a statement of the ideal of an education that will educate as could well be formulated. He says:

> Mental health and wealth do not depend upon a mere accumulation of single facts, but on solid ideas of what life is and ought to be, and what the world around us really means; it does not lie in confinement to a fragmentary life, limited in its range of view, and moving forever in the same monotonous routine, but in a large and free scope of experience; nor does it lie in the degree of variety and intensity to which we can bring our sensations and aspirations, but in acquiring the proper estimate of values, in calming the turmoil of temper and gaining at once sweetness and light, that gentle reasonableness which, though not less free to receive impressions than in the beginning of life, is at the same time matured by experience to a wiser judgment of their comparative worth. The true ideal of a fully developed personality does not consist merely in a keen intellectual acumen, nor in an intense but inactive susceptibility to the moods of happy feeling, nor in a perpetual unresting activity; it involves a balance of all these elements,

and this experience, these forces that play backward and forward, in school and out, touching the pupil in his every occupation; shall we not consider those that have the direct bearing upon his present and that can be appreciated by him, rather than attempt to introduce him to vague and indefinite elements? As I stood, some weeks since, beside the rude dwellings of a simple people in a western desert and watched the natives as they worked at rug weaving or in fashioning the basket, I recalled the question put to one of these people by an eastern woman: "Isn't it too bad," said she, "that you live so far away?" And the native woman returned a wondering glance as she replied, "I don't live far away, I live right here." While the work of the school must be such as to fit those who form the school community to adjust themselves to the society in which they individually may find themselves, it must not forget that the child can interpret only in the light of present experiences.

THE SPEAR

A VIKING SONG

Words and melody by the pupils of the Fifth school year, the University
Elementary School.

1. I made me a spear and called her Foe's Fear, I made her
2. A boat I made, too, I made her all true, I paint - ed her

strong, with a keen, sharp edge; She sings as she flies, "I am
red, with a fierce drag-on head; The waves dash her sides as

thirst - y," she says, So come, my foe, and fight.....
on - ward she strides; Go scare my foe a - way.....

EDITORIAL NOTES

It is told of Horace Mann that he walked into the office of a friend in Boston one day and asked him if he "wished to secure the highest seat in the kingdom of heaven; if so," he continued, "you may have it for fifteen hundred dollars." This was the sum needed by Mr. Mann to enable him to purchase a building at Lexington in which he wished to start a normal school. The friend produced the money and the opening of the school with three pupils on July 3, 1839, marked an important epoch in education in the United States. History, however, does not record that Mr. Mann was able to redeem the pledge made to his friend.

A Mortgage on Paradise

Since that time, normal-school training has passed through a number of important stages that correspond to certain epochs in our educational growth. At first it was inevitable that the normal schools should be largely academic. Especially in sections of the country where there were but few or no academies, and before high schools were generally established, the normal schools were compelled to assume the responsibility for non-professional work of a scholastic character. Having their origin in the pre-laboratory age, and their work, therefore, being exceedingly bookish, it was but natural, as the professional end of the curriculum gradually developed, that it, too, should be of a similar kind. It was abstract and theoretical, devoting much attention to detailed methods of teaching subject-matter.

Stages of Normal Training

No other agency has operated so powerfully as the normal school to stimulate general interest in popular education, and nothing else has done so much to elevate the intelligence of the public as to the necessity of having teachers specially trained for their profession. The time has come, however, when the normal schools and the schools of education must provide a new type of training. Academic training has been amply provided for and it must be, and hereafter it will be, assumed. The past generation has done practically all

New Type of Training

40

that need be done to place within easy reach of every intelligent teacher whatever it is necessary to know concerning special methods. Within the same period the subjects of psychology and child-study have been thoroughly worked over, and the results have been fully and clearly presented. It is well nigh impossible now to find a teacher who is not an interested student in these subjects and who does not have as a result a proper attitude toward his pupils and his work. This part of the teacher's training, hereafter, will not become of lesser importance, but it will be more and more assumed as a preliminary to the newer training which the public is now demanding. That the times are

New Type of Teacher ripe for a higher type of trained teacher and for a more thoroughly practical kind of professional training is evidenced by the following list of questions which was sent to me recently by a gentleman just elected to the school board in a suburb of Chicago. That community is evidently trying to find out something about educational values, and this officer made his appeal to expert teachers who might be supposed to be best prepared to make satisfactory answer. The questions are as follows:

1. Would you consider manual training, properly taught and

A Teacher's Examination properly related, as important to the best results in other subjects, or as something which might be omitted without detriment to the rest of the work?

2. Suggest briefly, and in a way intelligible to a layman, your idea of the function of manual training in the curriculum.

3. Has the fact that the country child deals with all sorts of concrete things anything to do with his superiority over the city child in filling important positions? Is manual training any substitute for the experience?

4. If writing, spelling, etc., seemed below par, would you think that the remedy might be looked for in the omission of manual training and the devotion of the time gained to drill in those subjects?

5. Would the fact that a large proportion of the pupils is from well-to-do families and that they do not have occasion to work with their hands, or do not expect to have occupations

requiring manual skill, have any bearing on the need of manual training in the schools?

6. Would you advise the introduction of domestic science into our schools?

7. Are public kindergartens desirable as a part of the school system?

These questions show distinctly what is needed in the teacher. IT IS POWER TO TEACH THE PUBLIC. The ability to teach the children henceforth will be assumed. Hitherto the people have passively submitted to whatever the teachers had to offer; now they have become sufficiently aroused to demand something like a demonstration. That demonstration is the main thing, therefore, which teachers in training must prepare for. That is why we need new curricula in our normal schools, and schools of education. There is not one in existence that gives its pupils half a chance to prepare for such an examination as that set in the foregoing questions. If this is doubted, try the questions on any class of graduating teachers you please; not one in ten nor twenty will be able to convince that community beforehand that it needs either him or his work. These are questions that no mere specialist in manual training can answer.

The new type of training will not be found in a further elaboration and intensification of book study and theoretical discussion; nor will it appear in a further development of specialization as that is now commonly understood. It will be based upon actual "field work" carried on in the community at large. That is, the teachers in training must study, in accordance with a plan analogous to that adopted in a science laboratory, the needs of a community as they manifest themselves in its daily life; they must, in fact, in some way become actual participants in that life. Whereas, heretofore, the school has been considered a part of the community, it is now necessary to make the community a part of the school. No other kind of training will ever equip prospective teachers to answer questions which the public is now asking. The school must go into the service of the community more directly, and the community must open itself up more freely to whatever service the school can render.

A New
Curriculum

Up to the present time the training schools for teachers are all modeled upon the plan and after the ideals of the older educa-

The School as tional institutions of an academic type, and these, **a Social** in their turn, grew out of the cloister. Most of our **Settlement** schools still hark back occasionally to the times when knowledge was chained to the desk of a priest, out of reach of the common people. The training schools for teachers, on the contrary, should be modeled rather upon the plan of the so-called social settlement, and the ideals of the teacher must become more nearly allied to those of the settlement worker. It is a huge mistake to suppose that the chief function of a "settlement" is to furnish slum districts with bath tubs, and that the principles underlying settlement work apply only to the socially submerged. There is as much real need in Hyde Park as there is in the Ghetto for the application of "settlement" principles to social and industrial life in the education of the children. Every school should be so organized as to draw the people together for the purposes of work, of study, and of recreation, as the public library now attracts people who wish to read. To this end, the studios, the workrooms, the laboratories, and the libraries of the schools should be open under the supervision of the teachers, as public libraries are under librarians, to suit the convenience of the people. The settlements in Chicago, following the leadership of Jane Addams, Mary McDowell, and a few others, are fair working-models of what our public schools should be in their relations to the people. A training school for teachers that could place its prospective graduates for at least a year in such intimate relations with community life as the settlements afford would give them the best possible preparation for undertaking with the people the joint task of educating the children. This does not mean, of course, that such training can be acquired only in the reeking and congested districts of the cities. Every locality in city, village, and country, should offer some opportunity for the practical training of teachers in the science and art of working with people. Until this art is thoroughly learned; until the social, the industrial, and the so-called educational interests of the community are organized as a single unity the education of the children will always be defective.

This kind of preliminary preparation for teaching would do much to solve the vexed question as to how teachers are to grow **Training of** in their work after they have become settled in their **Teachers in** profession. Every school should be a center for **Work** settlement work of the best type, and the life of the teacher should, and, under such conditions of service, would, naturally expand with the growth of the community. The greatest objection to the teacher's profession, at present, is that he is so hopelessly far removed from doing those things that the community is crying out to have done. His usefulness to the state at present is purely hypothetical. He may do some good in the world, but he can rarely claim the output. Righteous men and women do grow up on the earth, but heredity and every form of accident known in human development impudently filch from the schoolmaster the credit of their virtue. When we get down to the root of the matter, we shall find that it is this fact, more than the salary question, more than that of woman rule, more than all other causes combined, that contributes most to drive self-respecting men and women from **Teacher Must** the teachers' ranks. To go through a long course **Be a Citizen** of training, ostensibly for public service, only to find that the walls of the schoolroom are to bar him forever from the normal activities of a citizen interested in public life is more than self-respecting human beings in this day will tolerate. The schoolmaster's profession is still dominated by educational traditions of the Middle Ages, when the teacher was a monk who kept himself away from the affairs of the world as things unholy, and when the service of the state was chiefly in the care of the soldiers. No such division of function and shifting of responsibility can now exist. The teacher should take a leader's part in the debate of every question that relates to human welfare. It is only by the most active participation in public affairs that he can keep himself in proper training for the task of teaching the people's children. To give himself and the school over solely, or even mostly, to the petty routine of teaching reading, writing, and ciphering, or the mere details of subject-matter, is to devote himself and his institution to work that can be done almost equally well without either the teacher or the school.

When the teacher becomes a direct participant in the public service, he will then be measured and his place will be established

Promotion of Teachers

according to the methods and standards that are always employed in determining values in human character. When he is once placed in a position of responsibility toward the community, a responsibility that shows itself in some form that the public can understand, then he will take his place according to the law of moral gravitation. The teacher must have the opportunity and then he must be required to win his way to public recognition as every other citizen must do. The various promotion schemes now in vogue are mostly but weak makeshifts, prepared to fit unnatural and archaic conditions. The application of the marking system to the gradation of teachers as a means of fixing salaries has proven itself time and again to be just as vicious in its results as it is when applied to

Marking System

the gradation of pupils. Taking all things into account it possesses but little advantage over a system of grading based upon height, or color of the hair. It is equally factitious and unnatural to base salary or position upon length of service alone, that is, merely upon one's ability to draw his breath; for verily, there be many poor and useless teachers who are leather-lunged. When a physician loses too many patients, he is not deprived of his practice because somebody marks him forty-nine per cent.; and when a lawyer's practice falls away it is not because someone has graded him sixty-three—it is moral gravitation that gradually lowers these several servants of the public out of sight. We must come to the same thing with the teachers. No amount of politics or pull will make a man employ a physician or a lawyer whom he believes to be untrustworthy. When the responsibility of the teacher's place in the public service is equally well established, no more will politics or pull get votes for the incompetent teacher. *Moral gravitation is the thing.* If the teaching force were once brought under its sway, it would more quickly and more thoroughly purge the sys-

Law the Worthless Teacher's Opportunity!

tem of incompetents—by exclusion and by general improvement—than any system of legislation that could be devised. The one and only chance that a worthless teacher has for staying in the profession is that which is afforded him by some law that was placed on the statute books to exclude him. He merely tricks the law and is thereafter safe.

It is a fact of paramount importance which both the public and teachers are apt to overlook, that, in the end, it is of the most vital interest to the teachers themselves that there shall be not only some adequate and fair means of recognizing merit, and of estimating and suitably rewarding actual growing worth, but that there shall be, also, an equally effective plan for barring out those who are unprepared and for purging the school system of incompetent teachers. In the heat of discussion, the public and school authorities sometimes act as though, in their efforts to get rid of incompetent teachers, they cannot count upon the sympathy, much less the active support, of the teaching force. There are teachers, too, whose general behavior may seem to warrant this conclusion. But when in a calm and reasonable frame of mind all parties know that this is not so—that at this particular point there is a mutual interest of greatest import. When proper opportunity is given, therefore, the teachers may be fully relied upon to help work out some plan which will make their profession one that is practically self-purifying. If the responsibility for this were placed upon the teachers, it would at once key up the moral tone of the profession an octave above what it is today or what it ever has been. That is the way the responsibility for the character of the professions works in those of law and medicine. The most implacable foes of poor lawyers and physicians are the members of those professions who are reputable and worthy. The lawyers finally determine who shall be members of the bar, and the physicians determine who shall practice medicine. The responsibility for protecting the public against fraud rests practically upon the professions themselves. The teachers are in no wise so peculiar a people that they cannot or will not take care of their profession in a similar manner, when they have a chance to do so. Mistakes and abuses will occur; but these will be many times outweighed by the moral effect upon the teachers of being compelled to assume the responsibility for the character and work of their brethren.

Mutual Interest of Teachers and Public

What the details of such a plan will be must be left to the gradual processes of evolution to determine. It must be anchored **Plan Must** in some way, however, to a few fundamental condi-**Evolve from** tions: There must be a constantly rising standard **Experience** of training, which shall be modified to meet the growing demands of the community. This must be required of teachers before being allowed to enter the profession. The time is ripe for a great advance in this direction. There must be increased opportunities for the school to work out under the direction of the teacher a more intimate relationship with the life of the community. In this way, everyone will be able to get directly at the worth of the teacher. And, finally, there must be a due regard for length of service.

The encouraging feature in the present confusion of educational debate is that the teachers are commencing to think. They have been out of proper relation to the public all these long years, and now they are beginning to realize it. If they will hold steadfastly to the main question at issue until their true position is clearly defined in the public mind, most of the petty annoyances that now dog their footsteps will disappear.

W. S. J.

BOOK REVIEWS

School Days of the Fifties: A True Story with Some Untrue Names of Persons and Places. With an Appendix containing an Autobiographical Sketch of Francis Wayland Parker. By WILLIAM M. GIFFIN. Chicago: A. Flanagan Co. Pp. 137.

This little book gives a graphic pen picture of our public schools as Mr. Giffin knew them in his boyhood "in the old stone schoolhouse in northern New York, near the banks of the beautiful St. Lawrence." It is an interesting story, involving incidentally, an analysis of the motives and methods of teachers, good and bad, as teachers were before they had been reached by the transforming power of normal-school training. The book is reminiscent in style and abounds in anecdote and incident which show forth the thoughts and doings of lively boys and girls whose generally belligerent attitude toward teacher and school worked itself out in innumerable pranks. Mr. Giffin throws this picture of his youthful training up strongly against a background of the principles of teaching, and shows that many of the most serious difficulties of his early days might have been avoided if his teachers had been more careful students of childhood and less concerned with the intricacies of dry subject-matter.

The autobiographical sketch of Colonel Parker gives an interesting glimpse of the schools at a still earlier period. The book is rich in suggestion and serves more than to amuse; it furnishes to the serious-minded teacher much food for reflection.

WILBUR S. JACKMAN

VOLUME VII   NUMBER 2

THE ELEMENTARY SCHOOL TEACHER

OCTOBER, 1906

EDUCATION OF WOMEN IN GERMANY

RECCA DORMEYER

Principal of the Preparatory and Collegiate School, Chicago

One of the characteristic features of the nineteenth century was the constant progress in the education of women; and it still continues. Women are better instructed, and at the same time play a more important part in instruction. The history of education in this century will be notable for the great number of women who were educators—some real philosophers and distinguished writers, and others enthusiastic teachers.

There is no country where pedagogy has received a more philosophical and a higher development than in Germany. The German philosophers, Kant, Fichte, Schlegel, Schleiermacher, Herbart, Benecke, and Jean Paul, associated the theory of education with their speculations on human nature; even the great poets, Lessing, Herder, Goethe, and Schiller, have contributed through certain grand ideas to the construction of a science of education.

In the nineteenth century Germany took part in the great movement toward a more liberal education for women. There is no more an inclination toward the opinions of the over-courteous moralist, Joubert, who said: "Nothing too earthly or too material ought to employ young ladies—only delicate material should busy their hands. They resemble their imagination, and like it should touch only the surface of things."

Pestalozzi, Schlegel, Schleiermacher, and Jean Paul Levana stand for a higher and more serious education for women, but they conclude that their training should be for their own interests, their nature, and their proper destination—more a domestic education than for entering a public arena; they wish woman to remain woman. Bettie Gleim is the first who demands for girls, as well as boys, a public education; but she finds no general sympathy. Neverthless, it is considered necessary that women should be better instructed. The reasons given for it in the convention in Weimar in 1875 were:

1. In order that they may be able properly to raise their children, of whom they are the natural instructors.

2. In order that they may be the fit companions of their husbands—that they may feel an interest in their pursuits and participate in their life—such being a condition of conjugal happiness.

3. In order that they may not quench by their ignorance that inspiration of heart and mind which previous studies have developed in their husbands, but that they may nourish this flame by conversation and reading in common.

In the decree of 1875 for the higher girls' schools, which had been left until then to the management of private enterprise, ornamental and decorative elements predominated completely over that of use. Women should become pictures of a certain gorgeous attractiveness—not white sunlight, but a kind of rose-pink, artificial bedizement. It is true that woman is the companion of man upon earth, yet she exists also on her own account. She needs above all an education which prepares for direct self-preservation —not numerous accomplishments for the purpose of making conquests. It is a question of the true measure of value of knowledge to herself—not its effects on a husband. It is a question of not catching the shadow and losing the substance. In 1887 a petition was sent in from several women's clubs which had sprung into life, headed by H. Lange, saying that by the multilateral of the subjects of studies a solid education would be impossible, and only a superficial knowledge could be acquired. The first consideration would be to give women, not an ornamental domestic education, but a preparation for the vocation of life. Female educators, with Helene Lange and Luise Buchner as leaders, demanded a larger field in teaching and the instruction of the higher grades of girls' schools, which had until then been entirely in the hands of men who followed the teaching of Rousseau and polished the mentality and manners of girls, to the end, that they might become companions for husbands. The granting of the petition was partly due to the Victoria Lyceum in Berlin, an institute which since 1868 had been devoted to the accomplishments of women. In 1888 special scientific studies for teachers were added, and, with the permission of the *Kultusministerium*, female teachers who had been employed in the higher girls' schools for at least five years passed after a three years' course the examinations for principals. Step by step they fought their way; in vain men urged that female teachers for the higher grades were neither necessary, nor desirable, nor worthy to be admitted. The ice was broken, and there was no holding back any more. It had been easy enough to suppress the single woman; the women united had become a force. In 1894 the *Kultusministerium* reformed the *Höhere Töchterschule,* and at the same time the normal school, which had been in existence since 1875, was enlarged from a two- to a three-year course. In several universities preparatory courses were arranged, extending to six semesters, for principals' examinations.

Plato based his recommendations of equal education of men and women on equality of civil functions; in modern thought it is the conception of equal rights and of equal abilities that tends to prescribe the same course of intellectual training for both sexes. I have my doubts of its being advisable to pursue entirely the same course of studies. At all events, I am opposed to coeducation after the age of fourteen. While girls are endowed with a quick intelligence, while they divine and see more quickly than boys—Bronson Alcott says, "Divination seems heightened to its highest power in woman"—they lack in continuity and depth of thought. Prolonged attention wearies them; they are too mobile to be profound. There is no reason why they should have a less serious education than boys; but the methods employed ought to be different. Then, again, the period from fourteen to twenty years of age should be entirely given to study; but naturally the young man thinks more of the roguish eyes and laughing lips he sees at his side than of his mathematical formulas; his Latin might suffer less. He will without doubt be sure of his *amo, amas, amat,* and the girl cannot help to sympathize with the poor lad, and sighs *amemus.* Too early marriages are often the result; boys of twenty or still younger spoil their prospects in life by marrying, and in most cases, after a short time, they conjugate the past *amavi.*

Like mushrooms, teachers' associations have sprung up, many teachers' conventions have been held, and the general German teachers' association numbers now seventeen thousand members. They not only extend their arm all over the fatherland, but also reach into foreign countries. In England there is a German teachers' association, under the leadership of Helene Aldermann, and one in France, under the leadership of Miss Schliemann. It is their purpose to watch the interests of teachers and help them in every way—those who either wish to perfect themselves in foreign languages, or who come as teachers of German only. In London a home and sanitarium are connected with the association. In the year 1900 a new law for teachers' examinations was passed, and philosophy was added as a compulsory study. In 1889 was founded the first college—*Realgymnasium*—for girls, which was changed in 1893 by Helene Lange, its principal, into a *Gymnasium* preparing students in a four-year course for the university. This college corresponds to the collegiate course of four years, resulting in the conferring of the degree of A.B., in Chicago, Yale, Harvard, and Cornell universities. With the fifth year the conferring of the German universities begins.

With this the opening for women in the study of medicine and similar sciences was accomplished. Soon followed others and there are now fifteen colleges in Germany with a four- to a six-year course. They are in Berlin, Karlsruhe, Leipzig, Hanover, Königsberg, Stuttgart, Breslau, Munich, Hamburg, Frankfort, Cologne, Mannheim. In Prussia women provided with the certificate are admitted to hear lectures but are not matriculated as in other states.

Although nothing hinders German girls from entering universities, yet, since they are inclined more by nature for domestic life, or since German fathers are still opposed to that kind of education for girls, only a small percentage take advantage of it. Until 1903 there were only 122 graduates from the colleges, while from the normal schools there graduate yearly a large number without becoming teachers; which proves that the study of modern languages is preferred by women to the study of ancient, which is the greatest difference between the colleges and the normal schools. In Baden, Würtemberg, and Hessen many institutions have coeducation.

Compulsory education begins at the age of six and continues to the age of fourteeen. Negligent parents are liable to punishment by fines or even by imprisonment. There are five grades of instruction for girls, so that each one has the opportunity to receive the education adapted to her need:

1. Public schools, without charge for tuition—*Volksschule.*

2. Manual-training schools, also free—*Fortbildungs- und Haushaltungsunterricht.*

3. Public middle schools, where tuition is charged, and private schools—both called *Höhere Töchterschule.*

4. Normal schools—*Seminar.*

5. Colleges for girls—*Gymnasium.*

Both public and private schools are under the supervision of the state, and both receive from the state a yearly allowance.

In Prussia there are 36,138 free public schools, attended by five million children; the cost is $67,480,000 annually. Boys and girls receive the same instruction. They are attended by the children of the working classes, who receive not only free books, but are fed and clothed also if necessary. A bun and hot milk are provided for those who have had no breakfast at home before lessons begin.

Not more than forty pupils are permitted in one room. They have eight grades, and the instruction might be compared with the grammar schools in America. The curriculum is: reading, arithmetic, composition, grammar, religion, geography, German history, natural science, drawing, singing, gymnastics, and needlework for girls.

Connected with the *Volksschule* is the manual-training school for girls of from fourteen to sixteen years, where the instruction acquired is strengthened and completed, but principally domestic economy, cooking, washing, ironing, and serving are taught, This is compulsory only in about seven German states. In Prussia, Bavaria, and Würtemberg it depends on the parents if they will send their children after their fourteenth year.

In Prussia there are 213 higher public schools, attended by 72,932 girls. Connected with these schools are 3,347 male and 6,200 female teachers. This gives about 15 pupilss to every teacher. The teachers' salaries are: for male principals, $1,360; for female, principals, $550; for male teachers, $800; for female teachers, $460. The tuition of the higher public schools ranges from $30 to $50 yearly; for the private schools, from $50 to $100. The cost of conducting the higher public schools for girls is $2,098,230 annually, of which $1,251,950 is paid by tuition.

The *Höhere Töchterschule* adds to the curriculum of the *Volksschule:* literature, ancient and general history, rhetoric, geometry, French for seven years, and English for four years. The course is ten years for pupils from six to sixteen years of age, but, considering that Saturday is a school day—which adds two years—and that the yearly vacations are one month shorter —which adds another year—there are in reality thirteen American school years. This instruction might be compared with the education through high schools except that the membership in rooms being much smaller and the curriculum having been pursued throughout the school course, it is more individual and has more depth. The immediate object of the teaching of foreign languages is to enable the pupil to understand the easier French and English writers, to grasp easily the meaning when the languages are spoken, and to use them with some facility both orally and in writing when they are applied to the simpler forms of everyday intercourse. The more indirect aim of the teaching is that of introducing the pupils to an appreciation, as far as possible, of their mental development, and of the manners and customs of the two foreign nations named. Reading occupies a central position during the whole course. Grammar is not taught

systematically from the beginning, but is deduced from the read.
ing and gradually built up from concrete observations. Prac.
tice in speaking plays a great part in this course. German
history is taught for three years; ancient and general history, for
two years each; geography, for seven years. Physiography forms
an important part of the course. Natural sciences are taught for
six years; zoölogy and botany, for four; physics and chemistry,
for two years. In arithmetic special stress is laid on the "oral."
Literature and composition are regarded as of importance.

1. The *Seminar* is connected with the *Höhere Töchterschule,* and prepares girls from sixteen to nineteen for teachers'
examinations. These examinations are about the same as those
in the United States, with the difference that in the normal school
in Germany neither Latin nor Greek is taught, but French has
been taught for ten years and English for seven years, and both
languages are mastered and familiar. The *Gymnasium* is also
connected with the higher girls' school; it prepares girls from
fifteen to nineteen years for the university.

2. Girls who do not go to normal school or to college finish
their education mostly in a pension away from home, either in
Germany or in a foreign country. In these boarding-schools are
from ten to twenty girls who receive lessons from special teachers.

Education is now almost definitely systematized in Germany.
There have been vigorous efforts toward a rational pedagogy—
toward the science of education which, as Virchow says, "ought
forever to proscribe the gropings of an ignorant education whose
experiments are ever to be gone over anew." We live in a world
where much is to be done and little is to be known. A notable
step has been made to settle the important question of the end
and the means—what subjects of study and instruction shall be
chosen, and by what method the child can be taught rapidly and
well. The object is to teach as completely as possible the knowledge that is best adapted to develop individual and social life;
there is a dislike for glancing at subjects, for painting and tattoo-
ing the girls' schools with a little Latin and Greek, because they
form a part of the education of a gentleman. Boys study Latin
for nine years, eight hours each week, having about nine thousand

lessons altogether; in girls' schools it is considered more profitable to devote this time to modern languages. The comparative merits of classics are also revived in boys' schools; permission to enter the university is given to boys from the *Realgymnasium*, where no Greek is taught and less time given to Latin.

The education that comes through amusement dissipates thought. Labor of some sort is one of the great aids of nature; the mind of the child ought to accustom itself to the labor of study. You will teach a multitude of things to a child by means of pictures, but you will not teach him to study. Kant's idea of education for training, culture, and disciplining the mind, as distinguished from an education whose only aim is to impart knowledge, received recognition in Germany. Imagination is cultivated to a high degree. Mythological history and sacred history are taught before history proper, because their legendary and fabulous character offers a particular attraction to the child's imagination.

A very important factor in school life is discipline. There is a chaotic state of opinion and practice relative to government. Richter writes:

If a secret variance of a large class of ordinary fathers were brought to light and laid down as a plan for studies of a moral education, they would run somewhat after this fashion. In the first hour, pure morality must be read to the child; in the second, the chief matter is that you should succeed in the world; in the third, do you not see that your fathers do so and so; in the fourth, you are little and this is only for grown-up people; in the fifth, the eternal determines the worth of a man, therefore rather suffer injustice; in the sixth, but defend yourself bravely if anyone attacks you. Changing his morals during the twelve hours of the day, the father will never notice the instability of this twisted convex-concave mirror. As to the mother, she is neither like him nor yet like that harlequin who came on to the stage with a bundle of papers under each arm and answered, to the inquiry as to what he had under his right arm, "Orders," and as to what he has under his left arm, "Counter-orders;" but she might be much better compared to a giant who has a hundred arms and a bundle of papers under each.

The lesson drawn from this is: Do not lack consistency in discipline. There is no lack of consistency in German discipline. There is no lack of consistency in German schools. When the teacher commands, he does it with decision. The same offense is treated with like severity to all. But Richter says also: "The best rule in politics is said to be *pas trop gouverner.*" This is also true in education; and there is the rub in German schools. German children go to school because it is a duty, and because the German mind naturally is athirst for knowledge. American children go to school because it is a pleasure. Why? In America discipline is more adapted to produce a self-governing being than a being to be governed by others. The German teacher is too much of a passionless instrument; we must love children in order to know them, and we divine less by the intelligence than by the heart. The German teacher is too much of a pedant—he sits too high on a throne. Kant's book *Moral Catechism* is still followed too little. Kant wants to substitute in a child the fear of his own conscience for that of men and divine punishment, inward dignity for the opinion of others, the value of actions for the value of words.

In America I find that clandestinely copying from other pupils and deceiving teachers are considered mean and dishonorable acts not worthy of a gentleman or a lady. In Germany to pin the lesson which ought to be recited by heart on the back of the pupil in front, to read it from a handkerchief or cuff, to copy right and left, are considered perfectly proper. They do not deceive a friend, but only get even with a teacher. But worse than this is inconsistency, or the permission of rudeness and disobedience from pupils to teachers; better even is a barbarous form of government, carried out consistently, than a civil one, inconsistently. I hope this drawback will soon be removed. German teachers will find that they may descend from their throne, share the joys and little troubles of their pupils and be friends to them, without losing their authority. The more we study the body and the mind, the more we find both to be governed, not by, but according to, laws such as we observe in the larger universe.

The day has gone by for physically delicate women; this age demands Hebes and young Venuses with ample waists and veritable muscles. To procure them, public and private schools furnish playgrounds, and there is a fair share of time for out-of-door games and a recognition of them as needful. Germans always liked to produce a robust woman; they are somewhat like Spartans; they are hardened to all kinds of weather. Most girls not only walk to and from school, but also daily take at least a one-hour's regular walk in the park. Robust health and abundant vigor are not considered plebeian. German girls are well known for their red cheeks and healthy color. They are fond of activities in sport, and gymnastics are given by special teachers. Germans are "early birds." "Morgenstunde hat Gold in Munde!" Boys' schools are from seven to one o'clock; girls', from eight to one. Thus there is given the children plenty of time in the afternon for home work, music lessons, and at least from one to three hours for out-of-door games.

A great error—coloring, or rather discoloring, the minds of the higher and lower classes—has sown wide dissension and wider misfortune through the society of modern days; this error is the misinterpretation of the words "woman's rights." They do not mean, as many think, that women want to be less effeminate. The fact that there are some loud and bold women has nothing to do with "woman's rights," which do not mean vulgar assumption. Having opened a wider scope than home is not inconsistent with her cultivating the characteristics naturally expected in womanhood—a pleasant temper, a cheerful disposition, and the ability of making a lovely home. It does not take the charm from femininity if she should be quick to seize an opportunity and shrewd to find a point of vantage. If circumstances call her out into the fight for bread and butter, let her be prepared to rank with men and make ever so fine a name for herself in whatever vocation she chooses; it need not detract one whit from her womanliness, provided she keeps herself unsullied of soul and and tender of heart. German men do not respect rude or noisy women—nor do you. Girls should be trained to be jolly, warmhearted, impulsive, and independent; they should not bluster, but be quiet-voiced; they should be, in the orchestra of human life, a flute, not a trombone. Robert Browning gave, with one stroke of his pen, the most adorable portrait of a woman when he wrote of the beautiful Evelyn Hope: "God made her of spirit, fire, and dew."

THE NEW VOYAGE OF THE INNOCENTS

KATHERINE ELSIE CHAPMAN

One of the Innocents

[NOTE.—A group of Chicago people, some of them students of the University of Chicago, are spending three months in Paris this summer studying the French language. These students are under the guidance of Mlle. Lorley A. Ashléman, teacher of French in the University Elementary School of the School of Education. After a description of their voyage, which the want of space prevents printing here, Miss Chapman gives the following account of their studies.—EDITOR.]

Our final destination was the *pensionnat* of Madame Fauconnet at Fontenay-sous-Bois, a beautiful suburb of Paris which is, in fact, what its name indicates, a village by a wood. We reached our new home by omnibus. As we rambled and jolted past the old wall of Paris and struck out into the open country, with trunk, suitcase, handgrip, and bandbox piled atop, with the dames packed inside like herring until their voluminous drapery overflowed, and with the most aspiring maiden of the party perched aloft by the driver, we must have looked truly unique and distinctively American, judging by the wild-eyed astonishment of the natives. One very personable Frenchman stopped by the side of his spouse and stared after us until our plethoric vehicle vanished in the distance.

It was a warm, weary, dusty, doubting company which reached the *pensionnat* at seven-thirty in the evening. The first glance at our haven revealed nothing but a lofty iron fence shrouded in impenetrable foliage, and a tall roof arising amid the trees. But the broad iron gate stood wide open, and it was but a moment before our doubts and fears were dispelled by as warm and friendly a welcome, accompanied by as true an American handshake, as ever. enlivened the heart of a traveler. When Madame Fauconnet led us into the salon, and soon after into the *salle-à-manger* to an abundant dinner served with true French grace, we began pleasantly to realize that we were at last in France.

And here in this lovely retreat, amid these idyllic surroundings, amid conditions as perfect as could be found upon earth, the Chicago University Innocents are pursuing their various lines of study, and hoping to pass their examinations in three majors in the autumn. Refined and cultured French is the only language spoken around them. The beautiful garden, with its perfectly kept walks and full-blooming flower-beds, furnishes a daily rendezvous for study and recitation. Beneath the foliage, near the vine-clad fence, we sit at the little round tables, or traverse the pebbled *place* and imagine how naturally the peripatetic school of philosophers might have fallen into such deep contemplation and evolved such perfect systems of thought in surroundings like ours. And, moreover, the *bois* itself extends almost up to the garden, where, in shady retreat, the disciples may wander, book in hand, surrounded by shade cool and deep, and stillness so profound that thought may not only peep through her casement, but come out and walk, unmolested by the reacting currents of the world. Here the soul may expand her wings. Food for both is not lacking in the instruction presented. Besides the daily review in the principles and construction of the language, two hours daily are devoted to lectures by eminent scholars of Paris. Mr. Schrader, well known in America as professor of geography in the École d'Anthropologie, and officer of the Legion of Honor, speaks upon geography, especially in its relation to the distribution of the races and its influence upon civilization. Mr. Debussy, *licencié ès lettres,* is treating of modern French writers, especially in the drama. Mr. Paul Lesaunier, professor of history in the École des Roches, gives French history. All treat their subjects in a broad and academic manner, and with an ease of style which furnishes an agreeable variation to the formal limits of the college textbook.

In August we shall have the further privilege of lectures by M. Paul Fauconnet, *agrégé de l'Université* and professor of philosophy in the Lysée de Cherbourg. He is the son of Madame Fauconnet, our kind, intelligent, delightful hostess.

One delightful evening was passed in the company of Pastor Charles Wagner, who resides in Fontenay-sous-Bois, and who honored us by a call shortly before his vacation trip to Switzerland. In delightfully broken English he talked of his experiences in the United States, and of how much he had enjoyed them. Our first Sunday morning in Paris was devoted to attending the old chapel in which he was preaching for the last time before removing to the more commodious building which has been made needful by the increasing crowds which seek out his preaching. Mlle. Muller, who has given twenty years to conducting students about Paris, has charge of the grammar department of the instruction to the Innocents, and takes charge of all the excursions. Two days in the week are given to the palaces and the art gallaries, and usually two evenings weekly, by those who desire it, are devoted to hearing the purest French diction as spoken in the Comédie Française or other theaters of Paris.

The students already realize that they are beginning to absorb the subtle aroma which pervades the atmosphere of this interesting and highly artistic race. They are realizing that, truly to know a language, one must know the people who speak it; thoroughly to absorb it, one must breathe its native air and dwell in its native homes. It is a privilege extended to few to be received into the family life of a true French family. The charming affection, the easy cordiality, the lively expressions of interest, show that not in America alone are there happy homes, and that France, far from spending all her time in the cafés and boulevards, retires behind her high-walled gardens to experiences replete with all the joy of the family affections. Our Innocents feel assured that by thus mingling for a few months with their daily life they are absorbing more French from the French themselves than could be laboriously achieved by the same number of years over textbooks. To know the French people in their humanity, their achievements, their place in the wide circle of nations, is not only to know *French;* it is to know more broadly all life, all nations, all humanity; thus are the fine threads of sympathy woven which link all to each other in true comprehension. "For so the whole round world is bound in golden chains about the feet of God."

[*To be continued*]

THE SANITARY REGULATION OF THE SCHOOL-ROOM WITH REFERENCE TO VISION*

CASEY A. WOOD, M.D., D.C.L.

Chicago; Professor of Clinical Ophthalmology in the University of Illinois; President of the American Academy of Ophthalmology, etc.

If the ocular apparatus of the average child were by nature adapted to the amount and kind of eye-work that he is ordinarily called upon to do, it would not be so necessary for us, as physicians, to consider, as we often do, the details of school hygiene. In spite of the fact that the eyes are the organs, above all others, that are called upon to labor excessively in the effort to obtain an education, they would cause us little or no anxiety if there were any provision in them for an unusual amount of accommodative effort—for excessive focusing for near work in particular. In the great majority of cases the opposite is true. We are all of us born farsighted, i. e., with the vision and visual apparatus of our savage ancestors, and with these eyes we deliberately proceed to the school-work that civilization demands, which, for its easy accomplishment, necessitates quite a different type of eye, viz., shortsighted or myopic globe with an oculo-muscular system in correspondence with it. Happily, quite a few of us run the gauntlet of these dangers to our nervous and digestive apparatus and to our sense organs with little or no damage, but some of us experience ills from which we recover either partially or not at all.

In estimating the value of sanitary precautions in the regulations of the average schoolroom it must be remembered that a respectable percentage of children begin their shool life with congenitally defective eyes. Quite apart from the treatment of this aspect of school life, which I do not propose to discuss here, it follows that any advantage accruing to the merely farsighted

* Read at the Annual Meeting of the American Academy of Medicine, Boston, June 2, 1906.

pupil in easing the burden of his eye-strain is of manifold greater assistance to the boy or girl who assumes the tasks of study with astigmatic, diseased, or organically defective eyeballs.

Even if the eyes of every school child were, as they ought to be, carefully examined every year for the purpose of detecting and treating all errors of refraction, all defects in accommodation, and all anomalies of oculo-muscular balance, there would still remain many who, from incurable or only partially curable eye defects, need every possible aid to comfortable vision that can be afforded them.

It must also be borne in mind that there are numerous diseases of the other sense organs as well as of the system generally that, neglected or incapable of cure, reduce the effectiveness of the visual function. Even where the eyes are comparatively free of congenital defects or active disease, ineffective digestion due to poor food or other cause, acquired or hereditary diseases of many sorts, obstructed breathing, imperfect mental development, etc., not uncommonly serve to weaken one or more parts of the visual mechanism, and the child so affected is unable to continue his studies.

It is, consequently, not alone for the sake of preserving the eyesight of the ordinary healthy pupil that hygienic precautions are of supreme value in the schoolroom, but that we may not add to other considerable burdens the serious drawback of eye-strain.

In considering a few of these questions let me say that although the discussion of them has been going on since the early days of public education, they still present ever new, because ever changing, aspects, and this fact is another justification I offer for presenting them to you once more.

The illumination of the schoolroom.—This is the oldest of the questions relating to the hygiene of school vision. It seems strange that, although one of the simplest and most easily applied of the rules of school sanitation has been known for many years, it is so often overlooked. I refer to the *dictum* of Risley, that at any hour of the day in any season of the year it should be possible to read the finest (diamond) print in any part of the schoolroom. If this can be done the illumination is *sufficient*. It may, of course, be *excessive* (too strong light may be admitted to the school, or the artificial illumination may be unduly concentrated) or even too variable, but these are not the usual faults. Speaking for Chicago, I believe that, considering the rapid growth of the city and the constantly increasing demands upon us for school space, our school board has done wonders, yet there are many schoolrooms in which pupils and teachers strain their eyes, worry their nervous systems, upset their digestive apparatus and contribute to other forms of mental and physical distress by attempting to see by insufficient or improper illumination.

I do not, of course, say that in a crowded city with its atmosphere befouled with smoke it is always possible to secure, especially during the winter, an ideal illumination, but the continual agitation of this important matter has enabled us to obtain better-built and better-lighted schoolhouses. Largely due to this cause is the decent light in our public schools as compared with the generally wretched illumination of our federal, state, and municipal buildings. Everybody, even the proverbial schoolboy, knows that in the construction of the schoolhouse the distance that separates it from surrounding buildings should be at least twice their height and that the window space of the exterior walls having a northern or western exposure should be quite one-fourth the floor space, although it may be only one-fifth of the floor area when the schoolroom has an unobstructed southern or eastern exposure. Of course, I need not say that the application of this rule must be somewhat modified, as in the case of all rules, by individual instances. In small rooms with a generally clear atmosphere, or where the school buildings can be elevated well above their surroundings, a smaller proportion of window space may be allowed.

During winter, or where, as in some localities, it is a question of artificial lighting or no school at all, the respective merits of kerosene, gas, electricity, and the various forms of lamps are often discussed. I have had occasion to say, in this connection, and I repeat it here, that as a choice of evils I would prefer to have the pupil take an indefinite holiday than allow him to be immured during school hours in some of the educational dungeons that I have known to masquerade as recitation and study-rooms. I need not enlarge upon the physical, moral, and mental ills that come to children that are forced to study or even to sit all day in a badly ventilated, artificially lighted, interior schoolroom. Better a healthy street arab than a shortsighted, anemic, neurasthenic schoolboy.

If artificial lighting is unavoidable, the same law that governs the employment of sunlight should ever be borne in mind; *the illumination should resemble as nearly as possible diffuse sunlight; it should be sufficient to permit diamond print to be easily read in any part of the room, and it should shine upon the work to be done, and not, either directly or by reflection, into the eyes of the pupils.* After all is said and done, if the lighting, natural and artificial, of all schoolrooms realized these standards, we should have few excessively myopic and fewer nervous symptoms to treat among our child population.

Owing to recent improvements in electric lamps, to the fact that the electric light does not to any extent overheat or vitiate the atmosphere of the schoolroom, to the diminished danger of fire, and to its greater convenience, it is generally to be preferred to gas or kerosene. It is, however, capable of greater harm to the vision and much more likely to produce eye-strain unless judiciously arranged. As a rule, I prefer a sufficient number of 32 candle-power lamps placed, in ground-glass globes, near the ceiling. The dazzling, uncertain, flickering, arc-lights with their irritating violet rays should never be used for school lighting or, in my judgment, for any illuminating purposes when any close work is to be done.

That the sunlight should not shine into the eyes of the school children will require a proper arrangement of the seats, desks, and blackboards. Of course, this important detail in school-house building should receive the careful attention of the architect, but it can generally be satisfactorily arranged, it matters not what exposure the schoolroom may have.

Inasmuch as the great majority of pupils are right-handed, the rays of light from whatever source of illumination, from the left, or from the left and rear, should fall upon the desk, book, writing pads, etc., in near work, and from the rear or obliquely upon blackboards, maps, wall diagrams, or other objects required to be looked at by pupils from distant parts of the room. If windows are upon the right side of the room, they should, as in artificial lighting, be placed as near the ceiling as possible. It must be remembered that the eyes require *sufficient,* as well as *proper,* illumination to do without strain the work of ocular fixation. As Risley points out, these supplementary windows may, in summer, be used for ventilating purposes. He also suggests that where for any reason there is not sufficient sunlight admitted to a room, a second sash may be adjusted to each window on the left, which, when dropped to an angle of thirty-five or forty degrees, will act as a reflector and throw the light from the sky upon the desks of the pupils. I have myself seen such a device employed for directing the sun's rays upon a white ceiling and then by secondary reflection upon the objects in the room below. In this way the sun's rays were sufficiently diffused to render them effective and not irritating to the eyes.

While on this subject I am, of course, distinctly opposed to such means as Luxfer prisms for school lighting, valuable as these devices undoubtedly are in illuminating basements and other dark rooms of our city buildings, particularly. All schoolrooms in which pupils are expected to use their eyes to any extent should be properly lighted, outside rooms—for many reasons besides the fact that they are necessary for the ocular well-being of the children. Indeed, in the ideal school building the rooms in which pupils spend most of their time should have a south or southeastern exposure. Excessive sunshine could be regulated by double screens—the one semi-opaque and colored light green for bright summer days, and the other cream or light gray for the less dazzling though direct sunshine of winter. If this were done recitations and other occasional tasks could be worked out in rooms on the opposite side of the building.

The tinting of the walls.—Although much has been written on this subject and although the rules for successful mural coloration are easily remembered, there still exists some confusion in the minds of many educators regarding this important matter. As before stated, if the ocular apparatus is adjusted (especially during such near work as reading, writing, drawing, etc.) for diffused sunlight, the wall tints should be chosen in view of that fact. Each schoolroom should be considered by itself. If it be situated above the ground floor, has a southern exposure, faces a wide street or other large space, and particularly if there be no tall building to shut out the sunlight, the color chosen may be a light green, dull gray, or even a deep orange relieved by a lighter ceiling tint of the same color mixture. On the other hand, the walls and especially the ceiling of a recitation or study-room with a northern exposure, especially if the window space be insufficient or the view obstructed, should be papered or painted a light buff or, better still, dull white. To assist in lighting up such a room the walls should be regarded as reflecting surfaces and ought not to be unnecessarily covered with maps, diagrams, pictures, blackboards or figured wall papers. Where it is possible, dull paints on a smooth surface are preferable for use in such a room to burlap, calcimine, or wall paper.

A wider choice may be allowed in rooms and halls with a bright southern exposure; indeed, if for this reason alone it is a pity that *all* rooms cannot have either a south, a southeast, or an eastern outlook; it would permit of almost unlimited color schemes and mural decorations. Between the brightest southern exposure and the most obstructed northern view, we may then say that the mural colors should be chosen to suit the individual case. As you are aware, there are several photometric schemes devised to reduce color schemes in schoolrooms to a scientific certainty, but practically all that one needs to remember is comprised in the foregoing considerations.

Reading matter.—The size of the letters, the style of the type, the width of the printed columns, the spacing of the words and lines, the color and texture of the paper used in the make-up of schoolbooks are all important factors in the prevention of eye-strain and ought to receive more attention than they generally do. Without entering too deeply into these subjects I believe that the rules laid down by Cohn ought to be followed. He advises that the weight of letters like *n* be not less than 1.5 mm. and the down strokes be at least one-fourth of a millimeter thick and, that the the vertical distance between the lines be not less than 2.5 mm.

Inasmuch as the strain upon the eye muscles, both internal and external, is in direct proportion to the length of the lines, he suggests that the columns of reading matter never exceed 10 cm. Furthermore, as ocular fatigue is, other things being equal, more easily brought about in younger children than in those more advanced in years, these measurements should be increased for those of tender years. Edward Shaw proposes that for the first year in school the type should be 2.60 mm. high and the leading 4.5 mm.; for the second and third years the height ought to be at least 2 mm. with leading of 4 mm. For the fourth and subsequent years 1.8 and 3.6 mm., respectively. Considering the unavoidable variation in school lighting, I do not consider these figures unwarrantable.

A good deal of discussion and much difference of opinion is held as to the proper texture and color of paper in schoolbooks, but I do not think we shall be far wrong if we insist on a dull white paper printed with jet black ink. Likewise the copybooks, pads of paper used in school exercises, in the practice of hand-writing and as substitute for greasy, dirty slates (now happily things of the past) should be a "dead" white, the ink deep black and the lead pencils as black as they can be had. Where illustrations requiring a highly calendered or shiny surface are required, these should be in the form of "tips" or inserts; the fewer of them the better. I may say in passing that the fewer magazines printed on glossy paper the child is allowed to read the better for his eyes.

Handwriting.—As to the relative merits of perpendicular, intermediate slanting penmanship and the decidedly slanting forms of penmanship as well as the postures assumed in each, I have little to say. In choosing one or other, let us not forget that easy legibility is desirable both for the writer and for the reader, and that it is important that the pen strokes should be thick enough to be read without eye-strain. When properly arranged desks are used and the illumination is good, perpendicular penmanship (taught in the upright position) certainly presents ocular advantages over every other form of handwriting with which I am acquainted. Writers on this subject frequently speak of curvature of the spine as the chief danger to the child when he assumes the abnormal positions so long associated with the old Spencerian copybook. It is time to remind them once more that myopia, chronic headache, and other forms of eye-tire are much more frequent, if not more important, consequences. The strain upon ocular muscles in their efforts to make two eyes functionate for hours at unequal distances from the near point often produces those varied, complex and disastrous results that we are in the habit of speaking of as "eye-strain."

In all forms of writing and reading the book or paper should not be allowed to approach the pupil's eyes nearer than 35 cm. If he persists, with normal surroundings, in reading or writing at a nearer point, one may suspect an approaching myopia, or that he has a refactive (farsighted, a stigmatic, etc.), or accommodative error that demands attention.

A few words about *blackboards and maps*. The objections to many of the former are manifold. As long as they are dull finished and kept clean of chalk dust, they do not reflect the light into the eyes of the pupils. They are not objectionable except that they may interfere with the proper lighting of the room. All blackboards should be frequently cleaned with competent erasers and the writing upon them should always be large and heavy and be done with soft, white crayons. When colored chalks are used one must recollect that yellow and blue are the colors most easily recognized by pupils with defective vision and defective color-sense. Wall maps of all sorts ought to have a restricted use in the schoolroom, owing to the extreme difficulty with which a mass of names (some of them in small print) are made out by pupils some distance away.

Size of the schoolroom.—Apart from the question of air, space, ventilation, and lighting, the size of the schoolroom is very important from the visual standpoint. When pupils are seated at desks too far removed from blackboards, maps, specimens on exhibition. etc., they are likely to suffer from eye-strain, particularly if they have weak eye muscles or are slightly shortsighted. In these events the ocular apparatus makes an abnormal effort to overcome the defect and reflex symptoms result. Probably 25×30 feet are the maximum ground measurements. Such a room, with proper ceilings, window space, etc., will accommodate from 45 to 50 pupils.

Detection of disease.—I have already referred to the desirability of having school-children's eyes examined at the beginning of the scholastic year. Let me say briefly, in this connection, that the scheme first proposed by Dr. Risley and subsequently elaborated by my associate in medical practice, Dr. Frank Allport, provides that at least one teacher in each school be instructed in this work, that it can easily be carried out in practice, and it has been recommended by many Boards of Health and adopted by a number of School Boards.

In a few of the states these methods have also been adopted by the legislature, and in my opinion they ought to be further employed as the most practical and most useful means of detecting diseased eyes and ears that I know of. The examining teacher does not pretend to diagnose the case in hand; he or she merely applies certain tests and makes sundry observations that any layman may, to determine whether or not the services of a physician are desirable—whether further medical examination is indicated or not.

The school desk.—I am well aware that I am walking in slippery places when I approach the desk question, but it has a very important bearing on eyesight. As a proof that I am not commercially interested in any particular desk, I will say that there are, in my judgment, several good forms of that kind of school furniture on the market, the names of whose makers I shall refrain from mentioning.

First of all, I am in favor of *single,* adjustable desks with a sliding top, as better suited to the *minus* and *plus* distance required for the comfort and accommodation of the growing individual child. The desk should be adjusted vertically at the beginning and in the middle of each school year. It should be without foot rests; the lid should have a slope of 10 to 15 degrees as best fitted to the perpendicular or slightly slanting chirography. When, for certain kinds of work, it is necessary that the desk be almost flat, a couple of small supports from the interior of the box desk may easily be arranged to accomplish this end.

Length of time consumed in schoolroom study and recitation.—So far as ocular strain is concerned, surely experience will teach the observing educator that when the attention is for too long a period fixed upon a book, blackboard, writing pad, map, or other object, or if the class is too long bombarded with questions regarding the same, all kinds of fatigue, mental and physical, result. So is it with the oculo-nervous apparatus. It is of course difficult to lay down a rule applicable to every child. Edward Shaw believes, and I am sure most oculists will agree with him, that recitations should not for the first year exceed 10 minutes in length, for the second year 15 minutes, and so on, gradually increasing the study period until the highest grade is reached with a maximum of 45 minutes. Similarly, study hours in school should be frequently interrupted in the interest of eyesight and the nervous system.

Study out of school.—If I had my way, I would not allow any child to do reading (especially of newspapers and magazines) or studying out of school hours until he or she were at least ten years of age. "Oh! how will they pass their time at home?" and then adds the anxious mother with a sigh: "There is so much for them to read!" My answer would be: "Read to them yourself or have somebody else do it, or, better still, give them some constructive manual work to do in their playroom during the winter evenings, and turn them out into the air when the days are propitious." Especially for our precocious, over-stimulated, native-born American children exercise in fresh air, sound sleep, and healthful, interesting exercise are more desirable than rubies and—at least as far as the eyes are concerned—are in the end a better commercial investment.

In closing this incomplete study of the schoolroom and its influences upon eyesight for good and evil, let me draw your attention to the fact that almost without exception the laws of ocular sanitation are in accord with other rules of personal hygiene, thus furnishing evidence of the dimly recognized truism that ophthalmology is not an art or a science apart, but is merely one chapter of the whole philosophy of healing.

THE GROUP IDEA VERSUS THE GRADE IN THE ELEMENTARY SCHOOL

LUCY E. BROWNING
Chicago

"If the school were to be viewed in a strictly scholastic sense, its function might be briefly stated as the cultivation of thought and expression. If, on the other hand, an ethical point of view is to be taken, then the school's function might be summarized as the promotion of the best social life." It will readily be seen that these two views supplement each other and as a working plan may be viewed as one. The modern school is not only expected to give the pupil a knowledge of the three R's, but also to teach morality, train character, and make good citizens.

Present-day psychology considers that education is a process of growth; that, as Froebel said, the full and complete development of each stage is necessary for the development of succeeding stages. The child is a part of society. He is not fitting himself to be a member, he *is* a member, of society. The home and the school must not be separated. It is for the school to make its curriculum fit the child. The problem is not to give the child such material as he will need when he is grown. but what he needs now.

The school must recognize the great fundamental instincts and turn them in the right direction. The hunting and shelter instincts develop in the child as they did in the race, and should be turned to account by being used as motives for hand-work, stories, and reading.

In the recapitulation theory there is simultaneous and parallel development. Nowhere is there series or successive development. Our problem is to take the raw feelings and give them opportunities to grow in right directions. Children (and adults) must want the right things.

Growth is by pulses; it is not steady. This is seen in child play. The child becomes completely immersed in one thing and goes on with that until he has found all that he can in it. Then he plays something else in the same way. It seems to me that there might be times in school when an absorbing interest could be carried out in the same way. Mr. Burbank and others have shown that with plants there is a period of adaptation and mutation when new species are easily formed. After that period they cannot be formed. With human beings after the nascent period it is only with difficulty that new acquisitions are made.

It is true that the growing process is going on during the twenty-four hours, and not only while the child is in school. Does the school during a few hours give opportunity and means for the best development of each child? To some of those who have this aim in view the present system of grading seems detrimental. Mr. Jackman says that the children are graded according to age, knowledge, and skill, which he shows to be unnecessary. And still further, he says: "The influence of the grading system upon the pupil is necessarily bad. It retards his progress through the elementary school, and it fosters selfishness. Under the old ideals of education the children must exert themselves to excel each other. Under the new, members of a group must exert themselves to help each other."

Mr. Jackman presents a sociological problem that thinking teachers must face when he says: "The problem of grading and grouping of pupils will be solved when the children are permitted to plan work for themselves that demands co-operation." To achieve an ideal humanity there must be co-operation. "The future belongs to co-operation, or, if it is preferred, to the rivalry in social service. Co-operation means co-working; co-working develops community of feeling, which is sympathy, and sympathy is the basis of love." The knowledge of the school must be given a social value. The individual cannot live to himself alone.

The individual, the social unit, must be strong, if the whole is to be strong. It is through his rights that he learns there are duties connected with rights. The group idea carries out the social ideal. Mr. Scott advocates allowing the children some freedom in forming the groups. The strong and weak intellectually would in this way be brought together and help each other. The children would naturally group themselves according to liking for hand-work or by a natural sympathy. Mr. Search in *An Ideal School* shows how varied are the capabilities in an ordinary grade, and in his school each individual would do what he can and not be hindered by others. Every child should be placed where he is the happiest. Mr. Search gives every consideration to health, which he thinks of first importance in his plan for an ideal school. He does not emphasize the social ideal as does Mr. Henderson in his *Education and the Larger Life.* Perhaps there are in this work some ideas which may be laughed at, but there are many more which are inspiring and suggestive in the search for what is best in educational ideals.

In the School of Education the group idea is carried out especially well in the morning exercises and in the parties which are given to one room by another. There is co-operation, co-working, and sympathy. There is great incentive and help in carrying out all plans of the school in the co-operation and sympathy of the parents, many of whom are frequent visitors. In Pestalozzi-Froebel Haus children from the different grades are gathered together for the study of pictures. This grouping is to stimulate that of the family. The social idea is carried all through the Haus, each grade assisting another in some way.

It is essential for this change in grading that there be not only those who believe it to be wise, but also those who can effect it in the school. Teachers go into the schools to teach children —not reading, writing, and arithmetic. Perhaps more attention given to how to learn rather than how to teach would bring about the desired results. President Hadley thinks that more attention should be given to the mental types of pupils. There is the literary, the scientific, and the administrative type of mind. The teacher should realize that the scientific mind takes up every subject from the standpoint of the scientific investigator; the other types form the administrative and literary point of view. The recognition of these types will enable the teacher to understand and meet the needs of her pupils.

The pupils are to be guided into the life of moral freedom. Should not the one who guides have achieved this freedom? What is there in the good, the uplifting, the right to put into the mind to give it control? By moral freedom is meant complete control by ideas of right. This is an inner, not an outer thing. "Ye shall know the truth and truth shall make you free."

BIBLIOGRAPHY

P. W. Search, *An Ideal School.*

C. H. Henderson, *Education and the Larger Life.*

W. S. Jackman, "School Grade Fiction," *Educational Review,* Vol. XV.

W. S. Jackman, "The Year in Review," *The Elementary School Teacher,* June, 1906.

"Children's Self-Organized Work and the Education of Leadership in the Schools," *Elementary School Teacher,* Vol. VI.

A. T. Hadley, "Mental Types and Their Recognition in Our School," *Harper's Monthly Magazine,* Vol. CXI, p. 123.

Ira W. Howerth, "Education and the Social Ideal," *Educational Review,* Vol. XXIV.

F. Burk, "The Old Education and the New," *Forum,* Vol. XXXIII.

"The Curriculum of the Elementary School," *Teachers College Record,* Vol. V, No. 2.

John Dewey, "The Psychology of the Elementary Curriculum," *Elementary School Record,* Vol. I, p. 221.

W. H. Burnham, "Education from the Genetic Point of View," *Elementary School Teacher,* Vol. VI.

Josiah Royce, "Self-Consciousness, Social Consciousness, and Nature," *Philosophical Review,* Vols. III and IV.

APPLIED ART IN THE FRANCIS W. PARKER SCHOOL

In carrying on the hand-work in the Francis W. Parker School the ideal held is that of allowing the pupil freedom of choice in those articles which he makes for his home or for himself, instead of requiring him to make a prearranged set of models. His only limitations in his work are those fixed by his individual power and skill, as estimated by the teacher. To follow such a plan successfully, it is essential to have for suggestion a large number of examples of work involving the various typical processes of the crafts.

The somewhat fragmentary articles which follow are presented with the idea of making a few suggestions for hand-work which this school has found practicable in the various grades indicated.

Because work of this nature is comparatively untried in the elementary schools, it is thought that such detailed descriptions as are here given may prove valuable to other schools making similar experiments.

APPLIED DESIGN

KATHERINE CLEMENTS

The various crafts in the school—wood-work, copper, clay-modeling, textiles, and bookbinding—present a constant demand or motive for the study of design. The children work eagerly, applying original designs to the material as soon as they are able to produce anything worthy. This work develops to the utmost the child's creative ability and imagination, in terms of shapes, and cultivates the taste and skill in choice and arrangement of these shapes in beautiful relations. The children used *given* units first, the problem being to arrange these units in a beautiful design, in a given space; for example, a square, suitable for a tile. The units were: See Fig. 1.

The children used these to make original designs under the following regulations: Each form must be used at least once; the size of units may be changed, but not the shapes; each unit may be repeated as many times as desirable.

It was exceedingly difficult for some of the children to think in terms of forms of this kind, and most of them had to make several designs before they could produce anything satisfactory.

Figs. 1–5 show some of the results of this work.

Then more difficult groups of units were given, some of the results being shown in Figs. 6 and 7. These were used with much more ease, and some interesting designs were made. One student used a design made from these units to decorate a desk set (see Fig. 8). The set consisted of ink-well, stamp-box, and pen-tray, and each was ornamented with a design. (See full illustration and description of desk set under "Clay-Modeling.")

After the children had worked sufficiently with given units to enable them to think in terms of this kind, they were given vegetables, fruits, and flowers, which they cut into sections, and from these they found units for themselves. The vegetables, fruits, and flowers used most satisfactory were the tomato, carrot, lemon, apple, trillium, and wild carrot blossom. (See Figs. 9 and 10.)

A design (see Fig. 11) made by a boy in the tenth grade from tomato units was applied to a decoration or design for a handle for a table drawer, which he was making in the shop.

Having the knowledge of many shapes and the ability to see shapes in everyday, familiar things, the children can now work with simple curved and straight lines, arranging them in a given or chosen space; e. g., a square which is divided into four equal parts. These lines, when combined, make shapes that are interesting or commonplace, beautiful or ugly. The ability to arrange lines in beautiful and refined relations demands the best individual thought and skill, and the possibilities of beauty of arrangement of lines are unlimited.

The children wished to design pillow-cushions, etc., for Christmas gifts, and one group of children planned to furnish the rest-room with pillows and draperies, appropriately decorated.

Successful designs were chosen and carved in wood blocks, and these blocks were used to print the design in the textiles. Blocks of white pine were used of the desired size, two or three inches square and about two inches thick. Soft wood was used because it could be carved with sloyd knives at the desks in the class-room. There are many disadvantages in using soft wood, great care being necessary not to split the wood. Hard wood is much to be preferred if tools and the shop bench are available. A large level-surfaced board is necessary to spread the soft over before printing, and another smaller pad covered with felt or cheese-cloth for the color. The color must be thoroughly mixed with turpentine. Oil paints are most satisfactory and convenient to use and wash well in equal water and soap if handled carefully. Dyes can be used but must be mixed with a paste, any starch or library paste will answer this purpose. When two or more colors are to be used, as many blocks must be carved as there are colors, or if one block is used, the colors must be painted on the parts of the design with a brush before each print is made. See Figs 12 and 13.

METAL-WORK

GRADE SEVEN

Metal-work has been attempted at this school, up to the present time, only in grades above the 7th. Even in the sixth a comparatively small amount has been done.

There is perhaps a fair question as to whether work of this kind cannot be done by still younger children, but it has been the general experience of the school that work of the character described here—the shaping of small bowls and trays, and the decoration by raising and etching—may be begun more success-fully in the seventh grade than with younger children.

The description which follows tells somewhat in detail of the methods employed in making a few articles which are fairly typical of many of the things made.

To avoid the danger of discouragement at the outset of the work, beginners are usually permitted to make only the most simple articles, such as ash-trays, pin-trays, and plates of various sizes and shapes. (See Fig. 14.)

The metal most used has been copper, though a few pieces have been made of brass, and a few of a combination of both.

In planning an article, its construction is carefully considered; also the best materials for it, its proportions, the design for its decoration, and the tools which will be required in its making.

Working-drawings are then made, including the decorative design, special attention being given in the latter to proportions and space relations.

In every case where it has been practicable, especially with the younger children, wooden blocks and wooden hammers have been used in preference to the metal tools. This has been done because with the wooden tools the children are less likely to make ruinous dents in their work: because the metal hardens less quickly in the working, and so needs annealing less often: and because the pupils themselves can make much of their own apparatus.

The oblong trays (see Fig. 14) were shaped by hammering with a wooden mallet from the outside over a wooden block having a curved edge corresponding to the curve at which the piece was to be turned up.

The plates were fashioned by hammering from the face side on a wooden L-shaped block with metal hammers. Wooden mallets were used to flatten the flange and bottom of the plates.

The metal becomes hard after being beaten for a time, and must be annealed by heating to a bright red and cooling suddenly in water, after which it is as soft as at first.

The trays and plates are usually decorated, either on the flange or in the bottom.

If the design is to be etched, in the bottom of the tray, for example, it is first carefully drawn in pencil, then the raised portion of the design is painted with asphaltum paint. This must be most carefully done, as the paint is apt to spread over the line of design, and when etched leaves a ragged edge instead of a good, clear line. When the paint is dry, diluted nitric acid is used to eat away the background. When the acid has eaten deep enough, the paint can be removed with turpentine, and the metal cleaned and polished with powdered pumice stone and oil, and afterward with powdered rouge. The tray can then be colored either by acids or heat, or it may be left to oxdize naturally.

If the pattern is to be embossed on the tray, a pitch block is used. This is made by melting together equal parts, by weight, of black pitch and plaster of Paris with a small lump of mutton tallow, the mixture being poured into a wooden bowl while liquid. The tray is placed on the pitch block while it is hot, but the pitch must be allowed to cool before work is begun.

One of the simplest forms of embossing is done by using nails or blanks, each one filed to fit a unit of the design. These forms would necessarily be limited to such simple figures as rectangles of varying proportions, elipses, circles, etc. The tool is used like a die, being held in the proper place in the design and struck so as to make but a single impression of itself. Many attractive and original patterns can be made in this way, and it has the added advantage of being within the power of the sixth- and seventh-grade pupils, while the embossing done with tracers and punches requires greater control and care than children of these grades are apt to possess.

A number of pieces, such as match-safes, ink-stands, lamps (both base and shade), candlesticks, and shades, have been made by riveting the parts together. This is usual where the article is bounded by plane faces or is of cylindrical or conical form. The candlestick (see Fig. 14) is composed of three pieces. The round dish has the edge turned up to half an inch in height. This was done on a wooden block with an oval-faced metal hammer, from the inside of the dish.

The candle-holder was cut out of a single piece of copper of somewhat lighter weight than the dish, and when flat was shaped like a cross. After filing, it was riveted to the center of the dish, and then the four arms of which it was composed were bent into position. The handle was next cut out, shaped and filed, then riveted onto the bottom and rim of the dish.

Some of the older pupils have made watch-fobs and belt-clasps (see Figs. 15–17). Fig. 15 shows a sketch of one of the

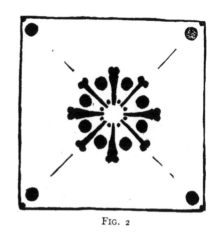

FIG. 1

FIG. 2

FIG. 3

FIG. 4

FIG. 5

FIG. 6

FIG. 7   FIG. 8   FIG. 9

FIG. 10.—Wild Carrot Unit

FIG. 11   FIG. 12

FIG. 13

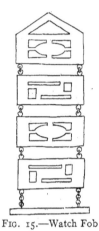

FIG. 17.—Belt Buckle

FIG. 15.—Watch Fob

FIG. 18.—Winnowing Wheat
2d Grade

FIG. 19.—Inlaid Tile

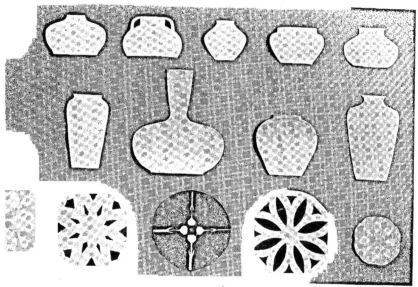

FIG. 20.—Designs for Inlaid Tiles
5th Grade

Model

18"

FIG. 22.—Desk Set
9th Grade

FIG. 23.—Pottery for Christmas Gifts
d to 11th Grade

fobs. This was composed of four pieces linked together. These pieces were one and three-eighths inches long, and five-eighths of an inch wide. The squares and oblongs were cut through with a fine jeweler's saw, after which the edges were filed smooth. The little rings to link the pieces together were then soldered on.

An enameled belt-buckle (see Fig. 16) was made in this manner. A piece of copper, larger than the buckle was to be, was put on the pitch block, which had been heated by the blow-pipe. The design was then transferred to the copper. A piece of steel blank was filed into a tracing-tool, and with this and a chaser's hammer the outline of the design was traced. Other tools were then made and used to push down the background. The copper was then taken from the block, annealed, and cleaned. The pitch was again heated, and this time the copper was put on face down, so that the part to be raised could be pushed up with rounded tools.

This process was repeated several times, first working from the face and then the back, until the design was as perfect as the pupil could make it.

Each time the buckle was taken from the pitch block the copper was annealed and cleaned before again putting it on the block. After the buckle was sawed out and filed, the back was put on. The completed front piece was clamped to a clean piece of flat copper. A wash of borax was painted around the joint as a flux, and little pieces of silver solder put near together around the joint. The blow-pipe was turned on, gently at first, from underneath, then on top with good force, until the solder flowed into the joint.

The enamels selected were green and blue. They were first ground separately in small mortars. When fine as sand, they were washed with clear water to take away dust or other impurities. The enamels were then put into the depressions of the design, and when they were dry the buckle was placed so that the heat from the blow-pipe would come underneath it. After the enamel was fused, the buckle was allowed to cool gradually.

When the enameling was finished, the back piece was sawed close to the joint, and filed until smooth and round. Then the buckle was cleaned and polished, and the clasp and loop were soldered to the back with soft solder.

CLAY-MODELING

HELEN PUTNAM

The following statements written by the children, tell something of what is being done in clay-work in the school. It is customary for the various classes to report from time to time to the whole school at the morning exercises about their work, and the accounts are reproduced here as nearly as possible as they were given at such times.

We were studying about threshing grain, so we thought that it would be nice if we should make models of clay for the second grade next year. The first thing I did was to make a tile of clay. Then I had to draw men pitching up wheat with forks to winnow it. When the men toss the grain up the wheat falls down; but the chaff blows away. After I got through drawing, I built on some more clay where my drawing was, to make the men stand out. I made the arm of the man highest because it was nearest to me, and the other parts that were further away I made lower. After we get through modeling, our tiles will be baked in the kiln, but not glazed. (See Fig. 18.)

A. H., Second Grade.

This is how I made my inlaid tile. First I made the tile. Then I drew the letters on it, and as soon as I got them to my liking I dug them out ⅛ of an inch deep.

Then I ground, sifted, and weighed the colors I wished to inlay. These colors were red and blue. For the red I used 10 grams of red under-glaze color and 20 grams of common clay. For the blue I mixed 7 grams of blue under-glaze color, 2 grams of green under-glaze color, and 35 grams of common clay. I ground them in a mortar, with water, and poured them out on a plaster tile to dry till they were no longer sticky.

Then I put them in the spaces I had dug out, using the red for the M and the blue for the C. When the letters were all filled in, I let the tile get almost dry, and then scraped it with a knife to make it even all over. Then it was ready for firing. (See Fig. 19.)

W. B. B., Fourth Grade.

Last year in the fourth and fifth grades we made our designs for pottery work by folding and cutting papers. The fourth grade made designs for jars or bowls, and they were limited to 5 inches in diameter and 3 inches in height. The upper row of patterns (Fig. 20) shows their work. Of course, they did not have as much variety as the fifth grade, who were allowed almost any size they wanted, but it was very surprising to see how many shapes they could get within those dimensions.

The fifth grade took pieces of manila paper and folded them in half; then they cut one side of the shape wanted. When they opened the paper, they had both sides symmetrical. A good many of us wanted drip glaze, and we had several different ways of representing it in our patterns. One way was to cut a piece of paper the shape of the drips, painting it the color we wished. Another way was to saturate the jar pattern with water, then paint it over the top with the drip color, letting this run down. This made a more satisfactory effect than the other. The second row shows these patterns.

The bottom row shows the way we made designs for inlaid tile. First we cut a piece of paper into a square or circle, according to the design we had in mind. Then we folded it into halves, then fourths, then eighths (or halves and sixths if our design called for that), with the folds always radiating from the center. Next we cut out different figures from the folded papers, and then opened them out to see the whole design. It was lots of fun, because we never knew just what was going to come out. We mounted these patterns on colored paper, the openings showing the places where the colored clay was to be. (See Fig. 20.)

D. P., Sixth Grade.

I began my desk set (see Fig. 22) by making drawings for the intended ink-well, stamp-box, and pen-tray. Then, from a few units, given me for use in the drawing class, I composed a design, and adapted it to the set. (See Fig. 8 under "Design.") Then I made the drawing of the copper corners and stand for the set. The ink-well, stamp-box, and tray are made of clay. The ink-well was modeled of a block of clay, and the well hollowed out. The stamp-box is of the same dimensions, but the sides were cut out of a slab of clay and welded on, instead of being modeled on.

The covers of the ink-well and the stamp-box are uniform, and are made with a rim at the edge, so as to fit onto the box and well.

The design on the sides of the ink-well, stamp-box, and tray was indented with a small tool. The design on the covers and the bottom of the tray was dug out.

The copper stand and corners were cut out according to design, and openings were left in which to place the various parts of the set.

The design on the copper consisted merely of dots in relief, made by hammering from the under side. Then the rough edges were filed off and the stains rubbed off with diluted sulphuric acid.

The blotting-pad is made of heavy tar-board, upon which I laid the blotter. Over these I slipped the metal parts, and then set the pottery pieces in place. (See Fig. 22.)

T. M., Ninth Grade.

Fig. 23 shows pottery made for Christmas presents by children from third to eleventh grades.

TRAINING IN GEOGRAPHY

F. P. GULLIVER

Geography has been taught for many years as an informational subject. Masses of facts are given, many of them undigested, and often these facts have no systematic relation to each other as they are given to the pupils to remember. Memory is made an all-important factor by this method of teaching the subject, and it is an undoubted fact that the memorizing of a mass of disconnected material is one of the most difficult accomplishments for the human mind, and one which is practically useless from an educational point of view. Most of the facts so learned are retained in the mind but a short time and are easily forgotten. This leads to the method of cramming for examination, which is always to be deplored.

Systematic training in the science of geography has demanded a good deal of attention during the past few years, and it is to this subject that attention is called in the following paper. The history of the development of systematic geography from the early work of Ritter and von Humboldt will not be discussed, but, assuming the fact that geography may now be considered a distinct branch of science, some of the more recent methods of teaching this important subject will be described and discussed as a valuable means of training the minds of pupils.

No one will doubt that every educated man should know a certain number of the important facts in regard to the geography of the world in which he lives, and of which he is a part. The relation of man to his surroundings is too important a subject to be lightly passed over in this age of great commercial enterprise. The boys of today will have to be the leaders of the world tomorrow. No one can successfully cope with the world-problems of trade and commerce unless he has some knowledge of the various portions of the world in which he is to become an important factor.

The difficulty lies in knowing just how to obtain this knowledge of the great world outside of one's own little sphere of activity. The ideal way, of course, would be to travel to all parts of the world, and see as minutely as one can the surroundings of other people in other climes; but, of course, this is possible for only a very few of us. The time necessary to obtain even a fairly accurate knowledge of the one hundred square miles immediately surrounding one's home makes it absolutely prohibitive to study the geography of the world by this ideal method. It is astonishing to find how few people have any adequate conception of even twenty-five square miles of territory immediately surrounding their home.

The method used, therefore, in systematic geography must be such that, with a minimum amount of actual travel, rational and intelligent ideas may be obtained of parts of the world which cannot be visited in person. Books of travel well written have always been interesting to boys, and it is undoubtedly true that a great deal of information in regard to other parts of the world comes from such books. The writer firmly believes that many more such books of travel, written particularly for young readers, will be of the greatest value as aids in the teaching of geography. This, however, is work which should be done outside of the class, as illustrative of class work rather than as the basis of systematic geography. The short stories written for children, such as have appeared in the last few years in the *St. Nicholas, Youth's Companion,* and other well-written papers for children, stimulate in the very young the thirst for more knowledge in regard to distant regions. These truthful stories of differing conditions have very wisely taken the place of the fantastic tales which used to be told in regard to monsters, goblins, and extinct animals. What is wanted is actual knowledge of the present conditions in the world in which the boy is to live.

There is very wide acceptance of the idea that the point to begin the teaching of geography is the home and its surroundings, the school, the school-yard, and the village, city, town, and country in which the pupils reside. Home geography then should undoubtedly be the starting-point for systematic training in geography. The great difficulty in the carrying out of this idea is the fact that no textbook is available for every school. In fact, no publisher would consider the idea of making a separate textbook for each town. In a few of the great centers of population this has been attempted; and, as far as the result of only a few years of application of this method warrant an opinion, it is undoubtedly true that this method has met with very great success.

A greater difficulty than the textbook is the teacher. Very few teachers are properly prepared to instruct their pupils in regard to home surroundings. The teachers themselves do not know the home in which they live; this is a strange fact, but very true. A good teacher, in sympathy with the surroundings of the home and school, can develop a great deal of interest among the pupils in home geography. Teachers are too often afraid to rely entirely on themselves, and hesitate to start out as explorers with the class in the immediate vicinity of the school.

Principals and superintendents also are not alive to the real situation in this matter. They know that the teacher is untrained, and they fear the criticism of parents that "time is wasted when not spent looking at a book." The fact, however, remains that time is not wasted by out-of-door work, even if imperfectly done. It is far better to get a fair knowledge of one's surroundings on this earth than to have no knowledge whatever of one's surroundings. Observational knowledge remains in the mind much more tenaciously than facts learned from a book, and if the facts learned about the home are so learned that they lead the mind into the greater affairs of the state, the country, and the world, it will be of infinitely greater value to the pupils individually, as well as to the state, the country, and the world in which these pupils live.

By a study of any industry located at home, a knowledge of that industry, as carried on in other parts of the world, may be rationally and easily obtained. This study of some special branch of agriculture or manufacture leads to the wider study of commerce. The commercial relations of the world depend on the facts of home geography in a great number of points. It is along these lines of commercial enterprise that the life-blood of the world flows. Until some reasonably accurate idea is obtained of the industries immediately surrounding one's home, it is practically impossible to give pupils any adequate conception of the great world-industries, of which his home industry is simply one small part.

Geography deals with many of the complex interrelations between man and the plants and animals which surround him. It is therefore important that he should study first the plants and animals surrounding him, before he can understand the great trade of the world in cotton and leather. A fairly accurate knowledge of the growth of the plants which surround him will enable the boy to form come rational conception of the growth of other plants in other parts of the world, which have an important relation to the life of man on the earth. A study of the habits and characteristics of the animals in any region will in a similar way enable the boy to conceive, in a fairly accurate way, the great facts in regard to many animals in different parts of the world, upon whose existence and developmen man so largely depends.

It may be safely said, therefore, that systematic training in geography should begin with the home surroundings; that a knowledge of the relative location of the home to the school, the school to the village, the village to the city, the railroad connections of county and state, leads to the state capital, to the state metropolis, and should lead later to a knowledge of the other states, and finally to the other countries of the world. The next step should be a study of the plants and animals surrounding the school, in order that the pupils may have a clear understanding of the great facts of animal and plant life which so closely affect the position of man on this globe.

No one will be bold enough to say that every school should take up systematic geography in exactly the same way. So much depends upon the locality, and so much on the individuality of the teacher, and upon the interest of both teacher and pupils, that the best scheme for each individual school must necessarily differ from the best scheme for other schools. There are, however, many important principles which should be studied in every school, and a textbook based on these general principles, written so as to stimulate observation rather than memory, may be so constructed that it will be of service for schools in very widely differing localities. It must emphasize those facts of local geography which are characteristic of the greatest number of regions. These exercises must, of course, be supplemented in each individual locality by the facts which appeal most to the interests of the pupils and the teacher.

Such a book should contain exercises based on the common animals and plants which occur in the greatest number of localities. When an exercise cannot be used in a given locality, another more suited to that individual school should be substituted in its place. Thus, after a few years of work in any given locality, a teacher will find those subjects which best stimulate the observational faculty of each pupil. The textbook will not be used as a cast-iron structure from which no deviation can be made, but will become an elastic structure which will simply guide the minds of teacher and pupils into the lines of thought best calculated to give the pupils such an idea of the immediate surroundings that they may then safely extend their conception to more distant regions.

For example, the study of meridians—that difficult stumbling-block for so many pupils—should begin with the idea of the shadows at noon of various objects. These shadows form the mid-day line for the school. Let this idea of mid-day line be extended until its significance is perfectly clear. At 12 o'clock the shadow of a pole forms the mid-day line for the school. Extend this mid-day line both north and south. When this conception is perfectly clear, introduce the idea that by following this mid-day line north and south the north pole and the south pole will be reached. Then state the fact that this is the meridian line of the school.

By the use of a small globe it will then be very easy to pass to the idea of the meridians of other places, and the false idea often obtained that meridians are only imaginary lines, drawn at stated intervals east and west from Greenwich, will never enter the minds of the pupils. Mid-day lines are everywhere. Meridians in the same way pass through all points on the face of the earth. Their real character is thus firmly established in the minds of the pupils, and the mathematical fact that lines may be imagined between any two points does not enter into the conception at all. An actual meridian line should be drawn on the schoolroom floor or in the school-yard, from which pupils may take their first conception of a map.

Map-drawing and map-construction should be among the earliest ideas introduced to pupils. Before maps of the county, state, country, and world are introduced, pupils should know from actual experience what a map is. Make a map first of what may be seen—the schoolroom, the school-yard, or the village. Let this map be constructed on different scales, so that pupils may realize what the change of scale means—the representation on a small area of a greater area. One of the commonest sources of misconception in geography is the lack of appreciation of what a map really represents.

When pupils thoroughly understand the meridian and the school map, the idea of representing a larger area should be introduced. This may be called *a route map*. The class should cover an area so large that it cannot all be seen from one point. A compass may be used to give direction; pacing, revolutions of a wheel, or time taken on a trolley trip may be used for distance. The route followed on the trip should then be represented on different scales. More than one such route map will have to be made before all the class gets a correct idea of what a map really means.

When the making of such a route map is impracticable, a very good substitute is to take the courses followed by different pupils from their homes in different parts of the town to the school. When each one has made a map of his daily walk to and from school, these lines may be put together on the blackboard by the teacher or pupils, and the map of the village is thus easily obtained. The school in this map may be represented by a dot, while in the first map constructed it is represented by four lines surrounding the space which represents the interior of the school building.   Only after these conceptions are fully fixed in the minds of the pupils is it safe to introduce a map which represents the village as a dot, with roads and railroads connecting surrounding towns, also represented by dots.

Along with the development of the idea of local geography a knowledge of what a village contains should be obtained by the pupils.   The writer firmly believes that it is the wisest plan to introduce with this study of locational geography a knowledge of what makes up a town—its people, business, manufactures, its railroads, its steamship lines—as well as the plants and animals which inhabit the region.

Geography truly includes the elements of various sciences. If the elements of the various branches of science are introduced at this early period as a part of the teaching of geography, the pupils gain a better conception of what geography really is, and at the same time get a conception of what the other sciences treat.   If the facts thus taught are wisely selected, geography will not become a mass of disconnected facts, but will be a natural foundation for scientific training, and a stepping-stone to the later study of the details of these other sciences.

ART AS RELATED TO MANUAL TRAINING[1]

JAMES EDWIN ADDICOTT
Principal of I. Newman Manual Training School, New Orleans, La.

It is my purpose to make clear two points: First, that art and manual training, as expressed in private, municipal, and national life, are one and inseparable, and consequently should be so presented in the industrial-arts courses for our public schools. Second, I shall attempt to show specifically what phases of art and manual training may be correlated naturally and advantageously.

This paper assumes that both art and manual training constitute essential branches in the courses of study of our elementary and secondary schools. The direct question before us is: Are they distinct branches having few common points of contact, or are they fundamentally related?

The answer cannot be safely settled by refering to texts on the subject; neither should opinions of successful teachers of the individual subjects be wholly relied upon, unless perchance they aim far beyond the technique and organization of school work. Rather let us look out broadly upon the necessities of the industrial world, and feel the pulsing needs of American institutional life, if we would answer the question rationally.

To be more specific, it must be admitted that, on the one hand, there may be a few individualistic artists whose work is so highly specialized as to be wholly unrelated to structural elements; and, on the other hand, there may be mechanics whose work does not, and need not, partake of any artistic feeling. It seems to me, however, that such specialists have no more right to expect that a technical preparation for their callings be given in the elementary schools than the lawyer has to expect a training sufficient to plead a case of criminality in the courts, or the surgeon that all pupils be qualified to treat a case of appendicitis, or the clergyman to request that each child be able to expound the doctrine of the Trinity.

[1] Read before the Department of Superintendence of the National Educational Association, Louisville, Ky., March 1, 1906.

In the past the manual-training movement in this country emphasized highly specialized technical and accuracy features as essential elements of a preparation for a few specific forms of handicraft. Likewise much of art in the schools has been and still is a series of drawings arranged in such sequence as eventually, after many years of effort, to prepare the pupil for some specific phase of so-called "refined art." The teacher who hopes to guide educational thought today must feel the relation of his specific branch to the world's work. Admitting the narrow specializing aims of art and manual training in the past, it is but just to say that they approached the educational idea as closely as other school branches; for we not only claimed, and could prove by the theories of the pioneer psychologists, that manual training and art trained all the faculties at one sweep, but we also invented some new, artistic, and mechanical faculties which were developed simultaneously with the commonly accepted list.

With such narrow and undemocratic ideals, and with such an inadequate theory of the aim of education, it was impossible fully to comprehend the fundamental relations which naturally combined the arts and crafts into a broad, unifying, educational movement.

Today the educational ideal has shifted. We look not so much to textbooks, not to the teacher, not to the rich heritage of the past; rather, we look out broadly upon the many needs of society, and to the great industrial and commercial enterprises, if we would know just what is best to teach.

The thoughts contained in texts, the ideas of the pedagogue, and the ideals of past generations are to be accepted only as they serve to fulfil society's present plans for physical, intellectual, and religious attainments and needs.

From this broad social standpoint let us first consider the arts, then the crafts, and then their union as expressed in private and public needs; and lastly the relations of the two in school as a preparation for, and as participation in, this private and public life.

In the past there has been an almost superstitious reverence for the highly specialized talents of the artist. Someone has described the artist as "heaven-taught;" for it is he that has led us to see and appreciate the beauties of ocean, of mountain, and of God's grandest works.

When the artist really does lead us through his work to a nearer

view, and a higher appreciation of the exquisite harmonies and beauties of nature, his work may indeed be styled heaven-taught, and
even heavenly; and he may be given credit for living up to his highest religious and educational ideals. Too often, however, we see the
painter of the picture glorified, rather than the works of the Creator
which inspired the artist and thus made the painting possible. We
have a suggestion here of the true nature and mission of art. Art
fulfils its highest mission only when it leads us to a higher appreciation of the beauties of nature, whether they be inanimate, animate, or
human. A taste for things beautiful in nature, a refined and delicate
feeling of pleasure in the sunset, the woods, the mountain streams,
and a sympathy for nature's creatures, are among the highest ideals
of art instruction.

When fine art becomes separated from all other arts, when fine
art ceases to be an integral part of the thoughts, actions, and inner
being of the individual, its grace, charm, and effectiveness are lost.

Instruction in fine arts is the creation of an atmosphere in which
the student breathes, moves, and performs every detail of his life's
work. Fine art should affect our taste for nature, for literature, for
music, for high companionship, and, in fact, for everything that may
be made lovely and holy.

Art is not a subject to be isolated from all other subjects, and then
subdivided into its various parts for special study and arrangement;
but rather a charming appreciation of all things beautiful, at all
times, and in all places. Consider for a moment the broad influence
of art in the modern home. Notice the simplicity of lines in the
woodwork and furniture; notice the color scheme of carpets, rugs,
tapestry, wall-paper, and decorations. While there are many things
in one room, the harmonious blending of colors and of simple
decorations impresses one with a unity and simplicity that are ex-
quisitely pleasurable. The darker tones of the floor gradually lighten
to the soft tints of the ceiling, producing a quietude in the individual
similar to that felt when nature supplies the restful dark green beneath, the woods and mountains in the background, and the light-
blue sky above.

An attempt to separate clearly the arts from the crafts in such a
home would mean annihilation to both. Without the delicate artistic touches to the structural and ornamental elements, there would be

little need or appreciation for much of the craftsman's work. Reciprocally, without the constructions of manufacturer and craftsman, how and where may the artist express his feelings or display his talents?   .

The union of arts and crafts is displayed in every department of a modern home; from the drawing-room to the kitchen, the principles of harmony, simplicity, and beauty are expressed by the correlated work of the artist and the artisan.

This correlation is strikingly manifested also in private, municipal, and national enterprises, though what has been accomplished is a very small part of what is to be. Elaborate preparations are on foot in many of our cities to adopt a style of architecture adapted to the climate and most fitting the natural environment; also to give such cities an arrangement of public buildings that will add architectural beauty, and at the same time suit the convenience of the public. The conception of artistic civic centers, with landscape gardening, boulevards, and parks, is growing in popularity every day, and evidences in a profound way the increasing public demand and appreciation for the union of arts and handicrafts. In many of our American cities the union of the beautiful and the useful is being expressed in every detail coming under municipal control. We find artistic feeling expressed even in the poles and fixtures for electric and gas lights, in billboards, shop fronts, fire-alarm boxes, plates naming the streets, letter-boxes, electric-light signs, pavements, fountains, monuments, and the arrangement of steps, flowers, shrubs, trees, and lawns.

Striking examples of this harmonious blending of the arts and crafts may be found in public buildings, such as the Boston Public Library and the Southern Pacific Railroad Depot at San Antonio, Tex. The latter has an entrancing architectural charm, and seems to bespeak the climate, history, and character of the Texan people. The simplicity, beauty, and unity expressed by the Boston Public Library are beyond description. One can simply breathe the atmosphere and receive the inspirations. Every minute spent within its walls only enhances the ennobling influences which administer to the spiritual emotion.

In government buildings, such as the Congressional Library and the new San Francisco Post-Office, we see indications of a growing national desire for the correlation of hand crafts and arts. Though these national buildings may not fully satisfy our ideals for unity and simplicity, nevertheless, when viewing them, the æsthetic element dominates ones feelings.

At the Louisiana Exposition much of the so-called arts and crafts was exhibited in the Palace of Fine Arts. Porcelain, glass and metal-work, textiles, and household furnishings were awarded honors and prizes on equal terms with paintings and sculpture. It is gratifying to note this national approval of the art-craft movement. It would seem in place not to ask the following questions: Should teachers of art or of manual training ignore the official position of the government in this matter? Should they ignore the desires and needs of society? Should art be taught largely for art's sake, and manual training largely for the sake of manual training; or should they both be taught wholly for the pupil's sake, and for the sake of society which we serve?

It is unfortunate that teachers of art and manual training have been slow to recognize each other's virtues; for the work of either is essential to the welfare of the other. If the fault lies unevenly, it would seem to rest on the side of those who are mechanically inclin-ed. The all-important thing at present is to harmonize these elements, and thus secure a reciprocal influence between art and construction. The most useful things are artistic, and the most artistic things are in the highest sense useful.

The artistic project is becoming the ideal of the artisan, while usefulness and fitness are being recognized by artists as concomitants of the beautiful. This meeting upon common ground of art and industry is due in no small measure to our changed and changing notions of education, thoroughness, and specialization. The specialist of today is not that person who knows one thing and only one thing, but rather that person who knows one thing in relation to all other things to which it is in some way related.

There is no adverse criticism of the artist who wishes to make a shelf or plant and care for a flower garden; on the contrary, we credit him with being an artist of the broader sort. The artisan in the same way is considered a more proficient man if he gives a touch of beauty to the form and color of his work.

The present tendency to introduce art and manual training into the already crowded curriculum of our public schools is due to this broader view of education, thoroughness, and culture. Both these subjects touch in a vital way the very heart-strings of every boy, girl, man, and woman. Each of these branches is related in some way to every other subject in the curriculum, and by denying either of them a place in the course of study we only weaken that course, and consequently the pupil; for we are thereby cutting off the full supply of experience which give life and motive to the thoughts and actions of normal children.

The school-teacher who objects to art and manual training, on the ground that there is not even time to teach reading, writing, and arithmetic thoroughly, is like the farmer who spent all his time plowing, harrowing, irrigating, and fertilizing; but, as he never found time to do these things thoroughly and perfectly, he therefore objected to planting any seed. This school work that is always *getting ready* for life, and forever says to the child, "Don't touch life till you are thoroughly prepared by studying textbooks," is like the experience of the farmer who refused to plant seeds until the propitious time had passed, or like the boy who was trying to swim before venturing into the water.

I have little patience with that form of education which is based wholly upon a preparation for life. If school work is not life, and life work, it is not worthy the name of education. Education means life. "I have come that ye may have life, and that ye might have it more abundantly." The life of every boy and every girl is an unfolding, a growth, a participation in some form of life's duties; and the process is internal application, not external. We have looked upon the child too much as we should a watch with all its wheels, springs, screws, and cogs, thinking that, as the watch-maker may adjust and lubricate till the perfect timepiece is produced, just so the teacher may force his ideas and impressions upon the child, regardless of the child's aptitudes, previous experiences, or attainments. If this theory were true, we should have found the perfect man long ago. We shall make educational progress faster and more naturally by thinking of the child rather as a plant which does and must develop largely according to its natural inclinations. We can nourish, protect, and guide, but we cannot safely force either the growth of the plant or the development of the child.

As a means of natural unfolding and self-expression we find both art and manual training to be safe and reliable agents. The correlation of these two subjects is the great need of each. This cannot be done by discussing the relative merits of each, nor by emphasizing the strong characteristic features of one for the benefit of improving the other. What we must do is to seek common ground, and work together along the line of least resistance for common ideals. We have already shown that there are certain fields of educational work, and of industrial enterprises, and of practical, everyday affairs which look to both art and mechanical skill for their highest and richest realization of success. Speaking broadly, we find that even remote and apparently unrelated branches, such as music, poetry, and literature, are dependent in no small way upon fine arts for a full and complete interpretation. The mechanical element, likewise, is necessary for any expression of cadence and rhythm in either poetry or music.

It is in the field of industrial arts that hand skill and fine arts are obviously related and interdependent. In the preparation and serving of foods, in the planning and making of clothing, in the construction of homes, business houses, means of transportation, and in the various other conveniences serving the æsthetic and practical needs of man, we find the common ground referred to, the workable field for both fine arts and manual training.

In considering the various sub-topics coming under the general heading "industrial arts," we find some lines—such as pottery, basketry, and metal-work—lending themselves most naturally to the artistic designer. There are other lines—such as textiles, cardboard, and wood-work, offering many limitations; while still other lines—such as joinery and machine-shop work—admit of every little art expression.

Let us consider what phases of art are best suited to manual-training courses. Both applied design and art interpretations may well serve the manual teacher; for the former deals with the size, form, and color of constructions, and the latter allows a universal application of art principles.

It is evident that other important lines of art—such as a study of pictures, of the life and works of artists, of historical and inspirational masterpieces, as well as the production of pure or modified representation—are less intimately related to structural work.

That branch of art known as "design" seems, then, to be most vitally related to hand-work. Indeed, it is an essential part of that work; for it deals not only with decoration, but also with construction and arrangements of parts. By "design" I mean the "conception and expression of form and color ideas, including all kinds of construction, arrangement, and decoration." The main purposes of design are to secure unity, simplicity, and beauty; the specific principles of balance, rhythm, harmony, variations, etc., are also to be ever kept in mind.

Every design must be influenced by, and must conform to, the ideas of *use* to which the thing is to be put, to the essential structure, to the materials of which it is to be made, and to its surroundings. It is in these last ideas that the artist finds his greatest difficulties, when trying to assist the manual-training work. The art teacher who has never made a basket can hardly be expected to direct the work in designing baskets. The same difficulties arise in designing for sewing, bent-iron work, cabinet-making, or any other line of hand-work.

The question naturally arises: Where may the teacher be found who is at once artist and mechanic? One rarely finds an artist with the accurate training of a mechanic; the artist rather deplores accuracy, as being destructive to art. On the other hand, how few technological students find real pleasure in fine arts; they rather look upon artists as visionary persons, who have a superstitious reverence for beautiful forms and color.

Occasionally we find an artist who sees how art may be applied to the work of securing and making food, clothing, and shelter, in such a way as to administer to the æsthetic feelings as well as to the material comforts of man. Occasionally, too, we see a manual-training teacher taking fine-arts courses, and getting the appreciation and spirit of art, perhaps as a controling influence over all he sees, and hears, and thinks.

While we are expressing our desires and ideals concerning the simultaneous teaching of hand-work and art, the fact still remains that the artist-artisan who is at once an artisan-artist is rarer than the four-leafed clover, I might say, after the frost.

What education wants today are men and women who are well balanced in these two related subjects, who appreciate both, and who can teach both without under- or overestimating either.

The teacher of design should fully understand the limitations of material to be used. Such knowledge is impossible to one who has not had much experience in the manipulation of substances involved in manual-training courses. The teacher of hand-work has the limitations of material well defined; he usually has his ideas of design well defined also; too well, in fact, for the straight edge and compasses are still used at the expense of free-hand designs, and consequently the æsthetic element is not given its rightful place.

It is practically impossible for the art teacher and the manual-training teacher fully to agree upon the design and structure of a given project, and this lack of agreement indicates the desirability of securing a teacher who is well balanced in designing and construction. Such combined qualifications, as has been pointed out before, are rarely found in one teacher. And this indicates the crux of the whole matter. When our training schools and colleges can send out well-balanced teachers of the arts and crafts—teachers who understand both, and teachers who love to teach both—the question before us now will not be a difficult one to solve. This does not mean that teachers without training in each line should be forced to teach both; for if the teacher is an artist, it is futile to try to get an exact balance of the two. If the teacher is a mechanic, the same is true. Let the teacher teach that which he loves, that which he feels and lives in, that which he has the power to enthuse his pupils with, and to give them a thirst for more.

To state briefly our conclusions:

1. Art and manual training are fundamentally related, and should be so considered in elementary and secondary schools.

2. In all lines of industrial arts hand-work and design may be advantageously correlated.

3. The double purpose of this correlation is to elevate and refine the work of the artisan, and at the same time to make the artist's work practical and essential.

4. From the pupil's standpoint, this correlation gives interest, reason, and motive to both art and hand-work.

5. Lastly, the ideal is to make of every teacher artist an artisan-artist, and of every teacher artisan an artist-artisan.

NATIONAL PURITY CONFERENCE

Arrangements for the National Purity Conference to be held in Chicago, October 9, 10, and 11, have been steadily going forward, and warrant the belief that we are to have very much the best gathering of persons interested in the promotion of purity that has ever been called in our country. ·

ITS IMPORTANCE

The importance of this conference cannot be overestimated. The time is ripe for united, national effort to be directed against the organized traffic in virtue. Events the past months of even more than usual boldness and flagrance have occurred to give publicity to this organized traffic. There is an interest in the purity movement, awakened, no doubt, by these facts made public, much greater than ever before noticed by our oldest workers. People are looking to us to lead in some united effort which shall bring relief from this awful debauchery of our sons and daughters.

NATIONAL PURITY FEDERATION

This conference is called by, and will be held under the auspices of, the National Purity Federation, which was founded at the National Purity Conference held at La Crosse, Wis., in October, 1905. The officers, executive committee, and object are as follows:

OFFICERS: President, B. S. Steadwell, La Crosse, Wis.; Vice-President, Miss Katharine Bushnell, Oakland, Cal.; Corresponding Secretary, Sidney C. Kendall, Long Beach, Cal.; Recording Secretary, Mrs. Rose Woodallen Chapman, Brooklyn; Treasurer, Dr. Carolyn Geisel, Battle Creek, Mich.

EXECUTIVE COMMITTEE: Mr. Anthony Comstock, New York City; Dr. Emma F. A. Drake, Denver; Mrs. E. M. Whittemore, New York City; Dr. J. H. Kellogg, Battle Creek, Mich.; Dr. Mary Wood-Allen, Brooklyn; Miss Belle H. Mix, Danville, Ia.; Professor Newton N. Riddell, Chicago; Miss Hattie Dickson, Marshalltown, Ia.; Mrs. Lenora Lake, St. Louis; Mrs. Elizabeth Andrew, Oakland, Cal.; Dr. Howard A. Kelly, Baltimore; Mrs. V. A. Barnes, St. Louis; Rev. Dr. H. Pereira Mendes, New York City; Mrs. Julia Kurtz, Milwaukee, Wis.; J. T. Upchurch, Dallas, Tex.; Mrs. Nora E. R. Perkins, Milwaukee.

OFFICIAL ORGAN: *The Light,* published at La Crosse, Wis.

The object of this Federation shall be to unite in national co-operation all those forces in the United States that are striving to promote purity in the life of the individual, in social relations, and in family life by preventive, rescue, educational, reformatory, law enforcement, and legislative lines of effort.

DELEGATES

Delegates from churches, reform societies, labor unions, temperance organizations, social settlements, and all bodies promoting purity, will be welcome at this conference, as well as individuals who are interested in the cause which it is called to further. The Federation, while distinctly and thoroughly religious, is not connected with any sect and is independent of any political party, philosophical school, and religious confession. All will be welcome. Come!

REDUCED RAILROAD RATES

The Western Passenger Association, Central Passenger Association, and Southwestern Excursion Bureau have each granted a rate of a fare and one-third for the round trip from all points in their respective territory. It is fully expected that all passenger associations in the United States will concur in these low rates. Local ticket agents can give all necessary information after September 1. Delegates should observe that these rates will be on the regular certificate plan. When purchasing your ticket for Chicago, ask your ticket agent for *certificate* (not receipt) duly filled out. If you cannot buy through ticket, get certificate for each ticket purchased. When signed by joint agent, who will be present on Wednesday and Thursday, and for which he will charge twenty-five cents each, the certificate will enable you to buy return ticket for one-third regular fare, provided one hundred delegates holding certificates are present at the conference.

LOCAL ARRANGEMENTS AT CHICAGO

The local arrangements at Chicago are in charge of a very able committee, composed of the following: Rev. William Burgess, Chairman, 6822 South Park Avenue; Rev. Jenkin Lloyd Jones, Bishop Samuel T. Fallows, Rabbi Tobias Schanfarber, Mrs. J. B. Caldwell, Dr. David Paulson, Rev. Dr. John Balcom Shaw, Professor W. S. Jackman, and Rev. Joseph F. Flint.

This committee has already performed much work and promises as every provision for the comfort of delegates and the convenience of the conference.

PLACE OF HOLDING THE CONFERENCE

Rev. Jenkin Lloyd Jones and his people of All Souls' Church have very generously and kindly offered the Abraham Lincoln Center for our conference. The offer was promptly accepted by the Chicago committee. Lincoln Center is located at the corner of Oakwood Boulevard and Langley Avenue (between Thirty-eighth and Thirty-ninth Streets, near Cottage Grove Avenue), and is conveniently reached from all parts of the city by street cars. The auditorium of Lincoln Center will accommodate nearly one thousand people, and there are ample rooms for rest, sectional meetings, and committee work. The management will serve supper each evening of the conference for the convenience of delegates, at a price of only twenty-five cents. It is possible that lunches will also be served. There are very excellent hotels located within convenient distance of Lincoln Center. Very reasonable rates have been secured for delegates which will enable them to keep expenses down to a low figure.

THE PROGRAM

The chief interest in a gathering of this nature centers in the program, and we are fortunate this year in having assured the very best program ever given at a purity conference. Men and women from all sections of our country who have attained eminence in their chosen work will present thorough discussions covering every phase of the purity question.

Delegates should plan to arrive in Chicago as early as possible on Tuesday morning, October 9. At 10 o'clock there will be a meeting of the Executive Committee, and at 1:30 o'clock there will meet in different rooms at Lincoln Center, two sectional conferences. The one dealing with "Purity Instruction in Schools" is in charge of a committee with Mrs. Elizabeth B. Grannis as chairman, while Rev. Sidney C. Kendall is arranging the sectional meeting on the "White Slave Traffic." At 4 o'clock a joint meeting will be held, being the first meeting of the general conference, at which committees will be announced and the president's address delivered. On Wednesday and Thursday three sessions will be held each day.

SPEAKERS

Space does not permit more than the mention of speakers thus far secured. A number not here given will appear on the program.

Rev. Wilbur F. Crafts, Ph.D., Washington, D. C.; Mr. Anthony Comstock, New York City; Mrs. Lenora Lake, St. Louis; Maria Lydia Winkler, Berlin, Germany; John B. Lennon, treasurer, American Federation of Labor; Miss Frances A. Kellor, New York City; Professor Newton N. Riddell, Chicago; Mary Church Terrell, Washington; Dr. J. H. Kellogg, Battle Creek; Rabbi Tobias Schanfarber, Chicago; Rev. Sylvanus Stall, D.D., Philadelphia; Rev. Father Coffey, St. Louis; Dr. Mary Wood-Allen, Brooklyn; Mrs. Rose Woodallen Chapman, Brooklyn; Theodore Schroeder, New York City; Ada Wallace Unruh, Portland, Ore.; Mrs. E. M. Whittemore, New York City; Delos F. Wilcox, Ph.D., Detroit; Mother Prindle, Boston; Miss Belle H. Mix, Danville, Ia.; Mr. J. B. Caldwell, Chicago; Mrs. Mary E. Teats, Los Angeles, Cal.; Mrs. Charlton Edholm Sibley, Tucson, Ariz.; Rev. Wiley J. Phillips, Los Angeles; Mrs. E. M. Adams, Mound City, Kan.; Dr. Hattie E. Schwendener, St. Joseph, Mich.; Dr. Emma F. A. Drake, Denver; Rev. Charles Mitchell, Guthrie, Okla.; Rev. George Rheinfrank, Le Mars, Ia.; Mrs. Sarah F. Bond, Oklahoma City; Rev. Albert Godley, Munice, Ind.; Mr. Richard R. Lee, Omaha.

FURTHER INFORMATION

The complete program, including full information relative to railroad rates, hotels, sectional conferences, etc., will be ready for mailing by September 15. These will be sent free of cost in any quantity requested to all applicants. Address further inquiries to NATIONAL PURITY FEDERATION, B. S. Steadwell, President, La Crosse, Wis.

You are most cordially invited to attend the National Purity Conference. The conference will represent the true federation spirit, and no matter what phase of the purity movement, the greatest cause on earth, you are interested in, you will find here people who are devoting their lives to the prosecution of just that work and ample consideration given to same on the program. Urge other interested persons to come and organizations to send delegates. No one truly devoted to the cause of purity can afford to miss this conference. Come anticipating that our fellowship together shall accomplish much for our movement.

LYDIA AVERY COONLEY

JESSIE L. GAYNOR

1. In - dian, in your blanket bound, In - dian, in your bead chains wound,
2. When to fish and hunt you go In the mountains white with snow,
3. Cun - ning lit - tle red pappoose, Tight - ly strapped in cradle noose,

O - ma - ha, or Sioux, or Crow, With your ar - row and your bow,—
When you pitch your point-ed tent Where the pan-ther late - ly went,—
With your moc-ca-sin on your feet, Blank - et for your robe complete;

Tell me, do you like to roam With the for - est for your home?
Can it be you nev - er fear Sav - age foes are hid - ing near?
This fair land was all your own Ere Co - lum - bus made it known.

[1]From *Songs in Season*, by permission of A. Flanagan, publisher.

EDITORIAL NOTES

Somebody should write a *Primer of Evolution* for the especial use of school-teachers. Everybody *says* nowadays that

Wanted:
A Primer

he bases his work with the children upon the principles of evolution, but practice soon betrays that very few clearly or fully appreciate how much is implied in their adoption. Our educational practice rests mainly upon a curious and a confusing blend of evolutionary theory with ancient tradition. Bound up in the same teacher's mind we can often find the most audacious guesses concerning the possibilities of growth and a whole code of superstitious rites as a proposed means of realizing them—hence the imperative need of a Primer.

The first lesson of this Primer should impress the point that the present never represents anything but a group of conditions

Chapter I

that is undergoing reorganization; conditions that are resolving themselves constantly into new relationships. Most teachers have gone no farther than dimly to realize that "the present is a transition stage"—meaning by this

Evolution vs.
Intermittent
Transition

that it represents a set of conditions in flux *which connect one fixed state with another fixed state that is soon to follow.* But this is not evolution at all; it is a nugatory blend of two diametrically opposed ideas, and the product is practically worthless as a foundation principle for school-teaching. Under this false idea, the teacher is continually trying to bring a living, moving, growing, thing, the child, into a state of rest. Without fully realizing it, he has his ideals fixed on the stage of quiet which it is supposed will succeed the period of transition. Present unrest is only to be endured for the sake of the repose that is to come. The teacher deals with it as a

Mistaking the
Permanent for
the Transient

temporary shifting thing preliminary to future stable realities. He recognizes the importance of present movement to the *growing* thing, but, after all, his interest is centered *in the thing grown up;* whereas, it is the fact that a fully grown-up stage is never reached. Evolution never predicts that for even our descendants. Here is a blend of the modern ideas of evolution with the ancient heathen notion of a state of endless quietude. This is at the root of most of the spiritual conflicts between pupil and teacher. Let the Primer make this matter clear.

The second lesson of the Primer should bring out sharply the fact that evolution involves elimination and extinction as well as conservation and propagation; that it involves degeneration as well as progress. It is the most serious part of the teacher's business to determine the direction and the value of a tendency. This was not always so. In the past all human tendencies were bunched together and assumed to be bad. In those days the science of teaching was an organized and wholesale warfare against nature. After the complete subjugation of nature, education was, then, something to be supplied. Under such ideals teaching was a matter of "main strength." Under the newer ideals the value of education will be determined largely, so far as the teacher is concerned, by his power of discrimination; that is, upon his ability to decide which tendencies are fading and atavistic, and which are growing and prophetic; which should be ignored and discountenanced, and which should be recognized and cultivated. A study of tendencies is the critical thing in education. As child-study and psychology have shown, they have their natural periods of appearance and disappearance. If the teacher misjudges and cultivates the wrong one, or neglects the right one at the proper period, irreparable mischief is done. Most teachers, blindly applying the "Recapitulation Theory," make too much of many selfish tendencies in childhood that are as rudimentary, socially, as the vermiform appendix is physiologically. It is no part of education to encourage growth in one more than in the other. Such tendencies must be reckoned with, but it is ridiculous to treat them as a help instead of as a hindrance in human development.

Illustrations are numerous; for example, take the question of

Chapter II

The Importance of Tendencies

ambidexterity. Is the gradual shifting of function to one hand,
Significance usually the right, a sign of progress or of degenera-
of Biological tion? How should the teacher deal with this tend-
Specialization ency of the pupil to localize functions in one of two
similarly constructed organs or members? That is, is the evident
tendency of man to change from a bilaterally symmetrical animal
to one that is unilateral, a tendency in the line of progress or
of deterioration? Until we can settle this question, our teaching
must be at random. The tendency to localize physical functions
seems to be almost irresistible. In teaching how to ride the
bicycle, most instructors were careful to train their pupils to
dismount on either side. Yet, once "out of school," not one rider
in a hundred, perhaps, continued to dismount indifferently on the
two sides—one or the other being permanently chosen. In
mounting a horse, one always does so from the left side—
though, but for the tendency toward unilateralism, there is no
reason why either side should have the preference. There are
many skilful horsemen who would even find it almost, if not
quite, impossible to mount from the "off side." The milking
of a cow from the right side is another concession in the same
direction. This has gone so far as to create a kind of corresponding habit in the bilateral cow herself, as there are few of
them, indeed, that will not kick—literally kick—if the milker in
absent-mindedness tries to perform the operation from the
"wrong side."

Now here is a biological tendency—what is its meaning? Is
it backward or forward? On the one side, the gist of the argument is that, if we can do well with one hand, we should be twice
as well off if the other hand were equally proficient—which may
be a statement of fact, but it is certainly not proof. On the other
side, it is claimed that the localization of function in one place
rather than in two results in a refinement of work that would not
otherwise be possible. This, also, is an assertion, but not proof.
In the meantime our teaching will be guesswork—each according
to his own guess.

The study of tendencies is not less interesting in other than strictly biological fields. At present we are trying to conduct the

Significance of Social Tendencies school according to the ideals required by the theory of social development. But there is in every school a tendency—now much in favor, too—that is diametrically opposed to those ideals. This is the tendency toward so-called specialization in studies and in teaching. The specialist—the type most commonly met—is one who turns his back upon the social theory. He sets himself off as one apart, hyena-like, to enjoy his bone alone. We cannot imagine a "social" body composed of different specialists. They could only form an aggregation. If one were to lock up in the same room, for example, a specialist in some department of chemistry

Specialists as Social Types with a specialist in some department of language, there would be but little chance for social organization, unless both were to forsake their specialties. By mutual consent—thus implying a social instinct—they would have to unite upon some common topic—say, the weather. But then they would be specialists no longer! They would be compelled to discuss a topic that neither knew much about, or else be doomed to a gloomy solitude. Here is a tendency, the value of which, as a means of education, should be carefully determined. In the social field there have been some examples which will throw light upon the subject. While in the biological world no strictly unilateral or bilateral prodigy has been produced, in the social domain it is different. Here nature is not always uncertain or atavistic. At times in chance creations of mind she is clearly prophetic.

A generation or two ago the world was interested in the musical wonder known as "Blind Tom." In the direction of

Blind Tom music Blind Tom seemed to have reached the limit of development. Into him, nature appeared to crowd the result of a thousand ages of musical education. Thru him, we were permitted to look into the distant future and catch a glimpse of what specialization in music may do. But Blind Tom was the extreme limit also of the anti-social type. He was absolutely senseless toward every social influence. From the social standpoint in him, degeneracy had reached the bottom; from that of the specialist he represented the climax—that pitch of perfection where all that we now call learning, knowledge and wisdom, in music, had become practically an unconscious instinct. For him, in the field of music, there was no more learning—no more knowledge.

We have examples of the opposite kind, too. Take Leonardo da Vinci; a mechanic, an engineer, an inventor, an artist, and a scientist; a scientist, in the dark ages, asking ques-
Leonardo Da Vinci tions upon which no twentieth-century scientist can improve. He was a man not only great in almost every field of human endeavor; he possessed an open-mindedness that far outran his day—that far outruns our own time. He was in no sense a specialist. Were he to come to life now, it would seem as though he should fall in at once with any and all of our many activities and immediately lead the way into new fields. He stands high as an ideal social type. There is no phase of society where the Da Vinci quality of life is not made welcome and which it does not adorn.

The human being when born is open to a wonderful variety of interests. For a brief period he is left in a measure unfettered,
Variety of Inherited Interests and he acquires skill, knowledge, and a breadth of interest to a marvelous extent. The school then takes hold, and with its dogma that "a few things well learned are better than a little of many things,' it begins the cramping, narrowing process, until in some cases it actually creates in the man a kind of pride in his ignorance concerning most things on the earth. It is as tho he used his vast ignorance of many things to represent obversely the depth and intensity of his knowledge of a few.

Now, if the present does foreshadow the future, and if the social ideal is the thing to be developed, we must draw the line somewhere on the specialist. If we want to develop
A False Scent the social type, we must treat with greater considera-tion and intelligence that love for breadth of knowl-edge that is the instinct of every child. The plea of the specialist is that, since one cannot know all or very much about everything, the general quest should be abandoned and he should try to know a great deal about a few things. But in the growth of the social type as a product of evolution, it is not the *amount of knowledge*

either of many things or of one thing that is important. It is that hospitality toward all things and interest in them which makes social organization possible. Nobody can transmit his knowledge to posterity any more than he can his money. But **Only Quality** his quality of character, his attitude toward all **of Character** things, including his fellows, whether it be narrow, **Transmittible** self-centered, and solitary, or whether it be liberal, sympathetic, and social—it is this quality of character that seems to go onward through the generations. Herein lies the real significance of the teaching of psychology, that the period of childhood and youth should be prolonged to the latest moment: not merely that the child may be kept in short clothes, may play with dolls, and may be fed with a spoon, but, rather, that the inborn and inherited breadth of interest may have the chance of unhampered growth as long as possible. This is important because **The Child** *it is in his early years that the human being most* **the Social** *clearly foreshadows the real social type of the far-* **Type** *distant future.* As instinctive and untrained children, we are truly social; as educated adults, we degenerate and become merely gregarious.

There is dire need for a reformation of specialists and of specialization. The universities must stop sending into the high school and elementary school their graduates as **Reform** specialists who have no knowledge of the tendencies **Needed** that sway childhood and youth, and consequently no appreciation of their tremendous significance. For an obvious reason, the kind of specialization now permitted in the universities leads the majority of teachers so prepared to begin with children just where they themselves left off in their postgraduate work. Such teachers bring into the schoolroom all the formulas of true scientific instruction, but these in their hands are as meaningless and ineffectual with childhood and youth as would be the rites and ceremonies of the sun-worshipers. It is another instance of a confusing blend of modern scientific method with the antiquated theory that early tendencies must be overcome, or, at least, may be ignored.

Here, then, are three chapters for our *Primer of Evolution.*

W. S. J.

BOOK REVIEWS

Agriculture for Beginners. By CHARLES WILLIAM BUNKETT, Professor of Agriculture, and FRANK LINCOLN STEVENS, Professor of Biology, and DANIEL HARVEY HILL, Professor of English in the North Carolina College of Agriculture and Mechanic Arts. Boston, New York, Chicago; London: Ginn & Co. Pp. xii+339. 12mo, cloth.

This is the best book on the subject for school children that has come to my notice. In their work the authors have happily combined nature-study of the "impersonal" or general kind with that of a utilitarian or economic type in an interesting and useful way. The headings of the chapters show the order of treatment and also the scope of the work. They are as follows: I, "The Soil;" II, "The Soil and The Plant;" III, "The Plant;" IV, "How to Raise a Fruit Tree;" V, "The Diseases of Plants;" VI, "Orchard, Garden, and Field Insects;" VII, "Farm Crops;" VIII, "Domestic Animals;" IX, "Farm Dairying;" X, "Miscellaneous—Foodstuffs, Tools, Birds, and Life in the Country;" XI, "Supplement on Horticulture, Market Gardening, etc."

The book should be a text in every county, village, and city school where there are opportunities for observing farm work or for participating in gardening either at home or at school. It presents farming and gardening as fascinating studies, and no pupil can follow its pages without developing a genuine respect for these greatest of human industries, as well as a wide knowledge concerning them. The illustrations, of which there are many, are well chosen and excellently executed.

The book is not merely a "reader;" it contains many suggestions for both teacher and pupil which, if heeded, will furnish a continuous line of work in observation outdoors and experimentation indoors. It is a good beginning for both pure and practical science.

WILBUR S. JACKMAN

BOOKS RECEIVED

AMERICAN BOOK COMPANY, NEW YORK AND CHICAGO

Wilhelm Tell, Schiller. E. C. ROEDDER, Editor. Cloth, 12mo. Pp. 352. $0.70.

The Golden Fleece. By JAMES BALDWIN. Cloth, 12mo. Pp. 288. $0.50.

Hernani, Hugo. JAMES D. BRUNNER, Editor. Cloth, 12mo. Pp. 264. $0.70.

Progressive Arithmetic. First, Second, and Third Books. By WILLIAM J. MILNE, Ph.D., LL.D., President of State Normal School, Albany, N. Y.

Am Sonnenschein, Storm. By Z. L. SWIGGETT. Cloth, 12mo, Pp. 78. $0.25.

Little Stories of France. By MAUDE BURROWS DUTTON. Cloth, 12mo. Pp. 176. $0.40.

THE MACMILLAN CO., NEW YORK

Macmillan's Pocket American and English Classics. Cloth, 16mo. $0.25.

King Henry V, Washington's Farewell Address, Passages from The Bible, Dicken's Christmas Carol, Church's Story of the Odyssey, Carlyle's Heroes and Hero Worship, Emerson's Essays, Bacon's Essays, Miles Standish, Homer's Iliad, Church's Story of The Iliad, Hawthorne's Wonder Book, Carroll's Alice's Adventures, Longfellow's Tales of a Wayside Inn.

How We Are Sheltered: A Geographical Reader. By JAMES F. CHAMBERLAIN, Ed.B., S.B. Cloth, 12mo. Pp. 184.

History of The English Language. By OLIVER FARRAR EMERSON, A.M., Ph.D. Cloth, 12mo. Pp. 415.

SILVER, BURDETT & CO., NEW YORK AND CHICAGO

Essentials of United States History. By WILLIAM Q. MOWRY AND BLANCHE S. MOWRY. Cloth, 12mo. Pp. xv+434. $0.90.

The World and Its People: Book VII. Views in Africa. By ANNA B. BADLAM. Cloth, 12mo. Pp. 443.

The School and Its Life. By CHARLES B. GILBERT. Cloth, 12mo. Pp. 266. $1.25.

B. F. JOHNSON PUBLISHING CO., ATLANTA

Playmates: A Primer. By M. W. HALIBURTON. Cloth, 12mo. Pp. 96.

Our Language: Second Book. By C. ALPHONSO SMITH, Ph.D. Cloth, 12mo. Pp. 240.

MAYNARD MERRILL & CO., NEW YORK

Graded Poetry Readers, Nos. 1, 2, 3, and 4. Edited by KATHERINE D. BLAKE AND GEORGIA ALEXANDER.

THE WHITAKER & RAY CO., SAN FRANCISCO

Lessons in Nature Study. By OLIVER P. JENKINS AND VERNON L. KELLOGG. Cloth, 12mo. Pp. 191.

CHARLES SCRIBNER'S SONS, NEW YORK

Occupations for Little Fingers. By ELIZABETH SAGE AND ANNA M. COOLEY. Introductory Note by Mary Schenk Woolman. Cloth, 12mo. Pp. 154.

PARKER P. SUMMERS, NEW YORK

An Algebra for Grammar Schools. By CHARLES A. HOBBS, A.M. Cloth, 12mo. Pp. 138.

VOLUME VII   NUMBER 3

THE ELEMENTARY SCHOOL TEACHER

NOVEMBER, 1906

NORWAY

A READING LESSON

GEORG THORNE-THOMSEN

Far to the north, stretching out toward the eternal snow and ice of Arctic regions, and in the latitudes of Greenland and Alaska, lies my native country, Norway.

Every year great numbers of foreigners visit this northern country in order to enjoy its beautiful scenery. And no wonder, for nature presents herself in Norway in a marvelous variety of forms.

To see Norway with its islands, fiords, glaciers, waterfalls, mountains, lakes, and forests; to see it all in the glow of a northern summer night, or under the flaming northern lights of its long winter, is to acquire a beautiful remembrance for one's whole life.

But there is something to be found in Norway besides its scenery, although this is all for which the country stands to the superficial traveler. The beauty of Norway lies, after all, in its people: they are the blossom of the country, and its beating heart; and in their character, in their mythology, literature, and art, the wonderful scenery is reflected as in a mirror. The people are the living and ever-changing expression of all that is beautiful and upright, as well as of all that is gloomy and melancholy, in this scenery, which has left its deep impress, not only upon the life of the individual, but also upon the whole national life of Norway.

Are you able to change your identity for a few moments in order to live with these people, to love and hate as they do, to enter into their longings and sufferings, into their hopes and yearnings? If you are, we are ready for our journey.

Let us imagine ourselves approaching the Norwegian coast in a steamer. Can you see the little white spot appearing on the horizon? As it comes nearer it proves to be a sailboat. A Norwegian pilot-boat has come to meet us and bring the first greetings from the country that we are to visit.

The weather is bright, but the sea is running high. At one moment the little sailboat seems almost hidden among the big waves; at another, it is high on the crest of them. The pilot-boat comes nearer and nearer, although continually dashed over by the rough sea. Soon you can distinguish the Norwegian red, white, and blue on the top mast, and discern two persons on the boat. At last the pilot is close enough to throw the line over to us on the steamer, and the next minute he is on board and takes command of the vessel.

The Norwegian pilot is the modern type of the old Norse viking. You find the same daring, the same undaunted spirit, in the two; for both belong to that stalwart stamp of man that among the old Norsemen was considered the ideal type of manhood. The pilot is one of the most interesting figures among the Norwegian people and embodies some of their best qualities. His home is found on one of the barren islands along the coast, where he is always watching for vessels in danger. The most furious storm never finds him unwilling to start out in his little boat and risk his life when other lives can be saved. When the pilot is on board and has taken command of the vessel, the pilot-boat is left entirely in the hands of the little pilot-boy, a lad of perhaps thirteen or fourteen years. He has to take the boat home all alone, but he knows every reef around; from the time he could lift an oar he has followed his father on his excursions. The boat was his cradle and only plaything; the boat is, perhaps, the last thing he sees in the world.

This is the way many a Norwegian lad is brought up, with his boat as his school-desk, and the sea as his schoolmaster. As the sea is, so is his life: it embraces his whole future with its joys and sorrows; he looks to the sea for every blessing that life can bestow on him, but also for every misfortune that can befall a human being.

But let us watch for land. We see a blue line on the horizon. Whether it be land or only clouds is hard to tell, and for hours we watch this blue line with the feeling that behind it is hidden something wonderful. As we come nearer, this blue line proves to be the continuous chain of islands that are scattered all along the Norwegian coast, protecting the mainland from the rough outside sea and forming a safeguard for navigation. You don't feel quite at ease as the steamer makes its way in among these rocky, barren islands and reefs. They seem to look at you with an evil eye, and you wonder how you can get safely through. But there is no occasion for fear. Look at the pilot with his firm grasp of the wheel. His weather-beaten face is perfectly calm; his whole life has been spent among these reefs and islands, and what seem enemies to you are old acquaintances of his.

Back of this fence of islands the mainland rises, weather-beaten, dark, like a huge giant. You do not expect to find human dwellings in this desert of sea and rock. The seabirds seem to be the only inhabitants here. However, once in awhile, as if emerging from the deep sea, and still wet from its embrace, a little village appears on the naked shore. You get only a glimpse of a few houses scattered about; some stores for fish down on the shore; some vessels in the little harbor—that is all. A moment later the little town is hidden behind the next promontory.

All along the coast numerous narrow entrances leading into the interior of the mountain mass are found. These narrow inlets of the sea are called "fiords," and constitute the most characteristic feature of Norway.

Let us enter one of these fiords. Islands and cliffs close the entrance behind us, and we see nothing more of the open sea. You are shut in by the almost perpendicular walls of the fiord, and it seems as if a door were closed between you and the rest of the world. The whole scene produces an entirely novel sensation, because you have had nothing in your previous experience with which to compare it. You look with awe at the rugged, savage mountains as they rise perpendicularly to a sheer height of five or six thousand feet, threatening you with avalanches of snow and rock.

The fiord is here very narrow and has a depth of, perhaps, more than five thousand feet. The few huts to be found cling to the mountain-sides like eagles' nests, and goats climb the mountains to seek their scant food.

Looking up, you may see a green spot thousands of feet above your head. By looking more closely you make it out to be cultivated fields, with some houses in between. You wonder how people and cattle ever can get up to these fields that seem to be hanging out over your head thousands of feet above. A narrow path leads up there, and whatever is needed in the house must be carried on horseback. Along the precipices, across the thundering torrents, the strong little horse has to be led. It happens often during winter that snow and ice block up the narrow passage; then the family will be for months separated from the rest of the world. During the long, dark winter they will see no human being except members of their own family. If during this time death should visit them, the corpse would have to be kept throughout the winter, to be carried the next spring on horseback to the far-distant church. Sometimes not even a path leads up to these green patches. I know instances where from a projecting ledge of a rock a rope has been tied; down this rope the peasant has to climb to cut some grass.

The waters of the fiord have a bluish-green color, and are almost fresh owing to the constant downpour from the glaciers and snow-fields. All is quiet and gloomy here, and a constant twilight prevails under the shadow of these mountains. Once in a while the silence is broken by the thundering of avalanches, which sweep down from the mountains and for a moment disturb the quiet waters of the fiord; or by the distant murmur of the cascades as they are precipitated in unbroken falls of more than two thousand feet. The surface of the water is perfectly smooth and shining like a mirror. If you look down into this abyss,

you will have a feeling as if you were suspended in the midst of
the vast blue space, hovering between two infinites. Fortunately,
not much time is left for us to look at this gloomy scenery, as
at the turn of the fiord a different view is disclosed. In the
previous scenery the snow-covered mountains formed both foreground and background. Here they recede and form the rocky
frame of a picture so sublime, so harmonious in composition, as
to defy description. Most of what the Norwegians have presented to the world in their poetry, music, and art has had its
germ here. Artists have tried to catch the coloring of this region; poets have celebrated it in song, and the music of its waterfalls has sounded the world over in the violin of Ole Bull.

The majesty and grandeur of the distant snow-capped mountains form a happy contrast to the foreground of the landscape,
blend with it and intensify it. Green shores stretch far out into
the fiord, and wind and bend in the most exquisite curves. Continuous orchards of pear, apple, and cherry trees on the banks of
the fiord lend, especially in spring, a wonderful coloring to the
scenery. Waving birch trees sing in the soft breezes, and bend
down to the fiord to see their images in its clear waters. White
brooks start out from the mountain-sides and wind among the
meadows to reach the fiord. Pretty houses and large barns tell
of the prosperity of the people, while white-painted churches
lift their steeples among the orchards. Behind the meadows the
pine forest rises dark and solemn against a background of rugged mountains. Most of these mountains are crowned with immense snow- and ice-fields, from which glaciers descend to the
meadows without reaching the waters of the fiord. You hear
the distant murmur of the waterfalls; swayed by sudden gusts of
wind, they sprinkle the dark rock with a silvery spray; many disappear in mid-air changed into mist, condense again, re-form on
projecting ledges, and once more evaporate before reaching the
fiord. The murmur from these cascades never ceases; like the
glaciers, they are fed by the snow-fields. You may travel all over
Norway from north to south, from east to west, and the music
of the waterfalls will follow you everywhere. It is interesting
to note that the beauties of this particular region seem to be re-

flected in its people. The peasant living here has reached a higher development than anywhere else in Norway, both physically and mentally. His features are intelligent and refined, his carriage dignified and aristocratic. The women are beautiful, and among them you find the characteristic Scandinavian type better preserved, more unmixed, than in any other part of Norway.

The fiord forms in a way an organic part of the life of the peasant living on its banks. It takes the fish from the sea right to his door many miles inland, while it is the shining highway between the surrounding districts.

On the little promontory stands the white church, and the chiming of its bells can be heard far among the mountains. As an infant, the peasant was taken in a boat over to this church to be christened; as a boy, he was confirmed in the same place. Then came an important event in his life, when the bells chimed on his wedding-day. Such a scene has been commemorated by four of our greatest artists in color, poetry, and music. The picture is called the "Bridal Festival in Hardanger," and is painted by two of our greatest artists. Inspired by this wonderful painting, a Norwegian wrote a poem, to which music was added. A bridal party is seen gliding over the fiord, returning from church. In the stern of the bridal boat sits the fair bride, who, like a king's daughter of old, wears the golden crown that has been kept as an heirloom in the family for centuries. The bridegroom swings his hat in ecstasy; he looks at his bride, in whose blue eyes his whole future life seems reflected like a continual bridal feast. The strains from the fiddle resound over the waters, guns are fired, and the echo is ringing among the mountains.

Again, and for the last time, the peasant has to be carried across the fiord. The church bells that rang out so merrily on his wedding-day now chime with a heavy, doleful sound. In the little churchyard, on the banks of the fiord that he loved so well, he finds his last resting-place.

Among these surroundings the old Norse vikings used to live. When the king's son had reached a certain age, his father furnished him with a vessel and warriors, and from that time on he

was a sea-king, with the sea for his kingdom. In the swift-sail.
ing dragon vessel he visited distant countries, conquering and
forming new kingdoms wherever he went. His whole youth wa:
spent to gain the riches and the fame without which he did not
dare return to his own country. And then, at last, he came
back, often with a king's daughter from a far-off country, and
with marvelous tales of all the wonderful things that he had seen
out in the wide world. But sometimes, even as an old man, the
viking would be seized with a longing for the sea. When spring
came and brought a message from the outside world through the
mild sea breezes, the fiord would seem too narrow for the old
sea-king; once more would he pick out his best men, and once
more the heads of the dragon vessel would be turned toward foreign countries. Often the supremacy of the sovereign became
too trying to the independent spirit of the viking; liberty and
independence were the laws of his being, and if not to be had at
home, he knew a realm where he could roam about wherever he
chose—the wide, open sea. On such voyages Iceland and Greenland were colonized. As is well known, the vikings even pushed
their way over to America, called by them Vinland. The small
sailboat in which a few daring Norwegians succeeded in crossing the Atlantic, and which attracted so much attention at the
World's Fair, was an exact model of the famous vessel that was
unearthed some miles away from Christiania a few years ago.

What is known as Jotenheim, or "home of the giants," formed
the wildest and highest part of the Scandinavian highlands.
The mountains are situated near the west coast at the middle
part of the plateau. Among their rugged peaks you will find
nothing to remind you of the plateau or of the wide mountain-
fields that are so characteristic of other parts of Norway. With
its sharp peaks, glaciers, lakes, and narrow gorges, Jotenheim
may be called the Norwegian Alps. In order to visit Jotenheim
we shall follow one of the many valleys which, forming the land-
ward continuation of the fiords, lead up to the mountains. The
scenery of the valley is strikingly similar to that of the fiord.
In the beginning the road is superb; it winds and twists in such
a way as to leave a gentle grade and make a very easy ascent.

At the bottom of the valley a furious river rushes along; the roar of its many cascades reaches your ear, while the spray covers the pine forests like a veil. At one moment, as if repenting its own wildness, it stops suddenly to form a quiet little lake; and then, again tired of this passive life, it makes a sudden plunge and disappears from your sight. If you stop a moment and look down the valley, you will perhaps get a glimpse of the fiord, whose shining waters lie thousands of feet below you. As we pass on, the farms become fewer and the valley narrower, while of the river nothing is left but a noisy little brook that jumps from ledge to ledge. We have lost sight of the fiord long ago, and now we follow a narrow path that grows more and more indistinct.

The forest is very thin here, and the few pines and birch trees seem to struggle for existence; at last only shrubs and dwarf birches can be seen; still higher up the vegetation disappears almost entirely—only moss and heather still linger, while a few Alpine flowers peep from behind angular stones and nod to you in their brilliant colors.

After some hours of climbing we have at last reached the plateau. Your chest expands as you feel the keen blast sweeping against you. In front of you, at a very short distance, as it seems, a snow-field sparkles in the sunshine. Its surface plays in all the colors of the rainbow as the clouds drift over it; now it is transparent and white like crystals, now it changes into green and blue. From its icy embrace a stream bursts forth and starts on its long journey to the sea.

These glaciers, seemingly dead and cold, send the very life-blood through that vast body of rock called Norway. The little fiery river, child of the glacier, sets all the factories and mills going; on its swift currents the timber, cut during the winter, rushes along; and down in the large valleys, where the whistle of the engine has not been heard, it forms the highway among the districts.

At a short distance we see a few low cabins nestling among the mountains, and hear the lowing of cows; we have reached the pasture-house, or what is known in Norway as *saeter*. At the barking of a dog, a young girl, dressed in the Norwegian peasant dress, comes out to bid us welcome. At her kind invitation, let us enter the house to rest a little. The interior is very simple and primitive, but neat and clean. On the shelves tubs of butter and cheese are placed in long rows; on the floor pine needles are strewn to give fragrance. From the hearth a blazing fire greets, and we soon feel at home among these kind, hospitable people.

The fresh mountain air has given us a ravenous appetite, and we notice with delight that a meal is being prepared for us. Let us see what they have to offer us: delicious trout fished from the ice-cold lake, cheese, cream, and fresh reindeer meat constitute the bill of fare in these pasture-houses.

Let us have a little chat with the saeter girls. It's a long time since they had visitors, and although they seemed somewhat bashful a moment ago, they are glad to have a gossip. Early in the summer the peasant girls take the cattle from the valley up to the high mountains, where they can roam about for miles and feast on the rich, juicy grass. The young girls stay here during the whole summer, many miles from the valley and the nearest peasant-house, tending the cattle and making cheese and butter. When Saturday comes around, everything is put in the best order in the staeter, and the girls put on their Sunday clothes, for on that day they may expect their lads from the valley. In the evening, when the setting sun makes the snow-fields and glaciers shine like gold, the saeter girl sits down on the lawn and looks down to the valley; she blows on the mountain-horn and listens; the strains from another horn are wafted up from the valley, telling that he is on his way.

Although living so far away from people, all alone among the mountains, I have never heard that a saeter girl was ever molested or insulted by anyone. They are brave girls, who are by no means afraid to use the gun when needed against the bear or the wolf. Of course, they feel lonesome sometimes, especially in the long light summer evenings; and on Sundays, when the chiming from the little church down in the valley is heard far and wide among the mountains, many a longing thought finds its way down to the parish. But they are so busy from morning till night that there is hardly any time for longing. They have the cattle to tend, and they do take good care of them. Every cow has its pet name, to which it responds when called; some of these pet names will sound queer to your ears. Here is an example of the way they call the cattle in the evening: "Come, all little children! Come, all children mine! Come now, Brynhilda; come, Morning Glory, Moonlight, Evening Praise, Ever Clean, Star White, Shining Black, Princess, Queen, Snow White! Come, all my little children!"

All during the long, dark winter down in the valley the people long to go to the saeter, and I think the cattle do, too. In the winter the cattle get little food; but when summer comes, they eat as much as they like among the mountains. When the field-work is done down in the valley, the whole family goes to the saeter. The key of the house is left under the threshold, and for about a month you may go from house to house without finding people at home. When the family is going to start for the saeter, the few necessary things are put on the back of the little mountain-horse, and off it goes. What a joy for the children, who have looked forward to this trip during the whole winter! What a delightful day! The wild cherry is in blossom, the cuckoo is calling, the birds are singing; summer has come at last. The little Norwegian mountain-horse opens the procession with all the things. He finds his way all by himself; since he was a colt he has been accustomed to walk in the mountains. On the narrow path he finds just the right place to put his feet above the most dangerous precipices. Then comes the whole family, and then the goats and the sheep. The children are exceedingly happy. They want to have every bird and every flower they see; they throw stones in the brooks, and call and shout. At last they get a glimpse of the saeter far off on the opposite mountain slope; they see the cattle; they hear the horns of the saeter girls, and the children answer. The echo rings among the mountains and seems to say: "Welcome to the saeter!"

[To be continued]

PESTALOZZI SCENES AND MEMORIALS

H. AUSTIN AIKINS

Western Reserve University

Switzerland, which has long been devoted to the honoring of men whose very existence is a matter of conjecture, has come of late to realize that it has the first right to honor one whose life and work have been of very real service to humanity everywhere; and memorials to Pestalozzi are beginning to take their place beside those erected long since to William Tell, Arnold von Winkelried, and other hazy heroes of the early days.

The most recent of these memorials is a statue in his native city of Zurich, the work of Hugo Siegwart; and it is, at the very least, most happily suggestive: A man in the garb of a century ago supports and leads along a poor boy, thin, barefooted, and ragged, who looks upon him appealingly, and in the wrinkled, homely face of the man one can see an answering look of sympathy and fostering care. On the granite base of the monument there is nothing but the name and date:

IOH. HEINR.

PESTALOZZI

1746–1827

I do not know whether it is by design or chance that the building behind this monument is a school; but the Pestalozzi represented is evidently not so much the successful teacher of the later years at Burgdorf and Yverdun as the friend of the poor and neglected at Stans and at Neuhof, in the neighborhood of Zurich itself.

Besides this statue, erected in 1899, there is also in Zurich a little room, down by the river, containing manuscripts and other mementos of him—a room, by the way, which should not be confused with the Pestalozzi room in the National Museum, which has nothing whatever to do with the great teacher.

It will be remembered that Pestalozzi married in Zurich and

took his wife to the oft-mentioned manor "Neuhof," which he had built, and where he hoped to make a model farm; and that his work as a teacher began when he took into it the most neglected children of the degraded peasants around him, and taught them to work and hope and respect themselves—until he himself was ruined; but he had begun to prove, first to Germany and then to the world, that education is for everyone; and, further, that the most effective education is something very different from mere book-learning.

Neuhof is rather hard to find. It lies three or four miles south of the railroad junction at Brugg, a mile from the lonely station at Birrfeld and half a mile south of the shabby old village of Birr where there is nothing but a few moss-grown roofs, an old hotel, a general store, and the desolate old graveyard where Pestalozzi is buried. This is a small, bare field with a row of weather-beaten headstones laid against the wall, a plain little church in one corner, a row of cypresses in memory of some French soldiers at the back, and in the other corner a combination school and fire-engine house, with a rather elaborate memorial to "Vater Pestalozzi" overlooking his grave. One would like to think that those whom the "father" called his children had put it there; but, alas, it was not erected by "thankful Aargau" until 1846, nineteen years after his death, and some sixty-five years after the last of the children (who *would* throw their flax out of the window until "Gertrude" weighed it) had been driven from Neuhof and the farm taken by the creditors; though for some reason or other the manor was left, and Pestalozzi and his family starved and shivered in it for eighteen years longer.

Thanks to a woman leading an ox-team, I had no difficulty in finding the house, and in that neighborhood, where paint is scarce and a single roof of moss-grown straw often covers dwelling and barn and stable with wood piled high around the house windows and the dung-heap in full view, it was certainly imposing with its red tiles and fresh, white paint and separation from the stables; and here, I suppose, one might shiver and starve with dignity.

Here, at any rate, half a mile from even the village church

MONUMENT TO PESTALOZZI—ZURICH

"NEUHOF"

and "The Bear," Pestalozzi wrote his *Evening Hours of a Hermit,* sprang into sudden fame with his simple peasant tale of *Leonard and Gertrude,* and pondered over the wretched condition of his neighbors, until at last he was called to Stans to work once more directly with unfortunate children. And hence to Neuhof, when the long life's work was nearly over, Pestalozzi returned and lived his last three years.

The conditions that produced such degradation among the children of Pestalozzi's neighbors have probably disappeared long ago; at least all the children I saw seemed clean and well cared for. But as I supped that evening at "The Bear," and an old man in unspeakable shirt-sleeves sat down near me for a bottle of beer, and talked unintelligibly to nobody in particular, then I did think of the shiftless mason in *Leonard and Gertrude,* who was always drinking and always in debt to the designing landlord, though, for all I know, my friend may have been the landlord himself. As for the landlady, she gave me butter for my bread when I asked for it, and my tall glass of milk, "fresh from the beast,' was warm and dripping and covered with an inch of foam.

From Neuhof Pestalozzi's destiny took him to Stans. This is one of the places that Cook's coaches take tourists out from Lucerne to see, and is in many respects as romantic as Birr is commonplace. The lake, though near, is quite invisible, and the mountains all around, with their grassy slopes and darker pines and steep palisades and painted rocks, combine to make a scene of loveliness. To the south there is a little bit of sky between the mountains, and for four months in the winter the village gets from it each day its single hour of sunshine.

The village itself is also interesting, with its Winkelried memorial, the convent and the Capuchin monastery, the church with picturesque tower and single-fingered clock beneath the spire, the fountains on the square below, where wooden shoes clatter over the cobblestones, and on the outskirts, up the valley, a warm and friendly little cemetery like an Italian campo santo, with flowers and cloistered walls—very different from the cold churchyard at Birr.

Then too, the time of Pestalozzi's advent was far from prosaic. On the mortuary chapel beside the church is a tablet erected to the memory of the "honor-worthy priests and the virtuous fathers, mothers, sisters, and brothers, to the extent of 414, who perished for God and their native land in the harvest month of 1798," when the French army of enlightenment massacred the people for their stubborn resistance. The orphans left by this horrible tragedy had to be cared for, and so the government turned the sisters out of a part of the convent and sent Pestalozzi, a liberal and a heretic, to take care of the children. Here he shut himself up for four long months in a single room with first forty and then more of the poor wretches, loathsome with disease and vermin, and incited by their elders to hatred and suspicion; and here he nursed them, taught them, disciplined them, and loved them through the dark winter days, with results that astonished the world; until at last the convent was required for a military hospital, the children were dispersed, and Pestalozzi took to the mountains to recover his broken health.

The wing of the convent which Pestalozzi and the children occupied dates back to 1730 (the chapel is a hundred years older), but it was renovated in 1897, and is now occupied by a girls' boarding-school. In the renovation the room occupied by Pestalozzi and the children was destroyed.

In the town Pestalozzi is not altogether forgotten. "He is thought well of," said one of the inhabitants; "he did good work with the children." But in bronze or stone he has no memorial there. The fountains on the square are still presided over by Winkelried and St. John; the local dealer in picture postal-cards can give you the church or the Winkelried Memorial and the inclined roads up the Stanserhorn and the Rigi, but he has nothing to remind one especially of Pestalozzi; and even the picture of the *pensionat* Santa Clara, into which the convent is converted, happens to show as little as possible of Pestalozzi's wing.

To follow Pestalozzi's movements, we must go west some twenty miles from Lucerne and Stans to Burgdorf, in canton Bern, only a dozen miles northeast of the capital city. Burgdorf is a busy town of some eight thousand inhabitants, with arcades

MEMORIAL TO PESTALOZZI ON SCHOOLHOUSE AT BIRR. CYPRESSES TO THE RIGHT

PESTALOZZI'S WING OF THE CONVENT—STANS

in front of the shops as in Bern or Bozen, good public buildings, and a beautiful view from the castle. Here Pestalozzi made a brilliant success with the two dozen children in the lowest grade whom his friends got him a chance to teach. He did not get along so well with the higher class to which he was promoted, perhaps because he was not so well fitted to deal with it—perhaps because he was thinking too much of universal principles. Finally, he joined forces in the castle with Kruesi and the poor children whom the fortunes of war had driven out of Appenzell. For what good is a castle nowadays, unless it can be turned into a school or a museum or a lunatic asylum? This, at any rate, was the beginning of the "Institute," and in the court of the castle the tourist can find Pestalozzi's portrait in relief on a commemorative tablet. But successful as the Institute was, it lasted scarcely three years; for in those days of war and revolution the central government broke up, and the cantonal authorities required the castle for their own purposes. Then came the short stay at Münchenbuchsee, and after that the more famous Institute at Yverdun, to which his wonderful genius, and the self-sacrificing labors of Kruesi and his other assistants, attracted children from all over Europe to be taught, and teachers to learn his methods. For Pestalozzi was no longer confining himself to work with the poor, as he did at Neuhof and at Stans; he was trying to "psychologize education" everywhere, and had for the moment the attention of Europe; so much so that Queen Luise declared she wanted to drive to Switzerland to see him; the Prussian government actually sent seventeen young men for a three-year course under him; and some years later, when things were not doing so well, and the Institute was actually degraded in the eyes of his fellow-townsmen, his name and word were still able to prevent the Austrians from turning the castle and other public buildings of the place into a military hospital, and the emperor himself treated him with marked consideration. But more important than all this, it was here at Yverdun that Froebel and Karl Ritter and von Raumer, the historian of education, got their inspiration. Ritter wrote:

I have seen more than the paradise of Switzerland, for I have seen

Pestalozzi, and recognized how great his heart is, and how great his genius; never have I been so filled with a sense of the sacredness of my vocation and the dignity of human nature as in the days I spent with this noble man. . . . . Pestalozzi knew less geography than a child in one of our primary schools, yet it was from him that I gained my chief knowledge of this science; for it was in listening to him that I first conceived the idea of the natural method. It was he who opened the way to me, and I take pleasure in attributing whatever value my work may have entirely to him.[1]

To be sure, the Institute was disgraced. Its very success was its undoing; for the "family" grew too large and heterogeneous to be governed merely by the love and tact of the "father," and things went from good to bad, and from bad to worse, until Pestalozzi was compelled to turn over the management to one Schmid, who was strong in "government," but who turned everything to gall and bitterness for his colleagues, drove away the faithful men who had had a common purse, and asked nothing for their work but food and clothes, and then finally proved himself to be a rascal and was expelled by the magistrates.

Here, then, Pestalozzi lived for twenty years, reached his highest success, lost in death his faithful wife, and met with his bitterest defeat, when the very foundations of everything were removed; for, as he said one New Year's Day, standing beside an empty coffin he had had carried in: "This work was founded by love, but love has disappeared from our midst."

If we visit the scene of this twenty years' work, the scene on which the drama of Pestalozzi's life was practically finished, we find Yverdun a quaint and interesting town only a dozen miles north of Lausanne; and the old castle is easily the most conspicuous thing about it. At the castle a sign at the head of a slight, wooden staircase says to ring for the *concierge,* and the ring is answered by a little old woman in spectacles, who tells you that the "infants"—for here everything is French—are at school; but if you return after four, you may come in.

So you have a chance to walk about and see what a magnificent and well-preserved old castle it is, with the dry moat faced with stone and the four great towers at the corners; a castle whose

---

[1] Quoted from Quick's *Educational Reformers.*

grim dignity could not be much impaired by the concrete bridge across the moat, the bottling business in the cellar, or the insult built against one wall. And there, facing it from the center of the square, was another beautiful monument to Pestalozzi.

At four the children pour out; the boys in long, loose, butcher-like blue blouses and knickerbockers, with their short stockings hanging down around the tops of their shoes; and the girls to match. Then we go in, and the old lady starts for her keys; but if you catch a glimpse of the room where she keeps them, you cannot help following her. It is a round room in one of the towers; the walls are eight feet thick, but the narrow slits from the windows run in on the bias, and so they seem even thicker. It is evidently her kitchen, and she has set a good-sized iron range right into the immense old fireplace. Then she tells you that it was Pestalozzi's kitchen too, and starts with you through the building.

The cobble-stoned court was once Pestalozzi's garden, and, see, there are remnants of a gallery that once went all around it. These beautiful old chapel windows had been walled up, and were discovered only last year when the walls were scraped. Here are some wonderful old door-latches. In this room Madame Pestalozzi had taught the young girls to work. In that room they had had school, and this upper room with the old porcelain stove had been his and her bedroom. She died in the one beside it and is buried in the cemetery not far away.

Our visit was not without its providential uses, for as the old lady unlocked the door of the old schoolroom, a small boy who had been most securely 'kept in' had a chance to slip out, and the old lady let him go.

If you ask to see some of the other rooms, where the children are taught now, you will find them interesting. There are new windows cut through beside the old loopholes, but on this day at least they had not been used very effectively for ventilation. The desks and benches are innocent of varnish; and the walls are decorated with family trees (nice real trees, too) showing the lineage of the Swiss confederation, with chromos of battles and scenes from Tell, and large printed sheets in which *mon enfant* is exhorted by the cantonal authorities to observe exactly thirty different rules. The poverty-stricken appearance of both children and rooms was very marked. Of course, it is far from being the abject poverty that Pestalozzi had to struggle with at Neuhof and at Stans; but frills are conspicuously absent, and the public schools of our American cities are models of elegance and luxury compared with this successor of the old Institute in the castle.

The monument outside can be seen from the windows of the room in which Madame Pestalozzi taught the young girls to work. It was erected in 1890 by popular subscription, and it has one advantage over that at Zurich—there is a girl as well as a boy. They cling to the teacher's legs, and both look up in his face. On the base of the monument one may read at one side a résumé of Pestalozzi's life, and on the other the words that give it a meaning: "J'ai vécu moi-même comme un mendiant pour apprendre à mendiants à vivre comme des hommes."

THE RELATION OF THE HOME TO THE SCHOOL

CORA HAMILTON
Training Teacher, Macomb Normal School

There are many definitions of education, each of which embodies the fulfilment of some need of the human soul. The varying opinions as to what life is, and is to be, leads to changing emphasis on what is important in education. Each group of people having common interests has a common ideal as to what the members of the community ought to become. This ideal growing out of the needs, experiences, and ideals of the group will be practically realized in exact ratio to the pressure of necessity. Since the group constantly enlarges its experiences and feels new needs, education has been a constantly progressive process. Education from this view-point becomes the socialization of the child. The uneducated child is a bundle of natural tendencies which constantly seek expression without reference to the rights or comforts of others. Education seeks to supply knowledge by which the conditions of life without the individual may be interpreted, and also to build up such habits of conduct and tendencies to behavior as shall best serve the needs of the group to which he is directly connected and the race with which he may at any time build up living relations.

In the beginning each family attended to the socialization of each of its members. When the group-idea became emphasized and duties multiplied as new relations were assumed, it became necessary for the home to delegate its power to some one individual who should perform for all the children of the group those duties which the family had heretofore performed for itself. Hence in the inception the school was a simple extension of the home. However complex and formal the administration of the school has become, its relation to the home has never changed. The teacher still, in legal phrase, is *in loco parentis.*

It is only too common to place the whole responsibility for

education upon the school, forgetting that it is only another phase of home life, and that while its sole purpose of existence is the socialization of the child, indirect influences, such as the industrial and political life of the community, its amusements, traditions, religion, and standards of morals and intelligence, are powerful enough to modify, and sometimes to counteract, all that the school can do. The home, therefore, must share the responsibility at least equally. The school has contact with the child one-third its waking hours, the home or community two-thirds. The stimuli received in the one-third the time will become evanescent unless the home offers some practical outlet for its application. It must be reinforced and supplemented in active living. This is all the more necessary since the group-ideals are sometimes narrow or mistaken and weakness exists in the school itself.

Since the school is organized to do the work properly belonging to the parents, the *first* necessity is personal contact between the parents and the school. It is most lamentably true that the major portion of the schools of Illinois are struggling to discharge their duty in socializing the children without the fundamental aid. The reasons for the lack of this contact are various. Some parents fear that their visits will be an intrusion. The teachers are strangers and they feel the same diffidence about going into the room that they would in calling on a stranger in any other place. The teacher need not be a stranger. I never refused an invitation to tea in the home of a pupil in my life. On the contrary, some of the dearest memories of my life cluster about the days spent in homes, sometimes elegant, sometimes very humble, where some mother who loved her children desired to know what sort of a woman had her child six hours a day and measured out in some degree the man that future days were to see. Again, some parents have no adequate conception of the meaning and purpose of human life. Spiritually they are blind, and look only toward the material things of life. Hence, education is purely something to be gone through with as a matter of habit. Social relationship and duties are ignored and efforts to socialize the child are met either with indifference or open ridicule. This is often quite as true of the well-to-do American parents as it is of the hard-worked and ignorant foreigners. A third class make no effort to establish personal contact because they believe education is the teacher's business for which they pay her a good salary, and she ought to attend to it. They really want their children educated and judge the progress they are making by such desultory tests as it occurs to them to make. Some parents feel their own ignorance of matter and method so keenly that they dread contact with the teacher lest they might be humiliated in the presence of their children.

On the other hand, some schools show very plainly that they do not want visitors. Sometimes their reasons are good. Some parents who have made no study of the progress of method in school have the old conventional idea of what a school ought to do, and discourage all attempts to make education *life,* instead of bare acquisition of facts. They are apt to discuss the methods of the school contemptuously in the presence of the pupil and so counteract all the teacher's efforts, unless the teacher can obtain a supremacy in trust and affection in the heart of the child, which is always an unnatural and pitiable thing. Again, some mothers idolizing the child at home, centering all family life around him, can never consider this child as a member of the community, and therefore demand special rights and privileges for the individual. This tends to de-socialize and defeat the very purpose of the school. Again, some few parents are absolutely meddlesome. So long as there is human nature, so long there will be people who delight in interesting themselves in other people's business even to usurping the rights of the school-teacher. Such people are the terror and despair of the teacher when they come to visit. There exists in my memory a picture of one visitor whose influence was felt for days afterward; who always humiliated me in some not-to-be-guarded-against way, and made me feel to the utmost that I *was* her *hired* servant and hardly worth my pay.

On the other hand, there are some teachers so lacking in social tact and self-control that while they are genuinely glad to see the visitor they have such unfortunate embarrassment of manner as to make the visitor feel awkward and unwelcome. Then, there is the teacher who *hates* visitors. She is doing poor work and does not care to do better. Visitors might discover it and her position might be forfeited. There is also the vain teacher who likes to get up a show, and who discourages visitors unless she has some spectacle on hand. In summing up these reasons it would appear that the lack of personal contact is due to fault on both sides which can only be overcome by a clearer idea of the benefits to be derived from conference between the interested parties.

Through the personal contact of parent and school the health of the pupil may be guarded. Since the school is the extension of the home, it devolves upon parents to see that defects in lighting, heating, and ventilating are avoided or corrected. It is the business of the home to see that proper seats are provided to avoid malformation and disease from this cause alone. We, as teachers, know that some terrible things are allowed in the name of economy, but our protests do not come to the building committee with the force of a complaint from a father and a voter. No housekeeper can manage her house without a working equipment, but thousands of teachers are turned into a bare room with nothing but their bare hands with which to work the miracle of transforming children from what they are to what they may be. If it were the sentiment of the homes represented that the school should be properly equipped, no school board could longer neglect or refuse to see that all necessary books and apparatus were furnished.

If parents really felt the school as an extension of the home, then there would be no such thing as putting the responsibility of progress on the school instead of on individual effort. They would cease to become the advocate of the pupil against the school. They would no longer attempt to save the pupil from the righteous consequence of his own misdeeds. They would realize that there are different types of children, and that there can be no such thing in a real school as "treating all pupils alike." Their differing characteristics and needs must govern all requirements. The help given a struggling, stumbling child would be an absolute curse to the lazy, able child. Mothers who have from one to ten children, and find their hands and hearts full of care for them, ought to have a deep sense of sympathy for her who handles all day in one cramped room forty-five to fifty children from as many different home environments.

The home in its present general relation to the school hinders its work in several ways. Too much work is often required of the growing child. The boy who gets up at three o'clock in the morning to deliver papers on his route till seven or after is in no condition to study after it. This is sometimes a necessity in family economy, but often an ambitious boy wants a little pocket money and is encouraged to get it in this way. On the contrary, I have in mind certain families where the pupils play *all* the time outside of school hours and have no duties or responsibilities to meet. They are so saturated with play that it is uppermost in their minds and supersedes all other interests. Again, the work of the school is interrupted and retarded by too many social diversions, and those of the wrong kind. I went recently to see a comedy, played by local talent, based on a wife's jealousy and a husband's lying attempt to shield himself. The moral was perhaps writ large to adults, but to the crowd of children from seven years to fourteen who witnessed it there were suggestions tending to lower their standard of life and of the eternal fitness of things, because they had no ground of experience from which to interpret the lesson of the play. My heart ached to put them to bed where they belonged, to tell them a story, sing them a song, and leave them to the sweet, youthful slumber that was their due. The dancing-school sometimes becomes the enemy of good, intellectual work. I believe in dancing for children as a form of physical exercise, but I object to the excitement, the formalism, and the suggestion of the ordinary dancing-class. We, as teachers, hail the advent of the gymnasium work in dancing for all children. There it becomes an ordinary school exercise.

Parents are awakening to the advantages of co-operation in many of the ways I have mentioned, but there is one great field practically untouched, and that is sympathetic knowledge of the course of study, its purposes and methods. Mothers have come to me again and again and have said: "I am humiliated in the presence of my child when I have tried to help him in his home work. I do not know what you teach, nor understand why you do the things the child tells me of. I am losing the respect of my child as an intelligent leader." I know a teacher who has organized mothers' classes in the common subjects, teaching them what the children were to learn that year, the purpose and method of the work.

With your permission, I should like to make a general summary of the course of study from a teacher's view-point for two reasons—one, that I may show where the home may help in carrying forward the work in the several subjects; the other, that you may suggest to me points where the suggested work does not meet the practical ideals of life from the home standpoint.

There was a time when the three R's made up the scope of subject-matter in the schools. In schools of the old stamp arithmetic still holds a prominent place. It may be that the wave of commercialism and materialism now sweeping our country may be traced to this very emphasis. Since we think in words and express the major part of our thinking in the same medium, language becomes the keystone of the new course of study. The child who comes to us at six has acquired by imitation such a vocabulary of, and use in, English as satisfies the needs of his immediate social group. But in socializing the child we make him a citizen of the world, past and present, instead of remaining a member of his own limited group. So we tell him the old tales of Troy, the Wagner opera stories, the Greek and Norse myths, the history of great heroes and noted events. We ask him to tell the stories back to us, and then to make sure that the language, the life, the meaning of the story shall enter into living experience, we have the story put into dramatic form and played in the schoolroom. If the home would encourage the giving of these same plays in the home yard by the neighborhood group, great aid would be rendered. If a story-telling hour might be inaugurated where the children would be expected to tell the family stories learned at school, the interest in the work would rest on the basis of satisfying real needs. We encourage the expression of children's own little experiences in story form, helping them introduce the dramatic elements that makes the story of each entertaining to all.

Believing that the feeling of rhythm helps the children in respect to thought and movement, we read to them as effectively as we can great poems full of rhythmic lilt and swing, even when they do not understand all the language. If on Sunday afternoon there might be an hour in the home when the child learns from the parent's reading the old Scotch version of the Psalms, it would mean power and joy in years to come.

History is the record of the life of man in contact with his fellow; literature is the record of the emotional and spiritual life of the race. The socialized child must have a knowledge of both these subjects, since until he knows how the race came to be, what it is, and how its standards and beliefs grew up, he can form no opinion as to what the future is to be or of his part in racial progress. Both these subjects are so great and the records so voluminous that the time spent with the teacher would be far too limited for such acquaintance with them as is an absolute necessity, so we teach the child to read to himself. Here the home should be our strongest ally. From the time the six-year-old can read anything, through to manhood, the home should see that proper subject-matter is provided and that some time every day is set apart definitely for reading. The boy who reads Cooper with his father won't sneak away to read "Bloody Dick, the Highwayman" in a barn with the boys. The child who reads much is laying up a great store of words, images, and convictions that become the materials of life in the future.

The child's relation to his environment is a never-ending source of interest to him. We call it geography, but it is no longer a formal study of the book. He studies the action of water upon the surface of the earth about him. The great physiographic fact of the leveling process going on all the time becomes a matter of real experience through which he interprets all similar action wherever it may take place. From a study of his own environment he passes to that of different children of the earth—Japanese, Eskimos, Indians, or Filipinos—interpreting each in the terms of his own experience. He watches the thermometer, barometer, and wind-changes till he is able to predict weather with as much success as the great Foster or his contemporaries. The sources of all materials for the satisfaction of human needs—food, fuel, clothing, material for shelter, tools, raw materials for, and processes of, manufacture are investigated. The influence of physiography on production and trade is suggested by experience in their own community and forms a basis for interpreting all they hear or read of the other lands.

Nature-study is a phase of this same subject, and gives rise directly to the most reverent thoughts of the Creator and created, if rightly handled. We sorely need the help of the home in this phase of education. If there could only be an effort to lead conversation at home into geographical channels; if parents and children would read daily papers together in search of knowledge of people and countries; if each child might have a garden where experiments might go forward; if parents could only have patience with the living animals the child likes to own—then the school would find its work vastly supplemented.

Sometimes it is necessary to make a record of some fact or observation so that it may be referred to at a later time; therefore the child must learn to write. This he does by imitation and visualizing, but by no formal drill. The home may assist greatly by giving opportunities for necessary writing, such as letters, notes, invitations to playmates, etc.

It is, perhaps, in the realm of mathematics that we most need intelligent help from the parents. The old days are passing away and new ideals have arisen. Since the race developed its practical applications of mathematical fact rather late in its period of development and then in answer to absolute need, we contend that the child in the lower grades has no reason for studying formal arithmetic, and that mathematics as the schools have known it may safely be left to the fourth year of school life. In the meantime, the child is acquiring unconsciously a great many notions of measure, value, and content, which enable him to do in a year what he would otherwise do in four. The content of the formal work itself differs widely from what I was taught in my youth. It does not consist of a series of rules with lists of

problems to be solved by rule, but furnishes a problem—so conditions the child that he needs to solve it, and leads him through
measurements and comparison to the result. The activities of
play and of the manual-training shop furnish many of the
problems. The home might furnish many more. Let the children help keep the family account book, having a duplicate of
yours, if necessary. Plan a house beautiful with your children,
and plan the furnishing, estimating all the costs. This is an
example of the way in which the home may help in this subject.
Believe me that the personal interest in these problems will give
a stronger grip on the application of mathematical principles than
any book problem could ever furnish.

History is also studied from an entirely new basis. The
teacher sets up some problem in human life which the child
endeavors to solve in the light of personal experience. When
he has come to a conclusion he compares his solution with the
actual facts as recorded by different authors. Individual reasoning is criticised, corrected, and enlarged in classwork with the
teacher. As an illustration of what I mean, suppose the lesson to
be taught is that of the resistance of the colonies to the tax laid
by England, particularly on tea. Here were the tea ships in
Boston Harbor determined to unload their cargo. Here were
the colonists determined it should not be landed. What would
you have done had you been a colonist? The children come to
class with an opinion, which is there compared with historical
record of what was really done. In this way the child comes to
feel that these events were living things, participated in by people
who were feeling and thinking intensely. Presently he begins to
realize the relation of cause and effect and to see how the great
movements of the race have contributed to the present state
of civilization, and to feel himself a debtor to those who have
struggled in the past to attain it. If the home would question
the child daily as to what problems were under consideration and
then add any personal touch of knowledge gained through experience or reading, the interest would be greatly enlarged.

On the art side of school-life we need help desperately.
Music is one of the great factors for culture, but it is a very

barren thing if it does not pass over into the home life of the child. There ought to be an hour in the week when the child sings his lullaby song to the dear home baby and all his songs to the members of the family, no matter how stumbling the performance may be. I know one home where the father is a busy physician and a very undemonstrative man, but Sundays just at dusk his little daughter sings to him and plays a simple tune on her violin, while her mother plays a simple accompaniment, and when it is over the father ceremonially kisses his little daughter as thanks for the music. In the child's mind, it has almost become a sacrament. We teach color harmony and design in our drawing classes. Why should not children make plans for house decoration, plans for gowns, and a hundred other things in which the home could utilize the lessons of the school? In so simple a matter as making flower-pots decorative even the seven-year-old can help.

In the manual-training work, the home may set the aims. Does mother need a shelf, a table, a breadboard, a box, a hall lantern—indeed, a hundred things? A simple suggestion of size and purpose leads to the most effective work that can be done—work which satisfies a real need. In the domestic science work there will be failure unless the children may work out the lessons. Let the child set the table as he is taught and cook the potatoes, even if it is not done according to your most cherished ideals.

In summing up what I have tried to say about home co-operation in the course of study, you will see that I have tried to show that *education is life* rather than a preparation for living, and that it is only effective when that which is taught finds an outlet in the home. Finally, we depend on you to help us to maintain the tone of the school; to set high standards of thought and life, believing that we grow by "admiration, hope and love."

TEXTILE ARTS AS SOCIAL OCCUPATIONS

CLARA ISABEL MITCHELL
School of Education

The study of textiles in the school is to be considered not merely as a form of manual-training, but as a fundamental social occupation. Spinning, dyeing, weaving, and needle-work give children opportunity for creative work in these arts and make them intelligent co-operatives in the clothing activities of society.

That the textile arts may be truly *social* occupations, it is first of all essential that all enterprises engaged in shall be social in their nature; that is, that the result desired, the work completed, shall have a definite social use, shall fill a need of the community in which it is made. Nor is it sufficient that such need exists. It is a necessary condition of truly socialized work that the workman himself clearly perceive this need and willingly co-operate in filling it. The acts of weaving paper mats, tying intricate knots in strings, and the sewing of models for a sample-book may all be very interesting in themselves, and no doubt develop a degree of skill in children. These are not, however, *social* acts unless every article made has a definite use, æsthetic or utilitarian —a use which has been so apparent to the children that it has stimulated them to enthusiastic effort.

Another condition of socialized work is that it shall benefit, not only the community, but also the worker himself, and it is primarily the function of the teacher as a social organizer so to plan community work as to make it of greatest value to the individual child. Much of the hand-work in schools has been planned upon the idea that *all work is education,* whereas it should, of course, be logically based upon principles which will make it of the highest possible value. Such principles have been promulgated by the leaders in education and have been recognized by students, but few of them are in operation in our school-rooms. The teacher who stands as guardian of a child's best good must recognize the fact that character-building is his function, and that this can come about only through properly organized community life.

The primal condition of right community life is that it should afford opportunity for and encouragement of voluntary individual service. The second is that the service performed shall be such as to react upon the individual offering the service to his best growth. To keep the knowledge of this scheme entirely outside the consciousness of the children; to order the affairs of the schoolroom in such a way as to bring about spontaneous, intelligent, and educative co-operation, is the work of the teacher.

The textile arts cannot fulfil their function in the educational scheme, therefore, unless they take their place in the community life in their proper order and under right social laws. As has been already pointed out, they must propose only such articles for making as can be used—articles for which the children see the need, and which they care to make. They must afford opportunity for the children's initiative, choice of material, taste in color, originality in design; in other words, that they may offer the highest development to the maker, they must give him the fullest chance for self-expression. Further than this, all textile materials and processes used must bring the users into close contact with the geographical and industrial sources from which they come; must lead him to large information regarding the origins and meanings of the things he is making and the materials he is using. It is therefore plain that the study in school includes more than the making of a series of objects. A most important part of the subject is the science, history, geography, and literature which interprets it and makes it applicable to life.

The course of study in textiles for the elementary department of the School of Education is an attempt toward socializing a part of the children's effort in school. Changing from year to year, to fit the changing conditions of the school society, a mere enumeration of the articles made conveys little meaning to a reader. But it is not possible within the space of this paper to indicate either process or much of the correlation with other subjects.

Following is an outline of work done throughout the different groups of the school, and later numbers of the magazine will
give detailed descriptions and illustrations of the results.

Mats, rugs, carpets, and curtains are woven or stenciled by
children of the first grade for their playhouses, and used in their
own games or in the games of the children to whom they are
given. The designing of them sets the children to work on
the problems of color, light and dark, proportions, and lines. The
cotton, wool, linens, and silks used are studied as the materials
of clothing. Specimens of each are mounted with pictures of
sources and processes, and all are labeled in written words and
sentences learned for the purpose. As a means of awakening
the minds of the children to the general subject of clothing, a
series of lessons is planned upon the clothing of animals, the
function of coverings and their adaptation to environment.

In the second and third grades mats and baskets are made
for picnics and luncheons, from primitive materials gathered in
the home locality. In the making of these greatest encouragement is given to originality and invention. To facilitate processes
of weaving, looms are invented, and spindles are made; wool and
linen fibers are twisted into thread and dyed by means of any
vegetable or mineral suggested by the children. With the discovery and invention of primitive methods in spinning and
weaving the children are given lessons upon the clothing processes of such primitive peoples as the cave-men, the North
American Indians, the lake-dwellers of ancient Switzerland, and
the Eskimos; also the shepherds of Arabia and of ancient peoples;
later of the Norsemen and ancient Greeks. Numbers, weights,
measures, and arithmetical processes are taught in the use of
dyeing and weaving materials.

Baskets and mats are woven of rattan and raffia; rugs of jute;
slipper bags are worked in original cross-stitch designs with heavy
linen floss in coarse canvas.

In the fourth grade one quarter's work is given to sewing—
selection and buying of material, use of scissors, design and
cutting of a pattern, basting, running, French seam, hemming,
blanket-stitch, feather-stitch, and joining of tape all come into

this problem. Several members of the class begin the use of machines in stitching the larger seams. Special study is made of cotton from specimens of plant fibers, and fabrics; also from pictures and printed descriptions.

The children of the fifth grade design a small pocket or belt, and weave it on a hand-frame invented and made by them from the knowledge gained from their second- and third-year's experiences. After this they design and execute in cross-stitch one article for household use—e. g., a pillow, table-cover, or bureau-scarf. Sewing is carried one step farther in the making of curtains, aprons, or some simple article needed in the school. Weaving progresses to the point of making a rag-rug. The materials used are dyed by the children with natural dyes. A special study is made of flax, silk, and wool fibers. The history of the early American colonists and of the textile arts of their homes accompanies this work, also a study of the spinning-wheel and the colonial loom.

In the sixth grade one quarter's work, two hours each week, is devoted to the designing of one decorative piece of household furnishing—a pillow, scarf, curtain, what the individual children choose—to be executed in stencil, appliqué, or simple embroidery. With this should be read or told stories of mediæval tapestry-working, and ancient embroideries, as part of the history and geography of the Middle Ages. Some mechanical drawing is needed in this design; dyeing is continued.

The girls of the seventh and eighth grades sew on muslin garments. Both boys and girls do some weaving in the Swedish loom in the making of scarfs and squares of simple design; both design and carve wooden blocks for block-printing; both study clothing and the clothing industries of their own town. They have industrial excursions, and learn the history of their own clothing as nearly as possible from original sources. They learn the history of special fabrics, light calicoes and cretonnes, for example; the routes of transportation for clothing fibers and fabrics, and something of the business forms involved in their manufacture and sale. The history of textile machinery, and a little of the story of the origin of the factory system, should also be part of this study of clothing. Besides the making of clothing, laboratory experiments give information in regard to the proper care of fabrics—that is, as to washing, cleansing, dyeing, and fading. Samples are studied, combined, and discussed. High standards of taste in dress are discussed and used as subjects for papers. Costumes are planned in a practical way, with some regard to prices as well as to taste and suitability.

The aim of this work is, first, to give children experience in all possible clothing processes, in order that they may become actually intelligent in regard to them; secondly, to give them an appreciation of the meaning of clothing from the scientific, artistic, industrial, and historic standpoints; thirdly, and most important, to make them willing and skilful co-operators in the work of the community.

DOMESTIC SCIENCE IN ELEMENTARY DEPARTMENT OF THE ETHICAL CULTURE SCHOOL

JESSIE P. RICH

Ethical Culture School, New York City

Although "domestic science" appears in the curriculum of the best elementary schools in the country, its meaning to many is yet obscure, and its work and function still unknown. For the last three years the Ethical Culture School has been struggling with the implied content and value of this branch, and offers here a review of the subject-matter selected—matter which at present seems best adapted to the work of the grade and the social development of the child, and material which allows a "technological" treatment of the subject rather than a technical.

The work finds its first value in the primary grades. Here it is an agent for the illustration or starting-point of some thought-idea, or the means of carrying out some social desire. It is a tool for the aid of building upon a foundation of experience. It is a means to an end—that end being such as to demand a means for expression.

In Grade I the work has been with the idea of bringing out a contrast of food and serving of peoples in different climates. The children are at work with their own home study and contrast it with the homes of the Eskimo and Japanese—peoples living in hot, moderate, and cold climates.

Work begins at home, and simple things are cooked, such as cereal, toast, apples, and garden vegetables; things familiar to the child, lacking in difficulty of technique, and of such type as can be done at home, if a little help be given. This is then contrasted with the Eskimo boy living in a cold, snowy country, filled with wild animals, where little or nothing is known of stoves, gas, utensils, etc., and only a little drift wood and steatite are available.

Method seldom furnishes a rule or recipe to be followed.

Such materials are chosen as lend themselves to a simple thought or mathematical relation, and appeal to the reason and number-sense of that age. Little work of an experimental nature is attempted; for the minds are yet too young to deduce from experiment, to realize the need for one, or to understand that growth often comes about by such means.

In Grade II the attack is to set the children, from the situation of today, back to the crude beginnings of things, and illustrate the evolutionary development of cooking and necessary utensils through the tribes of tree-dwellers, cave-men, Indians, and shepherd people. This at once puts the work on an experimental basis: We are here, and don't know what to do. Devise a way! For instance: the acorn (almost the only food of one of the Indian tribes) is bitter, bad to taste; the squirrels in the park and pigs in the pen refuse at the present day to eat it. The acorn was all they had. What could they do? Can we get rid of the bitter taste? After attempts, the facts are collected, and with a little side-light the way is deduced and manually expressed.

This work is contrasted and strengthened by present home-doings through simple cooking to be of value for Christmas, i. e., party or gift, and is of importance, as previously, in illustration and experience in mathematics, science, and English.

In Grade III the department is used to illustrate the early industries of the pioneer people, the "old-time" home manu-factures. The children find the people doing many things now delegated to the factory, and for more accurate understanding of present and early practices it is well to have a few worked up in detail. The kitchen becomes a pioneer fireside, and all members of the family help in making samp, candles, and soap.

It has been possible to repeat the early conditions in part. We got the lye from ashes of an excursion and picked enough bayberries to realize the source of wax for the candles.

In Grades IV and V this study has had no place. In Grades VI and VII the work continues. Here is the subject no longer a tool in the sense of the primary work. It is a branch with definite aims and ends of its own to satisfy. The object is to give the children (for boys could well take such lessons) the underlying facts in regard to food classes and their best preparation for use, with training sufficient to develop skill in manipulation at an age when it can most economically be fostered.

Grade VI studies the food materials, with a resulting idea of food classification on the basis of certain basic elements, and the underlying reason for right cooking. In other words, familiarity is given with the laws determining right cooking of the so-called "food principles."

"Cooking is the appliction of regulated heat to known material for a given period of time"—heat, material, and time, the three important factors. Each "food principle" is worked with to determine the truth concerning its relation to these three essentials. Then follows the application to foods which can be cooked according to a law of science rather than a rule of proportion— such as potatoes, rice, eggs, etc.

With Grade VI as a basis, Grade VII proceeds to deal with "food principles" in combination through a simple course in cooking, designed also to develop skill in manipulation and encourage responsible usefulness at home. Grade VI gave knowledge of food types and laws underlying this cookery; it is now only necessary to know how more fully to recognize the type in order to apply the law, and further to discover new laws of relation existing between materials. It reduces the work to a study of good tests and the scientific development of the recipe.

The tests are simple and easily applied: iodine for starch, Fehling solution for sugar, the grease stain for fats, and millous reagent for proteids. This occupies the first few lessons, after which cooking begins. A simple starchy food is taken for the beginning—Pettijohn. Its method of cooking is understood, but its quantitative behavior with other materials is required. The simplest relation is with water. "How much Pettijohn is required to thicken one cup of water?" (This experimentally.) Then follows: "How much rolled oats is required to thicken one cup of water when Pettijohn contains 72 per cent. starch and rolled oats 64 per cent. starch?" Following: "Deduce recipe for cooking farina if the composition is the same as Pettijohn but the weight 2 :1."

All recipes can be placed pretty largely under some type; the first of which is determined by experiment, and many others deduced by use of mathematical relations, common-sense, and thinking. Such work makes a thought series. It develops independence in the use of materials and puts the recipe nearer the requirements of a science.

The work ends with a simple luncheon or tea given to the mothers. Here the social value (a strong factor throughout) finds its ultimate expression, and the occasion gives opportunity to develop in the girls "grace in extending hospitality to others."

Thus has the brief outline interpreted the term "domestic science" of the curriculum in the Ethical Culture School. We do not claim ours to be the only interpretation, or even to be the right interpretation; but, in so far as we are able to judge, it certainly is a reasonable, logical, and seemingly educational use of the branch, and an attempt to rescue it from the popular opinion that domestic science aims only to teach a girl to stir up a "fit" cake, to set a table according to Hill, or to clean a dish with the latest patent of "ine."

A SERIES OF PRIMARY READING-LESSONS.   II

JENNIE HALL
Francis W. Parker School

INDIAN WEAVING

Long ago Indians had no sheep.
Some Indians could spin cotton.
They wove cloth and made clothes of that.
Other Indians wove cloth of their own hair.
But most Indians used skins for clothes.
When white men came, they had sheep.
They sold them to the Indians.
Then the Indians used the wool to spin and to weave.
The Navajo Indians made blankets of wool.
They wore them for clothes.
They are the best Indian weavers.
Other Indians get blankets from them.
They trade jars or baskets for them.

NAVAJO SHEPHERDS

The Navajo Indians have many sheep.
The men are the shepherds.
They want to take good care of their sheep.
Every shepherd cuts a little sheep out of stone.
He puts it into a little bag.
He hangs it around his neck.
"This will make my sheep safe," he says.
"It will keep wolves away.
"It will keep sickness away.
"It will bring little lambs."

NAVAJO DESIGNS

Navajo weavers make pictures in their blankets.
They make clouds and mountains and houses.
But they cannot make the pictures just like the things.
They must change the shapes.

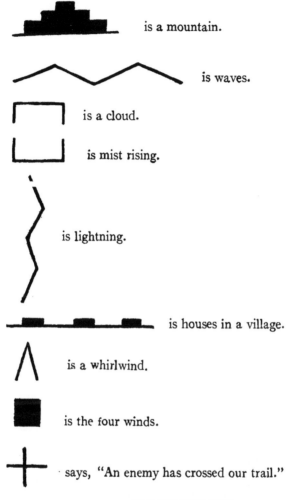

is a mountain.

is waves.

is a cloud.

is mist rising.

is lightning.

is houses in a village.

is a whirlwind.

is the four winds.

says, "An enemy has crossed our trail."

NAVAJO WEAVERS

A Navajo woman is sitting in her house.
The house is made of brush and poles.
There is no wall at one end.
The woman looks out.
The sun is very bright.
The ground is bare and hot.
Little bushes grow here and there.

Sheep and goats are eating the leaves.
A man lies watching them.
He has a bright blanket under him.
Far off are red hills of stone.
A few trees grow in the shade of these hills.
The woman turns again to her work.
A loom hangs before her.
Many little balls of yarn hang from it.
She is weaving a blanket.
Across the end of it she has made a line of mountains.
Above them she is making lightning.
Other blankets are hanging over a pole.
Skeins of bright yarn hang on the wall.
Baskets sit in a corner.
They are full of corn and flour.
Dried meat hangs from the roof.
Another woman sits at the open end of the house.
She is spinning.
She rolls her little spindle on her knee.
It is full of white yarn.
A pile of wool lies on the ground near her.
The weaver says:
"The bushes are bare.
"We must move soon."
"Yes," the spinner says, "tomorrow the men will thresh the wheat.
"Then we will go."
"It will be a long journey this time," the weaver says.
"Yes," says the spinner, "the next water is far away."
"I cannot weave for many days," the weaver says.
"I fear that I shall forget my pattern.
"The last time we moved I lost my yellow yarn."
Now another woman comes into the house.
She has been to the red hills.
She has a big basket.
It is full of leaves.

She drops it and sits down.

"Oh!" she says, "the sun is very hot.

"But here are the peach leaves for your yellow dye."

She gets up and takes a big kettle from a corner.

She puts the peach leaves into it.

She takes it to the spring and fills it with water.

Then she hangs it upon a stick and makes a fire under it.

"Take your yarn off the spindle," she says to the spinner.

"I will dye it soon."

A man rides up on a horse.

"Some Pueblos are coming," he says.

"They have three horses laden with jars.

"They will trade for blankets.

"Get them ready."

The women stop work.

They get all their blankets and spread them out.

They are glad the Pueblos are coming.

The women need clay jars, but they cannot make them.

But the Pueblos are good potters.

"Good!" the women say. "Now for a good trade."

BEDOUINS

How the Country Looks

There is a country far away. The sun is bright there. The land is made of sand and gravel and stones. It is hot and dry. But in March there is rain. Then flowers grow. You can see very far. The country looks like a garden. You see a big red place. It is red tulips and poppies. They grow wild here. You see a low green place. Wild oats and rye and barley grow there. You see yellows places. They are wild marigolds. You see other yellow places. They are sand. You see gray places. They are stones and gravel. Little bushes grow there. Pools of water shine in the sun. White flowers and purple irises grow in them.

The rain stops. The pools dry up. The flowers and grass and bushes die. The country is all dry, hot sand and stones and gravel.

The Animals

Rabbits and birds live in this country. Wild goats and sheep and camels and horses lived there long ago. They ate the grass and the flowers. They ate the wild oats and barley. They drank from the pools of water.

Men lived there. They were hunters. They killed the birds and the rabbits and the goats and the sheep and the horses and the camels. They ate the meat. They made clothes from the skins. Sometimes the men were very hungry. They went out to hunt. But often they could not find any animal. The children were very hungry. They cried. But there was nothing to eat.

Men Tame Goats

Once the men went out on a hunt. They killed many goats. They found one alive, and she could not run. She was hurt. The men took her home. They cooked the meat of the other goats and ate it. But they tied the hurt goat.

"We will eat it another day," they said.

They milked her. They tasted the milk.

"It is good," they shouted. The children tasted it. They liked it. The men said:

"We will not kill her. We will keep her. We will milk her every day. The milk is good. We must get other goats."

They went out to hunt again. This time they did not kill the goats. They caught them and took them home and tied them. The goats ate the grass and the flowers. After a while the goats had eaten all the green things. The men said:

"We must move. The goats must have more grass."

They went to another place. They always milked the goats. They drank the milk. They made butter and cheese from some of it. When the grass was all eaten, they moved again.

After a while they caught camels. They drank their milk. They rode on the camels. They made them carry things. They petted them. The goats and the camels were tame now. They did not run away. The men did not tie them up. Boys drove them to grass. They had dogs to help them watch the herd.

How the People Look

This country is Arabia. These people were Bedouins. They live there now. They are not tall. They have black hair and black eyes. Their noses are straight. Their skin is brown. They are good-natured, but they look cross. They frown. They do that because the sun is so bright. They try to keep it out of their eyes.

Tents

They still have goats and camels. They have horses and sheep, too. The camels and sheep and horses and goats eat very much. They eat all the grass and flowers in one place. Then the men drive them to another place. All the people follow. They are in that place for three or four days. Then the grass is all gone again. The people move again.

So they have tents, because they are easy to move. They make them of thick cloth. They make cloth of camel's hair. The women spin the hair and weave it. They color it black. They put up the tents near pools of water. The sheep and goats and camels and horses are near by. They are eating the grass and flowers.

Coming Home for Supper

It is supper time. Boys are driving the sheep home. There are fenced places close to the tents. The fence is made of branches of trees and of bushes. The boys drive the sheep into the fenced places. The camels come home alone. Nobody drives them. They stand near the tents.

The men come across the sand. They have no saddles on their horses. A rope is tied around the horse's nose. The man drives with this. These men have been to war. They have lances in their hands. They wave them in the air. They jump off and tie their horses to the tent. They give them oats and dates to eat.

These men wear long white shirts. They tie cords around their waists. They wear big blankets made of camel's hair, with stripes of red and yellow. They wear striped cloth around their heads.

Inside the Tent

The men go to their tents. A fire is burning inside the tent. It is in a hole in the sand floor. Lavender bushes are burning in the fire. They make a sweet smell. Saddles hang on the poles. They are for the camels. Ropes hang on the poles. Some wooden dishes and a coffe-pot are on the floor. A sword hangs from the cloth of the tent. That is all there is.

Cooking

Women are cooking. One woman has a big stone dish. She puts wheat into it and pounds it. She is making flour. She puts water with it and makes a round, thin cake. It is bread. She puts it into the fire and covers it with ashes. It cooks.

Another woman is pounding coffee. Another is churning. The milk is in a goat's skin. The woman rolls the skin on her knees. That makes the butter come.

One woman comes in from the pool. She has a bucket full of water. The bucket is made of leather. Other women come in. They are carrying little bushes. They throw them upon the fire.

Other women are out milking. They milk the goats and horses. They get big bowls of milk. They take this milk to the horses, and the horses drink it. Boys milk the camels. They get more milk than the women got. They take it to the tent for the people to drink.

Supper

Supper is ready. The men stick their lances into the sand. They go into the tent. A wooden dish is on the floor. It is full of camel's meat. There is a basket full of dates. There is a cup of soft butter. There is a big wooden bowl full of sour milk. There is a pot of coffee. The flat bread lies on a mat.

The people sit cross-legged on the ground. There are the father and the mother and one little girl and two little boys. The children do not wear any clothes. All the people take meat in their hands. They all drink the sour milk. They like it. They dip the dates into butter. They have not eaten today. They never eat any breakfast or dinner, but only supper. After supper they lie down on the floor and go to sleep.

Moving

It is morning. Everybody is up. The chief says:

"The pools are dry. The grass is dead. We must move today."

Women take down the tents. They tie the cloth around the poles. They tie the dishes together. They take oats and barley from a hole in the ground. They tie them up in a cloth. They take dried goat-skins and put water into them.

"We must carry water to drink," they say.

Men tie these things upon the camels. They put saddles upon the camels for the women to ride. A man sits on every camel. He drives it with a little stick. The boys walk. They drive the goats and sheep. Some men ride the horses. They carry their lances. They are ready to fight. They will keep the women and herds safe.

They ride for a long time. The sand is dry. The sun is hot. The horses are tired. The people drink water from the goat skins. Sometimes the women walk beside the camels. They spin as they walk.

At last they see trees. All the people shout with joy. They ride to them. There is a well here. Grass grows in the shade. The chief says:

"We will camp here."

Everybody gets down. The men take their things off the camels. The boys drive the goats and horses and sheep to grass. The women put up the tents. They get wood and build fires. They take a piece of steel and a hard stone and strike them together. A spark comes and catches the wood. The fire is made. The women bring water from the well. They get supper.

Herding

There is not much grass near the tent. The men say:

"Leave this grass for the horses and sheep. We will take the camels away. They will eat anything."

So they drive the camels off. They go a long way. At last they cannot see the tents. The camels eat, and the men watch them. It is not much work. They sit down. They sing songs. They tell stories. At night the camels lie down. They will not run away. The men lie on the ground. They put the blankets around them. It is very still. They look up at the sky. It is dark blue and full of stars. The stars are very big and bright. The men talk about them. They tell stories about them. They give names to them. They love them.

In a Town

But the other people stay in their tents. They live here for a week. They cut the wool from the sheep and the goats and the camels. They tie it in bundles. Then the grass is gone. The well is dry. There is no rain. The chief says:

"All the grass is dead. All the wells are dry. There is nothing but sand and stones. We will go to town and sell our wool."

They send for the men with the camels to come back.

So they all move again. They go to a little town by a river. They put up their tents there. They sell their wool. They buy wheat and dates and coffee. They stay for two months.

At last it rains again. The chief says:

"I can smell green things. In our desert the grass is green. The flowers are growing. The pools are full of water. We will go back."

They take down their tents and pack the camels and ride away. So they move all the time.

A Visitor

Often these people have visitors. When a stranger comes, he goes to the biggest tent. The chief lives there. The chief sees the stranger and goes to him. He says:

"Welcome. Are you well?"

He takes the stranger into his tent. He says:

"My tent is your tent. My bread is your bread. You are my friend."

The stranger eats and sleeps in the chief's tent. He stays there for a long time. He is poor. The chief gives him blankets. After a while another man comes. He says to the chief

"This man is a bad man. I will drive him away."

The chief says:

"No. He has slept in my tent. He has eaten my bread and salt. No man shall hurt him."

So the stranger is safe.

Games

The girls work. They get wood and carry water and churn. They learn to spin and cook. And the boys work. They milk the camels and drive the herds. Sometimes they take care of the herds at night. But they play games, too. This is one of their games:

They black their faces. Their mothers give them wool. The boys tie it to their chins. It looks like beards. One boy has a very large beard. He is their chief. The boys all go to some tent. They play they are black men from a far country. They look at things in the tent. They play that they do not know what the things are. They talk about them in a strange way. Then they run off.

They have another game. They play it after supper. It is not hot then. All the children run out of the tents. The big girls sit on the sand and sing. Little girls and boys play that they are horses. Every little boy gets a little girl. They take hold of hands. They play that they are a pair of horses. They run, they jump, they kick, they neigh. They chase other horses. Other horses chase them. They play for a long time. At last they are tired and lie down on the sand.

The boys like to play war. They get upon horses. They take long lances and wave them in the air. They make their horses run. One boy runs at another boy. He tries to push him off his horse. He hits him with his lance. Then he turns his horse and runs away. He must not let the other boy hit him. Then they do it again and again. They must be very quick. Sometimes the boy falls from his horse. The other boys laugh at him. Their fathers and mothers watch them. They say:

"They can ride. They are strong. They will be brave."

Story of Tellal

Tellal was a Bedouin boy. He was twelve years old. His father was chief. There were many tents in the village where he lived. Many people lived in the tents. One night Tellal's people were asleep. Other men came. They were very still. They drove away the sheep and camels of Tellal's people. In the morning Tellal's people awoke. They looked for their sheep and camels, but could not find them. The people said:

"Who did it?"

After a while they found out. Then they said:

"We will have war. We will get our sheep and camels back."

The chief said:

"Yes, take your lances. Get upon your horses. Tellal, get your lance. You shall be captain."

Tellal shouted with joy. He jumped upon his horse and made him run. He shook his lance. He cried to the men:

"Come on!"

The men followed him. They made their horses run. They shook their lances. They rode across the desert to the other village. They had the war. They got the sheep and camels and brought them home. The people shouted:

"Tellal is brave. He is a good captain. He shall be our chief sometime."

A DYER

A Persian dyer stands in front of his dye-house.

It is only a little wooden shed.

But he is a proud man.

His father and his grandfather and his great-grandfather were dyers.

They worked in that shed.

He knows all their secrets.

He can make beautiful colors.

His hands are blue with dye.

His baggy trousers are spotted with red.

His face and turban are streaked with purple.

His bare feet are splashed with green.
But he is proud of that.
"See my beautiful colors," he says.
"I can make them all.
"Come in and see."
The little shed is crowded inside.
There are baskets and little jars on the shelves.
They are full of onions and beets and berries and roots and
leaves.
All these things are used to make dyes.
Big copper kettles are hanging over fires.
Dyes are boiling in them.
Many big clay jars sit against the walls.
They are full of dye.
Yarn hangs over them dripping.
The dyer feels of some red yarn.
"This is ready," he says.
He takes it and goes to the end of the shed.
There is a ladder to the roof.
He goes up the ladder.
On the top the roof is flat and sunny.
There are poles for hanging yarn.
He hangs up the yarn to dry.
He sits down by it.
He watches it all the time.
One minute too long would spoil it.
"The sun is not too hot," the dyer says.
"The wind is right.
"My color will be beautiful."
After a while he takes it down.
"It is done," he says, and smiles.

A PERSIAN WEAVER

A Persian weaver is weaving a rug.
Another rug hangs on the wall.
It is very beautiful.
There is a vine around the edge.

In the middle is a tree.
There are flowers and birds around the tree.
It is a very old rug.
The weaver's great-grandmother wove it.
Now the weaver is making one like it.
It is almost done.
"This is my last row," she says.
When it is done she looks at it lovingly.
"You are very beautiful," she says.
She rubs her hand over it.
"You are very soft.
"You are made of lamb's wool. My husband spun the yarn,
and my father dyed it.
"I wish I could keep you.
"But you will bring me much money.
"I wonder who will buy you?
"Will your new master love you?
"I will send a letter to him."
She goes to a wise man in the village.
"Write me a letter," she says to him.
"Say, 'Be kind to me, Nahid took four years to make me.'"
The man writes the letter.
The woman takes it home and sews it to her rug.
"I wish you good luck, my rug," she says.

A RUG FAIR

Many Persian weavers do not live in big cities.
Some live in tents in the mountains.
Many live in clay houses in little villages.
The men are shepherds and dyers.
The women weave rugs.
These people seldom see big cities.
But sometimes the men go to fairs.
They take the rugs from their village and roll them up.
They tie the rolls to their horses.
They ride for many days.

They see other men who are going to the fair.
The roads are full of horses and mules and camels.
At night they stop at inns.
The inn is a large, low building.
There is a yard in the middle.
There are rooms around the sides.
The yard is full of camels and horses and mules.
The men make a bonfire in the court-yard.
They sit around it and talk and sing.
Some men tell stories.
Some men play tricks.
They all dance and run races and shoot at a mark.
The next day they all go on again.
At last they come to a big city.
Here is the rug market.
The men leave their horses at the inn.
They take their rugs to the market.
It is an open square.
There are houses around the sides.
The men unroll their rugs.
They lay them on the ground or hang them on the walls.
There are thousands of other rugs.
Many men are looking at them.
Some have come to sell.
Some have come from big cities to buy.
They look at the rugs and feel of them.
Everybody is talking.
After a few days the rugs are all sold.
Then all the men go home, and the fair is over.

A HOME-MADE POTTERY KILN

IRA M. CARLEY

Francis W. Parker School

This article is reprinted from the *Elementary School Teacher and Course of Study*, Vol. II., No. 5 (January, 1902), in response to many requests for information regarding the construction of a pottery kiln.—THE EDITORS.

During the session of the School of Education in the Kozminski School last summer (1901), a kiln for burning work in clay-modeling was built of brick, under the direction of Miss Antoinette B. Hollister. A kiln may be purchased for about a hundred dollars. This kiln of brick was built to demonstrate how cheaply a serviceable kiln can be constructed. The cost of the material was in the neighborhood of eight dollars. With the labor, a good bricklayer for two days and a helper for one day, the total cost approximated twenty dollars. The kiln may be built either indoors or out. Below are given plans of it and directions for building:

The kiln is built entirely of fire brick, laid in fire clay. The sides, floor, and top of the muffle, *M M,* are built of fire brick of half the thickness of those used for the outside.

Before beginning to build the kiln, if made out-of-doors, a hole about one foot deep, and of the dimensions of the ground space to be occupied by the kiln, should be dug and filled with loose stones and cinders. On the upper layer of cinders a floor of common brick is laid level with the ground.

Fig. 1 shows the ground plan, or, rather, a horizontal section an inch above the ground, the rows of bricks, *e e e e,* being simply to support the floor above. The opening and fireplace are at *A.*

Fig. 2 shows the horizontal section at *F F* (see Fig. 5); that is, the floor above Fig. 1. This floor is built of large fire brick. *H* is the hole by which the heat passes under and around the muffle.

Fig. 3 shows the floor of the muffle. The cut is a horizontal section at *O O* (Fig. 5). The floor of it is made of the thin brick, supported by pieces of brick, *so placed as to leave as much air space as possible under the muffle and yet support the floor.*

Fig. 4 shows the front elevation of the kiln, *K K* being the opening

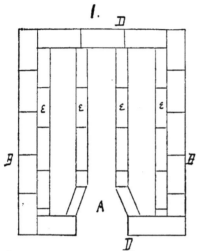

1.

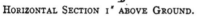

HORIZONTAL SECTION 1″ ABOVE GROUND.

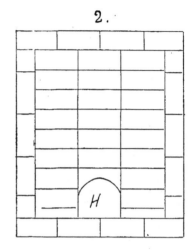

2.

HORIZONTAL SECTION AT *FF* (FIG. 5).

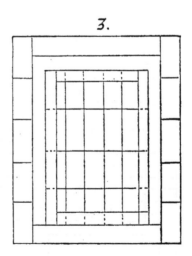

3.

HORIZONTAL SECTION AT *OO* (FIG. 5).
Scale $\frac{1}{8}″ = 1″$, reduced to $\frac{1}{4}$ size.

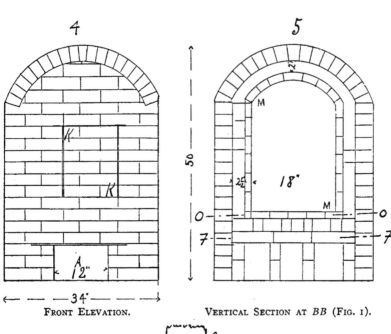

FRONT ELEVATION.   VERTICAL SECTION AT *BB* (FIG. 1).

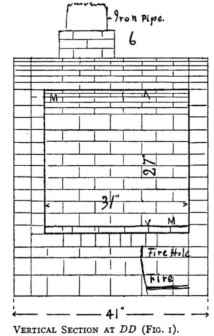

VERTICAL SECTION AT *DD* (FIG. 1).

into the muffle. The bricks are set loosely in this opening, so that they can be removed when the kiln is to be charged. When the kiln is charged, they are replaced and plastered over with fire clay. *A* is the fire opening. The bricks above it are supported by a strip of iron about three-sixteenths of an inch thick and one and a half to two inches wide.

Fig. 5 is a vertical section at *B B* (Fig. 1), showing shape of the muffle *M M,* and the air spaces through which the heat draws. Owing to the thinness of the bricks composing the muffle, it is well to extend a few bricks through from the outside wall to give support to the walls of the muffle.

Fig. 6 is a vertical section at *D D* (Fig. 1), showing the longitudinal form of the muffle and the location of the chimney. The opening of the chimney should be about five inches in diameter. It should be built of brick to a height of about two feet, and extended beyond that with sheet-iron pipe to a height of at least five feet above the bricks.

After the kiln is completed as shown in these plans, it is well to inclose it in one or even two layers of common, cheap brick, set in mortar.

The fuel used is kerosene. It is burned in a pan placed in the fire-place. The pan is fed by a pipe three or four feet in length and about one-quarter or three-sixteenths of an inch bore, having a funnel at its outer end into which a small stream of oil flows from a tank fitted with a small faucet.

The supply tank is placed above and somewhat to the side of the fire opening, the pipe being bent to fit location.

The pipe should enter the fire-pan at the edge and not from above, to avoid heating the oil in the pipe too much.

Fig. 7 is a plan of a clay-modeling stand which has been worked out by the pupils of the seventh and eighth grades.

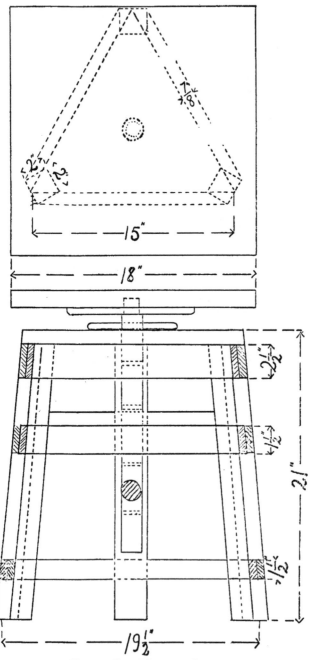

FIG. 7.—CLAY-MODELING STAND.

THANKSGIVING SONG

Words and melody by 9th year (Grade VII) pupils of the University Elementary School.

1. Thanks-giv-ing is here with all its good cheer, With
2. Out-side the trees spark-le and shine in the sun, With

tur-keys and pump-kins and cran-ber-ry pies; The
cheeks like red ro-ses, the chil-dren all run, Till at

chil-dren are gay on this beau-ti-ful day, And
eve-ning the fire's glow calls them with-in To roast

hap-pi-ness gleams from ev-'ry-one's eyes.
ap-ples and chest-nuts with mer-ri-est din.

EDITORIAL NOTES

Some seven or eight years ago Dr. Hermann Lietz, a German schoolmaster of fine insight, leased eighty acres of ground in the beautiful Isle-Thal near the Harz Mountains, for the purpose of founding a school. The only building on the premises, he told me, was an old powder-mill with but one door and no windows. Upon this he began work with a very small number of pupils, refitting it to meet the needs of a school and a home—for he called it "The German Country Educational Home." It was here that the boys were to live and learn.

Building a School

While the work on the building was progressing, a patron mother visiting the place was much concerned with the fact that she should have to pay a large tuition in an institution which the boy himself had to assist in building. She therefore asked Mr. Lietz to make a reduction in the fee. "More, Madam, more," he replied. "I should charge you more rather than less; for after the work of construction is completed, the educational advantages of the place will be greatly reduced."

There can be no question as to the soundness of the German schoolmaster's answer. A pupil can get from a school only the natural profit that accrues from an actual investment of self—not a whit more.

The attitude of Dr. Lietz's patron toward the manual work required in his school is very common. Parents, generally, are ready to attribute their own success in life to some form of labor which circumstances made necessary; but, curiously enough, they are usually anxious to shield their children from similar sturdy influences. They desire their children to have a smoother road than the one which they traveled themselves. Praiseworthy as this may appear, it ordinarily takes away from the children the most valuable opportunities for self-development. Mother-love is both natural and beautiful; but in the proper nurture of childhood it requires that judicious admixture of intelligence with instinct which will lift it well above the mere cub-licking impulses found in the fox and in the bear.

Education and Manual Labor

Ignorant Mother-Love

In a school, properly organized, there are as many duties to be done "around the house" as there are for the children to perform in a well-regulated home. There is no **Home Duties in School** *natural* division, in kind, between the work of the janitor and much of that which the pupils should do, if the highest efficiency of the school is to be secured. Circumstances make it advisable to assign certain duties to the former; but the latter should participate in all that pertains to sanitary conditions, cleanliness, and arrangement and care of the school's property. To this end the girls should be provided with large aprons and the boys with overalls, that they may meet these duties with dispatch and without the necessity of soiling their clothes. Every part of the building and grounds should be in charge of a group of pupils who are responsible for its condition, and there should be definitely appointed times when all such matters should receive attention. The development of a right disposition toward these homely duties is at the root of a true social organization, because they are all so intimately related to the welfare of the whole.

Objections to this kind of regimen for school children are based upon various grounds. Some people look upon manual labor as degrading. Their ideas concerning it are **Objection to Manual Labor** still tangled up with certain conceptions of that serfdom which once put the badge of the menial upon everyone who worked with his hands. It sometimes happens, for example, that these people file objections to cooking in the school on the ground that they do not wish to have their children trained for service in the kitchen! Since they themselves are in a more or less backward stage of social emergence, these objectors naturally regard such employment in the school as drags on their aspirations.

· Other parents profess a strong belief in manual labor— "manual training" would perhaps be better—but they object to **School Janitoring** their children doing the work which traditionally belongs to the janitor. They believe that the tuition which they pay, or in the case of the public school the taxes, should go for hired service as far as it may be necessary to relieve the pupils of all the burdens imposed by good house-keeping.

There is still another class of objectors who are deeply imbued with the idea that the school is a knowledge-shop where for coin **School Not a** of the realm intellectual commodities may be obtained **Knowledge** in snug packages from the teachers. Some of these **Shop** people are still in that rudimentary stage of intelligence which cannot grasp the significance of purposeful occupations in the training of children. Others, however, have their attention glued upon certain college-entrance requirements which so far have failed to give recognition in any tangible form to the manual labor required of young people either at home or at school. They look down upon the performance of all work not down in the "Requirements" as a waste of time.

There is still another group of people, too, who are mildly astonished that the "new education" should smack of anything like work which might prove disagreeable at times **School Not a** to children. They are accustomed to regard the **Toboggan** modern school as a frictionless toboggan into the fields of knowledge; as an organized means for systematically training people in the art of dodging the distasteful and difficult things of this life. Hence their inability to reconcile their ideas of education with anything that makes a demand for physical labor. These people are merely doing their share toward perpetuating the oldest and the crudest misconception as to the conditions necessary to genuine growth. The type of character the world most needs has for its corner-stone earnest personal effort on behalf of self for the good of the whole. Any other course leads him who purses it thru general uselessness straight toward imbecility, adipose, and apoplexy.

It is needless, however, to multiply words in the consideration of these objections and others that may be urged; for, at last, they must all be brought to the bar of a single princi- **A Deep-lying** ple. The end of education is character, and the in- **Principle** trinsic fineness of character bears a direct relation to service, It is unthinkable that a fine character may be built up

by any means whatsoever in anyone who is not continually expend-
ing himself to the utmost in service. The school is a recognized
means for character-building in childhood and youth, and it

**Character,
Thru Service**

follows that *it should exist for the sole purpose of
offering the children adequate opportunity for trans-
muting that service which they can bring to it into*
the character which they can take away. It is as inexorable as
gravitation that, if no service is rendered no qualities of character are acquired. Here, again, is where the oft-attempted
parallelism between education and merchandizing breaks down.

**Education and
Merchandizing**

Tuition and taxes are not sums of money paid for
something that can be weighed out over the counter.
They should be regarded as *fees paid for the privilege*
of participating in the opportunities for actual service which the
school offers the children. As a means of service the school stands
intermediately between the service required in the home and the
more extended and complicated service demanded by society at
large. It is service, service everywhere—from the kindergarten
to the grave—that nature extorts as the fixed price of life from
everyone who has emerged from the blindness of the "ape and
tiger" stage of existence.

It is happy for the school-teacher that children instinctively
respond to the general demands for service. Were this not so,

**Children Love
Service**

education would not be possible—at least what we
now believe it to be, could not be true. Since
schools began on this earth, children in various but
feeble ways have shown a devotion to their institution that has
been very little appreciated. The carving of a cross or other
symbol on his desk, or the scratching of his name on a window-

**Rudimentary
Service**

pane, is the child's rudimentary thru abortive
method of expressing an affection for the school
that might easily be fanned into the flame of worthy
service. What anyone actually lives with, into that he must and
will in some way put himself. The soft pine wood of the desks
and the smooth glass of the windows were the extent of his
opportunities for impressing himself in the schools of the past.

In one of the rooms at Eton they have not "cleaned house"

for some centuries, I was told, for fear they might rub from the
walls the names of some of its earlier students
House-cleaning
at Eton
who in their later years have made England famous.
Probably no boy ever scrawled his name on a
schoolhouse wall without at least a vague hope that some day
he might make that name illustrious; that in due time in some
way he might make it a beacon for those who were to come after
him.   The men of England performed a distinct service to
English life and education by merely scratching their names on
Eton's walls.   The luster of those names alone renders dear to
the hearts of young Englishmen a musty and gloomy old room
which to an American schoolboy, unacquainted with its traditions, would be but a place of durance vile.   These
Subtle In-
stincts Not
Insignificant
instincts of childhood which hitherto have been
allowed to express themselves only in punishable
offenses are the most subtle as well as the most vital
sources of character.   When teachers and parents become wise
enough to recognize them properly, these early impulses, directed
into channels of service for the school, will then become the root
of a true social organization.   As their lives gradually become
absorbed in its service the pupils will naturally forego the more
primitive pleasure of merely defacing the walls of the school.

The kinds of service that are possible to the school are not
all indistinguishable from those usually assigned to the janitor.
Beautifying
Schools
Besides those which relate to sanitation and order,
it is most important that the pupils should actively
participate in every effort made to render the house
and premises more beautiful.   The schoolhouses and grounds in
this country, as a rule, are notoriously unattractive.   Money could
hardly hire parents, no matter what the intellectual feast might
be, to sit day after day amid surroundings as barren as those
found in the average school.   Yet they consign their children for a
series of years to such conditions, and by force and cajolery endeavor to make them like it.   This, too, in the face of the fact that
as a depraver of the æsthetic sense and as a corruptor of public
taste there is nothing to beat the average American school-house!

Everyone of them, however, might be redeemed and be made

attractive, if the children themselves were free to work on the problem. The instinct which impels a little girl to

Give the Pupils a Chance trim and decorate an old store-box for her playhouse, if allowed its legitimate exercise in the schoolrom, would soon transform it, too, into something at least childishly beautiful. With children's well-known fondness for trees, shrubs, vines, and flowers, it is simply monstrous that school-yards should remain as unplanted as Sahara. This arid school environment of the young is chargeable directly and only to the colossal ignorance of both teachers and parents as to what constitute the essentials in character-building.

The compass of school life includes years of fine feelings, high aspirations, and great physical vigor. It is a period that

Potentiality of the School Period should be marked by considerable actual achievement. In the home this is frequently recognized, and the demand is made for helpful service in some form which the child can understand. If a bed which he should make up is left unmade, that is a fact that stands out for itself. The disorder and the discomfort which he inflicts upon the

Criteria in School and Home family place him at once in the focus of their attention, perhaps displeasure; and as this is repeated he gradually acquires a just measure of his worth to his social unit, the household. But in school, if he fails to recite well, it is very rarely that he charges it up to his own unworthiness. It is, indeed, difficult to prove that he should do so. It is not easy for him to see how anyone, even himself, is either benefited or injured by the character of his recitation. The teacher's measure of his worth is expressed thru a rattan or a mark or a frown or a smile. The inevitable outcome of this state of uncertainty is indifference, distaste, and hatred of the whole scheme of learning as set up by the schools—hence the truant officer and the juvenile court!

The relationship of service to knowledge is palpable. The loftiest service requires the highest skill and the most learning

Servicea nd Knowledge Accomplishment means exactness of knowledge when both doing and learning are controlled by motives pointing to useful service.

Schools, therefore, should be regarded as workshops. They

should be equipped with simple means for pursuing some phase of every craft that bears upon human welfare. One cannot over-estimate the boon that such arts and crafts as clay-modeling, pottery, woodwork, textiles, metal-work, book-binding, printing, drawing, and painting are to children whose artistic tastes are stimulated and whose efforts are booted and spurred by a worthy purpose. By these means our schools some day will be made beautiful thru the work of the childrens' hands, and their lives will be made fair thru their consecration to the school's service.

W. S. J.

ALBERT G. LANE

VOLUME VII   NUMBER 4

THE ELEMENTARY SCHOOL TEACHER

DECEMBER, 1906

ALBERT G. LANE (1841–1906)

ORVILLE T. BRIGHT

Josiah Lane, the father of Albert G. Lane, came to Cook County with his wife in 1836 and settled at Galewood on the old Gale farm a little northeast of Oak Park, then a long distance from Chicago, but now within the city limits. On this farm Albert Lane was born, March 15, 1841, and here the old farmhouse still stands. Albert was the oldest of eight children. When the Lane family came to Cook County in 1836, the total population of Chicago did not exceed two thousand, and the exports from the Chicago port that year amounted to $1,000.64.

Soon after the birth of Albert the family moved to Chicago and settled in a cottage on the site now occupied by Rothschild's department store. The cottage was later moved to 132 West Monroe Street, and is still occupied by the family. Upon the great open prairie, used as a cow pasture, the boy Albert ventured as far west as Ashland Avenue in the capacity of herdsman; and from this time the sturdy, independent character of the lad rapidly developed. When he began school, the entire school attendance of Chicago did not equal that of one of our largest schools at the present, and there was no high school.

As a carpenter, Albert Lane's father found difficulty enough in supporting his family of eight members on a dollar and a half per day, and at the age of twelve years it seemed necessary for the boy to leave school and go to work, as he could thereby turn in one dollar and fifty cents per week toward the family expenses.

177

Albert cheerfully complied, but his heart longed for his school, and he gained permission to return to it by offering to earn the dollar fifty per week out of school hours. He did it, of course— he never failed at anything—and by selling papers he carried himself through grammar school and into the first class of the first Chicago high school. With this class he would have been graduated from the high school under Mr. Charles Dupee in 1858 at the age of eighteen years, but he had to leave school a short time before graduation.

In the Lane family teaching was second nature, and to it Albert naturally turned. In the year that he left school he was placed in charge of the old Franklin School, and was its principal until 1868, a term of ten years, when he succeeded John F. Eberhart as superintendent of Cook County schools. With one interruption of four years he filled this office with distinguished ability until December, 1891—that is, for nineteen years. During the four years' interim he turned his attention to banking—and with marked success.

The year 1873 brought to Albert Lane misfortune such as tries the very souls of men and tests their integrity to the utmost. As county superintendent he had on deposit in the Franklin Bank school fund money amounting to $33,000. The bank failed, and the deposit was absolutely wiped out—a total loss. As a depository the bank had been approved by the county commissioners, and Mr. Lane was probably under no legal obligations to refund the money. To add to his perplexities, he failed of re-election as county superintendent the same year. Now his splendid conception of honor and his superb courage came to the front. No legal technicality for a moment dimmed his vision. To him the educational fund was a sacred trust, and without a moment's hesitation he entered upon the task before him.

Getting his bondsmen together, he called upon them to make good the loss, and pledged them that every dollar with interest should be paid back to them. He converted into cash whatever of property he had accumulated, applied it on the debt, and then for nineteen long years he labored and saved to wipe out the balance—and he did it—principal and interest amounting to

$45,000. It was my good fortune to call upon him at his office at the consummation of this struggle. I found him out of the office, but he came in soon after, and never shall I forget the sort of glory that seemed to envelop him, as, stretching to his full height, he brought his hand down upon my shoulder and said with the utmost intensity: "Bright, I have just paid the last dollar of it." In the annals of Chicago can be found nothing more thrilling than this heroic struggle of Albert Lane. His will be a name to conjure with in teaching civic virtue when that of many a Chicago millionaire shall have passed into oblivion.

The county superintendent was, ex officio, a member of the Cook County Board of Education. Acting in this capacity, Mr. Lane was largely instrumental in bringing Colonel Parker to the Cook County Normal School. This was a momentous event in the history of that institution, and the next few years made the school not only of national but also of world-wide importance. Mr. Lane fully appreciated the value and importance of Colonel Parker's work, and in all of the troublous times which followed he stood staunchly for the school and made possible its final triumphant success.

Beginning in December, 1891, Mr. Lane served as city superintendent of Chicago for seven years. They were the most arduous years of his life. Through the pernicious meddling of the city hall, politics became rampant in educational affairs, and the balking of his plans for the schools so added to the natural burdens of the office that even Mr. Lane's splendid health gave way. He never recovered from the strain of the last two years in the city office, and it was doubtless fortunate for him that he failed of re-election in July, 1898. Here again Mr. Lane's loyalty to Chicago schools shone forth, and with it a dignified manliness of character. He cheerfully accepted the office of district superintendent, and, in so doing, rendered a service to the city of Chicago which it would be difficult to overestimate. His intimate knowledge of school affairs of city, county, and state was unequaled by that of any other man. This, added to his sound judgment, his vast acquaintance, and his unselfish devotion to the schools, made him almost indispensable as a counselor to his successors in the city office. This service was freely rendered and fully acknowledged. He remained at his post until well into the last vacation, though often working under intense weariness.

Albert Lane had often expressed the hope that he might "die in the harness," and this desire was practically gratified. After a short vacation at Bay View with his family, and as the constant companion of his little granddaughter, he felt called upon to return to his post of duty; but his strength gave out on the return trip, and a very few days closed one of the noblest lives that have ever blest this city.

Albert Lane's work was not confined to Chicago or Cook County. For thirty-five years he was a potent factor in the State Teachers' Association, of which he was at one time president. No other man has contributed more than he to the success of the National Educational Association. For many years he was a member of its executive committee and was also its financial manager. In a recent letter Mr. Irwin Shepard, secretary of the association, said: "I do not see how we can go on without him." The National Educational Association accorded him its highest honor in 1893, when he became its president. Few men have enjoyed so general a personal acquaintance among prominent educators throughout the United States, and to none was accorded greater respect.

Albert Lane saw almost the entire growth of Chicago. He loved the city intensely, and he gave all the worth of his splendid manhood to her service. His impress upon the county schools was remarkable. He rendered to the city just as generous and devoted service as to the county. This service was fully appreciated by the teachers with whom he worked, and today thousands of them mourn his loss.

As a citizen Mr. Lane shirked no responsibility. He proved that a schoolmaster may be a man among men; for few enjoyed so generally or so genuinely as he the respect and confidence of his fellow-citizens. He was a devoted member of the Methodist church, and in its service his life was spent. Thousands of young men connected with the Young Men's Christian Association, of which he was trustee, knew Mr Lane, admired him as an ideal Christian gentleman, and emulated his example.

His devoted wife said of him the other day: "He was all that a son could be; he was all that a husband could be; he was all that a father could be; he was all that a church member could be; and you know what he was as a citizen and as an educator."

Yes, we know full well. His labors are ended, but the influence of a noble life can have no end. Albert Lane's cheerfulness, his devotion to duty, his courage, his unselfishness, his clearness of vision and fearlessness in living up to his convictions, the charming sincerity of his friendship, and his keen sense of right and justice, all added to the rarest integrity, made up a character which is our inheritance. We admired him, we trusted him, we loved him. We are better teachers because he labored among and with us.

Mr. Lane was married in July, 1878, to Miss Frances Smalwood, a teacher in the high school. Two children blessed this union.

To his sorrowing wife and daughters we express our warmest sympathy in their great bereavement.

SOCIAL SCIENCE

JOHN S. WELCH
Supervisor of Grammar Grades, Salt Lake City Schools

In the "Outline of Social Science" published in the April number of the *Elementary School Teacher,* an attempt was made to
indicate *how* first-hand experiences in social, industrial, and
political life, which touch the child on every hand, may be organized into a working force for intelligently constructing history and
also for defining the child to himself in terms of the great complex life in which he finds himself. The motive of the present
article is to deal with the *why,* and also to answer briefly some
of the objections that may be raised in opposition to the teaching
of social science in the elementary schools.

To get a reasonable working hypothesis it may be well to call
to mind the significance of a movement that is now a matter of
history. Here we shall find the genesis of the new movement
in modern education.

Not many decades ago educators had begun to realize that
the tendency of the school world was to divorce the child from
the real world. Instead of coming in contact with things—their
relations and interrelations—his whole energy and attention
were centered on learning many more or less useful, but wholly
unrelated, facts about things. The scholar was distinguished by
his ability to know—by his knowledge—regardless of his utter
failure, perhaps, as a constructive doer. He was so busily engaged
in memorizing the ideas and opinions of others that he had little
time and often less inclination to formulate ideas and opinions of
his own. Children of a larger, as well as those of a lesser, growth
were often prodigies in their ability to follow the calf-paths of
the mind, but they were often startlingly deficient in their ability
to blaze new trails. The whole idea at that time, controlling the
school and shaping the work, was to prepare for high school,
college, and going out into the world. The motto writ large, so

that he who would might read, was: "Be miserable now. Glory, fame, pleasure unspeakable, power and dignity of office, are just around the corner."

A few there were even in those good old days of settled opinions who had begun to think that life is growth; that it is with us always; that we are in the here and the now realizing a large, rich, full-orbed life; or a mean, petty, cramped, and dwarfish life; that the life now large or small is the precursor of the life that is to be—the foundation upon which it must be built. They had also begun to realize that every child born into the world is the center of his own universe. About him prairie and forest, mountain and stream, bird and beast, range themselves. About him planets, stars, and suns sweep and blaze and burn. In fact, all that he can ever know of earthly form and color, of heavenly splendor, of visible and invisible worlds, must be built out of and upon the ideas that are poured in through eye and ear and muscular sense. So nature-study was ushered—nay, forced itself—into the course of study. Thus a study of things became a necessary preparation for a study about things.

This is neither the time nor the place to comment on how this primary impulse and spirit of nature-study has been thwarted and deadened by the old show of things; how it became one more line added to the knowledge about things, nor of how it took the more practical, but equally deadening, point of view which may be summed up in: "What form of life interferes with you most? Kill it." It is better to deal with the spirit that ushered it in, however much blind leaders of the blind may have thwarted and deadened that spirit.

Nature-study, then, is a study of things: what they are; what they do; how they do it; or of what they have done, are doing, purpose to do; their motive. Thus the movement may be from groups of individuals to individuals in groups; a study of group relations and group conduct. Upon this foundation, and upon this alone, the world of science not present to the senses may be built.

Now this great realm of nature—this world—includes the child himself in his group relations. From this standpoint we must determine, not whether we *will,* but whether we *must* take note of social science in our school work. What is the significance of group study? It is the study and organization of the elements out of which are built every form and phase of human thought and activity. It comprehends all history, patriotism, citizenship.

To see this motive-force of history—society grouped and regrouped—in the present, and its significance in giving purpose and meaning to the past, as well as pointing to all the future, it may be well to consider for a moment an attitude of mind toward history.

Aside from the deep and permanent influence of Hebrew literature, it seems quite unnecessary to take much note of oriental civilization, as western civilization was only indirectly affected by it. True, the Persian invasion welded the people of Greece together in defense of home and country, revealed their power and resources to them, and had a tendency to bind them together by ties of common memories, if not common interests. Yet the tendency in Greece was ever toward individual freedom from the larger group interests, that is, *freedom for the free men.* It may have been this tendency which gave rise to the versatility of Greek genius, her sculpture and painting, her poetry and philosophy, which remain the wonder and the inspiration of all ages, and through which Greece bequeathed to the world the mighty impulse called progress.

The tendency in Rome was toward freedom in terms of Roman citizenship. This tendency gave rise to the great body of laws which sought to incorporate, interpret, and define the social and political rights of the individual and to define his obligations and limitations in his relation to the state. These laws, thus formulated and defined, form the basis of modern jurisprudence. The extension of citizenship through the vast cosmopolitan organization known as the Roman Empire, thus recognizing the political brotherhood of man; the fostering of the central idea in Christianity, thus recognizing the higher brotherhood; the extending of law and order and systems of political organization, have been Rome's contribution to modern civilization.

The Teuton attempted to solve the problem of representative government; of extending and enlarging the social and political rights of man; of instituting constitutional forms of government that grow directly out of, and rest upon, the consent of the governed; of proclaiming the doctrine that all men are created equal in their right to aspire to develop and to realize the best that is in them, an idea which must eventually leave no place in their thought for the bondman or the slave.

This tendency toward freedom, transferred to the untrammeled West, blossomed in this republic of ours. It is the expression of a people's thought and feeling transplanted to a new world and modified by the new conditions in the new environment. It is the thought and feeling of a people enacted into law as they were changed and shaped and fashioned on the anvil of experience by the hammers of toil and suffering, of privations and sorrow, of splendid courage and noble self-sacrifice during all of the years required to cause the wilderness to blossom as the rose. For the first time on a broad and comprehensive plan the rights of the world's down-most were clearly recognized, and a broader and a nobler meaning was written into the term "citizenship." This generic idea gave rise to the public-school system whose mission is "to preserve the past, conserve the present, and shape the future."

The foregoing is intended merely as an outline suggestive of the stream of history flowing into and shaping the life of the present. It is also intended to suggest that the permanent things of history, the ones that have endured, are those most worthy of study. All the facts of history which may lay claim to the student's attention are those which revolve about these vital principles, aiding or retarding their development, or adapting them to new conditions. Before he can appreciate this causal movement in history the child must first become conscious of the institutions which constitute his life as well as the life of society. That is, he must deal with the institutions that came to be before he can appreciate or intelligently understand *the processes by which they came to be.* Through the study of history, as he learns to appreciate the vast expenditure of time, men, and money required to shape these institutions to what they now are, a larger and a more significant meaning will be written into these institutions.

If the above assumption is even in a measure true, then the study of social science, the study of groups and group relations which touch the child on every hand—call it by whatever name you will— is just as essential a foundation for the purposeful study of history as is the study of nature as a foundation on which to build the sciences. Out of the material of the here and the now the child will rebuild the unseen past and construct the still more progressive future.

This is the *justification of,* and the *necessity for,* the study of social science in the elementary schools.

The objections and the objectors to that study may be dealt with briefly.

Of course, conservatism, which sums itself up in "our safe and sound leaders of educative thought," will stand aghast at the bare idea of adding one more subject to an already over-crowded and bewildering course of study. (They evidently overlook the fact that the principle of elimination applied to the husks in the overcrowded course would soon reduce it to a reasonable working basis.) They still earnestly plead for a better mastering of the *essentials* of an education, reserving the right, of course, to *name* the essentials. They will still continue to give little time or consideration to weighing the difference between what a child really needs to know and to do in terms of his own growth and development, and what is assumed ought to be known in terms of the subject-matter divided by the number of school years!

The teacher, now driven to the verge of distraction in a vain endeavor to "jam in, cram in" all of the facts now embodied in the outline for her grade, will groan in anguish of spirit at this added burden—this new thing to be held accountable for. The requirements, pressed down from above, won't let her realize even for a moment that the child is her only subject, the world of matter and idea, the material from which to choose her means; *what he is,* the only legitimate test of her work.

We as teachers must all learn to realize that, if the old subject-matter system lays claims to the man in the White House, it must with equal consistency lay claim to the individual who has reached potter's field by way of the gallows. We must also realize that scholarship is not, has never been, synonymous with character. We must come to know that the quality of knowledge, not the amount, determines the quality of the individual.

"It is the duty of each individual to be born a man of social tendencies which his communal tradition requires of him; if he persist in being born a different sort of man, then, as far as his variation goes, he is liable to be found a criminal before the bar of public conscience and law, and to be suppressed in an asylum or a reformatory, in Siberia or in the potter's field."[1]

It is at least one of the functions of the public schools to determine the ideals toward which the individual aspires.

Another class of objectors will be found among the educators who still long for the good old-fashioned education which taught children to know things and to do things, and which never worried either the teacher or the children with the why of the knowing or doing. Their philosophy may be summed up in a simple problem in subtraction, 21 − 9. "The child should be taught 9 from 1 I cannot take, so I borrow one from the 2. Nine from 11 leaves 2 and 1 borrowed from the 2 leaves 1, hence 12!" It is so simple! Such philosophy is born of the time-worn platitude: "The child learns to do by doing, and doesn't reason at first." Out of nothing something comes! He will reason after while! When he teaches school, perhaps!

The members of this class will also throw their hands up in horror at this new attempt to cause a child to realize himself and his functions in terms of others; to cause him to know that *humanity* and *service* are the largest words yet written in the vocabulary of man. Or they may hedge by saying: "All this is well enough after the child has mastered the essentials." They may assume the position of the authority on reading who says: "After the child has learned to read, the wise teacher begins to

[1] Baldwin's *Social and Ethical Interpretations.*

look about for reading matter that is worth while," and who evidently ignores the pertinent question: "Why shouldn't the wise teacher look about long before that interesting phase of development is reached?"

In spite of conservatism, time element, what-not, these new forces must dominate both schools and teachers. We may retard, we cannot stop, the new demand of a new time in our work.

With the course of study as now arranged, where shall we find time for work in social science? We shall take time from problems in arithmetic which have naught to do with the child's life and precious little to do with adult life. We shall take it from the time usually devoted to the reading of scraps of literature found in the average reader, selections which are utterly devoid of any thrill or stimulus toward a higher life. We shall take it from the time given to that portion of geography, as now taught, which has nothing to do with the heavens above, the earth beneath, or the waters under the earth. We may take some time from some of the handwork with great profit.

It may be permissible to digress at this point for a moment to make the meaning clear.

"The child epitomizes the race;" therefore, because his ancestors (considerably remote) gathered and selected grasses and made baskets under the stress of necessity, it becomes vitally essential that grasses be gathered and baskets be woven, willy nilly, by every child of school age from Maine to the Golden Gate until some of us shy at grasses and raffia in the school-room more than we did at the old-time birch!

This is no disparagement of handwork. It simply raises the question as to whether the handwork of today should be based, to any great extent, on by-gone conditions. The mistake, if one exists, lies in assuming that the simple is necessarily so to the child, though far removed in time and thought, instead of believing that the known and necessary are simple however complex apparently, and that the far-off, the unknown, is complex however simple it may seem.

In dealing with social science we must be careful to avoid one factor which has greatly disturbed the educational vision in some quarters, that is, the bugbear of environment. Some of us are prone to believe that environment merely refers to the little physical pocket in which we happen to find ourselves. It is well to recognize this physical environment, for, as has been said, it is a factor with which we must deal. We must build our world out of the material of every phase and form of life found therein. But we must not stop here. We must go on to realize the spiritual environment in terms of the accumulated treasures of the ages, preserved in song and story; in scientific discoveries; in bronze or marble or on the glowing canvas; and in the uplifting message of the poet, prophet, and seer. From the environment of the vicinity the child must be led to the contemplaton of the universe; from the world-wide, material environment, to the highest spiritual environment yet penned or pictured. On this basis, from this standpoint, must we settle the question as to whether the teacher shall be one of the group, or whether there shall be a group and a teacher requiring new groups with new leaders.

Shall we as teachers ever fully realize that there is but one subject for us to teach, that is, the child? Shall we ever realize that he is the exhaustible quantity, the subject-matter the inexhaustible quantity, so far as he is concerned? Shall we realize that we must finally turn from the subject as an end to regard it wholly as a means? Shall we, instead of assuming the facts that ought to be known, determine what will best meet the needs of the period of growth with which we have to deal? Shall we all finally realize that the self grows in the body as the plant grows in the soil, and that all the teacher can do in the process is to make conditions for the grower to have free access to the sunshine, light, warmth, soil, moisture, the factors of material and spiritual life and growth? When such an idea prevails we shall cease to worry over teaching all that the course of study contains as a minimum. We shall know that children, like ourselves, will continue to forget nine-tenths of all that we thought so essential for them to learn each day. We shall know that the growth toward a larger and larger self—*the is* and *the ought to be*—which sums itself up in conduct and character, in the ability to know and to do, to aspire and to be, is the end and aim of school and culture.

NORWAY

A READING LESSON. II

GEORG THORNE-THOMSEN

And now begins a merry life for the children. Up early in the morning to take the cattle to the best pastures, and then to pick flowers and berries the whole day: For the evening the best part of all is left—to sit around the hearth and listen to fairy-tales. In this way the short summer passes rapidly—altogether too rapidly.

Among the remembrances of a Norwegian boy none are dearer to him than those connected with the saeter. When school closes at the end of June, it is the highest ambition of every schoolboy to visit the mountains. How I used to long for them and look forward to the hour when I could put the books on the shelf and say goodby to the hot, dusty city!

With the knapsack on his shoulder, and with a very little money in his pocket, the Norwegian boy leaves his home and stays away for weeks during the summer. Wherever he goes, everyone is kind to him, and, thanks to Norwegian hospitality, he does not spend more than ten to twenty cents a day. In many places they receive him as a guest and are glad to have him. He has to walk most of the time, the railways being few and the rivers not very navigable. Of course, the wealthy foreigner travels all over the country in the cariol, a typical Norwegian vehicle for one horse. On the steep, narrow mountain-paths these rich people have the mountain-horse to carry them. But the schoolboy can afford no such extravagance. A pair of strong legs, a determination to climb all the peaks nobody else could climb, and fifteen to twenty dollars in his pocket are his whole outfit for a five to six weeks' journey. But he gets on all right. Maybe his feet are sore once in a while; perhaps he does not climb all the peaks that stand in his way; maybe he doesn't travel so very fast; but what he gains by this slow way of traveling is a thorough understanding and appreciation of his country and its people. Traveling on foot gives, more than any other way of traveling, a splendid opportunity of coming into close contact with the peasants and their lives; and the boy coming back from his journey brings with him a strong impression of the beauty of his country and a better knowledge of its people.

But it is not only in summer time that we visit the different parts of our country; the winter also gives us, perhaps, still better opportunities. From their earliest childhood, the Norwegian boy and girl become accustomed to the use of the *ski*—a kind of snowshoe, that, however, bears no resemblance to the Indian snowshoe. When the snow lies several feet deep, covering up every path and road, when the lakes are frozen, and with only a few hours of daylight, we visit the mountains and forests on snowshoes. All the saeters, the pasture houses, are closed, and we may be fifty to sixty miles away from any human dwelling; but on such trips we are generally supplied with reindeer bags, which furnish us shelter for the night. Usually two persons sleep in one bag; and, although surrounded by ice and snow, and at a temperature of twenty to thirty degrees below zero. this bag gives us a warm shelter for the night. Snowshoe-running is the typical national sport in Norway, and is indulged in by young and old, men and women. A Norwegian girl on skis is a pretty sight; health and independence are her main characteristics; and the boys, who on their skis jump ninety to a hundred feet, and lie out in the dark winter night far from home, grow to be men with a healthy mind in a healthy body.

As a young boy, with a knapsack on my shoulders, I climbed the Galdho Peak, the highest peak of Jotenheim, together with some countrymen and an English couple. Tied together with a thick rope and with axes and sticks, we first crossed the immense ice-field that stretches off for miles at the foot of the peak.

Finding our way over the many crevasses, the intense heat reflected from the ice burned our faces. In hot, but perfectly clear, weather we reached the summit, where our guide had built a small hut, after having first carried the timber on his shoulders all the way over the snow-fields. From this little hut we enjoyed one of the grandest scenes a person can look upon; one of the wildest, at any rate. On all sides of us nothing was to be seen but rock, ice, and snow; in the whole landscape you could discover neither grass nor forests, neither a bending river nor a glittering water-sheet. It was a perfect Arctic scene. All the valleys, the gorges, the fiords, were hidden from our view. The icy tongues licked the mountain-sides, and far west the sunshine sparkled on the Justedal bræ, the largest snow-field of Europe.

It was among these mountains that the god Thor, in the old days, fought the Jotuns, or the frost giants; it was here that he used his never-failing hammer. But on Christmas Eve Thor is again at the head of the warlike gods. In the furious winter storms they ride through Jotenheim on foaming black horses. The peasants from the surrounding valleys hear the terrible noise and tremble, and woe to him who has forgotten to put the sign of the cross on the doors of his house and barn. He may find his cattle and horses gone, or even he himself may be dragged by one of the valkyries up to Valhal. This ride of the gods on Christmas Eve is known as the *Aasgaardsridt.*

A sail along the northern coast of Norway, with its thousands of islands, is wonderful. The islands assume the most fantastic shapes and give rise to a rich folk lore; every rock and cliff has its story attached to it; islands, miles apart, act as characters in one drama, and whole series of cliffs and rocks are connected in the same story. There is a group of rocky islands called the Seven Sisters; at some distance another island is found known as the Horseman; with a stretch of your imagination you can make out the panting steed and the gigantic figure on his back. The giant was pursuing these seven maidens, so the story goes; but, unable to catch up with them, he lifted a tremendous rock and flung it after them; the stone passed through a large mountain, and the hole it left can still be seen.

Some of these rocks are teeming with life, and millions of birds use them as their roosting-places. At a distance you see only a moving mass, but coming nearer you will find that this mass consists of millions and millions of birds. To possess such a bird-rock is to be rich, because it yields annually immense quantities of the finest down.

Here, among these islands, the Lofoten Islands, are the most extensive fisheries of Norway. In the coldest part of the winter, people from the surrounding districts, even from regions far south, meet on these islands to attend the winter's fishing. If they fail, it means starvation to thousands; if they turn out well, families may become rich in a few weeks. But terrible storms rage here, and in a single night hundreds of boats may be upset, leaving families all along the coast unprovided for.

Imagine a scene here in midsummer, among these fantastically shaped islands, where the whales are playing and the birds are crying; you might think you had come to a fairyland. At night the light of the sun is very pale, weird, and drowsy, and the sky has every appearance of sunset. The birds seek their nests, the dew falls, all nature seems to go to rest. But this lasts only for a short time; the mellow light passes away, and the whole sky becomes brilliant as at sunrise. The sun rises; shortly afterward there is life everywhere. The birds begin to sing again and go busily to work; the northern summer is so short, and so much has to be accomplished before fall sets in; the young ones must be taught to fly, to be ready to spread their wings and go with their parents far south when the autumn storms begin.

Norway has a long and dark winter, but it has also a warm and beautiful summer. If you have missed the sun through the dark winter months, you enjoy its return so much more. The summer sends a message of its coming through air and water; you feel the summer in the warm breeze from the sea, in the blue sky. The ice loosens on the rivers and comes dancing down from the mountains. In a short time it is green everywhere, right up to the edge of the glacier. The sun seems to feel how cruel it has been in staying away so long, and tries to make up for all the dark winter days. How fast everything grows, and how rapidly the landscape changes! And no wonder; for many a week the sun shines without sinking below the horizon. Instead of a day of twelve hours, there is a day of three months.

Evening comes, but still the gleam of the sun is on the sea and among the mountains.

People up in the northern regions look forward to the return of the sun with the greatest impatience; they watch all the things that predict its coming. They notice with the greatest delight the high, flaming pyramid which it forms at the horizon while still being under it. When, at last, the mountains are burning in its beams, and it appears down in the fiord and valleys, there is then a joy that only those can feel that have missed its sight for nine to ten weeks. The guns from Vardohus, the most northern fort of Norway, are thundering, and the day of the sun's return is celebrated as a holiday. Forgotten are all the dark and dreary hours, and life seems beautiful again. Nobody thinks of sleep, but only of enjoying the short, beautiful summer.

After the last days of July the day grows rapidly shorter, and you see less and less of the sun, till at last it disappears. But although the sun itself cannot be seen, there is a bright glow in the eastern sky every day, which, as winter deepens, becomes dimmer and dimmer, until there are only a couple of hours at noon when you can see to work by daylight. When the weather is stormy, lamps are kept burning all day. However, most people overestimate the darkness of the winters far north. They are not so dark, after all; the stars, the moon, and the reflection from the snow and ice give much light, and, still more, there is the aurora borealis that makes the northern winter nights so beautiful.

From our earliest childhood we are nursed by folklore and mythology. All nature seems alive and speaks to us—the mountains, the lakes, the rivers and the brooks, the deep sea, and the forest.

When St. Olaf attempted to introduce Christianity and built the first churches in Norway, he had a terrible struggle; the old gods were not willing to give up their hold on the people without a battle. So they rose against the king with their hosts of Jotens, dwarfs, and other strange beings. It was for them a hopeless fight; nothing availed against the victorious king; their very efforts to obstruct him were turned into blessings, and their gigantic strength became an instrument in his hands. Soon the king's work was successfully accomplished; but, as a punishment for their obstinacy, many of the giants were turned into stone, and are now found all over the country as representatives of the old mythology in the fantastically shaped islands and cliffs, waiting for their final judgment. But most of these strange beings are still said to people the mountains and forests. Sometimes you hear the most beautiful music from within the mountains; or you see a castle in a place where you saw nothing before. A large crowd of people is gathered outside it, and music and noise are heard from within. Then you must be careful, or else these beings may get power over you; but if you make the sign of the cross, or say the Lord's Prayer loud enough, it will all vanish in a second, and nothing will be left of all the splendor. If you don't take this precaution, you may be drawn into the mountain where these beings live, and where all is gold and silver.

In the waterfalls the *fossegrim* lives. He plays the violin, and they say that Ole Bull and other famous violinists learned their art from him. Sometimes he plays so beautifully, so enchantingly, that you forget everything, and are tempted to throw yourself into the waterfall. Sometimes the tune is so heavy, so mournful, that you can't help weeping.

In the lakes and the fiords lives the *nökke*—a being who every year wants the sacrifice of a man or a woman; so that in the lake or fiord where there is a nökke a human being is lost every year.

The principal being in the Norwegian folklore is the so-called *huldre*. The huldre lives on the mountains and in the valleys. She has all the beauty and splendor of the Norwegian scenery; but she has also its deep melancholy, as revealed in her singing and violin-playing, and to which you cannot listen without tears; but by her beauty and love she weakens and entices people's minds.

In many hills around the country old kings have been buried with their goods and treasures. I have myself helped to dig up such a hill, in which we found old weapons, implements, bones, etc. In many a place immense treasure is said to be concealed, and the common belief is that a light is burning over it during the night. If you dig three successive Thursday eves, without uttering a word while digging, the treasure is yours.

A very familiar figure in Norwegian fairy-tales is the devil. As he appears in the Scandinavian folklore with horsehoof, plug hat, and swallowtail coat, he is rather a stupid fellow. All kinds of tricks are played on him, and numerous are the scrapes he gets into. The old Norse mythology did not know of any devil. Loke, however wicked, was no devil by any means. When Christianity was introduced, many features of the old belief were transferred to the new religion, and as they had to have a devil, Loke was favored with the position.

The hero in our fairy-tales is Askeladden, or "the cinder-lad." While the others are working he seems to be idle. He is laughed at and looked upon with contempt by his brothers and everybody else. He takes no active part in what goes on around him, but spends his time by the fireside digging in the ashes. But great powers and abilities are dormant in him. He is quietly observing, and knows that his day will come; and until then he is contented to wait. Then, when the country is in danger; when everybody else has tried and failed; when a great deed is to be done, and the whole nation is waiting for a man, then Askeladden appears, no longer in rags, but in all the splendor and confidence of a hero. Then, when the deed is done, when the king and his people are rejoicing, and the princess and half the kingdom are promised to the hero, Askeladden, again in his rags, returns quietly to his fireside. He knows the task has been done, and that appreciation will come, however late. Much of the Norwegian's way of thinking and acting is mirrored, and has found expression, in this hero of the fairy story. He is the embodiment of certain features in the character of the Norwegian, as much to his disadvantage as to his advantage.

The Norwegian loves the deed, and his whole life and labor are back of his love. It is generally agreed that the dwellers in mountainous countries are much less fit for the constant, monotonous labor, as found in factories, than the people in the lowlands

The life of the Norwegian is divided between indolent rest and fight for a scanty support. At one moment the sun shines brightly, the sea is unruffled and the sky without clouds; in fact, nature seems to smile on him. At another moment, nature in all her fury is arrayed in fierce battle against him; she no longer gives out of her abundance like a kind mother, but he has to put in his life for what he can get. At such times he is the man of deed, with his whole personality concentrated and expressed in a single act.

Along the western coast this life in calm and storm is more apparent than anywhere else. The extremes in nature have their equivalent in the character of the people. Look at the peasant ashore—a picture of indolence and inactivity. See him in his boat—all energy, daring, but at the same time self-possessed; he seems not like the same man. This is what makes up his real life—these flashes, these gleams of danger and action—while the rest of his life is only an intermission, an indolent waiting for the next deed.

The sailor's life is exceedingly attractive to the Norwegian, because it presents the unexpected, that living for the moment for which his nature has so great a craving. For this reason the commercial fleet of Norway stands fourth in rank among the nations; for this reason Norwegian sailors are met in every corner of the world. But these sailors would do only medium work in the large cotton factories. It is against our inmost soul to give our lives piecemeal. It is when labor is elevated to a fight, when work becomes a deed into which he can put all mental and physical powers, that you can count on the Norwegian. He may be slow to arouse, but when aroused, his whole being is put in for the issue. The history of the Norwegian people, from the vikings down to modern times, tells of the same tendency—this love of the deed. Their heroes have been those men who, in times of national calamity, put everything at stake to conquer all or lose all.

The Norwegian people are not a money-saving nation. What is gained in the fierce struggle is easily squandered in the quiet intervals. It is difficult for the Norwegian to get down to the business and routine of life. From childhood we are kept away from it by the enchanted world in which we lead a second life—a world of princes and princesses, of giants and heroes; a world in which wonderful feats are performed, where nothing is impossible for him who dares. Then in after years we measure life by this world full of impossibilities, but the measure seldom fits. When, instead of heroes and giants, in actual life we find mostly dwarfs and cripples, we are disappointed. Our eyesight has to be readjusted, and some never can get over this readjustment.

One will readily understand that people living in deep valleys, under the dark shadows of mountains, year after year, seeing only the black rock, wildly roaring ice-rivers, or blue glaciers; who are always being threatened by avalanches of stone and ice, must acquire peculiar traits of character. People who have their hopes out on a furious sea; who, in the dark winter, at every moment must risk their lives for a scanty support, must necessarily lead a peculiar mental life. This is the case on the west coast of Norway. Under such circumstances man feels himself powerless, although this feeling has a different influence on different individuals. Some give up the fight immediately and sink helplessly down to lead a life of misery. Others become cold and severe by the daily struggle, and believe firmly that life is ruled by an unchangeable fate, called in Norwegian *lagnad*, against which there is no use fighting. The latter are strong but stern men and women, who have neither hope nor illusion. They meet the danger with cold tranquility, and avoid all that makes life bright and beautiful. Their expression is rigid and immovable, and they think it the greatest shame for a man to show any outward sign of emotion. They resemble the heroes about whom the sagas tell, who, in exciting situations, grew ashy pale like withered grass, big drops of sweat bursting from their brows.

The national types, as you find them today, have had centuries in which to develop their own peculiar characteristics. Within its narrow limits, every fiord, every valley, has brought forth its own type. Separated by the vast mountain wastes, they developed dialects hardly comprehensible to people outside the valley. The national dress and customs of one valley are very much different from those in the adjacent valley. It is an interesting fact to notice that, owing to the structure—that is, the parallelism—of the valleys and the rivers, one peculiar type of people can be more or less recognized along the entire length of the valley. Although separated by hundreds of miles, the people in the upper part of the valley and those living in the lower part of the same valley are therefore more closely related than people only separated by a few miles of mountain waste, but living in different valleys.

The Norwegian rivers, however considerable, are joined by few tributaries and receive their drainage almost entirely from the narrow valleys through which they flow. It is the same with the national life pulsating in many valleys; it has for centuries flowed in the same narrow channels. No tributaries of outside influence have come in to blend their waters and add strength and freshness. On account of this seclusion, life in many a valley used to be stagnant, and a visit there would put you back centuries in civilization. In some corners you might find a superstition reminding you of mediaeval times, and a roughness in habits and ways of living that would be shocking to an outsider; a wildness and a lawlessness that would have fitted the times of the viking.

Drinking and fighting used to be the only worthy entertainment for men. At parties, and at their weddings and funerals, fighting with the knife was a fixed part of the programme. Such parties used to last for several days, and started very tamely; but as the strong home-brewed beer commenced to act on the men, and as the rhythmic dances made the blood flow like fire in their veins, the spirits of their ancestors would wake up in them. Wilder and wilder the dance would be; higher and higher the girls would be lifted by the strong arms; oftener and oftener the drinking horns would be filled and emptied. And then, when the eyes gleamed, and the jumps and turns became more and more daring and violent, one quarrelsome word would be enough to make old jealousy and hatred fresh again, and start a fight. A circle would be formed on the floor around the fighters, and then a dance would begin which, in most cases, proved fatal to one of the participants. In those days a wedding very often ended in a funeral.

This division of the country into deep, narrow valleys has had a marked influence on the history of the people. In ancient times, up to the year 800 A. D., the country was divided into numerous kingdoms, every valley and fiord having its own chieftan or king. Under Harold Fairhair the whole country became united, but only after a terrible struggle in which each valley and fiord had to be conquered separately. All through history a certain lack of unity has been apparent, the difficult task for the sovereign being to have these different clans work together as one unit, as one people.

It is not strange to find a deep longing in a people that lives in narrow valleys, with only a narrow strip of heaven above, shut out from the rest of the world. With the deep fiord below and the high mountains above, your home becomes a prison. Your longings and yearnings are thrown back by the rocky walls. This longing found an expression, in the olden time, in the life of the viking. His home on the bank of the fiord was to him but a place to which he could bring his prey; the wide sea was his real home. This longing for the outside world still survives in the Norwegian. Wherever you go in Norway, you will never be far from the sea; it hugs the thousands of islands around the coast and sends its arms into the very heart of the country. However much you are shut in, there is one exit—the fiord. And this sea—how it tempts! Sailors come home and tell the eagerly listening children wonderful tales about far-off countries where the sky is wide and blue, where there is always summer, nothing but sunshine and warmth, where palms sway in the soft breezes, and where life is easy. With every vessel that spreads its sail to leave the little harbor the boy sends a longing thought; every vessel that anchors brings him greetings from the world. To thousands of Norwegian boys this longing becomes too strong, and then they leave their homes often at the early age of thirteen or fourteen. This wild longing makes them give up home, school, and fireside; drowns all other interests.

But high above the narrow fiords and valleys there is another sea—the wide plateau. This sea has also its billows, with crests of ice and snow. And this sea had all my longings and thoughts.

The picture of Norway and its people is one of great contrasts, of high light and deep shade. The short, brilliant summer is succeeded by a long, dark winter. The open, fertile valleys of the fiords of the eastern part of Norway have their counterpart in the west, with rocky, gloomy chasms into which the sun's rays hardly ever penetrate. In the people the most liberal and progressive spirit is found side by side with the greatest narrowness. An exuberant joy of life is overshadowed by the deepest melancholy. In the mountain-fiddle this melancholy vibrates as a deep, weird undertone that never for a moment ceases, even when the merriest music is played.

The gloomiest fiord has, however, its gleams of light, and the darkest rock its spray from the waterfalls. With all the wildness and warfare of the sages there are woven into the dark pictures golden threads of friendship and love. Among the warlike gods of the Norsemen, with Odin and Thor at their head, Baldur lives fair and beautiful forever.

A STUDY OF THE ORIGINAL KINDERGARTENS

GRACE OWEN

University of Manchester

At the present time the principles and practice of the kindergarten are the subject of much discussion. There are those
who question some of the fundamental ideas underlying it, and
there are others who, while admitting the truth of these, differ
considerably among themselves as to the ways in which these
ideas may be best expressed in practice. This, then, is surely
an appropriate moment to look again with renewed attention at
some of the original kindergartens founded either by Froebel himself or by his immediate disciples during his own lifetime. From
these we can presumably learn the most concerning his own
ideas as to the practical outcome of the educational principles
which they embody.

We must not forget that Froebel did not claim to have said
the last word upon the education of little children. As Middendorf wrote: "Ein Mann kann nicht alles leisten; es ist genug,
dass Froebel die Bahn gebrochen und Mittel geschaffen hat."
Yet we may naturally expect to find in the records of the first
kindergartens indications as to how Froebel himself solved
some of the problems of which we are so conscious at the present
time.

Some of the questions which seem to rise most naturally, in
view of recent discussions, are the following: (1) How far
were Froebel's own kindergartens systematic and set? How did
he plan the work from week to week? What took the place of
the present programme? (2) Granted the truth of Froebel's belief
concerning correspondences between the world of nature and the
mind, exactly how did Froebel present these correspondences to
his children, or did he present them at all? (3) What was his
customary method of procedure with the Games, Gifts, and
Occupations? Do we find that he made use chiefly of dictation,

or suggestion, or imitation, etc.? In other words, how far did he impose his own ideas upon the children, and how far did he leave them free and undirected?

There are many other questions of perhaps equal interest, but to collect material sufficient to answer these alone is not easy. There are, however, numerous—if somewhat scattered—allusions to the practical carrying out of the kindergarten in the Froebel literature. Happily for us, moreover, there are detailed descriptions of the kindergartens of the time to be found in the writings of Middendorf and of Baroness von Bülow. These, with the collected statements from Froebel's writings, give us a fairly distinct picture of the kindergarten in its early days.

First, then, let us look for records of the more general characteristics of Froebel's own kindergartens. We find that they began on a small scale, and that this feature of the movement gave Froebel entire satisfaction; for he says in a letter to his cousin:

> Your recommendation, my dear cousin, to develop the kindergarten on a small, on the smallest scale, is quite after my heart; and, further, its development on a large scale, as a great institution, does not attract me in the least, for I know that a large undertaking . . . . often carries with it much that is empty and lifeless.[1]

It seems that the actual number of children admitted to a kindergarten was, as a rule, smaller than is usually the custom in the present day. Of the Rudolstadt kindergarten, which was one of the first to be opened, we read that the number was limited to twenty-six—only "for want of room," it is true; but there are other statements in the *Letters* which seem to imply that customarily the groups of children were not large; for example, Froebel speaks in one place of a particular game as follows: "It is . . . . written for a large body of children: at least thirty-two persons take part in it;" as though this were unusual. Later, indeed, we hear of Froebel working with "his forty peasant children;" but, on the whole, the evidence seems to show that the first kindergartens were probably smaller than the average kindergarten of today, and that Froebel himself considered this characteristic a desirable one.

[1] *Froebel's Letters on the Kindergarten*, edited by Michaelis and Moore, p. 49.

Was it on account of the comparatively small groups of children with whom Froebel worked and played that he was able to preserve the spontaneity and joy of which one receives such an irresistible impression from the accounts of those days? Be that as it may, we can be sure that, though the kindergarten system was then still in the making, its spirit was there in a freshness and wholeness that can scarcely have been surpassed since. Witness the following passage, written by Froebel himself, describing the opening of the kindergarten mentioned above:

On the first Tuesday of the present month, from two to four in the afternoon, the Rudolstadt kindergarten was opened with twenty-four charming children, varying from two to five years old, accompanied by their mothers, by some of their fathers, and by a few other relatives. It is a true Garden of Children: they are as joyous, as lively, as fresh, as vigorous as the flowers in a garden—and at the same time as lovable and gentle as mignonette and violets.[2]

Indeed, it may be said that the spirit of this passage is present whenever either Froebel or his contemporary helpers write of the children for whom they lived.

Let us now turn to the question of the "programme." In the sense in which kindergartens of the present day use the word— that is, the arrangement of the children's work in relation to a succession of selected interests, each being made the focus of attention for a definite number of days or weeks, and each being logically connected with the rest—we have as yet found no trace of evidence that in Froebel's kindergarten there was anything of the kind. Such remarks as we can find having any bearing upon the subject seem to indicate that Froebel's kindergartens were simple and informal, for he does not mention any continuous scheme. For example, in describing what took place in the Rudolstadt kindergarten, he says nothing further as to his general plans than that "every Tuesday and Friday we have games and occupations from two to four;"[3] and again: "The playtime is devoted half to building, and half to games."[4] Hanschmann, however, says that Froebel "drew up, as a basis of his first actual experiment, a complete Course of Games and Occupations,"[5]

[2] *Op. cit.*, p. 54.   [3] *Ibid.*, p. 54.   [4] *Ibid.*, p. 55.
[5] Hanschmann, *The Kindergarten System*, translated by Franks, p. 145.

but exactly what was here meant by the word "course" is not explained. It seems probable, from the description of Middendorf, as will be shown more at length later, that the general trend of work depended upon the interests of the children at the moment. Their surroundings were chiefly those of the country, and the point of departure seems to have generally been some occurrence noted in nature, in the home, or on the way to school, rather than any systematic plan of emphasizing certain experiences at any particular time.

In trying to picture to ourselves what the first kindergartens were like, we should make a great mistake if we failed to give an important place to gardening. Gardening was, in Froebel's eyes, not only a desirable feature of the kindergarten, but also a necessary one. He says:

If, now, this comparative study [that of development and growth in nature with the growth and development of man] is important for man, it is especially important for the embryo man-child. Thus an all-sided satisfactory education necessarily demands that the child be afforded opportunities for this comparison. . . . . The kindergarten thus necessarily requires a garden, and in this, necessarily, gardens for the children.[6]

In the Blankenburg kindergarten, accordingly, and apparently in the other regular kindergartens of the period, a considerable portion of the children's time was spent in gardening. Froebel held that each child should have a little bed of his own, and that there should also be two large beds common to all, one devoted to the culture of flowers, and the other to the raising of common grains and vegetables, fodder and oil plants; and this idea he carried out himself. At Rudolstadt he speaks of the garden as part of the necessary equipment:

Yet everyone expresses the wish that the work we have begun shall be carried on through the summer, and a garden and playground up in the hills are already offered us without charge.

On the whole, then, it would seem that we may think of the first kindergartens as comparatively small groups of children, playing together at their games and occupations, or working at their gardens with genuine freedom and spontaneity. We may surmise, too, that, had we been present in the kindergarten at

[6] Froebel, *Education by Development.*

Blankenburg or Rudolstadt, we should have been as much struck with the informality and simplicity of intention of the teachers as with the joyousness of the children.

At this point in the inquiry it may be interesting to quote at some length from the description of Middendorf alluded to above, to be found in a little book written by him in 1848, four years before Froebel's death. It is called *Die Kindergärten,* and was evidently undertaken with the purpose of convincing the general public of the need of kindergartens, as well as of acquainting it with its aim and character. One chapter is chiefly concerned with an account of a typical kindergarten, and it is from this that the following passages are quoted; these, however, have been freely abbreviated and summarized by the writer of this paper.

The chapter opens with a description of the children coming into the kindergarten in the morning, happy and fresh and clean —and bright and joyous, "like flowers in the sunshine." The older ones lead their little sisters and brothers by the hand, and they go up to the kindergartner, who is waiting to greet them.[7]

When all are arrived, they form a circle together, moving lightly and happily, and singing a cheerful song meanwhile. And since gratitude springs naturally out of joy, the children now reverently fold their hands and sing a morning hymn of thanksgiving: "It is Thou who hast given us our life: throughout the night Thou hast watched over us with fatherly care." . . . .
After the morning prayer, the children go to their little seats at a long table, and look around for some means of playing out the ideas which are filling their minds more or less clearly. At their request, little boxes of blocks are given to them, and they begin without delay to play eagerly. One child remembers how he has just had breakfast with his dear parents, and he quickly builds a table surrounded with chairs, using the leaves of the flowers he has brought to the kindergarten for cups, and the flower petals for bread. He invites the kindergartner to join the party with great friendliness, and she, reading his thought in his eyes and in his words, helps him to its expression in language by an appropriate little rhyme. For the kindergartner recognizes that the child's short separation from his parents is making him conscious of the happiness he experiences when he is with them.
Another child shows a fireplace which he has built, for he knows that his mother must be in the kitchen now, preparing the meal which he is to

[7] Wilhelm Middendorf, *Die Kindergärten* (Hoffmann & Campe, 1861), chap. 3.

enjoy with his father and brothers and sisters when all come home. . . . .
Yonder a child shows us quite a different idea. He has seen a shepherd
starting out in the early morning with his flock; and so he represents the
shepherd prominently, with the sheep obediently following him.

Thus each child follows his individual bent, according as the spirit
moves him. Here is a boy who has built an anvil; two men stand by it, and
forge the iron with a beautiful clang! He saw this as he passed the forge
in the morning, and the kindergartner now helps him to express what he
has seen in a little blacksmith song. . . . . There is a little girl who has built
a townhall. Her father goes there every morning when she comes to the
kindergarten. . . . . But now the kindergartner calls the attention of all
the children to something which one of them has made. When *this* little
child waked in the early morning, his mother pointed out to him the sun
rising above the mountain edge, and he has not forgotten its golden
brightness. So he has made a picture of the radiant sun, and seems very
happy over it. The kindergartner says to him: "I am not surprised that
you like it so much. The sun climbing in the sky is like your mother
coming to you in the morning. . . . . There is an old saying: 'Morgenstunde hat Gold im Munde.'" The children now take pleasure in making
a similar picture of the sun.

Meanwhile the kindergartner repeats a stanza of a hymn
which expresses simply a morning thanksgiving. She then asks
the children whether they like it, and suggests that they should
learn it all together. Accordingly they repeat it part by part
until it is known.

Again, one of the children represents with her blocks and
describes the meeting of her father with the family at home in
the evening, and another child, after listening a while, points to
a picture of "Christ Blessing the Little Children" and remarks
that the child's story is like the picture. The kindergartner
responds by telling the story of the picture.

Then comes lunch, and after lunch the children march in
order, two by two, out of doors, while they sing a marching
song: "Let us into the garden go." In the garden is a number
of little beds, surrounded by a long, big one, and among them
the children run to see how their seeds are getting on. They
dig and weed and water and plant their own gardens, and then
run to visit each other's, helping and receiving help.

In order to give plenty of scope for the love of activity, an inviting and
suitable playground is provided close to the garden. Here the children run

races two by two, the competitors being as nearly as possible of equal strength, while their companions cheer them on with singing and shouting. . . . . Then they all rush into the playground, jumping and wrestling like little gymnasts. Soon, however, they unite to play games. First they play a game of bees, which they have just seen hovering over their flower-beds.

Then bird games. The flight of pigeons over their heads suggests the pigeon game. Later, they play a circle game, the many circles finally uniting in one large one; and after this comes a series of ball games. Lastly the children go to their Occupation work. One group is occupied with paper-folding, making forms according to given rules—squares, triangles, rectangles, two squares, etc.; also in sequence, a number of objects—table, mill, boat, etc.; each being folded out of the last. Others are pricking pictures of flowers, figures, etc., on folded paper—so that the picture is made several times at once. This result is a joyful surprise to the children. Another group colors the work done with the idea of making out of it birthday presents for their parents. Some are cutting "forms of beauty" out of paper, following a single law and discovering to what results it leads them. Others weave; and others, again, make boxes for their seeds out of paper. A few are laying pictures on the table with sticks, which they themselves have procured and cut to the required length.

These also make pictures of the letters of the alphabet as a preparation for writing and reading. Others, by laying their sticks in ordered and numbered heaps, are preparing their way for the study of number in school.

This account, as coming direct from Froebel's own disciple and closest friend, must be of special significance to those who are interested in the origin of the kindergarten. There are many noticeable features in the description, some of which may be pointed out as follows:

1. The wide range of topics which the children touched upon during one morning, every one of which, however, was a part of their immediate experiences. Thus we have building in connection with shepherds, blacksmiths, and home-life, and games of pigeons, bees, etc., without any apparent grouping round a given

focus of interest. All seems to depend upon the individual experience of the child during that day, or every day at home.

2. In spite of this spontaneity and freedom from restriction, a certain order and unity are preserved throughout the morning. There are the morning circle, the united prayer and thanksgiving, the formal march to the playground. There is also a proportion of directed work—the folding of forms out of paper, the cutting of paper according to given rules, etc.

3. The significance, symbolical or otherwise, of the children's experience is never pointed out to them by the kindergartner. We find one apparent exception to this rule, however, where the kindergartner draws the attention of all to one child who has made a representation of the rising sun, and suggests the analogy between its brightness and his mother's morning greeting.

4. The kindergartner's office, especially during the building play, seems to be to encourage by her response the spontaneous self-expression of each child, and by means of suggestive conversations and songs to make his experiences fuller of meaning to himself.

5. The constant cultivation of the children's religious sense.

6. The co-operation indicated in the descripton of the gardening, made possible by the perfect freedom of speech and movement allowed the children, so that they could help and sympathize with each other.

7. The place given to competitive games, entailing vigorous physical exercises.

8. The occasional use of unprepared material for gift-work, as when the children cut their own sticks to the required length.

Turning now more particularly to our second question—as to the practical treatment in the kindergarten of the correspondences between the world of nature and the mind, we find that, in speaking of the practice as well as of the theory of the kindergarten, Froebel and his followers give great weight to the spiritual value of the plays and games. We read this in nearly every line. The joy of the children in their games is attributed, first, to love of activity. (Froebel says of his student-teachers: "What I want especially to teach them is how to develop the love of activity that children show between their first and sixth or seventh years."[8]) But, secondly, this joy is constantly and uniformly attributed to the correspondence of the activities of the outer world of nature with their own inner being; the former wake and feed the latter, etc. Froebel also looks for a gradual development of self-consciousness in the child. There is, however, nowhere any evidences that he ever tried by direct words to "stir premonitions" of universal truths. He certainly believed that the "mind anticipates in feeling the insight" it will later "consciously possess;" but, from what can be gathered from his writings, he never dreamed of forcing its normal activity by word or any other stimulus. The above description of the kindergarten game-hour—given as typical—points to great simplicity of treatment, and the following quotation from Hanschmann implies that those who watched Froebel with the children did not notice any tendency on his part to give a mystical touch to the game-hours; had this been the case, it would probably have been mentioned:

> He [Diesterweg] repeated his visit, and saw Froebel conduct some games in the open air; a large circle was formed, and eight or ten young girls took their places in it. The children, whose ages varied from two to eight or ten years old, were evidently very poor. Some were bare-footed, some bare-headed, and some in rags. They were playing with the utmost vigor and delight, however, and Froebel was a very child among them. Many of the games are now familiar to us—e. g., the Fishes, the Pigeons, the Cuckoo. When the games were over, the children were led off in procession, singing their closing song.[9]

With regard to the more special methods of procedure used in the first kindergartens, we may gather a few further hints both as to (1) the game-hour and (2) the gift-plays.

1. As regards the games, it was Froebel's practice to develop them from the free, undirected play of the children. An instance of how he did this is given by Hanschmann:

> There happened to be a slender support in the middle of the children's playground at Blankenburg, and children always delight in turning around a pole. This column seemed to have a magnetic effect upon them: the moment they were free to do as they liked, everyone wanted to get hold of

[8] Hanschmann, *The Kindergarten System*, p. 153.

[9] *Ibid.*, p. 190.

it, and there was a regular skirmish as to who could join the little crowd twirling round. Seeing this, Froebel devised a way of bringing order into the game without too much interference, and his suggestions were heartily welcomed. Four or eight children were allowed to grasp the column with one hand, while stretching out with the other to a little companion, who in turn did the same to another, making radiating lines round the column. . . . . They turned at first very gently and got gradually quicker and quicker; the little mill-song was added to regulate the movement:

> Blow, wind, blow, and go, mill, go,
> That the miller may grind his corn,
> That the baker may take it, and into rolls make it,
> And bring us some hot in the morn.

To Froebel's great delight he found the children playing this game again and again, and eagerly adopting any suggestions he was able to make, such as now and then turning the other way, changing miller or baker.[10]

Froebel, however, believed in connected series of games, and he describes a chain of ball games in one of his letters.[11] The chain starts with some perfectly free movement on the part of one child, passes through a number of games illustrating different kinds of movements, such as rocking, rolling, tossing, passing from one to another, etc., each with its appropriate song; and it ends with a quiet, closing song. This chain Froebel calls "a definite selection of games;" and he adds: "It may, *as long as the children find pleasure in it,* be repeated in some of the following play-hours."[12] He emphasizes, however, the dangers of rigidness, "which would quite destroy that fresh, merry life which should animate the games." He continues:

One rule must be, however, unfailingly observed: the games must always begin with the earliest and easiest ones of whatever selection may have been made, and must rise by development from simple to complex, according to the universal and never-to-be-forgotten law; but within this limit free choice and unhindered play of movement is allowed. Otherwise the games would cease to be games, and lose their full educational power.

In Middendorf's account we have no evidence of any selection being made by the kindergartner, but the choice of games in this case seems to have been determined by the spontaneous desires of the children in response to the natural life around them.

[10] *Ibid.,* p. 175.
[11] *Froebel's Letters,* p. 73. [12] *Ibid.,* p. 83.

2. In connection with the methods used in the gift-work, there are two chapters in *Education by Development* in which Froebel gives two specimens of gift-plays, word for word. In the first certain ideas of direction are developed by means of play with single sticks. Here the prevailing method is suggestion: "What can your sticks do?" and, "What is your stick to you?" the reply to the latter question being different from each child. In the second gift-play the idea of angles is developed, first from the jointed finger, and then from the use of sticks; and with the given suggestion of certain angles the children are led to think out all the instances in their own experience, which illustrate them.

Again, in Middendorf's account we have instances of perfectly free self-expression on the part of the children, the kindergartner not even suggesting to them what they shall make, but always helping them to express their ideas more fully, and sometimes lifting these up to a higher plane. Here, too, we find instances of the use of a different method. Certain definite directions as to the manipulation of their gift materials are given to the children. They are to repeat the same movement again and again, not aimlessly, but with the conscious purpose of discovering what new interesting or beautiful results may thus be obtained. These are often a joyful surprise when they come. This method seems to have been Froebel's nearest approach to dictation. Of dictation, pure and simple, we read nothing. And, indeed, we cannot conceive that it was by means of any rigid and unintelligent methods that he gained the success that prompted the following enthusiastic expression in a letter to his cousin :

I wish you could have been here this evening and seen the many beautiful and varied forms and lovely patterns which freely and spontaneously developed themselves from some systematic variations of a simple ground-form in stick-laying. No one would believe without seeing it how the child-soul—the child-life—develops when treated as a whole by some skilled kindergarten teacher. Oh, if I could only shout aloud with ten thousand lung-power the truth that I now tell you in silence! . . . . What keenness of sensation, what a soul, what a mind, what force of will and active energy, what dexterity of skill and muscular movement and perception, and what calm and patience, will not all these things call out in the children![18]

Although the material available for the present study had been somewhat scanty and inadequate, there yet stand out from it clearly certain characteristics which must have predominated in the kindergartens of Froebel and his contemporaries. We may sum them up briefly as follows:

1. The fresh, childlike spirit of the teachers, and the natural happiness and free activity of the children.

2. Comparative unpremeditation in the general sequence of thought.

3. The presentation of symbolic ideas through experience, and through that alone.

4. The scope given to the individuality of the children.

5. The habitual use of the following methods: undirected play, suggestion, imitation, and discovery by experiment of results following on obedience to given laws.

There are other writings of Froebel—notably the *Sonntagsblatt,* a periodical now out of print, which he published somewhat irregularly between 1837 and 1843, the first years of the kindergarten movement—which would undoubtedly throw more light upon this interesting subject. A true conception of what the kindergarten actually was under Froebel's own personal influence should be of value in helping us to understand more clearly his theory of education, and to avoid misconstructions of his words. To this end, further research would be surely worth while. It may be affirmed, however, even now, that a first-hand study of the writings of Froebel and his fellow-workers would lead those who complain of the rigidity and unfitness to childish thought of the modern kindergarten system to at least one conclusion—namely, that in the mind of the founder himself these limitations found no place.

[18] *Ibid.,* p. 145.

A VISIT TO A CHINESE KINDERGARTEN

MARY RICHARDS GRAY
Tonopah, Nev.

Wearily the kindergarten teacher plodded up the hill on Washington Street in Chinatown, San Francisco. About her flocked between thirty and forty children whom she had gathered up and was taking to the kindergarten in the basement of the Oriental Home. It is one o'clock—yes, past the hour—but all mission kindergartens have an afternoon instead of a morning session, the morning being too uncertain a time; for, with the Chinese, breakfast is a movable feast which rarely takes place before half-past nine, and may not come off until twelve or one o'clock.

We are acquainted with the teacher and greet her, then busy ourselves looking at the children in their queer costumes.

"You are late, are you not?" we ask.

"Oh, yes, I'm always late. I always have to wait for a few who cannot get-ready on time, for I cannot afford to jeopardize our future by offending seriously in leaving some behind."

"Which are boys, and which girls? Tell us the distinguishing marks", we beg, in the meantime observing enough details to be sure of several pairs of trousers, nondescript in color, patched, rent, and re-rent, which have about them an uumistakable masculine air.

"Why, those are girls with the gayer cambric trousers with stripes of pink, blue, and green around the legs. The style of dressing the hair and feet, rather than the garments which cover the body, gives the marks of sex. Both boys and girls have their hair shaven part way back, and wear a bang about an inch in length all the way around until seven years of age. Both have queues, but oftener than not the little girl's queue is drawn to the side and tied or festooned elaborately over her ear, and decorated with ribbons, strings, and ornaments. Oil is used plentifully in plastering every black hair down just where it is to stay. A long, heavy queue is a mark of beauty; and in the case of the girl, when Nature does not provide abundant tresses, the mother resorts to strands of cerise and green string, which she braids in with the hair until her daughter's queue assumes proper proportions. The process of hair-dressing is so elaborate that it takes place only now and then, say once in a week or ten days. There are other unfailing signs of femininity—earrings. The saying goes among the Chinese that a woman without earrings is like a pig without ears. This sort of feminine adornment is resorted to early, and also bracelets around the ankles."

We are now within the kindergarten quarters, a large room back of which is a yard visible through an open door. The swing out there has such attractions that a few cannot resist the temptation of making a dive for it, though they know perfectly well that the bell will ring in a moment or two. There are pegs on the wall for wraps and hats, but it is too warm for wraps, and few wear hats, the girls never unless they have arrived at the stage of assuming American attire. A band, ornamented more or less elaborately according to the wealth and position of the parents, is ornamental head-dress and hat at the same time. A few of the boys have American hats and caps to be disposed of, but it is a rare thing for a child to need an outside wrap. If cold, he or she puts on extra coats and wears them all the time.

The bell sounds, and obediently the children flock in, though loath to leave the swing which is a great treat to them, their only playground being the street or alley. They make a noise, but not the amount ordinary American children make under similar circumstances. The little chairs rattle, the American heels on the American shoes and the boat-shaped soles on the Chinese slippers clatter and shuffle until the assistant, a young girl from the Rescue Home, commands silence in Chinese. The words come out so explosively in a high nasal tone that it seems as if she were going to jump at every mother's child of the lot, but no one moves a muscle either in fear or surprise. They begin by singing "We Thank Thee, Our Father." What can this mean to children whose religion is ancestor-worship? Then the assistant takes the younger children and shows them how to sew little designs marked on a card-board, while the teacher gives the older ones a lesson on drawing a buttercup. They sing about the pretty buttercup, talk about it, and make a picture of it with green and yellow chalk. Wah Foy is restless and insists on wiggling about and talking; it being quite proper to talk out loud in Chinese schools, his inherited predilections in that direction now crop out. He is told several times to be quiet, but he forgets. Finally the teacher covers his head with a green cloth. This produces silence, and now that Wah Foy is good she takes the cloth off. All the buttercups are drawn, and each picture is commented on in turn. As a reward of merit each one is to take his work home. Wah is ominously still. This bodes something. What is it? He has busied himself drawing the leaves on the papers of those on both sides of him. Dependent, shy Minnie, alias Ah Sau, could not get the touch and he furnished it; likewise, George, alias Sing Fat. The teacher pronounces these productions spurious, and decides to tear them up, whereupon Ah Sau and Sing Fat assume doleful expressions bordering on tears. Wah continues to wiggle, and, on the explanation of his behavior, we conclude that a bath would not be a bad thing for him.

The assistant wishes three-year-old Sing Ling to put down his primer, which he holds with a death grip, and try sewing a card. Though this is his third day, he cannot be persuaded to part for an instant with this introduction to the learning of all ages. With his long Chinese trousers, once some bright color and now an indescribable merging of many, his Chinese slippers, and light-green coat over which he wears a bib with a big pocket squarely in front, he is a picturesque object.

"'He go say his a b c,'" quotes the teacher, explaining that when a child begins going to school, no matter what his age, he must have a book in which the alphabet occupies a prominent place.

"We put on no age limit. We have children of all sizes and ages here, our desire being to get them to come and to make them happy while they are with us. We say the alphabet every

Marching in from Recess

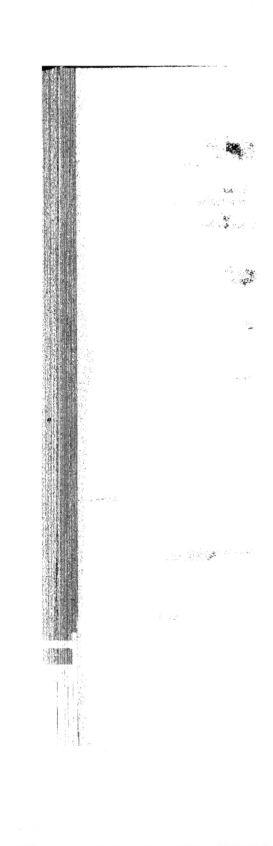

day. I understand modern pedagogical theories, but I've had experience, and try to join the two in loving embrace. We'll go through the alphabet now." The assistant explains what is wanted, and they begin, "*A-ah, b, c. . . . .*" All goes pretty well until they come to *r*—the Waterloo of Chinese of all ages. They stumble over it, storming it with a faint *l*, and continue.

When the ordeal is over, the teacher comments: "We've said *a b c;* and next we'll get in a circle and sing." It is a struggle to get all the children to toe the circle marked on the floor, and all the slant eyes on the teacher. Again and again the assistant repeats the command to those too immature to grasp what toeing the mark means. They decide upon singing "Pretty Dolly," and Mame, a Celestial barely four years old and not yet bleached out by the California sun, is asked to hold the "pretty dolly." She was the first to get her toes on the mark and keep them there, receiving from her teacher a beaming smile and the appreciative remark: "I like the way Mamie folds her hands and toes the mark." The little girl in blue Mother Hubbard with a self-satisfied smile on her face rocks the dirty rag doll (never by any wild flight of the imagination "pretty") without the slightest regard to its comfort, her mind being occupied with ways and means of procuring another toothsome compliment. She fastens her slant eyes on the teacher with a longing look of invitation. It comes: "I like the way that Mamie rocks the 'pretty dolly.'" Then someone else takes the dolly, while Mamie treads air as she goes to her place in the circle and again stiffly assumes the approved pose. The song drags. They march, have a language lesson on the orange, say some religious verses, then race out into the backyard for recess.

Playing horse and swinging are the favorite amusements. Round and round the yard the galloping horses run with danger to flying pigtails and slippers. Back and forth go the swings. Intently some of the older children stand and gaze at the flowers which they love, but are not allowed to pick or handle. The yard is such a delight.

Wah Foy has rearranged his toilet, and, as it is well to have him busy, he is called upon to drum in the recruits. They come. The horsy spirit has not had time to die within their demure little souls, and the boys do not behave any too well; that is, comparatively speaking. Usually they are so good. A few bump, jump out of line, struggle for the first place and gape about. Now they are soldiers, and "Here Come the Soldiers Marching." First there is a lesson on stringing beads and counting them, after which the children struggle through many explanations in getting ready to play "Flying Chickadees." To fly in proper numbers proves the tug of war. Then they "Hurrah for the Red, White, and Blue." (May these our native-born Mongolian citizens respond with equal vigor in the time of our country's need!) For "Clap, clap, clap" they muster much vim whenever the chorus comes in, but the words of the song spasmodically fade away and die, though the teacher's high soprano leads clearly and forcibly. The vigorous clapping has the effect of dwarfing vocal expression. All begin to act weary except Mamie, the model of deportment, who is still setting an excellent example. It is time to go home. All is quiet until Sit In's elbow hits a box containing beads, and away they go in every direction over the floor. Sit In hangs her head, and Wah Foy jumps at an opportunity to pick them up. He likes to be up and doing. His are the faded, rent, and patched trousers in which we first discovered unmistakable signs of Small Boy.

"Our final song—what shall it be?" queries the teacher. Half a dozen voices pipe up, "Jack Frost." Sweet inconsistency of childhood, the same in Chinatown as elsewhere! The day is phenomenally hot. Jack Frost, that merry little fellow, what can they know of him? California saw the one snowstorm which serves as a date in modern history on December 31, 1882. The suggestive description of his "nipping, pinching ways," however, gives the imagination delightful excursions into cool highways and byways. The teacher then asks the assistant to tell Ah Kum to bring two children who live in the same house with her to kindergarten the next day. Ah Kum replies: "They won't come. They're afraid of being put in jail." She promises that nothing of the sort shall happen, and as a token of her goodwill sends them some picture cards. The work is over for the

HIS FIRST DAY AWAY FROM MOTHER   "HE GO SAY A, B, C"
BRINGS TROUBLE

MOY AND "MAMIE"

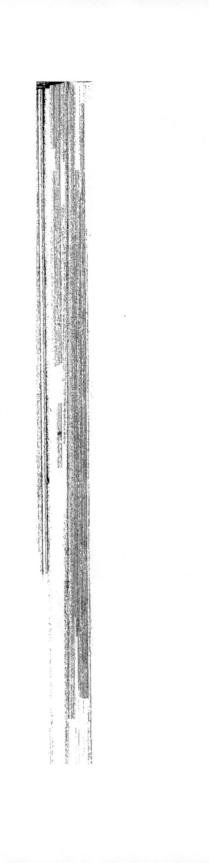

day, and the teacher again starts out with her flock on her rounds through Chinatown.

This sketch was written a few days previous to the disaster in San Francisco. These children are now in the Chinese camp in the city and in Berkeley, where teachers are doing what they can to reorganize schools and kindergartens in cramped quarters and under trying conditions. Motley relief costumes have taken the place of the picturesque native costumes, and all is changed, until such a time when the Chinese shall once more be installed in new Chinatown.

MATHEMATICS AND ITS RELATION TO THE STUDY OF HOME–ECONOMICS IN THE UNIVERSITY ELEMENTARY SCHOOL

I. CAROLINE MAY PIERCE
Critic Teacher

There is no subject taught in elementary schools which is more liable to deaden the mental growth and retard the development of the reasoning powers of the child than arithmetic. Unless an evident need exists for using number in order to make a mental picture more vivid, or to make a distinct problem more definite, mathematics becomes a working with symbols which are mere symbols, instead of standing for real quantities—for problems that tend to a close and complete adjustment of means to some end.

Without going beyond the mental grasp of the pupils, the working at problems should command their best effort, although it is not necessary that each child should understand every problem which arises in the class, unless it will make his individual work of more intrinsic value.

Last year, in the seventh year of the University Elementary School, the work in beginning fractions was based almost entirely upon the children's work in cooking. In measuring materials for their grape jelly, cranberry sauce, brown bread, and other articles of food which they were preparing for the Colonial Luncheon to be given at Thanksgiving time, the need for the knowledge of halves, thirds, and fourths of their cups was supplemented by a necessity for learning the divisions of those parts, and combinations of different values.

At first, when working at his problems, each child held his measuring-cup in his hand; later many of the children represented upon paper or blackboard the operations to be performed, and some very quickly learned that the quantities could be represented by symbols alone, and referred to their measuring-cups

220

only in cases of doubt, or in proof of work when the results had been challenged.

It is neither wise nor desirable that the measuring-cup should become a fixed and sole standard, and so it was displaced by the quart, peck, pint, foot, yard, and other standards.

This year the beginning work in fractions was also based upon cooking.

II. JENNY H. SNOW
Teacher of Home-Economics

The following article is written in response to a request that a definite illustration be given showing how mathematics is involved in the study of home-economics.

The papers are written by children of nine and ten years. The experimental work was done in the cooking laboratory; the mathematics, in connection with it, was carried out under the direction of the critic teacher, Miss Pierce.

The children were trying to find out how much sugar was needed to make jelly, and to solve the problem as to what difference it would make if varying amounts were used. They suggested that there might be a difference in the quality, amount, and cost of the jelly. The class as a whole seemed to think that the more sugar used, the greater would be the cost per glass of the jelly. The only way to decide this question was to ascertain the cost of each glass. Their papers show the amount of work necessary to do this, as well as the value of such a method in mathematics—a method which involves a problem the answer of which has a definite meaning to the children.

Following their papers is a summary of the work and its results.

SEVENTH SCHOOL YEAR
OCTOBER 25, 1906

GRAPE JELLY

I

The last time we made grape jelly each child used $\frac{1}{2}$ cup of grape juice and different amounts of sugar. I used $\frac{1}{2}$ cup of sugar to $\frac{1}{2}$ cup of juice and got $1\frac{1}{2}$ wineglasses of jelly. The way I found out my cost was to find out that a basket of grapes cost 20 c., and the 14 children that went up to cooking used $\frac{3}{4}$ of a basket of grapes, which must have cost 15 c. There are 7 cups of grape juice in $\frac{3}{4}$ of a basket of grapes. $\frac{1}{7}$ of 15 is $2\frac{1}{7}$, so $\frac{1}{2}$ cup would cost $1\frac{1}{14}$; and 1 lb. of sugar costs 5 c., and there are 2 cups of sugar in one pound. $\frac{1}{2}$ of 5 c. is $2\frac{1}{2}$ c., and $\frac{1}{2}$ of $2\frac{1}{2}$ c. is $1\frac{1}{4}$ c., and if you add them both together they make $2\frac{9}{28}$ c.

ALFRED ROGERS

II

In making grape jelly the question came up how much sugar ٤o use. So we tried to find out by experiment.

To find out, each child used a different amount of sugar to half a cup of grape juice. I used 6 tablespoons to half a cup of grape juice and boiled it to 220° Fahrenheit. I got nearly one wineglassful of jelly.

$\frac{3}{4}$ basket grapes cost	$0.15
Grape juice (14 people) cost	0.15
1 cup grape juice cost	0.02$\frac{1}{7}$
$\frac{1}{2}$ cup grape juice cost	0.01$\frac{1}{14}$
2 cups sugar in pound	
1 pound sugar cost	0.05
1 cup sugar cost	0.02$\frac{1}{2}$
6 tbsps. sugar cost	0.00$\frac{15}{16}$
16 tbsps. sugar in one cup	

$1\frac{1}{14} = \frac{8}{112}$

$\frac{15}{16} = \frac{105}{112}$

$1\frac{113}{112}$ or $2\frac{1}{112}$ cents cost of jelly

MORITZ LOEB

III

Grape jelly can be made without sugar.

I made grape jelly with half as much sugar as juice.

We started out to make grape jelly, when someone asked whether it could be made without sugar.

We tried many different ways. Some of us made it without any sugar and some with $\frac{1}{4}$ as much sugar. All jellied.

I got $\frac{4}{8}$ wineglass of jelly, using $\frac{1}{2}$ cup of juice and $\frac{1}{4}$ of a cup of sugar.

One basket of grapes cost 20 c.

$\frac{3}{4}$ of a basket of grapes cost 15 c.; we used $\frac{3}{4}$ of a basket.

There were 14 children in the cooking class that day, and each one had $\frac{1}{2}$ cup of grape juice.

One cup of grape juice cost $2\frac{1}{7}$ c.

$\frac{1}{2}$ cup of grape juice cost $1\frac{1}{14}$ c.

In grape jelly there is the juice and sugar. The juice cost $1\frac{1}{14}$ c. The sugar cost $\frac{5}{8}$ c. The sugar and juice together cost $1\frac{39}{56}$ c.

ARLINE FALKENAU

IV

Grape jelly can be made out of grape juice with different amounts of sugar. We started out to make grape jelly, and a question came up as to how much sugar we would use. I started out with $\frac{1}{2}$ cup of juice, and then I put in $\frac{1}{4}$ cup of sugar and let it boil to 105° C. When I had finished I had a wineglass full of jelly.

I used $\frac{1}{4}$ cup or 4 tablespoons of sugar and $\frac{1}{2}$ cup of juice. A basket of grapes cost 20c., and we used only $\frac{3}{4}$ of a basket, so that cost 15c. There were 14 girls and boys. And there are 7 cups of juice in $\frac{3}{4}$ basket, so one cup cost $\frac{1}{7}$ of 15c., or $2\frac{1}{7}$c., and $\frac{1}{2}$ cup would cost $\frac{1}{2}$ of $2\frac{1}{7}$c., or $1\frac{1}{14}$c. So the grape juice that I used cost $1\frac{1}{14}$c.

Sugar is 5c. a pound, and there are two cups in one pound. If sugar is 5c. a pound, a cup would cost $\frac{1}{2}$ of 5c. or $2\frac{1}{2}$c., and $\frac{1}{4}$ a cup would cost $1\frac{1}{4}$c. Both would cost $1\frac{1}{14}$c. and $1\frac{1}{4}$c., or $2\frac{9}{28}$c.

MABEL CHAMBERLAIN

V

One day we made some jelly. The question came up as to how much sugar we were going to use. I used $\frac{1}{2}$ cup of juice and $\frac{1}{4}$ cup of sugar. I boiled my jelly to 220° F. I had $\frac{4}{8}$ wineglass of jelly.

A whole basket of grapes costs 20 c. Three-fourths of a basket cost 15 c. There were only 14 of us, and we used a half cup each. My grape juice cost $1\frac{1}{14}$ c., because a whole cup cost $2\frac{1}{7}$ c., and it would cost half of $2\frac{1}{7}$ c., which is $1\frac{1}{14}$ c.; and I used $\frac{1}{4}$ of a cup of sugar, which is 4 tablespoons full. My sugar cost $\frac{5}{8}$ c., and my jelly cost $1\frac{29}{28}$ c.

ELIZABETH JOHNSON

VI

We wanted to find out how much jelly we would get using different amounts of sugar.

I used two tablespoons of sugar and boiled to 220° Fahrenheit.

I got $\frac{1}{2}$ wineglass of jelly.

One basket of grapes cost 20 c.

$\frac{3}{4}$ of a basket of grapes cost 15 c.

One-half cup of grape juice cost $1\frac{1}{4}$ c. That is the amount of juice I used.

One cup of sugar cost $2\frac{1}{2}$ c.

There are 16 tablespoons in one cup.

I used $\frac{1}{8}$ of a cup of sugar.

My sugar cost $\frac{5}{16}$ c.

My juice cost $1\frac{1}{14}$ c.

My jelly cost $1\frac{43}{112}$ c.

ROBERT LOVETT

VII

We started out with grape jelly.

Then the question came up whether we all used the same amount of sugar.

Some had $\frac{1}{2}$ cup of juice to $\frac{1}{2}$ cup of sugar.

I used $\frac{1}{2}$ cup of juice and no sugar. I boiled it to 220° Fahrenheit.

Then I took it off and let it cool, and then we studied out the different costs of our jelly.

I had ¼ of a wineglass of jelly.

One basket of grapes cost 20 c. We used ¾ of a basket, which cost 15 c. We had 14 people, and we used 7 cups. Each child had ½ cup of grape juice. I had ½ cup grape juice. I did not use any sugar at all. My grape juice cost $1\frac{1}{14}$ cents.

BERNICE SCHMIDT

VIII

I started out to make grape jelly. I made my jelly without any sugar. I got my jelly, and I put it on to cook. I cooked it until 105° C. I had ¼ wineglass of jelly.

1 basket of grapes cost 20 c.

¾ of a basket cost 15 c.

My jelly cost $1\frac{1}{14}$ c.

I made grape jelly without any sugar. I had half a wineglass of jelly.

SAM GOSS, JR.

IX

If a pound of sugar cost 5 c., a cup of sugar would cost $2\frac{1}{2}$ c., and half a cup would cost $1\frac{1}{4}$ c. We had one basket of grapes, and that cost 20 c.; and we used ¾ of the basket; that cost 15 c.; and for 14 people it cost 15 c.; and so one cup of grape juice would cost $2\frac{1}{2}$ c., and ½ cup would cost $1\frac{1}{14}$ c. If I did not use any sugar, my grape jelly would cost $1\frac{1}{14}$ c.

HELEN GRISWOLD

SUMMARY

1 cup = 16 tablespoons

Amount of Juice	Amount of Sugar	Number of Glasses of Jelly Obtained	Cost of Jelly
½ cup	8 tablespoons	1½ wineglass	$2\frac{9}{28}$ c.
½ "	6 "	1 "	$2\frac{1}{13}$ "
½ "	4 "	⅘ "	$1\frac{39}{56}$ "
½ "	2 "	½ "	$1\frac{48}{112}$ "
½ "	No sugar	¼ "	$1\frac{1}{14}$ "

Much to the children's surprise, they found that the more sugar used, the cheaper the jelly per glass.

VOLUNTEER FIELD AND CAMERA GROUPS IN THE SCHOOL OF EDUCATION

ROBERT K. NABOURS
School of Education

Last fall an effort was made to have the children of the Elementary School become better acquainted with the outdoor life in the Chicago area, and to secure their help in collecting specimens for the Museum and the vivaria in the Museum and the grade rooms. Hitherto, the collections had been made and the vivaria maintained almost exclusively by grown persons, and entirely without help from the students. However interesting the collections were, or the life-histories grown and preserved, or the forms in the various vivaria, the interest shown in them by the students and friends of the school was so small as to be very discouraging.

The effort was begun by announcing in morning exercises that a field trip would be made to some place the next Saturday morning and that the students were invited; and this announcement was made weekly, while the weather permitted, during the school year.

About seventy children and four mothers took part in these volunteer field trips. Most of them went more than once, and several were very regular. But this does not, by any means, represent all who helped, after it was seen that a great many interesting things were being brought in. No estimate can be made of the number of students who took interest in the vivaria, brought in specimens, cared for them, asked questions, but who could not go on the excursions because of parental objections, swimming- or music-lessons, or other Saturday morning engagements. There was also difficulty in having the trips properly announced as to time, place, and cost, as was shown by the frequent misunderstandings and disappointments. The number of volunteers ranged from three to seventeen each Saturday.

EXAMINING A SPECIMEN

Photo. by Botsford Young, Seventh School Year

OUTDOOR DRAMATICS—THE SLEEPING BEAUTY

Photos. by Dorothy Beman, Ninth School Year

IN JACKSON PARK

It is impossible to describe these trips in detail. They were usually made to some point on a stream or pond, and as much in the woods as possible, and at a low cost for transportation. The material was collected in Mason jars, pails, lunch boxes, etc., and placed in the aquaria and cages on the return to the building. The material consisted of many plant and animal forms, both aquatic and terrestrial: bats, lizards, snakes, turtles, fish, frogs (their eggs and tadpoles), salamanders, crawfish, fairy shrimp, mussels, snails, and many forms of land and aquatic insects and their larvae. They saw on these trips several of the larger mammals and birds in their natural habitats: woodchucks and their holes, chipmunks, squirrels, muskrats and their villages covering acres of the marshes, and nearly all the birds common to this area, and several of their nests, eggs, young, and care of the young. Considerable attention was given to physiographic features, such as dunes, beaches, ravines, streams, lakes, lagoons, the work of the waves, running water, and ice, and a great deal of attention was given to climate and the weather. There was a tendency toward specialization on the part of several of the volunteers—a few studying birds almost wholly, and some, insects or flowers; while others preferred to explore the ponds and streams.

The interest of the children in the forms found was far beyond expectation. They simply ran over each other in their eagerness to see and learn about them. It was not necessary to create interest, and everything was done in the most beautifully sincere manner. After going out into the woods and calling attention to a few things, or asking a few questions, or without saying anything, the main thing was to answer questions or listen to them. To appreciate the situation, it would be necessary for one to see them exploring some of the ponds and streams and woods visited. Photographs can do the scenes no justice at all. The sincerely inquisitive manner in which they entered upon the quest must be seen to be appreciated. The success in these quests was always surprising; nothing seemed to escape them. If the work had been simply to collect, they probably would have done as much as an equal number of grown people, or even better.

The co-operation in bringing in animals and caring for them, and the almost fellow-human sympathy, solicitation, and consideration bestowed upon them by the children, were a source of satisfaction and delight to every one who had the privilege of seeing them. Many of the students made regular daily observations, and kept themselves well informed concerning the growth and habits of the various forms. Some observed pretty generally, while others studied only one or a few things, as, for instance, the doves, snails, or the development of larvae. They saw in the vivaria corner a good many of Nature's operations—from the human-like care which the doves give their young to the horrible, relentless, merciless process of a snake's swallowing a live frog; and they displayed many emotions—from the wildest, unbounded joy in the good and beautiful to fearful indignation at the rapacity of the snake and pity and tears for the frog.

During the first few weeks, considerable difficulty was experienced in restraining the students, both elementary and high school, from disturbing the animals in the vivaria. It was not altogether through mischief that they handled them, but often through affection or desire to experiment. They became so annoying at one time that we were on the verge of reducing the number of animals to those that could be kept under cover. The situation was dicussed with the students who were bringing in and caring for the material, and each one agreed to make every effort possible to prevent the necessity of doing this by watching the vivaria and speaking to or reporting everybody who wrongly handled any of the forms, or disturbed things in any way. For many days everyone who was seen to be observing in the corner was asked to enlist in this work. Everyone was assured that he had a responsibility in the matter, and that it was not sufficient for one to refrain from disturbing the animals himself, but that he should restrain others, also. There were several who readily agreed, and others who were not decided, while still others freely argued that as long as they kept hands off no responsibility was attached to them. So there were many opportunities for discussing with them in terms of things immediately concerning all of us a very vexing moral question—a question

EXPLORING A STREAM

WHEN THE MOTHERS WENT; OR, LUNCH HOUR

which appears to branch out into a good many relations. The discussions nearly always turned to one's duty when he knows of graft or other violations of the law in business, labor, or politics. For instance, if one should see another student chasing a young alligator or frog around the aquarium with a stick which would pobably result in the death of the animal and therefore deprive those who captured it and others of the satisfaction and pleasure of observing it, and took no part in it himself, he was under no obligation to restrain the student or report his conduct. When the covering was torn from a pipe in the hall of the school building, making an unsightly condition, a boy acknowledged he knew who did it, but did not feel it to be his duty to disclose the perpetrator's names. The majority of a group of high-school boys saw no reason why they should call a contractor to account for placing flimsy material in a building and thereby making it dangerous, unless they expected to inhabit or use the building themselves. The discussions which brought out these points usually came about through somebody's being caught in the act or reported as disturbing the arrangements in the vivaria. However unsocial some of the views were, the questions were given surprisingly serious consideration throughout. The matter must have been gone over with more than a hundred students, individually and collectively, and, although it required a great deal of time, the results amply repaid us in the good to the vivaria, and in getting into touch with the ideas of the students and in securing their sympathy for the work. Although the Museum was without an attendant for hours at a time during the last two months of the year, and many students came and went—there were always from one to twenty-five—nothing was seriously disturbed.

The last was the climax to the volunteer field trips. Three mothers and eight children went, and it was the best of the year in the exploration of the stream and woods, and all of them apparently enjoyed it immensely. It would help the field work immeasurably if one or more of the parents would go on each trip, and in most cases they would enjoy it as much as the children.

The elementary school had the greater number of interested field-workers, but the number probably would have been only a very little greater had the same invitation been extended to the students of the high school. It is to be regretted that exact data were not kept showing how many high-school students took part, but a considerable number did. A few of them, with the permission of their dean, spent their study hours in the Museum and gave effective help in keeping order and protecting the animals. Several useful additions to the vivaria and preserved specimens were made by high-school pupils, and during the recess periods they visited the Museum in nearly as large numbers as the elementary pupils, and were apparently fully as deeply interested. It was impossible to observe any lines drawn between grades in this work—where the elementary ended and the high-school began.

In connection with the field club, and working hand in hand with it, there was a photography group, and several pupils belonged to both. In this work the enthusiasm was all that could be desired and considerable good work was done. From the time we started to the photography room till the last print was put in to wash there was a high state of tension. They appeared to be on edge in this more than in anything else. Although a few of them had great difficulty and accomplished very little, it was found at the end of the session that they were far from being discouraged. Several did extra work, so far as they could be accommodated, and a few went to great trouble to equip outfits for continuing it in their homes or wherever they expected to spend the summer. It would be hard to find anything which brings out the native resources of a student so much as an interest in photography.

While the group was for the most part mainly engaged in learning the technique of developing and printing, it made several interesting photographic records of field trips, social affairs, and other events in the school life. A good many records of the handwork, and changes in the garden and on the grounds and in the parks from winter to summer, were made. The children made lantern-slides of these records and showed them to the whole school in the morning exercises.

Through means of the vivaria, field trips, and especially the camera work, there was a limited opportunity for putting to practical test the theory that the common branches, reading, writing, etc., may be taught well, when there is need for them, to help in giving expression to ideas or work about which, in the opinion of the student, the community should know. On two occasions when we were to show lantern-slides in the morning exercises, boys handed in papers indicating what they were to say. The spelling and composition in two of the papers were especally bad. The boys were told that the papers must be improved before being read to others. In the one case, it was written twice, and in the other, three times, with great improvement each time. The last ones were passable, and as the time was short they were allowed to use them. It appeared from the eagerness and persistency with which these boys worked on their papers that a great force could be brought to bear on them could motives of this kind be kept before them. They were interested in and knew something which they were legitimately sure the other members of the school wanted to hear.

rai - sin ver-meil, Garde la cha - leur du so - leil,...... Et
corps des vieux Et le sou - rire dans leurs yeux;.....

1st & 3d verses.

verse la dans le Ton-neau. Rai - sin ver-meil,
Donne la joie aux braves gens. . . . . . . ,. .

2d verse.

rai - sin nou-veau.
. . . . Et l 'es-pér-ance aux in - di-gents.

EDITORIAL NOTES

The only kind of activity that has any educational value is that which yields a tangible result in some worthy product.

Educative Activity

The ordinary distinction drawn between the activity of play and the activity of work has neither meaning nor value in terms of growth. Both play and work may be good or bad, educative or otherwise; that depends alone upon the motive. The infallible test is found in the character of the output; it is a measure that anyone may apply with ease and directness when education is conceived to be a concern of the familiar things of life.

An educational activity, therefore, is one which expresses itself through some helpful work. This is not a machine-made definition—it depends upon the nature of things.

Lazy Children

It is rooted in the fact that every child is a born worker and a lover of work. To work, to do things, to bring about results, useful and beautiful, is just as natural as it is for him to breathe the air. There are no lazy children —naturally. Catch them young and treat them right, and they are all workers and lovers of work. A lazy boy is merely either one who is sick, or one who does not like to do something which a "grown-up" thinks he should do; his indisposition, if not a matter for the physician, should be placed to his credit. A big boy came to my office one day who was too lazy, the teacher said, to be allowed to remain in school. I asked him what he would like to do if he were left entirely free to choose, and he replied: "I would quit school and go to work!" I thanked him—inwardly—for his criticism, over which I have since deeply pondered. Doubtless the "work" which this boy would be able to pick up in the streets would be as little to his taste as were the tasks left behind in the school. For the average employer rarely considers the soul-life of the employed. So between the teachers who do not know enough and the business men who do not care enough the lazy boys are easily turned into the path of the transgressor. Laziness is the merciful invention of nature, whereby she holds them for a time at the parting of the ways, and enables them, during this period of wavering, to escape the stupidity of the schools on the one hand, and the heart-breaking conditions of business on the other.

It was a bad day for education when it got itself placed over against work; when it made work a penalty for the stupid **Education** and a punishment for the perverse who would not **vs.** become "educated"—and education is just finding **Work** out its colossal blunder. Figures from the fourth grade up show that, when it is solely a question of school *or* work, it is work that wins the contest, hands down. Of the hosts that enter the primary grade, practically all the children of all the people, by far too small a per cent. finish the eighth year; of these a still lesser per cent. go to the high school, and beyond this there is scarcely more than a negligible minority. This absorption of child-life by the world's work all takes place in the face of modern educational theory, our advanced views of culture, our legal enactments, and the truant officer!

The forsakenness of the schools is due in part to the bread-winning necessities of the family; but the deepest cause lies in **Education and** the attitude of the pupils toward what the schools **Labor Laws** now offer them. The children themselves are the most persistent enemies of the child-labor law. They all seem to have it reckoned up by the almanac just when they will be permitted to get a real job. That day is a prouder one and probably more significant to the boy than the one that gives him a vote. To gratify his ambition for accomplishment, he gladly leaves school to subject himself to long hours and often to much physical discomfort, in order that he may bring forth something tangible as the result of his own hand and brain. Of course, in the majority of cases he is grossly self-deceived and buncoed. Neither the school nor the home has given him any adequate opportunity to learn what his real earning power is, and neither has taught him how this compares with the actual cost of self-maintenance. He is apt, therefore, to overestimate the one and to underestimate the other—he is self-deceived. He has more than even chances of finding a place with a man who wants to extract more gold from wood and stone and iron and dry goods and groceries than nature has put into them, and he therefore tries to make up the deficit out of the boy. The latter, discovering the bunco, suddenly loses his taste for work and begins to reflect upon the fairy-stories which he heard while in school about benevolent old gentlemen who kindly give nice honest boys a chance to begin at the bottom—carefully concealing the conditions, however, which necessarily keep them there. The fable of the frog in the well which climbed up two feet in the daytime and slipped back three feet at night seems to point his own destiny, and the stammering schoolboy's conclusion as to where that frog was bound to land in less than a week no longer seems so funny.

The situation is scarcely improving. Better schoolhouses and equipment, more skilful teachers, and higher ideals have the same unequal struggle as of old, because the allurements of active life have, *pari passu,* also grown more numerous and tempting. The schools of the period offer little help in the solution of the child-labor problem, because they fail to recognize adequately the child's desire to work. On the contrary, they do much to thwart his love for it and thereby to transform him into a non-educable being.

The question above all others is this: Shall we permit the children to be driven by their irresistible instincts into the world of labor, immature and unprepared, where **School Industries and the Alternative** they will grow up under the starving and stultifying circumstances of the store, the factory, and the sweat-shop; or shall the school system be overhauled so that the inborn love of work may be gratified and fostered under normal and healthful conditions? To this there would seem to be but one answer: if work the children must, and, as the facts show, work they will, it is for the schools to provide the opportunities for it to be done under the highest educative conditions. The provisions for industrial occupations in the schools should be entirely comparable with the practical advantages of those found in the community at large which now lure the children to disappointment and despair, and infinitely above them in their influence for good upon physical, mental, and moral growth. In such an educational process all industrial reforms must have their roots.

It is difficult for people, generally, to understand that labor has anything to do with education; it is merely a means to a livelihood—a source of income—a road to money and wealth. Those who favor trade schools usually have in mind the *laborer* and not the *educated* man. Manual training has been fought for a generation because people have feared it would turn out workers instead of thinkers! Scientific and technical schools with their laboratories and shops have done something to dispel the illusion—although the S.B. degree is still hardly considered to be on the same scholastic level with its aristocratic neighbor A.B. A generation or two ago there were thought to be no educated men outside of the "three learned professions;" now we know there are legions of them. The conviction is growing slowly that there is a relation between labor and education, and in another generation we shall believe that they are inseparable. We shall have not only education for labor, but also labor for education.

Educated Men vs. Laborers

Labor as a means of education is rather a new idea, but it is a sound one. It may be, or it may not be, necessary for children to help support the family, but they should always have a chance to do something to support themselves, and the school should furnish, in part, the means. At no stage should education be wholly divorced from the question of self-support. Curiously enough, the validity of this principle has been established only in the best reform institutions and with the wayward class of children, most of whom have utterly repudiated the ordinary type of schools. We must put the occupations in the schools on such a footing that the children through their industrial and artistic instincts and ability may gradually acquire a correct notion of their own earning power. If the work of their hands and brains is *educative,* then *it has an objective value also,* either in the school, the home, or the open market; and it is due the pupils that *this value should be distinctly set over to their credit in terms of self-support.* It should be done in such

Education by Self-Support

a way that the children themselves will fully understand, appreciate, and prize the worth of their own work. The occupations which should at first engage the children in school **Essential** are those concerned in the establishment and the **School** maintenance of the ideal home. The human home, **Industries** so infinitely removed from the lair, is the very highest achievment of evolution. Individual worth, community life, and national welfare in a democracy will be forever determined by the qualities bred into personal character by the common home. Domestic economy, with its allied sciences and crafts, and the arts, and their relation to nature and history, must become more and more the dominant factors in early education; first, because the artistic and industrial instincts in childhood are commanding ones, and, second, because early and prolonged practical training in such subjects is essential to the upbuilding and the integrity of the home. The virtues of family life can never be overmagnified, can never be too deeply impressed upon the minds of the children. In these fundamental occupations the boys and girls should participate equally through- **Boys and Girls** out the period of elementary and secondary instruc- **and Industries** tion. The strong tendency at present to consider the home-making side of life, in school and out of it, a matter for the girls alone is entirely wrong. A home of the right type is an impossibility unless the husband and wife are both practically acquainted with the details of its make-up and equally intelligent as to its mission. The boys, therefore, should scrub and bake and brew as a matter of daily routine, and as a matter of course, until they know better than they know anything else what it takes to make a home and what their duties are in the making. Home-making depends upon the character of the woman; it hangs no less upon the character of the man; with either alone it is a lonesome and hopeless task.

How shall we keep the boys off the street? Let them scrub the front steps and back porch, sweep the rooms, take care of **A Question and** the furnace, care for a garden be it ever so small, **its Answer** keep chickens, sew on buttons. trim the lamps, mow the lawn; give them a work-bench in the basement and elect them tinkers-in-chief to the household, and on

Saturdays let them earn their shoes as errand boys for druggist or grocer. There is plenty of time for all this besides an hour or so for play each day, and a half holiday, too, on Saturday. A boy with less work or more free time than this will find it hard to keep clear of trouble.

What "home work" should the schools require of children? Let them help get breakfast, wash the dishes, dust the furniture,

Home Work for the School put cupboards and drawers to rights, make the beds and keep their rooms spick and span; let them talk over a few of the things that interest them in school, that they may start into the day's work with something of a purpose which the school can help them realize. It is only when we attain such vigorous action and reaction between the home and school that the educational ' process will become identical with the process of living.

W. S. J.

BOOK REVIEWS

Melodic Music Series. By FREDERICK H. RIPLEY, Principal of the Longfellow School, Boston, and THOMAS TAPPER, Lecturer on Music at the Institute of Musical Art of the City of New York. New York, Cincinnati, and Chicago: American Book Co. Cloth, 8vo.

This four-book course presents a graded collection of well-chosen songs, accompanied by a modicum of brief exercises. It carries the work through the grades, ending with three- and four-part selections.

The material is collected from the works of classical composers, from the folk-music of various countries, and includes also original compositions of well-known modern writers, as Margaret Ruthven Lang, Jessie L. Gaynor, W. W. Gilchrist, and others. The authors have evidently the courage of modern pedagogic convictions, that the preservation of the child's interest in the subject is of first importance. But few exercises are given, and these show concisely—sometimes in a couple of measures—the vital point to be mastered. Its elaboration is given in the song-form. The scale, its individual tones, intervals, measure, time-symbols, the minor mode, chromatics, rhythm, phrasing, two- and three-part singing, are introduced in turn with a skilfully brief exercise for drill, while emphasis is laid upon the song which illustrates the point under discussion.

The plan of the series is new and commendable and should be a boon to the inexperienced teacher.

M. R. KERN

The Mind and Its Education. By GEORGE HERBERT BETTS. New York: D. Appleton & Co., 1906. Pp. xiii+265.

This book is especially suited to teachers who, independent of an instructor or class, wish to pursue an introductory course in psychology and its application to educational problems. The book reflects standard and commonly accepted positions of contemporary psychology. Novelty characterizes not the subject-matter, but in a measure the treatment, which is at times so direct and personal that the reader is in a fair way of forming the pleasing illusion that the author is speaking directly to him. The style of the book is clear and attractive, remarkably free from burdensome technicalities, and abounding in illustrations that illustrate. The beginner in psychology, especially if he is undertaking a study of it by himself, could hardly find a book better suited to his needs, a more admirable crystallization of scientific doctrine and common sense.

W. C. GORE

BOOKS RECEIVED

AMERICAN BOOK CO., NEW YORK AND CHICAGO

Robbin's Plane Geometry. By EDWARD RUTLEDGE ROBBIN. Half leather, 12mo. Pp. 254. $0.75.

Introductory Course in Argumentation. By FRANCES M. PERRY. Cloth, 12mo. Pp. 230. $1.

Outlines of Ancient History. By WILLIAM C. MOREY, Ph.D., University of Rochester. Half leather, 8vo. Pp. 550. $1.50.

THE MACMILLAN CO., NEW YORK

The Washington Word List. By WILLIAM ESTABROOK CHANCELLOR. Paper, 12mo. Pp. 114. $0.20.

GINN & CO., BOSTON

Natural Reading: Primer and Manual of Instruction. By LEW A. BALL. Cloth, 12mo.

Moni, the Goat Boy and Other Stories. By JOHANNI SPYRI. Translated and edited by EDITH F. KUNZ. Cloth, 16mo. Pp. 211. Illustrated. $0.40.

Third Reader. By FRANCES E. BLODGETT and ANDREW B. BLODGETT. Cloth, 12mo. Pp. 259. Illustrated. $0.45.

D. APPLETON & CO., NEW YORK

The Culture Readers. By ELLEN E. KENYON. Edited by EDITH A. SCOTT. Cloth. Pp. 144.

HINDS, NOBLE & ELREDGE, NEW YORK AND PHILADELPHIA

Graded Spelling Books for City Schools. By W. J. MORAN and C. H. BRELSFORD. Books I–VII. Paper.

Geography Primer. By O. P. CORNMAN and O. GERSON. Cloth.

LAIRD & LEE, CHICAGO

English Spelling Simplified, as recommended by President Roosevelt, Andrew Carnegie, Mark Twain, Brander Matthews, and other distinguished men. Paper. Pp. 96.

VOLUME VII NUMBER 5

The Elementary School Teacher

January, 1907

PHYSICAL TRAINING A DEPARTMENT OF EDUCATION

CARL J. KROH
Head of the Department of Physical Training in the School of Education

The human body in its wonderful structure and marvelous mechanism is expressive of the highest that in art is conceivable. Its study, as an entity, as a living creation, invites the profoundest inquiry; it embraces the whole realm of human wisdom. To mold the living nature, as it were, is the matchless and priceless privilege of the teacher.

Three great art fields are distinguishable: that of the plastic art of the human body, as implied in all its developmental possibilities—in its activities; that of the cultural arts; and that of the representative arts.

This view, I believe, includes all the virility and elemental qualities fundamental to the modern superstructure of high culture.

The first, fundamental or preparatory field concerns itself with the physical as the basis of the psychical activities. Either, as power develops and matures, or both, constitutes the forces determining the harmonious adjustment necessary to success in all later endeavor.

The portrayal, indeed, of the living art-work constitutes the art of arts, and represents the highest aesthetical worth. Arguments for its emphasis, when presented on approved pedagogical principles, cannot be denied. The quickening influences, however, so essential to a recognition of its legitimate place and bearing in education, have been slow to materialize, overshadowed as they have been in our time by the hue and cry of huge endeavor. Discrepancies in methods, consequent upon an over-emphasis of what constitutes the popular conception of physical training, as contrasted with the legitimate aspects of the work, are also responsible in no small measure for the hesitancy of even some of our most innovating educators in turning the tide of their solicitudes in the direction of this fundamentally important work.

The general conception of an educational rationale has always been more or less tinged with the utilitarian hues of our material progress. The ideal of a product, mentally and physically superior in every respect, is with difficulty construed in terms of its proximate equivalent. The interpretation of the phrase, "physical, mental, and moral education," has been singularly one-sided. Broadly construed, physical training always has had a rather general significance. Specifically construed, it has not yet been satisfactorily or fully adjudged in its initial import as signifying a department of education, although its bearing upon education has been demonstrated beyond cavil and doubt.

There is as yet, it is true, no royal way to perfection. The inquiries bestowed upon the intellectual pursuits have not been focused in a like manner upon the purely physical. The sheer endless sources of profitable inquiry concerning the human organism and its adaptability, as affecting the superior qualities of conduct and habit, have remained more or less obscure, and, it may be said, despite our progress in the related sciences, that the present-day student is not enlightened with respect to his organism and its functions in a manner possible with the means and resources at hand. "Were it not for the marvelous self-adjusting and self-regulating power of the human machine," it has been pertinently said, "we should utterly fail in our faith in progress, as determined by the tardy application of the modern doctrine of the human body."

The very gradual elimination of confusion existing between truth and probability, however, has lent tone to the general endeavor. Not "what is," but "what should be," is the stimulating motive of the exponent of progress.

Physical training, as an agent in our modern development, has steadily advanced through the demands for its better organization. This advance has not been in every way satisfactory, nor in concord with the purposes of education, whenever it resulted in a régime designated merely hygienic or recreative. It has been satisfactory whenever it reflected the needs of the individual, physical nature in nerve-stimulating and regulating work, "garbed in youthful pleasure and merriment," based upon pedagogical principles, and governed by the laws of mind and body.

Some of the methods nurtured in the schools owe their origin to conditions quite different from those prevailing in them, and are at variance with the avowed purposes of education. But, between the tenets of an ever-ready reasoning and the unsolved problems of the positive people, they serve their purposes in lieu of something better to displace them.

The probing of methods under the prevailing conditions is as futile as the inoperative demand in some of our school systems that the regular teacher shall adapt himself to this branch of work.

The solution of the problem of what shall be subservient to the most profitable results in physical training or education is a matter that must appeal to the professional schools, warranted by virtue of their determining influences in organizing well-equipped departments of physical training for the better guidance of the prospective teacher, in order that his interest in the physical welfare of his charges may become enabled to reinforce the superior mental equipment demanded in our time in all lines of pursuit.

It is gratifying, indeed, that the synthesis of opinion of a steadily growing coterie of critical educationists at present is gravitating toward the conviction that the most fruitful interpretation of the nature, scope, and spirit of this very interesting subject rests with its organization as a department of pedagogical discipline. A desire is being urged for an evaluation of the correlated factors constituting the various aims advanced for physical training that shall conduce to a more pronounced general and rational progress. The enhancement of the work is demanded to the end that it be made more real and vital, rather than appear as an artificial makeshift—as content. As a legitimate agent in actual life it should find its enhancement in most subjects taught in the school curriculum, and notably in the biological sciences. Preferences for the quasi-approved procedures, whether hygienic, developmental, recreative, or remedial, are kept in abeyance pending this somewhat conservative stand.

Experiment and inquiry have proved much to augur this promising distinction. The growing conception of the value of pedagogy and personal skill, as applied to the intellectual unity presented in the child's body, for instance, must ultimately determine the course of true physical training, and obviate the vexatious uncertainties due to a lack of coherent procedure. The superficial notion of utilizing gymnastic instruction as a perfunctory means of recreation, and as an incidental expedient for remedial purposes, to the exclusion of its larger function in the curriculum, is rightfully viewed as somewhat narrow by all who have thought seriously of the matter.

Not only the steadily growing significance of physical training in our elementary schools, but the phenomenal interest in athletics in our secondary schools as well, confront the authorities, who must determine the policy of the schools with reference to the order of their importance, with an interesting situation.

Whatever the background of the underlying charm, the actuating motive, or the intelligence directing the respective activities involved in systematic physical culture and the qualities cultivated, the most salutary effects of this large, interesting subject can accrue only through a definite and comprehensive scheme, embodying all the factors determinative in the work— adaptation of physical culture to the youth of all ages. To become effective, such a scheme must find the teacher of the future indorsed for the views he holds with reference to it. This demand, already emphasized in many normal schools, will in time insure a policy more in harmony with our interests than is the present athletic spirit.

In the interim, owing to the scant ingenuity displayed in a dissemination of knowledge and information, conveying the scope of physical training, the personal element discounts the pedagogical. The athletic interest exceeds the interest for a scheme of educational merit, the discomfiture of occasional criticisms being offset by the verdict that nothing short of these practices in a like manner can conduce to the sturdier and more desirable qualities developed in aspiring youth. The last resource in innumerable schools is had in a recourse to the seasonable in- and outdoor sports, admittedly the best substitutes for educative physical training. The principles or prerequisites of proficiency, as they affect the body of our school youth, are left to solve themselves. The characteristic alternatives represent the extremes of procedure on the one hand, and stimulation to supreme effort on the other—the distinction claimed for purely corrective work.

What is the function of organized gymnastics in the school? The function of gymnastics in the schools is to further the attainment of the ideal of education. This ideal may be variously expressed in a robust manhood of superior mental and physical quality and fiber, representing the qualities fundamental to an ideal citizenship; or, it may concern itself with the remoter concept of an exalted nationality, when it engenders a deep-rooted and fervent patriotism—a sentiment always to be transformed into a determining principle. With such an ideal as a motive, gymnastics represents more than a mere diversion—it attains a newer significance and becomes an art. "Living, acting, conceiving" form the triple chord within the child of every man, though the sound of this chord, now of that, and then again of two together, may preponderate."

The gymnasium, as a school of self-realization, represents a social institution, where the "pleasure of being strong lies in the fact that others around us are strong, thereby furnishing us with companionship and healthy competition, the fuel of life." Under this conception "health becomes incidental, and not the deliberate object of exercise." The ever-increasing body of scientific knowledge concerning the formative and developmental shapes of early life determines the means to be employed in its preservation.

Means, purposive in a hygienic sense alone, cannot be conducive to that interest in activity which represents the source of all volition, nor do they beget an atmosphere of cheerfulness. Gymnastics proper, on the other hand, which deal with ever new and interesting movement-concepts that train, not only in careful observation and estimation of distances and objects, and in the exercise of comparative judgment, and to reason in countless ways, and to appreciation of symmetry and form-beauty, but also to reason for the great perspective, the remote and final outcome, and to avoid the dangers of unprofitable deviations—such gymnastics must represent the school that would bring into play all the faculties.

The gymnasium should represent the very essence of community life. Through its work, help, play, and companionship, it influences and strengthens character toward the larger opportunities of life. It is a place where the growing boy's heart is thrilled with the power of right and robust resolution; where he is constantly brought into new relations; where encouragement bears fruit quickest and becomes most lasting; where reproof touches to the quick; where the varied phases of life-activity preclude all dry mastery; where power is developed to think and reflect, to execute and originate, not through direction alone, but also through exercise; "where order and propriety go hand in hand; where wilfulness is restrained, energy stored, and skill developed." So regarded, the gymnasium represents a correlation of factors emphasizing to the fullest all conduct.

Can the aspects of this training become realized in a scheme of school gymnastics? Thought and action be so adjusted, and motive so instilled, as to enhance interest in physical education?

Can there be any question as to who should assume responsibility in the espousal of this tremendous factor in our school life?

FORMS OF INDUSTRIAL EDUCATION BEST ADAPTED
TO CITY CHILDREN[1]

CHARLES H. KEYES

Supervisor of South District Public Schools, Hartford, Conn.

The traditional subjects of the school curriculum aim to train the child through exercises the perception basis of which is either visual or auditory, or both. The child's seeing and hearing alone condition all his learning within the scope of the time-honored subjects. But manual training aims at the development of the individual through the introduction of experiences based on other sense-perceptions than those of sight and hearing. Touch and muscular resistance are called into play because they furnish, independently and in conjunction with the other sense-avenues, experiences which react in the development of nervous centers and forces otherwise left practically impotent so far as the training of the schools is concerned. In deciding what forms of manual training are especially valuable for the child of any determined environment, certain governing principles must be kept clearly in mind.

1. This training must develop capacity which is a new, additional, positive contribution to the child's unconscious endeavor at self-realization, and the school's conscious endeavor to transform his possibilites into powers.

2. This training should furnish him experience which enlarges his capacity to adapt himself more easily and efficiently to his life-work and environment when school days are finished. He should begin to learn as a boy things he must do as a man.

3. This training should not neglect to furnish him some experiences lying entirely outside the field of his prospective life-activity, and especially some of that class of experiences which will enable him to understand and sympathize with the endeavor and aim of large groups of his fellow-men whose surroundings

[1] Address before the Department of Superintendence of the National Educational Association, Louisville, Ky., March 1, 1906.

and occupations are decidedly unlike his own. He should begin to get the view-point as a boy of a position he will not occupy as a man, but which will be occupied by thousands of his fellow-men with whom the good of the commonwealth and the nation demands that he shall have intelligent sympathy.

4. This training is the resultant of exercises in which the pupil is making high endeavors at self-expression. He is writing himself into the drawing or the model he constructs. His ideals of strength, utility, beauty, and honesty are modeled in the clay, cut and carved in the wood, bent and forged in the iron, braided and woven into the raffia and reeds which he manipulates.

With these principles in mind, and a recognition of the fact that the immediate direction of the manual-training work of the great majority of city children must be in the hands of the regular grade teacher, we may proceed to make some specific answers to the question: What forms of industrial training are best suited to the child of any determined environment?

Obedience to the first and fourth of these principles will eliminate some of the common forms of manual training frequently used as pedagogical soothing syrup, under the name of "busy work," in many primary schools. It will do away with much of the work on hard and fast models in which the pupil has little or no choice or initiative, and which admit of only a comparatively low order of self-expression.

So far as the life of any particular city or class of cities is distinctive, its conditions must guide us in applying the second and third principles, which chiefly determine the forms proposed for our discussion.

Recognition of the principle that in manual training and industrial education the pupil should be taught to know and do, as a boy, things which he will have to do as a man is now widespread. We have ceased to apologize for any special form of manual training having educational value, because it gives a boy the skill of a craft in which he may later earn his living. We are no longer ashamed to acknowledge that many of our pupils are taught in our schools the very art or arts whose exercise in the business world gives them their support. This conclusion is the only justification for the large place that cooking and sewing have long enjoyed in the schools of our most progressive cities. Call it trade-school work, if you will; but remember that all our girls must be trained for the vocation of homemaker, and be skilled either in practicing these two arts or in the direction, supervision, and training of others, in their exercise.

I may probably best indicate by illustration what I deem to be wise operation of the law that the special character of the business life of a city should affect the forms of industrial education in its schools. My own city (Hartford) is known throughout the business world as a banking, insurance, and manufacturing center. We employ thousands of clerks, accountants, copyists, bookkeepers, typists, and stenographers in these offices of our banks, insurance companies, and factories. The factories are devoted largely to the production of high-grade metal manufactures. Our guns and automobiles, our tires and bicycles, our typewriters and automatic machinery go into every quarter of the world where efficiency is prized. In their production we employ thousands of machinists, pattern-makers, draftsmen, smiths, and other high-grade mechanics. The ranks of all these must be annually recruited from the boys trained in our public schools.

We recognize, accordingly, that penmanship has in our schools a place which it is not generally accorded or entitled to in many other cities. We deliberately teach it as an important manual art all through the nine grades of the grammar schools and in the high school as well. Similarly, work in wood and iron is begun as low as the fifth grade of the grammar schools and carried through the high school. Drawing and designing begin in the kindergarten and are available through every year to the end of the high-school course. Typewriting, stenography, and bookkeeping are taught in our high school. Our work in pattern-making, mechanical drawing, and machine-shop practice is more extended than might be justified in a city of different commercial life. Our evening high school has not hesitated to undertake the training in its shops and drafting-rooms of ambitious young men from the factories. Without conscious formulation of the doctrine that the schools of the community should teach whatever the business of the community demands in a large way, we have accepted it in our practice.

Because of recognition of the principle that every man's vocation, as well as his location, puts limitations upon his life and thought, we have always deemed it necessary to teach pupils many things in history, literature, and language largely for the purpose of enabling them to understand people far removed from them in time or territory. We know the moral value of the suggestion, "Put yourself in his place;" but we have not fully learned that due appreciation of the dignity of manual labor, and its possible intelligence and self-respect, cannot be gained without doing this in some practical way. No amount of reading and study will do this for most of us as efficiently as a little experience with the life-work of the class we would understand. How else can we account for the general attitude of the public toward manual and industrial education? We hear enough of its virtue, we read enough of the value of its contribution to the efficiency of the social and political life. But so long as only the neglected negro, the abused Indian, and the inmates of our reformatories and penitentiaries are made its chief beneficiaries, how can we avoid the conclusion that it is not truly understood?

Now, no one will deny that it is highly important that the city boy, who as a man is to live in the city, help form public opinion of the city, and express that in his vote, should have a sympathetic interest in the work of the farmer, the horticulturist, and the gardener. The good of the commonwealth demands it. In my own state the gravest hindrance to progress in helpful legislation for both city and country is mutual misunderstanding of the city view-point and the country view-point. We in the city think the shortcoming and the duty of our farmer fellow-citizen are manifest; but it is not our duty to give our children, not only tuition, but also industrial experience that shall make it easier for them to co-operate more intelligently and sympathetically with the great agricultural class?

And not alone in manufacturing states like Connecticut, but indeed throughout the Union, the city children need this opportunity to gain at least an elementary acquaintance with the life-endeavor of the great farming class. The best place to train our city boys and girls to this open-eyed and open-hearted co-operation with the millions of their farmer fellow-citizens is in the school garden. The school garden as an institution has, of course, large value as a nature-study laboratory. It may also prove a solution of the vexed problem lying between too many hours in school and too many hours on the street. But its chief value lies in the fact that it gives through its experience the moral and intellectual sympathy which I have urged is so needed in the civic and political life.

It may be urged that the garden on any adequate scale is not available in the city. It is not and will not be in the city on the day in which we do not insist on the minimum land interests of children. No man would undertake to rear a score of good Kentucky colts without ample grounds in which they might get their play and their training. To limit these would be to insure failure with the noblest quadruped the world has produced. But dozens of communities are essaying to rear a thousand American boys and train them on a school site but little larger than the building—a school site covered with a brick house, a concrete walk, and the grave of man-making play, above which rises the mournful epitaph, "Keep off the grass." Have we not reached the time when we know that blooming girls and bouncing boys are worth more than springing grass and budding bush? Whenever and wherever the physical rights of our youth are properly understood by the managers of our schools, we can trust the solution of the land question to the American father whose prayer today is still that of the Grecian hero before the walls of Troy: "May this, my son, be greater than his father."

Again let me illustrate by the example with which I came to be most familiar, and which involved all the type difficulties besetting the development of a city school garden. The Wadsworth Street School—the central school of the system for which I am responsible—is situated in the heart of a thickly populated district of our city. To it eighteen hundred boys and girls went daily. The unoccupied portions of the site were barely ade-

quate to the play purposes of the school. The proper appeal
to the school committee in the name of the open-air rights of
the children resulted in the purchase of the needed land con-
tiguous to the school site. All was uninclosed, and to the committee it seemed desirable to keep open to the public certain
walks through the property by which thousands of citizens daily
traveled to and from their homes. The land secured was enough
to furnish garden opportunity for from three to four hundred
children in one year. It seemed desirable to them to give the
garden opportunity to the children of the youngest grades. The
first year the gardens were given up exclusively to the children
of six kindergartens, under the leadership of an enthusiastic
kindergarten supervisor of limitless industry. Nearly all of the
kindergartners and the great mass of their children caught the
spirit of the work, and the gardens were a great success. The
boys and girls of the neighborhood, without any invitation, took
on themselves, out of school hours and during vacation, the duty
of protecting them from trespassers and marauders. Remember
that the whole tract was unfenced, and that from 5 P. M. to 6 A. M.
no teacher or school official, not even a janitor, was on the
premises. The morals of young and old in the neighborhood
were equal to withstanding all, or nearly all, temptation. Remember, too, that there were scores of children living within a
few blocks of this garden who were pupils in private schools,
and had possibly never attended public schools. Bear in mind,
further, that there was no special police protection given to this
block more than to any others in the vicinity. When the
watermelons approached maturity, and before the frost was on
the pumpkins, the watering of some juvenile mouths and the
longing for Jack-o'-lanterns became too powerful, and we lost
a good portion of these two crops. Otherwise flowers and vegetables were practically unmolested.

The next season four first primary grades were added to the
garden squad. Their teachers brought added enthusiasm,
energy, and thoughtful consideration to the managing and directing forces. We were fortunate in having in these departments teachers able to take up new problems intelligently, and

ready to follow them up persistently. The gardens were now a pronounced success. The work was practically all done by the children and their teachers. The highly efficient teacher or kindergartner could be picked out as readily in the garden as in the school. We had answered the question: Are the school hours too long for the primary children? Too long always for the wrong kind of work; never too long in the school that has the intelligence to recognize, the courage to stand for, and the freedom to serve the true interests of the growing child.

Other cities of varying industrial life and environment may furnish varying specifications in their answer to the question we have discussed. The principles which we have endeavored to enunciate must, however, be followed by all. The best forms of industrial education for the children of any given city must result in the development of power not adequately developed in the traditional curriculum, must train for industrial efficiency in the city, and must give sympathetic understanding and respect for the life-work of the millions in the country.

WEAKNESSES IN THE TEACHING OF ENGLISH IN OUR COMMON SCHOOLS

JEAN SHERWOOD RANKIN
Minneapolis, Minn.

The phrasing of this subject hints at an actual condition, not at mere theory; for we are facing a universal complaint, more serious in nature than any before laid at the door of the common schools. The colleges, of course, blame the secondary schools; the secondary schools in turn point to the grades; the grade teacher, already round-shouldered with the burdens heaped upon her, points to the home, to the street, or to the playground, and wearily asks: "How can I overcome in a few short hours the tremendous momentum toward faulty speech acquired before pupils reach my hands?"

Widely different sets of causes have co-operated to induce the prevailing lamentable failure in English instruction which has recently driven college after college to rule that entrance examinations shall hereafter be required in the very elements of English.

These causes of failure are either (1) external to the school itself, and in nature more or less permanent; or (2) due to causes within the school system, and not in nature permanent.

The first great cause is external to the schools, and is found in the heterogeneous character of our swarming emigrant population. In public-school buildings Armenian and Russian children touch elbows with Italians and Bohemians; while Germans, Scandinavians, and Poles are equally in evidence. This mixed foreign population forces upon the schools a wholly new problem, so far as language and literature are concerned, which problem is, however, scarcely yet recognized. In fact, there is a general purblind indifference to this most significant feature of the twentieth-century American schoolroom. However, the teaching of English to foreigners during the first two school years is a striking feature in New York City's new course of study; and, where New York leads, others will soon follow.

A second primary cause for poor work in English is but partly external to the school system. This is the survival in home and in school of an ancient false tradition as to the culture value of a knowledge of technical grammar. All worthy authorities now agree that grammar the science, while of considerable disciplinary value, yet has little, if any, effect upon speech the art; nevertheless the old tradition dies hard. That it is, however, moribund no one will venture to deny who knows whither the tide of educational opinion has been setting for the past several years. I quote from the annual report of the state inspector of graded schools for Minnesota for the school year ending July, 1901 :

> Technical grammar is still begun too early in many schools. In fact, the poorer the school, the earlier grammar is taken up. Very poor schools almost invariably put a textbook in grammar into the sixth grade. The worst feature of this sort of teaching is that it makes what might be a very useful and even entertaining study a task which children dislike and misunderstand. The reason that teachers put technical grammar into the sixth grade is generally because they have not the originality to interest a class in intelligent composition or language work.

Very significant is the fact that several normal schools have recently adopted a new course of study deferring all technical grammar until the eighth grade. In this common-sense procedure these schools are only a little behind several Minnesota graded schools, which are courageous pioneers in the cause of better teaching of English. Assuredly the time is near at hand when reputable schools will no longer teach "baby grammar" in grades below the eighth.

The third primary cause for the general weakness in English work results directly from the second just stated. It is strictly an internal cause which may be remedied, and is this : Grade teachers, almost without exception, have not themselves been prepared to teach language as art. Looking at the study of English as science, they have constantly smothered in their pupils germs of linguistic and literary power. Blue-glass grammatical spectacles have colored their entire horizon, and, teaching indigo grammar for the sake of indigo grammar, they have not been able to perceive the rose-colored skies over literary fields.

Let us face these causes singly, and consider where lies the responsibility for present conditions, and where the remedy which public, college, and press are all vehemently demanding.

Primarily, without doubt, the chief blame must be laid at the doors of our normal schools. As a prominent normal-school president truly remarks: "The difficulty here, and I presume in many schools, is the fact that our grammar teachers are wedded to the old technical system, and it is hard to make a change." As soon as our normal schools send out teachers prepared to give intelligent training in living English, just so soon will the general linguistic consciousness be quickened.

Obviously, we cannot hope that the foreign element in our schools will soon be less. On the contrary, it may be even greater in proportion than it is at present. For the increasing number of excellent private schools proves that the American parent who can afford it will quite probably place his children where they can have the benefit of personal supervision in small classes, in which their progress is not inevitably slowed down to that of the weakest feet. Whether or not private schools shall continue to increase will depend somewhat, no doubt, upon the efficiency of the public schools in giving elementary English training.

These two last-named causes of weakness in English teaching are interdependent and can hardly be separated. Reduced to their lowest terms, they may be formulated simply thus: *ineffective methods,* accepted for use because of tradition, or because laid down in textbooks and courses of study by supposed authorities.

Before considering the inadequacy of present popular language "methods," as means to the general end of education, let us inquire: Precisely what are the specific ends in view in so-called "language" teaching? But let us first of all steer clear of that common error which fails to distinguish between all-important final ends and the prerequisite means to those ends. We shall then admit at once that spelling, penmanship, and even reading itself, are not absolutely essential elements in a good command of language. For the great epics lived by word of mouth for centuries; the man born without arms may become a linguist skilled in a score of tongues; and hence the tedious writing and rewriting of what a child already knows is not only non-essential to his linguistic proficiency, but also, indeed, a serious handicap in the effort to gain this.

Can we not agree upon the following outline?

Results sought in modern "language work" — Direct: (1) Command of language in oral speech; (2) Command of language in written speech. Indirect: (3) Literary appreciation; (4) Character-growth through absorption of ideals

Doubtless not all teachers would admit that the last two aims are indirect. For example, Mr. Percival Chubb, of New York City, principal of the high-school department of the Ethical Culture Schools, which were founded by Dr. Felix Adler, would magnify these as most important of all, and I heartily indorse his position; but as a concession to the extremest utilitarian standpoint we may grant that command of oral and command of written speech are the sole direct aims of the language teacher. This granted, what elements shall we call absolutely essential as prerequisites to the obtaining full command over one's mother-tongue? I conceive them to be these:

The prerequisites to command of language are — in oral speech: (1) a wide vocabulary, so well possessed as to be promptly available; that is, a supply of *words* for the sake of expression, because words are the sole tools of thought; (2) an idiomatic and easy sentence-habit. in written speech: (1) and (2) as above *plus* (3) the mechanics of reading, spelling, and penmanship

If it be granted that a command of oral English speech is the single, most important, educational desideratum to English-speaking individuals, the question at once arises: How can this be most swiftly and thoroughly acquired? Common-sense as well as authority answers: *By emphasizing oral language work,* and by remembering that spelling and penmanship pertain solely to the less important division of linguistic attainment. Oddly enough, the fact seems to be constantly forgotten that *composition* belongs to oral language quite as much as to written. Mr. Chubb holds negatively that *neglect of ear-training* in oral work is one potent cause of poor results. He says truly: "It is the ear, and not the script or print, that is the first, as it is the final, arbiter and nurse of all lovely speech and song."[1]

He lists the following also as causes of the prevailing unsatisfactory results in English: (1) Too much written work is asked for; (2) this is too labored, as we press for an excellence in form not to be expected from the young; (3) the compositions are too long; (4) wrong topics are chosen, depriving the work of reality and interest to the child.[2]

I am glad to quote Mr. Chubb because his general treatment of this subject is so rational and satisfactory, especially as a provision for American-born children from homes of culture who are destined to enter the high school.

It can hardly be denied (1) that many teachers have expected the language period to atone for all defects in the work of the three periods given respectively to reading, to writing, and to spelling; (2) that much of the time given ostensibly to "language" is in fact either "busy" work—which very name is a pedagogical contradiction—or else belongs in some other period; (3) that the language lesson often becomes a catch-basin for the unfit and the impractical. Here in wildest disorder may be found an unorganized mass made up from disconnected bits of geography, physical geography, zoölogy, physiology, botany, astronomy, Greek, Roman, German, or Norse myths, biography, drawing, art-history, bird-study, ethics, spelling, diacritics, kindergarten-platitudes, and grammatical science.

I assert with all the positivism at my command that the following prevalent methods have no place whatever in a rational scheme of language lessons:

1. Desecration of literature through so-called "reproduction."

2. Unpedagogical puzzle-and-guess work under the form of "blank filling."

---

[1] *The Teaching of English*, p. 24.   [2] *Ibid.*, p. 106.

3. The learning of diacritics which indorses single dictionaries; because this never yet taught, nor ever will teach, English pronunciation.

4. Composition for the sake of practice in spelling and penmanship.

5. Dictation lessons which are planned neither as knowledge tests nor to train the eye in observation—these being the legitimate aims of the dictation as method, and, hence, adapting it chiefly to the spelling and writing periods.

6. Information lessons about birds, pictures, artists, astronomy, history, geography, natural products, manufactured objects —or anything else under the sun, save only *language for the sake of language* and *literature for the sake of literature*.

7. Any method, and every method, which fails to utilize that most powerful possible element in all educational gains, the child's own ambition and desire to excel.

I am glad to note that Mr. Chubb has condemned at length that least excusable of all bad methods called "the reproduction," and that he declares strongly against the evils of basing written work upon the literature which is being studied. This vicious popular method becomes wholly absurd when one realizes that *the best* (that is, the most literal) *reproduction is the worst* (because the least original) *language exercise*. For the verbal parroting of fine phrases shows neither originality nor power of thought; and under this monstrous method pupils of genuine literary ability quite often make the poorest showing, because lacking the spur of original and spontaneous interest.

That many children excel in writing "reproductions" we all know. That this implies a certain sort of skill no one will deny. But it is the same sort of skill which in other fields of meretricious endeavor wastes endless hours in fashioning paper flowers and wax fruits, "so true to life that you can hardly tell they are not real." Here lies the test of all art: it must be *creative*, not *imitative*. That prince of imitators, Robert Louis Stevenson, by just so much failed to be a genuine artist—so a recent noted critic justly remarks; for he gives us, in fact, not chiefly himself as original genius, but a succession of different writers whose personality he has successively and successfully copied. Let us away with Mrs. Jarley's wax works the moment they attempt to deceive the public by claiming to rank as fine art. Let us also away with that reproduction of literature which gives us only the paper flowers and wax fruit of literary art. Can it be that we prefer wax fruit and paper flowers to wild strawberries and nature's uncultivated meadow flowers? Then so much the worse for us and for the false ideals grown out of our wrong system of training.

No one, of course, will confound written lessons, or *knowledge tests,* with the well-known method here referred to. Nor does my condemnation include such work as the outlining of plots, the making of written abstracts, the oral and the written summary, all of which may fill a useful place in grammar-grade work. What must be abolished is the fad, *so dangerously easy for the teacher, but often entailing cruel nervous strain upon the child,* which stupidly and wickedly in the name of "teaching" permits the cheap folly called "reproduction." I am not sure, indeed, but that a society for prevention of cruelty to human animals might well forbid the excessive amount of writing which this method entails upon pupils in the grades. While written composition should increase in amount gradually from the lower grades to the higher, still at no time should it equal or even approximate in amount the oral work required; and yet under present methods the frequent order, "Reproduce the story," means usually that oral work is wholly neglected.

Should you inquire how much I include under the term "information lessons," I reply: All the dilute science of every sort commonly found as padding in the "language" texts of the day. These subjects include among others the following: the sun, the moon, stars, waves, tides, air, clouds, ice, snow, frost (and Jack Frost), hail, fog; coral, coal, the peanut and other nuts, fruits of all sorts, pepper and salt, cotton, sugar, flax, silk, linen, wool, the clock, the mill-wheel, flour, bread, yeast; moths, ants, katydids, grasshoppers, squirrels, earthworms, butterflies, the dog, the horse, the cow, the duck, the hen, sheep, farm life; George Washington, Christopher Columbus, Murillo, Millet, Van

Dyck, and other artists; cheap woodcuts of all sorts; Ceres, Apollo, Mercury, the Wanderings of Ulysses, and myths of all the earth.

These subjects, and others of similar character, have wasted time enough in most American schools to allow the teaching of a foreign language. While their ostensible defense is always the "provision of suitable topics for conversation and for written lessons," in point of fact they neither furnish accurate science nor inspire interest leading to good language work. They are not lessons in language, nor in literature, nor even about language. They are usually mere crumbs from the loaf of natural science, and stale crumbs at that.

As corrective to the poor practices everywhere carried on in the name of language study, I suggest that teachers no longer accept cut and dried lessons and courses of study, but that they challenge their every daily recitation with these questions: (1) Exactly what is this lesson intended to accomplish? (2) Is it adequate to that end? (3) Is it a means to a larger end, or is it an ultimate aim in itself? (4) Will it insure definite language gains, or is it merely an information lesson? (5) Is it articulated with the live flesh and blood of idiomatic English, or is it but the rattling dry bones of a fleshless grammatical skeleton? (6) Precisely what is to be my own method in using it?

To be sure, information is not necessarily excluded from legitimate literary language material, but early lessons looking toward language as art may well deal largely with linguistic subjects, especially with words, their meaning, and their right use. Hence, special instruction in English, looking toward vocabulary gains, must become a marked feature in primary grades. This is absolutely indispensable where there is a foreign population, and its omission is as extravagant financially as sinful morally. *How* to give such training is not a difficult question when the need is once recognized: (1) Reading, both oral and silent, must increase in amount; (2) attention to concrete objects and their names must have definite place; (3) the reading and telling of stories by teachers to pupils must be considered as necessary as the children's own reading—this last because we now recognize that the child who is read aloud to at home receives an ear-training in English which is even more imperatively needed by the foreign child; (4) oral story-telling by pupils must become a strong and prominent feature.

Obviously, the primary teacher will need time for all this, and to that end we shall gladly excuse her from much of the work now required at her hands, asking only that the linguistic sense of her pupils shall be quickened. In particular, she shall be excused from most of those senseless memory tests which, under the name of "examinations," are supposed to inspire her to "keep up," but which tend instead to drag her down mentally, morally, and physically.

For the grade teacher of today is a typical jack-of-all-trades. She is expected to be a specialist in reading, penmanship, arithmetic, geography, history, basketry, rug-weaving, drawing, water-color work, clay-modeling, music, physical culture, psychology, and in some states agriculture. On top of all this we are now demanding that she be literary. But human flesh and blood cannot much longer endure so tremendous a burden, and the strongest back will break under the last straw. Moreover, folly such as this cannot continue in an age of progress *whose keynote is specialization.* In the better day near at hand grade teachers will have one, two, or at most three subjects to teach, and they will do their work with the enthusiasm of the specialist, not with the dragging weariness of the general drudge. No longer exhausted and hopeless, they shall at last do "all with the joy of the worker" whose individuality is respected, whose power of initiative shall have scope, whose originality is recognized and rewarded, and whose labor is ranked as a worthy product of art.

THE EXAMINATION OF THE EYES OF SCHOOL CHILDREN

JOHN C. EBERHARDT
Optometrist, Dayton, O.

The development of the mental faculties depends largely, if not entirely, upon the functions of perception, and these should therefore receive critical attention during childhood. Professor Tait, of the University of Edinburgh, Scotland, in his treatise on *Light,* says: "All our other senses together, except under very special conditions, do not give us one tithe of the information obtained at a single glance, and sight is also that one of our senses which we are able most effectively and extensively to assist by proper apparatus."

The phonograph, reproducing the falsely pitched voice and nerve-racking discords of a distempered piano, graphically demonstrates the undulatory theory of sound; nor can we criticize the faithful reproduction of these sound photographs.

Sight is purely a mental phenomenon, for the image of external objects reflected upon the inner wall of the eye is transmitted over the million nerve-fibers composing this wall to the innermost recesses of the brain, where consciousness of vision is born, and where also, phonograph-like, mental impressions are recorded, which, even after the lapse of years, will enable the mind's eye to pass in review that which caused them.

In the phonographs we know the accuracy of construction and delicacy of adjustment essential to its satisfactory operation. We should certainly be equally critical in dealing with that choicest of possessions—the eye.

Environment largely influences the mind for good or evil. The deformed eye, therefore, which constantly transmits to the brain distorted images must undoubtedly have a demoralizing influence upon the mentality. That this is true is evidenced by the statistics of our reformatories, homes for the feeble-minded, inebriate retreats, and insane asylums, showing, as they invariably do, large percentages of visual defects in the inmates.

Allen Greenwood, M.D., in an address before the Boston Medical Society, recently urged that municipalities take up the investigation of the eyes of school children, emphasizing the fact that alarmingly large percentages of backward and feeble-minded children examined had been found to be afflicted with deformities of the eyes, impairing vision, all of whom evidenced marked improvement, mentally and physically, when defects of sight had been corrected.

The *Medical Review of Reviews* quotes the results of investigations conducted by Dr. Theodore Gelpe of Vienna, in which he states that 72 per cent. of feeble-minded children examined had been found possessed of extremely defective eyes, largely of a congenital character, capable of marked improvement by properly adapted glasses.

Dr. John J. Cronin, chief of division of school inspectors of New York City, reports that, out of 7,166 pupils examined, 33 per cent. were found to have defective sight; whereas in Philadelphia the health board recently recommended that the authorities provide funds for supplying suitable examinations and glasses to the large numbers of poor school children in need of them.

One of the frequently encountered defects is a marked deformity or subdevelopment of one eye, which, owing to the resultant low vision. and consequent non-use, leads either to its total loss, a condition of cross-eye, or the various phases of nerve-suffering and mental degeneration referred to.

During childhood, when development is as yet incomplete, nature sends to each function blood and nerve supply, not only for the purpose of enabling it to perform its work, but also to contribute to its growth. If, therefore, owing to a deformity or faulty development, an excessive activity is involved, a correspondingly excessive expenditure of nutrition and energy will result, depleting the part and interfering with its development.

The question presenting itself is, therefore: Can an effective and feasible means be provided by which these cass can be discovered? It has been found impracticable to accomplish this by means of specialists, as the task, owing to the large numbers involved, is a difficult, if not an impossible, one. Several years ago the speaker suggested a plan which, if carried into effect, would result in the discovery of at least many such afflicted pupils.

For this purpose the regular wall test-chart is used. As many pupils as possible are seated in two rows facing the wall, and about twenty feet away. The rest of the pupils leave the room. Each of these pupils is provided with a sheet of paper on which to write his name.

The pupils are now required to cover one eye with a handkerchief (or strips of muslin can be used), the teacher displays the test-chart on the wall, and the pupils are instructed to copy the test-letters thereon, holding up their hands when completed. Some will accomplish this task quickly, while others will hesitate and after considerable effort abandon the attempt. (The teacher can here obtain considerable information of their acuteness of vision.) When sufficient time has been allowed, the chart is removed, and the pupils are required to cover the other eye, when the reverse side of the chart, containing other letters, is displayed and copied in a similar manner. These papers will at once indicate the acuteness and accuracy of vision of each eye, those showing unsatisfactory results being later again submitted to the test.

Where one or the other eye is very deficient, the result will at once indicate it, and parents may be notified. The principal should always have this chart at hand for the purpose of investigating the eyes of the dull, non-studious, unruly, or truant scholar, which may frequently furnish evidence of inestimable value.

Experience has demonstrated that marked deformities of the eye are usually due to malformations of the skull, which the analytical observer readily learns to recognize; whereas those pupils having deeply wrinkled foreheads, or those complaining of periodical headaches, should always be suspected as being possessed of eye-defects, and be subjected to examination.

The following cases are typical and demonstrate possibilities. Two years ago a boy, thirteen years of age, was brought to me. His vision was stated to be satisfactory, but nerve disturbances, which had evidenced themselves since the first school year, had gradually become more marked, until they had developed into a well-defined condition of epilepsy, the boy having had several attacks of falling fits monthly. He had been under treatment for four years, without relief, whereas recently attacks had become more severe, and frequent. Examination revealed an extreme distortion of the left eyeball, with the vision in this eye very imperfect and accomplished at the cost of great strain, leading to acute headaches, if the eyes were used for any length of time. The correction of the defect by the requisite glass, and the enforced activity of the defective eye, gradually, not only brought vision in this eye up to the normal, but also contributed to such an extent to improved physical conditions that for the past eighteen months he has attended school regularly, which he had not been able to do for several years prior to this time, and the nerve disturbances have entirely disappeared, the boy not having had an attack in over a year, and his school percentage showing a marked advance.

The second case was that of a boy of twelve brought to me by one of our principals. He was the son of extremely poor parents, who ridiculed the idea of glasses. He was given to truancy, was difficult to control, was non-studious, and apparently was mentally deficient. The correction of an extreme anatomical deformity of both eyeballs by suitable glasses not only developed vision where he had been to all intents blind, so far as objects beyond ten feet were concerned, but also thwarted vicious tendencies, and he became fond of his studies, as was evidenced by the marked change in his percentages. He is now working after school hours, and his employers commend him and are interested in him, and I am firmly convinced that the boy's future has been largly influenced for good.

The third case was that of a young girl, aged sixteen, who, since her eighth year had suffered from periodical attacks of headache, which in recent years had been accompanied by digestive disturbances, evidencing themselves by acute nausea, which had defied medical treatment. An examination revealed the fact that, while the left eye was normal, the right was so defective in formation that well-defined vision was an impossibility. Upon being questioned, she insisted that her vision was perfect, since she was able to see test-letters both on the wall-chart and at reading distance. Upon being requested to hold her hand over her left eye, she for the first time realized that she had no vision in the right beyond the ability to perceive light. With the proper glass before this eye she could with difficulty vaguely discern letters one-half inch in size, when brought to within six inches of the eye, and these for only a minute, when they became blurred and then faded away. Why? Because, owing to the existing deformity, and consequent non-use, the visual functions in this eye had not devoloped. Spectacles containing an opaque glass before the normal eye, and the corrective lens before the deformed eye, were prescribed for exercise use. By this means the dormant eye was forced into activity for short periods at first, as exhaustion speedily evidenced itself. After the first week improvement was marked, and the eye could now read headlines in the paper for ten minutes. At the end of the second month the eye was able to read regular newspaper print for half an hour. At this time clear glass was placed before the good eye, and glasses have since been worn constantly. Recent examinations reveal the vision to be normal in the deformed eye through the corrective lens; but, what is most significant, headaches, nerve and stomach disturbauces have disappeared, and the general health is vastly improved.

This case would have been discovered instantly by the test suggested, because the girl could not see even the largest letters on the test-chart with the defective eye, whereas a study of facial proportions at once revealed a marked distortion of the right side of the face, due to a cranial deformity.

Can we contemplate these possibilities unmoved? How many children may be struggling on under your very eyes, condemned to live within a circumscribed mental as well as visual horizon, to whom science might give invaluable service, were it but appealed to?

Cultivate the ability to read aright the hieroglyphics graven by suffering upon the faces of the young. Note the faulty position assumed by some students, the extreme tilting to one side of the head, a disposition to squint until the eye is scarcely visible. Add to this the simple visual test suggested, and you will encounter, when you least suspect them, visual deficiencies, the correction of which will not only be of great value to the ones afflicted, but will also prove a fascinating and grateful field of research and lead to the discovery of new truths.

AROUND PARIS WITH THE INNOCENTS

KATHARINE ELISE CHAPMAN

As soon as you go to Paris, you begin to learn things. The discoveries which you make are not always put down in the guidebooks, but they are interesting. Among other matters, you view with wonder the seeming naïveté of the Frenchman in his affairs of locomotion: your railway ticket is demanded only *after* you have taken your ride; on the Underground you receive one which is never collected, and which you are blandly requested to put into a receptacle for litter; or you get your pocket-book filled with 'bus checks, which you keep awhile with the vague expectation that the inexorable law of France may some time demand them of you. All this has the zest of a new experience, although you may somewhat change your views when you become wiser.

You scale daily the steep height of the tramway, because in the attic you can best see the town, and see it at half-price; or you are tossed about on the upper floor of the two-storied 'buses. You are packed in with the crowd on the Underground, while you devoutly hope that the home-folks will never discover your crime in being a free-born American and traveling second class. You are hustled and jolted and bounced in a quiet and orderly Parisian way, but you enjoy every minute of it. You are seeing Paris. You are an Innocent, but you are learning. It is a most appetizing way of acquiring the French language, and it is a part of the course offered to the Chicago University Innocents.

The two strongest points in the instruction by Parisian teachers of the French language are the excursions and the lectures. As instruction in the tongue with them includes everything essentially French, their method gives opportunity for object-lessons on every hand. A merely tabular account of the excursions would read with as much exhilaration as a table of contents, or the dictionary, of which someone remarked that it was very informing, but the story wasn't good. For such information, see Baedeker.

M. Lesaunier, *professeur licencié ès lettres,* has for more than eight weeks been giving a delightful résumé of the times of Louis Quatorze, but the punctuation of these lectures has been the excursions. To visit Versailles and see the identical couch from which that Grand Monarch would rise to be robed in the full view of his awe-struck courtiers, makes the past very vivid, and gives one a nearer view of the character of the man. "No man is a hero to his valet," but somehow Louis Quatorze managed to remain a king, even if not a hero, in the sight of all his valets, which included his whole court.

To enter the crypt of Saint Dénis, and stand face to face with the white marble slab behind which hides the poor remnant of that arrogant pride which was brought low by the armies of Blenheim, is almost to stand within the shadow, at least, of the living form. The centuries drop away like a robe of gauze. You see the great Louis and Madame Maintenon. You see that flowing hair which graced the monarch's shoulders, to be super-seded later by the voluminous full-bottomed peruke—an orna-ment which must often have felt very warm about his neck and shoulders. You see him surrounded by his courtiers. You see Madame de Sevigné—"Ici est le tombeau de la reine, Marie Thérèse," drones the guide, and you shake off with a start the seventeenth-century wig which has somehow crept around your own shoulders.

As you pass through, the crypt of Saint Dénis throbs with the great heart-beat of those past centuries. They can almost be heard when you stand before the great central vault where the poor marred body of Marie Antoinette found a final resting-place, after the Revolution had spent its wrath on the kings and queens entombed within. But Saint Dénis is only one of the object-lessons which the student of French finds on every hand. There is the chateau of Vincennes, whose empty fosse and stern donjon tower now smile so peacefully in the sunshine. On its southern battlements the young trees are growing, and vines fall gracefully over the wall. Yet it has played its grim part in

French history from the time of Saint Louis until the *coup d'état* of Louis Napoleon in 1851. There is Fontainebleau and there is Barbazon; there are Versailles and the Great and Little Trianon, rich in pathetic memories; there are the Luxembourg, the Place Vendôme, the Place d'Étoile—to enter any one of which is to link the life of France today with the spirit of the past.

But this is not all. These lectures in French history are not merely records of kings and of wars. France gracefully turns another side to the world in filling her old, disused palaces with the productions of genius, as well as adding new structures to hold her wealth of art. Among these, one, of course, thinks first of the Louvre and the Panthéon, either of which might be made the mistress of one's life-devotion, and which it would be a mere impertinence to describe in a few inadequate sentences.

There is still another side. There are the churches and cathedrals of France, which, of all its constructions, are the most profound exposition of the life which has flowed and surged and throbbed along the years. To view from without the massive bulk of Notre Dame with its flying buttresses is to realize, as never before, that those mediaeval piles were the concrete embodiment of a prayer. The grotesque gargoyles do not look devotional, it is true; but they are the fitting form for the blind and ignorant petitions of superstition. Some twentieth-century prayers may seem as distorted to angel vision. But the impression as a whole is a great uplift. Then stand within, where the transept, in crossing the nave, is bathed in the smile from the great rose windows, and you will surely know that the thought of the architecture was only to provide the means to an end. Those old builders *felt* the worship for which they built the shrine. And they built better than they knew; for the reverent calm and holy awe of this still place could not have failed to leave its impress, not only upon the generations of worshipers, but also upon the tide of sightseers which has since swept through the great nave.

One of the first things which the Innocent learns in going about Paris alone is the real good-nature and kind-heartedness of the people. This is not mere surface varnish. The politeness for which they are famed is only the outward guise of the inner instinct. When a lady, on coming out of her own Catholic service on Sunday morning, goes a block out of her way to show you the Protestant chapel, and stands with voluble gestures until she sees you heading in the right direction, she has nothing to gain by it but a good conscience. The Parisian will reply to your blocked-up French in halting English, doing his best to make you understand, in the cheerful and ubiquitous "oui, madame," with the accent on the last syllable. Good-nature and kindness of heart may not be the loftiest virtues of humanity, but they are pleasant virtues with which to come in contact in a strange land. It is sometimes said that Johnny Crapaud has his business instincts and his eye to the main chance; but one meets the same condition everywhere in Europe. In fact, it is whispered that the United States is the only land where absolute disinterestedness reigns; where the pocket-book hath no charms, and the almighty dollar is only a figure of speech.

Such have the Innocents found Johnny Crapaud—and have liked him; shutting their unaccustomed eyes to the things which have looked to them decidedly "queer," and feeling that it is hardly possible to obtain an omniscient opinion of a great people in a few short weeks.

The art-life of France as shown in her literature could hardly find a better exponent than M. Debussy, who has been for a number of weeks working through the field of the modern French dramatists. In delicacy of touch and expression M. Debussy reflects so well the literature amid which he has lived that he is himself an artist in words. Both M. Debussy and M. Lesaunier are men of deep and broad cultivation, and speak such exquisite French that to meet each of them for four hours weekly is in itself a comprehensive study of the language. The same may be said of all the lecturers of the course.

M. Schrader, himself one of the eminent men of France, at the invitation of his long-time friend, Mme. Fauconnet, has most courteously contributed a few lectures upon ethnology in its relation to the physical features of the earth; illustrating them by such precision of gesture and such clearness of enunciation as almost to give ears to the deaf, and understanding to the incapable. In his last lecture he dwelt upon the fact, already recognized by sociologists, that population, having touched the extreme west of the American continent, was bound to overflow in other directions. Following the line of the least resistance, and ever stretching westward, he said, population and commerce would at last reach the golden zone where West becomes East again, and, sweeping over, would rouse the ancient civilization of China from its long sleep by more perfect intercommunion with younger races.

M. Schneider, of the Paris Conservatory of Music, also courteously gave an evening in the salon as a compliment to the "Jeunes Américaines." His subject was the development of the theme in modern music, with illustrations upon the piano. Curiously enough, nearly all of his interpretations were from German composers. Truly, there is no fatherland in music, but as it draws its inspiration from all peoples, so it unites all upon the common basis of its enchantment. Beginning with the first simple theme of a fugue by Bach, he moved down the line through Mozart and Beethoven to Chopin, weaving in and out, as he advanced, the intricate web of variations which have gathered around the theme. In concluding, he gracefully called the attention of the ladies to César Franck, asking them to carry back to America with them the recollection that France had now a composer who was destined to place her in the front rank of musical attainment.

It would not be possible to omit from the *Wanderjahr* story of the University Innocents a hint or two about the snug and quiet nest to which they flutter home after their journeyings. Any home in France must be an object of interest to an American; but the *pensionnat* of Mme. Fauconnet has attractions which are unique enough for even a news article. Ascending the stone steps from the garden all abloom, you enter an ample hallway, with a door at your right opening into Madame's office. Here you may see her at almost any hour in the day, busy among her papers, the competent woman of affairs; although after dinner in the evening she often appears as the graceful and cordial

hostess.   Passing through another door to the right, you come
upon the vestibule containing the staircase.   Springing from the
ground floor, a story lower down, it ascends in spirals, with its
two branches leading off in other directions, so suggestive of
something fascinatingly different—some hidden nook or charming corner.   From other doors near the staircase you may look
out upon the long school buildings with refectory and schoolrooms and music-rooms; and above, the dormitories, with their
seemingly endless succession of neat white beds, fitting snug-
geries for youth and innocence.   You may see the quadrangle
formed by the buildings, making the school-yard.   There in the
middle stands a glorious old tree, and other trees hang over the
graceful latticed fence which is the inner defense, so to speak, of
this green-walled citadel.   It would never do to let either prying
eyes or desecrating feet roam in these sacred precincts where the
daughters of France are kept like articles of Sèvres china.   So
we will turn our feet and our glances for a moment to the room
where the Innocents spend their morning hours at the lectures.
It is large and light, and the long French windows swing open
inwardly and look foreign and enticing.   Here the Innocents
are seated, with the slightly furrowed brow of deep thought and
attention, as the sentences flow out from the lips of the lecturer
in sonorous accents.   But the door opens, and Mlle. Ashléman
enters, accompanied by Mme. Fauconnet, who greets with a warm
pressure of the hand each member of the party.   The Innocents
have one and all agreed that they have been surprisingly fortunate
in coming into close contact with this lady, who, although of a
land so different from ours in its customs and traditions, displays such unusual breadth of mind and such genuine kindness
of heart.   Instead of censuring, she has been ever ready to
sympathize, fully recognizing the individuality and yielding,
when possible, to the wishes of each.   One of the pleasantest
recollections of this so fruitful summer in after-years will be the
charming hospitality of this woman of France, who sets forth
so beautifully the truth that womanliness need not be the
exclusive possession of one nation, but is rather the blessed
and universal gift to the race.

READING FOR LITTLE CHILDREN

ELSIE AMY WYGANT
Third Year, University Elementary School

The children in the second grade have made a portfolio to hold reading-slips, and under this cover the major part of the reading will be found.

These particular slips cover three general types: the words of the songs they are singing; some poems and jingles not found in any one book; and the first of a series of sketches taken from Waterloo's *Story of Ab,* published by Doubleday & McClure Co., New York. The sketches are taken from the original text, in so far as the necessary simplicity of the beginnings of reading will allow. A part of the *Story of Ab* is told or read to the children directly from Waterloo's story; then the children supplement this by their own reading of the following sketches. This brings to their efforts at reading the impetus which the dramatic element and literary quality in the story itself furnish, and only in so far as it calls up that larger background is it valuable.

Some of the rhymes are selected for memory-work; others (taken from Edward Lear's *Nonsense Books,* published by Little & Brown, Boston), for the sake of the fun they hold. Childish humor, because it is so far from subtle, so wearisome in its repetition, and so often pointless, bores, embarrasses, and teases the average grown-up, and is neglected not only in the home, but also in the whole educational system. It is as food for this very positive appetite of children that the Lear limericks are chosen.

The children will include also in their portfolio the selections made from Christina Rossetti's *Sing Song,* which appeared last April in this magazine. In addition to the reading-slips are used:

Heart of Oak Series, Vols. I and II (D. C. Heath & Co.).

Garden of Verse (Rand, McNally & Co.).

Eskimo Stories, by Mary E. Smith (Rand, McNally & Co.).

Tree Man and *Early Cave Man,* by Miss Dopp (Rand, McNally & Co.).

Stories for Children, by Mrs. Lane (American Book Co.).

Little Black Sambo and *Peter Rabbit* (Warne Co., New York).

The above volumes are used because they offer material helpful in the work that is being done. Few will be read through, but selections will be made from all.

Copies of Perry Pictures are used as illustrations in the portfolio.

I. WORDS OF SONGS

SEPTEMBER

(Music by Eleanor Smith in *Songs of Life and Nature*)

The goldenrod is yellow,
   The corn is turning brown,
The trees in apple orchards
   With fruit are bending down;

The gentians' bluest fringes
   Are curling in the sun;
In dusty pods the milkweed
   Its hidden silk has spun;

The sedges flaunt their harvest
   In every meadow nook,
And asters by the brookside
   Make asters in the brook;

From dewy lanes at morning
   The grapes' sweet odors rise;
At noon the road's aflutter
   With yellow butterflies.

By all these lovely tokens
   September's days are here,
With summer's best of weather,
   And autumn's best of cheer.

H. H.

HARVEST SONG

(French Folk Song found in *Natural Music Course for Elementary Grades,*
Published by Ginn & Co.)

O'er our fields the frost has descended.
　　Labor is done; gone is the sun;
Safely stored, the harvest is ended—
　　All in a ring, dancing we sing.

She who leads is innocent pleasure,
　　Ending the year gladly with cheer;
Joy and comfort, barns full of treasure—
　　Everywhere health, season's ripe wealth.

THE CHESTNUT

(Music by Frank Atkinson, from *Songs in Season*)

I live in a little brown house—
　　With velvet and fur it is lined.
I am hid like a little grey mouse,
　　And my door is tight-shut you will find.

But when I am really full grown
　　With a shell and a sweet little core,
And my house is as hard as a stone,
　　Jack Frost then will open the door.

ALICE'S SUPPER

(Music by Eleanor Smith, in *Songs for Little Children*)

Far down in the valley the wheat grows deep,
And the reapers are making their cradles sweep;
And this is the song that I hear them sing
While cheery and loud their voices ring:
" 'Tis the finest wheat that ever did grow,
　　And it is for Alice's supper, ho! ho!"

Far down in the valley the old mill stands,
And the miller is rubbing his dusty hands,
And these are the words I hear him say
As he watches the mill-stones grinding away:
" 'Tis the finest flour that money can buy,
　　And it is for Alice's supper, hi! hi!"

Downstairs in the kitchen the fire doth glow,
And the cook is kneading the soft, white dough,
And this is the song she is singing today
As merry and busy she works away:
" 'Tis the finest dough whether near or far,
And it is for Alice's supper, ha! ha!"

To the nursery now comes mother at last,
And what in her hand is she bringing so fast?
'Tis a plateful of something all yellow and white,
And she sings as she comes with her smile so bright:
" 'Tis the best bread and butter I ever did see,
And it is for Alice's supper, he! he!"

———

MISTRESS COW

(Music by Neidlinger, found in *Earth, Sky and Air in Song*. Words arranged)

Mistress Cow stands at the gate—
Every evening she will wait—
Calling slow, calling low,
        "M—m—m."

Now the boy calls: "So, boss, So!
Did you think I would not come?"
And she answers, "M—m,"
As he leads her off toward home.

There they milk the good old cow,
And she fills the foaming pail—
Butter, cheese, and cream for us
She will give and never fail.

Mistress Cow stands at the gate—
Every morning she will wait—
Calling slow, calling low,
        "M—m—m."

WAKE, VIOL AND FLUTE

(Music by E. Richter, found in Second Book, *Modern Music Series*)

Wake, viol and flute!
Gay horn, be not mute!
The harvest is over, the grain and the clover,
Ripe fruit from the tree,
All garnered have we.

Our broad fields we plowed,
We harrowed and sowed,
We toiled on together in fair and foul weather.
Our labor was blessed,
Now sweet is our rest.

Wake, viol and flute!
Gay horn, be not mute!
While dancing and singing sweet pleasure are bringing,
Let all the world come
To keep Harvest Home!

HURRAH, BOYS!

(Music by Angelica Hartmann, in Second Book, *Modern Music Series*)

Hurrah, boys, hurrah! the grapes at last have grown
    The ploughs and the harrows
    Lie still in the furrows—
Their labor is done, the harvest has begun.

Hurrah boys, hurrah! the grapes at last have grown
As purple and mellow as evening's dark shadow.
    The meadow is strown
    With hay but newly mown.

Hurrah, boys, hurrah! now comes to all the earth
A time of thanksgiving and sociable living
    Of innocent mirth
    Around the crackling hearth.

II. POEMS AND RHYMES

HOW THE LEAVES CAME DOWN

I'll tell you how the leaves came down.
  The great Tree to his children said:
"You're getting sleepy, Yellow and Brown,
    Yes, very sleepy, little Red;
    It is quite time you went to bed."

"Ah!" begged each silly pouting leaf,
  "Let us a little longer stay;
Dear Father Tree, behold our grief,
    'Tis such a very pleasant day
    We do not want to go away."

So just for one more merry day
  To the great Tree the leaflets clung,
Frolicked and danced and had their way,
    Upon the autumn breezes swung,
    Whispering all their sports among,

"Perhaps the great Tree will forget
  And let us stay until the spring,
If we all beg and coax and fret."
    But the great Tree did no such thing—
    He smiled to hear their whispering.

"Come, children, all to bed," he cried;
  And ere the leaves could urge their prayer
He shook his head and far and wide,
    Fluttering and dancing everywhere,
    Down sped the leaflets through the air.

I saw them on the ground—they lay
  Golden and red, a huddled swarm,
Waiting till one from far away,
    White bed-clothes heaped upon her arm,
    Should come to wrap them safe and warm.

The great bare Tree looked down and smiled,
"Good-night, dear little leaves," he said;
And from below each sleepy child
    Replied, "Goodnight," and murmured,
"It is so nice to go to bed."

Susan Coolidge

THE SNOWBIRD

In the rosy light trills the gay swallow,
    The thrush in the roses below;
The meadow-lark sings in the meadow,
    But the snowbird sings in the snow.
            Ah me!
            Chickadee!
The snowbird sings in the snow!

The blue martin trills in the gable,
    The wren in the gourd below;
In the elm flutes the golden robin,
    But the snowbird sings in the snow.
            Ah me!
            Chickadee!
The snowbird sings in the snow!

—Part selected from Hezekiah Butterworth's "Snowbird"

THANKSGIVING DAY

Over the river and through the woods
To grandfather's house we go;
    The horse knows the way
    To carry the sleigh
Through the white and drifted snow.
Over the river and through the woods—
Oh how the wind does blow!
    It stings the toes
    And bites the nose,
As over the ground we go.

Over the river and through the woods
Trot fast, my dapple-gray!
Spring over the ground
Like a hunting hound!
For this is Thanksgiving Day.

Over the river and through the woods
And straight through the barn-yard gate.
We seem to go
Extremely slow—
It is so hard to wait!
Over the river and through the woods
Now gandfather's cap I spy!
Hurrah for the fun!
Is the pudding done?
Hurrah for the pumpkin-pie!

LYDIA MARIA CHILD

A THANKSGIVING FABLE

It was a hungry pussy-cat upon Thanksgiving morn,
That watched a thankful little mouse that ate an ear of corn.
"If I ate that thankful little mouse, how thankful he should be
When he has made a meal himself to make a meal for me!
Then with his thanks for having fed and his thanks for feeding
    me,
With all *his* thankfulness inside how thankful I shall be!"
Thus mused the hungry pussy-cat, upon Thanksgiving Day:
But the little mouse had overheard and declined (with thanks)
    to stay.   OLIVER HERFORD

LIMERICKS

There was an Old Man of the Coast
Who placidly sat on a post;
But when it was cold he relinquished his hold,
And called for some hot buttered toast.

There was an Old Person of Rheims
Who was troubled with horrible dreams;
So to keep him awake they fed him with cake,
Which amused that Old Person of Rheims.

There was an Old Man of Dundee
Who lived in the top of a tree;
When disturbed by the crows he abruptly arose
And exclaimed: "I'll return to Dundee.'

There was a Young Lady of Bute
Who played on a silver-gilt flute;
She played several jigs to her uncle's white pigs,
That amusing Young Lady of Bute.

EDWARD LEAR

THE OWL AND THE PUSSY-CAT

I

The Owl and the Pussy-cat went to sea
  In a beautiful pea-green boat;
They took some honey and plenty of money
  Wrapped up in a five-pound note.
The Owl looked up to the moon above
  And sang to a small guitar:
"Oh lovely Pussy! Oh Pussy my love,
  What a beautiful pussy you are!"

II

Pussy said to the Owl: "You elegant fowl!
  How wonderful sweet you sing!
Oh let us be married—too long we have tarried—
  But what shall we do for a ring?"
They sailed away for a year and a day
  To the land where the Bong tree grows,
And there in a wood a piggy-wig stood
  With a ring at the end of his nose,
      His nose,
  With a ring at the end of his nose.

III

"Dear Pig, are you willing to sell for one shilling
   Your ring?" Said the piggy: "I will."
So they took it away and were married next day
   By the turkey who lives on the hill.
They dined upon mince and slices of quince
   Which they ate with a runcible spoon;
And hand in hand on the edge of the sand
   They danced by the light of the moon,
         The moon,
  They danced by the light of the moon.

EDWARD LEAR

CALICO PIE

I

Calico pie,
The little birds fly
Down to the calico tree :
Their wings were blue,
And they sang "tilly-loo!"
Till away they flew:
And they never came back to me!
   They never came back,
   They never came back,
They never came back to me!

II

Calico jam,
The little fish swam
Over the Syllabub Sea.
He took off his hat
To the Sole and the Sprat,
And the Willeby-wat;
But he never came back to me!
   He never came back,
   He never came back,
He never came back to me!

III

Calico ban,
The little mice ran
To be ready in time for tea;
Flippity flup,
They drank it all up,
And danced in the cup;
But they never came back to me!
    They never came back,
    They never came back.
They never came back to me!

IV

Calico drum,
The grasshoppers come,
The butterfly, beetle, and bee.
Over the ground,
Around and round,
With a hop and a bound;
But they never came back to me!
    They never came back,
    They never came back,
They never came back to me!

EDWARD LEAR

III. STORIES ADAPTED FROM STANLEY WATERLOO'S "STORY OF AB"

I. A LITTLE BROWN BABY

A long, long time ago a little brown baby lived in a forest.

He lived with his father and mother in a cave.

This cave was on the side of a river bank.

Above and about the cave was a deep forest.

A steep slope of 150 feet led down from the cave to the river below.

The front of the cave was blocked with great rocks; only a narrow entrance was left.

A fire burned in front of this entrance.

This was Ab the brown baby's home.

II. INSIDE THE CAVE

Inside the cave was a great rock room.

The room was 20 feet square and 15 feet high.

Ledges of rock jutted out into the room.

Ab's mother, Red-Spot, used these for shelves.

A beam of light fell on the floor.

The light came through a hole in the roof.

This hole was a chimney.

Ab's father dug it down from the level ground above.

It let in the light and it let out the smoke.

Below this hole a fire burned.

It lighted up the dark corners of the cave.

It showed a bed of leaves in one corner.

The bed was covered with skins.

Here Ab slept at night.

III. A MEAL IN THE CAVE

One day Ab and his father and mother had been out in the forest.

Toward night they came home.

The cave was dark.

Red embers glowed in the fire-place.

Red-Spot threw twigs and dried leaves on the embers.

Soon there was a roaring fire.

Little Ab rolled on the earthen floor and crowed in the fire-light.

One-Ear, Ab's father, pointed to something in the corner.

It was a hind quarter of wild horse.

Red-Spot laughed when she saw it.

She pointed to a shelf on the side of the cave.

There were nuts and berries and wild honey.

She had gathered them in the afternoon while Ab was asleep.

Now they would have a fine meal.

She tossed nuts on the embers.

Pop! pop! pop! the nuts began to roast.

One-Ear cut the meat in strips.

He stuck them on pointed sticks to broil over the fire.

How good it smelled.

Soon the meal was ready.

They ate and then lay down on the bed of leaves to sleep.

IV. THE FOREST AT NIGHT

It was still in the cave.

But outside it was not so still.

Great beasts glided through the dark forest.

The wild horse and elk and bison came from the forest to drink at the river.

The cave bear and the fierce cave tiger came out to hunt.

The rhinoceros trumped in the river.

The wolves howled in the darkness.

Yet all this time Ab and Red-Spot and One-Ear slept in the cave.

They were well-fed and warm and safe.

No beast larger than a wild cat could get through the narrow entrance.

And even they would not for the entrance was barred.

No beast that ever lived dared face that entrance—for it was barred with fire.

All night pine knots flickered and flamed at the narrow entrance.

So the three in the cave were safe.

LE JEU UN FACTEUR IMPORTANT DANS L'EN-SEIGNEMENT D'UNE LANGUE

LORLEY ADA ASHLÉMAN
School of Education

[The following *rondes*, the first three of an alphabetical series, are folklore of France and historical, adapted, however, to the needs of the School of Education, where they have been tested and have met with the greatest success.—THE EDITORS.]

"Le jeu est le plus haut degré du développement de l'enfant."—Froebel.

"Le jeu n'est pas une chose frivole pour l'enfant mais une chose d'une profonde signification. C'est dans le jeu, qui est sa principale occupation, qu'il donne librement carrière à toutes ses aptitudes. C'est là qu'il nous révèle les dispositions les plus intimes de son âme."—G. Compayré.

Les jeux et les rondes sont le développement naturel du besoin inné que l'enfant a d'agir et de se mouvoir, besoin qu'il faut satisfaire si la jeunesse doit développer ses forces et ses facultés.

Si un enfant doit apprendre une langue vivante, il est de toute nécessité de commencer de très bonne heure. Il y a pour cela des raisons physiques et psychologiques. Les enfants ont l'ouïe plus prompte, les cordes vocales ont chez lui, plus que chez les adultes, une tendance à imiter de nouveaux sons. Un homme, qui, avant sa maturité, n'a jamais appris à danser ne dansera jamais avec le même naturel et la même aisance que l'homme qui a dansé dès son enfance. Il en est de même pour l'étude d'une langue.

Les Français disent, que, passé seize ans, un étranger n'arrivera pas à parler français comme un Français.

L'enfant dans les conditions ordinaires, a un laisser-aller, je ne sais quoi d'inconscient, agent d une importance capitale dans l'étude d'une langue étrangère. Chez lui, il y en a un autre de non moindre importance, son amour pour l'action. L'enfant s'absorbe tellement dans son jeu, qu'inconsciemment il le met en pratique dans une langue autre que la sienne.

L'enfant ne peut apprendre une langue rien qu'en répétant ce qu'il a entendu. L'oreille seule ne peut lui donner la sensation du terme dont il s'agit. Par tous les moyens possibles, il doit

288

saisir une pensée et la faire sienne, en l'émettant au dehors, non d'une seule manière, mais par des modes divers et variés. Le maître doit donc se servir des jeux, comme d'un moyen qu'il a toujours à sa disposition. La mise en drame des sujets tirés de la vie scolaire et qui peuvent se prêter à cette forme d'expression, constitue sans aucun doute, le moyen le plus vrai, le plus capable d'éveiller chez l'enfant quelque intérêt pour une autre langue.

En outre l'enfant acquerra ainsi le vocabulaire employé dans la langue familière, la langue du foyer, la langue de la conversation dont Monsieur Cutting, Professeur à l'Université de Chicago, a montré la nécessité d'une manière si claire, si définitive. "Ce n'est pas dans les formes pompeuses de la littérature, mais dans le langage du foyer, des magasins, et dans les réunions de famille que se déroule la chaîne des idiomes, expression de la pensée nationale. N'embrassant q'une très minime partie du vocabulaire, la tendance nationale est le trait le plus significatif que rencontre l'étudiant des langues."

Les idiomes ne se prêtent guère à l'argumentation, il faut les acquérir à un âge où les choses s'impriment d'une manière naturelle et profonde. Le plaisir que l'enfant éprouve en s'exprimant au moyen de la musique facilite grandement l'association du son à la signification du terme. Il imite ignorant encore que les sons ont un sens. Quand l'expression de la physionomie, le geste, l'action lui font comprendre la signification, il désire encore plus ardemment produire des sons nouveaux.

Les jeux, les chants, et les rondes sont des genres d'activités qui conviennent aux enfants. Ces rondes, chants, etc., ne sont pas des choses artificielles. Non seulement l'enfant travaille, il y met tout son cœur et toute son énergie à les acquérir. Comme il comprend et exprime les actions des hommes et des animaux, non seulement, il exerce les organes aux moyens desquels nous apprenons une langue, mais il a une connaissance plus grande des faits qui les concernent. L'enfant, ayant ainsi travaillé mentalement et physiquement dans une société différente de la sienne, aura un intérêt qui s'élargira et le mettra à même de mieux comprendre ses semblables, quelle que soit leur nationalité.

"La langue qu'il a étudiée sans en avoir conscience, dans ses récréations et sous la direction de son maître, lui fournira un instrument de grand prix dans les études indépendentes qu'il fera plus tard.

A. AVIGNON

Le Pont d'Avignon

Les enfants entrent dans la salle deux à deux.

Ils chantent:

> Sur le pont d'Avignon
> On y danse, on y danse;
> Sur le pont d'Avignon,
> Tout le monde y danse en rond.

Les deux directeurs du jeu forment le pont en se tenant par les deux mains, qu'ils élèvent le plus possible, les enfants passent dessous, puis ils se tournent en rond en se tenant par la main.

> Sur le pont d'Avignon
> On y danse, on y danse;
> Sur le pont d'Avignon,
> Tout le monde y danse en rond.

Les enfants se quittent la main et en continuant de chanter les fillettes imitent les manières des belles dames, en saluant à droite, puis à gauche.

> Les belles dames font comme ça
> Et puis encore comme ça.

Les enfants se reprennent les mains, ils sautent en s'avançant vers le milieu du cercle.

> Sur le pont d'Avignon
> On y danse, on y danse;
> Sur le pont d'Avignon,
> Tout le monde y danse en rond.

On s'arrête en se quittant les mains. Les garçons imitent les manières des beaux messieurs, en saluant à droite, puis à gauche.

> Les beaux messieurs font comme ça
> Et puis encore comme ça.

Les enfants font volte face, les jeunes filles se placent devant les garçons et tout le cercle saute en avant, chantant:

> Sur le pont, etc.

On s'arrête et les fillettes imitent les manières des paysannes en saluant à droite, puis à gauche.

> Les paysannes font comme ça
> Et puis encore comme ça.

Les garçons se placent devant les fillettes et le cercle saute en avant.

Sur le pont, etc.

On s'arrête et les garçons imitent les manières des paysans en saluant à droite, puis à gauche.

Les paysans font comme ça
Et puis encore comme ça.

On se reprend les mains, avançant deux à deux.

Sur le pont, etc.

On s'arrête et tous les enfants font le salut militaire.

Les soldats font comme ça
Et puis encore comme ça.

On se reprend les mains. Les enfants sortent de la salle deux à deux en sautant et en chantant:

Sur le pont d'Avignon
On y danse, on y danse;
Sur le pont d'Avignon,
Tout le monde y danse en rond.

VOCABULAIRE

le pont, the bridge	*font*, do
on, they, people, we, one	*comme ça*, like this
danse, dance	*les beaux messieurs*, the handsome
y, there	gentlemen
tout le monde, everybody	*les paysannes*, the peasant women
en rond, in a circle	*les paysans*, the peasant men
les belles dames, the beautiful ladies	*les soldats*, the soldiers

B.   BERGÈRE

IL ÉTAIT UNE BERGÈRE

Les paroles de cette ronde sont simples, et par conséquent adaptées d'une manière toute particulière à l'enfance. Les matériaux et l'action elle-même sont si variés qu'ils affectent plus ou moins directement chaque enfant en particulier. Le jeu se pratique comme suit:

On forme un grand cercle. "Attention," dit le directeur du jeu. "Harold vous êtes le mouton, Catherine, la maman mouton et Frédéric, le bébé mouton."

Il n'y a qu'une famille entière qui puisse satisfaire les enfants, et le bébé est l'un des traits les plus importants.   Une partie du cercle doit figurer la colline.   Un banc d'école à l'autre bout du cercle représente la cuisine de la bergère.   Un grand altère représente la barette.

Le directeur: "Donald, vous êtes le chien de la bergerie— gardez bien les moutons!"

Le directeur: "Marguerite, vous êtes le petit chat."

Le cercle saute gaîment et chante la petite chanson qui imite le ron-ron d'un chat.

I

Il était une bergère
Et ron, ron, ron, petit patapon,
Il était une bergère
Qui gardait ses moutons, ron, ron
Qui gardait ses moutons.

Les moutons maintenant rassasiés s'étendent et s'endorment, et le chien les garde.   La bergère entre dans la maison et se met à faire le fromage.   Le petit chaton se glisse en tapinois et essaie de s'appprocher de la baratte.   Lé cercle danse en marchant en sens inverse.

II

Elle fit un fromage,
Et ron, ron, ron, petit patapon,
Elle fit un fromage
Du lait de ses moutons, ron, ron
Du lait de ses moutons.

Le cercle se sépare.

III

Le chat qui la regarde,
Et ron, ron, ron, petit patapon,
Le chat qui la regarde
D'un petit air fripon, ron, ron
D'un petit air fripon.

Le cercle s'arrête et la bergère chante:

IV

Si tu y mets la patte
Et ron, ron, ron, petit patapon,
Si tu y mets la patte

Tu auras du bâton, ron, ron
Tu auras du bâton.

La bergère se retourne pour chercher un fromage; le chaton s'approche de la baratte; il y met le menton.

Le cercle chante:

V

Il n'y mit pas la patte
Et ron, ron, ron, petit patapon,
Il n'y mit pas la patte
Il y mit le menton, ron, ron
Il y mit le menton.

La bergère revenant sur ses pas, aperçoit le chaton et s'empare de son bâton. Le chat très effrayé à la vue du bâton se sauve, la bergère essaie de l'attraper au grand plaisir du cercle.

VOCABULAIRE

l était, there was
une bergère, a shepherdess
qui gardait, who was minding
ses moutons, her sheep
elle fit, she made
un fromage, a cheese
du lait, with the milk
de ses moutons, of her sheep
le chat, the cat
la regarde, is looking at her
la baratte, the churn
la crême, the cream
le lait du beurre, butter-milk

d'un petit air fripon, with a mischievous air
la patte, the paw
mettre, to put
je mets, I put
si tu y mets la patte, if you put your paw in it
tu auras du bâton, you shall feel the stick
il y mit le menton, he put his nose (chin) in it.
le beurre salè, the salted butter
traire la vache, to milk the cow
lait écrêmé, skimmed milk

C. CHOUX

Une Chanson Mimée Qui Amuse Beaucoup les Enfants

Sur le devant de la salle se trouvent les solistes. Pas trop éloigné d'elles, on remarque cinq enfants. Devant le premier enfant se trouve un panier rempli de choux. Le chœur est au fond de la salle.

Première soliste: "Savez-vous planter les choux, à la mode,
à la mode,
Savez-vous planter les choux, à la mode
de chez vous?"

(Le premier enfant s'avance avec le panier de choux.)

Le chœur: "On les plante avec les mains, à la mode,
à la mode,
On les plante avec les mains à la mode
de chez nous."
(L'enfant sort les choux du panier, les plante devant les so-
listes, puis il se rend à sa place.)
Deuxième soliste: "Savez-vous planter les choux, à la mode,
à la mode,
Savez-vous planter les choux, à la mode
de chez vous?"
(Le second enfant s'avance, les pouces en l'air.)
Le chœur: "On les plante avec les pouces, à la mode,
à la mode,
On les plante avec les pouces, à la mode
de chez nous."
(L'enfant fait le geste indiqué, puis il se rend à sa place.)
Troisième soliste: " Savez-vous planter les choux, etc."
(Le troisième enfant s'avance, les coudes en l'air.)
Le chœur: "On les plante avec les coudes, à la
mode, à la mode,
On les plante avec les coudes à la mode
de chez nous."
(L'enfant fait le geste indiqué, puis il rejoint ses camarades.)
Quatrième soliste: "Savez-vous planter les choux, etc."
(Le quatrième enfant s'avance en sautant.)
Le chœur: "On les plante avec les pieds, à la mode,
à la mode,
On les plante avec les pieds, à la mode
de chez nous."
(L'enfant saute sur les choux.)
Cinquième soliste: "Savez-vous planter les choux, etc."
(Le cinquième enfant s'avance, l'index sur le nez.)
Le chœur: "On les plante avec le nez, à la mode, à la
mode,
On les plante avec le nez, à la mode de
chez nous."
(Il fait le geste indiqué.)

Toutes les solistes: "Savez-vous planter les choux, etc."
(Les cinq enfants s'avancent et s'agenouillent devant les solistes.)

Le chœur: "On les plante à vos genoux, à la mode,
                         à la mode.
                   On les plante à vos genoux, à la mode de
                         chez nous."

(Chaque enfant prend un chou et sort de la salle. Les solistes les suivent.)

VOCABULAIRE

les choux, the cabbages
planter, to plant
je plante, I plant, I am planting
on plante, one plants
on les plante, one plants them
savez-vous? do you know how?
je sais, I know how
je ne sais pas, I do not know how
la mode, the fashion; the manner
à la mode, in the fashion

à la mode de chez nous, in the manner
  of our country
à la mode de chez vous, in the manner
  of your country
chez nous, at home, in our house
le nez, the nose
le coude, the elbow
les pouces, the thumbs
les pieds, the feet
les mains, the hands

les genoux, the knees.

A WINTER SONG

Words and melody by pupils in Grade IV, the University Elementary School

1. The dear old win - ter - time is here, The
2. The wind comes whis - tling thro' the trees, With

happiest time of all the year. The chil - dren get their
flakes of snow in ev - 'ry breeze. The chil - dren all are

sleds and play All thro' the long and hap - py day.
hap - py and bright, Un - til they're snug in their beds at night.

EDITORIAL NOTES

"I shot an arrow into the air"—

There is great diversity of opinion as to what constitutes an Opportunity. There are those who say she is a skittish jade

Opportunity in Poetry
that dances for a moment before the dazzled eyes of bewildered mortals, and then vanishes into the ether never more to return. This was the view of the late Senator Ingalls from Kansas, who embodied his idea in the "Great American Sonnet." In this, he said she tinkles the door-bell but once, or words to that effect, and if Buttons happens to be off duty for the moment, she goes careering on her scornful way. Whether true or false, this notion works up well into poetry, and the senator caught his Opportunity when he dropped state-craft long enough to write that verse. The chances are that as "the tooth o' Time" gnaws his fame away, the part political will be to the part poetical as oatmeal to grapenuts.

Others say, though, this view is entirely wrong; that Opportunity wanders about in every neighborhood with the patience

Opportunity in Blank Verse
of a tithing-man and the persistence of a book-agent; that she all but batters in the panels of the front door, and, failing entrance there, she goes around to the back and kicks and bangs until driven off by the dog. These ideas, so directly opposed to each other, show that there is considerable guesswork concerning this elusive wench, and the ordinary man may be reasonably excused if perchance he sometimes misses *his* Opportunity.

It is the purpose here, however, to set forth a case about which there shall be no doubt; that is, to present an unmistakable

Opportunity in Prose
Opportunity. This particular one is not to be of the winged-heeled, nervous, thistle-down type referred to in the Kansas senator's poetry. It is of the stalwart, beef-fed, ruddy-hued, portly kind that takes an apartment and settles down to make the acquaintance of the solid citizens.

It is the Opportunity to found an institution, mainly for children, that shall embody the best that we now have in the school, the home, the library, the park, the business house, the bank, the prison, and the reformatory. This institution is to be founded, constructed, and maintained according to the following bill of particulars.

1. It must be free for all, from the goo-goo grade up, who have time to spare and a desire to make good use of it. Nobody will graduate, because no one will exhaust the possibilities of the place nor the chances for work. There will be just plain living on and on from day to day —no quitters.

Specifications for a School

2. It will be fitted for work in arts and in crafts to meet the taste and the several abilities of the people. The occupations found in human society at large will be born here and carried as far as possible.

3. The building, therefore, will partake largely of the workshop character in which each shop will be a studio of art. It will have its museum for collections, in which there will also be a warehouse and salesroom attachments through which the products of the place can be sold. It will have a library with study-rooms adjoining for the reinforcement of the work of the place with all that books can give. A gymnasium, baths, and rest-rooms will be ample, and an assembly hall will give Opportunity to hear in public some of the things that may be worth while.

4. Every worker, according to his capability, must be placed upon a self-supporting basis. Everyone from the first must begin to work out the relation of his honest earning-power to the cost of self-maintenance. Everything done, therefore, shall be planned under an ideal of the useful and beautiful for some worthy end, and hence it will have its price. This price must go to the worker's credit.

5. There must be half a dozen acres of ground or more about the building, worked and cared for by the workers in the institution. In this place every square foot shall yield, as farm, garden,

orchard, or lawn, as much as it can be induced to give up for the common weal.

6. The work needed for the care and maintenance of the building and grounds will not be classified by itself nor be deemed something apart from instruction. How to keep everything clean and sanitary will be an important branch of learning. For this, as for all other work in the place, the worker shall receive his price.

7. There must be a financial department or bank in the hands of the workers, where all the funds acquired through their work can be properly handled. Money values must be learned, and business ideals must be developed to stop the drain of the slot machines.

8. All the resources of history, science, art, and of the three R's as tools will be drawn upon as fully as possible to enrich and forward the development of the social and industrial life of this community.

9. The house will be open at all hours day and night—at least as many hours as the saloons—free to all children and their parents, who will have access to reading-rooms, library, workshops, gymnasium, and playgrounds.

10. This institution will be based upon the social settlement idea—not that of the monastery.

11. It will be a school in the broadest sense for all the people who will practically observe the adage, "It is never too late to learn." It will stand, not only for education for the sake of labor—the idea of our technical and trade-schools—but also for labor for the sake of education.

12. It will not be a free institution in the sense that its function will be to hand out blessings gratis, but to the end that it shall stand as Opportunity to all who desire to be industrious and who wish to fortify industry with education as long as they live.

13. This institution is not to be built in the slums, nor yet beyond their reach in a remote country place, but middle-wise where people like to live because of fresh air, convenience to work, and something of open spaces.

14. The institution will rest upon the principle that the productive types of labor are essential elements in the highest type of education; that it requires a proper union of these two factors to develop the highest type of life; that the highest type of life is that which is most highly productive. There will be, therefore, a careful estimate of the values of the different things produced in terms of market price, so that each worker will come to know himself through the application of a common normal standard fixed by the public.

15. To establish this school under present conditions will require the loan of some money in advance—say, about two and a half millions—to be applied as follows: (1) To purchase a site of sufficient size in a suitable neighborhood. (2) To construct and equip the building. (3) An endowment for the teaching-force, in the beginning, and until the institution itself trains up a body of instructors who shall be self-supporting through their own work in the school. As security for the loan, the lender must take a mortgage on the future, and he must be able to get along for possibly a generation without interest. As fast as the workers learn how, though, out of the production of each a fair proportion shall be set aside toward the maintenance of the institution as a whole. In the long run, the type of education that will survive will be self-maintaining. This institution will have self-maintenance as its goal—*education and self-support shall come together*—but as a beginning, in these days, it will take a large sum of money to found it.

Most of the money now contributed for educational purposes goes into one or another of three directions: (1) toward higher institutions of learning and research; (2) toward the very poor; and (3) toward reformatories and various types of rescue-work. The first have enough. In the second case it is often wasted—always so more or less—because it is used under impossible conditions; and in the third it comes too late to reach certainly those whom it was intended to succor, and it is in many ways the most extravagant waste of all.

Where the Money Goes

This OPPORTUNITY, however, is offered for the establishment

of a school for average people under normal conditions, where
the rôle that education should play in the life of a
Opportunity
in Real Life democracy may be actually demonstrated untrammeled by the traditions that hinder and hamper both
public and private schools. The public schools are tied up so
tightly within the coils of a great system that the flexibility
demanded by the individual in his natural development is almost
impossible. The school organization is simply a machine invented
and perfected for the purpose of holding a boy down while we
"educate" him.

On the other hand, although the private school seems especially
favored, since the necessary charge for tuition results in the
entrance of children of at least well-to-do folk, who are generally supposed to represent the "better class," in fact, this
is its chief handicap. We are apt to forget that the children
of emigrants and of the poorer classes, who by reason of expense
are excluded from the private schools, often repre-
Buried Genius sent an art inheritance that stretches back through
the centuries that made Italy, and other countries of
the Old World glorious. With no means for developing this
latent power in the public schools, and debarred by monetary and
social considerations from the private schools, the situation is
such that the world in general and this country in particular is
losing capabilities that cost the race ages to acquire. Any teacher
in the Ghetto vacation schools will cite instances by the score to
show that there is a latent talent in those dark-eyed,
Latent Talent ragged little children for music and art, which it is
criminal to neglect. Some Croesus who agonizes
over the fact that he may yet die rich ought to endow the
slums. Here is an OPPORTUNITY to establish an institution for
original research for the purpose of discovering and saving
to the world the all but faded genius of Michael Angelo, of
Raphael, and of Da Vinci. Money so expended would have far
more significance and potency in developing the newer artistic
life of our age and country than any amount spent in the more
fashionable procedure of tearing the art treasures from their
sympathetic environment in the Old World and setting them up

amid the mocking surroundings of the New. Ten thousand
dollars is a great price for a picture; it is but a small

**A Fine
Investment**

sum, though, to be paid for the education of a boy
who, incarnating the genius of an old master, would
glorify the spirit of his own day and our country in some great
work of art. Money is always forthcoming for those who wish
to delve in the buried ruins of the ancient world, where uncertain
hieroglyphs tell the broken story of a life long ago departed. The

**Wanted:
A Man!**

quest is now for a man with money, and with the
insight and the willingness to spend it in the search
for the living spirit of those vanished peoples which
yet survives among the unnourished bodies and discouraged souls
of those who land on our shores by the hundred thousand. Do
YOU KNOW THE MAN? THEN, HERE IS HIS OPPORTUNITY!

> "Long, long afterwards in an oak
> I found the arrow still unbroke."   W. S. J.

We have just fitted up a Printshop in the University Elementary School which has for its motto "THE BEST WORK WE CAN DO."

With this understanding, the University Elementary School has prepared a calendar in its Printshop for the good year Nineteen Hundred and Seven. Everybody in the school has had something to do with this calendar. The designs are original—that is, so far as things in this world can be original with anybody—and we decided for ourselves everything about it except the number of days in the year.

The price of this calendar is fifty cents; by mail sixty cents. We have printed one thousand copies, and no more will be printed for anybody. We are expecting to do two things with the money that we receive. First, we shall pay our honest debts; second, we know some children who do not have a fair chance, and we are going to give them a lift. If people send us their names and money, we shall send out the calendars, as long as they last, in the order the names come in. We shall get the word if you write to THE UNIVERSITY ELEMENTARY SCHOOL PRINTSHOP, UNIVERSITY OF CHICAGO.

BOOK REVIEWS

Elementary Education—Its Problems and Processes. By John Alexander
Hull Keith, Supervisor of the Training Department and Instructor of
General Method in the Illinois State Normal University. Chicago:
Scott, Foresman & Co. Pp. 316.

In this book the concrete, everyday problems that present themselves to the
teacher are considered, and, working from this material by analysis, description,
and argument to educational principles, a logical basis for good teaching is formulated. Emphasis is laid upon the successive stages of the child's mental development and the relation of this to his growth as a social being in process of adjustment to his surroundings. The various forms of motor expression are considered,
and the self-activity of the child as a means for securing experience is intelligently
presented. The art of questioning is also treated in its various fundamental
aspects in a way that will appeal to the student of scientific teaching. Altogether,
the book is expressive of educational ideals that are sensible and progressive.

H. E. P.

BOOKS RECEIVED

CHARLES SCRIBNER'S SONS, CHICAGO

American Explorers and *American Leaders and Heroes*. By WILBUR F. GORDY. Cloth.

The Robin Reader. By MINNIE T. VARNEY. Cloth. Pp. 117.

Elementary English Composition. By FREDERICK H. SYKES. Cloth. Pp. 328.

AMERICAN BOOK COMPANY, NEW YORK AND CHICAGO

Brooks's Readers. By STRATTON D. BROOKS. Cloth, 12mo.

The Action Primer. By THOMAS O. BAKER, Ph.D. Cloth, 12mo. Pp. 112.

The Indian Primer. By FLORENCE C. FOX. Cloth, 12mo. Pp. 120.

Experimental Physiology and Anatomy. By WALTER HOLLIS EDDY. Cloth, 12mo. Pp. 112.

Half Hours with Fishes, Reptiles, and Birds. By CHARLES FREDERICK HOLDER. Cloth, 12mo. Pp. 255. $0.60.

D. APPLETON & CO., NEW YORK

Builders of Our Country. By GERTRUDE VAN DUYN SOUTHWORTH. Book I. Illustrated. Cloth, 12mo. Pp. 254.

CENTURY CO., NEW YORK

The Palmer Cox Brownie Primer. Text by MARY C. JUDD. Pictures by PALMER Cox. Grading and editing by MONTROSE J. MOSES. Cloth, 12mo. Pp. 108.

GINN & CO., BOSTON

Second and *Third Readers*. By JOSEPH H. WADE and EMMA SYLVESTER. Cloth, 12mo. Illustrated.

The Sunshine Primer. By MARION I. NOYES and KATE LOUISE GUILD. Cloth, 12mo. Pp. 128. Illustrated in color. $0.40.

FREIDENKER PUB. CO., MILWAUKEE

200 Indoor and Outdoor Gymnastic Games. By MARIA GREY. Cloth. Pp. 63.

VOLUME VII   NUMBER 6

THE ELEMENTARY SCHOOL TEACHER

FEBRUARY, 1907

PLAN FOR OFFICIAL ADVISORY ORGANIZATION OF THE TEACHING FORCE OF CHICAGO[1]

REPORT OF THE SUBCOMMITTEE OF THE SCHOOL MANAGEMENT
COMMITTEE OF THE BOARD OF EDUCATION OF THE CITY OF
CHICAGO, APPOINTED TO TAKE INTO CONSIDERATION AND
REPORT UPON THE WHOLE SUBJECT OF AN ADVISORY ORGANI-
ZATION OF THE TEACHING BODY, SUBMITTED TO THE COM-
MITTEE ON SCHOOL MANAGEMENT AT ITS MEETING, FRIDAY,
DECEMBER 28, 1906

*To the School Management Committee of the Board of Educa-
tion of the City of Chicago:*

Your subcommittee appointed to take into consideration and
report upon the whole subject of an advisory organization of the
teaching body respectfully reports as follows:

I. Your committee finds that under existing conditions the
Board of Education and the teaching body are as widely separated
for consultative and freely co-operative purposes as if they had
no educational interests or duty in common. For the teachers
are inarticulate as a body, and the board, compelled to act without their direct advice and only upon reports of official inter-
mediaries, is forced into the position of governing by the mere
right of its legal authority and often in ignorance of matters
regarding which the teachers would be its best advisers. This
is manifestly detrimental. It tends especially to lessen the effectiveness of the teachers in their school-work, by destroying in
them that spirit of co-operation which is vital to a homogeneous
school system.

[1] From the *Chicago Teachers' Federation Bulletin*, January 4, 1907.

II. Even if it were true that all goodness and wisdom in affairs educational dwell in the school authorities, the fact remains that in the end their decrees must be executed by the teachers. It is the teachers, after all, and not boards, committees, or superintendents, that must be depended upon to give vitality to public-school education. Their cordial co-operation is therefore essential.

And inasmuch as teachers are neither soulless machines to be despotically manipulated by masterhands, nor soldiers with no other function than unquestioning obedience, nor mechanical producers of the inanimate commodities of the factory, but are the personal guardians and guides of the children they teach, and come into more intimate relations with these wards of the public school than anyone else in the system, their hearty and intelligent co-operation in promoting the educational policies of the board is not to be secured by methods of management which are or seem to them to be despotic. If they feel the weight of despotic hands, the less assertive among them will cringe in their official intercourse with superiors in authority, and be despotic in turn in their official intercourse with subordinates. Thus perpetuating itself, the despotic or decree-promulgating policy must inevitably react upon the pupils, tending to turn some of them into little learning machines and others into little rebels, instead of making eager students of all.

In the opinion of your committee, the teaching force must be sympathetically considered and trusted. If they are to do their best for the children, the teachers must be consulted about educational policies—not now and then and here and there, as real or apparent favorites of superiors in authority, but as a body of educators organically recognized by the board and its employees. Their cordial acquiescence in the wisdom, justice, and sincerity of the policies they are called upon to promote must be secured, or their work will fall short of its highest possibilities. In the nature of things, this acquiescence cannot be secured either by preventing discussion or by ignoring recommendations. To prevent discussion irritates; to ignore the results of discussion is disheartening. The important thing is not that the recommendations of the teacher shall be adopted by the board regardless of their merits, but that they shall be considered in good faith upon their merits.

III. One of the most important steps, therefore, which, in the opinion of your committee, the board ought to take, is the organization of the teachers into an official consultative and advisory body.

There is no implication here, nor have we learned satisfactorily of any demand from any source, that the teaching body should govern the superintendent or the board, or in any manner dictate to either. What is in principle proposed is (1) that the responsibility of legislative authority and final control should be reposed in the board; (2) that the responsibility of administrative authority and advisory direction should be reposed in the superintendent; and (3) that advisory authority and responsibility on educational subjects, and the relation of the teaching body to the school system, should be vested in the teaching body. And the teaching body in its advisory capacity, should it be thus organized, should have the fullest parliamentary freedom of expression. The common-sense of the teachers, far better than arbitrary rules or decrees from their superiors, would soon indicate to them the proper limitations of subject-matter for their discussion.

IV. The value of such an organization is obvious. The lack of it is a manifest detriment to the school system in many ways.

In the matter of the selection of school readers, for example, we have already had an instructive exemplification of the unwisdom of not having an authorized method of securing the advice of the teaching body on important questions regarding the work in which they and the board are in common engaged. When authoritative pedagogical advice was needed on this subject, a recommendation by a jury of teachers selected by the superintendent, whose names were kept secret from the board, and whose verdict was transmitted by the superintendent with only perfunctory approval, was the only method available. In saying this we condemn no one. It was the result of a system which should be changed.

We regard an authoritative organization of the teachers for consultative and advisory purposes, with reference to pedagogical subjects and their own relation to the school system, as an immediate necessity for the best interests of the public-school children.

V. This idea of an official organization of the teaching force for advisory purposes has long been urged by the Chicago Teachers' Federation—one of the most useful civic and educational organizations of the city—as a fundamental method of harmonizing and increasing the efficiency of all parts of the school system. It was approved in principle in 1900 by the executive committee of one hundred citizens organized by another civic body of Chicago, the Civic Federation, in a recommendation of an advisory school faculty which should represent all grades of teachers, from principals to kindergarten teachers, by delegates chosen on some established basis. Its value is recognized by the educational committee of the Charter Convention. It has, moreover, had the approval of some of the most distinguished educators of the United States; not only such as are accounted radical, but also such as are accounted conservative.

VI. [NOTE BY THE EDITORS.—Section VI embodies quotations from the leading educational authorities in the country, showing the need for representation, and giving their sanction to it. This section is omitted from lack of space.]

VII. Your committee therefore recommends the adoption of the following resolutions:

WHEREAS, The full power and responsibility for legislative, judicial, and executive action within the school system, now reposed by law in the Board of Education, should be intelligently and faithfully maintained, and no part thereof should be surrendered to any employee or employees of the board; and,

WHEREAS, The superintendent ought to have full power and responsibility for executive administration on the educational side, as the servant of the board, together with advisory power and responsibility relative to all its legislative, executive, and judicial functions; and,

WHEREAS, The teaching force ought to be so organized

officially as to invest it with advisory power and responsibility relative to executive, judicial, and legislative action, whether upon its own initiative or in response to requests from the superintendent or the board; and,

WHEREAS, A realization of these principles in practice is necessary to secure the best service from the superintendent and the teaching force, and to enable the board to perform its functions in the most intelligent and effective manner; and,

WHEREAS, The superintendent's assistance and advice are already available to the board at all times, but the necessary organization of the teaching body remains yet to be effected;

Therefore, to the end that the advice of the teachers as well as that of the superintendent may be available, and that complete and cordial co-operation of the board, the superintendent, and the teaching body may may be thereby established;

Resolved, That "The Educational Councils" of the Chicago public schools be, and they are hereby, invited to submit to the Board of Education a revised constitution for the purpose of placing the teaching body of the Chicago public-school system into direct advisory relations with the board;

Resolved, That it is the sense of the Board of Education that the basic principles of such revision should be along the following lines:

1. All teachers and principals in actual service should be *ipso facto* members of the council of their respective schools.

2. District Councils and the Central Council should be formed by representation from the respective School Councils.

3. Provision should be made for advisory or other co-operation with the councils in their deliberations, of the superintendent and other officials on the educational side, analogous to that which exists between the superintendent and the board.

4. Provision should be made for separate expression of opinion and action when desired, on the part of the high-school councils, of elementary-school councils, of principals, of specialty instructors, and of the grade teachers and high-school teachers, as distinct departments of or bodies within the councils.

5. Rules of order should be adopted for convenient and

appropriate consideration and action by the councils upon any question for the purpose of advising the board, whether at the request of the board or upon their own initiative; and,

Resolved, That, pending the above suggested revision of their constitution, the aforesaid "The Educational Councils" be, and they are hereby, officially recognized by the Board of Education as an official advisory organization of the teaching body.

Respectfully submitted

CORNELIA D. DE BEY, M.D., *Chairman*

REPORT ON SOME CONTRIBUTIONS TO THE BEITRÄGE ZUR PSYCHOLOGIE DER AUSSAGE

HENDRIK BOSMA

Chicago

The *Beiträge zur Psychologie der Aussage* is a German periodical magazine, edited by William Stern and a few other psychologists, among whom is the foremost psychologist of the Netherlands, Professor Heymans, of Groningen. The German word *aussage* means "to state, declare, report," and the *Psychologie der Aussage* is concerned with questions like these: Suppose a man on the witness-stand makes, even under oath, certain statements, how much of what he swears to be facts are we to believe? Or, suppose a newspaper man writes a report of an accident or event, how much of what he writes may we accept as true, granted that he has done his utmost to be as exact as possible?

To solve these questions several experiments have been made by various investigators: Stern experimented with 35 children of an elementary public school; Rosa Oppenheim, exclusively with 30 girls; Max Lobsien, with 4 classes of girls and 5 classes of boys; Rodewaldt, with 50 hospital soldiers.

Stern took from the lowest, the middle, and the upper grades two backward, two mediocre, and two bright pupils and led them, one at a time, into an empty schoolroom, where for one minute each had to look at the picture of a room in a farmer's house. Then the picture was taken away and the child had to report what it had seen. Afterward, 73 questions, previously written out, had to be answered: 4 referred to persons; 26, to things; 5, to activities of persons; 9, to localities; 18, to colors; 11, to qualities and numbers. Besides there were 12 *suggestive* questions, i.e., questions as to things that do not exist. Nine and a half weeks later the children were asked the same questions, without the picture being shown them.

The other investigators' experiments were not exactly like this, yet the general plan was the same.

Compare the following results:

	PERCENTAGE OF MISTAKES	
	In Reports	In Answers to Questions
Stern	6%	33%
Oppenheim	5	33-34
Rodewaldt	6	32-33

The experiments showed that no one reports without mistake, and that the *Merkfähigkeit,* the power of perceiving, increases with age; that a *spontaneous report without mistakes is not the rule, but the exception;* and that, even when people take an oath that certain statements are correct, the fact is that they make 10 per cent. mistakes. Those who will not swear make 20 per cent. As the above table indicates, in general, *the answers to questions contain four times as many mistakes as the reports.* From this we may conclude that for the sake of truth no person on the witness-stand should be interrupted by questions, and that it is wiser for the teacher to let the pupil say what he knows than to confuse him with many detailed questions. In reporting, a person disposes freely of his mental stock. What is clearest is reproduced. Images that are just beneath the threshold of consciousness are dragged up to the surface along with it.

Suggestibility.—To measure the suggestibility, Stern and Rodewaldt asked twelve, Oppenheim ten, questions with reference to non-existing things: for instance, "Is there not a stove in the room?" "What about the glasses on the table?" Of the answers to normal questions Stern found 66 per cent. to be right; of those to the *suggestive* questions, only 59 per cent. Rodewaldt had only 47.3 per cent. good answers to the latter.

Netschajew, of the Pedagogical Laboratory at St. Petersburg, experimented in the following way: He gave the pupils of all classes a sheet of paper and a pencil, and, after they had written down their grade, age, and name, he directed: "As soon as I have said *now,* write down some number; for example, 8;"

or, "Write a sentence on anything you like; for example, music." This experiment was carried out in all classes at the same time. The papers were collected, and it was found that many pupils had written down the figure 8 and a sentence with the word *music* in it. But there were some also who had put down 7 or 9; others had given a number containing 8, as 28, 18, 108, and 198; and their sentences were not exactly on music, but on something associated with music, as: "I like to play the violin."

In general, the experiments made clear that the younger the pupils, the more they follow *direct suggestions;* and that, as they grow older and become more masters of themselves, the ego begins to assert itself. That they are going to have a mind of their own is shown in their greater liability to *indirect suggestions.* The Russian experimenter's figures show that *pupils in the age of puberty follow more indirect than direct suggestions* (23–11 per cent.).

Discontinuity of mental development.—Extensive dynamometric experiments by Schuyten, of Antwerp, have shown that the energy of attention steadily increases from October on, is abundant until March, and then diminishes, reaching its low-water mark in July. The power of attention notably diminishes during the late spring and summer months, but muscular power increases in a remarkable way up to June or July. This is true both for girls and boys.

Stern's experiments show, not only that there is a *distinct discontinuity of development,* but also that *it is not the same in boys as in girls.* With girls between seven and ten years the extensiveness of knowledge—as shown by spontaneous reports and answers to questions—increases but little; the fidelity (percentage of *exact* problems) even decreases. Between the age of 10 and 15 both increase strongly. Boys are at their best between 7.3 and 11 years. After this, the increase as to extensity and exactness is comparatively little. Boys report more than girls; yet the girls are more exact in their reports. This does not increase with age. Boys and girls of 7 years made 6 per cent. mistakes; the pupils of a seminary, soldiers, and univer-

sity students made as many. As to the extensiveness, the sum-
total, of their statements we find:

> Girls of lowest grade report 12.6% of the facts
> Girls of highest grade report 29.8% of the facts
> Boys of lowest grade report 15.2% of the facts
> Boys of seminarian grade report 39.5% of the facts

The *Merkfähigkeit* (power of perception) *is also a function
that is capable of progressive development.*

From these investigations we may conclude that a child is
not a small adult, and that mental development is more an
additive than a proportional process.

The reports and answers contained many categories: persons,
things, actions, and qualities. Development does not proceed in
a way that the younger children answer of each category a few
elements, and the older pupils perceive of each category many
elements. No, the fact is: the younger children report *few,* the
older *many,* categories. Children 7 years old mentioned spontaneously only *persons* and *things.*

Interest.—Girls report more personal categories, boys more
those related to things. *Persons and their actions form one-
third of the total reports of the girls; with boys, it is one-fourth.*
The girls of the middle grades are most interested in the doings
of persons. With boys this stage lies between the lower and
middle grades. Girls remain longer in the stage of attending to
persons, things, and actions; boys reach sooner the stage of
quality and relation. Colors and qualities were mentioned last.
This is strange, as the colors on the pictures were very conspicuous. It is evidently not the vividness of a sensory impression that determines the choice of perception, but *interest.*
With reference to interest, knowledge, and exactness in stating
colors, the girls proved to be far behind the boys.

It is perhaps unwise at the present moment to draw from
these investigations practical pedagogical deductions. As far as
the experiments have been carried on, they plead against
coeducation, and it would seem that teaching which is of a
theoretical nature does not appeal very much to the girls. "Only
a teacher," says a German educator, "who by his or her person-

ality can greatly influence the girl may have results. The girl more than the boy is inclined to ask: 'How does the subject-matter affect my personal life?' Her courses of study, therefore, should be practical."

Safer inferences are these:

1. Questions of detail make a report worse.

2. The ordinary question has suggestive influence; the more so a suggestive question; and still more so when the questioner indicates what he thinks. ("Was not the dress blue?")

3. It is better to ask in this way: "Is among these persons or things the particular person or object?" than: "Is not this the man, the coat, etc?"

4. It is of importance to know whether a statement is spontaneous or an answer to a question. If the latter, how was the question put? "La question forme avec la réponse un tout indivisible."

5. The value of a statement *(Aussage)* also depends on what others have said, or the press has written. Especially the printed word is suggestive—a man on the witness-stand is often influenced by his daily paper.

6. In general, only those statements of events and things which a person attended to without strong emotional effects can be trusted. The results with descriptions of an action, of a process, are better than those of a locality or a space. The mind is less attracted by outward appearances and colors than by movements. Strong emotions tend to exaggeration.

7. Lapses of time under five minutes are almost invariably overrated and the more so the shorter the time. There is no tendency for over- and underrating times between five and ten minutes. Times over ten minutes are usually undervalued, although not much.

These conclusions were made by Otto Lipman, and are based on his own experiments as well as on those of Stern and others. For the teacher they may probably have practical value; but, above all, judges, lawyers, and members of a jury should take notice of them.

A REVISION OF THE RUDIMENTS AS CONCERNING NATURE-STUDY

WALTER J. KENYON

State Normal School, San Francisco, Cal.

The biographers of great men appear to take a mischievous delight in showing how their subjects came up through the period of childhood virtually untutored in those studies which pass with us as the essentials of education. We learn that George Stephenson at the age of eighteen could not read; and that at nineteen he was able "to sign his name, in a good round hand." Yet, by one shift or another, he managed finally to loom large in the pages of history as one of the world's considerable figures in the field of science.

Georg Ebers is said to have been withheld by his mother from a study of printed words until his tenth year, the interim being dedicated to a free wandering among studios and craftsmen's shops, or wherever knowledge might be absorbed at first hand. Yet this Ebers figures later in life as a man of famous erudition, the great Egyptologist.

The statesman Elihu Washburn, surnamed "the Watchdog of the Treasury," as early as his seventh year was making himself generally useful on a New England farm. Says his biographer: "He went to school for a few weeks in winter and again for a few weeks in summer, but, as may be imagined, he learned very little."

Peter Cooper "attended school only two quarters, altogether." His childhood was a constant struggle for existence. Most of it was taken up, in dehairing rabbit skins in his father's hat factory.

Sir Isaac Newton, says a biographer, "at the age of twelve showed little taste for study, and managed easily to stand at the foot of his class." This poor showing, however, was evidently occasioned, not by idleness, but by his constant preoccupation in various mechanical conceits.

In the case of Abraham Lincoln his very struggles for book-learning reveal how desultory must have been his early acquisitions, and how wholly innocent his period of actual childhood must have been of that formal knowledge which is the chief concern of our elementary school; and, conversely, how his early boyhood must have been passed in those unorthodox employments and experiences which go unrecognized by the accepted course of study.

Further inquiry discovers a similar hiatus, of greater or less degree, in the boyhood of Herbert Spencer, James Watt Whittier, Howells, and U. S. Grant. And the inference is that these cases, selected at haphazard, are typical of a great number of others.

The question then arises: If so many of these typically successful men of history came up through childhood with the merest smattering of letters and numbers, in many instances acquired in a most desultory fashion, just what were those other and major factors which must have entered into their early education, to bear so ample a fruition in the later life?

The inquiry thus gravitates into a question of the rudiments. And this, in turn, hinges upon our interpretation of life. All schoolmen seem to agree that (a) the school should prepare for life, and that (b) the elementary courses of study should deal exclusively with the rudiments. But there appears to be no agreement as to what constitutes life, nor as to what studies may properly be enumerated as rudiments.

Our public-school tradition has ever held stolidly to the idea that life is summed up in vocation, and too often vocation is by the same estimate interpreted as shopkeeping. From such a basis the deduction is easily made that the list of rudiments is complete in the three R's.

Against this sordid tradition innovators have ever arisen, and will arise, whose thesis is that life is something more than vocation, and that therefore the group of rudiments reputed directly to serve vocation may not be accepted as a complete inventory, provided the school is really to prepare for life.

This more liberal interpretation of the school's responsibilities conceives life as including five general phases, ranking as co-ordinate and indispensable factors, and exhibiting claims upon the public school which cannot be repudiated except by sheer evasion. These five phases are: (1) the physical or creature life; (2) the intellectual or psychic life; (3) the home life; (4) the civic or community life; and (5) the vocational life. Each of these implies certain rudiments of study directly appropriate to itself, although they indirectly serve the others also. A complete list of these co-ordinate rudiments would seem to be: physical culture;[1] nature-study (of an extensive but not intensive order, as hereinafter indicated); music; history, literature, and civics; geography; manual arts; domestic economy; arithmetic (in a diminished proportion); and formal language (without grammar).

Our caption calls for the discussion of only one of these rudiments; and the foregoing remarks have been necessary in an attempt to orientate this subject of nature-study in the general scheme of elementary instruction.

As regards the direct aim of nature-study, I should say it is: *to inform the growing mind with innumerable sense-products, which shall now and later afford an adequate basis for intellection.*

These sense-products are variously called by psychologists "sense-percepts," "elementary ideas," etc. I have no wish to become defendant in a wrangle over terminology, so let us agree upon the exact nature of these sense-products by citing examples: they include all the objective phases which function in our nouns, adjectives, and verbs; and all of the external situations whence arise our figures of speech. Thus, "green," "warm," "sweet," "heavy," "brittle;" "rise," "expand," "glow," "freeze," "grind;" "iron," "apple," "shovel," and so on, *ad infinitum,* as unnumbered as the fish in the sea. We say that "Mr. So-and-so is in buoyant spirits today." But these words can function in the

---

[1] Including attention by the school authorities to sanitation and hygiene.

mind of the hearer only as he has witnessed the suspension of a cork in the water or a balloon in the air. Now, this observation of the cork or the balloon is nature-study. Out of such observations, repeated without number and in infinite variety, we amass our intellectual small coin in which all the affairs of the mind are transacted. And let us observe again that the first step in the whole process is nature-study, and the first activity is sense-activity.

These sense-products, then, as innumerable as the leaves of the forest, are the currency of the mind, those units of imagery in the total absence of which no intellection could proceed. Absolutely our whole vocabulary functions directly or indirectly in them, and they instruct our every conscious act. In copious supply and intricate relationships they lie at call in the antechambers of the mind, instantly ready to come before the footlights into the focus of consciousness. The barren mind is barren in the degree of its poverty of this elemental equipment. No man can come to Shakspere, or Milton. or the Bible, with appreciation and understanding, except as he is richly equipped with these elements of imagery.

This raw stuff of. the imagination we must have, in no restricted measure, if we are to be numbered as sentient human beings. And it must exhibit those well-ordered relationships which facilitate judgment and choice. The raw stuff must not only be there, but it must also be mobilized with a degree of readiness that is brought about only through much use. Such a power has the artist, the poet, the general, the acrobat, the captain of industry, the statesman—each of them, as we say, "a man of imagination."

As to the origin of these elements of imagery there are just two possibilities: either we possess them as a heritage at birth, or we must acquire them by an untrammeled sense-activity continuing at least throughout the period of childhood. And this activity needs an exceeding range, but no particular intensiveness. The nature-study in vogue at present tends, I think, to reverse this proportion, through studies which are insignificant in their scope and, on the other hand, unprofitably logical and intensive. If we believe, with Comenius, in this connection, that "there can be nothing in the understanding which was not first in the senses," then it becomes our most immediate concern to consider by what means and method this mental stock may be most liberally secured to the pupil. Our public-school children do not finger enough substances with a discriminating touch; they do not gaze observantly upon enough colors and forms, and physical and chemical changes; they do not listen, in a conscious discrimination, to enough sounds; they do not lift enough weights, or constrain enough resisting bodies. We try to substitute the cold type of textbooks and readers for this foundation platform of sense-products. But the books are useless until an apperceptive basis of millions of interrelated sense-percepts is established. We trust to the god of chance for the furnishing of this apperceptive mass, and at that point education ceases to be a science. Right there we begin to elicit unfunctioned words from the pupil, and give him his first lesson in lying. That is the burden of psychological miscalculation which has ever weighed upon our teachers' efforts, and is weighing upon them today.

The remedy lies in less reading—or rather a postponed reading; less bandying back and forth of unfunctioned or only half-functioned words, and more of a constructive manipulation of objects, more intent looking at spaces, forms, and colors, more listening to characteristic sounds, and more language lessons based directly upon the resulting mental states. This enriching of the apperceptive data one man calls nature-study; another, manual training; another, object-lessons; another, industrial education; and so on. But what is there in a name? Call it what you will; it is simply letting the pupil loose once more into a normal environment from which it appears the school's chief business, at present, to withhold him.

I protest against this question being swept aside with the assertion that the mind becomes sufficiently informed with these elements of imagery before the child's entry into school, and during the recesses of the school life. It is in every probability far from the truth, more particularly in the great cities. And this view is amply borne out in the standard complaint of our various high-school teachers, who find the graduates of the elementary school vacant of mind and quite impermeable to the excellences of fine literature, or artistic presentations of any sort; while the laboratory men complain equally that the entering pupils display no gumption in the handling of materials and apparatus. In a word, the lower-school graduate has given so many of his eight thousand hours[2] to the mastery and re-mastery, and again the re-mastery, of the three R's that there are sounding echoes in those chambers of his mind which should be filled with working material. He breaks an inordinate number of test-tubes because he has a too vague conception of the frangibility of glass. His crude notions of weights and measures, and stresses, strains, and proportions, mark him as a very clown in those little exigencies where his benchmate, perchance, having the boon of a normal childhood behind him, proves adept. He mars the schoolhouse and its furniture with jackknife and pencil, and is arraigned for malicious mischief. But the truth of the matter is that he merely does not possess those standards of the general fitness of things which are acquired through much constructive sense-activity among the simple forms of the objective world.

The great obstacles toward the rationalizing of our public-school work are, first, the inordinate proportion of time given to formal language and number, and, second, the resulting popular cry of "overcrowded course of study." The latter is that destructive *vox populi* which frightens the superintendent out of the course which his common-sense dictates. It sanctifies the teacher of the traditional type, whose ideal of professional service is to live out a life-tenure with the least possible exertion. And it paralyzes the initiative of the opposite type, who struggles unconfidently against the rigidity of her circumstances.

If these reflections are at all in keeping with reason, they seem to imply the following steps toward a readjustment of the course of study:

1. Reduce the time allotment of the three R's. Give formal

[2] The public-school course consumes 8,000 hours: 8 years of 40 weeks of 25 hours.

language and number their due, but not three times their due. For the rest of the eight thousand hours either enrich the pupil's life by a recourse to the other rudiments, or turn him loose to seek that enrichment, as Newton did, in his own devices.

2. Disabuse the teacher's mind of the moss-grown fallacy that formal language and arithmetic are the only rudiments; or even that they legitimately take precedence among the rudiments.

3. In the enriching material introduced as the media of the other rudiments, correct that tendency toward intensive study wherein the adult reads his own special interests, aptitudes, and intellectual necessities into the mind of the child. Let the subject-matter of elementary instruction be more broadly inclusive than it has been, and in a less degree intensive.

This latter stipulation implies my final proposition, as to the content of nature-study. I limit the term to a diffuse and juvenile sense-activity, as something different from, and antecedent to, those intensive and logically pursued studies which fall under the head of natural science. The pupil must rove afield, and see grass and flowers, and hear the birds sing. He must sail a boat and fly a kite. He must whittle a stick and mold a lump of clay. He must draw and paint, in a hundred different aspects of form and color, and light and shade. He must construct, in paper and wood, and tin, and putty, and glass, and rubber, and all available sorts of matter. He must fashion the boat he sails, and frame the kite he flies. A good half of the manual arts, as available for the elementary school, will be merely these little constructive enterprises, in exemplification of his nature-study.

It is apparent that we can no more specify the exact number of sense-percepts to be secured to the pupil than we can designate the precise number of words which shall constitute his vocabulary. It would sound the knell of human growth if we could to this extent crystallize elementary study. The most successful teachers, those whose beneficence weaves itself into the lifelong remembrance and affection of their pupils, will probably say: "The more the merrier, and God save the little chap who gets least."

WHAT FORM OF INDUSTRIAL TRAINING IS MOST PRACTICAL AND BEST SUITED TO THE COUN-TRY CHILD?[1]

O. J. KERN

Superintendent of Schools for Winnebago County, Rockford, Ill.

It is to be regretted, perhaps, that we do not have a better term to express the thought of this afternoon's programme; for a great many most excellent people today moving along Educational Avenue, leading up to the public school, shy and stop still at the sight of the word "industrial" as applied to the work of the school. Any attempt to lead them closer for a more careful inspection of this word proves unavailing. To their thinking, industrial training means the elimination of "culture," whatever that may mean, and the substitution of the reform school or the trade school. For them the thought has not yet come that education should be for service as well as for "sweetness and light"; that the children in our schools should be able to do things, as well as to know about things. And in the doing of things there is as great opportunity for culture as there is in studying about what men have said and done, as revealed by the printed page.

The distinction between higher education and industrial education has no real foundation upon which to rest. It is a survival of the aristocratic ideas of the Middle Ages. The thought is not original with the writer to claim that farming and blacksmithing are just as high as law and theology. Whether it be better to be a blacksmith than a minister depends. As has been well said recently: "It is better to pound an anvil and make a good horseshoe than to pound a pulpit and make a poor sermon."

Quoting further from this same writer: "There is a real distinction between education for self-support and education for self-development; between what the Germans call the bread-and-

[1] Paper read before the Department of Superintendence of the National Educational Association, Louisville, Ky., March 1, 1906.

butter sciences and culture. In order, if not in importance, the bread-and-butter sciences come first. The first duty every man owes to society is to support himself; therefore, the first office of education is to enable the pupil to support himself." And, as has been said above, industrial education, if carried on aright, contributes to self-culture as well as to self-support. . . . .

My discussion calls for a consideration of "What Form of Industrial Training Is Most Practical and Best Suited for the Country Child?"

All those interests and activities that relate to agriculture in an elementary way, quite elementary for a while, are practical and suited for the training of the country child. The prosperity of this nation in its last analysis rests upon agriculture. A very great majority of the children enrolled in the country schools will remain on the farm, and the country school should help them to a better understanding of the new phases of agriculture. The number remaining on the farm will increase when right ideals prevail in the instruction with reference to the dignity, worth, and financial possibilities of the kind of farming that is "higher education."

To be specific, a study of the soil by means of the school garden is practical to a certain extent in every country school. To be sure, a live teacher will get more out of it than a dead one who does not yet even know that she is dead. But something is done and can be done. A start is being made. To wait till all the teaching force is ready is to do nothing.

Last year the Department of Agriculture at Washington surveyed over fifteen million acres of farm land. The state of Illinois is spending $25,000 annually in its soil survey and soil experiments. Thus far, sixteen counties have been surveyed, and the expectation is to continue till the entire 102 counties are surveyed. Every type of soil, as small as ten-acre lots, is mapped and described. A various-colored map is published and put in bulletin form.

Here is a map of one county [showing] which gives you an idea of the work of the Soil Bureau. You see the different types of soil for this particular county represented by different colors. The printed matter in connection with this map gives an accurate account of the early settlement, climate, physiography and geology, description of the types of soil, agricultural conditions, markets, transportation facilities, etc. Laying aside all thought of industrial training and the so-called elimination of "culture," and the alleged "making farmers" of our country chidren by "putting agriculture into the country school," just think how valuable this bulletin is in teaching home geography! Surely there is time for the study of geography in the average country school. A copy of this map and bulletin was put into the library of every country school of this county. The expense was nothing. And this map, so far as it goes, is far more valuable for the teaching of agriculture than the so-called agricultural charts for $40 which some school officers are buying of agents who are posing as apostles of agricultural instruction for the country school.

We are not quite accurate when we speak of "putting agriculture into the country school." Rather let us attempt to put the school into agriculture, into right relation to its environment.

A school garden is practical. True, it is in its experimental stage as yet. So was manual training for the city child, and is so to a certain extent today. But no one would eliminate manual training because teachers do not yet know all about matter and method. We do not know all about the school garden as a means of giving instruction with reference to soil and plant-life. We can learn, however, and learn by doing, even if the doing is crude for a few years. The best way to have a garden in the country school is to have it even if it is no larger than four feet square. A start can be made, and that is a great deal. To sit down and contemplate the difficulties is to remain seated.

School-garden work, manual training, and domestic arts for the country school will be put on a more intelligent and permanent basis when there are trained supervisors for this work, just as many city schools now have. This will come when the county superintendent can change the ideals of the country people so that they will regard the office for educational leadership, and not subject to the exigencies of party politics. The task of changing ideals in this respect is a fairly big one.

True, if we could have such gardens as the Macdonald gardens of Canada, better results would be obtained. If millionaires of this country would find it possible to do as this man is doing, doing something for the country child, a great educational uplift would come to all phases of country life. Here [showing] is a most interesting pamphlet describing the Macdonald gardens. There are special traveling instructors for these gardens, which are two acres in extent. One or two quotations are sufficient to reveal their character.

With reference to the place of the garden in school work:

The work of the garden is recognized as a legitimate part of the school program, and is already interwoven with a considerable part of the other studies. The garden is becoming the outer classroom of the school, and its plots are its blackboards. The garden is not an innovation, or an excresence, or an addendum, or a diversion. It is a happy field of expression, an organic part of the school in which boys and girls work among growing things and grow themselves in body and mind and spiritual outlook.

Of the advantages, the following summary only is given here:

1. Educationally, it affords a release from the dull routine of the schoolroom, and puts the pupil out into the fresh air and sunlight. It is a means of help by affording scope for motor activities that are natural to growing children. The garden work is correlated with much of the formal work of the school, as arithmetic, reading, composition, drawing, etc. It serves as an introduction to the development of literary appreciation, as the "ability to appreciate the charm of many of the best poems depends not a little on ability to form visual images of natural objects." In this respect, if the teacher in the country school is alert, the country child has the advantage over the city child; for "the urban eye of the town-bred child, who has never been interested in garden or field, must fail to catch the imagery of our best nature poems."

2. Economically, the school garden teaches the composition and care of the soil, best conditions for plant life, value of fertilizers, seed selection, etc.

3. Nationally, the school garden develops an interest in the fundamental industry of the country. There develops the sense of ownership and of respect for property.

In the care of their own plots the pupils fight common enemies and learn that a bad weed in a neglected plot may make trouble for many others. The garden is a pleasant avenue of communication between the school and the home, relating them in a new and living way, and thereby strengthening the public interest in the school as a national institution.

A study of plant-life is practical and suited for the country child. For years we have had the thoroughbred horse, the pure-bred cow, and now comes the high-bred corn. Here is an ear [showing] of high-bred corn raised by the president of the Illinois Corn Growers' Association. This was taken from a field that easily made one hundred bushels per acre. To be sure, to raise hundred-bushel corn there must be not only hundred-bushel seed, but also hundred-bushel soil and a hundred-bushel man. Our industrial training should teach the children in the country schools to strive for these three things: better seed, increasingly fertile soil, and more intelligent methods of operation. Here is an opportunity for the school to co-operate with the home and train children to study corn on experimental plots at home.

Likewise some training with reference to farm animal-life, and a consideration of some of the elementary principles of the business and of farming, is practical and suitable. Farm economics is practical arithmetic, and could well take the place of much textbook matter that is "taught at." Surely the average country school has time to teach the arithmetic that the pupils must use after leaving school.

With the country high schools—that is, the village high schools—and the country consolidated school as centers, manual training for the country child should begin. From these schools this educational activity will spread into a large number of one-room country schools. This will be slow; for the average farmer does not yet distinguish between manual training and manual labor. If all the data could be collected, it would appear that quite a considerable amount of manual training, elementary in form, is now being carried on in the country schools.

Here is a great opportunity for the school to co-operate with the country home; and through the inspiration and help of a live teacher a work-bench can be installed in the home workshop, if it seems impracticable to instal one in the country schoolhouse. The boy at home—and the girl, too, in connection with home economy—can make a small collection of simple tools, and from the teacher receive instruction as to processes of work, etc. The country school and the country home should come closer together. The lines of industrial work suited to the farm and farm home offer an exceptionally fine opportunity for this closer union for a common purpose. Most of the old farm activities have gone since the introduction of farm machinery of improved make. With this change have gone some elements in the training for the country child that must be supplied by the new country school and the new farm home, to meet the new conditions of country life in the age of telephones, trolley cars, daily delivery of mail, improved farm machinery, discoveries relating to the science of agriculture, and improved methods of farm operations.

For the boy this manual training will consist in a working knowledge of the care and use of tools for repair work on the farm, farm mechanics, the simple elements of carpentry, etc. Along with this will go a practical knowledge of materials.

For the girl there will be instruction in household economy and management, food materials and the preparation of food, sewing and a study of textiles, etc.

There need be no alarm that the country child will not receive culture along these lines. As has been well said:

To teach a boy the mechanics of home-keeping, to teach the girl the chemistry of home-keeping, is as much self-culture as to teach either what kinds of homes the ancient Greeks and Romans possessed. Our present self-development is too narrow. We need to broaden it. Manual training is necessary to make the "all-round" man.

We can take this culture to the country child, and in addition take to the country school good books, art, and music; and we need no longer be under the necessity of tearing up the farm home by its roots and taking the children to the city to secure the country child's rights, so far as an educational opportunity is concerned, to partake of all that is best the age has to offer.

SOME EXPERIMENTS IN GROUP-WORK

C. B. SHAW
Wells School

In 1904 Dr. Scott, of the Boston Normal School, gave a series of talks before the Dunton Club on matters pertaining to the education of children, emphasizing the value of self-organized group-work. I became interested in his accounts of work which had been done in the West, and resolved to allow my pupils to suggest some line of work they would like to pursue, and to give them a place on the regular school programme for carrying out their plans. I first consulted our principal, who readily agreed to our trying it.

The work was begun with a fourth grade of girls, the greater part of them the children of Russian Jews. The girls of this district are a very bright, interesting set, to whom getting an education means all that is pleasant; and perhaps this latter fact will account for their choosing at first some regular school-work like arithmetic, or writing compositions, during the half-hour which I offered them, instead of something which might seem more attractive to other children.

On the afternoon when they were to tell me what they would like to do, the list of things suggested was a long one. Some things were never attempted at all, as many girls gave up their own plans to join some other group. On the list were sewing, crocheting shawls, drawing, arithmetic, reading stories, playing house and store, elocution, etc.

Of course, the kind of work or play in which a child wishes to engage is largely influenced by his home-life and the resources which he has. Many of these children are very poor, and many of those who are not poor live at home very differently from our American children. Groups in photography, for instance, were not thought of where no child owned a kodak and few had ever seen one used.

Some of the groups carried on their work in different corners of the schoolroom, while some used an empty room in the hall, and others the teacher's dressing-room. The time allowed was only one half-hour a week, but through interest in the work much extra time was spent on it before and after school and at recess.

That year the group that remained practically unchanged from beginning to end, and that did the best work, was, surprising to say, the elocution group. I must admit that the word "elocution" alone was enough to arouse my doubts, and I frankly told the leader I had no experience in that direction. She didn't seem to need any assistance, however, for she told me she had a book which explained all about elocution. She gathered six or eight girls about her and taught them the appropriate gestures for grief, joy, surprise, supplication, etc. Then she gave them each a selection to learn in which the proper inflections and gestures were used.

After this things were rather at a standstill until the teacher suggested that they give a little play. The leader took a book from the library and selected the little drama "Cinderella," but after some work upon it they all decided that the songs and dances were too difficult, and, moreover, they didn't know what to do with the boys' parts. (We have since had many plays and tableaux in which the boys' parts have been well taken by girls.) Then a play called "The Little Needlewomen" was chosen. The parts were distributed and learned, and the rehearsals conducted without any aid from the teacher. When the group was ready for the final rehearsal, the teacher was invited to see it. There were some mispronounced words to correct and stage-setting to suggest, but their interpretation of the play was good. It was given for the class and for guests. At the end of the year, when their class and two others held their picnic at Franklin Park, the girls of this group entertained the three classes by giving a dramatic representation of "Bluebeard" and a little play called "The Coal Famine," which the leader had adapted from one called "The Bread Famine."

The following year the work was carried on in a sixth grade

by many of these same girls who had received a double promotion. Their experience of the year before had given them a better idea of the work. They began to get away from selecting the regular studies on the school programme, and were readier with ideas of their own.

Groups for acting plays and stories and poems, which they themselves dramatized, and for the presentation of tableaux, still held a prominent place and seemed to have the most attraction for these children. Of course, the dramatic instinct is strong at this age, and particularly among the Russian Jews. At Christmas time one of the groups presented "How We Caught Santa Claus," an original play written by the leader, a girl of twelve years; and another group gave "The House of Santa Claus," taken from a book of plays.

About this time we were asked by a friend what would help us most in our work, and we immediately said: "A curtain to go across the front of the room for our theatrical performances." The material was bought, and the girls made the curtain and sewed on the rings. Then our principal had a copper wire put up across the front of the room, and the curtains were hung when needed, and taken down and put away when not in use. The groups did not resort to the Elizabethan way of representing scenes by simply writing on the front board, "This is a street in New York," but always had as much stage-setting as they could collect. When an interior was shown, they brought rugs, table-covers, sofa pillows, etc., from home. Right here was the teacher's opportunity to help these children make a room look homelike, to put together quiet, harmonious colors, and to arrange flowers and books on a table. The only lamp we had offered for one play had seen better days, and there were some fearful and wonderful table-covers brought in.

Another original play given this year was "Patsy and Laura," written by a little eleven-year-old girl of French parentage. Several times during the year other classes in the building were invited to our room to see what a group had to present. In May our class gave a little entertainment on a Saturday afternoon in St. Andrew's Hall to raise money for a private charity. All of the twenty or thirty tableaux which were given were originated by a twelve-year-old girl, and were posed by her personally just before the curtain rose. The play, "Patsy and Laura," was repeated, and other plays selected by the teacher were given.

At different times during that year there were five or six groups for giving plays and tableaux; three groups in cooking; and groups in sewing, crocheting, and cutting and pasting to make scrapbooks. There were many difficulties in the way of the cooking group, but overcoming difficulties is one of the helpful features of this work. Our principal gave the first cooking group a gas stove, and it bought its own pipe. The other groups brought their own stoves from home. There was only one gas-burner in the room where a pipe could be attached, and, as all the groups had to use that, there was considerable waiting. Sometimes a group would make something that didn't need to be cooked, as stuffed dates. Among the different things that were made were cocoa, jells, farina, and several kinds of candy. One morning the first group made fudge which was too soft, and it immediately said it should make it again next time and get it right. The second group had a bad time getting started, and often tried things that were too hard with which to have great success. The leader didn't seem to have much ability in carrying out the work. After spoiling peppermints and muffins, the children meekly tried stewed prunes, which they prepared successfully. Later they brought in a freezer and ice and made lemon sherbet. The members of the cooking groups always passed to the teachers portions of whatever was made.

This fall my sixth grade has begun its work, but, as it had no opportunity for carrying it on last year, the results will probably not be so satisfactory as could be wished.

One group is at work in dolls' dressmaking. The first thing it did was to make little muslin or calico bags to hold thimbles, needles, etc. There are several groups for acting, and a group which is cutting out paper furniture and pasting it on sheets of gray paper in imitation of furnished rooms. The leader of one group, who had a book of Wordsworth's poems at home, wished to have some of them learned and recited. She

selected "To the Cuckoo" and "The Reverie of Poor Susan."
One little girl said she wished to make some drawings which
could be represented afterward as tableaux. "But," I said, "you
would have to make drawings of people; can you do that?"
(The school programme doesn't allow much time for pose drawing, and never for a *front* pose in our grade, I believe.) The
child was quite sure she could do what she had in mind, however, and I asked her to take a sheet of paper home and draw
something to show what she meant. Next morning she appeared
with a good drawing of a little girl standing at a table and
blowing soap-bubbles. The table was decorated with a fringed
cloth, and a bowl of water was standing on it. The little girl
in the drawing was facing full *front,* and, even to the buttons
on her shoes, her appearance was faithfully represented. There
are two little girls working in this group now. It is the first
work of the kind that has ever been suggested. The girls do not
copy their drawings, but "make them up" as they go along. The
titles of some of these pictures are "Saluting the Flag," "Taking
Dolly for an Airing," "Playing Telephone," etc.

At the teacher's suggestion one group is preparing to give a
representation of the old ballad, "King John and the Abbot of
Canterbury," and another the Lullaby for Titania from *A Midsummer Night's Dream.* The leader of this latter group, who
also belongs to the drawing group, has set the words of the
Lullaby to a little song which she had learned in school, and just
now she is carefully teaching it to the girls who are to take the
part of the fairies.

On Friday afternoon, November 16, we had our first finished
piece of work, an original play entitled "The Orphan," by a ten-
year-old girl. It was a simple little play of three acts. In the
first act a child is begging on the street. People jostle her and
speak to her rudely, and, as she herself says, no one seems to
care for her. At last, one woman stops and asks her some questions, and when she finds that the child is alone in the world
she asks her if she would like to go home with her and be her
little girl. The second act shows us little *Rosebud,* still in her
ragged clothes, eating her first dinner in her new home. The

third scene is the street before *Rosebud's* new home. The little girl, in pretty new clothes, is playing with other children. Among the passers-by is one woman who had spoken roughly to *Rosebud* when she was a beggar. Now she looks at her with eyes of envy, as one of the children expressed it, and tries to steal her away, but *Rosebud's* adopted mother appears just in time to save her, and they live happily ever after. The leader of this group has since written another play, which the teacher decided was too much of a tragedy to be given, and so she is now looking over some plays in books in order to select one.

On the following Friday the members of another group gave a collection of recitations and songs. The pasting group also hung up for examination the sheets illustrating furnished rooms.

The criticism of the class upon the work presented by any group is one of the most helpful parts of the work.

This group-work is not always carried on without friction between the leaders and those under them; the children's ideals are not always very high; and their productions, particularly the original writings, are very crude and faulty; but it seems to be all in the right direction. The children gain a great deal in power of independent thought and action; the desire for leadership is satisfied (which should make the teacher's work in discipline easier); difficulties are overcome; and work is often attempted and done easily and pleasantly which the teacher would think too difficult to give.

These are some of the simple experiments we have tried, and from results already attained we feel encouraged to continue the group-work.

GROUP-WORK IN THE HIGH SCHOOL

LOTTA A. CLARK
Charlestown, Mass.

A child, like everyone else, learns to *do* by *doing*. This is such a truism, and everyone knows it so well, that it would seem as though nothing more need be said about it. Yet the number of things which our pupils actually *do* for *themselves* in the schoolroom is very small.

With our crowded and hurried conditions it is not easy to see how it can be otherwise. Teachers feel that in order to get the necessary amount of work done they must plan it in detail carefully beforehand, must get all the material ready, and must put the pupils through the work in as systematic and orderly a way as possible.

Yet, with all our care, how much of this work, which seems so clear and simple to the teacher who has thought it all out— how much of it is clear, vital, or palatable to the pupil? Like the proverbial horse that can be led to the water, the pupil can be put through a certain amount of work; but, just as the horse will not drink unless he be thirsty, so the pupil will not make these facts his own unless he *feel* the need for them. Do our lessons in grammar make our boys and girls speak good English at home, in the street, or even in the classroom? How many of our boys in school learn to add and substract as our newsboys do on the street? How many lessons in history and civil government send better voters to the polls? How many of our boys and girls leave school with good rational habits of study and a *desire* to *continue* to study? Yet, if our young people do not learn to speak good English, to deal with figures accurately and quickly, to be conscientious citizens, and intelligent readers and thinkers of the world's problems, their education has not been as successful as it might be.

The question is how to make the work in the schoolroom of

the kind which will give our young people some of the same experience and training which they are expected to have when they leave school and go out into life. More than this, the school-work ought to give them a chance to express and use any natural inclination or talent which any of them may possess.

After a boy or girl has spent thirteen years in school and goes from the high school out into business, he or she is expected to assume *responsibility*, plan ways of doing things, make investigations, and talk to different sorts of people intelligently and forcibly. In the ordinary recitation in school, which has been planned and is conducted by the teacher, in which the business of the pupil is to answer the questions, the boy or girl takes no responsibility in the progress of the lesson, and gets no chance to plan, investigate, or discuss. If, however, the work is carried on by means of the social group, these are the very things that the pupils get an opportunity to do. I had learned the idea of the social group from Dr. Colin A. Scott, who had told us of the success with which it had been tried in some of the cities in the West.

It seemed imposisble at first to get a chance to try the group-work—the conditions in the high school make it difficult. Instead of having the same pupils for five hours each day, we have a different set each hour, and it is with us but forty-five minutes. Some of our classes we see only three times a week, and, as a number of the pupils is preparing for college or normal school, there is not a moment to be wasted. The group-work must be directly in line with the work laid down in the course of study, and, as it is expected in the high school that lessons shall be learned outside, the work in the classroom must test what has been learned.

In spite of all this, I determined two years ago to try the social group-work in the classroom. The class in which the experiment was tried was a beginners' class in ancient history. There were ninety-three pupils in the class, and it was divided into three sections, each of which recited to me three times a week. There were two things which I wished to give them an opportunity to do: (1) to co-operate—to work together; and

(2) to give each individual a chance to do the sort of thing which he *particularly wants* to do.

I talked the matter over with the classes, showed them why the lessons which we had been having were not satisfactory, and asked them how they would like to try the experiment of conducting their history lessons themselves. The novelty of the idea pleased them, and after considerable informal discussion we decided to carry on our recitations in the form of business meetings. A chairman was appointed from the class to take charge of the meeting, and there was something of a sensation when I exchanged chairs with him. He appointed committees to nominate candidates for a president, vice-president, and secretary. These officers were elected by ballot for one month, and their duties were decided upon by the class. We had an amusing time when they tried to decide what they ought to do with me. I told them I was going to do just as little as possible in the class, so that they might have all the time and opportunity there was. They finally decided to call me "the executive officer," with power to exercise full authority if necessity required.

It was surprising to see the change in the whole atmosphere of the recitations which this order of things brought about. The pupils were timid at first, and I trembled for the result; but after a lesson or two they became used to it, and the work went with far more ease and spirit than I had dared to hope it would. Here is a brief sketch of the order of the new kind of recreation:

1. The president called the class to order and called the roll.

2. He called for the secretary's report, which was corrected by the class and was then formally accepted.

3. The president asked if there was any unfinished business. If so, that was taken up first; if not,

4. The lesson of the day was called for. Whoever wished to, arose, addressed the president, and began to describe the historical events. If he made a mistake or omitted anything, any pupil who noticed it arose and, when recognized by the president, made the corrections he thought necessary. Sometimes these corrections were not correct or did not go far enough, and sev-

eral others entered into the discussion. When there were several pupils on the floor at once, the one who was recognized by the president first had the right of way, and the others had to do the same in turn. That prevented disorder. This part of the work proved to be of great value. The pupils questioned each other's statements; and, when they could not agree, the point was left over as unfinished business until the next day; and in the meantime they consulted authorities to be able to prove their points, and they used their reasoning power to good advantage.

There were all sorts of unexpected, interesting developments as the work went on. Whenever difficulties arose, we solved them together. My opinion was of no more importance than theirs. When we did not agree, I insisted that they should try their way, so they would have confidence in their own judgment if they succeeded, or so they could see its weakness if they failed. Sometimes they elected officers who were not efficient and who bungled matters uncomfortably. The pupils suffered immediately from the results and got some valuable lessons in civil government at first hand.

To tell all this sounds as if it must have taken a great deal of time. As a matter of fact, we soon found that we had time to spare. The time which had previously been taken up by the teacher's questions was all saved, and the pupils could easily recite in half an hour what it had taken them an hour to prepare. The reports of the secretary gave all the review necessary; and, as the class grew more critical of both the history and the English of these reports, the secretaries grew more careful, and very often we had reports read with which no fault could be found. The roll-call and report were sometimes finished in five minutes, the lesson of the day in thirty more, and we found ourselves with ten minutes to spare. There were various suggestions as to what we had better do with the extra time. One was, that they take longer lessons; and this led us into the habit of letting them assign their own lessons; and they almost always took longer ones than I had been in the habit of giving them.

Another suggestion was that the scholars collect pictures and show them to the class during spare minutes. One boy said he didn't have much luck finding pictures, but he would like to read things in other books and tell them to the class. A girl asked if she might draw some pictures from a book in the library, and still another boy asked me to get permission for him to go over to the Art Museum with his camera to take photographs of the casts there that were connected with our work. We did all these things, and many, many more; and these suggestions led to the richest development of all in the work of this year. The classes formed themselves into little informal clubs, met at recess and after school, and decided what each would do to contribute something interesting to the lessons. There were the drawing clubs, the camera clubs, and the clubs that brought in pictures, newspaper clippings, and told interesting accounts which they had read, calling themselves the "Sidelights Club."

We used the last half of the last history lesson each week for the reports of these clubs. They all did well for beginners, but the work of the drawing clubs was remarkable. A point worth noting is that some of the finest drawings were made by the poorest talkers.

The Sidelights Club did some fine work, too. They always had more to give than the time allowed. One boy who had tried several times without success to get a chance to talk asked me: "Do you suppose I shall ever get a chance to tell what I've found about Vestal virgins?" I told him to keep on trying, and finally he found his chance. Another boy wanted to describe a Roman house. He felt the need of a large plan to show the class, and, as he himself could not draw, he asked one of the girls in the drawing club to help him. She made him a beautiful pen-and-ink sketch of the ground-plan of a Roman villa. Still another boy, who had been specially interested in Pompeii, had been to considerable trouble to get a certain collection of Pliny's letters from the central library. He had read one of the letters describing the eruption of Vesuvius to the class, and some time afterward he said to me: "If we have time today, may I read another letter from Pliny?" "Isn't that book overdue?" I asked. "Yes," he answered, "but there's another letter in it that the rest ought to hear." He was willing to pay the fine so they might hear it.

The discipline of these classes was the easiest I have ever had, and became almost entirely unnecessary as the year went on. On one memorable occasion a boy forgot himself and was severely reprimanded by the teacher. The next day the secretary described the whole occurrence minutely in her report. It nearly took my breath away and met with a storm of protest from the class. We had the report carefully re-read, and, on finding that every word of it was perfectly true and proper, the class accepted the report, and it was placed on file with the rest. There was no more unsatisfactory conduct to report in that section.

And what was the teacher's part in this new order of things? She was learning the truth of the statement that "no teacher is equal to the dynamic force of the class before her." Her energy was taxed to the utmost to utilize all that the pupils produced, to help to get material for them, to find and suggest books to be consulted, and to give them credit for work done.

Our history work was completed two weeks before the school closed, and the extra time was spent in debates, reporting items of interest, and in making the notebooks which they were to take home as rich and attractive as possible. As the year closed, I felt that I had never done such a satisfactory year's work, and in all the classes the pupils asked if they might not be allowed to continue their work next year in the same way.

The following year (which was 1905) we tried the same method in our graduating classes which were studying United States history and civil government.

Every Monday they elected a president for the week by ballot. They changed officers often, in order that all might be able to hold position during the year. One member of the class volunteered to be secretary for the week, and four others to be assistant secretaries.

Any mistakes that were made either in history or in English were corrected by the class. Sometimes the pupil who was said to have made a mistake insisted that he was right and read the passage from the book on which he had based his statement. There were several kinds of books used in the class, and, as they often differed in statement, this led to comparison, keen discussion, and careful judgment by the class, before it could come to a conclusion.

As those who criticize are given as much credit as those who describe events, the attention of the class is constant, and, as time goes on, the pupils are careful not to make mistakes. Criticism by one of his own age means more to a boy than the criticism of a teacher. He knows very well that it is not fair to expect him to look at a thing from her point of view, nor to express it just as she does. But if one of his fellows points out his mistake, he is anxious to bring himself up to the mark at once.

If there was anything in a lesson or discussion that was not perfectly understood, the pupil who wanted an explanation felt at liberty to ask for it. This led to a most valuable kind of work. For instance, the class was discussing the administration of Monroe, and the Erie Canal was described. One of the girls arose and said: "Mr. President, I wish someone would explain to me how that canal works; I do not understand it at all." Several other girls nodded in sympathy. The boy answered: "It works by hydraulic pressure." "But just what is hydraulic pressure?" asked the girl. "I'll have to make a drawing to show it," the boy replied. He went to the board, put on the drawing, and succeeded in explaining it so the girls understood the *principle* very well. "Now, how do they use the hydraulic pressure at the canal?" was the girl's final question. Several boys tried to answer this, but none could make it clear to the girls, so they agreed to study it out more carefully and give it at the next lesson. Two of the boys investigated the matter and gave very satisfactory explanations of it.

Much of our civil-government work has been done at first hand. We had the state and city elections in our class. Previous to each election we found out what was being done in preparation for it. In connection with the city election this brought up the questions of the Luce law and the primary elections. We found we could get no help from our textbooks on these subjects, so a letter was written to Mr. Luce asking him for a copy of his law. He sent us, not only what we had asked for, but also some interesting literature in regard to the law, and told us where we could get more if we needed it.

After discussing how such things should be done, the class divided itself into two wards, appointed the proper officers, and every pupil registered exactly as he would if he were a voter. The voting lists were typewritten and placed on the bulletin board a day or two later; and, when election day came and the voters of Massachusetts were at the polls, each of our pupils had a ballot which he had prepared for himself and was ready for our voting.

All raised their desk-covers and retired within their desks as far as possible while marking their ballots. This was the best imitation we could devise of the Australian system, and it answered very well. The pupils then deposited their votes in proper order in sealed ballot boxes, and the polls were closed. The ward officers counted the votes, the result was written on the board, and the election declared.

The same thing was done several weeks later when the city election took place. The pupils entered into the spirit of· the thing, posted pictures of their favorite candidates on the bulletin board, and brought in interesting newspaper and magazine articles about them. It all seemed very real, even to the teacher; and if these boys and girls do not vote when they are of age it will not be because they do not know how.

The pupils this year (1906) have taken up the work very easily, and have been able to undertake some things which we were never able to do before. We have a Current Events Club, and among other things in which it was much interested was the coming exposition at Jamestown. Several magazines were brought in which contained accounts of it, and a discussion arose as to whether there really is a town of Jamestown now. In a similar way, a question came up as to whether or not William and Mary College is still in existence. One of our best histories states plainly that it is not, but some very good evidence was brought in on both sides. Finally one of the girls volunteered to write to a high school in Portsmouth, Va., and ask both questions. A letter came back promptly, and, in addition to the information we sought, there was sent us a plan of the exposition and some pictures of historic interest. These were posted on our bulletin board for the benefit of all, and we corrected the mistake in our textbook.

This letter which we received from Virginia will be the beginning of a Correspondence Club. Our school is on the Bunker Hill battle-ground. When we have finished studying about the battle and have collected all the historical material possible, the classes will incorporate what they have gathered and worked out in a letter illustrated by sketches and photographs taken by our Camera Club. The first copy of this will be sent to the Portsmouth High School. Others will be sent to schools in New York City, Detroit, and London, England. These schools in turn will send us letters describing places of historic interest in their neighborhoods.

We have a Library Club also, which has taken upon itself the work of beginning a students' history of Charlestown. There are few pupils who do not write well when they are writing for a purpose.

There is much more that I might say in regard to this method of carrying on our work, but enough has been said to show that work based upon the *social idea* can be carried on even with *our present school conditions* in a way, not only successful and valuable, but also quite delightful.

Pupils are glad to work when they know that whatever they are able to accomplish by themselves will be appreciated in school. In searching for material, they ransack their attics and libraries, and learn to know what there is at home better than they ever did before. They talk about their work with the family and friends, who also contributed items of interest, souvenirs of travel, and sometimes relics of value. Last week a friend loaned one of our boys a volume of London magazines published in 1776. The boy read us a thrilling account of the Boston Massacre from it.

In closing, let me say that I have recently heard from three teachers, who, though strangers to me, became interested in our work last year and tried the same method. The teacher in Detroit sends word of excellent results; one in the Medford High School says that one class of boys which was not at all interested in English history before carried the work along with life and spirit when it got a chance to conduct the class itself. I quote from the letter of the New York teacher. She says:

The class of older girls, which I had dreaded, had a life about it that *I* had never been able to arouse. The girls were full of interest in the subject, and I found they loved to talk provided I would give them a chance, and I did learn to keep my lips closed more and more. I had never realized before how much talking I had done.

As a final word, may I make a plea that we give our boys and girls a chance to work in ways more natural to them; that we learn to know them better; that we may keep their school-life so keenly in touch with the life outside that they may feel that *both* are vital parts of the social world in which they live?

AN INDIAN VILLAGE IN THE FIRST GRADE

BEATRICE CHANDLER PATTON

Training School, Los Angeles State Normal School

The school life of the twentieth-century child is complex in character and rich in opportunity for self-expression. The old limitations have been set aside, and his greatest need is unity of thought and purpose. Subject-matter can no longer be arbitrarily chosen nor fitfully pursued, but must center around some unifying idea. This unifying idea must be suggestive enough to admit of expression through many mediums; it must make a demand upon the whole power of the child; it must dominate his thought, so that he will use his reading, writing, and handwork as tools with which to express his ideas.

The Indian village set up in our sand tray by the children of the first grade has met these needs admirably and proved a source of endless delight. Longfellow's *Hiawatha*, with its vivid pictures and rhythmical measure, was taken as a basis of work, and, aside from the fascination which the story of the Indian boy holds for little children, three important points were emphasized: (1) the opportunity afforded for dramatic representation; (2) the ingenuity and skill developed by the constructive work; (3) the ease with which symbols were mastered and a reading vocabulary acquired.

A series of progressive lessons in history, reading, language, and literature was presented and met with hearty response from the children. The story of the Indian boy excited their sympathy, stimulated their imagination, and culminated in effective dramatic play. They followed every phase of the Indian boy's life with eagerness, and, in the dramatization of it, put in their own original conceptions, and expressed them in their own terms. With Hiawatha as the ideal type, the children were told in childlike fashion of the industrial side of Indian life in California. The Indian home was the point of departure, and

345

included the problems of food, clothing, and shelter in a local environment. Definite topics resulted, such as the kind of home, its equipment, the occupations of the men and women, and the play and work of the Indian boys and girls. The children delighted in the comparison with their own home-life and were quick to seize upon their own advantages. They lived in the Indian world for the time being. Tepees were decorated and set up, canoes built and launched upon the water, clay kettles swung upon sticks, and corn planted. The village needed to be inhabited, and a touch of reality was added by making clay figures of men and women in their various occupations. The men were represented smoking the peace pipe, hunting the wild animals, or fishing along the streams; while the Indian women were set up in front of their wigwams grinding corn in a mortar, or out on the hills gathering firewood, with the little Indian babies strapped upon their backs. The Indian costumes excited great interest, too, and the children worked out some original designs, repeating simple units and putting in the vivid Indian coloring with good effect.

The children's sympathies were aroused, and their minds were full of vivid images; consequently the symbols of the words which were needed to express them were quickly and easily acquired. The reading lessons were spontaneous and full of interest, and the children attacked their problems with enthusiasm and determination. With the youngest group, the lessons were presented entirely from the blackboard, and a limited amount of the material was used. A definite vocabulary was kept in mind, and sufficient amount of repetition was provided to impress the symbols presented. With the older group, who had already a fair vocabulary, the possibilities were much larger. The children retold in short, clear sentences what they had learned in the history hour, or described in simple language what they had made during the manual-training period. These short sentences, childlike in form, but full of meaning to the class, were written on the blackboard and used as reading lessons for the day.

The following are some of the reading lessons which were

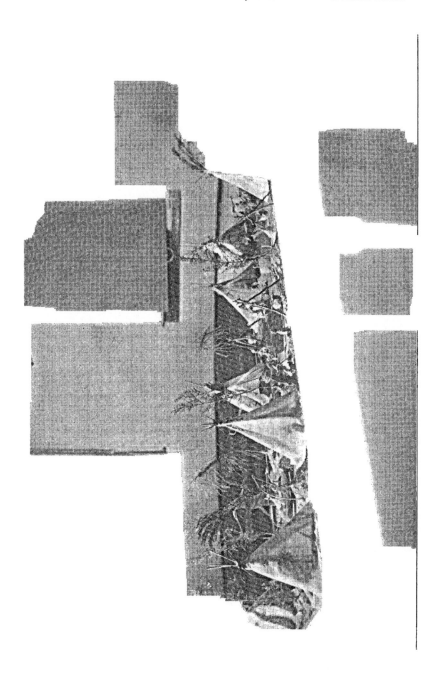

presented orally by the children and then read from the blackboard:

Hiawatha was an Indian boy.
Hiawatha lived with his grandmother.
Hiawatha lived in a wigwam.
Hiawatha slept in a cradle.

The bird sings to Hiawatha.
The squirrel talks to Hiawatha.
The rabbit plays with Hiawatha.
The big water sings to Hiawatha.
The tree bows to Hiawatha.

Hiawatha has a bow and arrow.
He will not shoot his chickens.
He will not shoot his brothers.
He will shoot a deer.

Hiawatha shot the deer.
Hiawatha will carry the deer home.
He will skin the deer.
He will make a coat out of the skin.

It was night.
Hiawatha was asleep.
It was dark.
It was very still.
Hiawatha heard an owl.
The owl was crying.
Hiawatha was afraid.
Hiawatha's grandmother told him not to be afraid.
Hiawatha heard his grandmother singing.
Hiawatha went to sleep again.

This experiment indicates that the time to teach the symbol of a word is when the image it describes is clear and vivid, and while there is an emotional response in the mind of the child. The topic has been full of poetic suggestion and childlike conceptions, but has been most valuable because it has kept a problem constantly before the children which required all their ingenuity to solve.

NATURE-STUDIES WITH BIRDS FOR THE
ELEMENTARY SCHOOL

ROBERT W. HEGNER

BIRD-PROTECTION

The necessity for bird-protection is shown in the results of an exhaustive inquiry made by Mr. William T. Hornaday, of the New York Zoölogical Garden.[1] He found that the decrease in bird-life in thirty states for the fifteen years previous to 1898 averaged 46 per cent. Nebraska showed the least decrease, with only ten per cent.; Florida the greatest, with 77 per cent. When we grasp the significance of these figures, we are appalled and at once seek the causes of this destruction. As soon as we learn the birds' enemies, we can begin to eliminate many of the causes of decrease and procure means for the reinstatement of our former feathered neighbors.

The best way to provide for the future is to teach the children the beauty of birds, and that they are not only harmless, but even of important economic value. Their worth as insect- and weed-destroyers will stimulate interest, especially if there is a garden where these pests are at work.

The lawmakers of the country have been made to realize the importance of protecting birds, and many laws have been passed imposing fines for killing birds and destroying nests and eggs. Unfortunately, it has not been possible to enforce these laws with enough rigidity to produce the desired effect. That further effort is necessary is obvious, and means that each and every one of us must be careful to live up to the letter of the law and use his influence on those with whom he comes in contact.

The subject of bird-protection brings forward the following questions: Why this absence of birds? How can we attract birds? How can we protect those already here? How can we best exert an influence on others?

[1] W. T. Hornaday, " The Destruction of Our Birds and Mammals," *Second Annual Report of the New York Zoölogical Society*, pp. 77–126.

The following are factors which account for the decrease in the number of native birds :

1. Cats.
2. Destruction by children.
3. Collectors who shoot birds and take their eggs.
4. Killed for wearing on hats.
5. Trapped for sale alive.
6. Hunted for use as food.
7. Poisoned by chemicals used in gardening, e. g., paris green.
8. Birds — some hawks, owls, crows, cowbirds, and jays.
9. Snakes.
10. Feet of cattle.
11. English sparrow.
12. Squirrels.
13. Cold, wind, and rain.
14. Telegraph wires.
15. Lighthouses.
16. Drainage of marshes.
17. Clearing away of trees and building of houses.
18. Lack of food.
19. Lack of water for drinking and bathing.
20. Lack of nesting-places.
21. Non-enforcement of laws.

The above list is very suggestive, but does not by any means include all bird enemies. It is intended to designate the more important ones.

Cats are very destructive, and particularly so during the nesting season, when the young are learning to fly and are easily caught. At this time an active cat includes tender nestlings in her daily bill of fare.

Children, especially boys, are accustomed to find pleasure in shooting birds with sling or air-rifle, just to try their skill.

Collectors shoot birds for birdskins or take eggs, thus destroying thousands every season. Collecting is a fad with most boys, and when a child shows a desire for gathering together a lot of birdskins or eggshells, he should be shown the evil of his ways, and his energy should be turned into other channels. Collections of skins and eggs are practically useless when they are kept locked away in dark drawers, and are of value only when on exhibition in public museums, where they are available for study.

Milliners supply a demand for birds as ornaments for hats, which is responsible for the devastation of vast colonies of nesting-birds. Of these the most abused is the snowy heron, whose plumes are commonly called "aigrettes." No woman would wear one of these plumes on her hat, if she knew the murder committed to obtain it. The heron is killed during the nesting season, which is the only time these plumes occur, and the eggs in the nest are left to spoil, or the young are left to starve. If women refused to wear feathers, the demand for them would cease, and no more would be sought.

Birds often turn upon members of their own tribe, and are responsible for considerable destruction. The hawks and owls prey upon smaller birds; the crows and jays are known to rob the nests of other birds; and the cowbird lays her eggs in other birds' nests, thereby preventing the successful rearing of the rightful owners. But by far the worst bird enemy is the English sparrow. This little pest, introduced from Europe, has proved to be a wolf in sheep's clothing. Brought into our country for its beneficial qualities, it has paid us for its protection by promptly driving away the robins, bluebirds, swallows, etc., and appropriating their nesting-sites in which to bring up its numerous progeny. It should be driven away from the homes of native birds, and every means possible should be used to hinder its increase.

Squirrels[2] have been known to destroy eggs and kill young birds. That they do much to harass our nesting birds is undoubtedly true, and we must choose between the squirrels and the birds.

Clearing away of trees and building of houses, and also the *drainage of marshes,* are factors in the decrease of bird-life, because they take away the nesting-sites and force the former inhabitants to go elsewhere to build houses.

---

[2] See Joseph Brunner, "The Devastating Squirrel," *Country Life in America,* Vol. VII, No. 3 (January, 1905), pp. 264–67.

1. Provide nesting-places, such as bird-boxes,[3] trees, bushes, etc.
2. Provide drinking- and bathing-places.
3. Put out food both winter and summer.
4. Drive out English sparrows.
5. Do not keep a cat.
6. Do not destroy nests or take eggs.
7. Do not use poison on garden vegetables.
8. Plant trees and bushes.
9. Provide nesting material.
10. Provide dust-bath.
11. Put out gravel and lime.
12. Hunt with a camera instead of a gun.

The bird-bath is an attraction without an equal, for birds need water, and will naturally build their nests where they can obtain it easily. There are a number of ways of providing them with drinking- and bathing-places. Where cats are common, the drinking-place should be situated above the ground, on a post or some other place where the birds are out of danger. Where there are no cats, the best bath is made on the ground. A hollow is dug three feet long and two feet and a half wide. This is lined with cobblestones laid in cement. When finished, it is three inches deep in the center and shallower toward the edges, so that birds of all sizes may bathe. If possible, the bath should be made near a water tap, where it can be filled easily and often. Bird-houses made of clay may also serve the purpose of drinking-cups, if a hollow is made in the top and kept filled with fresh water. Receptacles[4] for water which are placed in the limbs of trees excite the least suspicion.

Feeding birds is often necessary when the natural harvest has disappeared with the clearing away of weeds and trees. In winter a piece of suet or bone will attract nuthatches and downy woodpeckers. An elevated board may be supplied with seeds of the sunflower, pumpkin, hemp, timothy, remains from the hay-

---

[3] *Elementary School Teacher,* March, 1905.

[4] Mrs. F. W. Roe, "Some Familiar Florida Birds," *Bird-Lore,* December, 1904.

loft, cracked nuts, meat, and suet, and thus become a larder which will serve as a magnet for almost every variety of bird in the locality.

Hunting birds with a camera has of late become the pastime of many a birdlover who has discovered the fascination of this difficult pursuit. A volume of directions could be written on the subject, but only enough can be given here to start anyone wishing to enter the ranks of the initiated and become a true birdphotographer.

Before even the camera is purchased, one must have three things to become a successful bird-photographer. He must have a love for birds, much patience, and an abundance of time. The camera is then procured from a reliable dealer. It must be of the long-focus variety which enables the photographer to take pictures within a foot of his subject. The lens must be of good make, and the shutter must have a speed of one twenty-fifth or one-hundredth of a second in order to take successful views of moving birds. The phases of bird-photography that will be discussed below are, first, photographing nests; second, photographing birds at their nests on the ground; third, photographing birds at their nests in trees. Only the principal features of the processes will be mentioned.

The photographing of nests is very simple. The nest must be well lighted, and a small stop must be used to secure good definition.

Photographing birds at their nests presents many difficulties. Birds have learned to fear the presence of man, and will not return to the nest when anyone is near. The photographer, therefore, must be able to make the exposure from a distance. The process is as follows: The camera is securely fastened from three to ten feet from the nest, according to the size of the bird which is to be photographed. A string is attached to the shutter release and passed along the ground several hundred feet to a convenient hiding-place. The shutter is then set, a plateholder inserted, and the photographer retires to his hiding-place at the end of the string. The nests act as a magnet to the parent birds, and they will brave the terrible camera so close to the nest, in order to protect their eggs or young. In the course of an hour or two, the time varying greatly in different cases, the parent birds return to the nest. Then the string is pulled and a snapshot taken. Instead of a string, a long rubber tube with a bicycle pump on the end may be used. When the nest is in a tree, the camera is fastened to the limbs by straps and ropes, or by a clamp such as is used to fasten a kodak on the handle bars of bicycles.

The photographs of birds are not the most valuable results of bird-photography. It is impossible to keep watch hour after hour of a bird's actions while near its nest without learning something of vital interest about its home life, its food, its habits, and its song. And most valuable of all is the increasing love for all the feathered kind which must surely follow an intimate acquaintance with the most interesting and fascinating of all living creatures.

BIBLIOGRAPHY

The following references are selected as those most helpful for bird-students. The references given in the April (1906) number of the *Elementary School Teacher* also are useful in the study of bird-protection.

1. BAILEY, MRS. FLORENCE MERRIAM. "How to Conduct Field Classes." *Bird-Lore*, Vol. III, No. 3 (June, 1900), p. 83.
2. BAILEY, LIBERTY H. *The Nature-Study Idea.* New York: Doubleday, Page & Co., 1903. 159 pages.
3. CHAPMAN, FRANK M. *Bird Studies with a Camera.* With introductory chapters on the outfit and methods of the bird-photographer. New York: D. Appleton & Co., 1900. 218 pages, 110 illustrations.
4. CHAPMAN, FRANK M. "A New Device for Securing Birds' Pictures." *Bird-Lore*, Vol. III, No. 6 (November-December, 1901), p. 194.
5. CHAPMAN, FRANK M. *The Wearing of Herons' Plumes or Aigrettes.* Published by the Audubon Society of New Jersey and New York. Can be obtained from the Secretary of the State Audubon Society, Miss Emma Lockwood, 243 West Seventy-fifth Street, New York city.
6. HUBBARD, MARION E. "Bird Work at Wellesley College." *Bird-Lore*, Vol. II, No. 2 (April, 1900), p. 52.
7. JONES, LYNDS. "On Methods of Teaching Ornithology at Oberlin College." *Bird-Lore*, Vol. II, No. 1 (February, 1900), p. 14.
8. KEARTON, RICHARD. *With Nature and a Camera.* Illustrated by pictures from photographs by CHERRY KEARTON. London: Cassell & Co., 1899. 368 pages.
9. KEARTON, RICHARD. *Wild Life at Home: How to Study and Photograph It.* Many illustrations from photographs by CHERRY KEARTON. London: Cassell & Co., 1899. 188 pages.

10. PYNCHON, W. H. C. "Every-Day Study of Birds for Busy People." *Bird-Lore,* Vol. II, No. 1 (February, 1900), p. 19.

11. PRAEGER, WILLIAM E. *Birds in Horticulture.* From the *Transactions of the Illinois State Horticultural Society,* New Series, Vol. XXXIII, 1899. Reprinted for the Illinois Audubon Society, January, 1902. Can be obtained from Miss Mary Drummond, Secretary, Wheaton, Ill. Price per 100, $1.25.

12. United States Department of Agriculture. The following pamphlets have been published by the Department of Agriculture and will be sent on request.

A Review of Economic Ornithology in the United States. By T. S. PALMER. Reprint from the *Yearbook* of 1899.

Birds as Weed Destroyers. By SYLVESTER D. JUDD. Reprint from the *Yearbook* of 1898.

The English Sparrow in North America. Bulletin No. 1.

The Danger of Introducing Noxious Animals and Birds. By T. S. PALMER. Reprint from the *Yearbook* of 1898.

Some Common Birds in Their Relation to Agriculture. Farmers' Bulletin, No. 54, 1897.

The Crow Blackbirds and Their Food. By F. E. L. BEAL. Reprint from the *Yearbook* of 1894.

The Blue Jay and Its Food. By F. E. L. BEAL. Reprint from the *Yearbook* of 1896.

The Common Crow of the United States. By WALTER B. BARROWS AND E. H. SCHWARZ. Bulletin No. 6, 1895.

The Economic Value of the Bobwhite. By SYLVESTER D. JUDD. Reprint from the *Yearbook* of 1903.

Food of the Bobolink, Blackbirds, and Grackles. By F. E. L. BEAL. Bulletin No. 13, 1900.

Cuckoos and Shrikes in Their Relation to Agriculture. By F. E. L. BEAL AND SYLVESTER D. JUDD. Bulletin No. 9, 1898.

Four Common Birds of the Farm and Garden. By SYLVESTER D. JUDD. Reprint from the *Yearbook* of 1895.

MUSIC-STORIES FROM THE FIRST GRADE, ETHICAL CULTURE SCHOOL

SARAH M. MOTT
New York City

Teachers are more and more realizing the educative power of self-expression, and are finding many ways of turning to account this phase of the child's activity. Many avenues are already opened through manual training, art, dramatization, and kindred subjects. English composition, both oral and written, has received much attention, but another side of expression—music—has been lightly touched upon, or neglected altogether.

Many children live in a world of childish melodies, and the kindly sun of encouragement needs but to shine into this little world to make it bring forth a rich fruitage of "song-stories" as truly self-expressive as any other of their activities. The child sings his experiences almost as readily as he tells them, and early appreciates the kind of music necessary to convey his idea. If singing of sunshine, blue sky, or the flutter of birds, his music-story must be bright, light, and happy; if putting the baby to sleep, it must be quiet; if telling of the rough wind that bends the trees or brings the snow, it must be stirring and strong. Sometimes all words are omitted and only the tune is hummed, the other children guessing what meaning the music is intended to convey.

Along with the encouragement of the children's own productions goes other work in music intended to train the ear and voice, to lead to an appreciation of good music, and to give, though unconsciously, a comparative basis for original composition.

Whistles, farm calls, and sounds from nature are early introduced. Constant practice is given in singing rote-songs of merit. These songs are frequently tested by the child's own standards. He listens to the music of a wind-song, for instance, and tells

355

whether it adequately expresses the sentiment which the words
convey. Frequently the child makes his own song, comparing
it with the rote-song in process of learning. Composition and
memorizing go constantly hand in hand.

Sometimes a number of experiences are combined forming
a connected story, and all available material is used. At one
time the following "story" was told by children of the first
grade to those of the second and third, and the programme is
given just as it was arranged by them.

Several children who spoke of traveling decided they must
wear coats and hats; those who spoke of hoeing must have hoes;
the one who sang of the harvest must have a sickle; while the
dairy maids must have pails. Marion was chosen by the class
to tell the story because, after hearing others, it was decided she
could do it best.

Marion (spoken): "All of us have been away this summer.
First we took the ferry-boat. That blows a long whistle as it
leaves the dock."

I

oo......oo........

WHISTLE OF FERRY-BOAT

M.: "We passed a boat in the river and had to signal to it."

II

oo   oo

M.: "We saw another boat and it saluted us."

III

oo.....oo......oo

SALUTE (WHISTLE)

M.: "When we got to the other side of the river, we got on
the cars. Some of us had to go to sleep on the cars and ride
all night."

Said and acted by Peggy with eyes partly closed, while she played "train":

Choo-choo-choo
Choo-choo-choo

M.: "When we woke up, we were in the country. We had to drive to the farm. This is the way the farmer drove:"

(Acted by Jonas, who "clucked" and drove his imaginary horse with vigor.)

M.: "When we got to the farm, there were *so* many things to see. We looked at the sky."

Sung by Marie:

IV

The blue sky,   the blue sky,   the   pret-ty blue   sky!

M.: "We saw the farmers hoeing."

Acted and sung by seven children:

> "Hoeing, hoeing, here we go,
> Seven farmers in a row,
> Hoeing, hoeing, hoeing free,
> Farmer's life's the life for me."[1]

M.: "Nearly every day we went with the farmer to get the cows. This is the way we called them:"

V

Co - boss!   Co - boss!   Co - boss!

M.: "One day some little girls thought they would like to play they were dairy maids, and this is their song:"

(Eleanor Smith's *Music Primer*, p. 9.)

M.: "Laura liked to feed the chickens. This is her song that she sang when she fed them:"

---

[1] Adapted from Eleanor Smith's *Music Primer*, "Left! Right!", p. 49.

VI

Here, lit - tle chick-ens,   Come and   get   some corn!

CALLING THE CHICKENS

Several children impersonated the chickens and hopped right sprightly for the imaginary corn.

M.: "Peggy watched the bees and made up this little song:"

VII

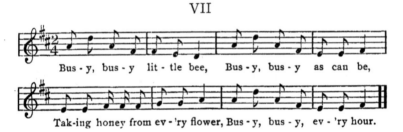

Bus - y, bus - y lit - tle bee,   Bus - y, bus - y   as can be,

Tak-ing honey from ev - 'ry flower, Bus - y, bus - y, ev - 'ry hour.

M.: "I saw a bluebird and made this rhyme about him:

    'I know a little bluebird,
    His back is all in blue,
    And when he sings a little song,
    I always think of you.'"

M.: "But we had to leave the farm and come back to the city. Robert will tell you how we said good-bye."

    "The coach is at the door at last,
    The eager children mounting fast,
    And kissing hands in chorus sing:
    'Good-bye, good-bye, to everything.'"[2]

M.: "While we were away, the things we had planted in our garden at school had been growing and growing. We went into the garden when we got back to school and found the corn was ripe and the stalks must be cut down. Louise made up this song:"

[2] R. L. Stevenson's "Farewell to the Farm."

Sung and acted by Louise:

VIII

Here is some corn growing up so high, I must go and cut it down.

SONG OF THE CORN

M.: "Herbert cut it down and made up this song:"

IX

Here is the sick-le, so stead-y and bright,

Let us cut it down, Let us cut it down.

M.: "Now our garden and the farm are all ready for winter. The wind is calling the leaves. They will play a little while and then go to sleep."

(' Come Little Leaves " — music by Horatio Parker, sung by entire class.)

While this programme is chiefly related to nature-work, other experiences are often sung. Games are originated, sung, and played. Dolly is lulled to sleep, and playmates are invited to join a game. In fact, every activity is carried along in song as well as in any other way. The children themselves are the guides, and their enjoyment of the work as well as their originality in it is a source of constant inspiration and help to the teacher.

AN ESKIMO SONG

Words and melody by children of the Sixth School Year of the University
Elementary School

The jol - ly lit - tle Es - ki mo. ....
Al - though his house is made of snow, Al-

Rides a - cross the ice and snow; He drives his dogs from
though the i - cy winds do blow, The furs he wears pro-

morn till night, And snaps his whip with all his might.
tect him so, That he's not cold at all, you know.

EDITORIAL NOTES

Everybody in Chicago is trying to help solve its educational problems. This is at once a source of hope and confusion; of The School hope, because out of a multitude of counsel will Question in come wisdom; of confusion, because in the babble Chicago of the masses there is apt to be some darkening of counsel "by words without knowledge."

The people of Chicago at this time are not to be satisfied by merely quelling the riot; when peace does come it will be because order has been established through the recognition of some new, or at least some more satisfactory, principles of school management.

At a recent banquet, the Merchants' Club took a hand in the discussion by securing some speakers from Boston, New York, and St. Louis who, as men interested in the public-A Notable school system, perhaps more strongly from the Banquet administrative side, told how educational affairs are managed in their respective cities. Of the addresses given, that by President Butler, of Columbia University, was most noteworthy, not only because of the speaker's large experience in shaping the educational affairs of a great city, but also because of the specific application of his remarks to the situation in Chicago. Concerning many of the points in his speech there can be no serious difference of opinion. But few thinking people will dispute his statement as to a school board's function which is found in the following quotation from his speech:

"The sole business of the board is to administer the finances and choose the best officer procurable to carry out a high educa-Dr. Butler's tional policy. If it goes farther than that, it will Ideas get into deep water. The work of the board is to legislate and supervise; when it begins to execute, then somebody will have to leave.

"Given a representative board of the best citizens you can get, citizens of common-sense and high-mindedness, the highest function they can perform is to choose an individual who can be the guide and inspiration of the public-school system. I say guide and inspiration because I hold ideas different from some others as to the superintendent of public schools. The best school system in America should have a big, strong, vigorous personality at its head, and you must create a big office to have a big personality in it.

"The superintendent should have a satisfactory salary. He is not a clerk to be brow-beaten and bullied, but a professional officer, representing cultural forces in your community at work upon the minds of the youth of the next generation. There is no man too great to be superintendent of the schools of Chicago."

It is doubtful if any "representative board of the best citizens" would ever wish to assume any other functions than those described by Dr. Butler, did not circumstances of **A Discretionary** unusual character force other matters upon them in **Board** their high capacity as a court of last appeal. The really best board of education, therefore, is one made up "of the best citizens you can get," who are willing, as a last resort, to ignore the limitations of their duties as fixed by a theory spun out of academic discussion, and who will carefully consider in a generous and impartial manner new duties which are born of new occasions. Nothing having the rapid expansive growth of our public-school system can be governed wholly by precedents.

Dr. Butler did not reach, in his remarks, the real cause of discontent in this city, and hence he failed to accomplish as much **The Real** as one could have wished. He dwelt mainly, in a **Cause of** critical manner, upon the present attitude and work **Trouble** of the Board of Education, failing to recognize that this is merely the necessary result of a deep-seated cause. This cause lies in a profound dissatisfaction on the part of a large number of teachers with the administration of the school system. In order, therefore, to have made the most of his opportunity, he should have dealt with the whole problem in a fair and an impartial manner. He, in common with the other speakers, made for the thousandth time the ancient blunder of treating the teaching force as a negligible factor. The dissatisfaction now existing, of course, cannot be said to be universal among the teachers and principals, if one chooses to make a count. That it does exist, though, among so large a number, and among so many whose motives must be respected, gives it a tremendous significance, which no one who attempts to grapple with the situation should overlook. The movement toward a better state of things in school affairs has been of slow growth, and it has developed from many and varied sources. It is the acme of narrowness to charge all the present difficulties in school matters against superintendents and boards of education. They have been the victims as often, perhaps, as the cause of the trouble that is now in an acute stage. Broadly speaking, it is the result of a lack of knowledge on the part of everybody, teachers as well as others, as to how a common-school system should be managed in order to keep pace

Whose Fault? with the unparalleled growth of the city. The more thoroughly one realizes his own ignorance as to how this should have been done, or as to what are the right things to do in the present crisis, the more humble he is likely to be in offering his advice. From the vantage-ground of the present one can see that in the past the mistakes have been pretty evenly distributed among all of those who took part in managing the schools. There is a great outcry for an administration of the schools on business principles. Yet, it is to boards with business ideas, probably, that Chicago owes the loss of her almost priceless public lands that were intended to support the schools. The men who composed those short-sighted boards were the business ancestors of the Merchants' Club. One cannot believe that they were all thieves or all dishonest. They simply failed to comprehend Chicago then, as the future will likely show that the Merchants' Club fails to comprehend it at the present time. People simply make mistakes; that's all there is to it.

The real educational question before Chicago is this: How can a village-school system of administration which is successful

Question at Issue with a couple of hundred of children, half a dozen teachers, and a principal be modified so as to work well in a city with some hundreds of thousands of children, half a dozen thousand teachers, and

a superintendent? Chicago is operated today under the
Overgrown village system, with this important difference: In
Village the village, while there is, in form, a one-man
System power, the fact that he is in close personal contact
with the work of each teacher makes it both easy and natural for
him to take the interests of all carefully into account. The
administration is essentially democratic. In the large city system the superintendent's sympathetic contact with the teacher is
wanting: he makes up his mind without this knowledge, and
the scheme becomes essentially autocratic. The gist of the Chicago problem is simply how to supply effectively this missing
link between the teachers' interests and the superintendent's
powers. If the speakers before the Merchants' Club had addressed
themselves to this point, they would, at least, have had the merit
of speaking upon the question at issue.

The most feasible plan for uniting the efforts and unifying
the interests of the superintendent and teachers would seem to
Representation be, then, some form of organized representation. If
Needed this were properly worked out, every other difficulty
in the case would be put upon "its passage" toward
solution. People generally seem to have the idea that teachers
desire such an arrangement because they want to drag things
to their ruin. Some teachers, indeed, may be possessed with
this idea; but the majority are fair-minded and do not have
such notions at all. They would be wholly satisfied if they
could but get freely and directly to the superintendent, before
he acts, a statement of what they believe to be for the
best interests of the schools. If this could be done officially
through regularly organized channels, in the end, it would be
sufficient. There is nothing—there can be nothing—in such a
plan of administration to prevent a superintendent from being just
the kind of a man Dr. Butler depicted—one "who can be the
guide and inspiration of the public-school system." There
is nothing in the operation of such a plan—there can be nothing
in it—that will interfere with the initiative or proper authority
of "the big, strong, vigorous personality" which he says a
superintendent should have. Dr. Butler told the Merchants'

Club to create a big office for a big personality; this is inverting the process. A personality with strength and breadth enough to grasp the situation from the side of the teachers as well as from the side of the public will make for itself an office larger than anything the Merchants' Club has yet dreamed of. A personality of the right kind will have no difficulty about his place.

In stating the functions of a school board, none of the speakers seemed to think that its duties need go farther than the election of a "big, vigorous personality" who by his own methods should "lick" the teaching force into "shape." Not only the teachers, but also, it is believed, the sober-minded element of the community at large, will adjudge Dr. Butler a bit harsh when he says in his address:

"If I were a member of your school board, I would do my best to have adopted a by-law which would remove from the school service any teacher who affiliates himself or herself **Rather Harsh** with a labor organization. If I were a member of your charter convention, I would have a vote and a roll-call on that question in the charter convention." These sentiments were received with "overwhelming applause."

Careful inquiry, however, into the origin and history of the teachers' organizations in this city will not justify either the feeling of the speaker or the enthusiasm of the **Why Teachers** audience. It is plain history, so recent that every- **Organized** body knows it, that this organization of teachers and its affiliations grew up only when, and simply and solely because, the great corporations, including some of Chicago's merchant princes, so persistently and so ravenously robbed the school treasury that neither the "big, vigorous personality" of the superintendent, nor the school board, nor anybody else in power could save the schools from what seemed to be 'utter demoralization, if not ruin. Then the common teachers—to their eternal honor be it said—rose in their righteous wrath, organized and beat the wolves off, and saved the schools to the people. Upon the necessity and the propriety of such an organization, the teachers themselves will heartily support any demand for a roll-call in the charter convention. Since Dr. Butler chose to deal specifically with Chicago conditions, it is a matter of regret that he did not give due credit to what the teachers have actually accomplished against tremendous odds.

Pursuing his subject with frightful logic, he said: "If the teachers of the public schools are to be organized, why not the firemen? If the firemen are to organize, why not **This is** the police? If the police, why not the army?" To **Disturbing** all of this the straight and obvious reply is that, long before they are subjected to the same humiliating conditions that beset the teachers four or five years ago, the firemen WILL organize; and so will the policemen, and finally so will the army! That is history; read it in the past in English, or read it in the present in Russian. The principle of representation **Principle of** in this country and generally in this age is incon- **Representation** trovertible. The theory that the people have a right to create a body of public servants who shall be denied an effective voice in the internal management of their own affairs, either directly or through their own properly accredited representatives, is out of date. This is the crux of the whole matter. The six thousand teachers of Chicago have grown up. They have got past the point where they will submit to a "big, strong, vigorous personality" who seeks to "guide" and "inspire" the school system with a club. They are not hirelings, applying Dr. Butler's apotheosis of the superintendent, to be browbeaten and bullied, but professional ladies and gentlemen representing cultural forces in the community at work upon the minds of the youth of the next generation. The present struggle should in no wise be construed as being a war **No Conflict of** upon the legitimate legislative functions of the **Functions** Board of Education or upon the proper executive functions of the superintendent or upon the rights of either to any initiative. It represents solely an effort on the part of the teachers to secure a voice in the educational counsels of the city which their close relations to the children and their practical knowledge of the needs of the schools may justify. They should have the right and the power to initiate and to recommend, by officially established means, legislation or anything else to either the superintendent or board or both that may in the judgment of the teachers seem to be wise. This is all that is needed at present to calm the intolerable turmoil and to start the school system on the road toward a safe, sane, and conservative management. The details of such a plan of administration will, of course, be numbered by multitudes that no one can foresee. In meeting these, time will develop wisdom, and wisdom will beget tolerance and patience, which alone are the sureties of progress and peace. W. S. J.

Note.—Since writing the foregoing editorial notes, and as we go to press, the copy of a report has been received which has been prepared by a subcommittee of the Board of Education. This report, somewhat abridged, is printed elsewhere in this issue. We are glad to submit it to the teachers of the country as being, perhaps, the most comprehensive and intelligent plan yet proposed anywhere which provides for a representation of the teachers in educational matters. The report is so clearly in line with the thought of the editorial, not only in this issue, but also in former numbers of the *Elementary School Teacher* (see the numbers for March, 1905, p. 439, and January, 1906, p. 265), that we are glad to make space for it. It deserves the closest study on the part of all the friends of public education. [THE EDITORS.]

BOOK REVIEWS

The School and Its Life. By CHARLES B. GILBERT. New York and Chicago: Silver, Burdett & Co. Pp. 259.

The above volume is a suggestive, disconnected, but not unrelated group of twenty-four short essays on subjects which are sure to be uppermost, at one time or another, in the experience of every school superintendent. The fact that the book lacks continuity diminishes its value, but the treatment of some subjects —e. g., chapter xv, of the judging and rating of teachers—shows a grasp of the real situation and a breadth of vision born only of real contact with a great system of schools. The benefits of co-operation applied to parent, teacher, and pupil are clearly shown.

Some of the strongest chapters in the book discuss the superintendent, his relations with teachers, and his social position in the community. If he is the right man in the right place, he can practically dominate the situation. If he cannot dominate the situation, nor secure enough power to make the board follow his leadership, he is not the man for the place. No system can be devised which can make a strong, successful man out of a weak one.

Mothers' clubs, parents' associations, and such efforts are commended as means of securing common, desirable information, and keeping the schools democratic. The last chapter sets forth "centralization of schools," elective or appointive boards, large or small boards of education, tenure of office for superintendents and teachers; the final test of all being the welfare of the individual children in schools. J. STANLEY BROWN

GABRIEL COMPAYRÉ

VOLUME VII NUMBER 7

THE ELEMENTARY SCHOOL TEACHER

MARCH, 1907

PUBLIC INSTRUCTION IN FRANCE IN 1906

GABRIEL COMPAYRÉ
General Inspector of Public Instruction, Paris

Within a quarter of a century the impulse of the republican government has modified our system of education to such an extent that it can hardly be recognized. Forty or fifty years later than in the United States, France has witnessed in its elementary schools a movement of progress similar to that period of development which has been called, in your country, the "revival of the common school." But in higher education also these reforms have been both numerous and important. Great innovations, veritable creations, have changed the face of things.

It is out of the question to enumerate them all in a brief survey, but we shall at least indicate the essential features of what has been done, and in addition make a few prophecies for the future.

FRENCH UNIVERSITIES

Prior to 1896 France had no universities. This country, which, during the Middle Ages, had held first rank in the establishment of these organs of higher learning, had, for a hundred years, been deprived of them. There were but few isolated faculties, scattered and without cohesion—faculties of law, medicine, science, and letters. Being under the direction of the government, these faculties were deprived of all individual liberty. They frequently lacked the spirit of initiative and of research. They were poor and without proper equipment. They were located in buildings which were old and inadequate. Their facilities were insufficient, particularly in the faculties of sciences, which had no laboratories and but little apparatus for research. Our most celebrated men of learning—Claude Bernard, for instance—have labored in garrets, in cellars, and in sheds.

On the other hand, the faculties of letters had no regular students, but only occasional listeners—amateurs who came for diversion rather than to derive benefit from lessons that were more oratorical than didactic. Instructors were few—but four or five in faculties that today number fifteen or twenty. There was not always an instructor to represent subjects of importance or sciences of the first order. And, finally, these faculties, which did not always deserve their title of institutions of higher learning, and the greater number of which were simply professional schools where public examinations were held, did not enjoy a life in common. They vegetated in the same city, separated from one another. As recently stated by M. Liard (who, as director of higher education, has contributed more than any other man to the foundation of new universities), even in Paris the members of the various faculties met but once a year at the "Messe du Saint Esprit."

Today everything is changed. The law of 1896 has established upon solid foundations the sixteen French universities. No doubt, all these are not of equal importance. A few of them comprise but two faculties: sciences and letters. But others are decidedly flourishing, and can now compete with foreign universities. The University of Paris takes the lead, and its pre-eminence is not contested. However, Lyons, Nancy, Lille, Bordeaux, Montpellier, Toulouse, and Grenoble also excel, and in some respects compete with, the University of Paris.

Perhaps the new law has not as yet been sufficiently liberal in its concessions to our universities. It may still be desired that they become more and more autonomous. But even now they govern their own destinies in a large measure, and are free in their movements. Under the presidency of the rector, who alone directly represents the government, a council of deans and professors—the latter elected by their colleagues—has charge of their management. This council, itself under the control of the minister of public instruction, regulates the order of studies, establishes the budget of the university, introduces new courses, etc.

Universities in France have not had the good fortune to be endowed by such generous benefactors as the multimillionaires in the United States—a Leland Stanford or a Rockefeller. Such great fortunes are not common in France. However, the Universities of Paris, Lyons, Nancy, and Bordeaux have in the past been favored with gifts, some of them amounting to two or three hundred thousand francs. On the other hand, their wealth accrues from year to year through increasing attendance.

It is true that foreigners do not respond as readily as we could wish to the invitation of France. Americans in particular are too likely to pass France by on their way to German universities. Progress, however, is marked and constant. Official statistics show that the enrolment of foreign students, who in 1900 numbered 1,779, has been as follows: 1901, 1,841; 1902, 1,862; 1903, 2,045; 1904, 2,094; 1905, 2,360, of whom 774 were women. With its 31,000 men students and about 1,000 women students—foreigners not included—our higher education, while not as yet on a par with that of Germany, occupies a very honorable position in the European world. The University of Paris alone has enrolled more than one-third of the total number of men students, French and foreign, or 12,496 in 1905, and about one-half of the women students, or 935, the total number of these being 1,922.

SECONDARY EDUCATION

The reform of 1902 has greatly modified the system of secondary studies in colleges and *lycées* for boys. This reform had been prepared by the extensive investigations of a committee, of which M. Ribot, former minister of public instruction, was chairman, in which the reports of the greater number of competent professional men had been collected. It consisted in creating four different types of secondary education, each having its own distinct curriculum, but with the same time given to each—

i. e.; seven years—and all of them leading to the baccalaureate. All of these four baccalaureates bear upon different subjects, but in rank they are equal and extend practically the same privileges to those who have obtained them.

At the close of his primary training, either in public schools or in elementary classes of colleges or *lycées* (for we have not, as yet, succeeded in effecting in the public or common schools the fusion of all the children of the nation), the French child enters, at the age of nine or ten, what is called the sixth class. There he may make his choice between two distinct courses of study, between two different paths: A, the classical course, characterized by the teaching of Latin; and B, the modern course, from which Latin is excluded and where the teaching of the sciences predominates. In the following classes—the fifth, fourth, and third, which, with the sixth, constitute what is called the first "cycle"—the same dual system is observed. Students go forth in two directions, which are parallel, with the exception that in the fourth class a new element of differentiation appears in Division A; the students who are in this division may, if they so desire, choose the study of Greek. Let us add at once that those who take advantage of this elective privilege are not numerous, and that Greek has not many adherents.

The subdivision into four sections does not occur before the second cycle, which comprises two years' study, the second and the first class. The first class is a substitute for that which in 1902 was called the class of rhetoric. Each of the four sections bears a sub-title: Section A=Latin–Greek; Section B=Latin–modern languages; Section C=Latin–sciences; Section D= sciences–modern languages.

Section A is nearly analogous to the old classical instruction. Students who in the fourth class, A, had chosen the study of Greek alone are admitted.

Section B comprises Latin given in the same proportion as in Section A, but is characterized by the larger proportion being given to the teaching of modern languages, German and English.

Section C retains the study of Latin and, of course, of

French and other literary instruction; but its marked distinction is the predominance of the sciences—it is the scientific section.

Finally, Section D of the second cycle, being the only one in which Latin is not taught, continues Section B of the first cycle. In this section sciences and modern languages predominate.

To the six years' study in the first and second cycle is added a last year of school-work in two parallel classes, one of which is called "philosophy," and the other "mathematics." Both are elective courses which may be taken optionally by students of the four sections A, B, C, D, provided they have passed successfully the first partial examination of one of the four baccalaureates.

To sum up, Greek is taught only in Section A; Latin, in Sections A, B, and C, and in the same proportions. As to the other subjects—sciences, French, and other modern languages, history, and geography—they appear in the programme of the four sections, but are given in various amounts in each section.

Such is the new programme of studies, as carried out during the last four years in our colleges and *lycées* for boys. In formulating this programme the elective system for many years past in vogue in the colleges of the United States has been suggestive. In organizing four series of instruction, while we formerly had but two, the classical and the modern courses, differences in the students' aptitude and plans for the future have been taken into consideration. Means by which to obtain the baccalaureate have been increased, and in order to excite the zeal of the students a greater variety of subjects has been offered.

But the reform of 1902 has also another aspect. It endeavors better to adapt secondary studies to the modern spirit and to the necessities of life at the present day. It tends obviously to limit the importance of the old classical studies, and to increase in the same proportion that of sciences and modern languages. In the latter particularly an important step forward has been made, not only because they are given broader attention in the curriculum, but also through the method now employed in teaching them. Formerly they were taught in the same manner as dead languages, by means of grammatical exercises through the explanation and written translation of text, so that even the best students, although able to read and understand German and English, were seldom able to speak these languages. It would seem that the application of the "direct" method now adopted, and which consists in conversational exercises between teacher and pupil—the method which imparts the languages through their practical application —has already produced far better results.

It is interesting to note how students of the *lycées* of France are distributed in the four new sections. It is far from being an equal division. Section D, in which no Latin is taught is the best attended, as was to be expected. According to official reports, this section was chosen in 1905–6 by two-fifths of the students, or, in exact figures, 39.15 per cent.; while the least-attended section (11.41 per cent.) is Section A, in which are maintained the traditions of Graeco-Latin humanism, now obviously in decline. Section C, the scientific course, which is in greater favor, recruits a large number of students—26.42 per cent.; and finally Section B, Latin–modern languages, enrols an almost equal number, or 23.02 per cent. No doubt these figures will fluctuate. At first there was, very naturally, some hesitation, some uncertainty. Owing to lack of experience or to insufficient information, neither parents nor students seemed to be able to decide which section to favor or to select. The situation was similar to that at a new railway station, where several trains are headed in different directions, and where the ill-informed traveler is much at loss to know which road to take. I do not believe, however, that the slight fluctuation which may take place from year to year will seriously modify the general aspect of the programmes just outlined.

From the point of view of school-work, the reform of 1902 seems to give good results; and, notwithstanding the usual instability of our laws relating to secondary education, there is reason to believe that this reform will last, with the possible exception of a few modifications in the curriculum, which is overcrowded in certain respects. The only material modification which may be prophesied for the near future is the suppression, or rather the transformation, of the baccalaureate. In accordance with a bill recently submitted to the chamber of Deputies by M. Briand, minister of public instruction, the baccalaureate, as it is conferred today, after examinations by the faculties of letters and sciences, would be supplanted by a certificate or diploma of secondary studies, which would be granted, one for each section, by the professors of *lycées* and colleges. It is true that the suppression of the baccalaureate has been so often demanded that it is permitted to doubt the success of M. Briand's proposition. However, let us call attention to the fact that a recent measure which admits the professors of *lycées* to the jury for the baccalaureate has, to a certain extent, prepared the way for the proposed reform.

SECONDARY EDUCATION FOR GIRLS

Coeducation, as you know, is not in favor with us, except in a few rural schools where mixed or "joint schools" still exist, owing to the fact that in the small communes resources are insufficient to warrant the luxury of two distinct schools, one for girls and the other for boys. As far as secondary instruction is concerned, the separation of the sexes still remains the absolute rule, and our *lycées* for women are institutions designed as exclusively for girls as are Vassar, Smith, Wellesley, and Bryn Mawr colleges in the United States.

It is only since 1880 that the French government has organized secondary instruction for girls. Prior to this date instruction was given only in private schools, generally in religious institutions, or convents. It is the law of 1880, named the Camille Sée Law after its promulgator, that has created the *lycées* and colleges for girls. Notwithstanding the opposition of the clerical party and the prejudices of certain families, these official establishments have continually prospered and developed as the result of the combined efforts of the government and the municipalities. Each year the attendance increases perceptibly, and each year similar institutions are opened in those cities which are not already possessing them.

At the present time we have forty-two *lycées* for women, aggregating approximately 12,500 students, and forty-two colleges, with 8,000 pupils. To these must be added eighty *cours secondaires* ("secondary courses"), which number also nearly 8,000 students. These so-called secondary courses, established by the municipalities from their own resources and with only slight aid from the government, are being gradually transformed into *lycées* and colleges.

In the secondary courses the course of study covers but three years, while in the *lycées* and colleges it extends over five. The curriculum offers about the same instruction as that of the *lycées* and colleges for boys, save that Latin is not taught and that special courses for women, such as sewing, domestic science, etc., are included. The diploma granted at the end is not the baccalaureate, but a special one called *diplome de fin d'études secondaires* ("diploma for completion of secondary studies".).

PRIMARY EDUCATION

It is in her primary schools, even more than in her institutions for secondary or higher education, that republican France has exerted her influence. The primary school, which is a lay school, free and compulsory, and which was created by the laws of 1881–82 and 1886, constantly grows, and the generation to whose development it contributes is more and more animated by the modern, democratic spirit. The expenditures for primary instruction are yearly increased by the government, which then makes further appropriations for this purpose: 140 million francs in 1896, and more than 202 millions in 1906. To these sums granted by the government must be added those contributed by the departments and the communes, so that the total expenditures for primary instruction amount to about 270 million francs.

Included in primary instruction in France are the schools called "superior primary schools," equivalent to the American high schools, with the exception that Latin is excluded and that the students are somewhat younger, entering the schools at the age of twelve or thirteen, to leave it when fifteen or sixteen years old. At present there are 304 of these schools, 204 of which are for boys and 100 for girls. While the progress of our superior primary schools has not been so rapid as that of your high schools, yet their development has been considerable. In the two years from 1903 to 1905, 43 new schools were opened, and from 1900 to 1905 the number of students increased from 28,000 to 50,000. The number is yet too small, and it is evident that out of the millions of children who leave the elementary primary schools at the age of eleven or twelve too few receive as yet a complementary education in regular courses of studies. We endeavor to remedy in part these conditions by increasing the number of courses called *post-scolaires*—such as courses for adults, popular lectures, etc.; but, whatever may be the success of these courses, we cannot expect to render to adults such services as the "schools of continuation" afford in Germany. Consideration has been given to making obligatory the courses for adults, which have hitherto been elective.

The French government is becoming more and more solicitous for the professional training of men and women teachers. A reform dating from 1904 has modified the régime of our normal schools in its decision that in the future the third year of study be set aside for the application of practical pedagogy and for the technical education of future teachers. There are today not less than 10,000 student-teachers of both sexes who are preparing themselves in our normal schools creditably to fulfil their future duties.

Retaining the traditional separation of the sexes in the primary schools as well as in the *lycées* and colleges and without adopting your favorite principle of coeducation, against which there exist in France all sorts of prejudices, the administration of public instruction seems disposed to favor mixed or joint schools at least in rural districts. A recent circular from the ministry of public instruction to the departmental authorities recommends that for the direction of these schools the preference be given to women, as if it were anticipated that, with us also, women teachers will to a large extent supersede men.

As a consequence of the recent laws for the suppression of religious orders, a number of private sectarian schools have been closed. The laity in education has not encountered in France so vigorous an opposition as in England, where the Education

Bill of 1906, although much more moderate than the French law, in that it imposed but slight restrictions upon religious, confessional, and denominational teaching, has been rejected in the House of Lords. Let us note, however, that the abolition of religious orders has not as yet been entirely effective. To all appearances the law is observed, but nevertheless it is evaded. In many cases the *Frères des Écoles chrétiennes,* who directed the larger number of the former confessional schools, have simply changed their costume. They have exchanged their ecclesiastical robe for the garb of the civilian, and, thus transformed in exterior appearance, although not modifying in the least their methods nor the character of their teaching, they continue to direct schools. Their number has decreased, however, their patronage has diminished, and the competition they exert against lay schools is less and less to be feared. With its 100,000 men and women teachers, France increasingly tends to bring together in the schools of the government nearly all the children of the nation, and also to establish the unity of national education.

PHYSICAL TRAINING—A QUESTION OF JUDICIOUS SUPPORT

A DISCUSSION OF PHYSICAL TRAINING IN ITS LARGER ASPECTS, AS AFFECTING SCHOOL YOUTH

CARL J. KROH
School of Education

Modern physical training as an operative and effective factor in education is unthinkable without the setting of an enlightened background. Its pedagogical-aesthetical and anatomical-physiological aspects involve more than mere disciplinary values and health-promoting influences—they represent the highest that is conceivable in art, and what has been achieved in the science of the modern doctrine of the human body as well.

So regarded, physical training depends for its best unfolding and maintenance on the attitude of the school, and on the exponents of its ideals. The school is the generative power and principal factor in the advancement of the universal interests to be subserved. Inquiry, therefore, reflecting the true function of physical training in a scheme of education, is necessarily of paramount importance in outlining a policy calculated to obviate unnecessary and unprofitable experimentation.

In the past, as in the present, inquiries into the merits of the multiform instructional procedures evolved and extant have been influenced by the character of the conceptions held with regard to it. Preconceptions, without the data of comprehensive experiences, have, in instances without number, been the rule in its organization. Declarations of mere intentional purport have availed naught, the most liberal provisions not unfrequently proving antidotal.

Uncritical conclusions have resulted in an overemphasis of extremes—huge effort on the one hand, and on the other the prominence accorded the ameliorative or remedial features of gymnastic treatment.

Wherever physical training was suffered to exist without the enthusiasm born of intelligent methods, and minus the co-operating factors of judicious support, its design became manifest in some tumbleform of gymnastics or in an emphasis of certain work-phases, curtailing the general and adequate concept of its import. Intelligently directed and supported, it became an ever-growing source of interest by virtue of its manifold aims and resources.

Conservatism and enthusiasm have until within recent times characterized the two phases of its development.

The status of physical training in some of the leading institutions of the country, not at all final, is the outcome of much thoughtful inquiry and consistent experiment. Psycho-physical in its modern aspect, its inherent quickening influences have become active and virile only since its advocates and expositors have persisted in reconciling the claims advanced in its behalf with those of the other interests included in educational pursuits. It was from this view-point that its demonstrable claims and relations advanced and became an integral part of educational work.

The question of a rationale of methods in physical training, as applied to the secondary school, was recently discussed by a small coterie of experts in educational work. The general argumentative trend of the following summary presents the attitude taken.

In an analysis of the present status of physical training, it was asserted that the popular concept with regard to it was directed principally toward the athletic features of physical activities. The public, as a rule, was influenced by what was presented in the burden of literature bearing on huge athletics, principally through the daily press. Systematic organization of reportorial staffs in the interests of universities, colleges, schools, and athletic clubs, devoted to field and track events, and to innumerable competitive sports, furnished the papers with the material at once welcome and necessary to sustain the large so-called sporting interests involved. The views concerning a rationale of physical education expressed in the public press were rare indeed in a comparison with this propaganda.

It was conceded that, however the aptitudes and predilections of normally constituted youth were directed and utilized for educational ends, the use and wont of the physical powers, *per se*, in the untrammeled exploitation and freedom of natural activities remained a matter of impulse and necessity, as distinct from the conventional routine of home and school occupations as is school formalism from the freedom of the playground. Instinctive desire prompted this use and wont, and the motive, if one could speak of a motive, was discerned in the cultivation of the sense of pleasurable experiences. Motive might represent a growing realization of what seemed practicable, advantageous, or helpful in the ordinary course of life-routine. The instinctive impulse, on the other hand, represented the alternative for the formalism of the school, sustaining the natural gift of cheerfulness and mirth. Both served the gradual preparation of the young aspirant for the larger responsibilities of a maturer life, and their encouragement was absolutely desirable—the question of direction of activities in the most profitable ways and in concord with prudence constituting the problem of the school. Therefore the most profitable school curriculum was the one based on a recognition of the facts evidenced in the daily life of school youth.

The charm of robust activity, characteristic of the display of skill and sagacity, witnessed in the individual and concerted action of field athletics during the recurring seasons of each year, had exerted a tremendous influence on the rank and file of our school youth. Outdoor recreation had received a mighty impulse. This was as it should be. Not only, however, were the seasonal in- and outdoor sports and games more popular than ever before, but a glance beyond the school gymnasium disclosed our young people disporting themselves in many interesting ways. Even our ten- and twelve-year-olds hurdle-jumped and danced to the shot-put in the most approved style. Our grammar-school boys and those beyond emulated the methods and practices of the seasoned athlete of the organized training quarters in the forms typical of the most successful record-breakers. The principles underlying proficiency were largely left to solution in interesting illustrations on the corner lot, back yard, and open-air playground. This was not as it should be.

The popular idea of our physical renaissance had become as distinct in its outward form from what it represented a decade or so ago as the onetime calisthenic drill, so variously provided for in innumerable manuals, appeared in a contrast with the huge athletics of today. Mere pleasurable activity for the sake of health and ample recreation had been augmented in a remarkable way by the enthusiasm for contests and competitions, the legitimacy of which was unquestioned in the acclaim of the interested multitudes.

The recognition of this very large factor in the life of our school youth had, with all educators who have thought of the matter, become imperative. Wherever, therefore, it assumed the proportions characteristic of organized competitions, we met with a pronounced demand for a better organization of physical training.

It was only reasonable under the conditions to assume that the opinions of a large and interested body of teachers must ultimately crystallize toward some definite and practical plan regarding such organization, since it was evident from past experiences that an effective organization of physical training without this general co-operation must fall short of its import.

These and other demands, wherever thoughtful inquiry had prevailed, indicated, if anything at all, that students should undergo a preparation for whatever specialization in athletics they might wish to engage in, and that there should be the fullest recognition of the regularly constituted authorities of physical training in determining the order of procedures for such training.

It was recognized that certain knowledge affecting the welfare of youth, which should be common possession, was not sufficiently emphasized in the school curriculum. There was felt to be much erring in matters pertaining to wholesome education. The mere stimulus of competition was deplorable, because pernicious. From the standpoint of the teacher, it was not enough to encourage the youth to exercise, and it was hazardous to encourage him to excel in athletics. With the superior boy this encouragement might, or it might not, lead to a proper regard for self. Many factors were constantly at play in strenuous, rather than in pleasurable, activities. The elements of time and energy in action were not merely estimated, but also generally considered—and unhappily for many boys—on the do-or-die side. It was not always a considerate estimate in the sense of prudence that characterized the sports of youth. Behind this demand for an appreciation of, and necessity for, the care of the body should stand the teacher. An intimate acquaintance with the structure of the human organism and its wonderful mechanism begets the appreciative faculty. This knowledge alone instils motives of the right sort into the aspiring student, and begets with the pedagogue concern for those he loves or should love well enough to guide aright in this very important and practical matter of the care of the body and its functions.

All educative pursuits involved certain fundamental considerations—the initial premise, the purpose and procedure, or, the principles, aims or problems, and methods. Principles as aims must always be based on pedagogy and aesthetics, the appreciation of the beautiful in nature and art. The emphasis of the aims under discussion is found principally in anatomical, physiological, and hygienic considerations.

To attain the "best estate," the inherent forces of the organism demand the cultivation of a robust physique through appropriate activities—healthy, strong, alert and enduring, beautiful in bearing and carriage—governed by a determining faculty, subserving these qualities. The question of conduct, of ethics in general, is an aim of education. That this executive faculty, the will, may become effective, in as far as the physical being can be considered, is the special aim of physical culture, implying physical education, training, gymnastics, and athletics, in the order of their importance. It must be regarded as nothing less than a perversion of aims to characterize physical training in its demonstrable scope and effects solely as a physical development, or as a purely hygienic procedure in the interest of health exclusively, or as a recreation, or as athletics pure and simple. Health should always be the incidental outcome. Athletics should be governed in accord with the principle which demands the prerequisites, not of special but of prolonged all-sided preparation, entailing a due regard for the factors of skill, strength, and endurance, based on a carefully nurtured vitality.

The larger aspect of the question, as it affects school youth, must deal with the psycho-physical phases of a large and interesting subject, based on the data furnished in the investigations available in the related sciences. Indeed, mere physical training does not include the whole scope of work in question. It is the emphasis of a preparation that will enable youth to live the most useful life, which is needed in our day. The hygiene of living involves so much that a school course which does not impart a knowledge of some of the fundamental laws involving nervous activities, often jeopardized in athletics, cannot be regarded as fulfilling its purpose.

Can this be denied in the face of what we see and hear in the contrasts of pure athletic competition—the uncouth and rude behavior, the slang witticisms as they re-echo, not only from our park commons, but also from our school halls? Are these accompaniments in concord with the dignity of the school? Should not these clamorous outbursts make way for a richer enjoyment, the result of a rational procedure more in line with the aims of educative pursuits? Form of character is always the result of preceding causes. The concept of a strong character must be ideally, if not the immediate, the remote outcome of such training. If we can fill our athletic fields with the school youth at hand, through proper methods, should not the results outweigh by far the results now advocated through our competitive methods?

WHERE AND HOW PHONETIC SPELLING SHOULD BE USED AT ONCE

GEORGE D. BROOMELL

Although in full sympathy with the objects of the Simplified Spelling Board, for the purpose of this article the reader will please regard the writer as opposed to any change in our spelling. Say, if you will, that any attempt to simplify or modify our present form of words would be sacrilegious, and it shall be undisputed here. Let the sole question under discussion be: What is the easiest, the best, the most advantageous way to learn to read and to spell English as it is?

All will agree that this is not an easy task. Every letter in our alphabet (and every combination of two or more used as a letter) has a variety of sounds. Webster says: "This letter *a* is employed for eight variations of sound." "This letter *e* has seven variations of sound." "This letter *i* has five variations of sound." "This letter *o* has seven sounds." "This letter *u* has six variations of sound." Here are thirty-three sound variations for five letters. And digraphs and other combinations are equally prolific of variety. Notice *ea* in *great, heat, head, heart, heard*. The versatility of *ough* is shown in *though, through, cough, hiccough, hough, tough, plough*.

If, now, we look at the matter in the opposite direction, we find that the difficulties seem even greater. Webster might have said: "*A* is employed for eight variations of sound, and its own name-sound is represented in fifteen different ways. *O* as a letter has seven sounds, and as a sound is spelled in fourteen different ways."

The reason is plain, then, why learning to read and write English requires a great amount of labor. The student is threading his way through a maze of irregularities and uncertainties. Much time and effort are required for him to get the clew even approximately.

CHILDREN OVERTAXED

And most of those engaged in this work are children. What is our customary way of teaching children a difficult thing? Do we not set them at exercises that are plain and simple, but leading toward the goal desired? They walk on smooth ground before they are required to tramp over rocks and hills. They learn to make plain seams before trying to do fancy work. They make simple drawings before pictures are expected of them. They learn the elements of music before attempting to play anything difficult. In manual training the student makes many simple things before he attempts anything elaborate.

But not so our present method of teaching a child to read and spell. He is given short words, it is true, but the complexities of English spelling are in his first lessons. From the beginning the letter *o* has its seven sounds, and vocal *o* its many spellings; and so of all the letters and sounds. Hence the process of learning is very slow and exceedingly confusing.

THE REMEDY

What is the remedy? This: Teach children to read in phonetics before putting them at our standard English. It is easy to devise a system closely resembling ordinary print in which each letter or digraph shall stand for but one sound, and each sound always have the same representation. Let such a system be used as an inclined plane or a scaffolding whereby standard English may be reached. All first reading-books should be phonetic. To master the alphabet would require about as much time and effort on the part of each one of a class of forty as to learn to recognize and call by name all his classmates, previously strangers. And, the alphabet once learned, simple reading will almost come of itself. It is only vocalizing the symbols as they present themselves to the eye, like calling the names of classmates when they are seen. All is plain and natural, and can be accomplished without mental confusion.

CHANGING TO STANDARD ENGLISH

Children should have enough of such reading as described to become thoroughly familiar with it, and to be able to call readily the most difficult words so spelled. Children six or seven years old would accomplish this in a few months. Then put into their hands primary books in standard English, explaining to them that, for reasons they will learn later, the spelling is irregular and the sounds of the letters uncertain. A large part of the words they will recognize readily by their resemblance to what is now familiar to them, and most of the rest they can get by study and attention to the context; and in a few months, with less help than children usually get from a teacher, they will read standard English as fluently as the phonetic. Several important consequences would attend this method of teaching. The first would be

A GREAT SAVING OF TIME

It is probable that children would learn to read standard English in one-half the time now required, thus leaving much more time than now for nature-study or any other of the numerous things that have been crowded into our school curriculums.

CHILDREN WOULD BE BETTER READERS

Because while learning they would not have to hesitate and puzzle over words on account of their irregular spelling, and hence could give their chief attention to expression. No one can read naturally and expressively unless he can apprehend the text without much effort. This the child cannot do as ordinarily taught; but, having formed the habit of reading expressively in simple text, he would carry it over into the more difficult.

THEY WOULD BE BETTER SPELLERS

Hon. William T. Harris said many years ago that children taught by the phonetic method made better spellers than those taught in the ordinary way. The reason for this is not far to seek. We learn to spell more by the eye than by the ear. and of what we see we remember what is striking. Our present spelling has a phonetic basis. Our words might be said to have an invisible phonetic line running through them, across which our current spelling zigzags. The child taught as indicated would mentally see this straight line, and the variations from it would be striking to him, often amusing perhaps, and would find a lodgment in his memory from the attention given to them. Children now learn spelling mainly by rubbing against it until it becomes somewhat familiar, with little either to guide or to stimulate the memory.

THEY WOULD BE BETTER SCHOLARS GENERALLY

The ripe scholar may see a reason for the irregularities of our conventional spelling, but the child can see none. There is a logical faculty dormant in every child, which must be brought into activity before much progress can be made in acquiring knowledge of any sort. The constant variation in the value of any letter or combination is irrational, and hence learning to read in the usual way tends rather to repress the reasoning powers than to stimulate them. But by the phonetic method the dormant logical faculty is appealed to from the outset, and just in proportion to its development will be the progress of the child in arithmetic and other studies.

THE HISTORY OF ENGLISH WORDS

Children taught as indicated are more likely to become students of English words. Knowing what letters represent the sounds in a word, the presence of silent and seemingly useless ones would tend to excite curiosity as to why they are there, and to gratify this children would ask questions and early learn to consult dictionaries.

OTHER USES FOR PHONETIC BOOKS

Every day hundreds of foreigners come to our country who know no English. These find our language very difficult to acquire, and men often become voters before they can read or speak it. The language in print is so different from what they hear that the eye does not aid the ear, nor the ear the eye, in acquiring it. But by the use of these phonetic books they could get the correct pronunciation as rapidly as they could master the meaning of words. The printed and the spoken language would each help in the acquisition of the other, and foreigners, like children, would soon learn standard English after getting it in its phonetic form.

THE CORRECTION OF NATIVE ILLITERACY

There are hundreds of thousands of adult native Americans who cannot read our language, many of whom speak it with a very imperfect enunciation. This is especially true of our southern states. Learning to read is so difficult that great numbers of the inhabitants are unequal to the task with such environment as they have. They are in great need of our inclined plane or scaffold by which to get up to our standard speech, both as spoken and printed. Give them these phonetic books, and many of them now illiterate would learn to read, and at the same time would perceive the inaccuracy of their speech and measurably correct their plantation dialect. Even if they got no higher than the scaffolding, it would be great gain, especially if some simple literature were printed in the same style, which could easily be done.

ENGLISH IN OUR FOREIGN POSSESSIONS

Such books would greatly facilitate the acquisition of English in our new possessions. It is desirable that all their inhabitants should learn as speedily as possible the language of the country to which they belong. Let them have it then in as simple a form as possible at first—that is, printed as it is spoken. Having learned to speak English, and to read and write it phonetically, no fear need be felt about their desiring to get it in its literary form.

ENGLISH IN ALL PARTS OF THE WORLD

It cannot be doubted that this scaffolding process of reaching standard English would be serviceable wherever throughout the world there may be occasion or desire to learn our language. Missionaries would use it in teaching those to whom they are endeavoring to carry the light of our religion and our civilization. It would aid and facilitate the acquisition of English everywhere, and thus hasten to make it a world-language.

MANUAL TRAINING IN THE GRADES

L. D. HARVEY

Manual training as a form of educational effort involves such a systematic training of the hand in construction work, through the use of tools and manipulation of material, as is adapted to the proper development of the motor activity of the hand, initiated, guided, and controlled by mental activities essential for the proper development of the mind.

It will be observed that by this statement the systematic training of the hand, in construction work, through the proper development of its motor activities, is made a definite end and aim of elementary training.

By the proper development of the motor activities of the hand I mean such a growth of power and control in the use of those activities through manual training as will enable the individual thus trained, and because of that training, more readily and more effectively to employ the hand in productive labor in the field of industrial effort. That such a result can be secured through this training is my belief, based upon the results of reasoning, of extended observation, and of experience in the administration of this line of work in the elementary schools.

To put it plainly, I find justification for that sort of manual training which aims at a systematic training of the hand in the increased power which it gives the individual to earn a livelihood through the use of his hands.

I am aware that this statement will invite criticism from some quarters; that it will be claimed that it is putting educational effort and aims on too low a basis. I would anticipate such criticism by saying that manual training is not all of education; that I do not claim for it everything that is needed for the proper development of those who attend our public schools; but I do claim that, if properly administered, it will increase the effectiveness of those trained as productive factors in society, and thus increase their capacity to earn a living and to support those dependent upon them.

Our public-school system is supported by public taxation. The right of the state to levy taxes for the support of a public-school system is found in the fact that the state has the right to do whatever is essential for its perpetuity; and good citizenship is essential for the perpetuity of the state.

The duty which the public school owes to the state is to train American citizens. The fundamental basis of all good citizenship is a trained intelligence which will enable the individual to earn a living, to become a self-supporting member of society. The public school which ignores this fact, through the quality of the training given, has no right to an existence.

That the individual trained in the public schools subsequently shows his capacity to support himself may be because of the training there obtained, or in spite of it. It should be because of that training. The public school should be an active factor in the development of this capacity to earn a livelihood. With this given, all things else may be added; but without it, nothing is possible.

Some years ago the secretary of the International Committee of the Y. M. C. A., after careful study of statistics relating to the subject of educational preparation of the young men of the United States between the ages of sixteen and thirty-five, reported as follows: "Of 13,000,000 young men in the United States between these ages, only five in every one hundred have been specially prepared for their occupations by education received at some kind of a school." He also found that of every one hundred graduates of our grammar schools, only eight obtain their livelihood by means of the professions and commercial business, while the remaining ninety-two support themselves and their families by means of their hands. If these statistics are correct—and an examination into the conditions existing in any community will seem to substantiate them—it must be evident that the education given in the grades below the high school which does not make provision for the training of the hand, as well as of the brain, is failing to do for these children what they have a right to demand shall be done for them, and what society and the state have the highest interest in demanding shall be done for them.

President Roosevelt has expressed, as the keynote of his administration, the sentiment: "a square deal for every man and every interest." If ninety-two out of every one hundred of the graduates of our grammar schools, and practically all of those who leave the elementary schools before completing the eighth grade, are to earn their living by their hands, I submit that the system of education which fails to give them during the most impressionable and formative period of their lives such a training of the hand as will fit them the earlier to become skilled in the different departments of manual labor in which they may engage, and thus to make their work more productive, is not giving "a square deal" to these future members of society, to society itself, nor to the state.

Thus far I have spoken of the systematic training of the hand as a definite end of manual training. But it is not the sole end or purpose. We must take note of the fact that the essential essence of all training is *doing;* of manual training, is *doing with the hands;* and that in systematic manual training, from start to finish, the motor activities of the hand must be set in operation, must be guided and controlled by the action of the mind; and the opening statement of this address calls for mental activities essential for the proper development of the mind—not all forms of mental activity, but forms which cannot be omitted, because of their necessity for proper mental unfolding.

Mental power comes through organized thinking. The mere memorizing of what others have said, or learning about what others have done, is not organized thinking, and gives little or no mental training. Organized thinking comes whenever the individual sets himself a definite task to do; and then determines and applies the ways and means necessary for the accomplishment of that task. This task may be the solution of a problem in arithmetic, or it may be the construction of a model from wood, iron, or other material, or the creation of a new and original design for such a model. I believe the latter forms to be of the higher value, because they demand the use of tools and material. The tools cannot be used successfully upon the material to produce the desired result, without the exercise of the closest attention and of those forms of mental activity leading up to an act of the judgment. There can be no training of the hand which does not involve mental activity, and the mental activity thus involved is of a kind which furnishes just the training needed for the practical concerns of life. It is a mental activity out of which grows skill in doing; and skill in doing as a result of intelligent thinking should be one of the chief purposes of education.

It is the ambition of every boy, at a very early age, to become the owner of a pocket-knife. The reason for this is that the pocket-knife is a tool which furnishes for him the largest opportunities for the exercise of his inherent desire to do. No one thinks of denying him the pocket-knife because of the fear that its use will result in his becoming a mere whittler; but, on the contrary, the thoughtful parent will furnish it because of its value as an instrument in the training of the child's manual and mental powers.

Because in the manual-training school the child learns to use a plane or a saw, it does not follow that he is to be a carpenter. Because the girl learns to sew, it does not follow that she must be a seamstress; or because she learns the value of foods and how to prepare them, that she must, therefore, be a cook. The use of the plane and the saw will be of value to the boy, should he decide to become a carpenter. The training in sewing and cooking will be of value to the girl, should she decide to become a seamstress or a cook, or should be compelled to take the place of either seamstress or cook, even temporarily. But, in any case, the training thus afforded will be of the highest value in the development of the individual, because first, it demands concentration of attention, and thus develops that quality so essential to success in any field of human endeavor; second, it requires organized thinking in the adaptation of means to ends, a demand which will be constant through life; and, third, it demands an exercise of the will-power, resulting in doing for the realization of those ends, and through the doing there comes a clarification of the thinking.

It is not claimed that this sort of training, and the knowledge and the skill which it brings, constitute all that is necessary in the education of the child; but the claim is made, and well made, that any system of education which leaves out this kind of training omits one of the essential requisites in the proper education of the child.

I believe that anyone who will analyze closely the mental processes involved in the mastery of a lesson in grammar, in history, in geography, or in any of the branches taught in the public school, and then compare them with the mental processes involved in making a working drawing of a model in wood, and then from that drawing, by the use of tools, reproducing that model, will see that for all purposes of mental training the latter is of no less value, to say the least, than the former. It has the added value in that it has developed control of the hand, and skill in its use, which will be of value in other fields of work where manual skill is required.

Systematic training of the hand involves a definite purpose and adaptation of material, tools, and processes for the proper accomplishment of that purpose. These determinations are, in every case, the result of mental activity. The selection of the material, the choice of tools, and even the specific purpose, at any given stage of the work, may be the result of mental activity and choice on the part of the teacher; but the setting in operation of the motor activities employed in the use of tools or in the manipulation of material, and the guidance and control of those motor activities to the accomplishment of the given end, are the result of mental activity on the part of the pupil. Hence it follows that the systematic training of the hand for the proper development of its motor activities involves an equally systematic training of the mind which initiates, guides, and controls those activities. The statement already given calls for systematic training of the hand for a proper development of its motor activities. The term "proper" is used advisedly. Under the limitations it imposes, the specific ends determined, and the exercises necessary for the accomplishment of those ends, must be selected with reference to the state of development of motor activity and power of the child being trained. It eliminates all classes of exercises beyond the strength of the pupil, at any given time, and also other classes of exercises requiring close work and too fine adjustments of motor activity at an early stage of the pupil's development. Since the training of the hand required by this statement involves mental initiative and control, it follows, that, when such a stage of skill has been developed as to cause the actions to become reflex, or when the stage is closely approached, they fall outside the demands here made, because then we have motor activity, but without the corresponding and correlated mental activity. Exercises thus continued may make for skill in a given narrow line of effort, but not for general development. The term "proper," as used in the statement, requires the discontinuance of any special motor activity when it has reached a stage where mental control is no longer an essential.

The *proper* development of motor activities implies an order of development which must be taken into consideration, and which must determine and control the character of the exercises which involve the training. The requirement that the motor activities involved in the manual training shall be initiated, guided, and controlled by mental activites essential for the development of the mind, makes it necessary that these exercises shall be selected with reference to the demands which they make upon the mind. It follows, therefore, that the mental capabilities of the pupil, at any stage in the process of training, must be considered. Work must be given of sufficient variety in the demand which it makes, for calling into play the varied forms of mental activity and in their proper order.

If this statement of the function of manual training in the public schools is accepted, it would seem to follow that there should be a definite course of training organized in the light of definite knowledge as to the motor and mental capabilities of pupils at different stages in their development, and that it should be systematic in its unfolding. It must grow out of careful study and scientific knowledge of what is necessary for the proper motor development of the child. It must not be left in its development to the sport and play of the child's impulses or temporary interests.

The problem is to present such a line of training as the child needs, and to interest him in something worth while, rather than to find some new thing which may appeal to each new and fleeting interest.   Training involves the shaping and directing of interests, and especially is this true in the training of the child whose interests are as varied as his impulses.

The exercise of the hand in manual occupations outside the school is not systematic; it is accidental, sporadic, fragmentary; and because the work is unrelated, unorganized, it is not of the highest value for hand-training, and the mental activity is not of a kind to give the best results.

The schools which do not give manual training give an incomplete training.   The sources of stimuli which they furnish are words mainly.   The words presented for the pupil's consideration are symbols.   The interpretation of the symbols depends upon the character and extent of the apperception mass in the pupil's mind.   It may be entirely adequate, or it may be partially or completely inadequate, in which case the mental product is imperfect, inadequate; the *impression* is faulty in that it is incorrect, vague, incomplete.   The *expression* of the results of this consideration of words is again chiefly through the medium of words.

The teacher under the present system of school organization, and with existing ideals of what is demanded of the pupil, too often is unable to test whether the pupil's expression is a remembered form of words without meaning, or, when other words are used, whether they are correct symbols of the correct idea.

In manual training, the sources of mental stimuli are things chiefly, and words secondarily.   The same thing is true in nature-study; but the former is of a higher form, because the mental stimulus leads directly to, and co-ordinates with motor activity, and results in an expression of thought in the completed products of the hand, guided and controlled by the mind.   This expression of thought is in permanent objective form, and furnishes an opportunity for comparison and correction of inaccuracies, which the fleeting word does not.

Book-study deals with words, and the character of the mental activity aroused is uncertain. Nature-study deals with objects of nature, their forms, structure, sources, and uses. Manual training deals with material things, their form, sources, and uses, and, in addition thereto, demands physical and mental activity in changing the raw material to the finished product; and this is exactly what the individual will have to do who earns his living with his hands.

We may say that education demands, on the intellectual side, the development, control, and training for effective use of the varied activities of the mind, through the action of stimuli of the right kind, properly applied at the right time.

The work of the teacher, then, in the development, control, and training of the intellectual powers of the child, is in selecting the stimulus proper in kind and time, and, through right methods of applying it, securing the kind and amount of mental activity, properly directed, required to meet the needs of the pupil at a given time for given ends.

It will be apparent that in the field now under consideration —the intellectual side of education—the nature of the mind determines what is essential in the educational process, and this without reference to environment. It will also be evident that the nature of the mind does not determine the choice of material available as to the source of stimuli for various forms of mental activity or control.

Sources of mental stimuli available in the work of the public schools are words and material things. In the actual affairs of life the great majority of human beings are engaged in productive activities of one form or another. These productive activities demand a knowledge of material things, and knowledge of and skill in the processes necessary for the transformation of the raw materials of nature into forms fitted to satisfy human wants.

To do the work with the greatest effectiveness, it is evident that there must be specific training for it. Such training is not afforded through the activities evoked by the mental stimulus of words alone.

The activities evoked by the stimulus of material things may be roughly separated into two classes:

1. Those which begin with observation, and, passing on through a consideration of their forms, sources, and uses, terminate in definite judgment, but which require no constructive effort involving processes resulting in change of form.

Nature-study affords an illustration of this type of mental activity. It has its place in a rational scheme of elementary education because it furnishes a necessary stimulus not supplied through the medium of words.

2. The second class of activities resulting from things as a source of mental stimulus is that shown in constructive effort through motor activities, controlled by the mind and directed to a change of form of the material things under consideration.

Since this is the class of activities which must employ the great mass of mankind, and since systematic training is essential for effectiveness in this line of effort, and since systematic training is not given outside the school during the school age, and because it can be most effectively given during that period of the child's life, it follows that provision should be made for giving it in the elementary schools.

Manual training under the implications of the introductory statement of this address furnishes this kind of training, and rounds out and completes the necessary forms of activity for the development of the child during the elementary-school age.

Let us consider briefly the part which constructive effort plays in the work of the world.

The magnificent cathedral, with its splendid proportions, adorned with paintings, mosaics, and statuary, embodies the highest creation of the mind of the architect and the artist. The splendid structure in its completed form existed in the mind of the architect as a mental product before it assumed material form. The breathing marbles and the speaking canvasses which adorn its walls existed in the mind of the sculptor and painter as products of the constructive imagination while the marble was yet in the unhewn block and the paints unmixed. Before these creations of mind could stand forth in embodied form to minister to the spiritual needs and aesthetic tastes of all, the materials of which its component parts are formed must be selected, assembled, and wrought upon by the cunning hand of the builder, the sculptor, and the painter in concrete constructive effort.

We may perhaps rightfully claim that the highest form of mental activity here involved is shown in the conception of the architect and artist, which preceded its objective realization; but we must not forget the debt they owe to the cunning work of the hand. Art, whether in architecture, painting, or sculpture, is an evolution. The builder's interpretation and embodiment of the constructive imagination of the early architect into an objective reality gave to that architect and others in concrete form that which had else remained a figment of the imagination. It now stands in form for study, for a determination of its defects and its points of excellence, of its adaptation or lack of adaptation to the purposes it was designed to serve. As a result of this study of the adaptation of means to ends, the imagination constructs a better mental product, which the builder again fixes in permanent form through the work of the hands. This process is continued, the work of architect and builder, each necessary for the other, each gaining by the other's work, until new types and higher forms of structure both in utility and in beauty are realized.

In the same way we might trace the development of art in painting and sculpture. The idea of the artist must take form through the work of the hand, and each creation of mental and motor activity, whether in statuary or painting, becomes a lesson and an inspiration for further effort.

Design, whether for decorative purposes, or in the production of new forms and combinations of materials adapted to the uses of man, follows the same line of development.

The modern printing-press is one of the most marvelous products of human ingenuity, but in its highest type today it is an evolution from the first crude press employing movable type, through the combined work of mind and hand. Each new type in the evolutionary process has come through a new conception of the mind, the outcome of a study of the defects and excellencies of an earlier type, and put into concrete form by the trained hand of the workman.

The more thoroughly the workman has been trained to conceive the end for which he works, and at each step to adapt wisely and skilfully his efforts to the accomplishment of that end, the more likely will he be to see the necessity for and possibility of improvement.

The more skilful the inventor is as a workman, the fewer the errors in his designs and in the complete product.

The course in manual training in the grades designed to meet the demands for training here set forth should have a content of its own, wrought out and determined by the capacities and needs of the individuals to be trained. The materials and tools to be used, the particular forms of constructive work and their order, and the processes employed in the construction, should be selected and determined with respect to their adaptation in furnishing the kind of training required.

Manual training should be given, not as the fag end of other subjects in the course, and not chiefly for the purpose of illustrating or enlarging the work in those other subjects. The question as to how far the exercises of manual training may be utilized to supplement other school work — geography, history, arithmetic, etc.— is of far less importance than the question as to how far these exercises are adapted to meet the demands for necessary mental and motor activity, essential for the development of the child and not otherwise provided.

It is not my intention to claim that the work in manual training should not be in any way related to the other work of the school. It furnishes opportunity for work of high value in connection with other subjects; and such opportunities of relating one line of work with another to the betterment of both should certainly be seized.

Enough crimes have already been committed in the educational world under the name of correlation, without still further extending the list in attempting to correlate every form of motor training with some phase of the textbook of the schoolroom.

Correlation in educational work should be natural and not forced. Indeed, it cannot be forced; and much of what goes under the name of correlation would better be called a conglomeration of disjointed and unrelated fragments of knowledge, with a resulting habit of mind of little value in effective and concentrated effort.

A course of study in manual training extending throughout the grades, and planned as above set forth, would furnish many opportunities for extending knowledge of materials and processes in industrial organization and administration lying outside the main line of training which the work is designed to offer. The extent to which these fields of knowledge may be explored must be determined by their value as matters of knowledge, their relation to other subject-matter of the course of study, and to the character of mental activity involved in their mastery. The exercises may frequently develop an interest in past or present industrial processes, the knowledge of which may be of value to the child.

I believe the children being trained today are far more concerned with the industrial processes of today than they are with the industrial processes of primitive peoples, and I cannot bring myself to the belief that nature has made so great a mistake as to bring children into the world at any given stage of the development of civilization, lacking the capacity to enter into that civilization without going through all the preliminary processes and steps through which it has been evolved.

I am not undertaking to argue the question as to whether the child in his unfolding must live over again in his development the development of the race, and must begin where the race began; but I do undertake to express my belief that, if this be true, he is at the time he enters the public school advanced far enough in this process of development so that some systematic effort may be undertaken for his training through the utilization of his immediate environment, and that it is unnecessary to attempt the difficult task of reconstructing the environment of primitive peoples which finds no proper place in the environment of today.

It is true that the industrial development of today presents complexities too great for the child of the public school; and yet I believe there is in it sufficient that is simple and elementary, and which leads directly and naturally to the more complex, to furnish ample scope and material for the activities of the pupil's mind and hand; and that the consideration of these simpler phases of present environment furnishes a better basis for the understanding and appreciation of environment as a whole than would a class of exercises growing out of a dealing with the supposed environment of a people remote in time and low in the scale of development.

I believe that in our effort to make the work in manual training serve as a point of departure in the accumulation of knowledge of that which is remote we have overlooked some opportunities which it affords, subsidiary to the main line of training, but which are of the highest value. I shall call attention to one instance of this kind which has been very generally ignored (so far as my observation goes) in the field of manual training. I refer to the opportunities it offers for exercises of the highest order in developing the use of language. In the completed products of the constructive exercises involved in manual training, and in the processes employed, we have materials which may be utilized for language-training in the two forms of description and exposition unexcelled by any other material employed in the public schools.

The child who is trained in accurately describing one of these completed products of his own hand, or who is trained in giving an accurate exposition of the steps in order, and processes employed in the construction of that object, has secured a power in the use of exact and definite language which he receives nowhere else in the public-school course; every such exercise in the use of language requires such a training of the observation, and a clarification and organization of his knowledge, as are demanded by almost no other exercise in any phase of the public-school work.

One of the greatest weaknesses of the pupils in the public schools today is in lack of power in definite, concise, accurate statement. Too often this lack of power is due to the fact that pupils are asked to talk when they have nothing to say, to write essays on subjects of which they know nothing except as they acquire the knowledge from the words of the book.

The constructive work demanded by the manual-training course requires close observation and adaptation of means to ends, an examination of effort and its results with relation to its success in realizing the desired end, a determination of what is lacking, further effort guided and directed by the increased knowledge of what is demanded, and again further comparison and study, followed by further renewed efforts. All this requires clear thinking. The work of the pupil's own hands is then a subject about which he knows something definite, and definite knowledge is the essential for definite statement. Here we have the raw material out of which accurate language in certain important forms naturally follows.

For the workman in the shop and elsewhere, the ability to state accurately and concisely what he is to do, or what he has done, or what another is to do, is an ability which has commercial value; and it is also an ability which has other value than can be measured in terms of dollars for the individual. Clear thinking furnishes the right conditions for clear statement. Clear statement begets clear thinking.

Too often in manual training we have left out all that is artistic. Motor activity may be developed and trained, and with it all the mental activity necessarily involved in such training when dealing with things beautiful as well as with things ugly in form. Artistic design is constructive work of the highest order. It is called for in the requirements for manual training set forth in the very first sentence on this address. But manual training is not a mere annex to artistic work, nor is it to be employed solely as a medium through which to display the results of constructive artistic design. Each should supplement the other. They are closely related. They should go hand in hand. Design for the mere sake of design in art has no value. Its value lies in its use; and ample scope is afforded in the field of manual training for effective and valuable artistic training in design and its applications to things useful.

A question of vital importance in the introduction of manual training into the grades is: Where shall it be begun, and how long shall it be continued? If I have correctly described its function, the question is answered in that statement. It should be begun when the child enters the public school, and it should be continued during his stay there.

There are still other reasons than those I have named, why it should be begun in the lowest grades and continued throughout the course. We have been making the mistake in our public-school work of assuming that the child can be taken from the home, where its activities before entering school have been concerned chiefly with things, and that during the school period each day we may entirely change the form of his activities and invoke the activities which come from the use of books. We are asking for mental activity, whereas the demand of its physical nature is for physical activity. We are demanding physical quiet, when its whole nature rebels against it. We have been asking him to deal with the abstract, when he wants that for which he is fitted and which appeals to him. We give him pencil and paper, and occasionally paints and brush, and expect him to find in these materials ample scope for the demands of his physical being for motor activity.

He should have during these early years just such scope for motor activity and systematic training as a well-organized course in manual training will provide.

I have sometimes heard it said that the claim made for motor activity carries with it the implication that manual training will make too great demands upon the mental activities of the child, and furnish no relief from the supposed mental activity involved in the use of books; but we must remember that change and variety in the form of mental activity invoked by material in use in manual training, which serves as a stimulus for such activity, afford the relief needed; and we must not forget that it is an impossibility to secure effective mental activity on the part of pupils in the primary grades, while holding them exclusively to a study of books and recitation work during the six hours of the school day. Manual training, then, is needed, in the very lowest grades, to furnish a form of activity which the physical nature of the child demands, and to utilize that activity through systematic, organized work for the development of the child.

While perhaps this reason may not be urged with the same force in the higher grades, it cannot be ignored with propriety in any one of the elementary grades. Manual training should be continued throughout the grades because a large number of pupils not only do not go beyond the completion of the work in the eighth grade, but drop out also before that time. All need the training, both motor and mental, which a systematic, well-organized course of constructive work gives when properly administered.

I shall not undertake now to discuss in detail, or even generally, the course of study in elementary manual training. This is not the place nor the time for such a consideration. But I do wish to say that, in my judgment, the large problem for those engaged in furthering the cause of manual training today is in the determination of the values of the different lines of work, material used, and processes employed in this field of educational effort; what motor activities are proper at a given stage in the child's development; what mental powers are valuable for the control of these activities; what materials, tools, and processes are best adapted to meet the needs of the child at the different stages of development.

Such an examination as this would result in material modification of the work done in almost any of our schools where manual training is in operation. We are as yet feeling our way. We shall make progress most rapidly when we throw aside sentimentalism, and consider the question of, not what showing we can make, but what can be done to meet the needs of pupils. We should stand ready to discard each and every pet form of work which cannot stand the test of such an examination.

The examination of the manual-training exhibits at the St. Louis Exposition showed some remarkable things. It showed work being done in the lowest grades in one system of schools, and exactly the same line of work in the highest grades in another system. It showed work too difficult for the grade in which it was undertaken in some schools, and not up to the capacity of pupils required to do the same work in the higher grades in other schools. It gave evidence in many cases that product was the thing in the mind of the school authorities rather than training. It showed that the relation of art to manual training was in most cases so remote as not to be discoverable.

All these conditions are what might naturally be expected. This entire field of work is comparatively new. But the time has come for deliberation, consideration, and examination, not only of the basis upon which it rests, of the ends which it is to serve, but also of definite plans of adapting means to ends. It is not the work of any one individual, nor of any short period of time. It must be undertaken faithfully, patiently, and systematically by all who are interested in this phase of educational work. Further, experiments must be tried; other failures will result; but out of failure will come new experience and better judgment.

I cannot close without considering briefly another phase of the subject, and that is: how to find a place for it in the course of study. We hear much of the overcrowded condition of the elementary course of study, and we hear perhaps as much more as to the meager results which come from the administration of this course of study. We are told that pupils from the public schools have no power in the use of language, are not able to use arithmetic for the practical purposes of life, know little of geography and less of history; and, in fact, that they are more noted for the things they have not learned than for those they have mastered. And many of those who make these complaints, doubtless with more or less of truth, argue that what is needed in the public schools is fewer rather than more subjects, and that manual training would only add to the burdens of teachers and pupils, and would detract from the quality and quantity of knowledge and kind of training to be derived from the study of the traditional subjects in the course of study.

The remarkable thing about these claims is that they are made just as frequently, and with just as much truth, where no work in manual training, or other of the so-called " fads," is found.

The trouble is, not that we have too many subjects, but that we attempt to teach too many things in these subjects which are not worth teaching, and are wasteful in time, method, and effort, with correspondingly poor results.

Those who argue against manual training forget that there is no other line of work in which the pupil can engage which calls forth mental activity of a higher order than manual training;

forget that this work can be introduced into the school and be used as a stimulus for mental activity, when books fail as such a stimulus, and when the time spent in the subjects studied is time not only wasted, but worse than wasted, because it results in the development of bad mental habits; they forget that this work gives physical activity, change of position, change of interest, change in the form of mental activity; and that the pupil goes from it to his other tasks refreshed instead of wearied, and that he is able in the remaining time to do more in the field of the common branches than he could have done had the effort been made to hold him to those lines of work continuously.

The mental power gained through this dealing with things, and in the direction and control of motor activities, is a mental power which manifests itself in greater capacity of the pupil for the mastery of his work and more rapid progress in that work. He sees in it practical utility. It holds him in school longer; and, if properly organized, it is pleasing to his parents from the standpoint of utility, if for no other reason. The influence upon the parents is to make them more cordial in the support of the public schools — and the development of such a sentiment in any community is one which should be encouraged, because the development of the public-school system depends finally upon the belief of the public in its efficiency.

SEVENTH-GRADE MANUAL TRAINING

V. M. RUSSELL

Director Manual Training, State Normal School, Platteville, Wis.

The central thought in planning the shop-work for the seventh grade this year was to get something around which as many as possible of the other subjects of study could be grouped naturally. The incubator and brooder were chosen because of the interest the pupils had in them; because of their close relation to the agriculture, geography, arithmetic, and composition then being studied; and because of the season—late winter, when the subject of chicken-raising suggests itself naturally.

Various styles of incubators and brooders were examined and studied. The ones best adapted to good work in the shop and easy to manipulate were selected. Plans were drawn, and specifications for lumber in the rough were made. The various pieces were cut to dimensions and assembled.

The work in agriculture, composition, etc., was done by practice-teachers under the direction of Miss Jessie Montgomery, principal of the grammar department.

The composition, following the outline used in the shop-work, was written by Archie Brugger, and chosen because it gives some idea of the knowledge the children gained about incubation and the raising of poultry.

Topics discussed in the shop:

1. Discussion of poultry-raising.
   a) Natural and artificial incubation.
   b) Profit.
   c) Good work for boys and girls.
2. Incubator.
   a) Selection of style; method of heating and ventilating; regulating temperature and moisture.
   b) Drawing plans and making bills for materials.
   c) Building: getting parts to dimensions, assembling and testing.

SPECIMENS OF WORK IN MANUAL TRAINING, SEVENTH GRADE

3. Operating incubator.
   a) Leveling apparatus.
   b) Quantity of water in tank; why tank cannot be filled.
   c) Lamp: filling; kind of oil; trimming; regulating.
   d) Regulating temperature: degree of heat; location of thermometer; dampers; adjusting regulator; time to run incubator before putting in the eggs.
   e) Care of eggs: turning; reasons for; method of; when to begin; how often; when to cease; time used.
   f) Moisture.
   g) Ventilation: at beginning of hatch; after forty-eight hours; during hatch; at time of hatch.
4. Selecting eggs.
   a) Defects: very large very small; poor shape; rough shell.
   b) Age: should be fresh.
   c) Care of, while in storage: temperature should be even and cool; should be turned once in twenty-four hours.
5. Brooder.
   a) Selection of style: hot-air and hot-water heating; ventilation; temperature; kinds of hover and runs.
   b) Drawing plans, and making bills for material.
   c) Building: getting parts to dimensions, assembling and testing.
6. Operating brooder.
   a) Filling tank; care of lamp.
   b) Temperature: during first four days; after first four days.
   c) Floor covering and food while in brooder.
   d) When to transfer chicks to coops.

AN EXPERIMENT IN INCUBATION

In the early part of our course in manual training the seventh grade decided to make an incubator and brooder, in connection with our course in agriculture. The incubator is heated with hot water and has a capacity for two hundred eggs. After it was completed, we spent a week in testing and regulating the heat-ing apparatus. We found that it would keep regularly the required temperature of 103 to 104 degrees. We purchased seven dozen eggs—two dozen Plymouth Rock, two dozen Black Minorca, and three dozen Brahma eggs.

Before we put the eggs into the incubator we tested them with an egg-tester to separate the bad from the good. Each egg was held before the flame of a lamp, and if it were dark it was bad. Then we placed the good eggs in the incubator on the thirteenth of March.

After the third day the eggs were turned and aired daily. About a week or ten days after they were placed in the incubator they were tested again to see if they were good for hatching.

When the chickens began to hatch on the third of April, we moved the incubator and brooder into the main room, because the shop was so small we did not have room in there. There were thirty-seven chickens hatched; seven of them died, but the remainder were healthy chicks. When they were about a day old, they were transferred to the brooder, which was heated by hot water and kept at a temperature of about 80 or 85 degrees. A hover which was made of felt was hung in the brooder, and the floor was covered with chaff for the chickens to scratch in.

The chickens were left in the brooder a day or so without being fed. Then we fed them baked corn which we crumbled up for them, and sometimes we gave them bread which we had soaked in water.

By this time the chicks became so noisy that they interfered with our studying, so we made a run for them in the basement. They were finally bought by a lady who wanted to have some early chickens.

As the incubator and brooder proved to be a success, we sold them to a friend who was interested in raising chickens.

Archie Brugger.

TYPES OF SCHOOL FESTIVALS

FRANK A. MANNY
Ethical Culture School, New York City

As one travels north from Naples through Italy and Germany, he is impressed, on the one hand, by the change in conditions of life and, on the other, by the continuity of the festival spirit under the changed conditions. The life at the south is so strikingly open, simple, direct. Farther north much of this aspect is lost, while there is more evidence of elements that make for cleanliness and progress. Yet throughout there is a greater reality to the festival side of life, whether it be of church or state, than one finds in America, where we have broken with the older tradition and as yet have not found a new life.

This festival spirit is so fully in accord with various phases of social and industrial activities in the best American schools that we may look to them for help even more than we can expect it from other social institutions. Our hope for a deeper enjoyment of the meaning of activities on the part of adults lies in making use of the fact that some value is attached by the adults to this phase for children in the plastic period. If we work out what we can for the children, the grown-ups may find that their own period of growth, and consequent enjoyment, are longer than they had thought. We need careful studies of the significant motives of what has been done. Dr. Dopp's *The Place of Industries in Elementary Education* has many illuminating suggestions. Someone of equal energy and experience ought to devote himself to "The Place of the Festival in Education."

Even a hasty view of the kinds of festivals now in use would be helpful, showing, as it would, the lines of least resistance or of chief interest in elementary, secondary, and higher schools. I wish that the *Elementary School Teacher* or some other leading journal would open a department in which reports of current endeavors could be recorded and evaluated. The difficulty in many schools is that a type of festival is learned or worked upon, and then, whatever is done, is made to conform to this type. Thus, in some places, the pageant is found to present less of subjective requirements than do other forms, and the entire supply of energy is spent upon certain spectacular effects. A study of the Venetian pageant and its influence upon art would help to prevent this one-sidedness which often results in nothing but display, or else leads either to the abandonment of the festival as an "extra," a "vanity," a "folly," or to a revolt in favor of plays with bare stage settings and no effort at costume effects, etc. I believe that both the pageant and the bare stage have their place, and each will be the better because of the use of the other.

In both these forms there is a high degree of participation and of product execution on the part of the performers. I have been giving some attention to the possibilities of more use of the process and of agents through which the performer works. This appears in the little pantomime plays in which objects cut out of paper or other material are used to make the shadows. The highest development we have of this method is seen in the marionette theater. After a performance in an Italian theater and an inspection of old models of the eighteenth century, now in a museum, I could better understand what these puppets meant to Goethe in his childhood. (I know of no book worth more to the student of the festival in aiding him to get the spirit of this phase of life than *Wilhelm Meister's Apprenticeship*.) There seems to be a utilizing in the puppets of one's tendencies to work through means, and a consequent objectification which is closely related to the socializing for which the school exists. This tendency is seen in normal boys and girls in playing with dolls, soldiers, paper animals, as well as with boats, engines, etc. "that will go." When there is added the element of improvisation, the value is even more evident, for by this means there is an avenue for that tendency to communicate oneself through a social situation so often seen in children and so often repressed. When there is this repression, the tendency feeds itself, in many cases, on day-dreams, poor love-stories. and cheap adventure tales. There is, of course, a danger in too great absorption in one's dolls or in pantomime or puppets or machines, yet an advance is made upon mere subjective fancies.

Another interest met is that which oppressed finds its main feeding in the serial pictures of the Sunday newspaper—Buster Brown, Happy Hooligan, the Katzenjammers, *et al.* One may well regret the devotion of many children to these unworthies, yet the need they depend upon for their vogue is natural. They are live characters, and week after week in new situations appear these old friends. It is often said that following them does no harm because the children are not led to act upon the suggestions they offer. While we certainly do not wish to have the tricks of the newspaper pictures become the acts of our children, yet there is some danger in cultivating the attitude of appreciation and enjoyment without participation and consequent relating of reader or seer to the material.

The festival work in most schools is still unrelated to other work, and is dependent largely upon chance opportunities and influences. It offers one of the most valuable tools available for the reconstruction now sought for. It deserves (1) careful study as a factor in social life past and present; (2) recognition as a definite factor in the curriculum and not as an "extra;" (3) division of labor so that all members of a school have experience both as doers and observers; (4) development of a variety of types; (5) relation to larger wholes of action, thus taking account of social and ethical possibilities (compare 1, 2, and 3).

VOLUNTEER SUMMER WORK OF THE FRANCIS W. PARKER SCHOOL

RUTH L. BRIBACH
University of Chicago

An interesting phase of the activities of the Francis W. Parker School is the volunteer summer work. Some account of it is here given in the hope that it may prove suggestive to readers of the *Elementary School Teacher*.

Just before the school closes in June a type-written outline of suggestions for voluntary summer work and reading is given to the children of all grades who desire it. Paper of uniform size, and of quality suitable for composition and for sketches in pencil and water-color, also is furnished. The outline, while serving somewhat to direct the interest of the children, permits of great freedom, and the idea of the work has been taken hold of enthusiastically. When the school opens in the autumn, the contributions are collected, and all are bound together, just as they are, according to grade. The best ones are used as material for the morning exercises of the school.[1] A programme frequently consists of a single topic—a summer spent in the mountains, for example—treated of by children in different grades. The description of various places; the handling of the topic from many points of view; the display of collected illustrative matter—photographs, pencil-drawings, and water-color sketches—both instruct and entertain the assembled pupils, faculty, and visitors.

An examination of the records of voluntary summer work for the year 1904 reveals interests of various sorts. Many children wrote of local industries. Several sent in creditable botanical collections, one of which consisted of blue prints of specimens gathered by an enthusiastic little girl who spent her vacation in

---

[1] Described by Jennie Hall, "Morning Exercises in the Francis W. Parker School," *Elementary School Teacher*, February, 1906.

England. Others sent in lists of wild and tame animals observed in their neighborhood or at places visited. There were some pupils who kept a record of problems solved. and of exercises written in German or French, and a few handed in original stories. The year of the Louisiana Purchase Exposition, a number visited St. Louis, and kept a diary, well illustrated. All of the contributions breathed the spirit of voluntary work.

The following "Suggestions" were brought together by different instructors in the school and were edited as follows:

SUGGESTIONS FOR VOLUNTARY WORK DURING VACATION

FOUR REASONS FOR DOING WORK DURING VACATION

1. To make a souvenir to remind one of the places seen and things done in the summer.

2. To add material to the school museum.

3. To furnish the school with valuable descriptions of places and industries. Papers which are good enough for class reading will be printed. They will also furnish interesting material for the morning exercises throughout the year.

4. To have the pleasure of the work. If the work is not a pleasure. it had better not be done.

I. *Suggestions for souvenirs.*
Keep a diary.
Make drawings or paintings of interesting places or things.
Collect plants, or minerals of locality.
If you go to the exposition. collect souvenirs which are worth while. (Advertising souvenirs frequently are valuable.)

II. *Suggestions for collections for the school museum.*
Only things which are of real value in showing the animal or vegetable life of some region. or the life-history of some animal, or stones and minerals of some special interest. can be put in the museum.
To make these useful. the animals. especially the insects, must be mounted (best inside glass cases). and the plants must be pressed and mounted on cardboard.

Everything must be labeled with its name, the place where it is found, and the character of the place—mountain, valley, prairie, swamp, beach, etc.

III. *Some subjects on which the school would like papers or sets of paintings or drawings.*

  1. An excursion.

    A description of a trip through beautiful or interesting scenery.

  2. The topography of a region.

    What are the most conspicuous features of the region? Hills; mountains; valleys; ravines; lakes; rivers; swamps; marshes; prairies.

    Make a map showing the relative location of the different features.

    Describe one or two of these.

    What forces do you see at present building up and wearing down the region?

    What forces do you think may have worked there in the past?

  3. Plants.

    Describe several trees and other plants.

    Use drawing and painting to show branching, the forms of the tops, and the shapes of the leaves.

    Tell in writing in what kind of place they grow, whether alone, or with others of the same kind, or of different kinds.

  4. Animals.

    Keep a list of any wild animals you see.

    Pick out one wild or tame animal, watch it as closely as possible, and write an interesting account of it.

  5. An industry.

    Watch the manufacture of some product or the growing or harvesting of some crop.

    Get as many pictures of the industry as you can, photographs or drawings.

    Secure samples of the material at various stages, when possible.

Write a description of the process.

6. The scene of a historic event.

If you visit the scene of any important historic event, tell the story of the event, describing carefully the place where each part of it occurred.

7. The exposition.

General description.

The exhibit which I liked best.

The music.

The different races of people.

IV. *Suggestions upon music for children who go to the exposition.*

1. Third and fourth grades.

a) Write description of musical instruments of various peoples, giving approximate measurements, and general character of the tone. For example, is it like a mandolin, a harp, a flute? Is it loud or soft, high or low?

b) Write short descriptions of players and singers, including the manner of playing and singing, and the *occasion*. For example, is it for dancing? Does it accompany work or play, or any special kind of activity?

c) Do they keep very good time? Can you count it? Is it beautiful music to you? Do they seem to like it?

d) Make drawings or paintings of instruments and players.

2. Additional points for upper grades.

a) What kind of time do they use most? Do they change the time in the middle of a piece?

b) Does the music mean much to you? Is it martial, sentimental, childlike, fantastic, savage, delicate, happy, sad? Is it varied or monotonous?

The following were among the contributions handed in, the autumn of 1904:

FISHING

The way they fish in Charlevoix is this. First they set the nets in Lake Michigan. About every other day some tugs go out loaded with nets, bring in the fish, and drop the nets that they brought out in place of the others. The fish are cleaned, sorted, and put in boxes on the tug so as not to waste any time. After they get back to the fishery, some of the fish they pack in ice, put in little cars, and ship. Some of them they put in the smoke-house to be smoked.

The smoke-house is made out of bricks, and in the bottom there is a hole for the fire. The walls and inside of the door are covered with tar. The door is made out of wood. They have a steel cover to put over the fire so the smoke could get only at the fish. The fish were hung on wooden rods, and they had sticks to hold the sides of the fish apart so the smoke could get at the fish. Over a hundred fish are smoked at a time.

The nets are washed in lime, and then hung on large wooden rods to dry so they would not rot. The bottom of the nets are weighted with lead, and the tops are floated with little pieces of wood, so the net will be in a perpendicular position. The fish swim into the net without knowing. The nets are made of fine string that looks as if it would break easily, but it is very strong. On the edge of the net there is a thicker and stronger cord, because it has to hold all of the fish.

LUCY DUNLAP SMITH, third grade

THE SAW MILL IN GLADSTONE, MICHIGAN

The lumber comes from across the bay and farther north than where we were. It comes in booms from 500 to 1,000 logs, and is towed by tugs. When it gets to the yards they untie it, and men with long poles with iron points on the end spear the logs and send them on a moving thing (made of iron with sharp points) that runs up to the second story of the mill, and keeps going around.

When the logs get to the top, a man with a shorter spear takes them off and puts the perfect or best logs on one side to make boards of, and the poor ones on the other side to be made into shingles. The good logs are pushed over to a sort of moving car with a big clamp on the side that catches up and holds the logs, then turns them over. There is a big saw at one end, and as the car moves it saws the bark off first, which they burn in the furnace. Then they saw the boards. The boards are pushed on to the next lot of men, where each board is placed in position and the rough sides are taken off.

Then they pass on to a set of four saws. If the board was perfect, just enough would be sawed off to even the ends; if not, these saws were worked by foot levers, and the board could be cut either 8, 12, 16, or 20 feet. The poor sides that were cut off were thrown to one side and sawed in just the same way as the larger board, only smaller, and were made into laths—two laths cut at a time. They were bundled and carted away as fast as made. Then the most imperfect logs that were thrown aside as they came up the shift were sawed into shingle lengths. This is very dangerous as the men have to hold the short pieces of logs so close to the saw that Mr. M—— said that they never knew until after it was over when a finger was off. They made three grades of shingles—shingles 1st, 2nd, and 3rd. I watched them bundle the shingles, which the men did very fast. We also watched them sharpen the big saws, which was very interesting.

FERDINAND BUNTER, fourth grade

GERMAN SONGS AND RHYMES FOR CHILDREN

ANNA T. SCHERZ

University Elementary School

There is, perhaps, hardly a country that has such a wealth of children's songs and rhymes as Germany. A great many of the rhymes are from six to eight hundred years old, but children still love to say them. Very extensive works have been published which contains numerous songs and rhymes of childhood, as, for instance, *Des Knaben Wunderhorn*, by Achim v. Arnim and Brentano, or *Das deutsche Kinderbuch*, by Simrock.

If children begin to study German when young, they take great delight in these natural little verses of childhood, and, as I have found them of great help to me in teaching the language, I present a few of the best ones which I have collected.

WIEGENLIEDER

I

1

Schlaf' in guter Ruh',
Tu die Äuglein zu!
Höre, wie der Regen fällt,
Hör', wie Nachbars Hündchen bellt;
Hündchen hat den Mann gebissen,
Hat des Bettlers Kleid zerrissen;
Bettler läuft der Pforte zu.
Schlaf' in guter Ruh'!

2

Schlaf', mein süsses Kind!
Draussen weht der Wind;
Häschen, Häschen, spitzt das Ohr,
Sieht aus langem Gras hervor;
Jäger kommt im grünen Kleide,
Jagt das Häschen aus der Weide;
Häschen läuft geschwind, geschwind.
Schlaf', mein süsses Kind!

II

Schlaf', Kindlein schlaf'!
Der Vater hütet die Schaf;
Die Mutter schüttelt's Bäumelein,
Da fällt herab ein Träumelein.
Schlaf', Kindlein, schlaf'!

III

Eia, popeia, schlag's Küchelchen tot!
Legt mir keine Eier
Und frisst mir mein Brot.
Rupfen wir ihm dann
Die Federchen aus,
Machen dem Kindlein
Ein Bettlein daraus.

IV

Schlaf', Kindchen, schlaf'!
Vor der Tür steht ein Schaf,
Ein schwarzes und ein weisses;
Und wenn das Kind nicht schlafen will,
So kommt das schwarze und beisst es.

KLETTERBÜBLEIN

Steigt das Büblein auf den Baum,
O, so hoch man sieht es kaum!
Schlüpft—von Ast zu Aestchen,
Hüpft—zum Vogelnestchen.
Ui!—da lacht es.—
Hui!—da kracht es.—
Plumps, da liegt es drunten!

WENN DAS KIND VERDRIESSLICH IST

Sag mir, du Siebenschläferlein:
Wie träumt das Maienkäferlein?
Mum, mum!
Wie lacht das Maienkäferlein?
Hum, hum!

Wie singt das Maienkäferlein?
Sum, sum!
Wie zankt das Maienkäferlein?
Brum, brum!

EIN LIED

I

Der Besen, der Besen!
Was macht man damit?
Man kehrt damit die Stuben,
Man kehrt damit die Stuben,
Die Stuben, die Stuben.

2

Die Rute, die Rute!
Was macht man damit?
Man klopft damit die Buben.

3

Warum denn nicht die Mädchen?
'Ne Schand' wäre das,
Die folgen schon von selber.

EIN LIED

Spannenlanger Hansel,
Nudeldicke Dirn'.
Gehen wir in den Garten,
Schütteln wir die Birn'.
Schüttel' ich die grossen,
Schüttelst du die kleinen;
Wenn das Säcklein voll ist,
Gehen wir wieder heim.

REIME AUS DER NATUR

I

Drei Rosen im Garten,
Drei Tannen im Wald.
Im Sommer ist's lustig,
Im Winter ist's kalt.

II

Blümchen am Wege,
Blümchen am Stege,
Blümchen blüh,
Frühling ist hier.

III

Es regnet, es regnet,
Es regnet seinen Lauf,
Und wenn's genug geregnet hat,
Dann hört es wieder auf.

IV

Es schneit, es schneit,
Es weht ein kühler Wind,
Es fliegen weisse Vögelein
Auf's Käpplein jedem Kind.

EIN LIED

A, a, a, der Winter, der ist da.
Herbst und Sommer sind vergangen,
Winter der hat angefangen.
A, a, a, der Winter, der ist da.

E, e, e, nun giebt es Eis und Schnee.
Blumen blüh'n an Fensterscheiben,
Sind sonst nirgends aufzutreiben.
E, e, e, nun giebt es Eis und Schnee.

I, i, i, vergiss des Armen nie.
Hat oft nichts sich zuzudecken,
Wenn ihn Frost und Kälte schrecken.
I, i, i, vergiss des Armen nie.

O, o, o, wie sind die Kinder froh.
Wenn das Christkind tut was bringen,
Und "vom Himmel hoch" sie singen,
O, o, o, wie sind die Kinder froh.

U, u, u, ich weiss wohl, was ich tu'.
Christkind lieben, Christkind loben,
Mit den lieben Englein droben.
U, u, u, ich weiss wohl, was ich tu'.

TANZLIEDCHEN

I

Tanz, Mädchen, tanz!
Die Schuhe sind noch ganz,
Lass dich's nicht gereuen,
Der Schuster macht dir neue.
Tanz, Mädchen, tanz!

II

Wenn ich zum Tanzen geh',
Tut mir mein Fuss nicht weh;
Aber o weh, mein Fuss,
Wenn ich arbeiten muss.

BALLSPIEL

Anne-Marie
Fall auf die Knie!
Steh wieder auf,
Mach einen Lauf!
Wasche die Hände,
Trockne sie ab!
Steck' sie in die Seite,
Ringel—Ringel—Reite!

STECKENPFERDLIED

Hopp, hopp, hopp!
Pferdchen, lauf Galopp!
Über Stock und über Steine,
Aber brich dir nicht die Beine.
Hopp, hopp, hopp, hopp, hopp,
Pferdchen, lauf Galopp!

DIALOGE

I

Ihr Diener,
Was machen Ihre Hühner?
Legen sie brav Eier?
Sind sie denn auch teuer?
"Stück für Stück ein'n Dreier."

II

Guten Morgen, Herr Meier!
Was kosten Ihre Eier?
"Ein' Dreier."
Das ist zu teuer,
"Einen Pfennig."
Das ist zu wenig.

TIERVERSCHEN

I

Storch, Storch, Langbein,
Bring mir ein kleines Brüderlein!
Storch, Storch, bester,
Bring mir 'ne kleine Schwester!

II

Muh, muh, muh,
So spricht die Kuh.
Sie giebt uns Milch und Butter,
Wir geben ihr das Futter.
Muh, muh, muh, so spricht die Kuh.

III

Rab', Rab', gräme dich!
Rab', Rab', schäme dich!
Kannst dir keine Stiefel kaufen,
Musst im Schmutze barfuss laufen.
Du stolzierst im schwarzen Frack
Und bist doch ein Bettelsack.

IV

Sperling ist ein kleines Tier,
Hat ein kurzes Schwänzchen,
Sitzt vor Häuschens Kammertür,
Macht ein Reverenzchen.

V

Schneck' im Haus,
Komm heraus!
Kommen zwei mit Stecken,
Wollen dich erschrecken;
Kommen zwei mit Spiessen,
Wollen dich erschiessen.
Schneck' im Haus,
Komm heraus!

VI

Kuckucksknecht,
Sag' mir recht,
Wie lange soll ich leben?
Will dir einen Groschen geben!
Belüg mich nicht,
Betrüg' mich nicht,
Sonst bist du nicht der rechte,
Ich verklage dich beim Spechte,
Der kriegt dich dann beim Kragen,
Drum musst du die Wahrheit sagen,
Kuckuck, Kuckuck!

WETTSTREIT

I

Der Kuckuck und der Esel
Die hatten grossen Streit,
Wer wohl am besten sänge,
Zur schönen Maienzeit.

2

Der Kuckuck sprach: "Das kann ich!"
Und fing gleich an zu schrei 'n.
"Ich aber kann es besser!"
Fiel gleich der Esel ein.

3

Das klang so schön und lieblich,
So schön von fern und nah;
Sie sangen alle beide:
Kuckuck, Kuckuck, ia!

—H. v. FALLERSLEBEN

REIMRÄTSEL

I

Welches Tier meint's nimmer gut,
Wenn es noch so freundlich tut
Und nur schmeichelt mit der Tatze;
Rate nur, es ist die ——

II

Wer kann mir den Vogel nennen:
Er ist grösser als die Hennen
Und geht ihnen stets voran,
Kennst du ihn? Es ist der ——

III

Was sitzt am Kopf und kleidet gut?
Errate schnell, es ist der ——

IV

Wer ist der Mann, er nähet Kleider?
Liebes Kind, es ist der ——

V

Es kann sich drehen, aber nicht laufen,
Es steht gewöhnlich auf grünem Hügel,
Es ist kein Vogel und hat doch Flügel;
Mit welchem Namen willst du es taufen?

VI

Wer hat einen Kamm und kämmt sich nicht,
Wer hat einen Sporn und reitet nicht,
Wer hat Sicheln und schneidet nicht?

VII

Was Zähne hat und doch nicht beisst,
Und auch nicht kaut;
Wer weiss wie's heisst?

THE VIKING

Words and melody by children of the Fifth School Year, University
Elementary School

King Har-old went a-cross the sea, To trade for sil-ver and gold; Three

ships to far-off Spain took he, With a hun-dred men right bold. One

night at sea a storm broke out, The thun-der roared and rang, The
hail to Har-old, glo-rious king, And hail to all his men, Long

Fine.

ships were driv - en all a - bout; The men but laughed and sang.
life and joy to them we sing, And vic - to - ries a - gain.

2. Out of the mist a drag-on came, It was a fier - y foe! The

swords and spears flashed like a flame, And hundreds "went be-low." All

Wilbur Samuel Jackman

Professor of the Teaching of Natural Science in the
School of Education of the University of Chicago;
and Principal of the University Elementary School

Born January 12, 1855
Died January 28, 1907

Editor of the
Elementary School Teacher
September, 1904-January, 1907

BOOK REVIEWS

Educational Manual Training. By WILLIAM C. A. HAMMEL, Director of Manual Training and Physics in the North Carolina State Normal and Industrial College. Richmond: B. F. Johnson Publishing Co. (No. 1, *Paper Folding,* pp. 45; No. 2, *Cardboard Construction,* pp. 48; No. 3, *Elementary Knife Work,* pp. 38; No. 4, *Advanced Knife Work,* pp. 45. Paper, illustrated.)

Mr. William C. A. Hammel has made a practical contribution to educational manual training in the above four paper-bound booklets. They contain drawings for a series of models in each material, together with explicit directions for carrying them out. The necessary equipments are simple, inexpensive, and permit the work to be done at the school-desk.

The purpose is to present an outline of work to begin in the third grade, leading finally to the wood-sloyd in the seventh, eighth, and ninth grades.

Some excellent models are presented, especially in the cardboard, but in some instances the drawings seem complicated in view of the age of the pupils for whom they are designed.

A. B.

BOOKS RECEIVED

A. S. BARNES & CO., NEW YORK

Simple Experiments in Physics. By JOHN F. WOODHULL and M. B. VAN ARSDALE.
 Mechanics, Heat, Fluids. Cloth. Pp. 142.
 Sound, Light, Magnetism, and Electricity. Cloth. Pp. 120.
Hints and Helps. Arranged by CAROLINE S. GRIFFIN. Cloth. Pp. 179.
Mary Kingwood's School. By CORINNE JOHNSON. Introduction by W. A. BEER.
 Cloth. Pp. 119.
Little Talks on School Management. By RANDALL N. SAUNDERS. Cloth. Pp. 68.
Composition in Elementary Schools. By JOSEPH S. TAYLOR. Cloth. Pp. 207.

LITTLE, BROWN & CO., BOSTON

Men of Old Greece. By JENNIE HALL. Cloth. Eight full-page plates and forty-
 three illustrations. Pp. 263. List price, $0.60.
Boy Blue and His Friends. By ETTA AUSTIN BLAISDELL and MARY FRANCES
 BLAISDELL. Cloth. Illustrated. Pp. 165.
Merry Animal Tales. By MADGE A. BINGHAM. Cloth. Illustrated. Pp. 217.
The Wide Awake Primer. By CLARA MURRAY. Cloth. Illustrated in color. Pp.
 111.
The Wide Awake First Reader. By CLARA MURRAY. Cloth. Illustrated in color.
 Pp. 128.

WILBUR S. JACKMAN

VOLUME VII   NUMBER 8

THE ELEMENTARY SCHOOL TEACHER

APRIL, 1907

WILBUR S. JACKMAN

ORVILLE T. BRIGHT
Chicago

Rarely has the educational world been so startled as on Monday morning, January 28, when without warning of any kind came the news that Wilbur S. Jackman was dead. He had been actively engaged in his work during the preceding week, and on Saturday evening was at a social gathering with the students of the School of Education until late in the evening. He seemed to rest well Saturday night, but early Sunday morning symptoms of the dread disease, pneumonia, began to show themselves, although it was late in the afternoon before his physician realized the serious condition Mr. Jackman was in. Even on Monday morning Mrs. Jackman could not believe there was any serious danger; but at eight o'clock, almost without warning and without struggle, his life slipped away. A private funeral service was held on Tuesday afternoon at the home, and a public memorial service, on Wednesday morning in Mandel Hall, which was crowded to the utmost with members of the faculty and students. The body was taken to his boyhood home in Pennsylvania for burial. I have heard him wish that he might die "in the harness," and this wish was literally fulfilled.

Wilbur Samuel Jackman was born at Mechanicstown, O., January 12, 1855. When he was four or five years of age his father returned to his own boyhood home on the ancestral farm two and one-half miles from California, Pa. This farm Wilbur's

433

grandfather had bought from the Indians, giving in payment a copper kettle, and it has been the family home for more than a hundred years. Wilbur's boyhood was spent on this farm, doing such work as offers for every farmer's boy, and attending the country school on the hill near by. It was while attending this country school, and while engaged in work on the farm, that he developed that passionate love for plants and animals which characterized his whole life. As soon as he was old enough, he attended the normal school at California, riding a horse to and from the school every day, and doing much of his studying on horseback. He was graduated from the normal school at about twenty years of age, and afterward taught there one year. It must be understood that all of the larger boys and girls from the country round about attended this school, and were the neighbors and friends of young Jackman. This familiar acquaintance led to some exciting experiences with the boys, and the first few weeks of his teaching were not altogether peaceful ones, but his great strength of character, backed up by physical strength just as remarkable, together with never-failing patience and common-sense, made him master of the situation, and his first students have been his lifelong friends.

After this year's experience, Mr. Jackman went to Meadville College for three years, and then to Harvard for two years, being graduated in 1884 in the general course. On his way home after graduation he stopped at Pittsburg at the time that Superintendent Luckey had charge of the schools, and before leaving the city had engaged to teach natural science in the high school. He remained in the position for five years, and during that time had worked out a plan for nature-study in the elementary schools. Here Colonel Parker found him in 1889.

While he was in the high school at Pittsburg, it was the custom of the principal to place thirty or forty young people in charge of each teacher for such personal services as could be rendered from the friendship standpoint. Mr. Jackman asked that the group assigned to him might remain with him for the entire four years. The result was remarkable in the strength of character developed among the students through this personal association. As men and women, these students refer to it today as the strongest and best influence of their lives. I have read some of the letters written by these men and women to Mrs. Jackman since Mr. Jackman's death. The heartfelt acknowledgments of their great debt of gratitude to their old teacher were most affecting, and this gratitude seems only to have strengthened with the years that have passed. They seem to realize fully that it was the wonderful character of the man, more even than what he taught, that had so powerfully influenced their lives. We are glad indeed that Mr. Jackman himself knew of this sentiment of his old pupils.

Mr. Jackman came to Chicago in the fall of 1889. Never shall I forget the elation with which Colonel Parker introduced Mr. Jackman and Dr. Giffin to the first gathering of parents at the school that fall. For years he had been in search of a teacher of natural science who could bring these subjects into rational touch with young lives. As soon as he saw Mr. Jackman at work at Pittsburg, he determined to have him at the Cook County Normal School. That he made no mistake in this selection I need not say to any teacher or pupil who was in the normal school from that time on.

As everybody knows who remembers the Cook County Normal School, the support of the school was very precarious, and its equipment wretchedly inadequate; but Mr. Jackman went at his work with remarkable enthusiasm and courage. No obstacles could daunt him. He took entire charge of the science, including chemistry, and within the next five years had, somehow or other, got into the school a very adequate apparatus, all of which could be, and was, constantly in use. His classes in elementary science, especially in nature-study, were wonderfully successful, and became celebrated throughout the country.

As a teacher, Mr. Jackman was an enthusiast, but a very quiet one. There was no bluster about anything that he ever did. He was a genuine inspiration to his classes, always insisting upon close attention and earnestness on the part of pupils; but at the same time he brought into his work so much of the charm of his personality and the rare sweetness of his disposition as to make these recitation periods the best of the day to all concerned in them. Every one of Mr. Jackman's recitations was a model of its kind. His preparation was ample, and every lesson showed the result of fresh study and thought. Many, many times have I enjoyed his classwork, and never have I seen any but clean-cut and effective teaching. His students were responsive—they could not be otherwise. Brightness and effectiveness were the rule of the hour, and this was always so.

Mr. Jackman was a thorough student, but not for the sake of hoarding knowledge. Aside from his love for study, there was always with him the hope that the knowledge acquired might be of service to his pupils. I have never known a teacher, unless it was Colonel Parker himself, who seemed so completely to fill a recitation, and yet to bring out the best results possible from every student present, and make every student feel himself to be a useful factor in the recitation through what he contributed to it. It seems to me that this is great teaching, and I believe that hundreds and thousands of Mr. Jackman's students would subscribe to the same sentiment.

When Colonel Parker resigned his position at the Chicago Normal School to organize and take charge of the Institute of Education founded by Mrs. Emmons Blaine, Mr. Jackman, as well as several other members of the faculty, went with him. The north side school could not begin operations for a year, and through the generosity of Mrs. Blaine several members of the faculty, including Mr. Jackman, were sent abroad for one year's study and travel. Later on this school was merged with the University of Chicago. For about a year and a half before his death, Colonel Parker was at the head of the School of Education, as it was afterward called at the university. The work was carried on in the temporary building provided for that purpose, pending the completion of the present beautiful building on the Midway. Two and one-half years ago Mr. Jackman was appointed dean of the School of Education, and took complete charge of the elementary school. His work was arduous and sometimes seemed almost beyond his strength, but from the time that he took the helm the school prospered beyond any previous record. President Harper expressed the greatest pleasure in the success of Mr. Jackman's work. This success became more marked each year until the school was crowded to the limit. During the present year from seventy-five to one hundred have been on the waiting-list all the time. As may be imagined, Mr. Jackman felt greatly elated over this success, and his plans and hopes for the future seemed almost boundless. He said recently: "If I can have just five years, I will show what this school can become."

Mr. Jackman was prodigal of his strength. He was a strong man, but the pace was too fast. He seemed never to rest. The School of Education was quite enough, but he edited the *Elementary School Teacher,* besides responding to constant calls for educational addresses and other literary work for the cause at large. He was a forcible and convincing speaker and writer. It is doubtful whether any other man in the country has done so much for the cause of rational nature-study and elementary science as Wilbur S. Jackman. He was also intensely interested in all sorts of hand-work available for elementary schools. The School of Education is more noted for these two lines of work than for any other, but only because it is so uncommon to find them effectively carried out. These two departments of education can ill afford the loss of so devoted and enthusiastic an advocate as Mr. Jackman. But the work he has done in them and for them will go on because he did this work so well.

Mr. Jackman believed in Colonel Parker heart and soul—rarely have I known a man to love and honor another so much. He generously acknowledged the great influence of Colonel Parker over his own aims and attitude toward educational work. To my mind the strongest proof of the correctness of Colonel Parker's educational principles was Wilbur S. Jackman himself, who studied and worked in them eighteen years, and never faltered in his faith.

It was my rare good fortune to know Mr. Jackman intimately during all the years he lived in Chicago, and to feel the full grasp of his friendship; and never a cloud has cast a shadow over this friendship. He never left a doubt in the minds of those whom he loved and trusted and honored. One can have very few such friends, because men of his pattern are not plentiful. He was a great teacher, but more than that—he was a noble, generous, loving man. His character was rugged and at need inflexible, but he was gentle as a woman and as full of fun as a boy. Perhaps his early Quaker training had to do with the wonderful evenness and sweetness of his disposition, his grandfather having been a Quaker preacher; but there was never a suggestion of weakness in this disposition. His decisions were remarkable for their quickness and correctness. It goes without saying that he was a great favorite with the faculty of the university, and that he was greatly beloved by all of the students in the School of Education.

And we who knew him best, how we loved him! His friendship was so sure and so beautiful. Of the old Cook County Normal School coterie, those who stood by in its trials and rejoiced in its triumphs, Colonel Parker, Albert Lane, and Wilbur S. Jackman have passed on. What a wonderful record they have left of all that is noblest and best in this world! Compared with such lives, how paltry and pitiful seems the mere scramble for dollars! Each of these men has gone just at the height of his usefulness, and when it seemed that he could not possibly be spared. Together with the death of President Harper in the prime of his manhood, does it not all give us pause for thought? We must wonder if it would have made a difference if they could have found time for rest and for play—if they could have known how to rest and to play.

But their lives and their work were noble and grand and beautiful. Perhaps they will seem only the more so that they were cut short in the full strength of manhood.

WILBUR SAMUEL JACKMAN[1]

A PERSONAL APPRECIATION

NATHANIEL BUTLER

Nineteen years ago the late Colonel Francis W. Parker, then at the head of the Cook County Normal School, was commissioned by the county board to go to Pittsburg to look up a man then teaching in the high school of that city, and make recommendation as to his appointment to take charge of the department of natural sciences in the Normal School. Colonel Parker made the journey, and, returning, called upon Dr. H. H. Belfield, a member of the board. "What success did you have?" asked Mr. Belfield. "Well," said Colonel Parker, "I am in rather an embarrassing situation, and I want you to help me out. I've engaged the man for five hundred dollars more than the board authorized." "We'll have to approve it, I guess," was the reply. Thus it happened that in 1889 Wilbur Samuel Jackman came to Chicago, to be associated with Colonel Parker. That association was continued in the Chicago Institute, founded by Mrs. Emmons Blaine, and still further in the School of Education of the University of Chicago. During this period of two decades Mr. Jackman has been an influential leader in education, well known in the National Association as a creative thinker and worker. To him more than to anyone else is due the position of nature-study in the elementary schools. His views, expressed in public meetings and in his editorials in the *Elementary School Teacher,* always uttered fresh, and often wholly novel, ideas in education. He thought vigorously and, for himself, and he certainly must be counted among those who have left a permanent impression for good upon American education.

Mr. Jackman's death occurred most unexpectedly on Monday morning, January 28. He had been suffering from a slight cold

[1] Read at the memorial service held in the Leon Mandel Assembly Hall, University of Chicago, January 30, 1907.

439

for a few days, but was able to be at his office all of the preceding week. On Saturday he attended an important meeting of the University Senate, and at noon lunched with some of his colleagues. In the evening he attended a social gathering at the School of Education. By three o'clock on Sunday somewhat alarming symptoms developed, but there was really no apprehension in the mind of anyone save his physician. Indeed, less than ten minutes before his death, Mr. Jackman in response to an inquiry of the doctor replied that he felt comfortable except for a slight inconvenience in breathing. Almost immediately a collapse followed, and he passed away without suffering.

Perhaps the first impression of which one is aware in our thought of him now is that of the difficulty in believing that he is no longer among us. This, I think, is due to the extreme suddenness of his death; to the fact that he was so vitally a part of whatever concerned him. He was a whole-hearted man, and his whole intellect and heart were fully enlisted in the thing he did. He was an embodiment of energy—mental, emotional, physical. His colleagues and his subordinates looked to him and relied upon him, so that he became an essential part of the activities in which he was associated with others, and in those activities he is still distinctly felt at the very moment in which he is so sadly missed.

No less distinct is the impression of the lovableness of the man. Affection plays a large part in our recollection. In the two years that I have known him intimately, he has not spoken one word to me, nor, so far as I know, to any of his colleagues, that can occasion regret. There were sharp differences of opinion, and even heated discussion. But differences of opinion never, with him, meant discord between friends. When the discussion was over, the friend, the frank, sincere, manly man, was there as before. And this impression of mine, resulting from my two short years of intimacy, is confirmed by the repeated testimony of others who have known him ten times as long. Faculty relations are a great test of a man's qualities. His colleagues knew him thoroughly, and they admired and trusted, often opposed and withstood, and always loved him. He thought clearly and positively, but he was always kind and courteous and cheerful. And in the relaxation of home and social life he was a charming companion, and in the most intimate association with his fellow-officers and his acquaintances these qualities were always in evidence.

Mr. Jackman was a peculiar compound of the autocrat and the democrat. By temperament he was a ruler. This was not so much a matter of vanity and self-will in the ordinary sense; it was, rather, a psychological necessity. He was ever at work upon a problem, and, when he saw its solution, all about him, as it seemed to him, must co-operate for its application. By creed, however, he was a democrat. He distinctly believed that others should enjoy all the rights and privileges that he claimed for himself. And he strove to bring his temperament into subordination to his creed. In this he succeeded, so that he grew ever more and more sympathetic and tolerant. Repeatedly he would protest against any legislation that would abridge the entire freedom of every teacher to work out his own results. For himself, in his work and friendships, he was a devoted, sincere man. Reasonable and sane, a seeker for truth, and a lover of beauty, he had in him both the scientist and the poet. His humor was a delight to his friends, and must have brightened for him many a hard experience. As was true of President Harper and of Colonel Parker, and of all large, free, kindly natures, he never outgrew the boy, and loved play and the outdoor world.

One would not quite say that his religion was the religion of work. Religion is certainly a far profounder thing than work. But work may properly be said to have been a vital part of his religion. These memorable words of Lowell may fitly be recalled as we think of Mr. Jackman:

> The longer on this earth we live ·
> And weigh the various qualities of men,
> The more we feel the high, stern-featured beauty
> Of plain devotedness to duty.
> Steadfast and still, nor paid with mortal praise,
> But finding amplest recompense
> For life's ungarlanded expense
> In work done squarely and unwasted days.

Of the deeper aspects of his religion let his own words speak, quoted from a recent editorial:

The ideal of every religion has at some time found its incarnation in a living character. . . . . Everyone acknowledges the tremendous educational effect produced by the study of a fine character. Our schools need now, and they always will need, the all-compelling influence of the life of Jesus. As the meridian sun seizes upon the seed lying in the darkened earth, and forces the expansion of leaf and flower and the ripening of the fruit, just so his teachings, as set forth in the Sermon on the Mount and in the parables, when learned and applied in the affairs of everyday life, must develop an irresistible spiritual control in the direction of righteousness.

Mr. Jackman's last active days were probably as happy as any that he ever spent. Saturday began with important discussion affecting the organization of the school. The subject had been one of considerable perplexity and anxiety, but on Saturday evening he expressed himself as well satisfied that the right thing would be done, and that good and wise counsels would prevail. So closed a day begun in university work; at midday, a luncheon with friends and visitors; in the evening, a social gathering of teachers and students. A happy Sunday at home followed, and as Monday dawned he passed peacefully away. Who would not, for himself, pray for an end like this? And yet not an end. Who can doubt that noble activities await him and all such as he, being

One who never turned his back but marched breast forward,
    Never doubted clouds would break,
Never dreamed, though right were worsted, wrong would triumph,
Held we fall to rise, are baffled to fight better,
    Sleep to wake.

No, at noonday in the bustle of man's worktime
    Greet the unseen with a cheer!
Bid him forward, breast and back as either should be,
"Strive and thrive!" cry "Speed,—fight on, fare ever
    There as here!"

THE SIGNIFICANCE OF MR. JACKMAN'S WORK [1]

JAMES H. TUFTS

It is at once a limitation and a source of strength, growing out of our common life, that no work and no personality can be judged in itself. We can estimate it rightly only as we see it in its relations to the larger human society, or the movement of human life in which it is placed. This is particularly true of the work and personality of the teacher. The teacher brings to the child or the riper student some part of the thought and life of society as it now is. In this he is therefore dependent for his resources upon the knowledge and culture of his time. But in what he selects and in his adaptation of this to the possible development of the child lies his opportunity to be in turn a contributor. If he can not merely apprehend the mass of material which civilization is constantly gathering and casting aside, but can also discern the movement, the direction, of the process; if he can sense, however imperfectly, what knowledge is of most worth; if he can glimpse what way progress lies; most important of all, if, amid the rival clamors of the liberal and the practical, of sciences and arts, of classicists and realists, he can remember that all these are for the child, and not the child for them, he has an opportunity to be of real service in the larger movement of humanity. However small his individual part may be, it gets permanence and worth as it becomes incorporate in the common life.

Mr. Jackman was connected with three great movements of education. The first claimed his activity when a teacher of science in Pittsburg—the movement to introduce the teaching of the newest science, already established in schools and colleges, into the secondary schools. To the second movement his work at the Cook County Normal School was an important contribution—

[1] Read at the memorial service held in the Leon Mandel Assembly Hall, University of Chicago, January 30, 1907.

the movement which included the study of nature as one of the agencies through which the school life was made to center its emphasis upon a free and full development of the child. The third movement is that for the bringing into mutual relation the work of the university with that of the training of teachers. Mr. Jackman had much to do with bringing about the union of the School of Education with the University of Chicago. This work, however, is still in its beginnings. It is to the work of the second period of his life that we naturally look at this moment, as it is the most conspicuous.

The introduction of nature-study into elementary schools had two aspects. It was, in the first place, a bringing of new material into a very meager and formal course of study. To any-one who has watched the active mind of a child the theory seems almost incredible that eight years, five days in the week, and five hours a day, were necessary to enable the child to deal with symbols of language and symbols of number, with perhaps a little geography and history that were necessarily almost as purely symbolic. To give the child some conception of the world in which he lived, of the material which has so enlarged and enriched all our modern views, was then in itself a sufficient reason for the introduction of the new study.

But this soon came to be only one phase of a larger movement. The average parent, as Mr. Jackman remarked in a recent editorial in the *Elementary School Teacher,* is too apt to think of his child's education as merely a process of fitting the child for something else—for college on the one hand, or for business on the other. There is undoubtedly a sense in which it is true that the life of the child is a preparation for the life of man or woman, but those who have lived with children feel that in another and very profound sense, if there is any part of human experience which pays as it goes—which is not a means to something else but is itself valuable and priceless—it is the life of the child. The biologists have recognized that it is an advantage for the evolutionary process that heredity is not too rigid. It is in the accidental variations, whether minute or large, that the opportunity for progress lies. Our educators have been slow to recognize that the same holds good in the field of social heredity and social progress. To impose upon the child all the learning and traditions of society in science, in art, in morals, in religion, is to leave too little room for the variaton of the child's own free spontaneity to assert itself; and it is in the happy variation that may be found in this child or in that child that the hope of human progress lies, as surely as it lies also in the painful and laborious conquests of the gradual advance of organized thought and purpose. When this began to be more fully appreciated and realized, the significance of studies in the curriculum took on a new interpretation. The study of nature came at once to have a prominent place, not merely because a knowledge of nature might be useful as a means to something else, but also because it was seen to be indispensable as a part of the necessary environment in which the child could live.

Mr. Jackman succeeded in his task because of three things. In the first place, he had a great love of nature and much ingenuity in finding ways to bring this home to children. In the second place, he loved boys and girls. These two facts made his work at Pittsburg so successful that Colonel Parker thought him the man for the new work to be done. In the third place, he had a large conception of the value of the study of nature. It meant, first of all, giving the child new material and imagery with which the mind might grow. Our schools, he said, squeezed the life out of children. They take them eager, full of questions, they give them only symbols and abstract, formal methods; they starve the minds and leave them poorer than when they came. The great variety which sky and earth, plant and animal, natural processes of change and movement afford, gives rich imagery and material, and suggests an expression in turn through a great variety of means. But, again, knowledge of nature means freedom from superstition. Our physical life is endangered, our mental horizon is limited, by ignorance of the world in which we live. The child has a right to be freed from these dangers and limitations. And, finally, the study of nature was by Mr. Jackman considered to be a means through which the child might come into actual, real, and moral relations with his universe; to obey the laws of nature through which we gain strength and power, to control the forces of nature and thus become master in some measure of our world, to recognize at once our limitations and our relations to the whole is of positive moral, as well as intellectual, value. It prepares one in some sense for the more effective relationship to human society through which we become efficient agents in its progress.

To one who, with Lessing, conceives all human progress from its rudimentary and barbarous beginnings up through its successive struggles and achievements as an "education of the human race" the work of the teacher has dignity and worth. When one has passed from the ranks his colleagues pay to the sincere co-worker their tribute of honor and respect.

AN INTERNATIONAL SUMMER SCHOOL IN FRANCE

WILL S. MONROE

State Normal School, Westfield, Mass.

Ten years ago a number of philanthropic gentlemen at Grenoble, France, induced the administrative board of the University of Grenoble to make provision for a special vacation session during the months of July, August, September, and October. It was the belief of these gentlemen that a city so exceptionally located as Grenoble, and with a splendid university plant idle during the summer months, furnished the opportunity of doing a needed piece of popular educational work—viz., furnish courses in the French language and literature to foreign students and teachers who might care to spend the summer vacation in the French Alps.

Grenoble, it will be recalled, is the ancient capital of Dauphiny. It is a city of seventy-five thousand inhabitants, and is situated at the juncture of the Isère and Drac rivers, on the western slopes of the French Alps. About it tower splendid mountain ranges and peaks, which are snow-covered throughout the year, and which attain elevations from eight to ten thousand feet; and within easy reach of Grenoble are the Grand Chatreuse, the Grand Goulets, Uriage-le-Bain, le Grève, and some of the other most picturesque sights in the Alpine system.

The University of Grenoble is one of the historic seats of learning in France. It was originally founded by a bull of Benedict XII in 1339, which was granted at the request of Humbert II, Count of Viennois. Its existence during the mediaeval period was precarious, but it ranks today as one of the best of the provincial French universities. It has faculties of letters, science, and law, and about three hundred students during the academic year, and with more than that number during the summer term.

The summer session is primarily for foreigners. Courses

are offered in the elements of the French language—phonetics, reading, and composition; French literature and history; geography of the French Alps; local arts and industries, and other subjects calculated to interest foreign teachers and students. There are courses suited to learners of all stages of progress in the language, and many illustrated lectures are given. A special feature is made of evening socials; and Saturdays are reserved for excursions among the mountains and to near-by places of historic interest.

The course of the past summer may be given as fairly typical of the work of the summer session. There were eight lectures on the relation of the French language to the civilization of France by Professor Besson, of the University of Grenoble; eight lectures on French lyric poetry by Mr. Brunet, of the *lycée* at Algiers; eight lectures on French fiction during the seventeenth and eighteenth centuries by Professor Joliet, of the University of Bonn; eight lectures by Professor Marillot, of the University of Grenoble, on French fiction during the first half of the nineteenth century; eight lectures on the romantic drama by Mr. Brunet, and two lectures on Victor Hugo by Professor Chabert, of the University of Grenoble. There were, in addition, lectures on the contemporary French dramatic writers, Gustave Flaubert, Paul Herviere, and other literary topics.

There were two courses of ten lectures each on French history; the first, on Michelet, by Professor de Crozals, and a splendid course on modern history—perhaps the most helpful course offered during the summer—by Mr. Mauric, of the Grenoble *lycée*. The course in geography included six lectures on the Mediterranean countries by Mr. Chabrol, of the Vaucauson School of Commerce, and seven on the French Alps by Mr. Henri Ferrand, of Grenoble. There were several lectures on contemporary science, and two noteworthy courses on the fine arts —the first on the art of Grenoble and Dauphiny by Mr. Marcel Reymond, the distinguished art critic and historian, and the second on music by Mr. Allix, a discriminating lover of the tonal art. Mr. Salmon, of the local commercial school, gave a series of lectures and lessons on commercial French; Mr. Rosset conducted a phonetic laboratory, and gave individual and class instruction in the syntax, morphology, and phonetics of French; Mr. Varenne gave a series of lessons on French vocabularies; Mr. Hardouin conducted composition classes, and there were classes in the translation of German, English, Italian, and Russian into the French. The German translation classes were conducted by Messrs. Besson, Herzog, and Joliet; the English classes, by Messrs. Mathias, Banjard and Jayet; the Italian classes, by Messrs. Hauvette, de Crozals, Guichard, and Matton; and the Russian classes, by Madame Koschkine. Thus, it will be seen, a very wide range of instruction was offered to those seeking to perfect their knowledge of the French language and literature.

The summer school is under the immediate direction of Mr. Marcel Reymond and a local committee of patronage composed of philanthropic citizens in Grenoble and professors in the different faculties of the university. But the extraordinary success of the vacation courses is very largely due to the devotion and untiring energy of Mr. Marcel Reymond. In the early history of the movement he was one of the most popular and helpful of the lecturers; but in recent years the administration of the school has consumed so much of his time that he has felt compelled to limit his lecture work to the art of Grenoble and Dauphiny, in which he is a recognized authority.

The expense of the school is moderate. The tuition for the summer is only eight dollars, and one may obtain good board in French families and boarding-houses for thirty dollars a month. One may enter or leave the school at any time. Those, however, who wish the certificate of the summer course must attend the school at least two months and take the required examinations. American teachers who contemplate taking the course may get the circulars of the summer school by addressing Mr. Marcel Reymond, president of the Committee of Patronage, Grenoble, France.

Three courses of the past summer were so significant that they justify special mention. I know of no course of lectures on French literature—Paris not excepted—to compare with the

excellencies of the lectures by Professor Marillot. He is one
of the best literary lecturers in France. The *laboratoire de
phonétique* of Mr. Rosset is one of the unique features of the
school. Phonographs and all other conceivable appliances are
utilized in teaching French to foreigners, with results that are
surprising. One of the most helpful courses of the past summer
was by Mr. Mauric, a professor in the local *lycée* and a comparatively young man; but his grasp of his subject, his mastery
of the pedagogic art, and his quiet and reposeful manner easily
gave him first rank among the lecturers of the last session.

As the title of the article suggests, the summer school at
Grenoble is distinctly international. Of the 435 students in
attendance the past summer, 181 were German, 62 Italian, 55
Russian, 42 English, 11 Scotch, 11 Irish, 26 American, 10 Austrian, 8 Polish, 8 Swiss, 7 Bulgarian, 5 Czech (Bohemian), 5
Swedish, with a scattering of Greeks, Armenians, Servians,
Canadians, Danes, Brazilians, Argentinians, Dutch, Spanish,
Portuguese, Finlanders, Roumanians, etc. For the student of
education, Grenoble is a good place to study comparative school
systems, since a large proportion of the students are teachers in
elementary and secondary schools, colleges, and universities in
their respective countries.

SELF-GOVERNMENT IN THE HIGH SCHOOL

P. A. WALKER
Shawnee, Okla.

The statement that "school is life" has been repeated so often that it is high time we were making it an active principle of our educational system, or were relegating it to the past as so much sentiment of the theorist. So long as the pupils are not permitted to do the things which make up the duties of the active citizen, our schools are failing to perform their true function in the community. With all the progress in the development of an educational system, we have done very little to raise the character of school government above the field of despotism, or to lay the foundation for practical citizenship. The principle of democratic self-government has been so long recognized in national governments that only the mediaeval institutions of countries like Russia and Turkey fail to permit of the participation of the individual in matters which affect the conduct of the community.

But while we have accepted republican government as a principle of our national life, we have made little effort in any practical way to inculcate the idea in our schools. What an opportunity we are missing for teaching practical self-government! We have not gone so far in the development of republican institutions that the pupil knows practical citizenship by instinct; on the contrary, the cry goes out that our citizens manifest a lethargy which bodes such serious ills to our commonwealth that some even say that popular government is doomed to failure. Nor is this wail uttered without some thought of the trend of the times. With our most prominent business men engaging in dishonorable practices, and our statesmen playing the part of the grafter, is it any wonder that the skeptic should cry "failure" at our system of government?

To the forebodings of the pessimist we answer that the hope of the state lies in the public schools. Then let us cease preaching theories, and make the school what it ought to be—a laboratory for the development of character and the practice of citizenship. And there is certainly no better way to begin than to allow the pupils to organize into a self-governing community. By self-government is meant the participation of the pupils in making, interpreting, and enforcing the laws of the school. Self-government does not mean that breaking-away from all authority of the school, any more than home rule in the city means the absolute relegation of the authority of the state. Just as the state holds the city responsible for the life, liberty, and property of its citizens, so the teachers hold the pupils responsible for the conduct of the school.

Self-government rests on the democratic principle that the interests of the community are best served by the participation of the individuals in the policies which determine the welfare of the community. It also recognizes the educational principle so well stated by President Eliot, of Harvard, that "the real object of education, so far as the development of character is concerned, is to cultivate in the child a capacity for self-government—not a habit of submission to an overwhelming, arbitrary, external power, but a habit of obeying the dictates of honor and duty as enforced by active will-power within the child."

Self-government places stress on the formation of the character of the pupil, instead of leaving to the executive the necessity of reforming him when he leaves school. It develops by imposing responsibility. Like the kindergarten, it educates by employing the normal and personal activity of the pupil. It trains by action, rather than by precept.

Self-government is expected to prevent in the pupils who practice it that civic apathy which is now a menace to popular government, because it will inculcate into them a feeling of personal responsibility, and a respect for law and order. What better training could there be for responsible citizenship than throwing upon self-governing pupils the responsibility of the proper care of the building and grounds? Let committees appointed by the pupils themselves see to it that the rooms are properly kept, that paper is not thrown on the floor or stuffed into the desks. Let a committee of pupils plan for the beautification of the school grounds.

Pupils rise to the responsibility placed upon them. In a night school in Mayayunk, a manufacturing suburb of Philadelphia, the discipline had got so poor that the discontinuance of the school was being considered; but Miss Chappel, the day principal, advised a trial of a self-governing plan. No sooner had the organization begun than the boys who had been going under assumed names, so as to escape publicity if brought into police court for the escapades in the school, came forward and gave their correct names, saying that if they were going to be intrusted with the government they wanted to by their own names.

Mr. C. N. Drum, of the Philadelphia schools, says: "The other day I stood in the halls of the Franklin School, where student government is in practice. No teachers were in sight. The children were entering the building in perfect order. Order seemed to be the first law in the school." Many instances may be cited of disorderly pupils who have reformed simply because they were intrusted with some responsibility upon being given a leading part in a system of self-government.

Other arguments might be brought up to show the advantages to be gained in civic and moral development. It is believed that the practice of self-government corrects a wrong attitude toward law and order by giving practice in law-making and law-enforcing. To quote from Dr. Frank Parsons, of Boston: "Habits of good citizenship are formed while the mind is plastic and open to the full force of considerations of right and justice, and free from commercial motives and other influences that in later life so often interfere with the duties of citizenship. The love of liberty is strengthened and ennobled by the recognition of the rights of others, and the necessity for mutual limitations for the public good."

But while the chief argument for self-government in the high school is based on that civic and moral development which makes for practical citizenship, the problem of how to secure good order must not be lost sight of. Self-government has brought order where all other attempts at government had failed.

In the previously mentioned night school in Philadelphia, order was immediately restored after the organization into a self-governing body. Principal French, of the Hyde Park High School, of Chicago, said that during the first year of the self-governing plan in his school an insignificantly small number of cases of discipline was referred to him, whereas during the previous years there had been an average of about three hundred.

Besides securing order, the self-governing plan will save the time of the teacher. To quote again from Mr. Drum, of Philadelphia: "The time formerly spent in duties outside of rooms saved to my teachers amounted in one day to five hours and twenty minutes; in one week, to twenty-six hours and forty minutes; in one year, to two hundred and fourteen school days. If the teachers are using that time in the preparation of lesson-work, at the present salary rate, the value to my school in one year is $642. In the Franklin School three hundred and twenty-one days are gained, amounting to $963 per annum."

Regarding the matter of the organization for self-government little need be said, for when the principle is once thoroughly understood its application can readily be made to any form of government with which the pupil comes into contact after leaving school. So far as its practical application in the school is concerned, the form is nonessential so long as the scheme is not made too complicated. Among the more recent practical attempts at self-government, the municipal form has been taken as a model, and school cities have been established. True, self-government has been tried more often in the grades than in the high school; but certainly, if pupils below the high-school age are capable of governing themselves, those in the high school should be more able to carry out a system of self-government.

The school-city idea originated with Mr. Wilson L. Gill. In 1896–97 Mr. Gill, who had been interested for some time in the teaching of practical citizenship, was consulted in regard to a New York school which had become so unruly that a policeman was permanently detailed to keep order on the school ground. Mr. Gill suggested that the school be organized into a self-governing body, with a legislature, executive, and judge of their own election. This was done. The boys and girls were delighted with the responsibility and quickly established order. Mr. Gill saw at once the moral and civic value of school self-government, and gave up important business affairs to introduce the new system of civic training wherever opportunity offered. He took for his model the city government. The organized school he styled the school city. Since 1897 Mr. Gill has introduced the school city into more than thirty Philadelphia schools, and in a few schools in other cities. He spent two years in Cuba, employed by the United States government, to introduce his system into all the public schools of the island.

Besides, the school city has been organized in a number of schools without the personal supervision of Mr. Gill. Among these are the schools of Syracuse and New Platz, N. Y.; Omaha; Chicago; some of the schools on the Pacific coast, as well as those of Hawaii and the Philippines. Says the pamphlet *The School City,* published by the National School City League of Philadelphia: "Wherever the system has been earnestly and intelligently applied, marked success has been achieved."

The success of the school city is due partly to two things: the pride and enthusiasm with which pupils take hold of a system of self-government; and the practicability of the scheme when once put into operation. From Mr. Gill's Cuban report we quote the following: "At half-past one, five hundred boys of the city of Guines filed into a hall down-town for the purpose of organizing a school city. The councilmen and other leading men of the city were there. The *alcade,* or mayor, made an address, explaining the purpose and importance of the meeting. After the speeches and the election of officers, I called the newly elected councilmen and the mayor to the stage. The mayor's name is Antonio Franqui. Young Franqui bowed, smiled, and thanked his fellow-citizens for the honor they had conferred upon him, assured them that he would try to be worthy of their confidence, and begged them to do their part to make theirs a noble city." The spirit and enthusiasm shown made the whole thing thoroughly dramatic. "The alcade said: 'I fear, Mr. Gill, that it may sound extravagant, but I say to you with deliberation, this is the greatest day of my life. It is the greatest event in the history of this town. I have seen the seeds of citizenship sown and take root, not only in the minds and hearts of these five hundred boys, but also in the hearts of the representative men of this city. One after another of the chief men of the city came up, and, unbidden, pledged me his support for the movement inaugurated on that day." The reports of General Leonard Wood and the statements of the Cuban press have attested the success of Mr. Gill's innovation in the school of the island.

Many prominent examples of the successful operation of the school-city type of self-government are to be found in the United States. In the John Crerar School of Chicago, composed of about eight hundred grammar-grade pupils, self-government has been in successful operation for about nine years. Its practicability is proved by the fact that it has been taken up by a number of the largest and best schools of the city, and by hundreds of individual teachers in other of the Chicago schools. When the school city was introduced into the Hyde Park High School, there was an enrolment of about fifteen hundred pupils. More than a year after the system had been put into operation, the principal, Mr. French, wrote: "We are using the municipal form in such a way as to acquaint the pupils with the principal functions of city government. We are thus able to teach most effectively lessons in sociology, civics, and ethics, as well as to secure a better self-control on the part of the pupils, and hence better order." Myron T. Scudder, principal of the State Normal School at New Platz, N. Y., says: "The school city, organized in this school five years ago, is increasingly vigorous, and is a powerful factor in our daily work. To me it is simply indispensable as an aid in school management, and I would not think for a moment of dropping it or of substituting some other form of organization."

Additional evidence could be quoted to prove the practicability of the self-governing scheme. Its success in the schools has called for the indorsement of semi-civic organizations, and of individuals like President Roosevelt; Chancellor E. Benjamin Andrews, of Nebraska; President Eliot, of Harvard; Professor Jackman, of

Chicago; and Dr. Albert Shaw. The Federation of Women's Clubs of Massachusetts and New York recommended the adoption of self-government in the schools of their states at their last annual meetings.

So far only the theory of self-government and its practicability as an organization for school management have been considered. By the adoption of self-government we begin a movement to make school a part of real life; to develop a higher and nobler citizenship; to arrest that dreadful apathy which keeps the best element in our community from taking any active part in the affairs of government, which prevents them from even registering to vote on a question like the sewer bonds, where the health of the city is at stake and the very lives of the people are in jeopardy. It is a movement to prevent that wantonness which allows corruption and selfishness to breed unchecked and to sap the vitality from our institutions.

In a state like ours, where advancement and democracy should be the keynotes of our existence, can we hesitate to hasten the adoption of a scheme which promises to give us a more rational and a more aggressive citizenship—a citizenship which shall ever foster the principles of liberty?

A LESSON IN GEOGRAPHY—FROM CHICAGO TO THE ATLANTIC

ZONIA BABER

School of Education, University of Chicago

The relative merits of teaching geography from books alone or from the earth itself is no longer a debatable question in any body of intelligent teachers. "Things before words" has become axiomatic. But in education we are prone to accept a principle in theory long before we put it into practice.

If any teacher cares to test the principle for himself, let him take a class into the field for several weeks of study. The teacher as well as the pupil will meet with many surprises. The teacher will detect even his best students gazing with unintelligent eyes upon a rich and interesting landscape, while the student will find that many subjects with which he had an intimate friendship in textbooks are indifferent strangers when met in nature.

Training in the ability to image from another's expression, to think through another's thoughts, to reason from premises established by someone else, does not develop initiative nor give power in action. It does not insure that a student can recognize even the things which he has described with satisfaction to the instructor, nor give him power to discover and organize a problem in the field—forming his own working hypotheses, discovering relevant data. But after a few weeks in the field the students seize upon a problem and follow it up day after day with increasing interest and enjoyment.

In reply to the question, "What of that called geography do the students learn on a field trip of a month or six weeks?" I submit the following superficial description of the region visited and the work done by a class of college students, School of Education, University of Chicago, during the second term of the last summer quarter.

The class was composed of fourteen teachers. Of the num-

ber, seven teach in normal schools, "teachers of teachers;" one
is principal of a public school in one of the largest cities of the
country; three are special instructors in geography in elementary
schools; two are grade teachers; one is a graduate student.

THE ITINERARY

The party left Chicago at nine o'clock, the morning of July
30, over the Big Four Railroad for Louisville, Ky. The day was
spent, as all others on the train, in making and recording observations on the topography, soil, rocks, vegetation, crops and
other cultural features of the region passed through.

The special problem for the first day was to determine the
limit and characteristics of the glacial drift along the route.

The first stop was made at Louisville to study the Ohio
River valley, the falls, and sink holes which are finely illustrated
here.

At Charleston, W. Va., the class made observations on the
form and terraces of the valley of the Kanawha River; studied
the sedimentary rocks of the Carboniferous period, the exposures
of which along the bluffs of the river show excellent examples
of the interbedding of coal; visited Malden, eight miles east of
Charleston, to see the salt-works which have been so potent a
factor in the history of this part of West Virginia; and studied
the region of Coon Skin Creek, which occupies a part of the
abandoned valley of the Elk River, a tributary of the Kanawha.

The next stop was made at Kanawha Falls for a study of
the falls, the foundry of an aluminum company, and the great
potholes in siliceous conglomerate exposed in the rock terrace at
Gauley Junction. The night was spent at Thurmond, which
boasts the only good hotel between Charleston and Clifton
Forge. At Thurmond a coal-mine was visited, after which the
party proceeded to Clifton Forge, Va.

On this journey the point of special interest, aside from the
study of the New River cañon, was the discovery of the beginning of the folding and crumpling of the rock, which had
appeared horizontally-bedded throughout the region previously
traversed.

A stop was made at Clifton Forge to study the great fold in the rocks called Rainbow Arch, which is exposed in the cañon of the Jackson River where it cuts through the Rich Patch Mountains. Just below the cañon, known as the Iron Gate, the Jackson River joins the Cow Pasture River to form the historic James.

South Glasgow was selected as the next stopping-place. It is a tiny village in the "Great Valley" just west of the Blue Ridge, at the beginning of the cañon which the James River has chiseled in its tortuous course through the mountains. From this village the Natural Bridge Region was visited. Mount Salling was climbed for a view of the "Great Valley." The contact between the sedimentary rocks to the west and the igneous rocks of the Piedmont was found about a mile below the village, exposed in the cañon of the James.

For a study of the Piedmont country and the tobacco industry, Lynchburg seemed the most desirable spot. From Lynchburg the James River was followed "on to Richmond." Here the Coastal Plain formations were seen lying just over the igneous rocks of the Piedmont; the contact was found in Shockoe Creek back of the Old Medical College; and visits were made to places of historic interest. On leaving Richmond, a part of the class went down the James River by boat to see the famous old homesteads—Shirley, Berkeley, Westover, Upper and Lower Brandon—and landed at the deserted spot where Jamestown once stood. The remainder of the party reached Williamsburg by rail, and drove the seven miles to Jamestown. After visits to some of the historic places in Williamsburg, and a boat trip to Yorktown by way of the wide tidal Queen's Creek and the York River, we journeyed to Hampton, where we were entertained at Hampton Institute, that excellent and interesting school for the training of Indians and negroes.

From here we visited the shipyards at Newport News, and went to Norfolk, Virginia Beach, and Cape Henry. At Cape Henry the fine examples of san-dunes were studied. The Jamestown Exposition Grounds are in plain view in crossing the Bay from Old Point Comfort to Norfolk, being just south of

Sewall Point, about five miles north of Norfolk. The trip from Hampton to Washington was made by boat, and while in Washington visits were made to the United States departments of geology, agriculture, soils, ethnology, entomology, and forestry. We were cordially received by the men in charge, who generously gave their time in instructing us as to the purposes of each of the departments and the character of its work. Through the special kindness of Dr. Hayes, of the Department of Geology, we were introduced to some of the interesting geological formations about Washington. After visiting Mount Vernon, Arlington, the Capitol, the Congressional Library, and other points of interest, we left Washington [1] for Luray, Va., over the Baltimore & Ohio Railroad to Shenandoah Junction, and the Norfolk & Western to Luray. A stop was made at Washington Junction,[2] about three-fourths of a mile east of "Point of Rocks," where the Potomac breaks through the Catoctin Mountains, twelve miles east of Harper's Ferry and forty-two miles from Washington.

On leaving Luray we continued up the Shenandoah valley to Basic City. After securing a magnificent view of the Shenandoah valley from the top of a hill, we crossed the valley to Clifton Forge, returning home over the line traversed in the onward journey, reaching Chicago, August 31.

SPECIAL POINTS STUDIED

General division.—The reason for selecting the special area from Chicago to the Atlantic Ocean was to give the students a view, although necessarily superficial, of the type land forms which constitute the eastern half of this continent, and which have played so great a rôle in the history of our people. These divisions are known as the Alleghany Plateau, which extends from the Alleghany Front to the Mississippi River; the Appalachian Mountain region, including the region from the Alleghanies to Blue Ridge; the Piedmont, from the Blue Ridge to the "Fall Line," which passes through Washington, Rich-

[1] A part of the class was obliged to return home from Washington.

[2] Within the distance of two miles along the railroad are excellent exposures of Juratrias, Cambrian, and Algonkian formations.

mond, Columbia, Augusta, and Macon; and the Coastal Plain, which extends from the "Fall Line" to the Atlantic Ocean. An attempt was made to trace the limit of each of these divisions along the route of travel. The rocks of the Alleghany Plateau are sedimentary, that is, made from materials deposited in water, which formed the sandstones, limestones, shales, and conglomerates of this region. The rocks are nearly horizontally bedded, looking like layers of a cake, as they are exposed in the bluffs of the numerous rivers which have dissected the plain.

The horizontal stratification of the rocks continues to a point near Hinton, W. Va., where slight tilting of the layers is first observed. Just east of Hinton, near Talcott, decided folding appears. The most perfect example of the Appalachian type form, however, on this route is the Rainbow Arch at Clifton Forge. Here the quartzite rocks have been forced up, forming a beautiful solid arch.

The sedimentary rocks, tilted, folded, and contorted, continue to a point just below a station known as Balcony Falls, Va. Here, in the Blue Ridge, the sedimentary rocks lie against the granite of "Appalachia," the old continent from which the sediments now made into the Appalachian Mountains were doubtless derived.

From Balcony Falls granites, schists, and gneisses are the dominant rocks to Richmond, Va., where the older rocks disappear under the Coastal Plain.

Besides making the acquaintance of these broader areas referred to above, opportunity was afforded for the study of certain of the earth-shaping forces, as the work of glaciers, surface streams, underground water, wind, waves, tides, ocean currents, and diastrophism. Stops were made where the most marked expression of any of these forces was exhibited. The vegetation, industries, and historic places were not overlooked.

Glaciated country.—The glaciated region was crossed between Chicago and Greensburg, Ind., a distance of about 240 miles. It was studied from the car windows only, but from even so superficial a view some knowledge of the topography and of the materials which compose the drift can be obtained. We left the level Chicago Lake plain near Homewood, Ill., going on to the rolling Valparaiso moraine. The surface of the glaciated region traversed is for the most part rather level, but relieved in places, however, by heterogeneously distributed hills, and dotted with swamps and ponds. Boulders are scattered aimlessly about, and the railroad and river cuts expose the clays, sands, and gravels which compose the drifts. The kind and condition of crops also told the story of the nature of soil.

Underground water.—The work of underground water, which, by reason of its concealment, is always surrounded with a certain mystery and fascination, reveals its "black arts" in the limestone region of southern Indiana, Kentucky, and the "Great Valley" in Virginia just west of the Blue Ridge Mountains. We stopped at Louisville, Ky., to study at close range the interesting depressions in the surface of the country known as "sink holes." In Cave Hill Cemetery, Louisville, are fine illustrations of this type of the work of underground water. When the rock has been dissolved until the roof of a cavern becomes too weak to support itself, it collapses, leaving these depressions in the surface. Sink holes are sometimes very shallow, and look like huge saucers; again, they may be elliptical in shape, while their depth may be measured in inches or in hundreds of feet. These pits or depressions are frequently filled with water, making ponds and lakes in regions whose surface drainage is otherwise well developed. Throughout the Blue Grass region and the "Great Valley" the eye becomes skilled in recognizing "sink hole" landscapes. At Luray Cave in the Shenandoah valley, about fifty-five miles southwest of Harper's Ferry, are very striking results of this wonderful agent. In these caverns are displayed the most beautiful formations of stalactites and stalagmites, rivaling exquisite tapestry in design and color. These remarkable deposits certainly suggest power no less than magic.

While the caverns of Luray are among the most beautiful of their kind, they are not more interesting to the student of the work of underground water than the region about Natural Bridge, Virginia. Not only the celebrated bridge, but also the caves, sink holes, calcareous deposits, and roaring "Lost River" all bear unmistakable evidence of the solubility of limestone. An interesting deposit of calcareous tufa, or travertine, may be found along the road about half-way between the famous bridge and Natural Bridge Station, three miles distant. The little stream flowing parallel to the highway is overcharged with calcareous matter which is precipitated in a beautiful terraced mound resembling, in form at least, that of the Mammoth Hot Spring in the Yellowstone Park.

Surface streams.—The work of running water upon the surface of the land is no less wonderful than that of underground water in its degrading and aggrading power; but its results are always before us, and hence become so familiar that they cease to stimulate the imagination, unless the grandeur of the scenery arrests the attention. In passing through the cañon of the New River from Kanawha Falls to Glades, W. Va., the Iron Gate near Clifton Forge, the cañon of the James at Balcony Falls, and through the gorge in Blue Ridge at Harper's Ferry, the aesthetic emotions frequently crowd out intellectual calculations, and it is not until the milder and more familiar type of landscape is reached that the meaning begins to be realized.

The description of the various results of the work of surface streams cannot here be given, but of the work of surface streams there is no form of wearing or building possible to rivers that is not well illustrated in some part of the region under consideration. There are valleys in every stage of erosive history, from the narrowest steep-sided gorge to the wide, level-bottomed, flood-plain; falls, terraces, islands, deltas, abandoned valleys, drowned valleys, with all the phenomena these terms imply.

Cultured influence of rivers.—The cultural influence resulting from the work of running water could not be overlooked. The magnetic attraction for railroads exercised by valleys was everywhere noted. From Ashland, Ky., to Richmond, Va., a distance of 373 miles, one is seldom out of sight of water. The distance of about twenty miles between Huntington, W. Va., and Scary, where the wide Teay Valley is traversed, must be excepted. This depression is believed to be the abandoned valley of the Kanawha River, but now only the insignificant Mud River flows through it for a part of its course.

When the Kanawha occupied this valley it is probable that the Ohio River did not exist, but that the Kanawha ran almost due west from just below St. Albans, instead of northwest as at present. It continued through the present Scioto River, and discharged toward the north. The subsequent ponding, during the glacial period, of the north-flowing rivers gave birth to the Ohio.[3] The effect of falls upon the human history was noted at many places. The falls or rapids in the Ohio River at Louisville were almost obliterated at the time of our visit by the high waters due to excessive rains; hence it took no little stretch of the imagination to realize the great influence these falls had had upon the development of the Middle West. But George Rogers Clarke appreciated the importance of this interruption of the navigation of the Ohio as early as 1778, and made the beginning of the present important city of Louisville.

The next falls of note are the Kanawha Falls, about a mile below the point where the clear waters of the Gauley River join the boiling chocolate of the New to form the Kanawha. These picturesque falls at the entrance of the beautiful gorge of the New River have as yet exerted little power as an urban stimulus, the result being the miserable little village of Stockton. Notwithstanding the insigficance of this hamlet, chromium from Turkey, Caledonia, Brazil, and Canada has found its way here to meet the coal, iron, and sand of the region, and armor plate for war vessels is the result.

The last falls seen going down the James River are of great importance, for they have given to Virginia her famous capital, and have stimulated many industries.

Of the numerous factories which line the banks of the James River at Richmond, we visited but one—a blotting-paper manufactory. We were surprised to learn here that American rags are not sufficiently worn to be used in making the finest blotting-papers, and that "best rags" are imported from Egypt, Turkey, Greece, and Germany. Whether our deficiency in this line is

[3] *Geologic Atlas*, Charleston Folio, 1901.

due to our wealth or extravagance may be a debatable question, yet either seems comforting when one gazes upon the great piles of unspeakable, evil-odored rags, and he wonders if the ten-hours' boiling in caustic soda will be sufficient to sterilize the impurities of Europe and Africa. .Apprehensive of the danger in such importations, one almost wishes, even in this free-trade-loving region, that there were a prohibitive tariff upon such imports.

While the rapids and falls stimulate manufactories and the growth of cities, the flood-plains of the rivers denominate the rich agricultural lands of many districts. The contrast between the fertile plains along the James River and the exhausted up-lands of Virginia is forced upon the attention of the most list-less observer. The value of rivers as giant excavators, laying bare the secret riches of the earth in the form of building-stone, minerals, metals, oil, and gas, is strikingly illustrated in the Kanawha and New River valleys from Charleston to Quinni-mont, W. Va., a distance of about seventy-five miles. Here the cliffs, almost perpendicular in places, rising seven or eight hundred feet above the water, are perforated from top to bottom with coal shafts. The buildings at the mouths of the shafts cling to the tree-covered rocks as woodpeckers to the trunk of a tree, while the coke-ovens make a necklace of fire along the seething . waters of the New River.

Tides.—The recent sinking of the Coastal Plain has so depressed the river valleys as to allow the influence of the tides to be felt many miles back from the sea. The ebb and flow in the James River reach as far as Richmond, eighty-five miles from Old Point Comfort. Even the creeks in the lower Coastal Plain are wide, navigable, tidal rivers.

Waves and currents.—The coast between Virginia Beach and Willoughby Spit affords an excellent opportunity for the study of the work of waves and currents as well as of tides. Willoughby Spit, which is about eight miles north of Norfolk, is a typical fish hook of sand, built by the waves and currents for almost three miles out into Hampton Roads. The end of the spit is about equidistant from Old Point Comfort.

Work of wind.—The coast also furnishes the best place for the study of the work of wind. A great amount of sand is brought up by waves and currents along the Atlantic in this district, providing material which can be easily transported by the wind. The best example of aeolian deposit is found at Cape Henry. The sand stretches for miles along the coast and reaches back from the famous Cape for about a mile and a half in beautiful cream-colored billows, whose crests rise eighty feet above the sea, burying the struggling forest under their smothering weight.

Diastrophism—rising and sinking of the land.—Changes of the surface of the land are not due to the agents of water, ice, and wind alone; for evidences of the internal movements of the earth are seen, not only in the displaced, folded, and contorted rocks of the Appalachian Mountains and the Piedmont, but also in intrusions of igneous rocks in the Piedmont. The records of recent changes in the relation of the land and the ocean are found in the "drowned" valleys of the Coastal Plain—the Chesapeake Bay and the tidal stretches of the James, York, and Potomac Rivers. Old pine-tree stumps, which now stand in the Chesapeake Bay at Buckroe Beach near Old Point Comfort, bear evidence of very recent encroachment of the sea in this region.

Historical geology.—The birthdays of landscapes are not marked by the dial of a clock, but by great changes in the surface of the land. When the land has risen after the encroachment of the sea, as seen in the Coastal Plain, a marine deposit is left over the valleys, plains, and hills.

From the evidences of such events, and the changes in life left as fossils in the rocks, geologists have been able to interpret a part of the history of the earth.

By examining a geological map of the eastern portion of the United States, it will be seen that in a trip from Chicago to the Atlantic Ocean one passes over rocks representing all the geologic eras and periods which man has devised for the classification of the great events of terrestrial history. The oldest rocks are called Archeozoic,[4] and are found between the "Fall Line"

[4] The Proterozoic are here included under Archeozoic.

and the Blue Ridge, a distance of 175 miles from Balcony Falls to Richmond. The rocks are mainly igneous, with some sedimentary deposits greatly changed or metamorphosed by pressure, heat, and moisture.

The next great series of rocks in point of age is known as the Paleozoic, and is found between Chicago and the Blue Ridge Mountains. The mountains and valleys, west of the Blue Ridge, in Virginia and West Virginia, the hills and plains of Kentucky and Indiana, as well as the area underlying the drift of Illinois and Indiana, were formed from these sedimentary deposits.

Great metamorphism, occasioned in the process of mountain-making, has changed the sandstones to quartzites, the limestones to marble, and the shales to slates, in many places in the Appalachian mountains.

The formations of the Mesozoic, the next great era, are represented in various places on the Piedmont (these were noted about Washington and Washington Junction), while the Coastal Plain exhibits the youngest sediments known as the Cenozoic. These newly formed rocks are but slightly consolidated sands, marls, and clays.

Vegetation.—The vegetation between Chicago and the Atlantic is characterized by a great sameness. Lists of trees and plants made at various places along the route are remarkable for their similarity, the differences being found in the addition or the subtraction of but a few species. Where trees abound one soon learns to expect oak, elm, maple, birch, sycamore, hickory, walnut, alder, willow, ironwood, ash, bass-wood, hackberry, beech, sassafras, chestnut, and pine. These are distributed along the streams or on the higher land, according to the habit of the tree. The holly, magnolia, and cypress, cultivated in Louisville, are abundant in the forests of the Coastal Plain. The wahu, whose fruit at this season resembles that of a small sour sop of the tropics, was common through West Virginia and Virginia. The pawpaw and persimmon, which appeared in central Indiana, continued in greater abundance into Virginia. The Ailanthus spreads from the Ohio to the coast.

The uniformity of vegetation due to natural causes of distribution was less surprising than the similarity of crops. From Chicago to the Atlantic one is practically immersed in a sea of corn. I believe that throughout the entire distance there is not a tillable area of any considerable size from which this beautiful tropical-looking plant is absent. The complete domination of corn was broken by an occasional field of wheat- or oat-stubble in Indiana, and by hemp and tobacco in Kentucky. Virginia, where once tobacco was riches and legal tender of the commonwealth, seemed to have submitted herself in servitude to King Corn. When inquiry was made as to the cause of the change in dynasties, the Virginian replied: "The exhaustion of the soil for tobacco, and the price of seventy-five cents per bushel for corn."

Notwithstanding the untiring efforts of the United States Agricultural Department in finding crops best suited to various soils, the average farmer knows and loves corn and wheat, and is slow to change his affections.

So much had we heard of the Blue Grass of Kentucky that our vivid imaginations pictured unparalleled horses and cattle standing side by side up to their necks in blue grass. A veritable agricultural and grazing fairyland! Hence the contrast with the reality was not a little disadvantageous to this famous historic, limestone district. In comparison with the fertile plains of Illinois, Iowa, and Indiana it yielded the palm to these rich prairie lands. Such must be the price paid for literary reputation. Even the famous Shenandoah Valley suffered in a similar manner. But after a few weeks spent in the less fertile regions of Virginia and the rugged, agriculturally inhospitable areas of West Virginia, the return to the Blue Grass district gave a much more favorable impression, for in comparison with hilly Kentucky and West Virginia it is rich beyond its enviable reputation. The acres of dark brown hemp tied up like shocks of corn, the tobacco curing in the fields and bulging from the great barns, and the golden corn were grateful to our eyes inured to rich western agricultural lands.

Other occupations.—Agriculture is not the only occupation the region supports. At Lynchburg we visited a tobacco manufactory, where chewing and smoking tobacco are prepared for the market. The sorting and stemming of the tobacco leaves by the happy, singing negro men and women, was a sight to be expected in such a factory, but surprises lay in the manner of improving the flavor of the cigars and the taste of the chewing tobacco. The brown plugs and twists, seen in the stores, give no hint to the observer that the leaves have been soaked in a brown, dirty-looking syrup, and that licorice, powdered peaches, plums, apricots, or locust fruits veneer the tightly pressed leaves to improve the taste. In a like manner those ignorant of the allurements of smoking never dream that the flavors are obtained by the addition of various perfumes.

Oyster industry.—The Chesapeake Bay region has long been famous for the production of oysters. The life and culture of these bivalves proved very interesting to the party of inland dwellers. The black stakes, peering above the water in the lower York and James Rivers, marked the limit of acreage rented from the state by the oyster farmers. We were told that the best seed oysters are obtained from the James River and are transplanted into the York, allowing from five hundred to a thousand bushels to the acre. After growing for about eighteen months, they are harvested and prepared in the factories for the market.

History.—The historic aspects of the region visited were in charge of Miss Emily J. Rice, head of the department of history in the School of Education. We saw the beginning of the Virginian comonwealth in the low church tower and the graveyard at Jamestown; followed its development at Williamsburg, Yorktown, and Richmond; reviewed the Peninsular Campaign; learned the meaning of Hampton Roads, Arlington, Mount Vernon, and the Shenandoah Valley; and traced the "Westward Movement" across the mountains into the wide, fertile plains of the Mississippi Valley.

Method.—The day was spent in the field, followed by a conference at night. At the conference the past observations and experiences were discussed and interpreted as far as possible.

The students prepared for the work of the following day by the use of maps or other material at hand. From information thus obtained they predicted the appearance of the country, the geologic and cultural aspects, suggesting problems which would arise for solution. Notes were kept in the field, and, after the close of the field course, reports of the entire trip were written.

Expense.—The expense for the trip was one hundred and five dollars. This is exclusive of the tuition fee.

MATERIALS USED ON THE TRIP FROM CHICAGO TO WASHINGTON, DISTRICT OF COLUMBIA, AND RETURN

INSTRUMENTS:
Hammers, clinometers, compasses, aneroids.

MAPS:
United States Geological Survey. Topographic. The maps are listed in the order in which they were used. Where ** appear the country is not mapped.

Chesapeake & Ohio Railroad—
1. Kenova Quadrangle, Kentucky, West Virginia.
2. Huntington Quadrangle, West Virginia.
3. Charleston Quadrangle, West Virginia.
4. Raleigh Quadrangle, West Virginia.
5. Kanawha Falls Quadrangle, West Virginia.
6. Hinton Sheet, West Virginia.
7. Lewisburg Sheet, West Virginia, Virginia.

Clifton Forge & Richmond Division, Chesapeake & Ohio Railway—
8. Natural Bridge Sheet, Virginia.
9. Lexington Sheet, Virginia.
10. Lynchburg Sheet, Virginia.
11. Appomattox Sheet, Virginia.
12. Buckingham Sheet, Virginia.
13. Palmyra Sheet, Virginia.
14. Goochland Sheet, Virginia.
15. Richmond Sheet, Virginia.
16. Bermuda Hundred Sheet, Virginia.

* * *

17. Norfolk Quadrangle, Virginia, North Carolina.
18. Washington Quadrangle, Maryland, Virginia, District of Columbia.

Main Line, Chesapeake & Ohio Railroad (returning from Washington)—
19. Mount Vernon Sheet, Virginia, Maryland.
20. Warrenton Sheet, Virginia.
21. Spottsylvania Sheet, Virginia.
22. Gordonsville Sheet, Virginia.
23. Harrisonburg Sheet, Virginia.
24. Staunton Sheet, Virginia, West Virginia.
25. Monterey Quadrangle, Virginia, West Virginia.

Baltimore & Ohio Railroad Shenandoah Junction, West Virginia (route to Luray)—

18. Washington Quadrangle, Maryland, Virginia, District of Columbia.

19. Harper's Ferry Sheet, Virginia, Maryland, West Virginia.

Norfolk & Western Railroad from Shenandoah Junction to Basic City via Luray—

20. Winchester Sheet, Maryland, Virginia, West Virginia.

21. Luray Sheet, Virginia.

22. Woodstock Sheet, Virginia.

23. Harrisonburg Sheet, Virginia.

24. Staunton Sheet, Virginia.

At Basic City the Main Line of Chesapeake & Ohio is reached, and maps read forward beginning with Staunton Sheet, No. 24, to No. 25.

25. Monterey Quadrangle, Virginia, West Virginia.

After leaving Monterey Quadrangle, return trip maps read backward from Natural Bridge Sheet, Virginia.

UNITED STATES GEOLOGIC ATLASES:

Folios—

Huntington, West Virginia.

Charleston, West Virginia.

Monterey, Virginia, West Virginia.

Raleigh, West Virginia.

Norfolk, Virginia, North Carolina.

Washington, District of Columbia.

Harper's Ferry, Virginia, Maryland, West Virginia.

Staunton, Virginia, West Virginia.

NOTE.—Topographic maps may be obtained by addressing the Director of the Geological Survey, Department of the Interior, Washington, District of Columbia, for three cents each by the hundred, or five cents apiece singly. Stamps are not accepted in payment. Maps should be described as in the list given above. Folios may be ordered in the same way, price twenty five cents.

Other Maps—

Geologic Maps of the United States.

State Maps of Illinois, Indiana, Kentucky.

Map showing occurrence of coal, oil, and gas in West Virginia by I. C. White, State Geologist.

Map showing the location of the battlefields of Virginia, Chesapeake & Ohio Railroad, 1906.

General Map of the Drift of the Northeastern United States, Sixth Annual Report, Plate XXIII.

BOOKS CARRIED FOR THE USE OF STUDENTS:

Geology and Geography—

Chamberlin and Salisbury, *Geology.*

Dana, *Textbook in Geology.*

Davis, *Physical Geography.*

West Virginia Geological Survey, Vol. Ia, 1904.

Froehling and Robertson, *A Hand Book of the Minerals and Mineral Resources of Virginia* (Richmond, Va.).

Shaler, *Dismal Swamp. Physiography of the United States.* (American Book Co.).

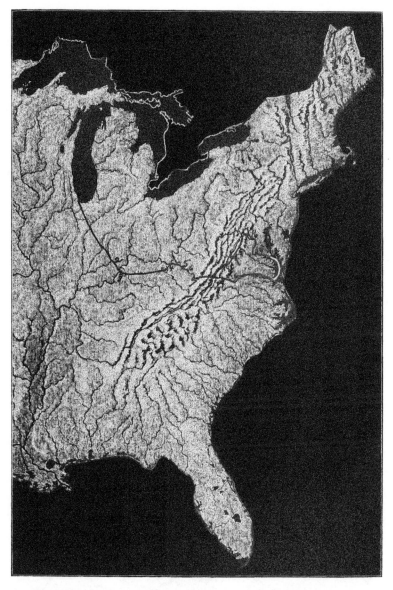

Georg Thorne-Thomsen

1. Chicago	7. Hinton	13. Old Point Comfort
2. Greensburg	8. Clifton Forge	14. Norfolk
3. Louisville	9. South Glasgow	15. Washington
4. Huntington	10. Lynchburg	16. Washington Jc.
5. Charleston	11. Richmond	17. Harper's Ferry
6. Thurmond	12. Williamsburg	18. Luray

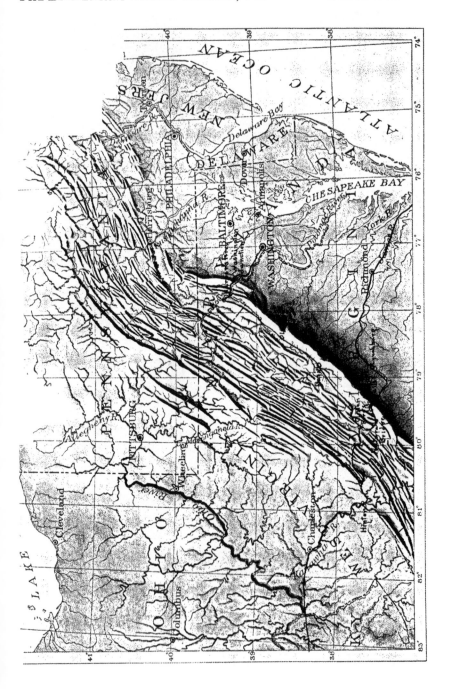

JAMES RIVER CAÑON—BALCONY FALLS

Rainbow Arch, Clifton Forge, Virginia

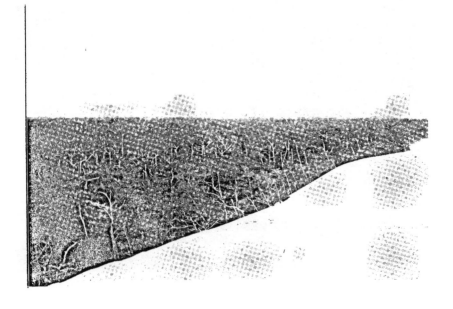

Botany—
Brittain and Brown.
History—
Semple, *American History and Its Geographic Conditions.*
Shaler, *Kentucky.*
Fiske, *Old Virginia and Her Neighbors.*
Cooke, *Virginia.*
Fisher, *Men, Women, and Manners in Colonial Times,* Vol. I.
Coman, *Industrial History of the United States.*
Other References—
Shaler, *Memoirs of Kentucky.*
Rogers, *Geology of Virginias.*
Keith, "Piedmont Plateau, Geological Survey," *Fourteenth Annual Report,* p. 366.
McGee, "History of the Piedmont Plateaus," *National Geographic Magazine,* Vol. VII (1895).
Davis, "Stream Contests along the Blue Ridge," *Bulletin Geographic Society of Pennsylvania,* April, 1903.
Semple, "Influence of Appalachian Barrier upon Colonial History," *Journal of School Geography,* Vol. I.
Fontaine, "Some Points in the Geology of the Blue Ridge in Virginia," *American Journal of Science,* Vol. IX (1875).
Keith, "Geologic Structure of the Blue Ridge," *American Geologist,* Vol. X (1892).
Dryer, *Studies in Indiana Geography.*
Gannett, *A Gazetteer of Virginia,* Department of the Interior, United States Geological Survey.
"Kentucky River Basins," *Journal of Geology,* Vol. IV, p. 671.
"Kanawha River Basins," *ibid.,* p. 669.
Randolph, "People of Virginia," *National Geographic Magazine,* Vol. VII.
McGee, "Geographic Development of the District of Columbia," *ibid.,* Vol. IX.
Brigham, *Geographic Influences in American History.*
Jefferson, "Atlantic Estaurine Tides," *National Geographic Magazine, Vol.* IX.
Puston, "Tides of Chesapeake Bay," *ibid.,* Vol. X.
Tight, "Drainage Modifications in Southeastern Ohio and Adjacent Parts of West Virginia and Kentucky" *Professional Paper 13,* United States Geological Survey.
Walcott, "The Natural Bridge of Virginia," *National Geographic Magazine,* Vol. V.
ILLUSTRATVE READING:
Allen, *Reign of Law.*
Churchill, *The Crisis.*
Dye, *The Conquest.*
Fox, *Little Shepherd of Kingdom Come.*
Johnston, *To Have and to Hold.*
Johnston, *Audrey.*
Glasgow, *The Battleground.*

A SERIES OF LESSONS ON WATER

MABEL M. DIMENT

During the fall quarter of 1905 the fourth grade in the School of Education began the study of the growth of Chicago from the historical and civic standpoints. On the historical side the approach was made through a study of the early French settlers and explorers of the Northwest. This included the story of LaSalle and his efforts to establish trading-posts and forts near the Great Lakes, and also the development of trading-posts at Kaskaskia, Vincennes, Detroit, and Fort Dearborn.

Fort Dearborn was taken as the real basis of the Chicago of today, and a model of it was actually constructed in class. Its evolution from that of trading-post to fort and to a village was compared with the Chicago of the present time.

On the civic side, the following problems were taken into consideration: the system of streets and bridges; the drainage system; the illuminating plants; the way the city is governed; and the city water system, and it was in this connection that the experiments for purifying water were given.

A study was made of the development of Chicago's great water system from the time it was simply dipped from the lake to the great crib system of the present time. The construction of the crib was studied, and expeditions were made to the pumping-stations. The methods of purifying water at the cribs were noted. The experiments given were to illustrate the means we have at hand for purifying the city supply, and to show whether it does purify it or not.

First there was a general discussion dealing with the general and specific sources of water, the cycle of rain to rain by means of evaporation and rainfall, leading up to the question of why we attempt to purify water, how we do it, and how we can prove it purified.

Then followed experimentation. Three kinds of water were used which could easily show any change: water plus a little sand or mud was taken as a type of substances in suspension in water; water colored with red ink, and water in which salt was dissolved, as types of substances in solution. One most essential thing is to have every flask absolutely clean before beginning an experiment, or the object of the experiment may be entirely lost.

Among the ways mentioned by the children for purifying water were boiling, filtering, and distilling, and we took these as three typical methods. We first boiled each of the three kinds of water, to see if boiling could purify it. The results were compared with some of the unboiled water; and as no change for the better was noted, the muddy water remaining just as muddy, the colored water just as red, and the salty water saltier than before on account of the evaporation of some of the water leaving the salt, it was concluded that boiling did not purify the water. (In the beginning of the lessons the children were all anxious to say that the object of boiling, filtering, and distilling was to kill the germs, so we took for granted that it did, and we were to see what the boiling, etc., did to the other impurities.)

It was necessary for the children to keep records of their experiments in order to compare results, and this necessitated reading, writing, and spelling. In the written lessons they followed this outline:

I. Why did we make this experiment?
II. What did we do?
III. What happened?

The drawing lessons consisted of drawing the apparatus, and these were used to supplement the written lessons. The spelling lesson consisted of words frequently occurring in the written lessons.

Filtering was the second experiment, and for this the apparatus was set up in the following way:

The funnels contained a layer of filter paper, and these were filled with clean sand, which should be saturated with clear water before the impure water is poured on. Boxes filled with sand, and having an opening to allow the filtered water to run off, could be used to good advantage to illustrate the use in many cities of filter beds for purifying water. When sufficient amounts had filtered through to show results, they were compared with the original water. It was observed that the salty water remained as salty as before, the colored water had not changed color, but the muddy water had become clear. From former work the children knew that colored and salty water were types of things in solution in water, and muddy water of things in suspension; so they concluded that filtering must take out things in suspension, but not things in solution. The written, drawing, and spelling lessons in connection with this experiment were given in much the same way as with the previous experiment.

The third way mentioned of purifying water was by distilling, and we were to find out if it really did purify the water. The apparatus for this experiment was a little more complicated than that for the others.

The water was allowed to boil some time to get a sufficient amount distilled over to show results. The children noticed the bubbles of steam come from the bottom of the flask to the surface of the water and break into steam; the steam rise and condense in the cold tube and fall as clear drops in the other flask. The distilled water was compared with the undistilled, and it was seen that distilling had taken out all impurities, things in suspension as well as things in solution; and so it was concluded that distilling was the best way to purify water. The written lessons were given the same as before, with the final question: "Which of the three ways is the best to purify water and why?" The drawing and spelling lessons were given as in previous experiments.

Many other little experiments had to be performed also further to convince a child of some statement, or to prove a statement of which he was not sure. For instance, one child did not seem to understand that boiling did not take out impurities; he thought they evaporated as the water evaporated. Therefore a little of each of the three kinds of water was boiled dry, and in one flask only the dry salt remained in the bottom, in another dry sand, and in the third the red coloring-matter of the ink looking like brick dust, showing that the water, but not the impurities, had evaporated in boiling.

SPRING POEMS BY A FIFTH GRADE

ELSA MILLER
Fifth Grade, Francis W. Parker School

Following is a report of some work in composition done by the pupils of the fifth grade of the Francis W. Parker School.

The class mentioned has heard and read, in its course through the primary grades, much of the best literature and poetry for children. They live in an environment where they come in contact with the best that a city park can give. They make frequent excursions to the woods and lake shore. Many spend summers out in the country, by lake or seaside, or in the mountains. Some hear good literature and poetry read aloud at home. These conditions form a wholesome, helpful fund of observation, experience, and imagination which must find expression.

The first of May in the Francis W. Parker School is a tree-planting day. The children choose some tree, shrub, or vine to plant in some spot on the school grounds which needs beautifying. The planting is attended by a festival with May queen, singing, and dancing. All the children in the school, who wish, write poems, which they read to the school and to the May queen on that day. She selects, with the aid of the teachers, the best one, and favors the author with a May basket. The chosen poem is set to music by some grade, or by individual members of the school, for the next May festival. Every song is sung to the school by the composer, or by a small chorus. Last year the chosen poem was sung with six different musical settings, composed in the regular music periods by the various children. Obviously this festival affords a very natural opportunity for poetical and musical expression, though necessarily the results are crude.

During the spring season the children had opportunity to talk about the numerous signs of spring, the beauty of the early spring flowers which they gathered, the sounds which they heard in the woods, the odors of the soft soil which they spaded in the garden and of the new moist grass which they uncovered, and the soft, delicate colors of the season which pleased them. All this work was done without mention of the writing of poetry; in fact, their desire to write came from these talks.

One day it was suggested that they write about what they liked best in the spring time, and, if they chose, write in verse. They immediately suggested that each child write a spring poem for May Day. They stipulated that these poems should be written without signatures and be placed in a basket on the table. They were to be read to the class by the teacher. The majority were eager and ready to write. They worked silently, without question to the teacher or to each other, to avoid influence and suggestion by others. They were allowed to write until they had finished. Some, as the results will show, had little to say, and others were more free in their expression.

Another day the poems were read aloud. After the first reading the children asked to hear some poems re-read. Some began to mark to meter, and detected faults and suggested changes. The teacher then wrote a familiar poem on the board and scanned it. The number of feet in a line was noted. The children scanned parts of many poems which they knew, and discovered how the number of feet in a line varied in different poems, how the length of lines in the same poem varied, and how corresponding lines of stanzas agreed. They wished now to mark their own poems to see whether feet or lines were missing. They consulted one another, and changed a line or a word here and there. *The work of every child in the class is given below, and as here presented stands in form as the children corrected it.* That is, no actual work was done by the teacher.

Several poems were chosen to be read to the May queen. Later every child read his verses to the school in a regular morning exercise. This required an introduction, which the children wrote with combined effort. The humorist of the class furnished the closing couplet.

THE POEMS

A MORNING EXERCISE

This morning exercise is begun,
We hope you'll all enjoy the fun.
We made some rhymes with many lines
To tell you of spring's happy times.
Some thoughts are of the birds and flowers,
And some of sun and some of showers.
We hope you'll think of shady bowers
Where you may sit in sunny hours.

—Read by DORIS; composed by the grade.

SPRING

The sweetest time of all the year
  Is the joyous time of spring,
When grass is green, and skies are clear,
  And birds are on the wing.

Now on the banks of laughing brooks
  The nodding violet grows,
And every pussy willow looks
  Like wee gray kitten's toes.

Hepaticae now push their way
  With all their tiny might.
And on their stems of hairy gray,
  Hang stars of blue and white.

—FRIEDA MAYNARD

SPRING

The days grow warmer and grow bright
And after them a nice spring shower,
To start the little plants a-growing
So's to be green some summer hour.

The mother tree puts on her leaves
To hide the nests the birds have made,
To give us sprigs both fresh and green,
In summer days to give us shade.

—LUCY DUNLAP SMITH

SPRING THOUGHTS

The trees are budding,
The flowers their winter caps throw off.
The bluebirds are singing,
The roses are sending sweet odors aloft.

The sky is blue,
Spring's sun is drying up the dew.
The grass is green
And yellow dandelions gleam.

—Elizabeth Beulah Beckler

SPRING POEM

This is the time of year
When birds and flowers are here
In all their beauty.
The buds on the trees burst forth,
Then tiny leaves appear,
And lo, they are dressed in lovely green!
Birds are on the wing,
They sing a carol of joyous spring.

—Carlton Prindeville

FOR IT IS MAY

The days are growing warmer,
The sun is shining bright,
The air is full of light—
For it is May.

The trees are swaying lightly,
Their leaves are growing green,
Then comes spring's joyous queen.
For it is May.

The robins with their nestlings
Are flitting through the trees
Mid sunshine and the breeze,
For it is May.

Mildred Zenos

MAY

May is best of all the year,
All things live and grow again;
   The tree sends out her baby leaves,
And birds build nests beneath the eaves.

All the seeds are in the ground,
Violets in the field are found;
Ducks are honking overhead,
The baby birds cry to be fed.

—JOSEPHINE PALMER

SPRINGTIME

Spring has come
And the children have fun.
   The sun is shining
   And the flowers are tiny.
The leaves on the trees are green.

—GRANT McDONALD

SPRING IN THE FOREST

   The grass is green,
   The robins are here,
And birds are thick in the air.

   The animals hunt,
   The wild bears roam
Far away from their native home.

   The fields look green,
   The trees make shade
In the far away, lonely forest glade.

—FRANK PACKARD

THE AWAKENING OF SPRING

The sleepy fields and meadows,
   At the call of spring,
Awaken after winter's doze,
   And the birds begin to sing, to sing
Of the spring, the glorious spring.

The cattle all are grazing
   In the pastures green,
Their smooth old heads are never raising.
   In every flower can be seen
The joy of spring, the glorious spring.

And when the spring is gone,
   Comes summer with her beauties
In the garden and on the lawn.
   But the spring is best for all.
Oh, the spring, the glorious spring!

                  —DORIS HUMPHREY

WINTER'S GONE

The cold and frosty winter's gone,
The warm and sunny days are here,
The little squirrels play all day long
And then we know it's spring.

                  —LESLIE VAUGHN

SPRING

I love the bright warm days of spring,
When the flowers come out and the birds start to sing.
   I love the bright warm days of spring,

                  —JAMES BRAITHWAITE

SPRING

With May-day comes the lovely spring
The ground is ready for the seed,
   The father bird begins to sing;
The mother bird her young does feed.

The robin red-breast, fat and round,
Is tapping softly on the ground,
The foolish worm the signal hears,
And from the ground he soon appears.

                —LEONARD MARSHALL

SPRING

When spring comes forth to smile at last,
Then winter must on his way.
When Herald Jonquil blows his blast,
The flowers and leaves awake to sway
In the first warm breeze of May.

Then the robin sings its joyous song,
And the wood-brook runs away,
The bluebell rings its ting-a-tong,
Oh! the thrush comes forth to stay,
Sings as he flies up the southward way.

The violet wafts its fragrance sweet,
The crow he almost sings, but mates
Last of all comes the bobolink late,
Last of all with his mate.

When spring comes forth to smile at last,
Then winter must on his way.
When Herald Jonquil blows his blast,
The flowers and leaves awake to sway
In the first warm breeze of May.

—KATHARINE TILT

SPRING

Spring has gone
And so has May.
Thus we have no more to say.

—FREDERICK GANSBERGEN

LE JEU UN FACTEUR IMPORTANT DANS L'ENSEIGNEMENT D'UNE LANGUE

LORLEY ADA ASHLÉMAN
School of Education, University of Chicago

Not in the more dignified forms of literature, but in the language of the fire side, of the market place, of the social gathering is revealed the genesis of the language.

Le chant populaire ne ment pas, c'est le miroir le plus fidèle de la société.

The series of popular rounds and songs characteristic of France that we are publishing represents the people in their various social conditions, in their occupations, professions, industries, in their fêtes. They give us their ideals of chivalry, their love for animals, birds, and flowers, and their deep appreciation of music and harmony.

ADDITIONAL RONDES[1]

DANSER

QUAND BIRON VOULUT DANSER

Cette chanson amuse beaucoup les enfants. Un des enfants de la classe joue le rôle de Biron. Sept ou huit autres lui servent de valets. Tous les autres forment le chœur. Le petit Biron assis majestueusement sur sa chaise s'écrie:

Biron: Mes souliers tout ronds!

Pendant que le chœur chante:

> Quand Biron voulut danser,
> Quand Biron voulut danser,
> Ses souliers fit apporter, (*bis*)
> Ses souliers tout ronds,
> Vous danserez, Biron.

Le petit valet, tenant dans chaque main un soulier tout rond, s'avance, salue profondément Biron, lui met les souliers, puis avec toute la dignité d'un laquais anglais, il se tient derrière son maître.

Biron: Ma perruque à la Turque!

Le chœur reprend:

> Quand Biron voulut danser, (*bis*)
> Sa perruque fit apporter,
> Sa perruque à la Turque.
> Ses souliers tout ronds,
> Vous danserez, Biron.

[1] See *Elementary School Teacher*, January, 1907.

Le valet s'avance avec la perruque et la lui pose sur la tête, puis il prend place à côté du premier valet.

Biron :

> Ma belle veste
> A paillettes !

Le valet s'avance avec la belle veste et la lui met.

Le chœur reprend :

> Quand Biron voulut danser, (*bis*)
> Sa veste fit apporter, (*bis*)
> Sa belle veste
> A paillettes,
> Sa perruque
> A la Turque,
> Ses souliers tout ronds,
> Vous danserez, Biron.

Biron :

> Mon habit
> De petit gris !

Le valet s'avance avec l'habit et le lui passe.

Le chœur reprend :

> Quand Biron voulut danser, (*bis*)
> Son habit fit apporter, (*bis*)
> Son habit
> De petit gris,
> Sa belle veste
> A paillettes,
> Sa perruque
> A la Turque
> Ses souliers tout ronds,
> Vous danserez, Biron.

Biron

> Ma cravate
> A la mode !

Le valet s'avance avec la cravate.

Le chœur :

> Quand Biron voulut danser, (*bis*)
> Sa cravate fit apporter, (*bis*)
> Sa cravate
> A la mode,
> Son habit
> De petit gris,
> Sa belle veste
> A paillettes,
> Sa perruque
> A la Turque,
> Ses souliers tout ronds,
> Vous danserez, Biron.

Biron: Mes manchettes
                    Fort bien faites!

Le valet s'avance avec les manchettes.

Le chœur reprend:

                    Quand Biron voulut danser, (bis)
                    Ses manchettes fit apporter, (bis)
                        Ses manchettes
                        Fort bien faites,
                        Sa cravate
                        A la mode,
                        Son habit
                        De petit gris,
                        Sa belle veste
                        A paillettes,
                        Sa perruque
                        A la Turque,
                    Ses souliers tout ronds,
                    Vous danserez, Biron.

Biron: Mon chapeau
                    A clabot!

Le valet s'avance avec le chapeau.

Le chœur reprend:

                    Quand Biron voulut danser, (bis)
                    Son chapeau fit apporter, (bis)
                        Son chapeau
                        A clabot,
                        Ses manchettes
                        Fort bien faites,
                        Sa cravate
                        A la mode,
                        Son habit
                        De petit gris,
                        Sa belle veste
                        A paillettes,
                        Sa perruque
                        A la Turque,
                    Ses souliers tout ronds,
                    Vous danserez, Biron.

Au dernier couplet, Biron se lève et suivi de tous ses valets, il s'en va
finalement au bal.

VOCABULAIRE

quand, *when*

voulut, *wanted*

danser, *to dance*

son, *his*, masc.

sa, *his*, fem.

ses, *his*, masc. and fem., plur.

les souliers, *the shoes*

le soulier, *the shoe*

ses souliers fit apporter, *had his shoes brought*

rond, *round*

tout, *quite*

vous danserez, *you will dance*

la perruque, *the wig*

à la turque, *in the Turkish style*

beau, *beautiful*, masc.

belle, *beautiful*, fem.

veste, *vest*

à paillettes, *spangled*

un habit, *a coat*

de petit gris, *speckled grey*

la cravate, *the necktie*

à la mode, *in style*

la manchette, *the cuff*

fort bien faite, *very well made*

le chapeau, *the hat*

le chapeau à clabot, *opera hat*

ENFANT

CADET ROUSSELLE

Cadet Rousselle a trois maisons,
Cadet Rousselle a trois maisons
Qui n'ont ni poutres ni chevrons,
Qui n'ont ni poutres ni chevrons;
C'est pour loger les hirondelles,
Que dire z-vous de Cadet Rousselle?
Ah! Ah! Ah! mais vraiment,
Cadet Rousselle est bon enfant.

Cadet Rousselle a trois habits,
Cadet Rousselle a trois habits,
Deux jaunes, l'autre en papier gris,
Deux jaunes, l'autre en papier gris;
Il met celui-là quand il gèle,
Ou quand il pleut, ou quand il grêle.
Ah! Ah! Ah! mais vraiment,
Cadet Rousselle est bon enfant.

VOCABULAIRE

l'enfant, *the child*

cadet, *the youngest boy*

a, *has*

je, *I*

ai, *have*

j'ai, *I have*

il, *he*

elle, *she*

un, *one*

deux, *two*

trois, *three*

maisons, *houses*

qui, *that, who, which*

ont, *have*

ne pas, *not*
ne, ni, ni, *neither, nor*
ils, *they,* masc.
elles, *they,* fem.
la poutre, *the beam*
le chevron, *the rafter*
ce, *it*
est, *is*
pour loger, *to lodge, to house*
les hirondelles, *the swallows*
mais vraiment, *but truly, but indeed*
bon enfant, *good, kind-hearted simple-hearted*

l'habit, *the coat*
jaune, *yellow*
gris, *grey*
l'autre, *the other*
le papier, *the paper*
met, *puts on*
celui-là, *that one*
quand, *when*
ou, *or*
il gèle, *it freezes*
il pleut, *it rains*
il grèle, *it hails*

FRÈRE JACQUES

CHANSON, EN CANON, À DEUX VOIX

Frère Jacques, frère Jacques,
Dormez-vous, dormez-vous ?
Sonnez les matines, sonnez les matines,
Din, din, don, din, din, don.

VOCABULAIRE

frère Jacques, *Brother James*
dormir, *to sleep*
je dors, *I sleep*
tu dors, *thou sleepest*
il dort, *he sleeps*
nous dormons, *we sleep*
vous dormez, *you sleep*
dormez-vous? *do you sleep? are you sleeping?*
sonner, *to ring; to ring the bell*
je sonne, *I ring*

les matines, *morning bells*
la cloche, *the bell*
comment, *how*
faire, *to do, make*
je fais, *I do, make*
il fait, *he does, makes*
nous faisons, *we do, make*
vous faites, *you do, make*
ils font, *they do, make*
comment fait la cloche? *how does the bell go?*

il doit, *he must*

APRIL SONG

Words and melody by children of the seventh school year, University Elementary
School

In the Spring-time of the year A - pril comes with all its cheer, Bring - ing back the birds and flow - ers, Gen - tle winds and sud - den show-ers. Buds are ope - ning

on the trees,   In   the   pleas-ant balm - y breeze;

Snow and ice are gone a-way, Spring is fair - er ev - 'ry day.

EDITORIAL NOTES

We are accustomed to congratulate ourselves upon living in an age of rapid advancement. We gloat over the marvelous achievements in commerce, in invention, and in social organization that have been effected in the last half-century. Our current opinion is that public-school education should share in this general laudation for its swift increase in extent and efficiency. And when we touch upon philanthropy or social progress, "What is there that has not been done?" we cry!

The Age of Rapid Progress

Truly we may marvel at the mushroom growth of ideas and at their spread throughout society—overnight, as one might say. Tip-toe we stand, expectant, ready to catch "the latest" in philanthropy, or in social endeavor, as the news flies from lecture-room to workshop, to office, and to the tea-table. We import and export not merely commodities, but ideas, schemes, reforms. Do we not learn how to make and mend municipal machinery from Australia, and how to equip an army from Japan? We snatch from our dailies intelligence of progress in war and in industry; the vogue in pleasure-making and theology; the newest in athletics and esoteric research, culled from Oxford to the South Sea Islands. We gasp and ejaculate over the measureless rush of social forces, and at the changes which have occurred "even in my time."

Dissemination of Social Reforms

And yet we might stop to ask ourselves whether the real movement toward freedom, and democracy, and opportunity for all is keeping the tempo of the *presto* march to which our pulses are beating; or, if the vaunted triumphal procession is a whizzing biograph to be understood, as in reality a weary *largo*.

Is the Movement toward Freedom and Democracy?

To the enthusiast, "initiated" is apt to spell "achieved," and for the speed-intoxicated it its well to call a halt now and then and count the milestones to come, as well as those already passed. If we should sum up the organizations in one great city that are instruments for social betterment,

Initiated is Not Accomplished

we could make quite a showing on the side of improvement. On the other hand, there would still stand a long roll on the debit side, which list is to be cleared away only by social education.

Here is a partial list of social machines that have sprung into activity during the last quarter-century. Every one touches the **The Growth** public school at some point:
of a Quarter School Children's Aid Society.
Century Day Nurseries.

Free Kindergarten Associations.

Social Settlements.

Religious Education Association.

Social Education Association.

Municipal Voters' League.

Consumers' League.

Neighborhood Improvement Associations.

Parents' and Teachers' Clubs.

Visiting Nurse Association.

Vacation School and Playground Committee.

Home-finding Association.

Public School Art Sciety.

Municipal Lodging-House Association.

Society for the Protection of Women and Children.

The Juvenile Court.

The Parental School.

The School Fellowship Committee.

Everyone of the above represents the effort of society either to adjust itself to the gaps that society itself has created, or to patch up failures that it has made. Each one is significant of the fact that social evolution is going on as rapidly as is commercial expansion; creating new necessities as each decade goes by.

And where does the school come in? Is it also dynamic? Is it accommodating its aim and its régime to the social milieu **Does the** of which it is a part? Certainly the school reflects **School Keep** to some extent the richness and movement of the **Pace?** age; but does it not falter a lap at least behind as it struggles on to maintain its position as nursery of civic virtues, and training ground for *any* opportunity which may open for *any* child today, or tomorrow?

Out of the list given above, four lines of work have sprung up to fill out essentials which the school has not been able to provide wholly out of public funds. These are the Free Kindergartens, the Public School Art Society, the Vacation School Committee, and the School Fellowship Committee. The Parental School and the Juvenile Court stand as indications of the failure of school and home together to do the work required of them.

If there is one thing that the present age should have taught us it is that the school cannot stand alone and apart. Especially **The School** is this true of the city school. We are finding that **Needs the Help** it takes all of the above-named institutions to accom- **of Social** plish the work which the school stands for, and we **Agencies** must press into its service a visiting nurse, a board of health department, a truant officer, and a Friendly Visitor before the school can get a chance to do its own work.

Here is a condition which is repeated over and over again in every city: The district is congested. The people are of the **A Typical Case** small wage-earning class, always liable to a cessation of income through accident or industrial depression. Two to five rooms, often dark, comprise the average home. There are no yards worthy the name. The playground is the street. Most of the parents and many of the children are foreign-born. The school has no yard large enough for games, nor has the building any playroom. It has neither room nor equipment for wood-work, cooking, or any of the industrial arts. Its walls are dull and bare. The numbers of children are so compacted that they must march from room to street in military file. No social interchange, no space, no adequate provision for play, athletics, or dancing. Yet these are the schools in which our future citizens are to be gaining the active experience which is to make them effective citizens, with honorable standards of living, and aspirations toward the best things of life!

But better things are being planned. The latest building plans of schools for Chicago have been drawn with a view to providing for just these conditions of effective citizenship. Indeed.

these plans of the architect of the Chicago Board of Education are

Another Type of Building such as would make one weep for the unlucky ones born too soon to spend their school days in them, in the happy time to come when public moneys will flow in to build and equip them. Color, space, shop equipment, ground floor, assembly hall, gymnasium, and plenty of playground are features of these last new plans.

Little by little a sense of the ineffectiveness of isolated scholasticism, in the face of our social problems, has forced itself

The Old Order and the New upon teachers and social workers. We owe to women's clubs much of the influence which has sprung up outside school walls to bridge over the gap between the school with its traditional aims and methods, and the pressing needs of the children of the people. Well it is for society that woman's sympathetic insight has run ahead of public legislation to give demonstrations of what art, and play, manual occupation, field science, and excursions can do for education in its elementary steps.

This has been the history of the movements for kindergartens, for manual training, vacation schools, and for playgrounds:

From Private to Public Support by pushing and pulling, by force of argument and appeal, by direct begging, by bazaars, and by subscriptions, support has been guaranteed until the worth of these things has been so fully demonstrated that the public school has been moved to incorporate them to some extent; but rarely have means been found to adopt them in a full and complete sense. For example, there are not funds enough to put kindergartens in all the schools, manual training in all the grades, or vacation schools wherever they are needed in most of our cities.

As yet we can only say that the activities which guard the health, secure regularity, and call out a full and free use of

The City School Yet to be Evolved intellectual and social power in school life are but in their initial stages. The school of the future is yet to be evolved—as the school building is on the eve of realization.

This new school is to be represented on the side of educa-

tional organization by the demand and supply of teachers who
are professional in training and in outlook. It is
Central Ideal is Activity to hold at its center the idea of activity as expressed
in investigation, in creative occupation, and in group
life. It is to treat children, not in mass, but as social units which
will cohere in comparatively small groups from their own co-
operative energy. It is to rely upon the larger mass-meeting
for building up that *esprit de corps* which it will be still a duty
of the school to supply.

On the side of control, there will be for many years to come
an increasing need in crowded city districts of agencies for find-
Highly Special- ing out home conditions, for relieving slight illnesses
ized Control by the visiting nurses, for protecting the mass against
Necessary contagious diseases, for keeping watch over minor
delinquents by the probation officers or school visitor; and yet
—how much of truancy and delinquency can be eradicated by
making the school, so far as work goes, as desirable, as—well
let us say Parental School? The report of an investigation of
truancy in eight public schools made by compulsory education
officers, visiting nurses, and a Hull House worker, and published
last autumn, makes most interesting reading, and it shows the plain
necessity of supplementing a child-labor law by a system of school
pensions to take the place of the earnings of the child-laborer
when others dependent upon him are absolutely reduced to want.

Here, then, is another avenue of effort. Paternalism!
you will probably cry! To this the answer may be quoted:
Paternalism "You can never pauperize a little child by helping
Not to be him to an education." The report referred to
Feared in shows also that in poor districts the school nurse
Education is an imperative necessity. School luncheons must
supplement the insufficient home fare, if children from the poorest
homes are to have vitality enough to take up the work offered in
the schoolroom.

Yes, the school must be dynamic. It must take on as
organic functions many phases of activity that once ranked as
philanthropy. It must be an exponent of the highest social forces
of the day. B. P.

BOOK REVIEWS

Men of Old Greece. By Jennie Hall. Boston: Little, Brown & Company. Cloth. Pp. 263; 12 full-page plates and 43 illustrations in the text. Listing price, $0.60.

In this book the men of old Greece live again, and the young readers live with them. The stories are told charmingly, with a beauty and simplicity well suited to a review of the "lovely land" and the "beautiful Greeks." The "men" are Leonidas, Themistocles, Phidias, and Socrates. The first story tells of "Leonidas," from his first day away from home, when he becomes a member of a boy's club to learn to live for Sparta, until the day he gives to her his life at Thermopylae. The movement is good throughout, and the interest well sustained. The story of "Themistocles" is the story of Athens, with her statesmen, her heroes, and her people meeting the Persians. And as the Athenian was more graceful, more artistic, than the Spartan so is the second story more beautiful than the first. "Phidias and the Parthenon" is a chapter breathing the spirit of civic beauty, which makes the reader long for the beautiful Athens of Phidias. Pericles says to Phidias: "These pupils of yours will go back to their cities and fill them with beauty." The children who read this will wish to make the most of the possibilities of beauty in their city. The story of "Socrates," in its lovely simplicity, brings the book to a close. One does not think of the story of the philosopher as one for children, perhaps; but, in reading this presentation of it, he knows it to be as happily chosen as that of any of the old heroes.

The book is full of pictures of the *daily life* of the Greeks. The reader *sees* the boys at home, at school, in the games, at the mess; he *hears* the men talk in the forum, and *sees* Phidias at work on the Acropolis. Socrates' father goes out from his low-plastered house, whose door half fills the narrow street, and invites his neighbor to the nameday feast of his baby son; and Socrates grows to boyhood and manhood—all before the reader's eyes.

Miss Hall has not told stories *about* the Greeks, but has made the Greeks *live again* for the children, and in this her book is really valuable.

The full-page plates are beautiful and the text illustrations are numerous. The binding is attractive.

The book is a delight to children from eight to eleven years of age, and older children enjoy it. It may well be given a place in our school and home libraries for boys and girls.

Annas Higgins

THE ELEMENTARY SCHOOL TEACHER

MAY, 1907

THE COMMON SCHOOL AND THE STATE[1]

J. H. T. MAIN
Iowa College, Grinnell, Ia.

The wisdom of Plato is nowhere more clearly proved than in the introductory passage to his treatise on education in the *Republic,* in which he makes, in a seemingly casual way, this profound remark: "In every work the beginning is the most important part, especially in dealing with anything young and immature." He then proceeds to discuss the system of education for his ideal state. There are two points to note: first, that he begins his discussion with the children; and, second, that he emphasizes the importance of the elementary instruction, and discusses with the greatest care its constituent parts. Nowhere are we permitted to lose sight of the central point of his system, that the children and their education are the fundamental units on which he bases his hopes of righteousness, happiness, and perpetuity for the state.

No educational reformer or theorist has got beyond the position of Plato, and in any system of general or popular education we must, consciously or unconsciously, pay our respects to him. Looking at the matter in a theoretical way, there are probably few here tonight who would venture to gainsay the view of Plato. The majority would accept it as educational gospel. On the other hand, there are few here perhaps who have given themselves concern that it should have practical realization, or

[1] President's address, Iowa State Teachers' Association, December 26, 1906.

who have considered how remote our practice is from our approved ideal.

Of course, this state and others have their public-school systems. Money has been given generously for school purposes, and there is, no doubt, warrant for a good deal of enthusiasm over what we have done for the education of our children. But we may safely leave it to the politician "to point with pride," as he eloquently reviews the benefits of free and universal education. It is the serious business of the earnest student of educational conditions to state as clearly as possible what the facts really are.

The state seems to have given its chief attention to the higher grades of secondary education rather than to the lower ones. The conspicuous building in the village or town is usually the high school, and the special provisions, if any, for the cultivation of the practical interests of the youth, are there and not in the lower grades. It would be anomalous for anyone to call attention to a rural-school building and grounds as evidence of the state's generosity in education. The rural school, or the grade school, rarely shows evidence of personal concern on the part of anybody for the children. The stream of revenue from the funds apportioned for educational purposes is reduced to innumerable small rivulets before it reaches the lower grades in the common schools, whether they be in city, town, or country. In thousands of rural schools, and often in town and village grades, the teacher is an immature and inadequately trained boy or girl without the gift of teaching, in the work for the meager pay, and without love for the children or ambition for the school. Nothing else is to be expected; and we have no right to criticize teachers or pupils because results are unsatisfactory. There never will be any improvement till we criticize ourselves a bit, and assimilate for use that portion of educational gospel which gives the place of chief honor to the children—the little children —and their education.

The chief problems of education are from the high school down, and not from the high school up. Below the high school, and not in it and beyond it, are to be settled finally the scope and character of the education for the majority of our fellow-citizens. In the grades will be determined in some degree their quality as men and Americans. It is a tremendous problem which as yet we have not done much toward solving. This much is certain: the duty of the hour calls for a development downward rather than upward in the public-school system. There may be something to say for the six-year high school, but it is little as compared with the call of the children in the lower grades. When they are reasonably well provided for, it will be time to talk and plan for added years in the high-school course. Development upward in the public-school system is an interesting question, but is purely academic when considered in relation to the needs in the schools below. I have nothing to say against advanced high-school development as an abstract proposition; but practically we are not ready for it, whatever may be said of the proposition one way or the other. The demand of the hour is for improvement of the schools we now have—high schools, and especially the schools below them.

If the state is to have a chance at its future citizens, it must take it when they are children. Only a small percentage of them reaches the high school; a still smaller percentage reaches the colleges. There are more than 25,000,000 children in this country between the ages of five and fourteen. Set this number over against the number in high schools, and the difference is appalling. Still more appalling is the fact that not one-half of the number is counted as attendant at the schools below high-school grade. Thirty millions or more of the people of this country are bread-winners and work with their hands chiefly. The common school in country and town must provide all the education they can hope for, if indeed they hope for any. But it is the business of society, through the medium of the state, to bring down to them education of such value and quality that they will hope for it, and find in it a way of approach to the practical life they are to live. We are not doing our duty by the children. In view of these simple but astounding platitudes, it seems strange that someone who has insight and vision has not recognized the implicit demands that economic principles and genuine patriotism are making—leaving out of sight all other motives—that educational legislation, to provide larger opportunities, is needed at the bottom more than at the top. We have many problems to deal with in this country, but none that approaches in importance this one, because this is fundamental to all the great problems. It is the problem of problems. If we deal with it adequately, there is hope that we shall be able to manage the others.

The magnitude of the problem is so great that private benefactions could not deal with it. It is the problem of the state and the nation, and hence your problem and mine. Since it is so, the responsibility that rests upon society in relation to it is not to be shifted, even if it were possible, upon others. Private beneficence, as has been wisely suggested before this association, in individual cases might serve as a spur to the public conscience, but it could never meet the social need or discharge the social obligation. It would indeed be a sorry day for the state if it should have reason to assume that its delinquencies might be made good by the benefactions of private individuals.

The duty of the state toward higher education is not so inclusive nor so insistent as that toward elementary education. It has discharged its duty better toward higher education, perhaps because it is a simpler duty and one much easier to deal with. The state has worked as the patron of education inversely to the real needs of the people. The state university is its most notable achievement, the high school is next in order, the common schools bring up the rear. The state university in the Middle West has achieved its place of distinction as an institution that meets in a noteworthy way the real needs of the people, because there have been leaders with initiative and ability to press its claims; in some similar degree, though after a long interval, the high school has had the advantage of the same sort of support. For the common schools there has been no organized or definitely continued advocacy of any kind, the result being that the provisions for them, good and generous enough for the time when they were made, have been left to take care of themselves. The state deserves the highest praise for its intelligent treatment of the problem of higher education. There is still much for it to do in that direction, but there should be no delay in taking up, with the same careful and detailed consideration, the common-school problem. The condition now existing illustrates almost a total lack of adjustment between the common school and present-day needs. And this lack of adjustment is chiefly due to the fact that the public-school system is governed by laws that have been practically unchanged for years, while society that needs the schools has been growing with the rapid growth of this age, and deserves, even if it is not conscious of the fact, a response from the schools that they are not able to give. The response to the call of the people has been through the institutions of higher learning—a response which is only for the select few.

The state universities actually do respond to public demands. They have specialists to study and report movements in education and in public life. They hold to the past, but are quick to detect special and local needs. They have a forward look. Their organization is such that with reasonable quickness they can adjust themselves to the constantly growing requirements of the people. These same ideals, which the state university aims to realize in its work, are also the ideals of every standard institution of higher learning. They are the ideals of education a democracy should aim to realize. Educational leaders understand this, and these same ideals are common matters of conversation and discussion in educational conferences and assemblies. But it is a notable fact that these discussions relate themselves to the higher institutions, and very rarely, or never, include the grade school and the rural school. The ideal that has in some measure realized itself in the higher institution is needed—sorely needed—as a revivifying force in the lower school. Are we alive to this fact? Do we know that the ideals of public service at work in the higher must also have a chance in the lower schools? The call of democracy today—the most insistent, the most urgent call—is just this, that the lower grades in our education system be given a chance to realize in their sphere of public service the same ideals that are effective in the higher institutions. Incidentally, the achievement of such a result, even in a very imperfect way, would be the greatest service that could be conferred upon the higher institutions. It would give them an educational constituency, larger in numbers, more able in material resources, and more intelligent and appreciative of educational and social needs than it is now. What greater benefits are there for an institution of higher learning?

School legislation in the early days (I have in mind particularly the Middle West) was directed almost wholly to the more external and material phases of the question. This is natural, for the first question in organizing a system involving great expense is the question of financial support. In a new state the school fund, the method of its collection and apportionment, provision for its enlargement, teachers' examinations, and questions of like character, consume all the time and interest that can be given to school legislation. Action is based upon the generally accepted belief that the common school is an essential constituent of a democratic society and should be generously provided for. The results secured by legislation, prompted by this noble sentiment, are magnificent in Iowa and in the western states generally, so far as the material basis for the development of an educational system is concerned. The trouble is, we have not in our educational product got on very rapidly. There has been much school legislation, but the equipment for the school is not very different from that which our fathers knew. Nor have the spirit and method changed as much as we should expect from the growth in resources and the larger demands of the people. Reading, writing, and arithmetic, with a little grammar, still form the staple intellectual diet for multitudes of young people in the common schools. They are taught practically as they were a generation ago, as subjects which the pupil must take as he might take medicine, with this difference, that there is no attempt to make a diagnosis of the youth's individual needs.

Measured by the rapid changes and advances in general social movements, the common-school system is in a state of standstill. This is chiefly due to the fact that, having given a material basis for a system of schools, we have not proceeded seriously and insistently to the more difficult questions of educational policy. We have not provided for adequate co-ordination and integration of all the interests involved; we have not given sufficient care to the personnel of the administrative officers; we have not recognized the importance of adjustability and plasticity in the system to meet enlarging demands as they arise; we have not given to our supervising officers sufficient opportunity for personal initiative in controlling and directing school affairs; we have not felt deeply enough that the chief end of our system is the care of some hundreds of thousands of boys and girls who will never see a high school. It is no easy task to deal with problems such as these, but we must deal with them.

The fact that there are such problems is no criticism of the public system. It has done an incalculable service for the people. But there are duties still to perform which are beyond it, through no fault of the system, but through fault of us who are the citizens of this and other commonwealths. The time has come for a new spirit and a new initiative in common-school education; when some of the personal and creative energy that belongs to present-day society must be put into it. On the splendid material basis, which has been maturing for more than a half-century, we must superadd the elements necessary to make the school system a more vital part of the public life. We are under obligations to do this, and we are under contract to the world to do it. If we do not do it, we are contributing to those elements of confusion and discontent which are likely to prove a menace to the permanency of our free institutions.

We have based our faith in the permanency of our institutions on the capacity of the people to govern themselves and direct aright affairs of state. The task we undertook in the infancy of our government is vastly greater than we anticipated. The difficulties of the task are multiplying with unexpected rapidity. Our appreciation of the difficulties is not growing with equal rapidity. Aliens are coming at the rate of a million a year to become citizens of this republic for good or ill. We have entered into tacit contract with ourselves and with them that they shall have the rights of free citizenship. The nations of the earth are looking at us and are wondering what is to become of our experiment in democracy; and we may well ask ourselves whether it is possible for us to give the newcomers adjustment to the ideals we cherish and make them one with ourselves. I believe we can do it. Whether we shall do it or not depends chiefly upon our willingness to study the problem of elementary education with a view to making, as far as possible, our education one of adjustment to practical life, and one of participation in it. More directly is it a problem of education because the real problem of the immigrant does not begin with the first, but with the second, generation. Hence the solution of the problem centers in the rural and grade schools. It is not a new problem the immigrant brings us; he simply emphasizes the old problem—the problem we have in connection with our own children.

All that has been said points to the boy and girl. Discuss any educational proposition, and sooner or later it reaches the boy and girl—the school, "only a lot of boys and girls." There is found the basal ultimate in educational theory and practice. Future school legislation, without question, will give greater emphasis to the boy and girl, and greater stress to enactments that look to their development as a real part of the community and state. We may not expect to legislate adequately till we see in the needs and capacities of the boy and girl the purpose and the end of the whole process of public-school education. If we consider their needs and capacities, and provide ways and means to treat them, we of course improve their value as social, political, and economic units in a free commonwealth. We do it for foreign-born and native-born alike. Education of this sort for all the boys and girls is a political and an economic necessity. It is the first duty of the state to provide it as a means of self-preservation. This would seem to be self-evident, but what legislative body in this country has emphasized with any insistence the patriotic and the economic motives for school legislation? The careful development of the dormant economic value in the millions of school children who will never have the opportunity for higher education would bring immeasurable spiritual and material returns to society.

We have need to consider the fact that permanent success and stability in our public affairs are not so much—by no means so much—dependent upon tariff legislation, the regulation of inequalities, nor upon any symptomatic treatment of special irregularities, as they are dependent upon the treatment of the fundamental problems of practical life—patriotism, economic value, and the like—which center in the public school. Germany has grasped this fact, and is the first European nation to give it practical illustration in a large way. She is securing industrial and commercial supremacy among the European nations because she has been developing the long unused and neglected economic values belonging to her youth. Her educational reports and her trade reports are complementary documents which show without question the source of her rapidly enlarging sphere of influence. The Kaiser, early in his reign, insisted on this new motive in educational legislation, and nothing better than this illustrates the sagacity and wisdom of the man.

Japan was quick to recognize the same fact, and the results achieved by her have taught a lesson to the whole world. She did not have many men. She understood that her success in war and in peace would depend on developing to the fullest extent the values of those she did have. She won in her struggle with Russia, and in her struggle for recognition among the nations, on this practical but fundamental principle.

The best way to increase the agricultural value of a state, or the commercial value, or any value, is to increase the value of the youth who are to be its citizens, by giving them acquaintance with their own powers and with the life and the materials of the life they are to live. It is easier to give them only reading, writing, and ciphering, and to let them go with the contribution these subjects can make; it is easier and cheaper, but it is not so wise nor profitable. It would cost much money to instruct the child in such a way that he would come into real touch with the life he is going to live; but, however much it might cost, it would not be expensive, because the returns would be more than commensurate with the expenditure of time and pains and money. If we give the children an interest in things, and give them adjustment to their environment, social and material, large results are sure to follow, both material and spiritual. This is spiritual law. This is economic law. Finally, it is education—education in the only true sense.

A youth is made up of a bundle of sympathies and native powers calling for cultivation. The chief object of elementary education should be to bring the youth to consciousness that these qualities are within him, and that they are there for enlargement and use. There is little to show that our system of elementary education has taken this very simple proposition into account. The educational food we are giving the child is good so far as it goes, but the method of giving it does not aim at the fundamental educative process.

What the child calls for are both subjects and method through which there may take place some constructive development of his latent powers. He can't be educated in any real sense without it. A child's education and a child's reformation, if he happens to be an irresponsible, take place along exactly similar lines. There is no hope that we shall improve a child on the street by telling him he has done something wrong and that he must not do it again. It wouldn't help the matter much if he were arrested and put in jail. The only hope for such a lad is a place where he may have a chance to practice and realize right principles of conduct, a place where the good in him is called into play by sympathy and encouragement. He must have a place where he can work out his own redemption under suitable guidance. The same is true of any boy in the school. The giving of a book and a teacher to explain rules will not insure educational results. The child should have the chance to reproduce, so far as possible, for himself, and to participate in the educating process. The school—rural school or grade school in town—should be a shop, a garden, a laboratory, should be a place where boys and girls come in contact with life and form personal acquaintance with the rules and principles which govern it. In short, there should be a creative atmosphere in the school from the lowest grades up. Manual training and domestic science are lines of educational activity which afford suggestions for use in all grades of school work.

I know a school in Iowa where the idea I am trying to emphasize has had beautiful illustration. A large number of triangular spaces in the town, due to an unusual manner of platting, have been taken in hand by grade pupils. Shrubbery and flowers have been planted, and places that were at one time very unsightly are now the beauty spots of the town. The children are enthusiastic about it, and have learned much about plants, seeds, and soils. Incidentally they have acquired a sense of beauty and order. This is education of the highest value. It comprehends the whole individual—gives information, excites interest, gives vital contact with the outer world, and develops a sense of social obligation. It epitomizes elementary education as it ought to be.

The value of any subject, or any method whatever, is directly proportional to the use that can be made of it in developing what is within the child and bringing it into a vital relationship with the world without. Looked at from this point of view our educational system, especially as realized in the grades and rural schools, is in its elementary stages. As yet we have merely announced our intention of educating our children, without appreciating the magnitude of the task and its ever insistent demands. A schoolhouse at every "cross roads," and a large school fund, are only suggestions of possibilities. With these provided, we are just ready to ask: What are we to do with the boy and girl in the schoolhouse? They are alive—they require immediate and constant attention. There is a teacher—alive also. Now, the consideration we secure for these living parts of the system will determine wholly whether it was worth our while to build the schoolhouse and vote a tax for its support. The difficulties of our educational problem begin here—and end here—in the living pupil and in the teacher. They are difficulties that will always be with us. They are not to be disposed of by a single act of legislation. The elements of these difficulties are variable and require provision for some continuous process of legislation, to be followed up by most careful and competent administration.

A forward movement in the interests of our educational system with especial reference to schools below the high school, particularly rural and village schools, should include emphasis on the following points:

1. An improvement of the plant—schoolyard, building, and equipment—with a view to the reasonable comfort and convenience of the pupils. There should be an appeal through an improved plant to the pupil's sense of order and beauty.

2. A determined effort to secure greater permanency and efficiency in the teaching force. The teacher's value will determine the value of every other element in the school. The teacher is a medium of communication between state and pupil, and is to be "philosopher, guide, and friend." A right adjustment between the child and his environment, social and material, is not to be expected unless the teachers have a reasonably good understanding of the obligations resting upon them. Teachers of this type are to be had in larger numbers, if the state will ask for them and provide a reasonable support. The teachers in our common schools sorely need the stimulus of encouragement and appreciation. There would be a quick response to such stimulus. A demand for greater efficiency would quickly secure greater efficiency.

3. Opportunity for practical acquaintance with the material and social environment. The boy and girl that grow up in the country should have an intelligent acquaintance with trees, birds, plants, and soils. There should be some provision for instruction in such subjects, and others of local importance. There should also be provision for elementary instruction in questions of social obligation and relationship. An attempt in each case should be made to prepare the child for the life he is to live as a fellow-citizen with many others, and as an active contributor to the needs of his community and state.

4. At various places in every county, perhaps in every township, there should be a consolidated school. This school should give what no single school could give, should have a richer course

of study, and larger opportunities for establishing connections between school-work and life-work. This arrangement is practical, and is an established success in several states, particularly in Indiana.

5. The status of the county superintendent should be improved. The office is one of immense possibilities, and under adequate legislative protection will have great practical value in the development of an improved school system.

6. A closer supervision by the state of all the schools, including, of course, the high school.

7. The appointment of an educational commission by the legislature to review all school legislation, to unify it, and to propose ways and means of improvement, with a view to placing the schools into close touch with life.

In conclusion, it cannot be overemphasized that the school is not to be the special interest of the teacher alone. It is also the special interest of every citizen who has the welfare of the nation at heart and appreciates the meaning of the common school in our social and national life. In the hope that we who are here may do something to focus attention upon this part of our educational problem, I have made these remarks. Apropos are the words of Walt Whitman:

> And you, America,
> Cast you the real reckoning of your present?
> The lights and shadows of your future, good or evil?
> To girlhood, boyhood, look, the teacher and the school.

CHILDREN'S DRAMATIC INTEREST AND HOW THIS MAY BE UTILIZED IN EDUCATION

HELEN ELIZABETH PURCELL
Illinois State Normal University, Normal, Ill.

The education of the child, as usually planned, sets at naught every natural tendency, and seeks to impose upon him certain tasks, the skilful performance of which the human race has decided shall be the standard for the educated man. The right of the race to decide its standard of excellence none will deny, but the will of the child is a matter which we are forced to consider, in bringing about the completion of this aim, if the end is a realization of the intention. For ages he has resisted the effort to educate him, and, in spite of free schools and truancy laws, a large proportion of the whole has eagerly answered the first call of the world of work and has joyfully left behind both school and books. Even now, in spite of our boasted progress in psychology and pedagogy, the fact remains that the average school is hateful and distasteful to those who should be its most zealous patrons.

Now, if the call of the world of industry is so alluring to the child that it is a successful rival to the schools, we must concede that in it the child finds something that his nature demands and which the school does not furnish. To me the answer to the situation lies in our outrage of every natural instinct of the child. Interest is born of instinct, but, instead of building our educational principles upon this fact as upon a rock, we put down, by force of arms, every attempt of the child to assert himself as heredity intends that he shall. The world outside of the school gives him freedom to follow those natural bents of the race. He is not considered a vessel of wrath and a favorite abiding-place of the evil one. Instead, he becomes a member of the great world-society, and is at once a giver and a receiver. He has a motive and he sees an outcome.

If we were to consider all of the instincts or impulses and their value in education, a book of many volumes might be written. To me belongs the task of setting forth briefly the claims of one impulse—the natural tendency of the child to engage in the dramatic. The date of the first play can no more be set than can the date of that first sound that heralded the birth of language. We only know that the play is as old as communication, and helped man to express his embryonic thoughts long before words had been wrested out of chaotic gutteralness. When prehistoric man had been successful in the chase or in conflict with his enemy, his savage mind naturally delighted in communicating this fact to others. At first language was entirely lacking, and only through pantomime and gesture was the transmission of his thought possible. After this first dramatic production of his act for the purpose of communication, we can easily conceive how the mere pleasure of the doing might incite him to a repetition of the performance. Since imitation is so deeply rooted an impulse, even in that prehistoric era, we can imagine the children, or even the elders, finding a joy in the imitation of this presentation, until it became a set play in which several might take a part the more successfully to work out the real act. Finally, as language and invention grew, changes that added to the pleasure of the act were made, and at last original performances were invented whose aim was the indulgence of more pleasure than mere repetition of a once-performed act could give.

Thus we see that the first drama had a social origin and grew out of imitation. Today man's dramatic interest is so vital a pressure that to gratify it he annually spends millions of dollars, and a great play makes for public sentiment and influences ethical relations as all the sermons of the world cannot do.

The child is born with a strong dramatic impulse which shows signs of development at a very early age. He plays horse as soon as he can chirp, and there is no surer guide to the growth of a child's experience than the diversity of his dramatic performances, for he reproduces everything that with any force presents itself to his consciousness. He is father, and his sister is mother. They set up housekeeping, and she attends to the home affairs while he goes to the office. Or perhaps the girl's doll is ill, and the boy is the doctor and visits the sick baby, who, he is assured, has a fever and a bad cough. He feels its pulse, examines its tongue, and prescribes with all the gravity of the regular family physician. A little three-year-old girl, who gives me many happy hours, and in whom the dramatic impulse is especially strong, invades my room almost every evening, and, after choosing a leading part for herself, assigns to me the other rôle necessary to the production of a drama. Storekeeper, as with most children, is a favorite, and, standing behind a chair, which serves as a counter, she assumes all the airs and expressions of the man who wishes to sell. I come to buy, and I am often hard-put to keep up my end of the play with anything like the spirit which she puts into her part. Taking a trip is another favorite of the little lady. Sometimes we go to Pike's Peak, where some of her friends have been. Sometimes we go to Chicago, where she has visited many times; but wherever we go *she* goes, and I am merely the conductor who punches her ticket and calls the stations. For the child naturally accepts no minor parts in his drama. Impulse is strong within him, and he has not yet learned to control it. In fact, our first memories of things are many times not of the thing in its reality, but as we played it. I have no memory of a funeral which preceded the death and burial of one of my dolls, and yet such an experience must in some way have preceded this act. What I do remember is that for several days my doll died with great frequency, and was buried with all the pomp attendant upon a funeral, in which the hearse was my brother's express wagon, and decorations were quite as likely to be weeds as flowers.

The dramatic impulse being admitted, the question of the methods by which we can take advantage of it in our training of children naturally presents itself to the teacher. To me the most convincing argument in favor of its full development lies in the attitude of the girl to her doll. This is not entirely an exhibition of mother-instinct, as we are so often assured. The mother-instinct truly asserts itself in the care and love which the mother bestows upon the child. The little girl plays at being a mother, and by the exercise of her dramatic impulse gains an immediate pleasure, and at the same time reinforces her maternal instinct, and prepares herself more fully for the real work of motherhood.

If the dramatic exercise of the mother-instinct is a preparation for the real condition of motherhood, it follows that the dramatic exercise of the ethical will tend to produce correct ethical relations, and that the dramatic exercise of judgments in life-situations will prepare the child for actual living as will no other means at our disposal. The curriculum of every school, dry and bare as it sometimes appears to be, presents living material for dramatization. Reading, geography, and history afford endless opportunities for work in this direction. Perhaps the discussion of some plays' recently written and produced by fifth-grade pupils under my charge will prove the most practical means of arriving at a way in which this work may be managed, and of reaching a summary of the benefits derived from it.

Part of the work of one class in history this autumn was a study of the Pilgrims. The children have no textbook, and the work of presenting the subject falls entirely upon the teacher. This is usually done by word of mouth, and it takes a skilful story-teller to keep awake a class of boys and girls, by the mere oral presentation of a series of events which happened three hundred years ago. For several days the recital of the woes of the Pilgrims went on, and at intervals the children were called upon to repeat the tale as adorned by the teacher in charge. Those who had good memories and inactive imaginations managed to pick up a few facts. The others were blasé. I suggested that we write a play about the Pilgrims, and that we present it for their parents and friends. There was a quick awakening. We could not decide then what part of the history of the Pilgrims we would take as the subject of our play, as we had studied but a small portion of it. You can see that there was an immediate incentive for further investigation, especially as the subject was to be decided by the children. I have never seen more interest displayed by a class than that which those children possessed. They ransacked the library for books, and even dry autobiographies were eagerly read and passed around. The teacher was no longer a reciter of a monologue. There were end-men and middle-men, but mostly men who wanted to talk all the time. The subject-matter was soon covered, and by a majority vote the children decided that the title of their play should be "The Treaty between Massasoit and the Pilgrims." We then considered the things that we ought to know in order to write and present the play—accurate historical facts, Pilgrim customs, dress, topography of the region about Plymouth, etc. Everyone became a zealous student. Pictures were brought out that had not seen the light of day for years. The news of the proposed presentation of the play soon spread to the other rooms in the school, and, as the actual historical facts would permit of a greater number of children taking part than the total enrolment of our room, applications for a place in the cast came in from children in the other grades. In fact, when the play was ready for presentation, I was obliged to allow initial performances to be given to the other children in the school, to their great satisfaction and the glory of the fifth grade.

Part of the plan was to encourage free oral expression, and a considerable portion of the play was written with this object in view. A pupil suggested what he thought would happen in the given situation, who would speak, and what he would say. This the teacher wrote upon the blackboard. Other pupils gave their thoughts, and these also were placed upon the board. Then we considered the merits of each thought presented. Often there were spirited discussions as to why a certain thing was not good or why something else was better. No effort was necessary to induce them to talk. In fact, the difficulty lay in knowing the point at which it was best to stop and take up another step. Finally, a decision as to which one we would use was decided by a majority of the class. Then we turned our attention to the language of the sentences, and it was corrected by general discussion. When a written lesson seemed desirable, often the entire class was sent to the blackboard, and each one wrote what he thought would come next in the drama. Then the class considered each one, and acted upon it as previously described. At other times each member of the class wrote out his thought upon paper and handed it to the teacher. The correction and discussion of the work was then taken up in various ways. It was slow work.

The play is short, taking perhaps less than ten minutes to present it when finally written. We were nearly three weeks writing it, but it was worth the time. The number of judgments which the children formed cannot be estimated, while the value of the spirit of fair consideration of a subject is beyond estimation. Added to the logical and ethical results mentioned, they had an excellent knowledge of the Pilgrims, their imaginations had been exercised, and yet had been held within bounds by the strictly historical, and their oral and written expression showed vast improvement.

When the work of writing the play was completed, the children decided who were best fitted to take the parts of the principal characters, and such was their interest in its successful presentation that I did not see the slightest evidence of a wish for personal aggrandizement. The remaining pupils in the room all became either Indians or Pilgrims without speaking parts, so that every pupil in the grade took part in its presentation, although but one class was engaged in the writing of the play. The immediate socializing influence of this fact is too evident to admit of discussion.

The play opens in Governor Carver's house. The governor is sitting at a table writing. Miles Standish enters and addresses him:

"Governor Carver, there were two Indians on Watson's Hill a while ago, brandishing their weapons as if for war. They have disappeared now, but I believe they mean to come again with others."

Governor Carver: "Beat the drums and call our men together."

(Miles Standish retires a moment, and the drum is heard outside. Then the Pilgrim men, women, and children pour into the governor's office. The women appear to be frightened, but the men form around Miles Standish. As they come in, some conversation takes place.)

Mr. Warren: "What is all this fuss about?"

Mr. Hopkins: "Captain Standish saw Indians on Watson's Hill, and he thinks they mean war."

(By this time the men have quietly formed around Miles Standish, and he addresses them.)

Captain Standish: "Two Indians stood on Watson's Hill a while ago, and I think others will come. (Indians appear on top of the hill.) There are a half hundred of them now, and I believe they mean to fight. Come! Let us drive them away!"

(Squanto is seen approaching.)

William Brewster: "Wait! Squanto comes. They may mean to be friendly."

(Squanto enters the room and addresses the governor.)

Squanto: "The great chief Massasoit and his brother Quadequina want to smoke the pipe of peace with the pale faces."

Governor Carver: "Go, tell Massasoit and his brother Quadequina to bring to us the pipe of peace, and we will smoke with them."

(While Squanto is gone the women express their fears, and the men reassure them.)

Mrs. White: "I am so frightened."

Mary Chilton: "I am afraid they will scalp us."

Mr. Winslow: "Don't be afraid. We will take care of you."

(Squanto returns.)

Squanto: "The great chief Massasoit will not come down into the valley, but wishes one of the pale faces to go up on the hill and talk to him about the land which they have taken from one of his vassal tribes."

Governor Carver: "What! Is Massasoit afraid?"

Squanto: "Massasoit fears the white man's thunder-and-lightning stick."

Governor Carver: "The great chief need not fear us. One of us will go to the top of the hill and talk to him. Who will offer to go?"

Mr. Winslow: "I volunteer to go!"

Mr. Bradford: "I offer to go!"

John Alden: "Let me go!"

Mr. White: "Let the governor decide."

Governor Carver: "Mr. Winslow may go. Get some presents for Massasoit and Quadequina."

(Priscilla goes to her house and comes back.)

Priscilla: "Mr. Winslow, here is some biscuit and butter to take to Quadequina."

Captain Standish: "Here are two skins that you may give to the chief Massasoit."

(Gilbert Winslow hands a package to his father.)

Mr. Winslow: "What is it, son?"

Gilbert Winslow: "A knife, an ear-ring, and a copper necklace."

(Mr. Winslow accepts the package and goes up Watson's Hill with Squanto. Massasoit and twenty warriors return with Squanto to the brook. Squanto takes six warriors into the village to be kept as hostages until Mr. Winslow returns. Gilbert Winslow sees Squanto returning without Mr. Winslow and runs forward to meet him.)

Gilbert Winslow: "Where is my father, Squanto?"

Squanto: "Massasoit left your father upon the hill with Quadequina. These six warriors will stay with you until Mr. Winslow returns."

Captain Standish: "Mr. Winslow is worth more than a thousand Indians!"

Squanto: "Massasoit waits across the brook. He wishes to talk to the governor."

Governor Carver: "Eaton and Crakstone, take these Indians and give them something to eat. Captain Standish, go meet Massasoit and bring him into the village. Mrs. White, will you please see that the house is ready for the Indian king?"

Mrs. White: "I shall be glad to do it. Remember Allerton and Elizabeth Tilley, will you help me?"

Elizabeth Tilley: "Yes, I will help you."

Remember Allerton: "I will help you."

(The women busy themselves preparing the room, talking vigorously. To the beating of the drum Miles Standish brings Massasoit and his warriors into the house and seats the chief. Governor Carver enters attended by the military band and an escort of Pilgrim men. Massasoit stands up, and Governor Carver kisses his hand.)

Governor Carver: "Welcome, King Massasoit."

(Both sit down, and Massasoit offers the governor his pipe. The governor smokes and returns it.)

Governor Carver: "We rejoice to see the great chief, and wish to be his friends. We promise that if our men take anything from your tribe we will give it back to you. If any Indians attack your tribe and it is an unjust war, we will help you."

Massasoit: "I promise that I will help you in war with any other Indian tribe, and if any of my people take anything from you I will make them give it back, and I will punish anyone who does anything to the white people. When we come into Plymouth we will leave our weapons outside. We will live as brothers."

(The pipe of peace is then smoked, and Miles Standish escorts the Indians to the brook.)

As Thanksgiving approached, the school was asked to consider some form of entertainment as our part of a general plan that had been arranged. They unanimously decided to write another play. This time they chose as their subject "The First Thanksgiving." The method of writing it was much the same as that already described, and the play was quite as entertaining.

In preparing the plays for stage presentation little practicing was necessary. By the time the writing of the play was completed almost everyone had it memorized. The expression of the parts was natural and spirited. It was *their play; they* had written it; and I am sure that Shakespeare never trod the boards with more pride in his own production than they felt in theirs.

In conclusion, I wish to lay emphasis upon the ethical side of the question of a subject for a play. In the formative period no child should play the part of a villain. We become by doing, and his part should be that of an ennobling character. Massasoit and his Indians were kind to the Pilgrims. The sentiments expressed by him are just and friendly ones, and the attitude of the Pilgrims toward the Indians was sincere and kindly. I would have no child take the part of a blood-thirsty Indian. The dramatic feeling in children is too strong to be directed unwisely. Used with proper aims, the child through its influence is helped to develop morally and intellectually toward the perfection of social existence.

THE TEACHING OF THE CONTINENT OF EURASIA

ZONIA BABER

The following outline is intended primarily for the use of students in the College of Education who are preparing to teach. It is meant to be used only as suggestive in the direction of study. Since it is impossible for a student to cover the entire subject, even in a superficial way, during a course of three months, opportunity is given each student to choose regions or problems in which he is most interested. This secures a more intensive study of fewer subjects and training in the organization and presentation of certain material. In order that the students may acquire freedom in drawing as an aid in teaching, each is required, as he presents his report, to draw upon the blackboard relief maps and type scenes of landscapes of the region under consideration.

The reports of the class, when related, should give a general view of the entire continent. The problems which arise with individual students or teacher are brought before the entire class for discussion.

After the students have had sufficient experience in dealing with the sources of the geographic knowledge—the field, books, charts, maps, globes, reliefs, pictures, and the laboratories—opportunity is given for discussion of the methods of using the various materials to find, if possible, that which is educative and that which is waste. With a similar motive they discuss the effect upon thinking of the various forms of expression—modeling, painting, drawing, writing, and speech.

The last few weeks of the quarter are given to observation, discussion, and teaching of some aspects of the subject to the sixth grade in the Elementary School. This is for the purpose of studying the response of children to given material.

OUTLINE OF THE COURSE IN THE STUDY OF EURASIA

Eurasia is studied as the home of the three great civilizations which have persisted to the present time, and which today are the great teachers of the rest of mankind—European, Indian, and Chino-Japanese.

The geographic influences which have produced and pre-served these civilizations are traced as far as can be discovered. This necessitates a special study of the peninsula of Europe and its attendant islands, China and associated islands, India and its related regions.

The remainder of the continent is considered as related to these three important regions.

EURASIA

I. What we owe to Eurasia. What we have given Eurasia.

II. LOCATION: Terrestrially; in relation to other continents. *Extent.*—Influence of great latitudinal extent upon the development of a country. Influence of great longitudinal extent upon its growth. Is there a preferred continental size?
Shape.—Compare with that of other continents. Is there a preferred continental shape?
Coast-line.—Compare coast-line with that of the other continents. Value of indented coast-line. Give reasons. Cause of indented coast-lines.

III. TOPOGRAPHY: Location, extent, and altitude of the mountains, plateaus, and plains. Is the arrangement of mountains and plains most advantageous for man's occu-pation? Suggest better distribution.

IV. DRAINAGE: Great continental slopes. Locate Arctic, Pacific, Atlantic, Indian, and inland drainage systems. What effect have the drainage systems had upon the development of the continent? What river valleys of Eurasia have been "cradles" of early civilization? Why? Which are the most important for irrigation? If the rivers of the Arctic system flowed south instead of north,

would their value to man be increased or diminished?
Why? What would be the effect if the inland drainage
became oceanic? Advantage and disadvantage of inland
drainage?

V. CLIMATE: Trace isotherms from 80° to — 50° for winter.
Give reasons for position. Trace isotherms from 80° to
40° for summer. Give reasons for change. Effect of the
movement of isotherms 32° over the continent. Prevailing winds; monsoons. Cause of monsoons. Locate
areas of great rainfall; of little precipitation. Account
for conditions.

VI. VEGETATION: Locate and give approximate area of tundra, forest, prairie or steppes, and desert regions. Give
reasons for position of each. General effects of each.

VII. PEOPLE: Locate regions where important civilizations
have developed and persisted down to the present time.
Give some conditions favorable to the growth of the
European civilization; to the Indian and its attendant
civilization; to the Chinese and its tributary civilizations.
General conditions favorable or unfavorable to the development of the remainder of the continent.

VIII. Model relief of Eurasia in sand. Draw relief on blackboard. Write general description of Eurasia adapted to
sixth grade.

REFERENCES

MAPS (WALL): Sydon-Habernich (physical).
    Rand McNally (physical).
    Rand McNally (political).

ATLASES: Longman, *New Atlas.*
    Diercke, *Schulatlas.*
    Bartholomew, *Macmillan's School Atlas.*
    Bartholomew, *Physical Atlas,* Meteorology, Vol. III.
    Andree, *Handatlas.*
    Century Atlas.
    Rand McNally, *Indexed Atlas of the World* (foreign countries).
    Statistical Atlas of India (1895).
    Constable, *Hand Atlas of India.*

BOOKS (general description of Eurasia): Mill, *Realm of Nature:* "Eurasia," pp.
    288–301; "Other Continents," pp. 271–88.

Mill, *International Geography:* "Europe," pp. 123–37; "Asia," pp. 422–38.

Keane, *Compendium of Asia,* Vol. I, Introduction, pp. 1–33.

Chisholm, *Compendium of Europe,* Vol. I, Introduction, pp. 1–58.

Reclus, *Earth and Its Inhabitants:* "Asia," Vol. I, pp. 1–33; "Europe," Vol. I, pp. 6–35.

Draper, *The Intellectual Development of Europe,* pp. 23–37.

Universal Cyclopaedia; see "Europe," "Asia."

International Cyclopaedia; see "Europe," "Asia."

Encyclopaedia Britannica; see index, "Europe," "Asia."

Herbertson, *Asia,* Introduction.

Herbertson, *Europe,* Introduction.

Murray, "Drainage Areas of Continents," *Scottish Geographical Magazine,* Vol. II (1886), pp. 548–55.

Knox, *The Spirit of the Orient* (1906).

Dana, *Manual of Geology:* "Europe and Asia," pp. 31–33.

Freeman, *Historical Geography of Europe* (2 vols., 1881).

More detailed outline—

III. TOPOGRAPHY.

1. *Mountain ranges.*—Appearance, location, approximate extent and height of Himalaya, Kara Korum, Kuen Lun, Thian Shan, Altai, Yablonoi, Stanovoi, Khingan, Hindu Kush, Elburz, Caucasus, Balkan, Carpathian, Transylvanian Alps, Dinaric Alps, Alps, Pyrenees, Apennines, Ural.

Locate ranges which are never free from snow. Give reasons. Causes of differences in appearances of sky-lines.

Regions of beautiful scenery; effect upon settlement. Influence of the above-named ranges upon neighboring regions—drainage, climate, animals, plants, people.

Formation of mountain passes; location of important passes.

Origin of mountain ranges.

2. *Volcanoes.*—Locate regions of volcanic activity in Eurasia. Regions where earthquakes have been important agents of geographical control.

3. *Expression.*—Draw characteristic sky-lines of important mountain ranges in Eurasia. Characteristic mountain scenes.

Draw map locating ranges named above. Write

description of a selected type mountain range adapted to the sixth grade.

REFERENCES

Mountains—

Gilbert, *Universal Encyclopedia:* "Mountains."
Universal Cyclopaedia; see special ranges, as "Alps," "Himalaya," etc.
Mill, *International Geography;* see index, names of special mountain ranges.
Reade, *Origin of Mountain Ranges.*
Reclus, *The Earth,* Vol. I, pp. 103–30.
Reclus, *Earth and Its Inhabitants;* see index of special ranges.
Encyclopaedia Britannica; see index of special mountain ranges.
International Cyclopaedia.
Keane, *Compendium of Asia,* Vol. II, "Himalayan-Orographic System," pp. 64–77.
Conway, *Climbing and Exploration in the Karakorum Highlands* (1894).
Hooker, *Himalayan Journal.*
Gordon, *In the Himalayas.*
Holdich, *India, Kashmir and the Himalayas,* pp. 102–29.
Turner, *A Record of Travel, Climbing and Exploration* (1906; Altai Mountains).
Smith, "A Journey through the Khingan Mountains," *Geographical Journal,* Vol. XI (1878), pp. 465–92.
Conway, *Climbing in the Himalayas.*
Partsch, *Central Europe:* "Alps and the German Danube," pp. 16–47; "Central Carpathian and Hungary," pp. 47–57.
Freshfield, "The Sikkim Himalayas," *Scottish Geographical Magazine,* Vol. XXI (1905), pp. 173–82.
Wells, "Across the Elburz Mountains to the Caspian Sea," *ibid.,* Vol. XIV, pp. 1–9.
Umlauft, *The Alps.*
Lubbock, *Beauties of Nature:* "Mountains," pp. 203–47.
Lubbock, *The Scenery of Switzerland.*
Herbertson, *Man and His Work:* "Mountains, Plains, and Coasts," pp. 43–49.
Herbertson, *Europe:* "Alps," pp. 94–97; "Balkan," pp. 149–52; "Pyrenees," pp. 238–41.
Huntington, "The Mountains of Turkestan," *Geographical Journal,* Vol. XXV, pp. 22, 139.
Adair, *A Summer in High Asia.*
Dingelstedt, "The Caucasian Highlands," *Scottish Geographical Magazine,* Vol. XI, pp. 273–99.
Obruchef, "The Geography of Central Asia and Its South Eastern Borderland," *ibid.,* XII (1876), pp. 75–87.

4. *Plateaus.*—Location, appearance, approximate extent, altitude, and general characteristics of Pamir, Tibet, Gobi, Deccan, Iran, Arabia, Balkan, Scandinavia, Iberia, Switzerland. Topography: hills, mountains, plains, valleys. Influence of plateaus on adjacent

regions. If the great extent of plateaus had been located in the northern part of the continent, what would have been the probable result? What is the effect of high plateaus upon the development of its inhabitants—physical conditions, industries, commerce, homes, government; upon climate; upon drainage? *Expression.*—Draw type scenes of plateaus. Draw map showing plateaus and mountains.

REFERENCES

General plateaus—
  Mill, *International Geography;* see index: Tibet, Arabia, etc.
  Universal Cyclopaedia; see index: Tibet, Arabia, etc.
  International Clyclopaedia; see index: Tibet, Arabia, etc.
  Encyclopaedia Britannica; see index: Tibet, Arabia, etc.
  Keane, *Compendium of Asia,* Vol. II: "Asia Minor," pp. 299–329; "Syria and Palestine," pp. 368–404; "Arabia," pp. 405–61; "Persia," pp. 462–510.
  Chisholm, *Stanford's Compendium:* "Europe," Vol. I, see index.
  Murray, J., "On the Height of the Land and the Depth of the Ocean," *Scottish Geographical Magazine,* Vol. IV (1886), pp. 548–55.
  Reclus, *Earth and Its Inhabitants;* see index.

Tibet—
  Hedin, *Central Asia and Tibet,* Vol. I, pp. 457–608; Vol. II, pp. 413–569.
  Larat, Chandra Das, *Journey to Lhassa and Central Tibet.*
  Markham, *Narratives of George Bogle and Thomas Manning* (London, 1879).
  Rockhill, "Exploration in Mongolia and Tibet," *Annual Report,* Smithsonian Institute, July, 1892, p. 659.
  Williams, *Middle Kingdom,* p. 239.
  Hooker, *Himalayan Journals,* pp. 408–10.
  Bishop, Mrs., "A Journey through Lesser Tibet," *Scottish Geographical Magazine,* Vol. VIII, pp. 513–28.
  Bower, "A Journey across Tibet," *Geographical Journal,* Vol. I (1893), pp. 385–404.
  Taylor, Annie, "My Experience in Tibet," *Scottish Geographical Magazine,* Vol. X, pp. 1–8.
  Abbé Huc, *Travels in Tartary, Tibet and China during the Years 1844-46.*
  Herbertson, *Asia,* pp. 105–11.
  Knight, *Where Three Empires Meet.*
  Younghusband, *Heart of a Continent.*
  Younghusband, "Journey through Central Asia," *Proceedings of Royal Geographical Society,* August, 1888.
  Wellby, "Through Tibet and China," *Geographical Journal,* Vol. XII (1898), pp. 262–78.
  Littledale, "A Journey across Tibet from North to South," *ibid.,* Vol. VII (1896), pp. 453–78.

Pamir—
Dunmore, *The Pamir*.
Gordon, *The Roof of the World*.
Delmar, "Pamir: A Geographic and Political Sketch" (map), *Scottish Geographical Magazine*, Vol. VIII (1892), pp. 15–23.
Reclus, *Asia*, Vol. I, pp. 165–71.
Knight, *Where Three Nations Meet*.
Hedin, *Through Asia*, pp. 170–83, 380–96.
Curzon, "The Pamir and the Source of the Oxus," *Geographical Journal*, Vol. VIII (1896), pp. 15–59, 97–120, 239–64.
Morgan, "Pamir: A Geographic and Political Sketch," *Scottish Geographical Magazine*, Vol. VII (1891), pp. 15–23.

Gobi—
Hedin, *Through Asia*, Vol. I, pp. 465–623; see also Hedin, "Takla Makan Desert, *Geographical Journal*, Vol. VIII (1896), pp. 264–79, 356–72.
Hedin, *Central Asia and Tibet*, 2 vols.
Littledale, "A Journey across Central Asia," *Geographical Journal*, Vol. III (1894), pp. 445–76.
Hedin, *Central Asia and Tibet*, Vols. I and II.
Younghusband, *The Heart of a Great Continent*.

Iran—Persia, Asia-Minor, and Palestine (see references above)—
Arnold, *Through Persia by Caravan* (1876).
Hogarth, *The Nearer East*; see index.
Bishop, Mrs., *Journeys in Persia and Kurdistan*.
Curzon, *Persia and the Persian Question*.
Curzon, *Persia*, 2 vols. (1892).
Wills, *Persia as It Is*.
Wills, *The Land of the Lion and the Sun*.
Goldsmid, "Geography of Persia," *Geographical Journal*, August, 1895.
Brown, *A Year among the Persians* (1893).
Hamilton, *Afghanistan* (1906).
Newton, *Travels and Discoveries in the Levant*.
Goldsmid, "A Railroad through Southern Persia," *Scottish Geographical Magazine*, Vol. VI (1890), pp. 617–23.
Vaughan, "Journey in Persia," *Geographical Journal*, Vol. VII (1896), pp. 24–41, 163, 175.
Ainsworth, "The Sources of the Euphrates," *ibid.*, Vol. VI (1895), pp. 173–77.
Syhes, "Recent Journey in Persia," *ibid.*, Vol. X (1897), pp. 568–97.
Yorke, "A Journey in the Valley of the Upper Euphrates," *ibid.*, Vol. VIII (1896), pp. 453–74.
Whisham, *The Persian Problem*.
Chisholm, *Hand-Book of Commercial Geography*, pp. 315, 316.
Le Strange, *The Lands of the Eastern Caliphate*.
Buist, *A Ride through Persia*, Vol. IX (1893), pp. 1–6.
Ransey, *Historical Geography of Asia Minor*.
Wilson, *Hand-Book* (Murray) *for Asia Minor*.
Mausell, "Eastern Turkey in Asia and Armenia," *Scottish Geographical Magazine*, Vol. XII (1896), pp. 223–40.
Smith, George, *The Historical Geography of the Holy Land*.

Daly, "Palestine as Illustrating Geological and Geographical Controls," *Journal of American Geographical Society*, Vol. XXXII (1900).
Libbey and Hoskins, *Jordan Valley and Petra.*

Arabia (see general references above)—
Hogarth, *The Nearer East;* see index.
Doughty, *Arabia Deserta.*
Doughty, "Travels in North-West Arabia and Neja," *Proceedings of the Royal Geographical Society*, July, 1887.
Harris, *Journey through Yemen.*
Mill, *International Geography*, pp. 451–56.
Hirsch, "A Journey in Hadramaut," *Geographical Journal*, Vol. III (1894), pp. 196–205.
Bent, "Expedition to the Hadramaut," *ibid.*, Vol. IV (1894), pp. 315–31.
Bent, "Exploration of the Frankincense Country of South Arabia," *ibid.*, Vol. VI (1895), pp. 109–33.
Miles, "Journal of an Excursion in Oman, in South West Arabia," *ibid.*, Vol. VII (1896), pp. 522–41.
Schweinfurth, "Recent Botanical Explorations of Arabia," *Scottish Geographical Magazine*, Vol. IV (1888), pp. 212, 215.

Balkan—
Hogarth, *The Nearer East;* see index.
Partsch, *Central Europe*, pp. 228–40.
Freeman, *The Ottoman Power in Europe.*
Herberston, *Europe*, pp. 142–68.
Wyon and Prance, *The Land of the Black Mountains* (Montenegro).
Moore, *The Balkan Trail.*
Guerber, *How to Prepare for Europe*, pp. 316–45.
Murray, *Hand-Book of a Tour in Turkey.*
Poole, *People of Turkey.*
Abbott, *Tale of a Tour in Macedonia.*
Baedeker, *Constantinople.*
Black, *Constantinople.*

Greece—
Hogarth, *The Nearer East;* see index.
Smith, *Glimpses of Greek Life and Scenery.*
Symonds, *Sketches and Studies in Italy and Greece.*
Mill, *International Geography*, pp. 344–49.
Reclus, *Europe*, Vol. I, pp. 36–85.
Bury, *History of Greece* (geography), pp. 1–5.

Italy—
See cyclopaedias.
Fischer, *International Geography:* "Italy," pp. 352–65.
Reclus, *Europe*, Vol. I, pp. 183–283.
Gallenga, *Italy Revisited* (2 vols., 1876).
Gallenga, *Italy, Present and Future* (2 vols., 1887).
Hare, *Walks in Rome.*
Hare, *Days near Rome.*

Hare, *Cities in Northern and Central Italy.*
Hare, *Cities in Southern Italy and Sicily.*
Taine, *Italy:* "Rome and Naples."
Baedeker, *Italy:* north; central; southern.
Guerber, *How to Prepare for Europe,* pp. 199–229.
Piexotte, *By Italian Seas* (1906).

Switzerland—
Lubbock, *The Scenery of Switzerland and the Cause to Which It Is Due* (1896).
Partsch, *Central Europe:* "The Alpine Countries," pp. 203–07.
Taylor, *Picturesque Europe:* "The High Alps," pp. 345–79.
Tschudi, *Sketches of Nature in the Alps.*
Herbertson, *Europe,* pp. 90–109.
Umlauft, *The Alps.*
Chaix, *International Geography,* pp. 256–65.
Murray, *Switzerland.*
Whymper, *Scrambles amongst the Alps.*
Dent, *Above the Snow-Line.*
Baedeker, *Switzerland:* "The Eastern Alps."
Guerber, *How to Prepare for Europe* (1906), pp. 170–98.

Iberia—
Cyclopaedias.
Reclus, *Europe,* Vol. I, pp. 370–465.
Fischer, Mill, *International Geography,* pp. 368–85.
Sime, *Geography of Europe,* pp. 71–102.
Adams, *Commercial Geography,* pp. 298–304.
Amicis, *Spain and the Spaniards* (1895).
Baedeker, *Spain and Portugal* (1901).
Hare, *Wanderings in Spain.*
Hay, *Castilian Days* (1899).
Gallenga, *Iberian Reminiscences.*
Wigram, *Northern Spain* (1906).
Guerber, *How to Prepare for Europe* (1906), pp. 230, 231.
Seymour, *Saunterings in Spain* (1906).
Macmillan's Guide: western Mediterranean.

Scandinavia—
Sundbärg, *Sweden, Its People and Its Industries.*
Thorne-Thomsen, "Norway," *Elementary School Teacher,* Vol. VII (1906), Nos. 3 and 4.
Hansen, *Norway* (Official Publication, Paris Exposition, 1900).
Bradshaw, *Norway, Its Fjords and Fosses* (1896).
Forbes, *Norway and Its Glaciers* (1853).
Taylor, *Picturesque Europe:* "Norway," Vol. I, pp. 1–20, 95–124; "Sweden," Vol. I, pp. 200–209.
Taylor, *Northern Travel.*
Arnold, *A Summer Holiday in Scandinavia.*
Chisholm, *Hand-Book of Commercial Geography,* pp. 278–82.
Redway, *Commercial Geography,* pp. 310–19.
Sime, *Geography of Europe,* pp. 282–99.

Forrester, *Rambles in Norway.*

William, *Through Norway with a Knapsack.*

Herbertson, *Europe*, pp. 1–28.

Andersen, *Picture of Sweden.*

Neilsen, "Scandinavian Kingdoms," *International Geography*, pp. 197–208.

Adams, *Commercial Geography*, pp. 258–68.

Du Chaillu, *The Land of the Midnight Sun* (1882).

Ballou, *Due North; or, Glimpses of Scandinavia and Russia* (1887).

Spender, *Two Winters in Norway* (1902).

Baedeker, *Norway, Sweden and Denmark.*

Murray, *Hand-Book for Tours in Sweden; Knapsack Guide to Norway; Norway, Sweden and Denmark; Norwegian Rambles among Fjords, Mountains*, etc.

Guerber, *How to Prepare for Europe* (1906).

Reclus, *Europe*, Vol. V, pp. 47–168.

5. *Plains of Eurasia.*—Great continental plain; plains of China and Manchuria, Indo-Gangetic, Tigro-Euphrates, Hungarian. Location; approximate extent. Compare with plains of other continents. Position with reference to highlands. Effect of size and location of the great plain of Eurasia upon the development of Europe; of Asia.

Effect of riparian plains on Eurasian history. Which have contributed most to European culture? Which have apparently retarded European development? Formation of riparian plains. Origin of the great plain. Forces which have in recent past shaped, and are at present shaping, the plains.

REFERENCES

Formation of plains—

Davis, "Plains," *Universal Cyclopaedia.*

Gilbert and Brigham, *Introduction to Physical Geography:* "Siberian Marine Plain," pp. 154, 155.

Herbertson, *Man and His Work:* "Mountains, Plains, and Coasts," pp. 43–49.

Chamberlin and Salisbury, *Alluvial Plains*, pp. 175–93.

Reclus, *The Earth*, pp. 78–89.

A. *Glaciated area.*—Excursion to Stony Island, Glencoe, and Cary, to see phenomena of glaciation. Extent; appearance; value or detriment of glacial period to present Europeans. Work done by continental glacier.

REFERENCES

Glaciated region—

Reclus, *Europe* (*Earth and Its Inhabitants*), Vol. V, "Russia," p. 186; "Region of Great Lakes (Finland)," p. 209; "Ural Mountains," p. 344; "Scandinavia," p. 87.

Chisholm, *Compendium of Europe*, Vol. I, pp. 25–30, 35, 36, 646–48.

Geikie, *Prehistoric Europe*.

Geikie, *Ice Age in Europe*.

Penck, "Climatic Features of the Pleistocene Ice Age," *Geographical Journal*, Vol. XXVII, pp. 182–86.

Geikie, "Recent Researches in Pleistocene Climate and Geography," *Scottish Geographical Magazine*, Vol. VIII (1891), pp. 351–62 (map).

Prestwich, *Geology*, "The Glacial Deposits of Europe," Vol. II, p. 455.

B. *Black-earth region.*—Position and approximate extent of. Characteristics of. Value for agricultural purposes. Effect upon the development of Russia. Origin.

REFERENCES

Black earth ("chernoziom")—

Dokuchaev, *The Russian Steppes: A Study of the Soil of Russia, Its Past and Present* (Public Library).

Reclus, *The Earth*, p. 67.

Reclus, *Europe*, Vol. V, p. 269.

Mill, *International Geography*, pp. 402, 405.

Herbertson, *Europe*.

Geikie, *Prehistoric Europe*, p. 243.

C. *Steppes.*—Appearance winter and summer. Cause of; industrial aspects. Probable future.

REFERENCES

Steppes—

Brehm, *From North Pole to Equator:* "Asiatic Steppes and Their Fauna," pp. 86–120, 568–71.

Hedin, *Through Asia*, Vol. I, pp. 36–46.

Wright, *Asiatic Russia*, pp. 539–69.

Stadling, *Through Siberia*, p. 23.

Herbertson, *Asia*, pp. 7–11. See also Brehm, *From North Pole to Equator.*

Chisholm, *Compendium of Europe*, Vol. I, p. 635.

Reclus, *Europe*, Vol. V, p. 269.

Seebohm, "The North Polar Basin—Steppes," *Geographical Journal*, Vol. II, p. 337.

D. *Deserts.*—Location; approximate extent; appearance of rocky, stony, sandy, clayey areas. Cause

of each.   Probable effect of the large desert areas
upon the development of European civilization; of
Asiatic.   Value of deserts.   Detriment of deserts
to neighboring regions.   Probable future of deserts.
Excursion.—Dune Park, to study sand dunes.

REFERENCES

Deserts—

Hedin, *Through Asia;* see index.

Hedin, *Central Asia and Tibet,* Vol. I, pp. 63–442; Vol. II, pp. 3–190.

Dingelstedt, "Irrigation, Natural and Artificial in Samarkand and Bokhara,"
   Scottish Geographical Magazine, Vol. IV (1888), pp. 642–54.

Kropotkin, "The Desiccation of Eurasia," *Geographical Journal,* p. 722.

Herbertson, *Man and His Work:* "The Hot Desert," pp. 32–37.

Annenkoff, "The Physical Condition of Central Asia in Relation to Russian
   Occupation," *Scottish Geographical Magazine,* Vol. VII (1891), pp. 75–79;
   "Löss," p. 77.

Reclus, *The Earth,* pp. 70–89.

Reclus, *Asia,* Vol. II, p. 64.

Cornish, "On the Formation of Sand Dunes," *Geographical Journal,* Vol. IX
   (1897), pp. 278–309.

E. *Forest regions.*—Approximate extent; appearance
in winter and in summer.   Cause of forest belt.
Products of forest.   Value of great forest belt to
remainder of continent.   Do forests invite or retard
the development of civilization in the tree-covered
areas?   Probable future of the great Siberian
"Taiga."   What determines the limit of forests?

REFERENCES

Forests—

Keane, *Compendium,* "Taiga," p. 205.

Stadling, *Through Siberia,* "Taiga," pp. 38–223.

Nordenskiöld, *The Voyage of the "Vega,"* "Taiga," p. 121.

LeRoy-Beaulieu, *The Awakening of the East,* "Forest," p. 6.

Herbertson, *Asia:* "The Forest Zone," pp. 4–7.

Wallace, *Russia* (1905): "In the Northern Forest," pp. 24–33.

Brehm, *From North Pole to Equator,* "Forests and Sports of Siberia," pp. 120–
   68, 571–73.

Schimper, *Plant Geography,* pp. 166–73.

Seebohm, "The North Polar Basin," *Geographical Journal,* Vol. II, "Forest,"
   pp. 336, 337.

F. *Tundra.*—Location; approximate extent; appearance of stony and swampy tundra in winter; in

summer. Appearance of the aurora borealis. Condition of plant and animal life. Life of inhabitants; industries. Effect of the introduction of the reindeer upon the habits of the people. Probáble effect of the exhaustion of game and ivory upon the people of northern Asia.

REFERENCES

Tundra—
Brehm, *From North Pole to Equator:* "Tundra and Its Life," pp. 63-86 , 566, 567.
Herbertson, *Man and His Work,* pp. 7-15.
Herbertson, *Asia,* p. 384.
Herbertson, *Europe,* pp. 30, 31.
Nordenskiöld, *Voyage of the "Vega,"* p. 132.
Stadling, *Through Siberia:* "Across the Tundra," pp. 201-47.
Nansen, *Farthest North,* pp. 69-77.
Reclus, *Asia,* Vol. I, p. 311.
Reclus, *Europe,* Vol. V, p. 34.
Reclus, *The Earth,* p. 69.
Seebohm, "The North Polar Basin," *Geographical Journal,* Vol. II, "Tundra," pp. 335, 336.
Seebohm, *Siberia in Asia.*
Schimper, *Plant Geography.*

Expression.—Draw type scenes of steppe, desert, black-earth region, glaciated area, forest, tundra. Draw map indicating area of each. Write description of one region selected from the above list adapted to sixth grade.

G. *Drainage of Great Plain.*—Compare inland drainage with area of oceanic drainage. Advantage and disadvantage of inland drainage to the region drained; to adjacent areas? If the Volga flowed into the Black Sea instead of into the Caspian Sea what would be the advantage or disadvantage to Russia? What would be the probable effect upon Russia in Europe and Asia if the waters of the Caspian should rise so as to flow into the Black Sea?

Characteristics of the Arctic system of river basins. Effect of the constantly frozen areas upon the

erosive history of the rivers. What is the effect of
the debouchere of rivers within the Arctic regions
upon the work of the rivers? Value of the Arctic
system of rivers as highways. Present commercial
use. Probable future use.

Value of the Atlantic system for commercial
purposes. Which have been of greatest importance?

REFERENCES

Arctic rivers—
Stadling, *Through Siberia.*
Kropotkin, "Siberia," *Encyclopaedia Britannica.*
Mill, *International Geography,* pp. 426, 399–401.
Reclus, *Asia,* Vol. I, pp. 329–93 (Ob. Lena, Yenisei).
Reclus, *Europe,* Vol. V, p. 341 (lands draining into the Arctic).
Herbertson, *Asia,* pp. 11 (Ob. River), 12 (Yenisei River), 63 (Angara River
    and Lake Baikal).
Seebohm, "The North Polar Basin," *Geographical Journal,* Vol. II, pp. 331–50.
Wright, *Asiatic Russia,* pp. 75–77, 492, 493, 103 (Lena River).
Inland drainage system—
Chisholm, *Compendium of Europe:* "Aral and Caspian Depression," Vol. I,
    p. 639.
Reclus, *The Earth:* "Caspian Sea," pp. 335–40.
Reclus, *Europe,* Vol. I, pp. 363–420.
Wright, *Asiatic Russia:* "Aral and Caspian Depression," Vol. I, pp. 25–54.
Mill, *International Geography,* pp. 390, 395–97.
Hedin, *From Lake Aral to Tashkend,* pp. 47–65.
Herbertson, *Europe,* p. 43 (Volga).
Atlantic drainage—
Universal Cyclopaedia; see "Rhine," "Elbe," etc.
International Cyclopaedia; see "Rhine," "Elbe," etc.
Encyclopaedia Britannica: "Europe," "Rivers."
Reclus, *Europe,* Vol. V, p. 256.
Chisholm, *Compendium of Europe,* Vol. I, pp. 383–92, 482–89, 650.

H. *People.*—Division of the Great Plain by various
nations. Large landowners; small landed nations.
Would it be better if all the nations in the plains
were confederated? Why? Advantage of large
land areas to a nation; disadvantage. Which
nations possess the best agricultural part of the
plain? Why best? Prevailing crops. Forest products. Hunting regions; products of the hunt.

Region of dense population—cause of; of sparse population—càuse of. Important cities. Account for location. Give brief story of the history of Russia in Europe and Asia, showing geographic influences

I. *Trans-Siberian Rairoad.*—Location; length; reason for location. Influence upon Russia in Europe; on Siberia, China, Korea, Japan; on the United States. If another trans-Asiatic railroad should be built, where would it probably be located? Why?

REFERENCES

Trans-Siberian Railroad—
Stadling, *Through Siberia,* pp. 273–83.
Beverage, *Russian Advance,* pp. 68–81.
Norman, *All the Russias,* p. 102.
Lynch, *The Path of Empire,* p. 193.
Singleton, *Russia Described by Great Writers,* p. 223.
Beaulieu, *The Awakening of the East,* pp. 64, 71.
Great Britain—
Mackinder, *Britain and the British Seas* (1902).
Hull, *Contribution to the Physical Geography of the British Isles* (1882).
Jukes-Brown, *The Building of the British Islands.*
Geikie, A., *Scenery of Scotland.*
Geikie, *The Rivers of Great Britain.*
Geikie, *Geological Sketches:* "Geological Influences Which Have Affected the Course of British History," pp. 307–32.
Ramsay, *Physical Geography and Geology of Great Britain and Ireland* (1894).
Industrial Rivers of the United Kingdom (1891).
Houghton, *Descriptive, Physical, Industrial and Historical Geography of England and Wales* (1898).
Cunningham, *The Growth of English Industry and Commerce.*
Anderson, *The Book of British Topography.*
Reclus, *Europe:* "British Isles," Vol. IV.
France—
Reclus, *Europe,* Vol. II.
Universal Cyclopaedia; see "France."
Mill, *International Geography,* pp. 233–55.
Chisholm, *Compendium of Europe,* Vol. I, pp. 359–428.
Chisholm, *Hand-Book of Commercial Geography,* pp. 233–40.
Adams, *Commercial Geography,* pp. 228–42.
Herbertson, *Europe,* pp. 212–54.
Guerber, *How to Prepare for Europe,* pp. 91–100.
Hare, *North East France; South East France* (1896); *South West France; North West France* (1904).
Taine, *Journeys through France.*

Netherlands—
Partsch, *Central Europe*, 298–312.
Universal Cyclopaedia; see "Netherlands."
Sime, *Geography of Europe:* "Low Countries," pp. 249–70.
Picturesque World, Vol. I, pp. 304–27.
Mill, *International Geography*, pp. 216–23.
Reclus, *Europe*, Vol. III, pp. 450–58.
Gannet, Garrison, and Houston, *Commercial Geography;* see index.
Griffis, *The American in Holland.*
Baedeker, *Belgium and Holland* (1905).
Hare, *Sketches in Holland, Belgium, the Rhine*, etc.
Guerber, *How to Prepare for Europe* (1906): "Belgium and Holland," pp. 256–85.

Belgium—
Reclus, *Europe*, Vol. III, pp. 337–447.
Mill, *International Geography*, pp. 223–32.
Encyclopaedias; see "Belgium."
Baedecker, *Belgium and Holland* (1905).
Guerber, *How to Prepare for Europe.*
Chisholm, *Hand-Book of Commercial Geography*, pp. 240–44.
Adams, *Commercial Geography*, pp. 242–50.

Germany—
Partsch, *Central Europe:* "The North German Lowlands and German Seas,"
pp. 112, 241–98.
Chisholm, *Compendium of Europe*, Vol. I, pp. 467–554.
Schierbrand, *Germany.*
Chisholm, *Hand-Book of Commercial Geography*, pp. 246–58.
Sime, *Geography of Europe*, pp. 146–211.
Herbertson, *Europe*, pp. 59–87.
Reclus, *Europe*, Vol. III, pp. 157–225.
Guerber, *How to Prepare for Europe*, pp. 146–58.
Baedeker, *North Germany; Southern Germany.*

Russia—
Wallace, *Russia.*
Rambaud, *History of Russia:* "Geography," pp. 13–23.
Mill, *International Geography*, pp. 386–421; *The Industries, Manufactures and
Trade of Russia* (5 vols., published by Minister of Finance for World's Colum-
bian Exposition, 1893).
Reclus, *Europe*, Vol. V, pp. 183–480.
Seebohm, *Siberia in Europe: Visit to North East Russia.*
Englehardt, *A Russian Province of the North.*
Rambaud, *Expansion of Russia.*
Norman, *All the Russias.*
Dokuchaev, *The Russian Steppes: A Study of the Soils of Russia: Its Past and
Present* (published for the World's Columbian Exposition).
Dingelstedt, "The Musselman Subjects of Russia," *Scottish Geographical Maga-
zine*, Vol. XIX (January, 1903), pp. 1–20.
Tolstoi, *What to Do?* (New York, 1877).
Morley, *Sketches of Russia.*

Smith, *Universal Cyclopaedia*, "Russia."

Milyoukov, *Russia and Its Crisis.*

Villari, *Fire and Sword in the Caucasus* (1906).

Taylor, "Russian Kurds," *Scottish Geographical Magazine*, Vol. VIII (1891), pp. 311–22.

Freshfield and Sella, *The Exploration of the Caucasus* (1896).

Hare, *Studies of Russia* (1904).

Morgan, "Little Russia," *Scottish Geographical Magazine*, Vol. IV, pp. 536–44.

Dingelstedt, "Russian Laplanders," *ibid.*, Vol. VI, pp. 407–11.

"Glaciers of Russia in 1896," *Geographical Journal*, Vol. XII (1898), pp. 184–86.

Guerber, *How to Prepare for Europe.*

Siberia—

Kropotkin, "Siberia," *Encyclopaedia Britannica.*

Stadling, *Through Siberia.*

Beaulieu, *The Awakening of the East.*

Nordenskiöld, *The Voyage of the "Vega."*

Brehm, *From North Pole to Equator:* "A Journey in Siberia," pp. 390–416, 510, 540; "Forests and Sports," pp. 120–68.

Wright, *Asiatic Russia.*

Kennan, *Siberia and the Exile System.*

Kennan, *Tent Life in Siberia* (1870).

Keane, *Compendium of Asia*, Vol. I, p. 167.

Mill, *International Geography*, pp. 399–401.

Seebohm, *A Visit to the Valley of the Yenesei* (1879).

Harrington, *Universal Cyclopaedia;* see "Siberia."

Turner, *Siberia: A Record of Travel, Climbing and Exploration* (1906).

EAST EURASIA CIVILIZATION

CHINA, JAPAN, KOREA

JAPANESE EMPIRE

EXCURSION: Visit Nickerson Collection, Art Institute. Japanese stores.

I. LOCATION: Effect of great latitudinal extent. Relation to China, Korea, America.

II. AREA: Arable and untillable regions. Effect of small amount of arable land upon agriculture; upon other industries.

III. NATURE OF COAST-LINE: Effect upon fishing industry. Position of fishing industry in Japan.

IV. TOPOGRAPHY: Location of moutains, rivers, and plains in Saghalin, Kurile, Yesso—main island or Hondo, Kiushu, Shikoku, Luchu, Formosa. Brief story of formation of the islands.

V. CLIMATE: Prevailing winds. Temperature winter and summer. Rainfall winter and summer; snowfall. Time and region of typhoons. Compare with climate of Spain; with that of British Isles.

VI. VEGETATION: Extent of forest land; compare forests of Formosa with forest of Yesso. Forest products—woods, camphor, lacquer, wax. Describe process of obtaining camphor, and lacquer.
Agriculture: Rice, millet, barley, tea, cotton. Describe culture.

VII. INDUSTRIES: See above. Other industries: silk culture; manufacture of lacquered ware; cloisonné; ceramics; paper; colored prints.

VIII. ARCHITECTURE: Domestic; religious—Shinto, Buddhist. Influences which have affected architecture—building material; earthquakes; ideas from India and China. Adaptation of plastic arts and color to architecture.

IX. PEOPLE: Language; dress; government; schools. Location of principal cities; give reason for position. History —brief sketch of Japan's past. Effect upon Japan of the Russo-Japanese War. Probable future of Japan.

REFERENCES

Japan—
Rein, Japan.
Keane, Compendium of Japan, pp. 445-511.
Mill, International Geography, pp. 545-54.
Brinkley, Japan Described and Illustrated by the Japanese (5 vols.).
Chamberlain, Things Japanese.
Murray, Hand-Book of Japan.
Griffis, The Mikado's Empire.
Norman, The Real Japan.
Sandow, "A Journey around Yesso and up the Largest Rivers," R. Geological Survey, Vol. III, p. 517.
Blakiston, "Zoölogical Indications of Ancient Connection of the Japanese Island with the Continent,"Transactions of the Asiatic Society of Japan, Vol. XI (1883), pp. 126-46.
Brown, "Winds and Currents in Vicinity of Japanese Islands," ibid., Vol. II (1874), pp. 142-82.

Bishop, Mrs., *Unbeaten Tracks.*
Keane, *Compendium of Asia*, Vol. I, pp. 445–511.
Marshall, "Notes on Some of the Volcanoes in Japan, *Transactions of the Asiatic Society of Japan*, Vol. VI (1878), pp. 321–43.
Reclus, *Asia*, Vol. II, pp. 355–475.
Scidmore, *Jinrikisha Days in Japan.*
Younghusband, *On Short Leave to Japan.*
Weston, *Japanese Alps.*
Stead, *Japan by the Japanese:* "Agriculture," p. 413; "Seri-Culture," p. 415; "Rice," p. 418; "Tea," p. 421; "Forestry," p. 425; "Marine Products," p. 428; "Problems of Far East," p. 573.
Beaulieu, *Awakening of the East* ("Agriculture," "Fishing," p. 125).
Davidson, *The Island of Formosa, Past and Present* ("Camphor," pp. 398–443).
Hearn, *Out of the East.*
Adams, *Commercial Geography*, pp. 406–14.
Satow, "Cultivation of Bamboo in Japan," *Transactions of the Asiatic Society of Japan* (1898).
Haton, "Destructive Earthquakes in Japan," *ibid.*, Vol. VI (1878), pp. 249–91.

ART

Dresser, *Japan.*
Gonse, *Japanese Art.*
Bing, *Artistic Japan.*
Strange, *The Color Prints of Japan.*
Anderson, *Description and Historic Catalogue of Japanese and Chinese Painting in the British Museum.*
Huish, *Japan and Its Art.*
Alcock, "Japan," *Encyclopaedia Britannica*—"Pottery and Porcelain," "Lacquer Ware," "Metal and Bronze," "Carving," "Textile and Fabrics."
Chamberlain, *Things Japanese*, pp. 45–55.
Quim, "Lacquer Industry of Japan," *Transactions of the Asiatic Society of Japan*, Vol. IX, pp. 1–80.
Griffis, "The Corean Origin of Japanese Art," *Century Magazine*, December, 1882.

ARCHITECTURE

Murray, *Hand-Book.*
Chamberlain, *Things Japanese*, pp. 34–41.
Brunton, "Constructive Art of Japan—Relation to Earthquakes," *Transactions of the Asiatic Society of Japan* (1873).
Cawley, "Some Remarks on Constructions in Brick and Wood and Their Relative Suitability for Japan," *Transactions of the Asiatic Society of Japan*, Vol. VI (1878), pp. 291–317.

KOREA

Present Relation to Japan.

I. LOCATION : Advantage and disadvantage—climatically, politically.

II. AREA: Tillable land; coast-line; difference between eastern and western coast-line; location of good harbors. Influence of tides.

III. TOPOGRAPHY: Position of highlands and lowlands; advantage and disadvantage in development of people. Rivers, use as highways; for irrigation—Yalu, Tumen, Han, Nak Tong. Compare topographies of Korea and Italy.

IV. CLIMATE: Prevailing winds; rainfall, temperature winter and summer. Compare with climate of Italy; reason for differences.

V. PEOPLE: Dress; language; education; government. Present state of art and architecture. Cause of decadence. Industries: Agriculture; principal crops; manner of cultivation. Cities: Manner of building; walls; streets; houses; lights; water. Seoul, Chemulpo, Mukpo, Fusan, Gensan, Hi Chin. Reasons for position. Result to Korea of the Russo-Japanese War. Brief story of Korea's past.

REFERENCES

Korea—

Griffis, *The Hermit Kingdom.*
Bird-Bishop, *Korea and Her Neighbors.*
Bishop-Mill, *International Geography,* pp. 542–44.
Lowell, *Chosen* (1886).
Gilmore, *Korea from Its Capital* (1893).
Reclus, *Asia,* Vol. II, pp. 334–55.
Keane, *Compendium of Asia,* Vol. I, pp. 323–41.
"Corea, The Hermit Nation," *Bulletin of American Geographical Society* (New York, 1831), No. 3.
Ross, *Corea: Its History, Manners, and Customs,* Vol. I, p. 464.
Lilly, *Universal Cyclopaedia.*
Richthofen, "China, Japan and Korea," *Geographical Journal,* Vol. IV (1894), pp. 556–61.
Hulbert, *The Passing of Korea* (1906).

CHINESE EMPIRE

EXCURSION: Visit Nickerson Collection, Art Institute, and Chinese stores.

I. LOCATION: On the continent of Eurasia; the relation to

other great nations. Advantages and disadvantages of position.

II. SIZE AND SHAPE: Influence of the size of the country on its development. Advantage and disadvantage of size.

III. TOPOGRAPHY:

1. *Plateaus.*—Tibet, Pamir, Gobi. Value to China. Characteristics of country and inhabitants.

2. *Mountains.*—Himalaya, Kuenlun, Altyn Tagh, Tian Shan, Altai, Yablonoi, Khingan, Tsin-Ling-Shan. Influence of altitude, position, and extent upon the climate, products, and people. Aesthetic value. Influence of the highlands upon the lowlands of the empire.

3. *Plains of China.*—Origin; relation to the Pei-Ho, Hoang-ho, Yang-tse Rivers. Relation of the great plain to Chinese civilization.

4. *Rivers.*—Yang-tse-Kiang, Hoang-ho, Si-Kiang, Pei-Ho, Tarim, Amur. Influence of the rivers on industrial and commercial development of China. Should the Hoang-Ho be considered a blessing or a curse to the Chinese empire? Story of its shifting its course in 1887–89. Rate of land-building in Gulf of Pechili.

IV. CLIMATE:

1. *Winds.*—Prevailing direction in summer, in winter. Influence of high plateau on the direction of the wind; influence of the deserts on the direction of the wind. Season and track of typhoons.

2. *Rain.*—Account for summer rains. Influence of fringing islands. Parts of the empire liable to drought. Tension regions of rainfall.

V. SOIL:

1. *Loess region.*—Extent; theories of its origin; influence on agricultural development of China. Homes in loess. Influence on concentration of people.

2. *Red-earth region.*—Extent. Account for productivity.

3. *Alluvial plain.*—Formation; influence on agriculture;

influence on transportation; effect of the deserts on the soil of adjacent countries.

VI. PRODUCTS:

1. *Agriculture.*—National standing of farmers; encouragement given by the emperor and mandarins; manner of cultivating the soil. Rice, cotton, tea, indigo, millet, cane, poppies.

2. *Forests.*—Account for small amount of forest products.

3. *Minerals and metals.*—Known extent of coal, gold, silver, copper. Probable influence of the development of coal mines in China.

4. *Manufactories.*—Home manufactures; how carried on; influence on education and commercial life of the people; introduction of factories; probable influence on China of change from home industries to factories.

VII. PEOPLE:

1. *Race.*—Appearance; dress. Account for high commercial standing of Chinese in the Orient; influence of religion on the development of the people.

2. *Location of principal cities.*—Peking, Tientsen, Cheefu, Shanghai, Hangchau, Hong Kong, Canton, Nanking, Hankow. Give reason for location. Plan of building cities; pavements; domestic and religious architecture; means of procuring water, light, and heat; transportation facilities in north and south China. Account for primitive conditions in transportation, home and city comforts.

3. *Education.*—Describe a Chinese school. Describe examination in Peking or Canton. Influence of education on government; on commerce.

4. *History.*—Short story of China's past. What constitutes China's greatness? What causes China's weakness? What can the Occident learn from the Orient? What justification is there for England's control of Kowloon, Hong Kong? Germany's occupation of Kiao Chow? France's claim to Hianan? What was the influence of the Chinese-Japanese War? What

was the influence of the Russo-Japanese War upon China? What do you predict for the future of China? Movement toward introduction of occidental culture. *Expression.*—Model relief map of China in sand. Draw relief map. Draw typical landscape of China. Write a plan for teaching China in the sixth grade.

REFERENCES

China—

Williams, *Middle Kingdom.*

Huc, *Chinese Empire* and *Travels in Tartary, Thibet and China.*

Milne, "Journey across Europe and Asia;" Part II, "Across Mongolia to Peking;" Part III, "Peking to Tientsen," *Asiatic Society of Japan,* Vol. VII (1888).

Ball, *Things Chinese.*

Beaulieu, *Awakening of the East.*

Williams, *History of China.*

Richthofen, *China,*

Baber, *Travels and Researches in Western China.*

Douglas, *China.*

Fergusson, *History of Indian and Eastern Architecture,* Vol. II, pp. 300–25.

Mill, *International Geography,* pp. 521–42.

Stanford, *Compendium of Asia,* Vol. I, pp. 243–444.

Reclus, *Asia,* Vol. II, pp. 58–334.

Holcome, *The Real Chinaman.*

Smith, *Village Life in China; and Chinese Characteristics.*

Hedin, *Through Asia.*

Reclus, "Vivisection of China," *Atlantic,* Vol. LXXXII (1899), p. 329.

Hart, "China Reconstruction," *Fortnightly,* Vol. LXXV, pp. 99–103.

Bird-Bishop, *Yang-tse Valley.*

Yan Rhon Lee, *When I Was a Boy in China.*

Norman, *The Far East.*

Scidmore, *China, the Long-Lived Empire.*

Wilson, *China.*

Keane, *Compendium of Asia,* Vol. I.

Adams, *A Commercial Geography;* see "China."

Bishop, "A Journey in West Sze-Chuan," *Geographical Journal,* Vol. X (1897).

Carles, "The Yangtse Chiang," *ibid.,* Vol. XII, pp. 225–40.

Dickson, "Voyage In and from Canton," *ibid.,* Vol. VI (1870), pp. 354–73, 393–407.

INDO-CHINA

EXCURSION: Visit South Park Conservatory for tropical vegetation.

I. CONTINENTAL POSITION: Relation to India; to China. Advantages or disadvantages of position.

II. AREA: Compare with size of China and India.

III. TOPOGRAPHY: Relation of mountains to plains; to climatic conditions; to rivers. Formation of plains; value agriculturally. Rivers: Characteristics of Irriwaddi; Mekong, Menam, Salwin, and Red Rivers; value as highways; for irrigation. Compare the topography of the peninsula of Indo-China with that of other peninsulas of Eurasia.

IV. CLIMATE: Temperature; account for condition. Cause of season of rainfall. Effect of climate upon condition of people.

V. PRODUCTS: Manner of obtaining principal products. Principal imports.

VI. PEOPLE: Relation to Chinese; to Malays. Appearance; language; religion.

VII. GOVERNMENT: Area dominated by France, by England; independent.

A. *French Indo-China.*—Location of Annam, Tonquin, Cochin-China, Cambodia. Topographic and climatic condition. Principal native products.

How is the region governed? Effect upon the people of French occupation; advantageous or otherwise from the point of view of the European; from the point of view of Indo-Chinese.

Compare density of population with that of the United States. Principal cities: Saigon, Touran, Hanoi, Haiphong. Location and characteristics of? Language of French Indo-China. Religion.

B. *British Indo-China.*—Burma: Upper Burma, Lower Burma; Straits Settlements. Location; topographic and climatic conditions. Native products.

Nature of British rule. From the standpoint of the British; from that of the Burmese.

Characteristics of the Burmese people; appearance; dress; habits of life; education; religion.

Cities: Advantage of location of Rangoon; Mandalay; Moulmein; Singapore; Penang or George Town; Malacca. Characteristics of Burmese cities; of cities of the Straits Settlements. Architecture—domestic and religious.

C. *Independent Indo-China.*—Siam: Compare the topography, climate, products, cities, and people with those of the other Indo-Chinese. Relation of the Siamese to their present ruler. Would it be advantageous or otherwise to Siam if it were governed by some European power? If by Japan? How can Siam maintain her independence?

REFERENCES

Indo-China—

Keane, *Asia*, Vol. II, pp. 210–98.
Harrington, *Universal Cyclopaedia.*
MacMahon, *Far Cathay and Farther India.*
Reclus, *Asia*, Vol. III, pp. 420–500.
Bradley, *Travel and Sport in Burma, Siam and in the Malay Peninsula* (1886).
Younghusband, *1800 Miles through Burma, Siam and the Eastern Shan States* (1888).
Lamington "Journey in Indo-China," *Scottish Geographical Magazine*, Vol. VIII (1891), pp. 121–35.

Burma—

Murray, *Hand-Book for India, Burma, and Ceylon* (1898), pp. 413, 414.
Bird, *Wanderings in Burma.*
Hall, *The Soul of a People.*
Cuming, *In the Shadow of the Pagoda.*
Spearman, *Gazetteer of English Burma.*
Caine, *Picturesque India*, pp. 613–54.
Universal Cyclopaedia.
Scott, *Burma* (1886).
William, *Through Burma to West China.*
Colquhoun, *Among the Shans* (1885).
Forbes, *Burma.*
Oertel, *Notes of a Tour in Burma* (1893).
Straits Settlement and the Protected Malay State.
Norman, *The Far East: A School of Empire*, pp. 37–71.
Lucas, *Historical Geography of the British Colonies* (1894).
Denny, *A Descriptive Dictionary of British Malaya* (1894).
Mill, *International Geography*, pp. 511–15.
Clifford, "A Journey through the Malay States of Trenggam and Kelantan," *Geographical Journal*, Vol. IX (1899), pp. 1–38.

Siam—

Mill, *International Geography*, pp. 508–11.

M'Carthy, "Siam," *Proceedings of the Royal Geographical Society*, March, 1888.

Scott, "Hill Slopes of Tonking," *ibid.*, April, 1886.

Smyth, "Five Years in Siam," *Geographical Journal*, November-December, 1895.

Vincent, "The Land of the White Elephant," *ibid.*, May, 1896.

Bowring, *The Kingdom and People of Siam*, pp. 183–87.

Grindrod, *Siam: A Geographical Summary* (1895).

Black, "A Journey around Siam," *Geographical Journal*, Vol. VIII (1896), pp. 429–49.

Smyth, "Journey in the Siamese East Coast States," *ibid.*, Vol. II (1878), pp. 455–92.

Curzon, *Journeys in French Indo-China.*

Norman, *The Far East:* "France in the Far East," pp. 71–141.

Zimmerman, Mill, *International Geography*, pp. 515–20.

INDIA AND CEYLON

I. LOCATION: In relation to China; to Russia; to other neighboring countries. Value of position from a commercial standpoint.

II. SIZE: Compare with China; with Europe; with United States. Coast-line: Entire; few harbors. Influences of entire coast-line?

III. TOPOGRAPHY:

1. *Mountains.*—Position of Himalaya, Hindu Kush, Kara Korum, Sulaiman, Vindhya, Aravalli Hills, Western and Eastern Ghats, Satpura Hills. Influence of the mountains upon the development of India. Value to the administrative Englishman. Influence of Khyber, Kuram, Gomul, Bolan passes on the history of India. Formation of the passes.

2. *Plains.*—Indo-Gangetic, Carnatic, Northern Circirs, Malabar plains, and plains of Deccan plateau—position of; influence of these plains on India's progress.

3. *Rivers.*—Characteristics of Ganges, Indus, Brahmaputra, Nerbudda, Kistna, Godavari, Tapti, Cauvery, Uses of for irrigation; as highways.

IV. CLIMATE: Trace isothermal line from 80° to 60° for winter and summer. Explain changes. Locate regions of rainfall above 100 in.; from 50 in. to 100 in.; 30 in. to

50 in.; 10 in. to 30 in.; below 10 in. Give reasons for location. Describe rainy season; dry season. Describe monsoons; cause of? Influence of climate upon natives; upon Europeans.

    V. GEOLOGY: Areas of alluvial plains; Deccan basalt; Archaean rocks; influence of each upon landscape; upon agriculture, soil, water. Alluvial plains—irrigation by rivers and wells. Archaean by tanks; basalt little or no irrigation. Give reasons.

    VI. INDUSTRIES: Agriculture—principal crops; manufactures —principal native manufactures; cause of decadence of native art.

    VII. PEOPLES: Number of languages spoken; appearance of different peoples. Education; religion; art; government. Architecture: domestic; religions—Buddhist, Jaina, Saracenic, Dravidian; characteristics of each.

What has been the value to the Indians of British occupation? What has been the detriment to the Indian of British occupation? Can Europeans permanently colonize in the tropics? What is to be the future of the Eurasian in India? What has been the value of India to England? What detriment to England?

REFERENCES

India—

Holdich, *India.*

Bartholomew, Constable, *Hand-Atlas of India* (1893).

Keane, *Asia*, Vol. II, pp. 53–199.

Statistical Atlas of India (1895).

Barnes, Mill, *International Geography*, pp. 469–502.

Oldham, "The Evolution of Indian Geography," *Geographical Journal*, Vol. III (1894), pp. 169–96.

Hunter, *Imperial Gazetteer of India.*

Oldham, *Manual of Geology of India* (1893).

Murray, *Hand-Book, India, Burma, and Ceylon.*

Memoirs of the Geology of India.

Caine, *Picturesque India.*

Wallace, *India in 1887.*

Lyall, *The Rise and Expansion of British Domain in India.*

Reclus, *Asia*, Vol. III, pp. 1–361.

Taylor, *A Visit to India, China, and Japan* (1859).

Holdich, *Indian Borderland.*
Holdich, "The North-West Frontier of India," *Geographical Journal*, May, 1901.
Holdich, "Tirah," *ibid.*, Vol. XII (1898), pp. 337–61.
Hooker, *Himalaya Journals.*
Black; *Memoirs on the Indian Surveys* (1875–90).
Fergusson, *History of Indian and Eastern Architecture* (2 vols.).
Birdwood, *Industrial Arts of India.*
Wheeler, *A Short History of India.*
Arnold, *India Revisited.*
Scidmore, *Winter India.*
Cyclopaedia of India (1885; 3 vols.).
Oldham, *Geological Survey of India* (edited by Mackenzie).
Bailey, "Forestry of India," *Scottish Geographical Magazine*, Vol. XIII, pp. 572.
Hunter, "Historical Aspect of Indian Geography," *ibid.*, Vol. IV (1888), pp. 623–42.
Hamilton, *Afghanistan* (1906).
Vambery, "British Civilization and Influence in Asia," *Scottish Geographical Magazine*, Vol. VIII (1891), pp. 289–98.
Duncan, *Geography of India* (1876).
Buch-Deaker, *Irrigated India.*
Blanford, *Practical Guide to the Climate and Weather of India.*
Royle, *The Productive Resources of India.*
Brandis, *The Forest Flora of India.*
Hooker, *Flora of British India.*

Ceylon—
Tennent, *Ceylon.*
Fergusson, Mill, *International Geography*, pp. 503–7.
Fergusson, *Ceylon.*
Cave, *Picturesque Ceylon.*
Haeckel, *A Visit to Ceylon* (1883).
Cave, *Ruined Cities of Ceylon* (1897).
Herbertson, *Asia*, pp. 179–86.
Official Handbook of the Ceylon Court (St. Louis Exposition, 1904).

COMPARISON OF EUROPE, INDIA, CHINO-JAPAN

Compare the civilizations of Europe, India, China, and Japan. Appearance of people—stature, color. Habits; home; cities; agriculture; mining; stock-raising; manufacturing; fishing; commerce; art; government; education; religion.

What is the chief characteristic of European civilization? Of Indian? Of Chino-Japanese?

To what extent are the respective civilizations due to the geography of the regions? What have been the chief factors in geographic control? What are the present chief geographic influences? What future do you predict for each civilization? Will the Occident greatly influence the Orient, or will the eastern civilization influence the western? When railroads make easy intercourse with the various parts of the continent, what changes do you predict? Is homogeneity of Eurasian civilizations desirable? Why?

What is our special oriental interest? What do you predict will be our position in the Orient in the future? Why?

How can the Occident and Orient come to a better understanding of each other?

REFERENCES

Hall, *The Soul of a People.* Knox, *The Spirit of the Orient. Letters of a Chinese Official.*

PEDAGOGIC ASPECTS.—What does the study of geography do for the child mentally and morally?

How can geography be taught to result in the development of initiative, observation, reason, judgment, memory, imagination? Can one faculty of the mind be cultivated alone? What is the value of field-work aside from the information gained? What are the disadvantages and limitations of field-work? How and when should laboratories be used?

What is the influence upon geographic imagery of drawing maps and landscapes? Of painting landscapes? Of modeling maps? Of oral descriptions? Which form of expression is least difficult for sixth-grade pupils? Most difficult?

When would you use the various forms of expression in teaching geography? Why? How can maps be made to perform their proper function as symbols? What is the effect of memorizing maps?

REFERENCES

James, *Talks on Psychology and Life's Ideals,* "Necessity of Reaction," p. 33.

Dewey, "Principles of Mental Development as Illustrated in Early Infancy," *Transactions of Illinois Society for Child-Study,* Vol. IV, No. 3 (October, 1899).

Thorndike, "Hand Work," *Teachers College Record,* Vol. II, No. 3 (May, 1901).

Parker, *Talks on Pedagogy:* "Modes of Expression," pp. 223–60.

CLAY-WORK IN THE UNIVERSITY ELEMENTARY SCHOOL

HARRIET JOOR
Instructor in Clay-Modeling

In the Elementary School the work in clay is always closely related to the other work in each grade, so that all forms of the student's activities may be brought into harmony.

The pottery is, in every case, built up by coils from a working drawing made by the pupil, and the decoration is incised in the wet clay, or modeled in very low relief; the whole piece being then covered with an opaque glaze. Very rarely, and then only in the higher grades, the design is painted on with a clay of a different color, or with slip in which color has been mixed.

The motives for the applied decoration are chosen in correlation with the pupil's school-work: thus, when the children of the third grade were studying Norse history, they decorated their bowls with arrangements of Norse shields, spears, bows, or writhing dragons.

Clay, as a medium, appeals most strongly to the younger children. It is so sensitive and pliable a material that it does not tire the smallest or weakest fingers; while the sturdiest little worker learns by degrees to control his nervous energy when he realizes that too great pressure destroys his work. That his fingers are his servants, and must learn to obey his will and work gently, even when most eager and excited, is one of the truths that the smallest clay-pupil learns very early; though his untutored muscles may be slow in rendering the obedience.

This year the pupils of the first grade began their work in clay by modeling farm animals. Later in the spring, the horses and cows and chickens will stock a miniature farm in the school garden. The same children have made in the wood-work department the barns for this farm. The animals were modeled from plaster casts and pictures; the children were questioned as to the animals they saw on their trips to and from the school, and were asked to note the relative sizes of the different creatures, and the proportion the head and legs (as well as any peculiar or beautiful feature, as, for instance, the splendid chest of the horse) bore to the body. In November their Christmas work was begun: very simple bowl shapes to hold nuts or short-stemmed flowers, the only decoration being an opaque glaze. In January, in connection with their study of Eskimo life, these children modeled Eskimo houses in clay; then little fur-wrapped Eskimo children, with their sleds and dogs.

The second grade, early in the school year, in connection with its study of the food-supply of mankind and its transportation, modeled fruits and vegetables in clay, then the trains, wagons, and boats used in the transportation of food-stuffs. In November it began the Christmas gifts: violet vases, low fruit bowls, candlesticks of very simple design, and teapot tiles, round and square. For decoration, some simple arrangement of leaf or berry was incised in the clay; the tiles being painted in underglaze colors; the bowls and candlesticks being simply color-glazed.

The third grade, which has been studying the story of the *Odyssey,* is to model during the winter quarter a series of tiles in low relief, telling the history of Ulysses' wanderings. These tiles are afterward to be set in a frame above the black-board in the classroom.

The fourth grade devoted the earlier portion of the year to the making of vases and jardinères, using for decoration whatever plant-forms were found growing in the open at the time the jar was ready for the design: berries, seed-pods, and thorny sprays, such as could be seen in the parks and vacant squares, together with the few leaf-forms that still lingered with us. During this midwinter term the class is busy making tiles for a window-box for its classroom. These tiles are later to be joined by copper frames which the children are themselves making in the metal department.

The sixth grade has been busy with Greek history and Greek literature; and for its clay-work has studied the shapes of the

Greek vases, choosing, for decoration, motives from Greek borders. This class has had rich opportunity for the study of lines of simple dignity, and shapes of purest beauty.

The eighth grade in its history work has been tracing the origin and development of chivalry; and in its clay-work in the spring quarter will illustrate this theme in simple compositions in low relief on rectangular placques.

The fifth and seventh grades have no clay-work during the present school-year.

In the lower grades no high degree of accuracy is expected; the chief aim being to awaken a sense of proportion, and train the inexperienced fingers to obey the child's will so that his artistic impulse may find expression.

But from the fourth grade, up to the eighth, not only is more accurate craftsmanship required, but the pupil is also led to note subtle differences in lines, and to feel the charm of harmoniously varied curves; while the sheer beauty of simple, lovely forms is more fully dwelt upon.

That there is in every soul an instinctive preference for those things that are enduringly beautiful is proved again and again by the fact that in spite of the distorted and unlovely creations with which, in this commercial age, we are all surrounded, the students usually choose vase-forms of simple dignity and grace. Sometimes there is revealed a rare sensitiveness to the charm of texture, or to the pure beauty of lovely shapes. One pupil in the sixth grade gives to the surface of her vases a certain veiled quality of delicately elusive charm; while, again and again, the finer quality of appreciation is revealed in an instinctive preference for the pure shape of the jar itself, which makes the worker shrink from cutting the line of the vase by any applied decoration whatever.

ANIMALS MODELED TO STOCK A MINIATURE FARM IN THE SCHOOL GARDEN
FIRST GRADE

PLANT-FORM DECORATIONS. FOURTH GRADE

GREEK VASES MODELED IN CONNECTION WITH THE STUDY OF GREEK HISTORY
AND LITERATURE. SIXTH GRADE

THE CO-OPERATION OF THE PARK COMMISSION AND THE ELEMENTARY SCHOOL PUPILS IN PLACING BIRD-HOUSES IN THE PARK TREES

ROBERT K. NABOURS

School of Education, University of Chicago

The careful pruning to which the trees of the Chicago parks are subjected makes them entirely too open for the birds to use as nesting-places. Comparatively few of the songbirds use the park trees, and so one must go entirely outside the city limits, into the brushy areas, in order to study the birds to any extent,. or to hear their music during the nesting season. This condition, therefore, prevents many of the birds from ever visiting the parks in the numbers natural for this region, and many of those that visit us at all are here only during the most uninteresting period of their stay in this climate.

Many people have observed and deprecated the condition, and a few have done something in a small way to encourage the birds to build in their private yards by placing a few boxes up in the trees. Professor W. S. Jackman, of the School of Education Elementary School, had thought that it would be a good thing to get the school children of the city interested in this work, and agitated the question for a number of years. But it was not till the latter part of 1905 that an opportunity was found. Upon application to Superintendent Foster, of the South Park Commission, he was able to arrange for the beginning of the work to the extent of placing about three hundred wren and bluebird houses in Washington and Jackson Parks. The commission did its part well by purchasing the lumber and having it cut, and the pupils of the Elementary School finished the work. The experiment of getting the park superintendent and the children to co-operate in making the houses and placing them in the trees was entirely successful. The extent to which the birds used the houses so generously provided for them, and the further extension of the movement, only remain for the future.

The spirit in which the children went into the work, from carrying the lumber to the fourth floor, to the more pleasant part of nailing the pieces together, could be nothing less than an inspiration to even the most pessimistic. There was no complaint about the kind of work to be done. When all the hammers were in use, the four or five boys who were left volunteered to bring up the several hundred pieces from the basement with as much eagerness as if they were nailing the pieces together into the finished home. The whole point with them seemed to be to have a hand in the enterprise.

SHEPHERD SONG

Words and melody by children of the fourth school year (Grade II) University
Elementary School

1. The shep - herd watch- es his flock with care
2. He leads his flock to a past - ure green Where a

All thro' the day and night; His dog pro-tects them from
stream is flow - ing cold; And, when the sun sinks

dan - - ger, And barks with all his might.
down in the west, He drives them home to the fold.

EDITORIAL NOTES

At the meeting held in Chicago last fall, under the auspices of the School Board, to discuss ways and means of lessening truancy and delinquency, it was shown that the root causes were, in the main, three: the failure of home influence, need and want in the home, and a failure of the school to supply work which would appeal to a child as worth doing from his own point of view.

A little pamphlet issued in advance of this conference affords most interesting data on this question. It is entitled "An Intensive Study of the Causes of Truancy in Eight Chicago Public Schools, Including a Home Investigation of Eight Hundred Truant Children." The investigation was made by a Hull House worker, three members of the Visiting Nurse Association, and four members of the Compulsory Education Department of the School Board. The investigators hunted down every case of truancy, found its real cause, and relieved the cause as far as possible.

Some children were found who never had been in school, of ages ranging from eight to twelve years. There were others who had managed, through their parents' shrewdness, to evade the compulsory-education law by transferring from a public to a parochial school, and then dropping out. The summing-up of causes of absences in one school tells the story:

Indifferent parents	36
Poverty and ignorance of parents	21
Illness of child	57
Illness in family	14
Wilful truancy	15
Incorrigibles	2
Total	145

In the majority of cases of illness of the child himself it was found that the attention which could be given at school by the nurse was sufficient to enable him to stay. In other cases attention at home by the nurse reduced the period of his home-staying. Out of 209 children reported ill in one school, during the month of April, 156 were found ill, 13 were not found at all, and 40 were found to be well; while 107 children were cared for in school. These conditions are not unusual, and show plainly that the services of a trained nurse in school districts of this character are of great importance as a means of keeping a certain percentage of children in school.

Where families are too poor to pay for help in the home, and the child's labor is needed there, or when he is the only bread-winner, the recently proposed plan of founding scholarships for such cases seems to be the only way of keeping the child in school without causing greater hardship at home. This scholarship means that a sum equal to that which the child would otherwise earn is paid into the home during the time of his attendance at school. Here is another of the many ways in which surplus wealth may spend itself to the betterment of social conditions without pauperizing; for money spent in elementary aid to education can never pauperize. The following quotation from the report shows a case of extreme need:

School Pensions

Louis B.—This child of nine years, whose parents were dead, lived with his grandmother and grandfather, neither of whom could speak English. The grandfather, besides having lost an arm, was ill and unable to work; the grandmother helped the family by picking up coal and wood on the railroad tracks, and occasionally picking and selling dandelions. Though fairly strong, she was too unskilled to do any sort of profitable work. The boy, the only other member of the family, paid the rent and supported his grandparents by the sale of newspapers. This he did entirely outside of school hours, having been absent only one day during the whole year, and this day he went with his grandmother to interpret for her while she was trying to get a job picking rags on Canal Street. Louis finishes the fourth grade this year. They lived in one rear room, for which they paid two and one-half dollars a month, and which was in fair sanitary condition. It is needless to say that all the members of the family were without sufficient clothing to keep them warm and clean. What clothes the boy had were always in good repair, being generously covered with patches of different colors. He wore nothing under his little coat, not even a shirt. In the more prosperous days the family had owned a white table-cloth, which was cut up into kerchiefs to be worn around the neck of the boy to conceal the absence of the shirt. This is not cited as a case of school neglect, as the boy was doing well in school and was anxious to keep on, his ambition being to finish the school. It is plain that such a household is on a most precarious footing, and that the boy's education and future usefulness are threatened by the hard work, the insufficient food and clothing, and general scantiness of his life. A school pension for this fatherless child should be obtained. In the meantime an arrangement has been made by which the monthly expenses for rent and coal have been met. The effects of his unchildlike struggle with poverty was shown by the boy's attitude toward the new suit of clothes which was provided for him. It was a gray suit, and he objected to the color, preferring a black one because it would save a new suit in case one of his grandparents should die, an event which he thought quite likely to happen, as they were both very old.

Where children are not sent to school because of the indifference of parents, personal visits, with patient explanation, are needed; where this will not suffice, and parents are still indifferent to the claims of the school, the law provides for prosecution and a fine, which is effective.

Now we come to the last items on our list—"wilful truancy" and "incorrigibility;" and this is where the school itself must

Cure for Truancy face the defections and assume at least a part of the responsibility. It is something of an anomaly to wait until children are sent to the Parental or Reform School before giving them the kind of work that makes school seem worth while to them. Wood-work, metal-work, designing, and all forms of shop-work furnish incentive and motive to the boy in Reform or Parental School. All children need these creative occupations; but it is the boy who is either more self-willed or with less good-will who balks at a course of study in which these occupations are left out. It is he, therefore, who eventually wins what he needs, whether he knows he needs it or not.

The more even-tempered, the less explosive, the better-balanced, obedient children follow the programme offered, and merely grow up through the school with less of initiative and less social training than they would have had if brought into contact with real problems and encouraged to face practical tasks. For it happens that we are so constituted that we find joy in achievements the worth of which we ourselves can measure.

Again to quote from the report:

JIMMIE H.—A little Greek boy of eleven years, has reached the second grade only; both father and mother are educated people. They were married in Paris, where the father was employed by the Greek gov-
One Kind of ernment. Misfortune brought the family to America. When
Backwardness we first visited them, the father had been ill four months, and the family was in a state of abject poverty, the mother having sold every salable article for herself and her boy. They lived in a basement of five rooms, three of which were dark. For these rooms they paid twelve dollars a month. The boy, Jimmie, is very backward in his school-work, for which, undoubtedly, poverty and insufficient food are partly responsible. He does not give the impression at home of being a stupid child, for he is very fond of playing with a little tool-chest, and will work all day long making things with his saw and hammer. *This ability he has no opportunity of utilizing in school, and there he ranks as a backward child.*

The truant boys frankly owned for the most part a lack of interest in the school curriculum. In several instances they were
Laziness or found, not running the streets, but at home, and
Love of engaged in occupations which suggested the idea
Work—Which? that, had they an opportunity for constructive work in school, they would not have turned into truants. One boy spent his time in doing carpentry of all kinds, another milked cows and cleaned the stable and yard, both without any compulsion from their parents. This tends to confirm the impression gained from former experiences with schoolboys that they shirk school for the sake of employments more interesting.

What a testimony this is to the uselessness of offering merely formal studies to children whose strongest bent is toward concrete activities! In our endeavor to make the curriculum so broad that they may be fitted for anything, are we fitting them for nothing? We say, and truly, that the elementary schools should not aim to train a wage-working class simply for artisan work; but it has been demonstrated again and again that children can get a general culture and instruction in the formal knowledge of reading, writing, and arithmetic, by and with work on concrete problems. These problems are found in construction work of all sorts; and the virtue that is in them cannot be replaced by dealing with motiveless abstractions.

A good story comes from the principal of the Jewish Manual Training School. Mr. Milliken was sitting in his office one day, when an officer came in with a boy who had been **Indirect Methods** sent there by the judge of the Juvenile Court. The boy had been an incorrigible truant, was in his fourteenth year, and would neither stay in school nor learn anything while there. The judge had decided to try the effectiveness of a large proportion of manual work. Doubtless he would have been surprised at the mode of initiation which followed:

"Well, so you don't like to go to school?"

"Nope."

"What's the matter with school?"

"Nothin' in it."   .

"Well, do you think you'll like this school?"

"Nope."

"Don't want to try it, eh?"

"Don't think I'll like it."

"What do you like to do?"

"Nothin'."

"Ever try to make anything?"

"Nope, never tried that."

"Well, my boy, you got here this morning on time, at least, and that's something. Now I'll tell you what I'll do. You need not do anything here if you don't want to. Just come here with me, and I'll show you a nice comfortable place where you can watch other people work. You'll like that, perhaps."

"Well you just bet I do—nothing better!"

So the head of the school picked up an easy office chair, carried it to the wood-working shop, and deposited it in a sunny corner. Here the boy was ensconced, with the injunction to make himself comfortable as long as he liked. The next day the principal came around to where he sat.

"Say, this is swell."

"You like that, do you?"

"Like it! Why, it's the softest thing I ever struck."

After having tasted the sweets of ease for three days, the boy was seized with a desire to make something that was wanted at home. This wish was indulged, and very soon it became necessary to do a little measuring. Measuring meant some arithmetical procedure, which came very toilsomely, but was achieved finally with the assistance of the teacher of the arithmetic class. His immediate problem solved, the boy decided to go on in the arithmetic class. Another piece of work was begun in the shop, and in the course of this a book of designs and descriptions was offered to help him to make a choice of pattern. Obstacle no. two: he could not read well enough to find out what he wanted. His kind friend, the principal, again solicited a place for him in a reading-class. Again the boy decided to stay on in it after he was in possession of the particular printed facts that his shop-work called for. According to the chronicler of these events, it took the boy about three weeks to take upon himself a full scholastic curriculum in addition to his shop-work. All of which he kept up for the year of his stay, which ended in his going to work.

These revelations of the relation between truancy and a lack of constructive occupation have resulted in an experiment. This experiment is the establishment of industrial rooms for boys of the intermediate grades in some of the public schools. It is in these middle grades that the desire to roam and explore seems to conquer the boy's supposed thirst for knowledge. These rooms are not in any sense branches of a reform school, but are intended to offer such a combination of manual work and formal instruction as will make the bond stronger between the restive boy and the school. The success of this experiment will depend, not only on the inherent charm of productive work, but also on the sagacity and tact of the teachers assigned to this charge.

Another Experiment

The natural docility of girls, as compared with that of boys, keeps them from committing the same rebellious acts, and hence the powers that be are not forced to give them the same advantages—a condition which has gained for boys always much that would otherwise have never been thought of for them, and is now not thought of for the girls, because not demanded. But it is well to state right here that what is needed by the boys is quite as imperatively needed for the girls, and would lead to the desired result of making better-equipped and less frivolous women.   B. P.

BOOKS RECEIVED

AMERICAN BOOK CO., CHICAGO

Little Stories of Germany. By MAUDE BARROWS DUTTON. Preface by F. LOUIS SOLDAN. Cloth, 12mo. Illustrated. Pp. 192. $0.40.

Nature Study on the Farm. By CHARLES A. KEFFER. Cloth, 12mo. Illustrated. Pp. 154. $0.40.

Jingle Primer. By CLARA L. BROWN and CAROLYN S. BAILEY. Cloth, 12mo. Illustrated. Pp. 128. $0.30.

GINN & CO., CHICAGO

Earth and Sky. By J. H. STICKNEY. Cloth, 12mo. Illustrated. Pp. 128. $0.30.

With Pencil and Pen. By SARAH LOUISE ARNOLD. Cloth, 12mo. Illustrated. Pp. 127. $0.35.

A Second Reader. By CELIA and HARRIET ESTELLE RICHMOND. Cloth, 12mo. Illustrated. Pp. 134. $0.40.

LAIRD & LEE, CHICAGO

Modern Penmanship. By C. L. RICKETTS and G. F. HERHOLD. Board covers, cloth back, stamped in two colors, $0.60 ; seal-brown cloth, gold stamping, $1. Illustrated. Pp. 96.

LITTLE, BROWN & CO., BOSTON

Daniel Webster for Young Americans. By CHARLES F. RICHARDSON. Cloth, 12mo. Pp. 216.

EDUCATIONAL PUBLISHING CO., CHICAGO

Drawing with Colored Crayons. By D. R. AUGSBURG. Illustrated. Pp. 64.

SILVER, BURDETT & CO., CHICAGO

Guide Books to English. Books I, II. By CHARLES B. GILBERT and ADA VAN STONE HARRIS. Cloth, 12mo. Illustrated. Book I, pp. 307, $0.45. Book II, pp. 366. $0.60.

FOR SALE: A limited number of copies of *Nature Study* by Wilbur S. Jackman, late of the Chicago Normal School and of the University of Chicago Elementary School. For parent, teacher, or student. $1 postpaid. Address MRS. W. S. JACKMAN, 7006 Perry Ave., Chicago.

VOLUME VII   NUMBER 10

THE ELEMENTARY SCHOOL TEACHER

JUNE, 1907

THE UNIVERSITY ELEMENTARY SCHOOL

INTRODUCTION

The University Elementary School, with the University High School, is the laboratory of the School of Education. Here educational theories are tested, and educational problems are developed. Consequently the organization of the school must be such as to give to its pupils the greatest opportunity for a healthy, normal growth.

In order that the children may work as individuals, rather than as a mass, the school is divided into comparatively small groups. Usually there are sixteen pupils working together. The small group tends to develop power of initiative, thoughtfulness, and intelligent co-operation with others, instead of blind obedience. It is believed that only by a social organization of the work of the school can a social spirit be developed.

The curriculum is planned to direct the creative activities of the children, and therefore a large place is given to the social occupations, work in the most fundamental of the handicrafts. These occupations give experience, as well as knowledge, and cultivate an active attitude toward learning in place of the passive attitude characteristic of schools conducted according to older theories of education. There are well-equipped workshops for woodwork, clay-modeling, textiles, cooking, metal-work, printing, and bookbinding. A large school garden furnishes an out-of-door workshop of great importance. The ordinary school-rooms have desks that are not fastened to the floor, and they are regarded as workshops as well as study-rooms.

If the handwork of this school were given without relation to nature-study, geography, history, and literature, it would lose much of its significance, but these older subjects of the curriculum are considered as not less important in this school than they have been in the past. It is not handwork in itself that is of value, but handwork which is done with an intelligent understanding of its scientific and social background. The problems which arise in work at school and at home, everywhere in the daily life, should drive the children to books for their solution. Study based upon experience is done with the desire for knowledge in order that it may be used. This motive is productive of better results, even in the gaining of knowledge, than the motive of learning lessons set by the teachers, and it trains the children to habits of independent and vigorous thinking.

It is the aim of this school to develop such skill in reading, writing, and other forms of technic, as is needed for the purpose of expression of thought. If every advantage is taken of the needs of the children for the use of these various forms, they usually acquire the necessary skill. However, wherever skill fails to keep pace with thought, this is taken as an indication that drill must be given upon the mechanical processes.

Since play is of as great importance as work in the child's life, play is so directed as to give it its full value. Care of the physical well-being of the children is made the first consideration.

The school endeavors to secure right conduct from the pupils through such an organization of work and recreation as cultivates habits of thoughtfulness and industry. Its tests of success are to be found not in mere knowledge, important as this is, but in the intelligent application of knowledge, and in the ability to use it for social ends.

HISTORY

History regarded as the study of social life begins with the first school year. Its purpose is to deepen the child's consciousness of the meaning of his own activities and relations, rather than to give him a fund of information about the past. With this motive in view, the material selected for each year's work is closely related to present experience, and the problems of the past are presented as far as possible in such a manner as to make them vital questions of the present. Gradually the children should be led to appreciate their place in a wider and wider circle of social relations.

While children in the lower grades are in contact with the complex forms of modern society, they are able to appreciate very little of what they see. Their own activities are of the simplest kind, and it is only the beginnings of industrial and economic processes that they can understand. For this reason the early history work centers around the evolution of the most fundamental processes, those of obtaining food, clothing, and shelter in primitive ways. In such history lessons there is a constant interplay of the child's activities and the activities of the past. He interprets the past in terms of his own experience, and he learns the meaning of his own experience by seeing it in its relations to the experiences of others.

The early settlements of our own country furnish material which in complexity is a step in advance of primitive industrial history, and which is in many ways well adapted to the needs of the middle grades. The biographies of the pioneers satisfy the love of adventure strong in this period. The story of their struggles with their environment organizes for the children the relations of geography and history. The habit of tracing the causes which underlie the movements of events is the one of most importance to cultivate. Here, as in the earlier work, the emphasis is upon the quality of thinking rather than upon the quantity of information.

The evolution of American history from the time of the earliest pioneers illustrates the steps in the development of modern conditions in social and political life. This story is suitable in its simplest forms for the upper classes of the elementary school and should be completed in the high school.

While the core of our course of study in history is found, as outlined here, in the story of our own country, it is intended that this story shall be placed in its proper perspective. The horizon of the children is widened by studies of European history which give background to subjects from American history. They thus have an opportunity to see that our nation is but carrying on the development of ideas and ideals which had their beginnings with other nations, and that our welfare and enjoyment are the result of what other people have wrought out for us by patient and heroic effort. Fairness in judgment and freedom from prejudice should be the results of this work.

In the social occupations of the school, the children come into contact with the materials and forces of nature, and many problems arise in regard to the ways in which these have been utilized in the past. The plan in history takes this fact into account and is in close relation to the occupations. Many problems which have been suggested in the workshop are solved in the history lessons. In this way the evolution of the industrial arts is made a part of the subject-matter of the course and the interest in construction is added to that in history. Often ideas that are developed in history are carried out in constructive ways, and the children are helped to form the habit of putting thought into action. The history course gives a social background with its larger significance to the handwork of the children, and it gains for itself the advantage of application to the immediate problems of life.

The aims of this course in history are primarily the cultivation of an appreciation of social life and the ability to meet social responsibilities.

GEOGRAPHY

The aim of the work in geography is to aid the student in gaining power to interpret his physical and social environment. The ability to understand his surroundings is obtained through a study of the physical forces which have shaped and are shaping the earth's surface and are determining its life; and through an appreciation of man's response to his physical and social surroundings. Opportunity is given even to the young children to observe the results of the work of the great forces of nature, and, when possible, to see these forces in action. This is done through field-trips to the country within a radius of thirty miles of the school. The work of waves, wind, rivers, and glaciers is well illustrated within the above limits.

Through gardening and visits to farms a touch of the fundamental industry of agriculture is gained; and through visits to the manufacturing centers an appreciation of man's control and use of natural materials and physical forces is obtained. The knowledge gained in the study of the building of this city becomes the basis for the understanding of all urban populations; the imported materials, both natural and manufactured, and the foreign peoples, if traced to their origin, lead to all the countries of the world.

The proper study of foreign peoples in relation to their physical and social environment develops a sympathetic appreciation of their relative position in the world's families of nations. It also affords an opportunity to see our own people from the view-point of the foreigner, thus broadening our horizon, placing our virtues in a rational perspective, and giving a consciousness of our faults, which is the first step toward correction and improvement.

The germ of interest in processes is nurtured from the beginning by simple experiments and explanations. This interest grows until in the fourth and fifth grades its satisfaction leads to the study of many of the simple phases of physiographic processes that are more fully developed by the older children.

During the elementary-school period the children are alive to all knowledge, regardless of utilitarian values which for the most part dominate the adult. This is the time to bring them into contact, as far as possible, with the various phases of the earth and the heavens.

In the early grades, from the first to the fourth, when interest in causal relations does not carry the pupils far from simple picturing of conditions, the children gain fundamental geographic imagery of type regions through a study of primitive peoples living in regions of extreme geographic control, as the Eskimo or Chukches of the Arctic regions, a Brazilian Indian tribe in the tropics, the Arabs in the desert, the Norwegians in the mountains, and the Indians of the plains. Through stories of travel the earth is circumnavigated, resulting in the discovery of the continents and seas.

The ideas gained in the earlier grades are organized and expanded above the fourth grade by the study of continental land-masses, islands, and seas. North America is studied as a type, in its aspects of human control and simple physiographic expressions; South America, as a tropical continent; Eurasia, as the home of civilization; Africa, as the continent of present colonization; Australia and New Zealand, as seats of important civic experiments.

The fundamental geographic principles and to a great extent the type-imagery are repeated in the study of each continent, thus giving the desired review of important ideas related to new situations.

Current events are always a source of vital interest and lead to a survey of various parts of the earth. They also furnish a needed review of the world, for memory retains in strong definition little that is not in constant use.

When the nature of the unknown can be realized by such experience, all problems arising in the study of geography are solved by experimentation. To this end a laboratory has been constructed where running water, rain, and waves may be controlled in action upon sand. The garden and the physical and chemical laboratories are also called into requisition in the solution of geographic problems.

NATURE-STUDY

The aim of nature-study is to keep the children in touch with the larger aspects of nature, through the school garden, the care of flowers, shrubs, and vines on the school grounds, and field trips to various interesting regions within the Chicago area. It is believed that this contact acquaintance with nature-phenomena and materials during the early period of childhood reacts strongly by deepening and enriching the whole emotional life, and that out of this experience gradually evolve the true intellectual interests of the child's more mature school life. The varied char-

PREPARING THE BEES FOR WINTER. THIRD GRADE

GYMNASTICS. THE BOYS

acter and content of our local landscape determine the range of our nature-experiences. The seasons and their accompanying changes direct the movement of the study. This great picture of the landscape and its seasonal changes when presented through its panoramic aspects becomes a subject with those dramatic elements which are so strong in their hold upon the imagination of the children. Much attention is given to drawing and painting, which offer, perhaps, the best means of recording these changes and of stimulating interest in nature. The detailed problems relating to minerals, soils, plants, and animal life, growing out of this field experience, are worked out in classroom and laboratory.

In addition to these direct experiences, nature-study finds a practical application in many of the other studies of the school. It opens up endless resources of materials worked over in designs used in the various crafts. Those aspects of nature-study which fall under the head of "applied science" are of especial interest. In cooking, in the dyeing of textiles, in mechanics, and especially in the application of electricity, the interest is great and persistent.

With our progress toward a truer understanding of the biological and psychological laws of human development, we are seeing more clearly that education, that is, development, while depending upon subject, is still more dependent upon the interest and initiative of the individual; and in the light of this knowledge it is beyond the need of demonstration that nature-study exists in the school as a necessary character-building force.

<hr>

HOME-ECONOMICS

Home-economics includes the subjects of food, shelter, and clothing. In the University Elementary School a study of shelter and clothing is made in different years as part of the work in history and textiles, so that the chief topic of home-economics, except in the last year, is food—its preparation, serving, composition, nutritive value, and purity—with the science problems that are involved in its study, and the related work in number, reading, writing, geography, and history.

The work is so planned that during the course the children become familiar with all the ordinary processes of cookery and with the different food principles. They gain skill in the combination of food materials and some knowledge of the composition and nutritive value of food. That this knowledge and skill are carried over into the home and practically applied is shown by experience. The lunches served from time to time are planned to develop in the children both the spirit of hospitality and grace in extending it.

In the earlier years cooking is considered chiefly a social activity, and finds its justification in its contribution to the social life of the school and in its relation to the home. It is so closely connected with the everyday life of the children that it makes a strong appeal to their interests. Largely because of this interest the number, reading, and writing constantly demanded by the work are handled more easily by the children than where there is a less definite motive for it.

In the upper grades the scientific aspect of the work is uppermost. Problems in physics, in chemistry, and in botany are constantly suggested by the processes that are carried on, and are discussed in their simpler aspects or solved by such experiments as are within the grasp of the children. Many experiments are necessary in working out the proportions or methods to be used in the preparation of different foods, and these, though not always dealing with the subject-matter of the sciences, involve the scientific method and develop a scientific attitude. In some years the work in other sciences is reinforced, since it is approached from a different point of view. In others some phase of history or of geography is illustrated and emphasized by the cooking. In the last year both the study of the house and the work with food adulterations, while essentially applied science, belong also to civics, since their direct aim is the development of a sense of social responsibility.

MATHEMATICS

The distinguishing trait of children of the kindergarten and first grade is a hunger for sensations—an all-consuming *curiosity*.

They reach out in every direction and through every avenue of sense for materials to gratify this curiosity. Their spontaneous impulses are to see, to play, to talk, to act, and to "try out" every way of acquiring sensations about things. There is but little reflection as yet and almost no disposition to weigh and pass judgment on the relative values of these external stimuli. Among the objects of their interest are the "whats" of concrete mathematics.

This is the period of *sense-perception* mathematics. *Experiential* arithmetic, i. e., actual measuring and counting of things, and *attuitional* or *purely observational* geometry, with little or no reference to the ulterior purposes of the work, are valuable and pleasurable here. The work is made incidental and contributory to the games, constructive exercises, and rhythmic activities of the children. Only such notation is given as is needed to facilitate recording the children's own findings. The aim is to secure many germinal ideas of arithmetical number and its combinations, and many image cores for later enrichment into geometrical concepts.

Second- and third-grade children manifest a marked desire for *efficiency*. They are no longer merely curious. They now desire to do well what they attempt. They are critical not only of their own degree of skill in doing, but also of the worth of results. Work that does not demand so high a standard of excellence as they feel capable of attaining cannot long hold their interest or attention. The pupil here craves only such knowledge as will enable him to do better what *he* deems worth doing. He is willing to submit to drill, if he feels that it will heighten his skill in ways that are worthy. He is self-centered, measuring all things, both efforts and results, by their value to himself. Social problems and interests appeal to him as yet but feebly.

Mathematical work must now make stronger and more systematic demands upon the attention and effort of the pupil. Knowledge is now of value to him because, and in so far as, he can use it. The useful is to him whatever will make him able to understand better and to deal more intelligently with problems having to do with food, clothing, and shelter. Problems of the grocer, the butcher, the baker, the merchant, etc., as they impinge upon home activities and interests, seem real and valuable to him. Such problems as those arising out of the school industries are used here to impress the pupils with the need for the tabular machinery of arithmetic—to lead him to see that he must learn the tables if he will become skilful in his work. The tables are built geometrically and the work of learning them is well advanced by the end of the third grade.

The chief working capital of children of the fourth and fifth grades is *industry*. Self-centered estimates are still dominant, but matters of social concern are awakening. Drill has become to them a need and a pleasure, and all they need is the opportunity and direction. They are now much more influenced by others' estimates of what is worth learning than they were formerly. The opinions of their parents, teachers, and school-fellows are now of worth to them. They reflect much more than heretofore on the consequences of learning and skilful doing. They are not averse to some generalizing. Many important truths can now be reached by them by the aid of inductive procedure.

Problems dealing not only with matters which touch community life in a large way, but also growing out of industrial history and commercial geography, which gather about the study of the growth and condition of the nation, constitute the main source of the mathematical subject-matter for these grades. The multiplication table, much factoring, and short division are done in the fourth grade; while long division, the fundamental processes applied to fractional number, and a beginning in the formal study of decimals, together with many mensuration truths, are given in the fifth grade.

Fractions are used, informally, as occasion calls for them from the first grade, but their formal mastery is undertaken in the fifth grade. Throughout the grades such use is made of letters for numbers as will aid in arithmetical generalizations, and such use of geometry is made as will illuminate the arithmetic. A very considerable body of geometrical truth is worked out in the fifth grade in the teaching of fractions and in mensuration. Scale drawing is also taught.

The chief agency that is available for teaching children of the sixth and seventh grades is their interest in *achievement*. Most of all, they desire to accomplish results that they can see. To maintain permanence of interest in educational work they must be allowed to carry through their undertakings. They cannot here long endure disappointment and failure in their efforts. Success is the sunlight needed to bring out their educable qualities. The executive faculties of the soul now possess them. They care only for such knowledge as is power for them. Their power of concentration has grown to a stage in which they desire to remain with a subject or topic until they have made an appreciable point—until they have accomplished something definite. The topical mode of study is now the only successful one with them. The so-called spiral method is now antiquated. Experimental methods are effective with them only when the experiment leads to a successful issue—to a positive outcome. Their problems in experimentation must eventuate in affirmative answers, rather than in negatives.

The mathematical work now consists mainly in applying the knowledge gained to such questions in valuation as are called for in the more technical business activities of American communities. The topics called for in mathematics are percentage and interest, and their applications in discount, profit and loss, commission, taxes, insurance, and the experimental and metrical geometry of the builders' trade. These topics, of course, demand a knowledge of decimal fractions, and this subject, together with compound numbers, is given a formal treatment in the sixth grade. Factoring is kept up through both grades, and a special feature of the work is "short cuts" for economy and methods of checking, not for accuracy, as is generally urged, but for *independence* and *self-reliance*. Percentage is applied to problems in nature-study, geography, mensuration and not to money problems, exclusively. Topical studies from commercial geography and industrial history are made a feature of the work of these grades, and graphs are extensively used. Scale drawing is continued.

Eighth-grade pupils manifest with marked emphasis *self-consciousness, diligence,* and a disposition to have regard for *social standards.* What grown-up people talk about and occupy themselves with appeals to them now as never before. They are looking forward and outward upon life with a feeling of personal interest in what is ahead as well as in what now is. They realize that some preparation for future duty and responsibility is worth their while. They desire to know how to bring their knowledge to bear upon the real questions of life. They are ready and able to work under motives more remote than appealed to them formerly. They are looking forward to employment or to the high school with a genuine interest and concern. The drill period is now well past and reason is strongly operative. They are ready for work of both an inductive and a deductive nature. In short, they are beginning to feel themselves to be little men and women. They are anxious to gather together and to get under control for use the knowledge and skill they have been acquiring.

In mathematics, the eighth grade reviews common and decimal fractions with especial reference to the discovery of mathematical truths, and carries forward the applications of percentage and interest to more difficult questions. Some graphing of the laws of percentage and interest is given. Mensuration and metrical geometry are extended, through the use of algebraic number to denote dimensions, or parts, of geometrical figures. Some attention is given to the graphing of statistical data, and square and cube root are new topics in this grade. Much indirect measurement, or geometrical surveying, and considerable work on similar triangles, are given. This work is always closely correlated with the regular work of the grade. When time admits, a "bowing acquaintance," at least, is made with common logarithms and their use.

Through the study of type-problems, through much summarizing and generalizing, the eighth-grade work gives both an easy working control of what has been learned and a firm, rational basis for the work of the high school. The concept of signed number is worked into the pupil's possession, by informal uses, beginning as early as the sixth grade, and gradually passing in the eighth grade into the formal uses in algebra. No systematic technique for either algebra or geometry is undertaken in the eighth grade. What is attempted here is a rational, conceptual basis in arithmetical number for high-school mathematics.

***

LANGUAGES

English.—The work of the school in English includes training in expression through language, and cultivation of an appreciation of literature. Since language implies thought to be expressed, it is impossible to consider it without taking into account all the other interests of the children. Language in the school is therefore used as an aid to accurate thought in all the subjects of study and as a means of organizing knowledge. Here, as in the arts and occupations, there is an opportunity for a co-ordinate development of thought and expression.

The earlier work is chiefly oral, and, as the children gain in ability to write, the amount of written work increases. Whereever there is a genuine need for writing, that is, a necessity for conveying thought to others, the children put forth their best efforts, and in such work they gain rapidly in skill. Writing done merely as an exercise fails to secure good results, either in spirit or in form.

The value of literature in presenting ideals of life and appealing to the emotional and spiritual nature cannot fail of recognition in any school. It is true that ideals of conduct have in themselves no saving grace, and the school which would cultivate right habits in its pupils must give them not only ideals but also opportunities to act in accordance with those ideals. However, ideals stimulate to right action and, given proper expression, refine and elevate the character.

In the kindergarten, the literature is rhymes, jingles, verse, and story, carefully selected. Much freedom is allowed in dramatic expression, and special attention is given to accuracy in spoken language.

In the first and second grades, the study of verse and story continues, with drills in phonics and the rudiments of reading and writing.

Beginning with the third grade, longer stories give opportunity for greater continuity of thought. Around one of the great hero tales or cycle stories—for instance, that of Ulysses or Siegfried—the literature of each grade groups itself. The study of stories and poems continues. It is thought that these years are those best adapted to the gaining of skill, and in the middle grades the children give much attention to the technic of oral reading and written expression.

In both the seventh and eighth grades formal grammar is studied, and in the eighth alone the study of the literary drama is begun.

The pupils of the school are publishing monthly a magazine, *The School Reporter.* They themselves do all the work and meet the financial obligations. The special value to the school of this interest lies in its effect upon the work in English.

Speech, oral reading, and dramatic art.—It is the aim of this work, first, to bring about freedom and expressiveness of voice and body; clearness, distinctness, and beauty of speech—good spoken English—by training the ear to hear, and the speech organs to form, well-shaped vowels and distinct, clear-cut consonants; second, to train the children to read intelligently and with a purpose; and to read aloud simply and naturally, with a clear perception of meaning, emotional content, and form. This will be done through the interpretation of literature, by means of extemporaneous speaking, and by the writing and acting of original dramas. Whenever possible, the literature being studied in English, French, and German is utilized for these purposes. The aim throughout is so to organize both the study and expression that the children shall acquire, not only independence in the use of reference books and literature, and freedom and spontaneity in expression, but also ability to think and do—that persistence and continuity of thinking which enables them to handle new material—new literature—with intelligence, purpose, and increased power.

With the majority of children real, living interest in reading seems to develop rapidly about the fourth year of school life. If up to this time the background has been well filled in by the constant functioning of words when the child felt the greatest pressure for their use, he has a key to the situation. Technical difficulties are mastered under the new impulse with marvelous ease and skill. By the time he reaches the ninth school year he not only can read for his own pleasure and entertainment, but also has developed gradually a definite motive for reading, and is able to use books intelligently in the study of subject-matter.

The organized social life of the school, the daily morning meetings, the special-day exercises, and the festivals of the year give motive and opportunity for practice in oral and dramatic expression.

With the purpose of laying the foundation of an abiding love for what is noble and beautiful in our literature, the teacher interprets a limited number of suitable selections to the children which they can understand and enjoy, but cannot read for themselves.

It is the aim to note every speech-defect, to watch the child, and, at the proper time, to give him the necessary help toward overcoming his defect.

French.—The acquisition of the French language in the Elementary School is not sought as an end in itself. The language of a people embodies their spirit. To learn French is to know the spirit of its speakers, and to be eager to know all that concerns and expresses them, their manners, their customs, their literature.

The study of French is begun in the sixth school year. The folk-lore of France, beginning with the simplest occupations of family life, forms the basis for the study of language. The singing of rounds and songs, the playing of historic games, and simple dramatic representations are activities suited to childhood. *"Play is the poetry of childhood."* In the play the little American and the little Frenchman feel alike and thus are united. *"L'enfant qui joue m'est sacré; je vois en lui l'homme travaillant à se rendre digne de sa destinée."*

In play the child feels the need of a large vocabulary with which to express ideas that are real to him. Furthermore, the constant repetition made necessary in the playing and singing of the rounds and songs is the best training for the ear to hear the foreign language, and a most natural and excellent drill in pronunciation.

The following are a few of the games and rounds characteristic of the French people: "Le cache-objet," "Le cri des animaux," "Le pont Lévis," "Le jeu de fruits," "Le gastronome," "Il était une bergère"—shepherd life; "Sur le pont d'Avignon" —buildings, customs; "Avoine, Avoine, Avoine"—sowing and reaping; "La tour prend garde," "Malbrough s'en-va-t-en guerre"—war; "Au clair de la lune," "Quand Biron voulut danser"—dress; "Qu'est-ce-que passe ici si tard?"—chivalry; etc.

Following and almost in connection with these games and rounds, stories and plays are taken up. Dramatic methods are used for several reasons. The strength of dramatic appeal is great because of its wide range—the stimulus coming through the eye, the ear, and the muscles. The close attention which comes from the pupil's interest and absorption in dramatic work is the strongest foe of self-consciousness. In no other way can such vivid impressions, both historical and linguistic, be produced. And finally, through dramatic dialogue idiomatic phrases can be most readily and naturally learned. The following are a few of the plays that have already been represented in the school: *Noël, Les Vendanges, St. François d'Assisi, Charlemagne, Guillaume, le Conquérant, La Salle, Versailles, Louis XVI, Lafayette en Amérique*, etc.

Throughout the writing, memorizing, and acting of the play careful attention is given to the memorizing of grammatical forms, but the effort is made to make this part of the work incidental, and to lay emphasis on *substance*. A breath of life enters the dry bones of grammatical construction when the lessons are the outcome of a real need. The plays are based upon French festivals, events in French history, and things characteristic of the French people. The rich, picturesque kind of history involves the study of manners, customs, appropriate settings, and national music. The child, having lived for a time in a community other than his own, should have that sympathetic interest which makes the narrowness of provincialism impossible, and which broadens, enabling him to comprehend more fully his fellowmen.

German.—It is the aim in teaching German in the grades, to give the children as large a vocabulary as possible, to enable them to use this vocabulary, to give them a good pronunciation and a fair understanding of the spoken language, and above all to make the German language a living thing to them. That is, this new subject must enter into their lives; they must realize that there are children who feel and talk and play as they, although they speak German. This aim may be reached in different ways.

In the earlier years the German must stand for everyday occurrences and actions, or for ideas in which children are especially interested and which they fully understand. It is perfectly safe, however, to go back, as far as thought is concerned, two or three years. For instance, sixth-year children are delighted to learn rhymes, etc., the thought of which really belongs to the kindergarten age. Another means of making the language real is the correlating of the German with other subjects. This is being done whenever deemed profitable. A third way is the use of plays. A play surrounds the children with the natural condition of the language, and is therefore the best substitute for a sojourn in a foreign country. Moreover, the frequent repetition of phrases, which is the best possible training for the ear, loses in a play all of its monotony because of the intense dramatic interest. It is hardly necessary to mention that subjects of plays given to children for the purpose of learning a language should be taken from the realm of children's ideas. That is, the children must represent what foreign children of their age in a foreign land would do. They must not use language expressing ideas which are foreign to them, for then again the language becomes unreal.

ART

Introduction.—The modern educator regards aesthetic development as neither more nor less than a part of the social problem of the age. A peculiarly decadent period has resulted from the rapid transition to the factory system. Among both the rich and the poor is apparent the need for standards which demand character, honesty, and simplicity in the materials of home and civic life. This universal lack denotes ignorance, an ignorance which reformers have attributed to the fact that the new order of things has deprived society of valuable educative agents. The home and village industries of the past made universal the consciousness of the meaning of construction and the qualities and limitations of material. Elaboration represented real rather than fictitious labor—the labor of love joyfully given to dignify and enhance the value of a worthy object. The carpenter, the weaver, and the smith were artists in their way, and the artist was all of these. In this great period the fine arts have marked the climax of a growth which drew its nourishment from the soil of the common industrial life.

There is but one way in which these fundamental truths can be handed on to the men and women of today. The school must supply social deficiencies. It must afford experience similar to that in which the human family has by slow steps come into possession of its technical and aesthetic standards. Pottery, textiles, metal-working, and woodworking are crafts which have most universally contributed to this development.

Art-training which attempts only the pictorial interpretation of human interests does not adequately meet its responsibilities. Art education should include the making-over of raw material into technically well-constructed and beautiful products. It must put meaning into the term "decorative construction," as well as "decorated."

The Art Course in the Elementary School is organized with this end in view. The crafts form the basis of design. The use in this capacity of clay, textile fabric, metal, or wood is governed by the character of the aesthetic contribution of each, as well as by the ability and interests of the children.

In order to gain the degree of control necessary to the realization of experience such as indicated, these crafts must be developed in an orderly way and continued through a number of years. It follows that they would parallel each other in many ways. There are certain stages in the evolution of every craft when it does for the individual what the others cannot do as well. These special contributions seem to be about as follows:

Clay through a plastic medium encourages creative effort and gives opportunity for the instinctive play with material which leads to the beginning of decoration. Textiles develop a consciousness of proportion, of color intensities and color values, and establish a rational basis for such formality as the naturalistic assumes when in terms of a concrete material it is adapted to a decorative purpose.

Metal, offering greater resistance, stimulates an interest in technical skill. It enlarges the ideal of good workmanship.

Wood shares with metal, pottery, and even with textiles, in certain content values, but it seems to make its greatest and most distinctive aesthetic contribution rather late in the elementary course. This contribution is the consciousness of the scientific principles of mechanics. It is the last of the sequence of experiences by which the child passes from the free play of barbarism to a form of expression which is architectonic. This sequence forms a background against which the man of today is able to interpret the machine.

A detailed statement of the art course is included in the group outlines. It is only necessary in concluding these remarks to summarize the technical sequence in design.

By technic is meant the control of material and the ever-increasing consciousness of the elements which enter into a structural and visual art. From the standpoint of mental development and art development it seems to proceed about as follows: (1) Rhythmic expression through free play and experimentation (in clay); (2) the naturalistic unit as a symbol of associated ideas. Through the limitations of weaving the interest is transferred to the unit as a decorative element; (3) color, dark and light, as in textiles or pottery; (4) proportion, form, shape relations, as in pottery, metal, wood, textiles, or bookbinding; (5) mechanical principles of construction. The harmonious co-ordination of technic and aesthetic qualities the ideal of industrial art.

Drawing and painting.—For the work in drawing and painting in the Elementary School, water-color paints, charcoal, and pencil are used.

In the selection of subjects there is a close connection with the interests arising in the school, as is indicated in the outlines for each year. In this is offered the opportunity to enrich by expression in form and color the impressions of a particular subject in the curriculum, and this expression involves special technical and general aesthetic improvement.

Close analytic study of models, which can be carried on with older students, is not generally possible with those in the elementary groups, but there is developed an appreciation of the aesthetic attitude of mind toward the subject to be represented.

In dealing pictorially with the subjects suggested in the outlines, the emphasis is placed on the technical and aesthetic phases which are within the grasp of the pupil at the time. Through this emphasis there is possible a growth in the power of visualization and muscular control in recording these observations. Aesthetic motives become dominant factors in the selection and arrangement of the subject in the pictorial panel. With the younger children, frequent change in the subject to be expressed pictorially is desirable, and interest in the subject may well dominate. Children in the older groups, however, are not only able to retain a prolonged interest in a given subject for such art expression, but also prefer such an opportunity. Accompanying this is an interest in the technique itself and a growth in aesthetic feeling which leads to realization of the conventions of pictorial art, and of its existence as a thing apart from the subject which inspired it.

Clay-modeling.—As a medium for art expression, clay seems almost ideal for the children of the lower grades. It is easily manipulated and renders possible a great deal of free expression without involving the troublesome problem of perspective. It is therefore used most extensively in the first four grades, serving as a medium in which are recorded observations made in the field and impressions of incidents in history and literature which especially appeal to the imagination.

A GROUP IN WOODWORKING

A GROUP IN CLAY-MODELING

The pottery which is made in the lower grades is the simplest unglazed ware and is decorated, if at all, with nothing more complicated than a rhythmic arrangement of some unit of ornament.

The making of vases, flower-pots, and other articles needed in the school, since it has a social value, serves to put the children in touch, in a very vital way, with the history of the evolution of the industrial arts as well as to furnish an opportunity for the development of the aesthetic sense.

In the upper grades the making of pottery becomes a serious study of applied design, involving the problems of shaping an object which shall serve the purpose for which it is made, of planning an ornament which shall be suitable for this shape, and of arranging a harmonious color-scheme for the object as a whole.

For the study of the figure in the upper grades a living model is used, and an effort is made to help the children in solving the technical problems which arise in the more elaborate compositions without depriving them of the freedom which they have had in the lower grades as to the choice of subject, etc.

Textiles.—The subject of Textiles in the Elementary School covers the study of clothing and household fabrics, and deals with them from the standpoints of economics, hygiene, history, geography, and design.

The object of the study is to give children experience in the textile arts of spinning, dyeing, weaving, basketry, and sewing, and to so relate that experience to lessons in history, geography, biography, and design as to give the subject its fullest educational value.

All work done is social in its character, that is, it is to fill genuine social need which is recognized and felt by the worker; it also is planned in such a way as to call for the exercise of the children's individual taste and initiative.

Regarding clothing and home-making as subjects of fundamental race importance, it is hoped through the years of continuously related training to give to the children skill and taste in the crafts; logical sense of textile arts as race activities; an appreciation of the work done in them, and an intelligent understanding of the workers who have wrought results in these arts.

In the kindergarten and the first and second grades, the textile work is connected with the making of playhouses, and consists in the study of colors, proportions, and qualities of rugs, curtains, and portières for the different rooms. It calls for weaving, dyeing, study of fabrics; classification of four different fibers and fabrics made from each, and discussion of the clothing of different plants and animals as well as of peoples of different climates.

In these grades also there are braiding and weaving of baskets, mats, bags, and small hammocks of primitive materials collected by the children themselves; discovery of primitive processes in spinning and weaving, as well as invention of primitive spindles and looms.

In the third grade there are the designing and making of a bag or other useful article in cross-stitch.

One-quarter of the fourth year is spent in sewing, in which are taught a little of cutting from a pattern; use of scissors and thimble; holding of needle and thread; care of materials; selvedge; basting; running; hemming; joining of tapes.

The articles made are simple and for immediate use—towels, aprons, or bags.

During three-quarters of the fifth year two periods a week are spent in working out more advanced methods of spinning and weaving; dyeing of materials; weaving of small articles on hand frames, and rag rugs on large looms; study of fibers; biographies of textile inventors.

In the sixth year two hours a week of one quarter are spent in designing, making, and using stencils as textile decoration, and in stories of the weavers' guilds of the Middle Ages.

In the seventh year the girls spend two hours a week of one quarter in household sewing, care of linen, making of muslin underwear, and drafting of three patterns. The boys design, make, and use the block print as a type of textile decoration.

The boys and girls together in the eighth grade spend two hours a week for one quarter in studying the fabrics in common use; in designing simple and everyday costumes; in industrial excursions, and in learning as much as possible of manufacturing and trade conditions; in the history of the development of textile industries in the United States.

Metal-working.—Metal offers a material by means of which the child may make objects that are both useful and artistic. Working with it develops a control unlike that found in the other handicrafts. This material has a very intimate place in daily life, and the use of it suggests questions in science and history which, if answered, show the development of the metal industry from the first crude operations of prehistoric peoples to the more complex processes of today.

The work in this school is now in its beginning, as it has been carried on the last two years only in the sixth and eighth school years. There will therefore be great similarity in the processes throughout the school for next year.

Metal-work has many possibilities, among them the following: (1) it is a simple article for social use, on which decoration may be etched, pierced, chased, or engraved; (2) it may be used as decoration on woodwork or in connection with pottery; (3) it is the material best adapted for jewelry, as brooches, belt buckles, hatpins, etc., including all the processes necessary to the jeweler's craft.

Woodworking.—All the children in the Elementary School go to the manual-training room for their woodwork. Each child, from the first to the eighth grade inclusive, averages two hours a week for a period of at least three months.

The work does not follow any of the well-known systems of manual training, but depends, rather, upon the plan of the grade. For instance, the work of the first grade centers about domestic life. Playhouses are made in the manual-training room. Each child furnishes his own playhouse, or helps in furnishing a group playhouse. The work in textiles lends itself to the making of rugs for the floors, and the lessons in drawing and painting are devoted to the designing of wall-paper. Thus the different departments of the handicrafts co-operate not only with the grade teacher, but also with one another, and in so doing discover the kinship of their special subjects and develop the correlated plan.

It is through correlation as a medium that the handicrafts, instead of being presented formally as so many isolated subjects, really become to the child methods of easy and natural self-expression.

Another use of woodworking is the making of Christmas presents. The children are alert for this chance and each autumn in all the grades the pupils select, design, and make with great care and great secrecy the presents to be given on Christmas.

Other uses of woodworking are the making of things for the grade room, the school, the school grounds, or for the children themselves. This work represents group or co-operative planning, and individual work.

If, however, the plans of the year do not especially call for illustration, and if the immediate needs of the school have been supplied, the children follow, under guidance, their own wishes in the choice of things to make.

In these years there are (a) freehand drawing for proportion and design; (b) reduction of these drawings to working drawings; (c) blueprints of these mechanical drawings—gradually introduced according to the skill of the pupils.

All, in proportion to their development, study (a) the history of the growing tree; (b) the process of lumbering; (c) something of lumber physics, and (d) myths of trees.

Throughout the work there is growing emphasis on technique, with instruction concerning the care of wood, finishing, the mixing of stains, and polishing.

Bookbinding.—The work in bookbinding is closely related to history and art. The pupils make suitable bindings for their written work and their drawings, and also furnish bindings for magazines, etc. The following outline gives a course planned for one year, for a group of ten children in the tenth year, and also the equipment needed:

First process: (1) Making a portfolio. (2) Case-binding: folding; sewing; putting in boards; covering; blind tooling.

Second process: Putting a book into a half-leather binding:

tearing apart and mending book; sewing; backing. Putting into boards: head bands; covering; tooling.

Third process: (1) Putting a book into full-leather binding: different kinds of sewing; backing; putting into boards; head bands; covering; tooling. (2) Library binding.

School equipment: 5 sewing-frames; 3 letter-presses; 1 cutting-press; 4 finishing presses; 1 photograph-cutter; 4 sets of backing-boards (can be made in manual-training shop); 4 lithographic stones, blocks of marble, or squares of cut glass; 4 knocking-down irons (flat-irons can be used); 1 glue-pot; type and pallets; simple tools for finishing. This equipment will cost about twenty-five dollars.

Individual equipment: Folder, cutting-knife; scissors; straight edge; square; leather knife; bodkin; hammer; 4 tins; 2 pressing-boards; paste brush; library paste. The total cost of this outfit is about three dollars and a half. A number of the things are already owned by the children, or can be borrowed from other departments.

Stock: Leather; cloth; paper; boards; sewing-cord, tape, and thread; silk for head bands; glue; paste.

Books: Aldrich, *Friar Jerome's Beautiful Book* (Houghton, Mifflin & Co); Brassington, *History of the Art of Bookbinding* (Stock); Bouchot, *The Book: Its Printers, Illustrators, and Binders* (Grevel); Crockrell, *Bookbinding and the Care of Books* (Appleton); Davenport, *English Embroidered Bookbinding* (Dodd, Mead & Co).

THE PHOTOGRAPHY GROUPS

The photography groups for the most part are mainly engaged in learning the technique of developing and printing, but make many interesting photographic records of field-trips, social affairs, and other events in the school life. Records of the changes in the garden and on the grounds from winter to summer are kept. Lantern slides made by the children are used to show these records to the whole school in morning exercises.

THE MUSEUM AND COLLECTIONS

The school grows through the study and criticism of its own work. To afford better opportunity for this, the pupils place in the museum, for the purpose of study, the various articles of handwork which they have completed in any quarter, and these remain there in the custody of the school during the next ensuing quarter. A photographic record of such work is kept for future reference.

The museum is also made the center of appropriate working collections, gathered on field-trips and otherwise, just as the library is the center of interest in books. The work in history, geography, and the arts is supplemented by exhibits which show something of the industrial and artistic development of the race.

It is not the chief aim to fill the museum with the unusual, the rare, or the curious, but rather to make it an illustrative adjunct to the common things that are studied. It contains a large number of mounted specimens, which illustrate the chief topics in nature-study, physiology, zoölogy, botany, geology, and mineralogy.

A museum field-trip is made each Saturday throughout a greater part of the year by someone connected with the museum and volunteer students. Probably no other school enterprise has more enthusiastic helpers among the students than this. During the fall many aquaria are filled with interesting aquatic plant and animal forms and kept in good condition throughout the winter in the museum, and in the various recitation rooms. Several forms are caught in the act of hibernating late in the fall and are brought in to be observed during the winter. The work of watching and preserving many life histories goes with the collecting.

In connection with the volunteer field-work, the children have prepared museum exhibits showing the life-histories of the ant lion (with its feeding habits), cabbage-butterfly, cecropia-moth (with its parasite), crane-fly, dragon-fly, wasp, snail, and salamander. These cases of museum material are used for illustrative purposes throughout the school. Two or three pairs of doves, a pair of rabbits, and a few other pets are kept and cared for in the vivarium corner, and in the classrooms. The children observe the full life cycles of a good many forms—mammalian, avian, batrachian, and on down to the protozoan.

Photo by Eldredge Hamlin

EXPLORING A SWAMP

Photo by Robert Stilwell

A GROUP IN BOOK-BINDING

In the museum continuous records are kept of the weather conditions, such as temperature, barometric pressure, wind velocity and direction, rainfall, and sunshine. In connection with this the Weather Bureau's daily, monthly, and annual records and publication describing apparatus are posted or conveniently filed. In addition, an excellent clock of the world, hydrographs, apparatus for taking soil temperature, and a skiameter in the garden are available.

A large camera obscura is placed upon the central tower. This throws a six-foot picture of the surrounding landscape for a radius of several miles with all its moving objects upon a stage in a dark room underneath. It is used in the study of physics, nature-study, and art.

During the past year a number of groups representing the vast life-history of the bald-faced hornet, yellowjacket, life-history of moths, ant lions, salamander has been added to the collection.

_____

MUSIC

The aim of the music work of the school is to awaken in the children a love for good music, and to enable them to get at the meaning of the printed page.

Exercises for ear-training, sight-reading, and part-singing are used through the grades, but are invariably subordinated to the musical ideal. Since but a small percentage of school graduates become musical performers, the drill in technique is never allowed to degenerate into drudgery that might stifle the growing interest in musical content. Even the so-called unmusical children leave the eighth grade prepared to be intelligent listeners.

Song-composition.—Each group in the first six grades is encouraged to write at least one complete, original song on a topic connected with school interests. These original songs are composite, each member of a class offering a phrase or line for the text, and afterward a musical phrase, until the song is finished. The children are usually desirous of having a copy of their song to show at home, so the work of notating it becomes of vital interest to them and is proportionately useful. This notation begins in the third grade. The original songs, with a piano accompaniment added by the teacher, appear from time to time in the *Elementary School Teacher*. The children make covers in which to preserve their written work, and have opportunity to note progress.

SONGS USED IN 1906-7

"The Goldenrod Is Yellow"..............................*Eleanor Smith*
"O'er Our Fields".....................................*Vial de Sabligny*
"Thanksgiving Hymn" ....*Sir George Elvey*
"The Happy Little Eskimo".............................*Eleanor Smith*
"The Indian" ....*Jessie Gaynor*
"Ye Shepherds, Arise"......................................*C. Reinecke*
"The Christmas Tree" ....*E. Grieg*
"Why Do Bells for Christmas Ring?".......................*F. W. Root*
"A Christmas Carol" (canon)................................*C. Reinecke*
"Fatherland Psalm" ....*E. Grieg*
"Betty Ross" ....*F. Atkinson*
"Flag Song" ....*F. W. Root*
"Aurora Borealis" ....*Rheinberger*
"To Thee, O Country"....................................*Julius Eichberg*
"Austrian National Hymn"..*Haydn*
"The Angel" (two-part).......................................*Rubinstein*
"Wanderer's Night-Song" ....*Rubinstein*
"Mother-Goose Songs" ....*J. W. Elliott*
"Santa Lucia" (two-part) ....*Italian*
"Spring Greeting" ....*Schumann*
"Greeting" ....*Mendelssohn*
"Early Spring" (four-part) ....*Mendelssohn*
"Come, Happy Spring"..*Giordani*
"Maypole Dance" ....(Seventeenth-Century English)
"The May Breeze" (two-part)..................................*J. Kreipl*
"The Wanderer's Song" ....*Schumann*
"Goodnight to Dobbin"...*E. Grieg*

PHYSICAL TRAINING

The physical training of the Elementary School seeks the achievement of four different values—a postural, a corrective, a recreative, and a training to quick and definite reactions.

Growth, development, and functional activities are considered in their physiological relations, and from this training for health mental and moral qualities result. As pride in personal appearance distinguishes cultivated people, it is the intention that other resultants shall be correct habits of bearing, carriage, and poise in address. Individual interest, and cheerfulness of mind and manner, as well as volition, are necessary if these results are to be obtained. The teacher can lead and direct, but is barred from going across the line beyond which only the individual holds sway.

Both system and method provide an opportunity for the more comprehensive motor activities denied in the ordinary school curriculum, and, as a result, backward children are often stimulated to mental activity.

The direct and indirect effects of all forms of school work are carefully noted, a normal development of the body is constantly kept in view, and class work is so judiciously arranged as to cover all common defects. For those children who upon observation, or as a result of the physical examination, cannot be considered members of classes for concerted work, individual corrective instruction is given. Among those fitted to take regular concerted work, those to whom corrective work would be advantageous, are given the option of joining such a class.

Physical exercises in the gymnasium are given each group twice a week and between recitations in the schoolroom whenever needed. Plays, games, and athletics under the direction of the department staff form a part of the regular daily program.

Regularity and system are required in this as in any other work, as it ranks in dignity and importance both in the curriculum and daily arrangements besides other work of the school. All children, with the exceptions previously stated, are required to take the class work, which is of such a character that it need not overtax the strength of a child who is in physical condition to attend daily school duties.

Parents are earnestly requested to take careful and watchful interest in the physical development of their children in and out of school.

MEDICAL INSPECTION

A plan of medical inspection is in operation which enables the school to ascertain and control the various forms of infection, to determine the amount of mental and physical training work to be done by each pupil, and to see that the best sanitary conditions possible in the buildings are provided.

The medical examination of each pupil is comprehensive, including a general survey of personal history, measurements of the body, conditions of eyes (errors of refraction as well as diseases of eyeball and lids being noted), ears, nose, and throat, and conditions of skin, glands, bones, joints, heart, lungs, abdominal organs, and general diseases and injuries.

The amount of physical training to be given each individual in class is based upon the findings in these examinations; all eye, ear, nose, and throat defects found are brought to the attention of the parents.

The building is regularly inspected to see that the light, heat, water, and ventilation are of the best. All seats and desks are readjusted at least twice a year.

Every child, after an absence of more than one day, is sent to the physician's office on his return to school, and is allowed to return to his room only after the examiner is satisfied that he is well. Any child taken ill in school is also sent to the physician, and, when necessary, is advised to go home for care and treatment.

The following rules in regard to the various infectious diseases are in use here:

Scarlet fever.—A child having had scarlet fever must not return for six weeks after all symptoms have disappeared. If other children in same house, attending school, are immediately removed, they may return in two weeks: if not removed, must remain away during entire case.

Measles.—May return at end of third week after disappearance of all symptoms.

Chicken-pox.—Must not return until crusts have disappeared, generally at end of third week.

Mumps.—May return at end of third week.

Whooping cough.—May return at end of sixth week, unless cough persists.

Diphtheria.—May return when a bacteriological examination shows no bacilli in throat; or in default of this examination, at end of third week after disappearance of all symptoms.

DANCING

Dances are shown to be one of the earliest and most natural expressions of man—to be, in reality, a form of language. Instruction in national dances is based upon actual experience of the teacher among peasants of Ireland, England, France, Germany, and other countries, and upon a psychological and historical study of their dances.

Children of the second, third, sixth, seventh, and eighth grades have lessons once a week and for three-quarters of an hour. Those of the fourth and fifth grades have instruction twice a week, each lesson an hour in length. This is because children of about ten years are peculiarly well adapted for this kind of exercise. They are ready for the more complex adjustments which the national dances require. These are taught as a whole—not by preliminary steps—and while they are being taught their history is explained.

TEXTBOOKS

THIRD GRADE

Literature: Robert Louis Stevenson, *Child's Garden of Verse* (Rand, McNally).

Arithmetic: Myers and Brooks, *Rational Elementary Arithmetic.*

History: Jennie Hall, *Viking Tales.*

FOURTH GRADE

History: Jennie Hall, *History of Chicago.*

Arithmetic: Myers and Brooks, *Rational Elementary Arithmetic.*

Geography: Carpenter, *North America.*

Literature: Hamilton Mabie, *Fairy Tales Every Child Should Know.*

FIFTH GRADE

History: Moore, *Pilgrims and Puritans.*

Geography: Longmans' *New School Atlas;* Carpenter, *North America.*

Literature: Irving, *Rip Van Winkle* (paper cover).

French: *Jeux, chansons, et rondes populaires de France.*

German: Foster, *Geschichten und Märchen.*

Dictionary: Webster's *Academic.*

SIXTH GRADE

History: McMaster, *School History of the United States.*

Arithmetic: Myers and Brooks, *Rational Grammar School Arithmetic.*

Geography: Tarr and McMurray, Book III, Longmans' *Atlas.*

Science: Walter, *Wild Birds in City Parks.*
French: *French Dramatic Reader.*
German: Guerber, *Märchen und Erzählungen,* Vol. I.
Dictionary: Webster's *Academic.*

SEVENTH GRADE

History: Sparks, *Expansion of the American People;* Roosevelt, episodes from *Winning of the West;* McMaster, *School History of the United States.*

Arithmetic: Myers and Brooks, *Rational Grammar School Arithmetic.*

Geography: Tarr and McMurray, *Complete Geography;* Tarr and McMurray, *North America;* Longmans' Atlas.

French: *French Dictionary; Dramatic French Reader.*
German: Guerber, *Märchen und Erzählungen,* Vol. I.
Dictionary: Webster's *Academic.*

EIGHTH GRADE

History: Harding, *The Story of the Middle Ages.*

Geography: Herbertson's *Descriptive Geographies; Asia, Europe, North America, South America;* Longmans' *Atlas.*

Literature: Shakespeare, *Julius Caesar.*

French: L. Bonneville, *Le petit Robinson de Paris-Foa; Brès Mon; Histoire de France.*

German: Seligmann, *Altes und Neues.*
Grammar: Scott & Buck.
Dictionary: Webster's *Academic.*

OUTLINE OF WORK FOR THE YEAR 1907-8

The children of the kindergarten period are interested in reproducing the life about them, the familiar occupations of their homes and immediate environment. In the play spirit, all their images find expression in action, and they are satisfied with the action for its own sake, and care very little about a definite result. It is by means of this play that they explore their surroundings, and experiment with materials, and gradually gain control of their own powers.

The work of the kindergarten consequently centers in the home life, and in a few of the activities most closely associated with the home.

The arbitrary divisions into subjects, as history and nature-study, are made only to connect more closely the work of the kindergarten with that of the other groups of the school.

History.—Autumn Quarter: Subject—homes. (1) Our own homes—inside and out. (2) Homes of animals: (*a*) domestic animals for which homes are provided, such as dogs, pigeons, chickens, horses, cows, sheep, pigs; (*b*) animals which find their own homes, such as rabbits, squirrels, bees, birds. (3) Relation of farm to the home.

Winter Quarter: Subject—baker (kitchen and shop), grocer, milkman, postman.

Spring Quarter: Subject—market gardener—close relation to grocer and to our life. Our own garden—in relation to that of the market gardener. Plans in sandpans of yards, gardens, playgrounds, and setting for stories.

Nature-study.—Autumn and Winter Quarters: The areas around which the year's work centers are: (1) garden, (2) lake-shore, (3) the Midway and playground, (4) the parks. Observations: Seasonal changes—effect of frost on plant life, animals, and people; habits of late birds; gathering seeds and noting how they are distributed; study of nuts, fruits, and vegetables, according to the way they may be preserved and stored for the winter. Care of animals.

Spring Quarter: Effect of warm winds and sun upon the earth; effect of moisture, heat, and light upon growth of seeds, incidentally noted; return of birds and insects; watching the bees at work in the garden. Watching the appearances of plants in the garden and in vacant lots. Noting leaves of these plants and trying to find others like them, incidentally learning the names of plants and flowers.

Cooking.—Used only as a social industry, and employed by the teacher with the children as a mother in the home would use it. The special function of the cooking in the Autumn Quarter is the preparation of grape juice, jelly, and cookies for a Thanksgiving celebration.

Mathematics.—Number used constantly as a limitation in building; in choosing children for games; in construction; in designing; in gardening; in taking measurements, and in allotting space.

Literature.—Rhymes and Poetry: From Lear, *Nonsense Rhymes* and *Mother Goose:* "Hickory Dickory Dock," "Sing a Song of Six-pence," "Little Jack Horner," "Mary, Mary, Quite Contrary," "Hey, Diddle, Diddle," and others; Christina Rossetti: "Mix a Pancake," "What Does the Donkey Bray About?", "What Does the Bee Do?" (from *Sing Song*); Robert Louis Stevenson: "The Rain Is Raining," "Birdie with the Yellow Bill," "When I Was Down beside the Sea," "The Swing," "My Shadow."

Stories: From *Six Nursery Classics,* edited by O'Shea: "The Old Woman and the Six-pence," "Chicken Little," "The Three Bears," "The Little Red Hen;" from Aesop, "The Lion and the Mouse;" from Dasent, *Stories of the Field:* "The Pancake," "The Pig and the Sheep," "The Lad Who Went to the North Wind;" from Dasent, *Popular Tales from the North:* "Billy Goats Gruff," "The Gingerbread Man;" from Thaxter, "Peggy's Garden and What Grew Therein;" Helen Hunt Jackson, "St. Chistopher;" adapted from Cary, "Peter at the Dike."

Dramatic work: "Playing out" the Mother Goose Rhymes or any simple story that suggests action of the simplest, most childlike kind.

Gift work.—Building with large and small blocks: animal houses, bakeries and furnishings (for bakeroom and shop), tile floors and show-windows for the shop; gardener's wagons and toolhouse, chicken yards and coops with sticks, marking off gardens with lentils.

Handwork.—Christmas presents: work incidental to the celebration of Hallowe'en, Thanksgiving, and Christmas. Animal houses of cardboard. The furnishing of a bakeshop and bakeroom made of a box. Construction of market gardener's tools and toolhouse (arranged in a box top), with small wagon or wheelbarrow for carrying tools. Making, or seeing made, some kind of raised bread (merely to interest them in the way that yeast affects dough). Cardboard baking-pans, ovens, and measuring-cups.

Art.—Autumn Quarter: (*a*) Painting. Fruits, vegetables, and other subjects of interest to the group. Paper-cutting for decorative purposes. Opportunity is given in both the clay- and color-work for the unconscious exercise through play of the rhythmic instinct; (*b*) Modeling. Dishes, kitchen utensils, flowerpots, tea-rests, marbles, seeds, and fruits.

Music.—Exercises in tone placing, in imitation of whistles and bells, and in humming simple melodies; simple scale songs; songs of question and answer. Appropriate songs from kindergarten and primary songbooks by Eleanor Smith, Jessie Gaynor, Mrs. Crosby Adams, Patty and Mildred Hill, Neidlinger, Alys Bentley; Elliott's *Mother Goose.*

Rhythm and Games.—Skipping and marching; simplest ensemble dances. Romping Games: skip and hop tag; changing chairs; "Chickeny, Chickeny, Craney Crow," "The Little Mice Are Hiding," "Cat and Mouse," "Going to Jerusalem," "The Farmer in the Dell," "Three Circles;" beanbag races. Rhythmic Games: skating, seesawing, swinging, windmill, arm rhythm, rockingchairs, pendulum, and boatrowing movements.

FIRST GRADE

In this section the children begin to find satisfaction in activity which has some definite result. They learn gradually to work with an object in view. They select something to be done, and show some power to adapt means to ends. They begin to compare the results obtained with the ideal which they had in mind in undertaking the work.

The material for study must still be based upon immediate experience, but now more than before use may be made of comparison and reflection.

The constructions of the children have rather more lasting value to them.

History.—During this year as in the kindergarten period, the activities and interests of the children still center largely around their homes. However, they are able to branch out a little farther into the sources of some of the necessities of their own home life.

In the autumn the groups take up the study of the farm as the source of supply of our grains, fruits, vegetables, and dairy products. They construct from blocks, boxes, or cardboard the houses, barns, and various animal shelters, and make miniature farms in large sand-tables. They make butter and cheese, and grind wheat into flour and corn into meal. General activities of farm life are reproduced in dramatic plays and games.

With the cold weather the immediate consideration of farm life is dropped until spring. The children build up some idea of the domestic occupations and surroundings of the Eskimos. As far as possible they make their pictures of the northern conditions through the similarity to our own most extreme cold. They have Eskimo pictures and stories, visit the excellent exhibit at the Field Museum, and construct summer and winter scenes of Arctic life.

With the study of Indian life they again have the benefit of the museum. The occupations of the people are also primitive, but differ from those of the Eskimo on account of physical environment. Possibly the study of the shelter, food, and clothing of these people lends more color and significance to the children's thoughts of their own homes.

During the spring the children again work at farm life, laying out and planting a small farm in the garden. They use such buildings on this farm as are in good condition from the previous year, and renovate or replace old ones.

The play center, the make-believe home around which the rest of the work circles, is the large playhouse constructed by the older children during the previous year and partly furnished by the younger ones. Whatever furniture, rugs, curtains, and wall paper, are needed are made early in the autumn. This playhouse, together with the sand-table constructions, affords a basis for the imaginative dramatic play still so near to the six-year-old interest.

Geography and Nature-study.—The children are taken on such trips and excursions as bring them into strong and close relation with various forms of nature which are as yet rather new to most of them. In the fall they go to a good farm, the lake-shore at Windsor Park, Beverly Hills, and Lincoln Park. In the spring they again visit these places, possibly substituting Thornton for Beverly Hills at the time of violets and crabapple blossoms. Most children know the woods in summer; but few know the autumn colors or spring flowers.

Especial attention is paid to animals of all varieties. At the farm are seen the domestic horses, cows, sheep, pigs, and fowls and some of the provisions for their comfort. At school there is a circulating series of pets: rabbits, squirrels, doves, turtles, mother cat and kittens, and possibly a lamb in the spring. These must be observed as to the care they need, and the children are made responsible for their welfare.

Some wild animals, polar bears, and seals in connection with Eskimo life, and deer, buffalo, and foxes with Indian, may be noted especially at Lincoln Park and seen stuffed at the museum.

In the fall the children set out bulbs in the east yard and in flower pots for winter forcing. In the spring they plant in their small farm in the garden, lettuce and radishes to mature in the early summer, and wheat, corn, potatoes, and onions to be harvested the following fall.

When for any reason in connection with the study of harvesting, planting, Arctic conditions, or everyday experience, the question of "weather" enters, simple observations are made and recorded. In noting direction of wind, children learn the points of the compass and when they are in relation to school, home, and lake.

With the study of the Eskimo, the children gain some notion of the barren, treeless snow fields and ice bound country of the North. With the Indians, they picture the grassy prairies and forested hills. These have to be closely connected with their own experience, but it is a beginning of geographical imaging.

Cooking.—In addition to the actual cooking the children have two lessons a week devoted entirely to the formal side of the work. They read and write the recipes and work out the number problems involved in them.

Their cooking consists in preparing: baked apples; apples cooked in syrup; dried fruits, stewed; lemonade; fruit lemonade; sherbet. Different ways of thickening liquid: by gelatine, as illustrated in lemon jelly; by sugar, in cranberry jelly; by eggs, in baked custard; in making cocoa, sandwiches, and other articles demanded by the social life of the children; and the beginning of the care of the house in the setting of tables and serving of simple luncheons.

Mathematics.—The making of furniture and wall paper for the playhouse, cardboard buildings for the farm, and book covers requires constant number work, especially with the ruler as the instrument for measuring. With the beginning of cooking they use another unit, the cup, and become familiar with one-half, one-fourth, one-third, three-fourths, and two-thirds. Most of the number work is incidental to the making and cooking, and it is only when the opportunity seems fitting that certain facts are fixed by special drill.

English.—(1) Literature: (*a*) Rhymes and poetry: Lear's *Nonsense Rhymes* and *Mother Goose;* repetition of those given in kindergarten; Christina Rossetti: "What is Pink?", "Brown and

Furry," "If a Pig Wore a Wig;" Robert Louis Stevenson: "Bed in Summer," "The Wind," "Foreign Children," "The Whole Duty of Children," "The Cow," "Singing;" "Little Gustava," Celia Thaxter;" "I'll Tell You How the Leaves Came Down," Susan Coolidge.

(*b*) Stories: From Dasent's *Popular Tales from the Norse:* "Boots and His Brothers," "Princess on the Glass Hill," "Gudbrand on the Hillside," "Why the Bear Is Stumpy Tailed;" adapted from Grimm: "The Wolf and the Seven Young Kids," "Cinderella;" from Grimm's *Fairy Tales:* "The Shoemaker and the Elves," "One Eye, Two Eyes, and Three Eyes," "The Town Musicians;" from Howells' *Christmas Every Day in the Year and Other Stories:* "The Pony Engine," "Christmas Every Day in the Year;" "The Sleeping Beauty," Perrault; "The Gingerbread Man;" Whittier's *Child Life in Verse;* "The Bell of Atri," from Baldwin's *Fifty Famous Stories Retold;* "German Legend of the First Christmas," *St. Nicholas;* "The Birth of Christ," read from Luke; *Fables of Aesop:* "The Wind and the Sun," "The Lion and the Mouse."

(*2*) Reading: (*a*) The work in phonics begins immediately and continues throughout the year. The children learn the sounds of all the consonants and combinations of consonants, the simple vowel sounds, and also some of the more unusual combinations as *oy, aw, ight,* etc. At first the work is largely in the form of games, but gradually the attempt is made to bring the knowledge thus gained into working use in reading.

(*b*) On the blackboard the children see constantly words and sentences in connection with their work. Through much repetition they learn to recognize words and are able to follow simple written directions. Recipes are written, and sometimes printed, for them. They also have printed short reading lessons or records of what they have done in connection with their history or science. (*c*) Books used in reading are-*Heart of Oak* No. 1, *Aesop's Fables, Hiawatha Primer,* and *Eskimo Stories* by Mary E. Smith.

(*3*) Writing: The writing at first is almost entirely confined to blackboard work. Later it is extended to paper with crayon or charcoal.

Art.—(*a*) Drawing and painting. At six the seeing is indefinite and general even at its best. It seems to be important to introduce the children to a wide range of visual material, rather than to force the accuracy of observation in any one direction. The subject-matter includes the seasonal coloring of plants and landscape, the illustration of the dramatic incidents of the history and literature and the decoration of such articles as the children have occasion to make during the school year, as portfolios, Christmas presents, valentines, invitations. The materials used are water-colors with large brushes, chalks, and charcoal. The technique of the year includes the use of large washes, mixing of green, orange, violets, recognition of at least two values of light and dark, and the co-ordination necessary to render the action in silhouette of animals and the human figure. While the dominant motive of this age is the utilitarian, there is an unconscious exercise of the aesthetic instinct, and it is the intention to develop this in all of the work which has been indicated.

(*b*) Clay-modeling. Fruits, animals, etc., to illustrate work in nature-study, history, and literature; bowls, cups, trays, etc., for Christmas gifts. The aim is to give much opportunity for expressing freely in so plastic a medium as clay, and incidentally to develop a more definite feeling for shape.

Music.—In the first year of formal music-work, emphasis is laid upon song-singing, that the children may join with the older primary grades in assembly singing.

They are taught to sing the scale by syllable, to write the scale on the staff, and to write exercises based upon portions of the scale. Two, three, and four-pulse rhythms are discussed, the children being led to recognize these different rhythms, to clap them, and to picture them on the blackboard in time to rhythmic music.

Gymnastics.—Marching, running, body movements and breathing, jumping, and games; short daily periods; work arranged to require little form or application; largely imitative; proportion of formal work to jumping and games one-third.

Music accompanies all parts of the lesson. Games of sense, inexact imitation, of no purpose, of variety of motion, and games involving all the players. One lesson each week in rhythm. Relation of directions and the different parts of the body discovered; their relation to various musical rhythms.

SECOND GRADE

The children in this year are able to go still farther than in the First Grade in comparing their own activities and surroundings with those of other peoples. Experience shows that they are easily led to trace the early steps in the evolution from past conditions of some of the industries of their environment. Here, then, the study of history, properly speaking, may begin. More careful observation than before may be expected in nature-study and geography.

Industrial History.—The history, woodwork, cooking, and nature-study for the first half of the year group themselves about the idea of food-getting. The industrial history attempts to put before the children the interrelation of the acts by which food comes to our table, first by seeing the process in Chicago, second by giving meaning to this very complicated process by stories of simple and primitive life.

The children visit a farm, South Water Street, a wholesale grocery, a bakery, a milk depot, a grain elevator, express depot, and a dock, to see the source and distribution of food in Chicago.

In order to focus and utilize the observations made upon these trips the children build in the woodshop toy representations of a grocery, bakery, milk depot, grain elevator, freight depot, dock, boats, train, and bridges.

Waterloo's "Story of Ab" is told with such detail that the children may work out primitive methods of getting food, making fire and weapons, pottery, clothing, and shelter. Field-trips are taken to gather such foods as the Indians about Chicago may have relied upon (*see* Nature-Study).

In the second half of the year dyeing, weaving, and garden-making determine the interest so that the history, textiles, and nature-study center in these activities.

The history here as in the first half of the year serves to give perspective to the immediate occupations. Stories are told of the great shepherds and weavers, those of Palestine, Arabia, Persia, and Greece (for stories and poems *see* Literature).

Trips are taken to a carpetweaver's, Marshall Field's rug department, and the Field Museum. To intensify children's images of these people and their environments models are constructed and pictures are drawn.

By April work in the garden begins. As the children prepare the ground and take care of the garden, the food-getting of hunter and shepherd people is recalled, and for the first time there dawns a consciousness of a time when agriculture was unknown. Then stories are told of people in the early agricultural stage, the Lake Dwellers of Switzerland being chosen as the type.

Geography.—The experience in typical areas and with natural materials gained in the field-trips forms the basis for geography.

After the trips the children make plans in sand or on paper of the routes followed and areas visited. No attempt is made at conventional mapmaking, the teachers' problem being to discover when and how children make the transition from purely picture records to the conventional representation.

Trips to the lake shore furnish collections of the common pebbles, and limestone, sandstone, quartz, chert, greenstone, granite, and iron pyrites become familiar. The children make crystals from various substances and this work culminates in our rockcandy for the Christmas tree.

As a background for the stories told in the history period the following regions must be pictured: a temperate forest area with caves and swift flowing river; the desert, and portions of Persia, Greece, and Switzerland. Stories, reading-matter, visits to the stuffed-animal section of the Field Museum and to the "zoo" at Lincoln Park feed that absorbing child-interest in wild animals.

Nature-study.—Trips are taken to Thornton at the time that the fruit trees are in bloom, to Ravinnia to see autumn coloring, to Clark Junction to gather swamp material, to the sand dunes at Miller's, to Flossmoor, and to Cheltenham Beach.

Upon these trips the children learn to know the common wild flowers and the familiar birds of the region.

A pair of rabbits and a pair of carrier pigeons have been selected as the particular care and property of the second grade, and homes will be made for these animals in the enclosure outside the grade room.

We find in the immediate vicinity of Chicago that the Indians depended upon the following list of wild things for their vegetable food: acorns, roots of arrow leaf and roots of water lily, tips of cat tails, stems of reeds, roots of wild hyacinth, wild rice, cranberries, chokecherries, wild grape, nuts, and sunflower seeds. We take trips for the purpose of gathering these foods, and prepare them for eating as nearly as possible as the Indians did.

In a similar way we go out to gather those vegetable materials which the Indians and early settlers used for dyes. Grasses, sedges, bulrushes, and reeds are gathered for experiments in weaving.

The children in this grade in the past have shown such interest in buying, rigging up, and playing with electrical apparatus that we furnish the material necessary for play with magnets and frictional electricity.

Cooking.—The social cooking provides luncheons alternate weeks in which the serving and setting of the table are taught. The children prepare grape juice, fruit lemonade, sherbet; they learn to thicken liquid by gelatine as in lemon jelly, by sugar as in cranberry jelly, by egg in baked custard, and by flour in tomato soup. They make rockcandy and cream candies for Christmas.

The children experiment with primitive processes. They make a fire out-of-doors, trying to do this without matches, and on this bonfire they boil water by means of hot stones, boil meat and eggs in this water, roast meat on the end of a stick, roast chestnuts, and make cakes of various meals which they have prepared from acorns, wheat, oats, and wild rice.

Mathematics.—The aim in this work is to put mathematical power into the hands of the children just so far as they have use for this power. Drill is given at the time that a need for a fact or process arises.

The following processes are demanded and should be so mastered as to be used with skill and accuracy: (1) addition of two columns of figures, and subtraction of quantities under 100; (2) recognition of pieces of money; (3) use of halves, fourths, thirds, eighths, twelfths, and sixteenths; (4) addition of simple mixed numbers; (5) making of plans to a scale; (6) use of gram, ounce, pound, gill, pint, quart, linear, square, and cubic inch, foot, and yard as standards of measurement; (7) construction of square, oblong, right-angled triangle, equilateral triangle, circle, and hexagon; (8) counting by twos, threes, fours, and fives.

These principles and relations are involved in the actual work as follows: (1) and (2) in keeping accounts (a blank book has been devised on the principle of a check book. The children deposit with the teacher one dollar, and she keeps on hand the school supplies, furnishing them to the children on presentation of check. The children retain in the check book a stub showing the material purchased, cost of same, and balance to their credit); (3), (4), and (5) in construction with wood and cardboard, cooking, and planning garden; (6) in scientific experiments, making beanbags, cooking, and construction; (7) in making circular and rectangular garden beds, valentines, maybaskets, candyboxes, and weaving; (8) planting gardens, cooking, and keeping accounts.

English.—(1) Literature: (*a*) Rhymes and poetry: Repetition of Robert Louis Stevenson's verses given before; the following ones added: "The Lamplighter," "Young Night Thoughts," "The Sun Travels," and "Nest Eggs." "Clouds," Frank Dempster Sherman; "Snow-Storm," Sherman; "Hunting Song," Coleridge; "The Lamb" (first stanza) and "The Shepherd," William Blake; "Fairy Folk," and "Wishing," Allingham; "Seven Times One," Jean Ingelow; "March," Wordsworth; "The Wonderful World" (three stanzas), William Rand; "The Birds in Spring," Thomas Nashe; "Seal Lullaby," Kipling; "Ariel's Song," and "I Know a Bank whereon the Wild Thyme Grows," Shakespeare; "The Swallow's Nest," Edwin Arnold; "The Sun with His Great Eye" (a fragment), John Keats. Most of the poems mentioned above may be found in *The Posy Ring,* edited by Kate Douglas Wiggin.

(*b*) Stories: Adapted from Grimm: "Snow White and the Seven Little Dwarfs," "The Enchanted Stag;" from Hawthorne's *Wonder Book:* "The Golden Touch," "The Miraculous Pitcher," and "The Chimera;" "Little Thumbling,' Perrault; "Old Pipes and the Dryad," Stockton; "Muleykeh," adapted from Robert Browning; "Mowgli's Brothers" and "Toomai and the Elephants," Kipling.

(2) Oral reading and dramatic art: The poems given above under "Literature," and the selections to be printed for the children's reading, listed above, offer opportunities for gaining skill in reading aloud. Certain of these are memorized for morning exercises and festivals, and are used as a means of entertainment at our social periods.

(3) Reading: The children's own reading is from books, printed slips, and script. Each child has at the beginning of the year covers for printed slips. These include the following subjects: Sketches and stories of shepherd life and descriptions of the desert, by Jennie Hall; stories of hunter life and adaptations from Waterloo's *Story of Ab;* descriptions of Arabia, Palestine, and Switzerland; "Threshing in Greece," by Jennie Hall; selections from children's poetry, some rhymes of Christina Rossetti, and the words of the children's songs. We use "Little Black Sambo" and "Peter Rabbit," and selected articles from the following readers: *Lights to Literature; Heart of Oak,* Vols. I and II; *The Blodgett Reader; The Culture Reader; Dopp's Tree-Man* and *The Cave-Man; Stories for Children.*

(4) Writing: The aim in the writing is to gain freedom and legibility. The drill comes through daily demands for written expression. An alphabetically classified list of words which have been used frequently is kept by each child as a means of independent reference and as a record of progress. The above-mentioned daily written expression together with general conversation gives opportunity for the teaching of English.

In the written work the definite points to be made are: the feeling for a sentence; use of capitals at the beginning of a sentence, in proper nouns, and in direct address; use and meaning of question mark, apostrophe, quotation mark.

Art.—(a) Drawing and painting: The children of this year are strongly imaginative. Free from the self-criticism which later retards creative effort, they are fearless in the pictorial expression. Conditions are favorable to the emphasis of imaginative drawing at this age. The interest in the idea should be the means of developing a closer observation of natural phenomena as the symbols of expression.

The technique of the year includes use of large washes, three tones of dark and light, expression of plane relations by variations of size and value, in landscape work, and action of figure. The aesthetic qualities emphasized are rhythm and balance. (b) The more formal design is developed in the weaving, and includes the use of symbols, two values of dark and light colors of two intensities.

Clay: The modeling is largely illustrative. The children make figures to use on their models of the Arabian village, "Fire-country." They make typical scenes from shepherd life in low relief and pencil trays, flower-pots, tea-tiles, or other pottery which can be made without the use of a glaze.

Textiles: The children make marblebags or belt-pockets, couch covers, portières, hammocks, or rugs for the playhouse. They dye the raffia, wool, cotton, silk, or linen, with which they weave, making simple experiments with vegetable dyes (*see* Nature-Study). They invent the necessary change in plain weaving to introduce stripes, squares, diamonds, or other simple patterns.

We have cotton balls, a sheepskin, flax from our garden, and silk-worms' cocoons with which to experiment, spinning these fibers.

In the spring the children construct out-of-doors a primitive form of loom, on which is woven a large mat of rushes or wool.

Woodworking: The first month the children make a very simple thing, as a Christmas gift.

By November they have made their industrial trips and have plans to build toy reproductions of the places visited. Children work in groups, making a grocery, bakery, milk depot, grain elevator, freight depot, dock, boats, train, and bridges. The grocery is approximately three feet square by two and a half feet high, and the others are built in proportion.

Music.—Work in musical rhythm is emphasized—simple melodies are given which the children are led to notate on the blackboard, and afterward copy on paper to be preserved in their notebooks. The names of lines and spaces are taken up; also the time-symbols (whole, half, quarter, and eighth notes). Rote songs are taught for assembly singing.

Gymnastics.—Beginnings of formal work in marching and running; odd fancy steps; postural work and breathing still imitative; beginning of exercises on apparatus (hanging); games. Short daily periods. Proportion of formal work to apparatus and games, one-half. Music accompanies all but apparatus and games. Begin games of exactness of motion.

One lesson each week in rhythm. The simple rhythms—walking, running, skipping, hopping, sliding, etc.—woven into combinations and combined with rhythmical movements of the arms and body.

Dancing.—First five positions for the feet; bows; grand right and left; beginning exercises leading to the waltz and two-step; galop square; marking the rhythm by hand; clapping in the waltz, two-step, and galop.

THIRD GRADE

In this grade there is not only an interest in results obtained from work but also a growing interest in the means by which ends are reached, a dawn of desire for skill. The child takes pleasure in doing things well and sets up a standard by which to measure the excellence of his work.

This is accordingly the time to emphasize the various forms of technique, as reading, writing, and drawing. If the child feels the need of these as modes of expression, or as a means of gaining knowledge, he overcomes with comparative ease the difficulties in the way of acquiring them.

Activities and occupations to be carried on during the year are: (1) walks in the park and excursions into the surrounding country; (2) gardening; (3) cooking, baking, preserving; (4) pottery; (5) textiles; (6) woodwork; (7) housekeeping and care of rooms, halls, and grounds; (8) a store, as a distributing point of supplies; (9) celebration; (10) parties and daily morning exercises.

The children are encouraged to acquire knowledge from every available source in order to carry on these activities in the most effective manner, and also in order to appreciate some of the social activities which they see around them. For this purpose it is necessary to visit shops, factories, markets, docks, and wharves in the vicinity, where similar occupations are engaged in, and to visit museums and collections of all kinds. It is necessary to perform experiments, to use books and pictures for information, as well as objects and specimens from the school museum. Each activity has a scientific and social aspect, both of which receive due attention. ·Records of the work are kept in the form of finished articles, plans, collections of objects studied, written notes, essays, drawings, and paintings.

History.—Basis: (1) observations of trade conditions; South Water Street; boats and freight-cars loading and unloading; stores; children's own desire to barter and exchange; (2) children's occupations in making boats and carts, and keeping a store for supplies.

Topics: Beginnings of trade, of exploration, and of travel; development of means of transportation and of a diversity of arts; expansion of industrial, social, and political life. As concrete illustrations of the era of early trade and discovery, some phases of Greek and Norse history are selected for study.

Geographical conditions which encourage early navigation and commerce—islands, harbors, overproduction of some commodity, desire for other products. Industries and occupations of the early Norse and Greek. Development of trade. How trade was carried on; means of transportation by land and water. Discoveries and expansion of geographical knowledge. The Vikings, their mode of life. Discovery of Iceland, Greenland, and America (Vinland). The Homeric Greek—based on a study of the *Odyssey*.

Standards of measurement, currency, use of metals. The children make furnaces, melt metals (lead and tin), make molds, and carry on the whole process of molding in lead and tin. Arrow-points, spear-points, battle-axes, money, weights, etc., are made. Social condition of the people, classes of people, the king, the assembly, games and sports, warfare and warlike conditions; ideals of the time, and religious beliefs.

The story of Columbus is told as embodying the spirit and aims of exploration. For comparison stories are told of modern explorers, as Nansen, Livingstone, Stanley; their equipment and aims as compared with those of the ancient explorers.

Geography.—(1) The neighborhood.· On all excursions the natural features are observed. The lakeshore—shore line, bluffs, different kinds of beaches. Beverly Hills—the ravines, brook-basins. Swamps—ridges with trees. (2) Typical environments. Mountain landscapes: Norway and Greece as types; narrow valleys, rapid rivers, falls, lakes; forest-covered, barren, and snow-covered mountains. Coasts: bays, headlands, fjords, islands, harbors. Animal life in the northern forests; animals of the northern seas. Study of such typical environments with relation to their social occupations, fishing, lumbering, hunting, trade (*see* "History").

Given typical physiographical features, the children plan routes of travel by sea and land; construct maps in sand and on blackboard. These maps are made to record first imaginary trips, and later the journey of the Norsemen to America, the caravan travel through the deserts, Columbus' discovery of America.

Children picture Arctic scenery with Nansen's journey, and tropical scenes with Livingstone and Stanley. The earth as a ball is introduced with the study of Columbus, and the different oceans and land masses noticed with relation to one another. The children construct simple compasses, and learn to use them on their excursions.

Nature-study.—The children have charge of the beehives in the garden. This responsibility necessitates a close study of these insects as to cleaning hives, winter conditions, removing honey, making new hives. This work interests the children in the life-history of bees and other insects; the bumble-bee, ant, and butterfly are studied especially.

Garden: This year is responsible for three flower beds in front of the school building in which tulips bloom in the spring and asters in the fall (transplanting); also for planting ivy and climbing-roses. Window-boxes in the house allow care of plants during the winter; the children are encouraged to have gardens and window-boxes at home, they themselves supplying the seeds. Note is made of trees that blossom early (food for bees). Sweet alyssum is planted for the bees.

Excursions: To Jackson Park, Wooded Island, South Shore, Beverly Hills, Lakeside. The special interests of the children are noted and followed up as far as demanded by them. Birds, bird-notes, building of nests, some ways of food-getting; the woodpeckers, kingfisher, swallows, robins. Materials gathered on these excursions are cared for, and different kinds of seeds mounted to show seed distribution, classified as to means of dissemination; insects and cocoons are placed in an insect case; frogs' eggs, tadpoles, salamander eggs, snails, larvae of mosquito, dragon-flies, etc., in an aquarium in the room; turtles, snakes, and toads are cared for in the school museum. The habits of the animals with which the children have become acquainted during the summer are discussed, such as the squirrel, chipmonk, bat, muskrat, and others. Stories of the same are told and read.

Temperature is studied in relation to bees, and to bulbs and other plants out-of-doors. Barometers are made and compasses constructed (see "History"). Phenomena of the Arctic day and night (history) compared with our own conditions lead to more interested observations of the sun's position. Experiments on evaporation (see "Cooking") are made. Paintings are made of out-of-door scenes often enough to be a record of the changes of the seasons.

Home-economics.—(*a*) Cooking: Drying of grapes; grape jelly; sugar cookery; Christmas candies; starch cookery; making of white sauce; cooking of starchy, sweet-juiced and strong-juiced vegetables; vegetable soups; making of bread. Study of fat in the making of butter. (*b*) Science: Quantitative work in evaporation; effect of the skin of the fruit on evaporation found, through the comparison of grapes and apples; study of individual food plants, parts of the plant used for food. Classification of vegetables according to their composition and the parts of the plants used; starch and cellulose obtained from potato; appearance of starch under the microscope. Iodine test for starch; determination (roughly) of the amount of water and starch in some foods; observation of the change of starch to sugar by the sweet taste developed in the chewing of starchy foods. Comparison of yeast used in bread-making with other plants. Density of different liquids from the study of milk and cream; determination of the amount of fat in milk through butter-making.

Mathematics.—If the children are actually doing work which has social value, they must gain accurate knowledge of the activities in which they are engaged. They keep a record of all expenses for materials used in the school, and do simple bookkeeping in connection with the store which has charge of this material. In cooking, weights and measures are learned. The children also keep accounts of the cost of ingredients. Proportions are worked out in the cooking recipes. When the children dramatize the life of the trader, in connection with history, they have opportunities to use all standards of measurements. Number is demanded in almost all experimental science work; for instance, the amount of water contained in the different kinds of fruit, or the amount of water evaporated from fruits under different conditions (in drying fruits). All plans for woodwork are worked to a scale and demand use of fractions. When the children have encountered many problems which they must solve in order to proceed with their work, they are ready to be drilled on the processes involved until they gain facility in the use of these. The children should be able to think through the problems which arise in their daily work, and have automatic use of easy numbers, addition, subtraction, multiplication, short division, and easy fractions.

English.—(1) Literature: Poems: Robert Louis Stevenson, "The Land of Story Books," "The Little Land," "North-West Passage," "Travel," "Where Go the Boats," "Escape at Bedtime," "Windy Nights," "Foreign Lands," "Fairy Bread," "Farewell to the Farm," "Looking Forward;" "The Fairy Folk," Robert Bird (Posy Ring); "Is the Moon Tired?", C. Rossetti; "The Wind and the Moon," George MacDonald; "Robert of Lincoln," Bryant.

Stories: the saga of King Harold the Fair-Haired, the Volsunga saga, and the sagas of Eric the Red and Leif Ericson told and read to the children; the *Odyssey,* parts read by children from Palmer's translations, parts read or told by the teacher; Norse myths: "Thor's Journey to Jotunheim," "The Death of Balder," "The Gifts of the Dwarfs," and others (Mabie's *Norse Stories* are recommended); Greek myths and hero-stories: "Apollo and the Python," "Hermes and the Cave of Winds," Perseus, Theseus, and Hercules (Hawthorne's *Wonder Book* and Kingsley's *Greek Heroes* are used. Fairy-tales to be told: "The Land East o' the Sun and West o' the Moon," "The Twelve Wild Ducks," Dasent's *Popular Tales from the Norse.* Fables: "The Country Mouse and the City Mouse," "The Man, the Boy, and the Donkey," "The Fox and the Grapes," "The Shepherd and the Wolves," and others from Aesop.

Poems and stories with which the children are familiar from previous years will be used constantly in the story-telling time.

(2) Oral reading: Poems and stories, of the greatest literary value, which at the same time are easy enough for the children to read, are selected for oral reading; they are studied especially with a view to rendering them in a beautiful way to others. All of the selections from *A Child's Garden of Verse,* some of the fables, the selections from the *Odyssey,* and the sagas are included in the oral reading.

(3) Reading: For some of the children considerable phonic drills and reading of very simple stories are necessary. Others use silent reading mainly for study in science, history, and geography, oral reading being used only for social purposes. At the end of the fifth year in school (third grade) the children should have acquired ease in reading whatever thought-matter

is adapted to them, and in giving an intelligent oral rendering of the same.

(4) Writing: The children have many opportunities to feel the need of writing, which cause them to use it for reasons which they themselves think valid. Written expression is used in the following instances: (1) note-taking (a) while experimenting, (b) while on excursions, (c) while studying books; (2) notes written up to present to the class; (3) dictation: (a) recipes for cooking, (b) directions for experiments; (4) original stories and verses; (5) invitations, letters; (6) to give direction for work to other children. In writing, the pupil needs many words which he cannot spell. The teacher writes them on the blackboard, or the child looks them up in his "dictionary"—a notebook in which each child writes the words he has misspelled or asked for in previous lessons. This dictionary, consisting of words which the child actually needs and uses constantly, becomes a spelling-book, if so it may be called, the children often taking it home to learn the words. When a paper is read aloud and the class does not gain the thought which the writer desires to convey, the language is reconstructed by the help and criticism of the other children. The use of punctuation marks is discovered, and rules for the use of capitals, etc., are established. The oral as well as the written language of the pupils is constantly corrected.

Art.—Drawing and painting: This is a year when the children make a rapid transition. Up to this period they put meaning into crude symbols, showing but little discontent with the crudeness of the effort. After this age they rapidly take an objective interest in their drawings. Their imperfections discourage and disgust them. It is important that the subject-matter should lead to a closer visual analysis, and that it should be of such a nature as to enable the children to "check up" their results by comparison with real things. The nature-study, with its wide range of interests, offers a class of subjects by which visual as well as aesthetic powers may be developed.

Clay-modeling: Vases, jars, and bowls for flowers. Having become familiar with some characteristic Greek and Norse designs, the children often choose these for their own purposes. Statuettes illustrative of the work in nature-study, history, and literature are made.

Textiles: Making of bags for school purposes, field excursions, etc. Designing and making of portière or window curtains with design in appliqué. Further experiments in dyeing and pattern-weaving.

Woodworking: At the beginning of the second half of the year the time scheduled for woodworking is devoted to the construction of portfolios—an exercise valuable not only for the concrete result, but also for the careful measurements involved. As a natural sequence, library fittings may follow, and penholders, trays, paper-knives, desk-boxes, blotting-pads, and paper-files constructed from wood. These are the personal property of the children who make them, and may be taken home or donated to the school for use. The tools involved in the construction of these articles are the plane, ruler, trysquare, saw, hammer, gauge and mallet, bit and brace, spokeshave, and file. The children are expected to have acquired a fair degree of skill in the use of tools previous to this year, and the articles are designed with reference to a natural sequence in the use of the tools and the increasing power of technic on the part of the child.

Music.—Sight reading is introduced in this grade by means of short and simple exercises. A musical value is given these by the addition of a piano accompaniment after the reading is accomplished. Phrases chosen from familiar songs are notated. Rests, whole, half, quarter, and eighth are used. Rote songs are taught for assembly singing.

Gymnastics.—Marching, running, fancy steps, postural work and breathing, and jumping and games. Work still imitative, but increasing importance attached to proper respect for command and response to it. In increasing the emphasis upon the advantages of method and system, begin methods of formally placing the class on the floor for postural work. All formal work still accompanied by music. Begin games of low organization, and simple games of competition and co-operation.

Dancing.—First ten positions with the feet; bow; grand right and left; waltz and two-step in couples; galop in couples; galop square, polka square.

In this year the improvement in technique should be marked. The basis of this improvement is to be found in the growing power of the children to criticize their work and in their desire for increased skill. Skill in reading, writing, and number is now sought as a means to an end—that of acquiring knowledge of history, geography, and natural science. It is also in itself a source of satisfaction.

During the previous years the children have studied some of the conditions that bring people together in a city. In the sixth year they trace the growth and development of their own city, Chicago. It is necessary to make a study of the present physiographic conditions; for Chicago represents man's struggle with his environment.

History.—The approach to the study of Chicago is through the consideration of the early French explorers and early settlers of the Northwest. This continues the study of explorers made in the third grade.

First half-year: (1) Early French settlers—their motives: (*a*) religion, (*b*) adventure, (*c*) acquisition of territory. (2) Industries naturally developed on the St. Lawrence: fishing, fur-trading, and trapping. (3) Story of Marquette and Joliet. (4) Story of LaSalle and his attempts to establish a chain of forts in the country south of the Great Lakes, and to control the fur trade; development of trading-posts at Kaskaskia, Detroit, Vincennes. (5) Fort Dearborn: (*a*) development of trading-post; (*b*) building of fort; (*c*) coming of pioneers.

Construction work: (1) Marquette's at Michillimachinac: (2) Fort St. Louis at Starved Rock; (3) Fort Dearborn.

Second half-year: Civics. Chicago as a village—development of the city: (1) streets and bridges; (2) water supply; (3) sanitation.

Geography.—First half-year, first six weeks only. Special point: agencies which change topography. Excursions to (1)

South Shore: (*a*) formation of sand bars, lagoons, swamps, and ridges; (*b*) reasons for piers; (2) swamps: conditions for formation and change; (3) Dune Park: (*a*) formation of dunes and swamps; (*b*) cause of succession of dunes; (4) Beverly Hills: special features—forests, wide ravines, swamps, and prairies.

In connection with history: (1) the St. Lawrence and Mississippi basins; (2) geography and topography of Illinois: (*a*) the old river routes; (*b*) appearance of the country; (*c*) routes to the East.

Lumbering (*see* "Woodworking").

Second half-year: (1) study of mining (*see* "Metal-Working"). (2) Study of clay (*see* "Modeling"). (3) Special study of Mississippi basin industrially considered: (*a*) cotton belt, (*b*) grain belt, (*c*) sugar-cane belt, (*d*) rice belt, (*e*) grazing belt, etc. (4) Excursions.

The last six weeks will again be devoted to excursions. Special point, ravines: (*a*) Thornton, (*b*) Beverly Hills, (*c*) Fraction Run, (*d*) Glencoe—character of beach.

Note.—For reference each child owns Carpenter's *North America*.

Nature-study.—(1) Animal life: The children build squirrel boxes in the garden and have special charge of a pair of gray squirrels. The question of taming them leads to a close study of the habits of these and kindred animals. , (*a*) Prehension of food, comparison of prehensile organs, nature of food, ways of obtaining it, are some of the points for comparative study. (*b*) Birds: habits of winter birds, children placing suet, meat, and grain for them; relation of claws and beak to food-getting. (*c*) Insects: grasshoppers, lady-bugs. (*d*) Spiders. (*e*) Earthworms: place in boxes; observe relation to soil.

(2) Garden: The children have charge of our flower-beds, the ivy and climbing-roses in front of the school building, one flower-bed and an herb-bed in the school garden, bulbs for spring and winter blooming, six large window-boxes outside the windows, and three boxes inside. In explanation of problems which arise, the following experiments are performed:

Those explaining (*a*) the relation of light and heat to growth under perfectly natural conditions; (*b*) germination and rate of growth in various soils with similar conditions; (*c*) effect of roots on rock; (*d*) ways of getting moisture; (*e*) relation of moisture to growth of root. Buds: examine; note modes of protection. Grafting fruit trees and house plants. Twigs of common trees: (*a*) find comparative growth for several seasons; (*b*) note modes of protection.

(3) Excursions: Excursions are made to (*a*) the Wooded Island, (*b*) South Shore, (*c*) Glencoe, (*d*) neighboring swamps, (*e*) Beverly Hills. Special points for observation: (*a*) plants— recognition of known species, identification of some new ones, where found, the nature of the soil, mode of growth, relation of seed to plant, meaning of color in fruit, meaning of shells on nuts; (*b*) observations of animals' life as noted under the first heading.

(4) Meteorology: (1) Slant of sun's rays; measurement taken weekly. (2) Average temperature; daily record taken at 9, 11, and 1 o'clock. (3) Direction of wind at the time noted above. (4) Relation of direction of wind and slant of sun's rays to temperature.

Mathematics.—In the correlation necessary to the general work, the following should be the outcome in arithmetical knowledge:

1. Familiarity with the use of the multiplication tables through the 12's. These tables should be learned through use and by building them upon compound numbers, as (*a*) 4 quarts = 1 gal., how many quarts in 2, 3, 4, 8, etc., gallons?; 4 pecks=1 bu. etc.; (*b*) use of clock-face; (*c*) dozen and half-dozen; (*d*) ounce and pound. Extending the multiplication tables by means of checked paper (graphs) to the conscious use of the simplest algebraic expressions as : There are 7 sq. in. in 1 row, 2×7 sq. in. in 2 rows, 4×7 sq. in. in 4 rows, on to $x \times 7$ sq. in. in x rows. Also: There are y sq. in. in 1 row, on to $7y$ sq. in. in 7 rows. Possibly this may extend to xy sq. in. in x rows.

2. Analysis of numbers: factoring, addition and subtraction facts. These may also be shown on checked paper (graphs).

3. Study of U. S. money in accounts, making out simple bills, bill forms, and receipts.

4. Averages: This may be taught in two ways: $\frac{a+b}{2}$ and $a-\frac{a-b}{2}$, $b+\frac{a-b}{2}$; shown by checked paper (graphs).

5. Simple fractions and decimals in connection with manual training and nature-study.

6. Linear, square, and cubic measure in study of ventilation and gardening.

7. Ability to add, subtract, multiply, and divide whole numbers as rapidly as is consistent with the general development of the individual.

English.—(1) Literature: Story of Siegfried. This is read and told by the teacher from William Morris, *Sigurd the Volsung.* The children also read "Aladdin, or the Wonderful Lamp," "Ali Baba, or the Forty Thieves," "Sinbad, the Sailor," from Mabie, *Stories Every Child Should Know;* Hawthorne's *Wonder Book* and *Tanglewood Tales;* Kingsley, "Greek Heroes;" and Kipling's *Jungle Book.*

(2) Reading in connection with history and geography: Catherwood, *Heroes of the Middle West;* Baldwin, *Discovery of the Old Northwest;* Eleanor Atkinson, *History of Chicago;* Jennie Hall, *History of Chicago;* Carpenter, *Geographical Reader: North America.*

(3) Special oral reading, and dramatic art: (1) dramatization of a part in the celebration of the yearly festivals. (2) Study of a group of celebrated horse-back rides in literature: (*a*) "John Gilpin's Ride;" (*b*) "How the Good News Was Carried from Ghent to Aix;" (*c*) "Sheridan's Ride;" (*d*) "Paul Revere's Ride." (3) Other poems and dramatic stories which develop the power to express intelligently the reader's interpretation of the author's meaning.

(4) Writing: The demands for writing are numerous. Papers are written for (1) records of (*a*) science work, (*b*) excursions, (*c*) cooking; (2) stories; (3) letters; (4) invitations; (5) expense accounts; (6) songs. The skill to be acquired through this demand is: correct use of capitals, periods, interrogation point, and quotation marks; the use of the apostrophe; some uses of the comma; simple paragraphing. Spelling: the plan suggested in the third grade is followed.

Art.—Drawing and painting: (*a*) Subject-matter. (1) Landscape: *a.* immediate landscape, showing weekly change; *b.* typical areas visited. (2) Trees and plants—from these areas. (3) Illustrative work in history, etc. The technic is constantly improved, or there is dissatisfaction with the work. (*b*) Design. The crafts in which the children engage form the basis of the design. The emphasis is placed on the following technical points: form, proportion, and spacing; the decoration of the rectangle and the circle; straight lines and simple units used in borders.

Modeling: (1) Pottery—i. e., vases, jars, tiles, etc. (2) Tiles illustrating in high or low relief a scene from literature. Excursions: Marshall Field's and Burley's, to see pottery exhibits; Art Institute; Teco potteries at Terra Cotta. (3) In connection with prehension of food each child will model some animal in the round. (4) Tiles for window-boxes in frames of metal or wood.

Woodworking: First half-year: (1) Desk-boxes, fernstands, doll furniture, etc., for Christmas presents, made in hardwood, in which the child meets the same problems of previous years; (2) a hardwood screen and other articles needed by the school.

Science: A collection of woods representing the trees of the environment is cut and polished to show the graining. Lumbering: (1) life of the people engaged in it; (2) their work; (3) the preparation of the wood for use; (4) trees used for other purposes—rubber, maple, etc.; (5) location of the great forest areas of the world.

Metal-working: Second half-year: The third grade has studied the use of metal in the beginning of trade and barter. Here it is taken up as a material in which the children can express themselves socially and artistically. They (1) hammer from sheet copper such articles as bowls and trays; (2) or make articles which call for sawing and etching, as bookends, letter-files, calendar-frames, picture-frames, etc. Science: Simple experiments in smelting. Geography: Mining; the life of the miner; the source of the ore; the preparation of metal for use; the location of mines.

Music.—Sight reading of the simpler songs is introduced. Familiar songs are notated. A preparation for two-part singing by means of rounds and scale exercises is given. Emphasis is laid upon time problems in exercises. Arbitrary rules for finding the keynote with any signature are given as preparation for later scale-analysis. The more difficult songs are given by rote.

Gymnastics.—Lesson plan same as for third grade. Proportion of lesson given to formal exercise increases. Shorten reactions by the addition of commands while running. Dumb-bells and wands introduced in postural work, also combination of movements demanding finer discrimination and co-ordination. Begin games of a higher type of co-ordination.

Dancing.—Waltz; two-step; polka; galop; folk-dances; clap dance; sailor's hornpipe.

FIFTH GRADE

The children in this grade are still very active and their interest continues to center in people, and in people in action. They have a keen love of adventure. Their work should give deeper meaning to their own activities by contrast with the activities of others.

History.—The Pilgrims in America, their relations with the Indians, and their life amid primitive conditions appeal to the child's spirit of adventure. Not only is the life amid these conditions of vital interest, but the beginnings of the improvement of them are equally interesting, and the substitution of the candle for the pine-knot, and of the rug for the sand floor, leads to a study of colonial industries and investigation as to the best methods of production. The greatest value of interest in work is secured by presenting to the pupil subjects for study in some relation to his own life and experience. He expends effort, and realizes to a degree the effort which must have been made by all pioneers to produce more comfortable living; and this is a great factor in enlarging his social interest.

By repeating the experience of other peoples, he is not only interested in their life, but in weaving and cooking, and in candle- and soap-making, he satisfies his own desire for activity, also. The mere doing generally satisfies him, and care in manipulation comes only after he has failed by careless work to produce good results.

Study of the Pilgrims: Plymouth Harbor is modeled in sand, and the town constructed on the sand-table, including Governor Bradford's house, the fort, the town brook, Leyden Street, Priscilla's home, and Burial Hill. The story continues with Governor Bradford's "Journal" as a basis, and the children read Nina Moore Tiffany's *Pilgrims and Puritans*. The study of the New England home includes the houses and furniture, fireplaces and furnishings, preparing and serving meals, spinning, dyeing, weaving, and making candles and soap. During the study of Pilgrim life, and because of the historical setting obtained, Longfellows' *Courtship of Miles Standish* is read.

The Virginia colony: The study of the Virginia colony begins with the plantation as contrasted with a New England farm. After describing the large plantation, with its great fields of tobacco, many laborers, mansion house, river, wharf, and the ship from England with its freight of manufactured articles, the causes for the difference between the life in Virginia and in New England are seen. This leads to the reasons for the introduction of slave labor, and the effects upon later history are very simply traced. The causes of the colony and events connected with the history of its founding are studied. The children construct a miniature plantation.

The New York colony: Hans Brinker furnishes a vivid picture of life in Holland, and the siege of Leyden illustrates the character of the people. The characteristics of the colony are studied and compared with those of New England and Virginia—occupations, classes of society, labor, education, government. A miniature New Amsterdam on the sand-table, and drawings of scenes in old New York, illustrate the work. The *Legends of Sleepy Hollow* and *Rip Van Winkle* are read, and the latter dramatized by the class.

Some functions of our own civic government are contrasted with similar functions of colonial government: the work of the fireman with that of the "bucket brigade;" the work of the policeman with that of the tithing-man and other officers. The development of modes of illumination from the use of the pine-knot to electricity is traced. This continues the civic study of the sixth year.

Geography.—The general work in geography is a study of North America. During the first half-year the geography is closely allied to history, which is a study of the colonies (*see* "History"). A general study of glaciation is made with special application to New England. From a knowledge of the rocky soil, and also through the use of pictures and descriptions, the class studies the rivers, forests, hills, boulders, water power, and climate of the region, in relation to the principal industries —manufacturing, agriculture, and fishing. Excursions are made to Stony Island, where the influence of the glacier on bed-rock and glacial drift can be seen, and to Purington and North Shore for larger deposits. The location of many towns and cities, as determined by topographic causes, is noted. Other sections of the country are studied by different groups of children, who work out characteristic occupations of the areas and present to the class the results of their work.

During the second half-year the study of the entire continent, including the polar and tropical regions, is continued. Visits are made to industrial plants in or near the city, which supplement the work of the classroom. A part of the work in home-economics is cooking of cereals, and the work is supplemented by a study of the location and areas devoted to the raising of the grains which the children cook. In the work on New York history, constant reference is made to Holland, and, in order to make this work more vivid, the general geography of Holland, including the subjects of erosion, formation of islands, and transportation of soil, is studied.

During the entire year current geography has an important place in the curriculum, and a period each week is devoted to current events.

Nature-study.—This class makes a special study of a swamp in its different aspects and relations. There are several low swampy areas near the Midway, and more extensive ones within easy reach along Stony Island Avenue. The children visit the swamp often, taking note of the changes in plant and animal life from time to time, and explaining the changes by showing the interdependence of the various forms of life. Frogs, toads, snails, snakes, and fishes may be introduced into the vivaria the children may establish in the schoolroom. The study of the swamp involves such topics as: the food of the swamp animals and their dependence upon plants; the "balance of life" between animals and plants; the changes in the flora and fauna due to changing character of the swamps; the ways in which swamp animals and plants survive the winter; the temperatures of the ground at different depths; the temperatures of the air; etc. The children, as far as possible, solve their problems by experimentation, as well as by reference to the books in the school library and at home.

The expression of the changing phases of the swamp takes the form, among others, of paintings, made at regular intervals. The complete set of these is a history of the swamp in color for a year.

Many problems in meteorology grow out of the work; the application of the principles learned is made to the country as a whole, in the study of the geography of North America.

Home-economics.—1. Cooking: (*a*) Preparation of food for winter use; making of jelly, canning of tomatoes, drying of corn and beans from garden, making of vinegar; (*b*) Preparation of dishes to illustrate colonial history; as hominy, corn pone, baked beans, brown bread, baked Indian pudding, succotash; (*c*) Review of starch cooking in the preparation of cereals and of vegetable soups, and of sugar cookery in the making of maple sugar and Christmas candies; (*d*) Cooking of eggs to illustrate the principle of proteid cookery. Combinations of eggs with starchy foods.

2. Science: (*a*) Study of cereals as an important food product of our own country (*see* "Geography"). Their value as food; distribution; conditions of growth; cultivation; milling. Visit to flourmill. (*b*) Review of starch test and finding of starch in foods. Sugar test and finding of sugar in vegetable

foods and milk. Cooking temperature of albumen. (*c*) Soap-making: leach lye for food ashes; test properties; let it combine with oil to form soap. The class makes hard soap and soft soap. Visit soap factory. (*d*) Candles: Work out conditions under which oils and fats burn, and study different kinds of wicks as to volatilization of oil. Make candles of tallow and paraffine. Discover use of chimney. Visit a candle factory.

Mathematics.—The number work of the year is correlated with other studies. The four fundamental processes are studied especially, and simple problems performed in fractions, common and decimal; garden: linear and square measure; material for looms and Christmas gifts—linear and square measure; cooking—addition, subtraction, multiplication, and division of fractions; dye for textiles—fractions and metric weights; supplies for school use—United States money. In the study of areas and of factoring the cross-section paper is used.

English.—(1) Literature: The literature of this grade is Pyle's *Robin Hood,* Irving's *Rip Van Winkle* and *Legends of Sleepy Hollow. Rip Van Winkle* is dramatized by the pupils and put upon the stage at one of the morning exercise periods.

(2) Writing: By means of the writing in cooking, history, and science, it is expected that the class gain a free and correct use of English. The pupils formulate simple rules for punctuation, capitalization, and spelling, and write them in their notebooks. By analysis of the thought of their work in history, geography, and literature they gain a knowledge of sentence structure. In this year the children begin to use the dictionary —Webster's *Academic.* They also write simple verse and original stories.

Speech, oral reading, and dramatic art.—The interpretation of *Miles Standish* by the teacher; study and dramatization of *Rip Van Winkle;* dramatic training in the staging of the French and German plays. Poems of the seasons are interpreted to the children and some of them are committed and recited at morning exercises. This class takes an active part in the Thanksgiving festival.

French.—Songs and games illustrating manner of living, customs, and festivals in France; dramatizing of French Christmas play. Reading material is taken from *Jeux, chansons, et rondes populaires de France.* Masculine and feminine of nouns and adjectives, singular and plural forms, agreement of subject and predicate.

Beginning German.—Instruction oral to a great extent. Special stress is laid upon ear-training, pronunciation, etc. Special drill in phonetic spelling. The vocabulary to be acquired in this grade is based upon actions that can be executed by the children, or upon rhymes, riddles, songs, and games.

Formal work: Attention is called to the use of the definite and indefinite articles, the different pronouns, the verb endings in the present tense, the singular and plural of nouns which occur.

Art.—The work is the beginning of a somewhat more conscious study of the aesthetic elements of art expression. These are developed in both the formal decoration of wood and textiles, and in the drawing and painting which arise from various subject-matter. The use of color opposites is studied .

First half-year: Weaving, on small hand-looms made by the children, belts or hand-bags or table mats. This problem includes the designing of the pattern to be woven and the dyeing of the yarn. In connection with this work the children study the processes used in weaving and dyeing by the early American colonists and make experiments in spinning wool and flax on spindle and wheel.

Second half-year: Making of portfolios, for cooking recipes or French and German exercises, covered in linen with decoration stenciled on cover. The children make a study of the different materials used in clothing, of the manner of production and preparation for use.

Woodworking: Second half-year: The use of woodworking is especially to re-enforce the other subjects. With the Dutch history as a basis a study is made of the characteristics of the Dutch house and furniture. Excursions are made to furniture shops for purpose of identifying Dutch furniture, and simple illustrative articles are made in the manual-training room. Simple mechanical drawings are made by the class.

Music.—Rote singing is continued; the singing of rounds begun in previous year is continued, both by note and with the words, and simple two-part songs are introduced throughout the year; the beginning of scale structure is taught, and a development of the rules for finding keynotes in the sharp keys; original songs are written and notated.

. *Physical exercises.*—Further development of volitional control through problems in new co-ordination in postural and apparatus work and jumping are sought. This age of children demands the addition of antagonistic and competitive work which requires special adaptation of running, vaulting, and jumping exercises. Games involve increased endurance and skill.

Dancing.—Waltz, two-step; galop; polka; three folk-dances: London dance; sailor's hornpipe; clap dance.

SIXTH GRADE

The children are interested in the many industrial and commercial problems arising in the city around them. Their father's business appeals to them; they visit his office or shop; they do shopping, and have a general interest in commercial values. The alien peoples about them suggest questions that carry the children into geography and history and civics with real zest. Questions of government are becoming interesting to them. They have a tendency to generalize in this as in much of their thinking. They are organizing their artistic and aesthetic tastes.

Civics and history.—This group of children helps very materially in making beautiful the school grounds, having charge of the flower-bed and urns in the court. Out of this grows an interest in the general work of beautifying the place in which we live. At this time children are alive to the problems of government in the concrete, and are beginning to enjoy something of the science of government. The outcome of these interests is a study of the work of our "civic improvement" societies, and Athens is taken as a type of the "city beautiful."

The children's interest in our own problems of government, and their desire to know more of the foreign people around them (which is given at length under "Geography"), make desirable and profitable a study of a people other than the English in the exploration and settlement of America. The French life in the early days in Canada and the Mississippi Valley is full of many simple, beautiful stories of the hunter, the trapper, and the priest guiding his own people or teaching the Indian, which give the children a feeling for the French people, and an appreciation of the difference between the French life, social and political, and that of the English and our own.

History.—A study of civic beauty; how to make our city beautiful; what the civic improvement societies of our city are doing. Greek history: Athens as a beautiful city; Greek education, music, art, games; Greeks' struggle for liberty. The *Iliad* is used as the foundation for this work.

The French in America: conditions, geographical, social, and political, that led to their coming; their fishing industries in the New World, Cartier on the St. Lawrence, at Stadaconé, and Hochelaga. Fur-trade monopoly, DeMonts and Champlain in Nova Scotia. Champlain on the St. Lawrence; Quebec, Montreal, summer fairs; trapper, soldier, explorer, missionary; church, school, seigniorage. Spread into Great Lake region and Mississippi Valley; contact with the English in the Ohio Valley. In much of this work the children are in touch with the original papers, journals, diaries, and letters of the Frenchmen as found in Champlain's Journals and other source material.

Comparison of French and English colonial life; account for difference in government. French and Indian War—the importance of its results.

Growth of English colonies: industrial development; hand and home manufacture; growth in factory system; lumbering; ship-building; manufacture of barrels, linen, paper, etc.; trade with West Indies and Europe; Navigation Acts. These acts and internal taxation lead to the Revolution; results, the birth of the nation.

Sand-modeling, map-drawing, clay-modeling, painting, and story-writing help the work. In the Greek work the clay-modeling is significant (*see* Clay under "Art"). Woodwork helps toward an appreciation of colonial homes, through study of furniture and building of the times.

Home-reading: Andrews' *Ten Boys on the Road from Long Ago to Now;* Guerber's *Story of the Greeks* and Hall's *Men of Old Greece;* Kipling's *Captains Courageous;* Martineau's *Peasant and Prince,* Weir Mitchell's *Hugh Wynne.*

Geography.—The children are coming in contact with foreign people at school, at home, and in the great city outside; they are seeing products of foreign countries in the stores as they go shopping alone or with their parents; they or their parents have traveled abroad, or are anticipating such travel. The scope of their interests is great enough now to include the many people and countries contributing to the life around them. They are ready to see the interdependence of peoples; to appreciate the contributions of nations to progress, material and otherwise—are really very open-minded and sympathetic in this direction. At this time much can be accomplished by a somewhat thorough study of foreign people here in our city, and in their own countries abroad. If this study is deferred a year or two, the children's questions are answered haphazard outside; the children make abstractions and come to wrong conclusions, which the truth, learned later, does not always eradicate. So, to satisfy the demands of the children at this time, Eurasia is studied.

Eurasia: Physical features: great mountain systems, plateaus, plains, and rivers. Climatic features: tundras, forest belt, steppes, desert belt; characteristic products of each; effect of each upon human life. Regions of wheat, flax, etc.; grazing, mining, etc. A general picture of the great continent.

We see the three great civilizations: the European, pressing ever on and on over the great western peninsula, and even across the sea to the New World; the Chinese (Japanese, Corean), clinging in the past to its own soil and looking backward, with its wonderful background of written history; the Hindu in the southern peninsula, looking to the spiritual, living in the future life, as it were, leaving only buildings to tell its past.

A study of France, England, and Greece, somewhat in detail,

is made in connection with history. The European is studied as a traveler, a discoverer, an explorer.

Our commercial relations with the leading countries of the continent are emphasized, and a study is made of special food products.

Sand models, chalk models, maps, drawings and paintings, and excursions to the Field Museum, Art Institute, Stony Island, and Dune Park are an integral part of the work.

Nature-study.—1. This class makes a study of birds. The children make frequent excursions to the Wooded Island of Jackson Park. Other wooded areas, such as Beverly Hills, are visited occasionally. Attention is paid to the changes in the nature picture, and frequent records in color are made. The children make a bird calendar, showing the date of the first appearance of each kind of bird, and explain as far as possible the migrations of birds by discovering the nature of the food of the birds.

Arbor and Bird Day is a special feature of the spring work. Excursions to Stony Island, and Dune Park (*see* "Geography").

2. Mechanics: Simple machines in use at school, at home, and on the streets; universal principles in machines; find lever in many phases; construction of simple machines.

3. Garden: Study of fertilization. Care of beds of flowers and strawberries.

Home-economics.—First half-year: 1. Cooking: Canning, preserving, and pickling of fruit as a beginning of the study of fermentation. Yeast bread as a type of fermentation.

Other methods of lightening doughs and batters: by air in sponge cake, steam in "popover," baking-powder in biscuit, shortcake, and cake. Use of soda with sour milk and molasses, as in gingerbread.

Making of tea and coffee: Study of tea, coffee, and cocoa—their cultivation, conditions of growth, and commercial importance, as illustrating the contribution of other lands to our food supply (*see* "Geography").

2. Science: Yeast, molds, and other germ life; conditions of growth of yeast, as food, temperature, moisture. Yeast seen under the microscope. Products of fermentation; carbon diox-

ide. Acid and alkaline substances (in connection with baking-powder). Expansion of gases; change of water into steam. Uses of water in cookery. Determination of the amount of gluten in flour. Visit to bakery.

Mathematics.—Mensuration: rectangle, triangle, trapezoid, parallelogram, polygon, circle—their perimeter and area. Work in geography will demand knowledge of ellipse, foci, horizontal, vertical, and perpendicular, angle, degree, use of compasses and protractor, measure of latitude and longitude, difference of time between places on earth's surface. How to draw lines parallel to each other, how to bisect a line, how to find the center of a circle, are problems that have a place here.

Business problems—how business is done, values, gain and loss; geographical problems, scientific and commercial; simple discount expressed in per cent. This last arises in home-economics. Common and decimal fractions; emphasis laid upon the free use of the latter. Mathematical language, the equation; generalized number with formal statement of principles.

The work is strengthened by graphs on cross-section paper.

English.—1. Literature: The *Iliad* is the principal selection of literature for the year. We use Bryant's translation. The children read and tell stories from the *Iliad,* from books they may have or find in the library. Some books of the poem are left untouched, and others read only in part.

Prose and poetry of the seasons are read. Burroughs' "Signs and Seasons," "Wake Robin," "The Apple;" parts of Thoreau's *Excursions*; extracts from Bradford Torrey; Riley's "Dream of Autumn;" Whittier's "Fisherman;" and "Paul Revere's Ride."

2. Writing: Writing is part of the work in every subject; the aim is toward legibility, ease, and rapidity.

3. Spelling: Oral and written spelling of words heard and used; some attention to simple rules of spelling.

4. Composition: Composition in its various forms—narration, description, character sketch—grows out of the wealth of material in history, geography, nature-study, and literature, and in excursions, travels, and other experiences. The heroic in

history and literature and the beauty of nature often appeal to the poetic in the children, and the result is simple verse. The aim is to foster a desire to express, and to gain the power to express, interestingly and beautifully what one has to tell. Clearness and conciseness are emphasized in appropriate places. Choice of words, flow of sentences, style, in a simple way, are noted. Letters and invitations are written. Records of experiments, and recipes are written.

Speech, oral reading, and dramatic art.—Parts of the *Iliad* interpreted by the teacher to the class. Construction of a drama founded upon some of the incidents of the *Iliad*; the selection is determined by the feeling of the class. Dramatic training in French and German plays. Oral reading of parts of *Hugh Wynne,* of *Paul Revere's Ride* (review), *King Olaf's Christmas* and other Norse sagas, and Browning's "Herve Riel." Interpretation by the teacher of season poems. Some of these are committed and recited by the children. Interpretation by the teacher of Browning's "Pheidippides" and other poems; also of "The Ship That Found Herself."

This class takes an active part in the Christmas festival.

French.—Dramatizing scenes from the life of Francis I; original play of Jacques Cartier's visit to Hochelaga at Mount Royal. Scenes from the life of Samuel de Champlain, Pontrincourt, and Lescarbot at Port Royal. Reading of Lescarbot's *Adieu à la France.* Reading of historical and literary anecdotebook printed by ninth-year pupils. Christmas work taken from illustration of play. Reading and grammar work taken from *Jeux, chansons et rondes populaires de France,* and *The Dramatic French Reader.* Emphasis is laid on the first and second conjugations in the indicative and imperative modes, pronouns of the first, second, and third persons; demonstrative and possessive adjectives and pronouns.

German.—Vocabulary of the Fifth Grade is reviewed and enlarged. Topics: Activities of the day, meals, house and its different rooms, stores, animals, etc. Sight reading of stories from Foster's *Geschichten und Märchen.* Retelling and dramatization of stories.

There is more dictation work. The writing of original sentences is encouraged as well as the writing of memorized sentences, since this is found to be the best means of getting accuracy. Formal work: The principal parts of verbs are taught in connected sentences, singular and plural of occurring nouns, possessive pronouns and their use in singular and plural.

Art.—Drawing and painting, and design: Landscape, to show change in nature. History, geography, and literature call for expression in pencil and color. Notes taken on excursions are material for composition in color; particular trees and flowers are studied in detail. Designs for pottery, textiles, and wood are worked out. Emphasis on invention; composition of plant and animal forms. Clay-modeling: First half-year: Building of pottery, modeled after Greek vases. The figure in decorative composition after Greek studies.

Textiles: The children make a study of primitive forms of weaving, used by the Zuni and other Indians. They have a general summing up of the knowledge gained in previous years, in order to realize something of the evolution of clothing, and the arts of spinning, weaving, and dyeing, and to compare primitive with modern methods. They may also design costumes for dramatic work—Greek, colonial, French, and Indian.

Woodworking: Second half-year: The study of colonial history by the children of this group suggests the opportunity of making a brief study of colonial furniture. Its chief features are taken up: (*a*) the principal articles of furniture in a colonial house; (*b*) the kinds of wood used; (*c*) the characteristics of the "colonial style." An excursion is made to a leading furniture store for the purposes of further illustration and identification of colonial furniture. It is hoped that in some of the articles which the children make for the schoolroom, or the school, or for their own use, it will be possible to carry out simple outlines and designs suggested by the study of colonial furniture.

Free-hand sketches for outline and proportion precede the making of all articles in wood. These are followed by a working or mechanical drawing. A few blueprints are made by the children of those designs which the class, as a whole, considers the best.

Music.—Considerable attention is given to sight-reading, both in unison and two-part songs; thorough drill in signatures and keys, and in scale writing; original songs written and notated; some rote singing is done. The children of this grade, in connection with their historical study of the ancient Greeks, have opportunity to hear some of the music of the Greek people, to help them in their understanding of conditions in early times, and in the writing of the original songs for the Greek play.

Gymnastics.—Lesson plan the same as that of the fifth grade. Additional control of distance and direction in running and marching; increased mental and physical values through tactics executed without music at command. Training for increased dexterity and alertness through introducing insistence upon form, as well as uniformity in the details of changing the direction of facing or position of the class upon the floor. Games still involve all players, but emphasize the elements of additional choice.

Dancing.—Waltz; two-step; galop; polka; square dance ("Prairie Queen"); Highland fling; lilt; gymnastic dancing for girls: (1) Highland fling; (2) cachucha; (3) Greek dance; (4) nursery rhymes.

SEVENTH GRADE

At the age of eleven or twelve the child is not so much interested in activities for their own sake as in their relation to the world-activities about him. In studying the different phases of the development of the United States, such as the development of the steamboat or the railroad, he constantly refers to the present and tries to interpret the significance of the present in the light of the past. This is the keynote of the work in history: the study of some of the social and economic questions of the past, in order to be able to interpret present-day problems. To be able to understand this, and to appreciate what is going on around us more fully, there must be a study of geography and the physical sciences. In all this study there is a constant demand for mathematics, which must become, if it is not already, an efficient tool. The children are not yet able to generalize broadly, but are able to organize their knowledge in the solution of a problem. At this age interest in adventure is strong, and the reading for home and school follows this interest and seeks to develop a greater love for the good in literature.

History.—The history of the United States from the Revolutionary War to the present time is the year's work. Special features of the work: the geographical, industrial, and social phases of the expansion of the American people; the great westward movement which began with the early emigration to Kentucky and continued across the continent to the Pacific Ocean.

Pioneer life: The child's conception of life on the frontier is built up from a study of such topics as the following: the migration of a family across the mountains to Kentucky; the cause of the migration; the possible routes across the mountains; the geographical factors involved in choosing a tract of land for a farm; the clearing and tilling of the land for a farm; the necessity for some form of community life; Daniel Boone as a type of the early explorer and pioneer; the governmental problems presented to the pioneers and their solutions; the settlement of Kentucky and Tennessee; the work of George Rogers Clark in saving the Northwest territory to the United States; the settlement of the Northwest Territory; the Ordinance of 1787; the Ohio Company and other land companies in the settlement of Ohio.

Reading: Extracts from original sources; two of the following: Thwaites, *Daniel Boone* and *How George Rogers Clark Won the Northwest;* Churchill, *The Crossing* (first part).

Economic and industrial conditions in the West. Topics to be considered: the demand for a market, and for the right to navigate the Mississippi River; the purchase of Louisiana Territory, improvements in transportation by invention of the steamboat, and the building of national and local roads and canals; the War of 1812, a struggle for commercial independence; the expedition of Lewis and Clark; the growth of the slavery questions, including the Missouri Compromise and the annexation of

Texas; the development of railroads; the effect of railroads and steamboats in the development of the trans-Mississippi country; the discovery of gold in California; the Oregon country; the economic conditions leading up to the Civil War; the geographic factors in these conditions; the Civil War; the great industrial revolution following the Civil War; the factory system; the industries of the North and South.

Reading: Extracts from original sources; three of the following as home reading: Lighton, *Lewis and Clark;* Kinzie, *Wau Bun;* Brady, *The Conquest of the Southwest;* Parkman, *Oregon Trail;* Irving, *Astoria;* Hale, *The Man without a Country;* Taylor, *Eldorado;* a biography of Lincoln.

Excursions to a farm, railroad shops, and other industrial plants, are made.

Geography.—1. North America: The study of North America begun in the Fifth Grade is reviewed here from the standpoint of the relation of the geography of the country to the history of the development of the people. Points considered: topography of the continent as a whole; the topographic divisions; the climate of each in connection with the daily weather maps of the United States Weather Bureau (*see* "Science"); the agricultural, mineral, and commercial advantages of each; state of development; the effect of these geographic factors upon the life of the people; the relation of the geography to the history. Blackboard chalk-modeling of topography; field trips and the geographic laboratory are used as aids in the study of physiographic processes. Maps, pictures, lantern slides are also used.

2. South America: A continent similar to North America in structure, but differing in its climatic conditions, hence differing in its agricultural, commercial, and social relations. The same general plan is followed as in the study of North America. The museum collection is used to illustrate the trade relations between Chicago and South America.

3. Africa: "The continent of contrasts" (Keane); a continent differing in structure from those already studied; a continent greatly retarded in its development because of its desert conditions, plateau formation, and slightly eroded river valleys.

Points to be considered and purpose to be attained are the same as in the previous study.

4. Australia: A continent similar to South America in location, but differing from it in climatic, industrial, and commercial features.

A study of current events continued during the year serves to unite all continents with our own. References for pupils: Carpenter, *North America, South America, Africa, Australia;* Shaler, *The Story of Our Continent;* books of travel; magazine articles. For textbooks, see list of textbooks on another page.

Nature-study.—This class makes a special study of trees, their habitats, and the character of the wood. Frequent visits are made to Washington Park and to Jackson Park to study trees. Each child keeps a history of the year in color, showing by frequent paintings the changing aspects of nature.

The class studies the principles involved in making hotbeds, and makes hotbeds and coldframes in the garden for the use of the whole school. The pupils plant new shrubs in the garden, including raspberries, blackberries, currants, and grapes, and are responsible for their care.

The nature-study and forestry bulletins of the United States Department of Agriculture and of the state experimental stations, as well as other books in the library, are of great use. A special study of the meteorological instruments of the school is made. Weather charts are kept for a while and the weather maps of the United States Weather Bureau are used in making out the weather and climate of the United States (*see* "Geography"). The principles thus learned are applied to the determination of the climate of the other parts of the world studied.

The longer excursions are to Dune Park, Glencoe, Palos Park, and Thornton.

Applied Science: First half-year—Electricity. Chief among the children's interests at this age is electricity. This is especially true of the boys. Because of this and its many applications along industrial lines it is given special attention at this time. Static electricity is not given much attention except from a historical standpoint. Each pupil is expected to plan and construct electrical apparatus with which to experiment. Any of the following may be constructed: wet and dry cells, storage cells, batteries of both electro-magnets, a simple telegraph instrument, electric switches, buttons, motors, signals, a small trolley-car system, or an arc light. The telephone, the telegraph, wireless telegraphy, the submarine cables, the X-ray, the phonograph, and other electrical achievements, and the part each plays in our complicated social and industrial life receive as much attention as the children can appreciate.

Each pupil is encouraged to work along individual lines according to interest, previous experience, and ability. As the classes are working in wood in the shop at the same time that electricity is studied they are encouraged to execute their plans at school under supervision as well as at home in their own shops.

Excursions are made to the University electric plant, the Western Electric Company at 269 S. Clinton Street, and the annual electric show.

Hygienic physiology: Second half-year. A study of the respiratory, circulatory, and digestive systems with special reference to the application of the experience gained in the work outlined under "Home-Economics;" a study of the effect of gymnastic exercise, games, out-of-door life, and pure, wholesome foods, upon the growth and functions of the heart, lungs, and stomach.

In connection with the respiratory system we study experimentally the air: its composition; carbon dioxide; oxygen; and impurities. This leads up to (1) the problem of the proper ventilation of our homes, schools, street cars, and public buildings, and (2) the dust and smoke problems in cities.

This study does much to make the pupil (1) realize the value of his work in physical training, (2) reach a higher ideal of physical development, and (3) consciously apply some of the simplest and most fundamental laws of right living.

Meteorology: Constituents of atmosphere; effects of changes in temperature and air-pressure; the barometer; the United States Weather Bureau; the weather-recording apparatus in the

Elementary School; weather records kept by children as a basis for study.

Home-economics.—Second half-year. A study of different foods leading to the classification of food as: (1) carbonhydrates, (2) fats, (3) proteids. Application of heat to each of these food principles, and temperature at which each is cooked. Different processes of cookery reviewed with more definite organization of previous experience. Study of the principles of cooking apparatus, especially of gas and electric stoves.

Science: Heat, and methods of transmitting it. Comparison of conducting-power of different materials; effect of pressure on the boiling and freezing points of water. Tests for different food principles. Simple food analysis and the study of the composition of food with special reference to its nutritive value and the use of food in the body (*see* "Physiology").

Mathematics.—The subject-matter for mathematics is selected as far as possible from the pupil's experience: from problems growing out of his activity in and out of school, and problems growing out of his study of the commercial and industrial life about him. This involves work in (1) arithmetical processes, (2) geometrical constructions and applications, and (3) algebraic representations of arithmetical processes and equations.

Arithmetical processes: (1) Through a study of the organization and operation of modern business institutions the pupils become familiar with the commercial transactions involved in banking, handling stocks and bonds, loans, promissory notes, interest, taxes, discount, insurance, and commission. This requires the solution of numerous problems demanding a knowledge of operations in percentage. (2) Ratio and proportion as related to field- and shop-work. (3) Constructions in cardboard and paper, and drawings and diagrams, to work out methods for field-work. (4) Volumetric mensuration: calculate cost of digging foundations, tunnels, and canals, filling for railroad constructions and elevations; finding area and volume of bins, boxes, railroad cars, and tanks; finding area and volume of cones.

Geometrical constructions and applications: (1) Working-drawings for manual training. (2) Representative drawings to scale of tracts of ground; of farms, maps, field measurements. (3) Designing for simple electrical and mechanical appliances. English and metric systems of weights and measurements used.

Algebraic work: (1) Syncopated algebraic laws of number and of mensuration formulated into equations by abbreviating words into letters, the resulting equations being read as sentences. (2) The use of the equation in percentage and interest. (3) Equations in ratio and proportion. (4) Solution of problems by both arithmetic and algebra.

Sufficient emphasis is given terminology for a clear and intelligent use of it. In all cases enough practice is given to fix the mathematical principles and processes involved.

English.—1. Literature: King Arthur Legends: the children read Lanier's *The Boy's King Arthur,* and selections from Mallory's *Morte D'Arthur.*

2. Reading: The books named under "History" for home reading.

3. Writing: When the children reach this year, they are expected to have the power to write legibly and easily. There is constant demand in history, geography, science, and literature for written reports, stories, and descriptions. The correction of these papers by the children requires a knowledge of the simpler rules of grammar. The papers are filed and furnish a record of the individual work.

Care is exercised to present the oral and written expression that should accompany the growth and complexity of idea. Drill is given in the forms and their use whenever the pupil feels a need for it, or whenever it is apparent that the form will not be learned without it.

Some facts in grammar are taught incidentally. The outcome of this work during the year should be a knowledge of sentences and sentence structure; subject and predicate; words, phrases, and clauses and their functions; parts of speech, with emphasis on nouns, pronouns, adjectives, and verbs, and functions of each.

Speech, oral reading, and dramatic art.—Old English and Scotch ballads, autumn lyrics, Browning's "Herve Riel;" Kipling, "The Ballad of East and West.' Interpreted to the children: Kipling, "The Explorer;" Longfellow, "The Building of the Ship;" Lowell, selections from *Bigelow Papers.*

The reading and recitation of poems, orations, and other selections for the school festivals. The dramatic training required for the presentation of the children's English, French, and German plays.

French.—Printing of historical and literary anecdote-book for the seventh and eighth years from material prepared by pupils of the seventh and eighth years. Dramatizing and writing of scenes characteristic of Breton sailors and fishermen in connection with the reading of "Herve Reil;" photographs and postal cards from Brittany to be used as illustrations. Reading of French historic sketches selected and printed by tenth year; review of sixth, seventh, and eighth years' grammar record-book. First, second, and third conjugations, indicative, conditional, and imperative modes; gender and number of nouns and adjectives; exceptions to the general rule. Reading-lessons and grammar work taken from *The Dramatic French Reader.* La Fontaine's *Fables.*

German.—Topics of conversation; the activities during the different seasons; the holidays, as Christmas. Later the geography of Germany is taken up and in connection with this legends and historical tales or anecdotes referring to certain places in Germany.

Writing exercises as in previous years, with more stress upon careful reproduction of sentences for the sake of accuracy. This class will probably read Guerber's *Märchen und Erzählungen,* Vol. I.

Formal work: Review of the work done in previous grades, future of verbs, genitive case of nouns.

Art.—Drawing and painting: (*a*) Subject-matter. While the subject-matter of the grade is the source of the interests which are expressed pictorially, it seems wise not to attempt a wide range of subject. It is better to select such material as is suited to the technical ability of the class and affords opportunity for prolonged and concentrated effort. In this way the result attains a dignity which is demanded by the more critical attitude of students of this age.

The technique of the seventh grade does not differ in kind from that of preceding grades. It represents an effort toward greater forcefulness.

(*b*) Design. This is based upon the experience which has been gained previously in the crafts, and hence does not depend entirely upon the initiative of those subjects. Creative exercises are organized so as to make the students conscious of the laws of pure design.

Clay: Second half-year. Making of pottery and the modeling of statuettes illustrating typical scenes and incidents in the life of the pioneers.

Metal-working: First half-year. The children hammer from sheet-copper and brass articles of social use, such as trays, bowls, candle-sticks; or cut and blend into shape such articles as book-ends, calendar-frames, picture-frames, candle- and lamp-shades. Designs are applied by means of etching, piercing, or perforating. This work necessitates riveting, and possibly soldering.

Woodworking: First half-year. Method: working-drawing for each construction; a careful study of plans and principles involved. Articles made for use in home or school, the pupil given a choice when practicable. The class designs electrical machines and apparatus (*see* "Applied Science"), demanding part of the construction in wood.

A study of the history and distribution of some important cabinet woods; characteristics of bark, branching, and leaves, by which trees may be recognized; grain and finish of woods; lumbering.

Music.—Two- and three-part songs read. Review of scales and key signatures is given. Chromatic scales are sung, analyzed, and written. Chromatic exercises are used. Songs with strong, musical inspiration are chosen for assembly singing. Pupils are encouraged to play or sing for one another in class, an opportunity for this exercise being given once each week. ·

Gymnastics.—Lesson plan the same as in previous grades. Girls and boys in separate classes. Marching and running as well as postural exercises and apparatus demanding increased volition and concentration of attention; rhythmic exercises for the girls developing into folk-dances; tactics introducing an increasing number of evolutions, calling for greater concentration and alertness. This is a period of rapid growth—new functions develop, as well as large amounts of new tissue. Hence all exercises tend to special development of heart and lung actions, care being taken to avoid strain. Games of higher organization are added which prepare for team play and require endurance and develop judgment.

Dancing.—Waltz, two-step, square dance ("Prairie Queen"); Irish washerwomen; rejane; gymnastic dancing for girls: (1) Swedish weaving; (2) Spanish dance; (3) Greek dance; (4) lilt.

EIGHTH GRADE

It is planned to meet the needs of the pupils of this grade by presenting studies more reflective and comparative in character than those previously chosen, and by strongly emphasizing the social aspect of the work.

History.—The European history immediately preceding the discovery of America: Following the American history of the ninth year, the tenth year takes up that period of European history which immediately precedes the discovery of America. The work which centers about the Renaissance is selected because it is the background of American history; because it may be used in solving some of the social and governmental problems which appeal to these pupils; because the spirit of chivalry, service, and heroism finds a ready response in the adolescent years; because knowledge of the conditions which surround modern labor shows the value of the freedom in work which resulted in the art and architecture of the thirteenth, fourteenth, and fifteenth centuries. The subject is presented according to the following outlines:

1. The period of discovery and the growth of geography: (*a*) Geographical knowledge previous to the fifteenth-century voyages; ideas of the Greeks and Romans. (*b*) The Crusades;

their effect upon the routes of travel. (*c*) The journeys of the Polos; increase of geographical knowledge and the breaking-up of routes of trade. (*d*) The invention of printing; books of the Middle Ages; mural paintings; effect of printing upon knowledge.

2. Feudalism and chivalry; the growth of feudalism; the life of the people; the growth of the church.

3. The guild system of labor contrasted with our modern factory system. Art: (*a*) The towns of the Middle Ages; their position on lines of trade; trade guilds. (*b*) Florence and Nuremberg—typical expressions of the thirteenth century; the cathedrals of Europe, illustrations of Gothic architecture. (*c*) Results of the guild system of labor—compared with modern factory system.

Geography.—In this year the class sums up the geography of the preceding years, including the physiography and political geography, but from a new point of view. The geographical conditions under which man is living on the earth, and the effect of these conditions upon his life, form the background of the work.

Starting with the world as a whole, attention is directed to the distribution of land and water on the earth, the mountain masses, the great plains, river basins, deltas, flood-plains, and coastal plains, the glaciated areas, tundras, and forests. This involves the study of the distribution of sunshine and heat on the earth, and the terrestrial winds. The children review their work of former years on weather and climate, and learn by experiment more definitely the principles of governing atmospheric pressure and winds and rainfall.

The class visits several of the large commercial stores and manufacturing plants, to learn what the different countries are sending us, and what we are sending them in return. This involves a thorough review of the commercial and political geography of the preceding years.

In the study of climate the class uses the meteorological instruments and records in the school museum, and makes a visit to the United States Weather Bureau Station in the Federal Building.

In studying the relation between the nature of a country and the lives of a people, constant reference is made to the books in the school library, to magazine articles, and especially to Herbertson's geographies, which are a series of extracts from the best books of travel.

The excursions are to the following regions: (1) Glencoe; (2) Fraction Run, near Lockport, and the Drainage Canal; (3) Dune Park; (4) Thornton (see "Nature-Study"). On these excursions the class uses the contour maps of the United States Geological Survey (see "Mathematics" and "Geography").

Nature-study.—This class has general oversight of the garden, with the specific work of mulching the beds in the fall, pruning the shrubs and trees, and guarding against injurious insects; it also makes a study of the relations of insects to plants. The beneficial relations are studied through the work of the bees in pollination, and the injurious effects through a study of the scale insects, the rose beetles, and the different moths. The depredations of the harmful insects are combated with the various spraying mixtures, and in other ways.

During the year the class makes frequent excursions to Jackson Park to observe the changes which are taking place, and to make sketches of the landscape. Last year these sketches gave the *motif* for a large mural drawing in the classroom.

In the spring longer excursions are made in connection with the geography: (1) to the North Shore, to study the action of running water in making ravines, and the action of the waves and of the wind; (2) to Thornton, to study river valleys of a later stage, with broad flood plains; (3) to Fraction Run, a rock ravine; (4) to Dune Park, to study the action of the waves and the wind in making sand-dunes. The pupils study the development of the topography of the regions, the distribution of plants and animals found there, and the factors which control it. They also draw contour maps (see "Mathematics"), on which they locate these life-areas. They study the borderland which lies between these vegetation areas, to emphasize the constantly changing conditions—physical evolution and the influence on life.

Home-economics.—First half-year: Beginning with the

homes of the Middle Ages, and instituting a comparison between them and the homes of the present day, the class makes a study of the modern house. The plan of the house and its furnishings; the methods of heating, ventilating, and lighting; the water supply and the plumbing are considered and studied experimentally. Visits are made to buildings in process of construction. The study of the care of the individual home leads to that of municipal housekeeping, and emphasis is laid upon the responsibility of each household in helping to secure healthful conditions throughout the city, and in making the city beautiful. .

Second half-year: The householder's responsibility—for pure food, as part of municipal housekeeping. Study of the pure-food laws; consideration of the interests of the manufacturer as well as of the consumer; household tests for food adulteration.

Mathematics.—1. Algebra viewed through arithmetic. By means of the equation, solve simple arithmetic problems, force problems, laws of simple machines, and mensuration laws, lead up to work with purely formal equations, and justify all reasoning by the five laws of the equation.

2. Mechanical drawing: Scale plans and elevations of accessible objects; scale drawings in 'manual training; representative drawings of accessible and remote tracts of ground; topographic work from data taken in the field; construction of ornamental designs; study of government land surveys.

3. Geometry: constructive, experimental, and quasi-demonstrative; relation of angles of polygons, shown experimentally and by measurements; construction of square corners on paper and in the field; running parallels and laying out curves; staking out lines at any angles to given lines; proofs of principles by actual superposition of representative figures; laws of similar triangles and their uses in field-work.

Literature.—Shakespeare, *Julius Caesar;* Aldrich, *Friar Jerome and His Beautiful Book;* Arnold, *Little Flowers of Saint Francis;* Henry Van Dyke, *The First Christmas Tree;* Tennyson, *Gareth and Lynette* (selected parts) ; Lowell, *The Vision of Sir Launfal;* Scott, *Marmion and Douglas,* and selections from **Ivanhoe.**

Home reading: As throwing light upon the history, the following poems and books are recommended for home reading. Some of the poems may be read with the class. Longfellow, "Venice," "The Belfry of Bruges," "Nuremberg," "Giotto's Tower," "The Sermon of Saint Francis," "Walter von der Vogelweide;" Scott, *Ivanhoe, The Talisman;* C. M. Yonge, *The Little Duke;* Pyle, *The Story of King Arthur, Robin Hood, Men of Iron;* Lanier, *The Boy's King Arthur;* Gunsaulus, *Monk and Knight;* Pitman, *Stories of Old France;* Harding, *The Story of the Seven Hills;* Brooks, *Historic Girls, Historic Boys.*

Pupils are expected, before completing the work of this grade, to have acquired the habit of spelling correctly, skill to write legibly, and power to express their thoughts clearly in both oral and written language. Systematic instruction in grammar to this end is a part of the work in English. There is a study of the sentence (subject and predicate, modifiers, phrases, clauses, kinds of sentence, forms—simple, complex, and compound). The parts of speech are learned, and some work is done in inflection. Scott and Buck's *Brief English Grammar* is used as a textbook.

Speech, oral reading, and dramatic art.—Subjects for oral reading are chosen from the general work in nature-study, history, and geography, from the subjects listed under "Literature," from Julius Caesar, and selections from Scott, and from other orations and dramatic selections to be used in the morning exercise. The oral reading of subject-matter bearing on these general topics is used to give the class information not otherwise to be obtained. The study of oratory has for its object the training of the pupils to speak with purpose and power to an audience.

French.—Selecting and printing of brief sketches of French history, dramatizing of scenes from *La Chanson de Roland* and *La Vie de Charlemagne.* Christmas work: Writing of scenes from *La Vie de Sainte Geneviève,* illustrations of Puvis de Chavannes used; Panthéon. Reading lessons and grammar work taken from *The Dramatic French Reader.* Review and printing of grammar record-book of the fifth, sixth, and seventh grades.

Reflexive and impersonal verbs; a few irregular verbs in common use; rules of past participle.

Latin.—Pupils who have previously studied French or German continue that study. Any who are not studying a modern language may begin Latin. The syntax of these languages, by conscious comparison and contrast, is used to aid in the understanding of English syntax. Latin in this grade consists of simple exercises planned in accordance with Professor Hale's *First Year Latin* lessons.

German.—The oral work in this grade is based upon the geography of Germany; the most important places of that country—especially those of importance in the Middle Ages. Poems and songs referring to these places are learned.

The formal work of the previous years is gathered up in the form of grammar this year. Conjugation of verbs, declension of nouns, adjectives, and pronouns. Special attention is paid to the correct use of these forms in the written exercises, as dictations, retelling of stories, answering of questions, etc. As a reader Seligmann's *Altes und Neues* is used.

Art.—Drawing and painting: (*a*) The pictorial work of the eighth grade is devoted to one or two large problems, such as a mural decoration representing a subject of class interest. The technique centers about the large problem and consists of the various preliminary studies required.

(*b*) Design: The summing-up of the principles of design is continued this year. More emphasis is placed on its historical elements.

Modeling: Second half-year. Illustrations of various phases of the life of the Middle Ages, emphasizing the spirit of chivalry and the work of monastic orders. Illustrations to be in the round or in relief, and colored when that is deemed advisable.

Textiles: Second half-year. Study of fabrics for clothing and for household use; classification of fabrics; some practice in fabric analysis; chemical tests for the different textile fibers; use of aniline dyes in the preparation of embroidery materials; preparation of maps, charts, and illustrative samples for the school museum to show the textile centers of the world, and regions of production and manufacture; history of the evolution of textile machinery.

Metal-working: First half-year. This group has had two quarters of metal-work, and is able to design more intelligently for this material. Designs are applied to all pieces, either in etching, piercing, chasing, or in combinations of the three ways. The process of soldering and riveting may be freely used. Very simple buckles, hatpins, or brooches are possible.

Woodworking: First half-year. The making of articles for use in the school. The making of articles for individual use, with emphasis upon staining, polishing, and care of wood. In drawing there are: (*a*) free-hand drawing for proportion and design; (*b*) reduction of these drawings to working-drawings; (*c*) blueprints.

Bookbinding: First half-year. The work in this department is extremely simple, but effort is made to acquaint the pupil with a general knowledge of book-construction in forms suitable to his hand training. Various blank and printed books are bound in pamphlet, case, and library bindings, using materials best adapted. Various deviations from a prescribed outline are made, as the individual needs of the children in the school arise. The beginning French lessons have been put into simple but substantial form by some members of the bookbinding class, and a few copies of the curriculum have been bound for the library.

Excursions are made from time to time to some large printing and binding establishment to see and compare machine methods, and to smaller hand binderies to view the work from the more artistic side. In the history of bookbinding as an art, the work correlates with the study of the mediaeval arts. A visit to the Newberry Library is then made.

Music.—No technical work is done. The pupils meet for chorus-work twice a week and are taught unison and two-part songs of high musical worth. Those who are wholly unable to sing in tune are excused from the work.

Physical culture.—Results more than ever depend upon the attitude and interest of the pupil. The training should begin to show dexterity and co-ordinate action and power of endurance.

Proportion of formal exercises to games now becomes two-thirds. Rhythmic work largely folk-dances. Exercises chosen for direct bearing upon the growth and development of the period. Exercises of skill and precision with hand apparatus. Fundamental exercises on hanging and resting apparatus. The best games of the previous years are used for the free play at the close of the lesson, and, in addition, preparatory work for the highly organized competitive games.

Dancing.—Waltz, two-step, square dance ("Prairie Queen" or "Samson clog") ; buck and wing; lilt.

Lightning Source UK Ltd.
Milton Keynes UK
UKHW021614051118
331792UK00010B/2119/P